W9-BWJ-406

160

$ 25.00

The Traditional Arts of Japan

The Traditional

Arts of Japan

A Complete Illustrated Guide

H. Batterson Boger

DOUBLEDAY & COMPANY, INC. · GARDEN CITY, N.Y. · 1964

LIBRARY OF CONGRESS CATALOG CARD NUMBER: 64-11726.
ALL RIGHTS RESERVED.
THIS BOOK IS FULLY PROTECTED BY COPYRIGHT
UNDER THE TERMS OF THE INTERNATIONAL COPYRIGHT UNION.
PERMISSION TO USE PORTIONS OF THIS BOOK
MUST BE OBTAINED IN WRITING FROM THE PUBLISHER.

DESIGNED BY LIBRA STUDIOS, INC.

PRODUCED BY CHANTICLEER PRESS, INC., NEW YORK.
PRINTED BY BRÜDER ROSENBAUM, VIENNA, AUSTRIA.

DOUBLEDAY & COMPANY, INC.
GARDEN CITY, NEW YORK.
1964

Acknowledgments

MUCH OF THE SUCCESS I may have attained in compiling the material for this work is due to the generous assistance accorded me at various stages of my interest in Japanese art by friends and associates in the United States and abroad. In the course of time a great number of photographs was gathered, and a careful selection was made to give this collection a true æsthetic value.

I wish to record my gratitude for the courtesy extended to me by various staff members of the photographic service at the Metropolitan Museum of Art, New York.

I take pleasure in expressing my most sincere appreciation for the generous assistance and cooperation given me by staff members of the Museum Extension Services at the Victoria and Albert Museum, in England. I am most grateful to Mr. Soame Jenyns, Deputy Keeper of the Department of Oriental Antiquities at the British Museum, for his helpful criticism and suggested emendations.

I have long been indebted to my many Japanese friends and acquaintances who have so graciously opened to me their stores of special knowledge. I must mention the kind assistance given by Mr. Takeo Takamatsu, editor-in-chief of the Japan Travel Bureau, who has supplied such beautiful pictures. Several of the fine photographs of domestic architecture were given to me through the kindness of Mr. Jiro Harada of the Tokyo National Museum. And I am indebted to Mr. H. Vere Redman of the British Embassy in Tokyo, who, as a director of the Asiatic Society of Japan, has graciously permitted me to make use of uncommonly fine line drawings that appeared in their journal *Transactions* many years ago. For illustrations of the art of floral arrangement I owe my deepest appreciation to Mr. M. Nishikida of the Ikenobo Floral Art Institute at the Rokkakudo temple at Kyoto, where the Ikenobo method has been handed down from one abbot to another for the past thirteen hundred years.

I wish to thank Mr. K. Imai of Kyoto, and Yamanaka and Company of Osaka and New York, for their kindness in allowing me to use certain illustrations from their collections. As for the color plates, I am deeply grateful to Mr. John A. Pope, director of the Freer Gallery of Art; Mr. Sherman E. Lee, director of the Cleveland Museum of Art; Mr. Richard E. Fuller, director of the Seattle Art Museum; Miss Dorothy L. Smith, *Life* magazine; Mr. and Mrs. Shizuo Nomura, New York and Kyoto; Mr. Kazuo Iwata, director of the Japan National Tourist Association; and Mr. Charles A. Greenfield, New York.

My wholehearted appreciation is due the staff members of the Tokyo National Museum, who have given such valuable material assistance and supplied me with so many choice illustrations that selection of those to be used has been most difficult. And to Mr. Nagatake Asano, director of the Tokyo National Museum, who was so kind as to read the original manuscript of this work and who so generously offered his assistance and guidance, I extend my deepest expression of gratitude. His suggestions and criticism were of the utmost importance, as was his supervision of the photographic illustrations, which are of immeasurable value to the text.

Finally, I am grateful to Mr. Henry La Farge for his discerning help in the preparation of the manuscript for publication.

Preface

THE PURPOSE of this book is to promote a fuller understanding and appreciation of the arts of Japan. It was developed, and most of the pertinent material was accumulated, during an established residence in Japan. The writer was especially fortunate in having several Japanese collector friends whose refined taste enabled him to cultivate their cultural approach and the æsthetic appreciation necessary to an understanding of the subtle beauty of their art.

The book is designed for the student as well as for the general reader and enquirer seeking to gain a more intimate insight into the unique culture that has developed in Japan throughout the centuries. It provides a complete introduction to the arts of Japan, surveying their evolution from the earliest times through the period of their greatest development. By art is meant not only the arts of painting and sculpture, but every form of artistic expression, including such æsthetic pastimes as the tea ceremony and flower arrangement, which the Japanese have raised to the dignity of an art. Emphasis is given to the popular arts, for the charm of Japan is found in the daily life, customs, and familiar beliefs of its people, and the many arts which play such an important role in them.

Because the book is planned as a comprehensive guide and the subject is broad in scope, the treatment is necessarily compact. Each chapter presents a particular Japanese art form and traces the chief influences which have affected its development. Such historical and æsthetic aspects as are necessary for an appreciation of the arts are also provided. Emphasis is likewise placed on the evolution of religious traditions, because art in Japan is so closely connected with religion that it is impossible to obtain an understanding of it without some knowledge of the beliefs which it reflects. A brief outline of certain pertinent aspects of the cultural history is the subject of the first chapter, which also includes some of the more familiar motifs occurring in Japanese art. The final chapter is devoted to the history of the Shosoin, a unique repository of Oriental culture.

There has been no attempt to extend this work beyond the periods of indigenous traditions into modern times, since contemporary art in the main has followed the dictates of conformists to international fashions originating in the Western world. While it is true that contemporary work portraying Japanese subjects suggests its native origin, much of it, showing little evidence of Oriental derivation, follows the precepts of international movements. To go further than the arts of design that are known and appreciated as traditionally Japanese, seems beyond the scope of this book, for a definitive history cannot be written until sufficient time has elapsed to allow the subject to fall into its proper perspective.

In all their arts the Japanese have been satisfied with nothing less than technical perfection, whether the work was on a minute scale or of heroic proportions. In that respect each branch of Japanese art merits universal interest. The symbolism which permeates the life and behavior of the Japanese has been recorded in an enduring manner in their arts. It is not a fixed and formal symbolism but rather a fine network of subtle associations giving it a unique appeal. Although Japan received the initial inspiration and guidance in her art from China, this island nation through the centuries has added a rich vocabulary of her own created to express native traditions and the æsthetic ideals of her people. Because the Japanese possessed the innate artistic sense to assimilate and adapt, to absorb and nationalize that which they borrowed, the art of Japan displays a sufficient degree of originality to be regarded as a national art and as such to take its place with the art of other nations in the history of the world.

It is hoped that this book may not only increase knowledge of the arts of Japan, but do much to promote an informed understanding of the people who created it and thus gave to the world a great art heritage.

New York   H. BATTERSON BOGER

Contents

Chronological Outline

PREHISTORY AND PROTOHISTORY

c. 7000 B.C.	Jomon culture (Neolithic age).
660 B.C.	Japanese Empire founded by Jimmu, first Emperor.
c. 300 B.C.	Yayoi culture (Bronze age).
first–fourth century A.D.	Ancient Burial Mounds; Haniwa culture.
A.D. 220	Empress Jingo invades kingdom of Silla; beginning of Korean influence.

ASUKA PERIOD (552–645)

552	King Paikche of Korea sends gift of gilt bronze Buddha to Japanese Emperor. Buddhism introduced.
593–628	Empress Suiko reigns; affairs of state vested in Prince Shotoku.
607	Construction of Horyuji temple, Nara.
621	Prince Shotoku dies.
623	*Sakyamuni Triad* bronze icon by Tori. Earliest example of lacquer in Tamamushi shrine.
645	Taika Reform edict issued to reorganize life and government on Chinese model. Gigaku dance drama introduced from continent. Incense burning introduced by Buddhist priests.
552–794	First period of Chinese influence in architecture.

HAHUKO PERIOD (673–685)

672–685	Emperor Temmu reigns. Decrees rebuilding of Ise Shinto shrines every twenty years.
c. 668–672	Tenjo era. Invention of folding fan.
670	Horyuji destroyed by fire.
701	Taiho code. Guild of Needleworkers and Weavers instituted.

NARA PERIOD (710–794)

Strong influence of Chinese T'ang dynasty culture.

710	Empress Gemmyo establishes Nara as permanent capital and court. Heijo built; *Amida Triad* bronze icon cast.
712, 720	*Kojiki* and *Chronicles of Japan*, first books written in Japanese.
724–749	Emperor Shomu, 701–756, reigns.
742	Shinto and Buddhism assimilated; Konkomyo sutra written.
745–752	Construction of Todaiji monastery, Nara.
749	Emperor Shomu abdicates; his daughter ascends throne as Empress Koken.
752	*Great Buddha* of Nara consecrated.
751–52	Construction of Shosoin.
755	Empress Koken institutes festival of Weavers' star.
756	Empress dowager Komyo (Shomu's widow) makes initial Deed of Gift of Imperial Treasures to Shosoin. *Bugaku* dance drama introduced from continent.

HEIAN PERIOD (794–1185)

794–897	Jogan or Konin (Early Heian) period.
794	Heian-kyo capital moved to Kyoto.
894	Suspension of relations with China. Native themes make their appearance in secular painting. Introduction of esoteric Buddhist sects and painting.
897–1185	Fujiwara (Late Heian) period. Spread of Amida Buddha cult; *raigo* ceremonies.
early eleventh century	*Amida Nyorai*, famous wooden icon statue.
980–1011	Emperor Ichijo reigns; flowering of brilliant aristocratic society.

c. 1020	*Tale of Genji* written by Lady Murasaki Shikibu.
1053	Construction of Hoodo, or Phoenix Hall of Byodo in temple; sumptuous lacquer decorations. Great age of scroll-painting; Yamato-e style of painting developed. *Animal Scroll* by Toba Sojo (1053-1140).
1180	Hall of the Great Buddha at Nara destroyed by fire.
794-1185	First period of nationalization in architecture.
tenth-twelfth centuries	*Shinden-zukuri* style of domestic architecture developed.

KAMAKURA PERIOD (1185-1333)

Minamoto Yoritomo establishes capital at Kamakura. Reconstruction of monasteries damaged during civil wars. Penetration of Zen Buddhism.

c. 1191	Zen sect founded by Eisai; tea planted for first time; tea ritual initiated.
1252	*Great Buddha* of Kamakura, bronze icon.
1274, 1281	Kublai Khan attempts conquest of Japan.
1309	Scroll-paintings of Kasuga temple. The No plays written and No masks perfected.
1185-1573	Second period of Chinese influence in architecture.

MUROMACHI (ASHIKAGA) PERIOD (1338-1573)

1479	Gingakuji, or Silver Pavilion, built by Shogun Ashikaga Yoshimasa. New dependence of Chinese models. "Higashiyama" age. Tea cult formalized by Zen monk Shuko, 1422-1502, who built the Dojinsai tearoom at Silver Pavilion. Incense ceremony founded by Shino Soshin. Lacquer by Michinaga Koami. Development of the new Suiboku (monochrome) style of painting, with Sesshu Toyo, 1420-1506, its greatest exponent. Tosa school of painting, led by Tosa Mitsunobu (1434-1525). Kano school of painting, founded by Kano Masanobu (1434-1530). Goto Shirobei (1439-1512), master metalworker for sword mounts.
1567	Hall of Great Buddha at Nara again destroyed by fire.

MOMOYAMA PERIOD (1573-1615)

1582	Rise to power of Toyotomi Hideyoshi.
1576	Construction of castle at Azuchi.
1584	Construction of castle at Osaka.
1573-1591	Tensho era, during which *karaori* (Chinese weave) textiles were introduced from Ming China. Raku pottery ware began to be produced. Kano tradition in painting continued by Kano Eitoku, 1543-1590, and Kano Sanraku, 1559-1635.
1596-1615	Keicho era. *Kirym* silks for warrior banners. Puppet shows developed, to accompaniment of *jojuri* chanting.
1598	Death of Hideyoshi, on expedition to Korea. Korean immigrant potters start kilns in Kyushu, making first glazed pottery.
1573-1867	Second period of nationalization in architecture.

EDO (TOKUGAWA) PERIOD (1615-1867)

1615	Tokugawa Ieyasu, 1542-1616, appointed Shogun. Edo becomes the Shogun's capital.
1616	Beginnings of Japanese porcelain. Ninsei, 1596-1666.
1624-1644	Kan-ei era; luxurious mode of living develops. Sotatsu, 1589-1651, painter active 1630. Beginnings of Kabuki, popular drama.
1637	Christian Rebellion at Shimabara.
1639	Cessation of intercourse with outside world. Revival of Confucianism. Rise of Ukiyo-e art. Development of the woodcut print. Hishikawa Moronobu, 1618-1694; Ogata Korin, 1658-1716.
1688-1704	Genroku era; prosperity and dissemination of culture.
1661-1673	Kambun era; feud between the Machi-yakko and the banner knights of Edo. Development of *kambun* textiles with bold designs for dress. Korin, 1658-1716, painter.
1720	Introduction of the Nanga school of literati painters.
1716-1736	Kyoho era of affluence and extravagant living. Master printmakers: Suzuki Harunobu, 1725-1770; Kitagawa Utamaro, 1753-1806; Saito Sharaku, active 1794-95; Hokusai, 1760-1849; Ando Hiroshige, 1797-1858.
1764-1772	Meiwa era.
1830-1844	Tempo era; economic reforms.
1853	Arrival of Commodore Perry.

MEIJI PERIOD (1868-1912)

Table of Provinces and Prefectures

THE EARLY TRADITIONAL DIVISIONS of the Japanese empire were in the form of regions known as *kuni*, or provinces, but during the Meiji period the country came to be divided into prefectures designated as *to*, *do*, *fu*, and *ken*. Of the 46 prefectures there are one *to* (Tokyo-to), one *do* (Hokkaido), two *fu* (Kyoto-fu and Osaka-fu), and 42 *ken* or rural prefectures. In the following table are listed the names of the provinces with the names of the prefectures that approximately correspond to the same geographical regions.

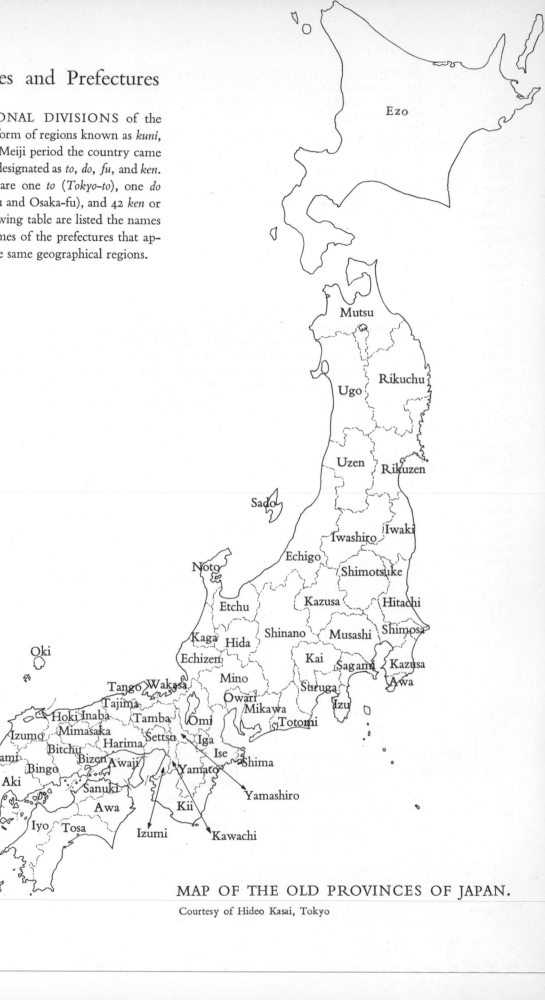

MAP OF THE OLD PROVINCES OF JAPAN.

Courtesy of Hideo Kasai, Tokyo

PROVINCE	PREFECTURE	PROVINCE	PREFECTURE
Aki	Hiroshima	Kozuke	Gumma
Awa	Chiba	Mikawa	Aichi
Awa	Tokushima	Mimasaka	Okayama
Awaji	Hyogo	Mino	Gifu
Bingo	Hiroshima	Musashi	Tokyo, Saitama and
Bitchu	Okayama		Kanagawa
Bizen	Okayama	Mutsu	Aomori and Iwate
Bungo	Oita	Nagato	Yamaguchi
Buzen	Fukuoka and Oita	Noto	Ishikawa
Chikugo	Fukuoka	Oki	Shimane
Chiuzen	Fukuoka	Omi	Shiga
Echigo	Niigata	Osumi	Kagoshima
Echizen	Fukui	Owari	Aichi
Etchu	Toyama	Rikuchu	Iwate and Ishikawa
Harima	Hyogo	Rikuzen	Miyagi and Iwate
Hida	Gifu	Sado	Niigata
Higo	Kumamoto	Sagami	Kanagawa
Hitachi	Ibaraki	Sanuki	Kagawa
Hizen	Saga and Nagasaki	Satsuma	Kagoshima
Hoki	Tottori	Settsu	Osaka and Hyogo
Hyuga	Miyazaki	Shima	Mie
Iga	Mie	Shimosa or	
Iki	Nagasaki	Shimofusa	Chiba and Ibaraki
Inaba	Tottori	Shimotsuke	Tochigi
Ise	Mie	Shinano	Nagano
Iwaki	Fukushima and	Suo	Yamaguchi
	Miyagi	Suruga	Shizuoka
Iwami	Shimane	Tajima	Hyogo
Iwashiro	Fukushima	Tamba	Kyoto and Hyogo
Iyo	Ehime	Tango	Kyoto
Izu	Shizuoka	Tosa	Kochi
Izumi	Osaka	Totomi	Shizuoka
Izumo	Shimane	Tsushima	Nagasaki
Kaga	Ishikawa	Ugo	Akita
Kai	Yamanashi	Uzen	Yamagata
Kawachi or Kochi	Osaka	Wakasa	Fukui
Kazusa	Chiba	Yamashiro	Kyoto
Kii	Wakayama and Mie	Yamato	Nara

MAP SHOWING THE PREFECTURES OF JAPAN.

Courtesy of Hideo Kasai, Tokyo

11

I The Cultural Heritage

OR OVER thirteen centuries of recorded history the arts of Japan have served to transmit her customs, myths, legends, and religious beliefs, besides chronicling the everyday life and scenic beauty of the land. This represents one of the longest aesthetic traditions in the history of art. Architecture, sculpture, and painting are not the only manifestations of this extraordinary legacy; account must also be taken of the picture scrolls and color prints, besides many other categories usually rather arbitrarily classified as "minor" or "decorative": objects of use and virtu, such as lacquers, textiles, ceramics, metalwork, masks, miniature carvings, sword mounts. Because of the extraordinary craftsmanship traditionally lavished by the Japanese on these objects, the Western distinction between major and minor arts does not hold in Japan, and these works must be regarded as art of the first order.

Aside from their high artistic quality and exquisite workmanship, many of these arts offer an inexhaustible repertoire of subjects and associations. There are scenes of the daily life and occupations of the people, epic battle scenes, episodes from the lives of Chinese sages and poets, folklore, legendary stories, Buddhist and Shinto gods and symbolism, scenes from the theater, mythical animals, heraldic motifs. These subjects are often treated in a style of such subtle and suggestive simplicity that their meanings are apt to remain veiled to the uninitiated Westerner. This is partly also due to the antiquity of their motifs, with derivatives and attributes that reach back to the earliest times. The stream of consciousness of this fabulous art, appealing essentially to the taste of noble and warrior patrons, resides in the life of its traditions descending from prehistoric times.

PREHISTORIC CULTURE

Although there was no written literature in Japan before the introduction of the Chinese characters early in the fifth century, there existed narratives in verse and stories of past events and the circumstances connected with them. These were carefully committed to memory and handed down to posterity by a class of historians called *katari-be*, or story-reciters, who were charged by the Imperial court to keep a clear and pure history of the nation's early traditions. From these treasured accounts the first written chronicles were compiled by means of Chinese characters successfully applied to the Japanese language. The records still exist and are known as the *Kojiki*, or *Record of Ancient Matters*, and the *Nihon-Shoki*, often abbreviated to *Nihongi*, or *Chronicles of Japan*, compiled in A.D. 712 and 720 respectively.

The chronicles begin with the story of the creation of the universe. After heaven and earth were formed from chaos, all the celestial deities presented a jeweled spear to the god Izanagi and the goddess Izanami, commanding them to give birth to a land. Standing upon the Floating Bridge of Heaven, they stirred the cool blue waters of the sea with the spear until the land appeared. This was named Onogoro-jima, or land-which-appeared-of-itself, now called Nihon or Nippon, meaning Sun Origin. From this land the two deities gave birth to the eight islands which constitute Japan, called Oyashima, or great-eight-islands, as the Japanese often call their country.

The first ancestress of the Imperial family, according to the chronicles, was Princess Amaterasu-o-mi-kami, literally heaven-shining-great-deity, or the sun goddess, daughter of Izanagi and Izanami, whose radiance was such that she was sent to dwell in Heaven. There she ruled with her brother the moon god. The next child born to Izanagi and Izanami was Susano-o-no-Mikoto, a fierce and cruel deity who brought much misfortune to the earth. It was because of the offenses of Susano-o that Amaterasu hid herself in the Cave of Heaven, throwing the whole world into darkness as the sun disappeared.

According to the legend, eighty myriads of deities assembled before the Cave of Heaven to persuade the sun goddess to come out and bring light back into the world. They gathered together many offerings and recited prayers, and even made merry with singing and dancing until the sun goddess in curiosity opened the door of the cave just a bit to see what was going on. At that instant one of the deities seized her by the hand and flung the door wide open to make the goddess come out and cause the sun to shine again upon the world. Susano-o was banished to the Land of Darkness, and the gods stretched a rope across the entrance of the cave to keep Amaterasu from re-entering. This has since been used as the Sacred Rope of Shinto, called *shimenawa*. Amaterasu then commanded her grandson, Ninigi-no-Mikoto, to descend to the land below as its first ruler. Leaving the Plains of High Heaven, he thrust apart the many-layered clouds with his sword and descended to the land of Japan. Amaterasu entrusted to him three objects, a mirror, a sword, and a jewel or necklace, as tokens of his divine mission, with her prophecy that his dynasty should flourish and rule forever. These are the Three Sacred Treasures that constitute the Imperial Regalia of Japan, the mirror being enshrined at the Daijingu shrine of Ise, the necklace preserved in the Imperial palace in Tokyo, the sword venerated in the Atsuta shrine at Nagoya. The early chronicles further record the genealogy of the Imperial line, whose prehistoric portion concludes with the Emperor Jimmu, the great-grandson of Prince Ninigi, who founded the Empire of Japan in the year 660 B.C. Emperor Jimmu's dynasty has continued for 124 generations until the present time.

Archaeological evidence indicates that Japan possessed one of the most advanced Neolithic cultures in the world, especially in the making of weapons, tools, and utensils, and in creating unusually intricate designs on pottery. Prior to the Christian era her civilization had been fairly homogeneous, but gradually there developed relations and traffic between Korea and Japan, which probably began even before the first century B.C., and there appears to have been a constant flow of immigrants. These were Koreans, and also Chinese who had fled to Korea because of wars in their own country, and most of them were skilled artisans, potters, weavers, scribes, men of learning, painters, farmers, and specialists skilled in the raising of silkworms. *Emigré* artisans and specialists appear to have come over in fairly large numbers, and a strong element of the early population of Yamato, as the region around Nara was called, consisted of foreigners. These talented immigrants stimulated the cultural development of Japan to such a degree that the high order of civilization brought from the mainland in the form of Chinese learning was quickly assimilated.

Of great importance in this development were the early military expeditions to Korea and Japan's political relations with the three kingdoms of the peninsula: Kokuli, Paikche,

and Silla. Around the end of the fourth century A.D. the Yamato court established friendly relations with Paikche, whose envoys were constantly trying to please the Japanese sovereigns by bringing tribute and skilled craftsmen with each of their missions. Among the learned men to come on one of these missions was a Korean named Achiki, a student of the Chinese classics. He was petitioned to recommend a man of outstanding literary knowledge to remain at the court and instruct the heir apparent, and at Achiki's suggestion a scholar named Wani was brought over who was said to understand all the books of classics. This event took place in the year 405, and although both the Chinese language and Chinese script were known in Japan prior to this date, the arrival of Wani with his assignment at court marked the official introduction of the Chinese written language. Not only did this make possible a more rapid absorption of Chinese culture, but the descendants of Wani and other scholars from Korea and China formed a nucleus of learning, and with the aid of the Chinese ideograms, a method of writing Japanese was evolved. The earliest surviving work written in Japanese is the *Kojiki* (712), although the first book in Japanese—now lost—was a chronicle compiled in 620.

ARRIVAL OF BUDDHISM

A further impetus to learning and cultural development was provided by the introduction of Buddhism in the year 552, when the King of Paikche sent an image of the Buddha, with a number of volumes of the sutras and a message recommending the adoption of this new religion. This message stated that although the religion of Buddhism was difficult to explain and its meaning was hard to apprehend, it was most worthy and excellent, bringing to its followers a beautiful conception of deliverance from all desires. These gifts from Paikche were soon followed by priests and nuns, besides temple architects, image carvers, and men learned in medicine, calendar-making, music, and divination. The Emperor, upon receiving the image of the Buddha and the sutras, decided to submit the merits of this new religion to his ministers for consideration. This decision brought about a conflict between two powerful factions at court. On the one hand were the Mononobe clan, who were the leading military family, and the Nakatomi clan, the hereditary liturgists; on the other, their common rival the Soga family. When the question was put before them, Soga, who had been appointed O-omi or Chief of Chieftains, favored Buddhism; therefore the Emperor presented him with the sacred image, which Soga set up in his own house. The opposing faction strongly objected on the ground that the worship of foreign gods would only bring down the wrath of native deities, who had been worshipped since the founding of Japan. Shortly thereafter, an epidemic of sickness spread throughout the land, and the Emperor, believing it was caused by the anger of the native gods, ordered the image to be thrown into the canal at Naniwa, now called Osaka. However, with the succession in 572 of the Emperor Bidatsu, who was learned in Chinese literature, the new faith was successfully re-established with the powerful assistance of Soga-no-Umako, who had followed his father as an ardent believer in Buddhism.

During the following decade the fortunes of Buddhism waned under the pressure of opposing factions when another pestilence occurred. These trying times proved the merits of Buddhism, for it emerged as the great new religion in the year 587, when the Soga family attained the most powerful position after a brief civil war. At that time the Emperor Yomei, a believer in the law of Buddha as well as in the native Shinto, fell ill and avowed his faith in the new religion. With this expression of devotion to the new faith by the Emperor, a great impetus was given to the progress of Buddhism. Soga-no-Umako, having reached a position of great power in Japan, placed his resources behind the movement, and the result was a rapid advancement of all forms of culture, with Buddhism as the source. More holy images and other religious articles were brought from Korea, along with sculptors, bronze workers, painters, temple carpenters, monks, and other learned men. The building of monasteries and the making of images advanced with great strides, particularly with the advent of Empress Suiko to the throne in 593, when affairs of state were vested in Prince Regent Shotoku Taishi.

Shotoku is considered the real founder of Buddhism in Japan. At an early age he became learned in the doctrines of the faith and in the Chinese classics, and as Regent he not only made Buddhism the religion of the court, but also issued a code and organized the government on the basis of Buddhist teachings. Along with his propagation of the moral and intellectual advantages of Buddhism, he built temples, monasteries, and religious houses of charity. Buddhism provided a new medium for learning the Chinese script and studying Chinese literature, as all the Buddhist sutras or scriptures were written in Chinese. A continuous stream of priests, monks, scholars, artists, and specialized craftsmen from Korea now settled in Japan, creating the most important nucleus of Japan's cultural foundations. The beginning of the Asuka period (552-645), named after the seat of the Imperial court near Nara, marks the initial stage of refinement and greatness of Japanese art with the introduction of Buddhism and the influence exerted by Chinese culture. The art of the Asuka period was principally sculpture in bronze and wood. In the applied arts there was metalwork. Painting showed little

progress, as most of the work in this medium was confined to the decoration of temples and images. Temple architecture quickly showed unusual development in its freedom of style in comparison to the Chinese prototypes, as indicated by the few splendid monuments that have survived the ravages of fire and the elements. The most celebrated are those of the Horyuji, near Nara, the oldest existing temple nucleus in Japan, besides being the most ancient wooden structure in the world. It was founded in 607 by Prince Shotoku in obedience to a command by Empress Suiko, and in its buildings are preserved images and other treasures of this great age of Buddhism.

All through the seventh century great numbers of missions were sent to China to acquire a knowledge of the cultural and administrative institutions that flourished under the T'ang dynasty. The envoys and staffs of these official embassies were selected with great care as to their rank and learning, the leader having a whole staff of subordinate envoys including artists, craftsmen, founders, carpenters, smiths, doctors, and diviners, frequently numbering as many as five hundred in a single mission. One of the important aspects of the new culture adopted by the Japanese was a modification of the Chinese administrative system, incorporating most of its categories, from the formation of a court hierarchy based on official rank distinguished by titles and costumes, to specific details as to land reform and taxation. Travelers returning from China with detailed accounts of the splendors of the T'ang capital at Ch'ang-an and of the stupendous scale on which the most magnificent undertakings were effected, inspired their countrymen to create even greater things for Japan.

During the second quarter of the seventh century efforts were made to carry out reforms and to complete the great work of compiling a code of laws and regulations, which finally resulted in the Taika Reform edict issued in the year 645, and the Taiho code completed in 701. An important feature of the Taika edict was the provision for a capital to be regulated by a complete system of municipal government. Until this time it had been the custom for the Emperor at the time of accession to erect a new palace on some new site, usually in one of the Imperial domains. Because the capital was transferred with each new reign, no great towns or cities developed, such as had been the case in China. It was not until the year 710 during the reign of the Empress-Regnant Gemmyo that the first permanent seat of court and government was established in the province of Yamato and called Heijo-kyo, which was later called Nara. The new city was laid out in accordance with a plan based upon the Chinese capital of Ch'ang-an, with palaces and mansions erected on a magnificent scale in the Imperial "inner city." The plan of the city itself was also on a grand scale, symmetrically arranged and classified in the Chinese manner in a great rectangle intersected by broad, straight avenues. So strongly did the influence of Chinese culture exert itself in every phase of Japanese life that not only were the temples and palaces in the style of Chinese architecture, but even religious texts were read in Chinese; and poems, chronicles, and official documents, and even court etiquette and costumes were modeled after T'ang precepts.

THE NARA PERIOD

The construction of Buddhist temples in and around Nara continued at an almost frantic pace as long as Nara remained the capital, many being moved from nearby locations, such as the Kofukuji temple from Asuka. The latter became one of the seven great temples of Nara and, at the height of its prosperity as the tutelary temple of the Fujiwara family, had as many as 175 buildings within its precinct. Among the other principal architectural survivals of the Nara period is the three-storied pagoda of the Yakushiji monastery, outstanding for its delicate and graceful proportions. The Nara period was the golden age of Buddhist art and architecture in Japan, and although most of its buildings have been destroyed by fire or other destructive elements, a great number of their art treasures have been preserved. The art of the Nara period consisted chiefly of bronze, wood, and dry-lacquer images of divine personages, religious articles in fine metalwork, and some mural painting of Buddhist themes. Its architecture became increasingly Japanese in style, with many great monasteries being erected in the new capital, each having numerous buildings within its compound.

Symbolic of this golden age in the Imperial city is the Todaiji, or Great Eastern Monastery, headquarters of the Kegon sect and well known for its chief object of worship, the *Daibutsu* or *Great Buddha*, the largest bronze image in the world. Construction of the Todaiji was begun in 745 by command of the Emperor Shomu, and its Great Hall was completed in 752. For generations the Todaiji not only constituted one of the seven great temples of Nara, but also was regarded as the center of Buddhism, the state religion during those times, with various provincial temples as its branches. Following the example of the Chinese Sui and T'ang Emperors, who had set up a Buddhist temple and a shrine for Taoist rites in each provincial capital, an Imperial edict in 741 prescribed the erection of a temple and a seven-storied pagoda together with a monastery and nunnery in every province.

The Todaiji was conceived on a stupendous scale. Its compound wall enclosed an area more than two miles square, with numerous subordinate buildings, the largest and most magnificent being the Great Hall, or Hall of the Great Buddha. This Hall was of enormous proportions, originally 284 feet long, 166 feet wide, and 152 feet high. Twice it was reduced to ashes as the result of conflicts between powerful feudal lords, in 1180 and again in 1567, and each time it was carefully restored. Although its present dimensions are only about two-thirds the size of the original building, the height remains 152 feet, and it is still the largest wooden building under a single roof in the world. The seated figure of the *Great Buddha* which it enshrines is 53 feet high.

RECONCILIATION OF BUDDHISM AND SHINTOISM

The erection of a great image of Buddha in the Japanese capital presented a difficult situation which was to have a profound effect on the religious life of the Japanese. The problem was to find a way of assimilating Buddhism and Shintoism, for the great image was to become an object of national worship with counterparts in all the provincial temples, presenting in substance an affront to the native gods worshipped by the people since remote antiquity. Foreseeing this, the Buddhist priests gave much thought to the problem of reconciling the two faiths and developing a doctrine which would be universally acceptable and allow Buddhism and Shintoism to coexist in perfect harmony. This reconciliation was achieved by a distinguished Buddhist priest named Gyogi, who became patriarch of the Hosso sect. He conceived the idea of syncretizing Buddhism and Shintoism by defining them as different forms of the same belief, and as an Imperial emissary he journeyed to the sacred shrine of the sun goddess at Ise, to solemnly request her opinion. After seven days and seven nights of prayer at the threshold of the shrine, Gyogi received an oracle from her sacred lips proclaiming her desire to unite and harmonize the principles of the two faiths, and obtained recognition of the native deities as manifestations of the Buddha. The overwhelming ascendency of Buddhism over Shintoism culminated in the creation of Ryobu, or Double Aspect Shinto, the theory that the Buddhist pantheon in general represents the indestructible parts of the gods, while the deities in the Shinto pantheon are their partial appearances or incarnations.

Shinto, or Way of the Gods, is the native cult of Japan, combining nature and ancestor worship in a pantheon of "eight million gods," with the sun goddess Amaterasu-o-mikami as its principal deity, enshrined in the Naiku, or Inner Shrine, of the Daijingu shrines at Ise. Shinto is as old as the country itself, having gradually evolved from an unorganized worship of nature and the spirits of the dead in the dim past of legendary times. This early cult had a pantheon of many nature gods and goddesses—of the sea, rivers, winds, fire, and mountains—besides many deified historical personages. It has no founder, no creed, and no teachings; it is simply the Way of the Gods, and a Shinto shrine has no image venerated in it, but its *kami* or deity is represented by a symbol of some kind, such as a mirror, a sword, a gem, a tablet, or other similar object. Most Japanese are both Shintoist and Buddhist without contradiction, and almost every Japanese home has its Shinto family altar or shrine where a god is symbolically venerated.

The oracle reconciling the two faiths occurred in 742, and the edict announcing that a Buddha image would be made was issued in the following year. Although the casting of the *Great Buddha* was completed in 749, it was not until 752 that the dedication ceremony took place, at which the eyes of the image were touched to symbolize bringing it to life. The occasion presented a fabulous spectacle of Oriental splendor amid great rejoicing; there were performances of the ancient *gigaku* (dance-drama), and a maigre feast was provided by the court for 10,000 priests. The solemn ceremony of the opening of the eyes of the *Great Buddha* was performed in the presence of the Empress Koken, who had ascended the throne in 749, and her Imperial parents, the former Emperor and Empress Shomu. Many articles used at the "eye-opening" ceremony are preserved in the Shosoin, the Imperial Repository, a famous wooden treasure house a short distance behind the Hall of the Great Buddha. The Shosoin was built about 751 or 752 to preserve several thousand objects of art and other belongings of the Emperor Shomu, donated at his death to the Todaiji temple by his consort Komyo-kogo and their daughter, the Empress Koken. Preserved for more than a thousand years, these treasures of the eighth century, the classical period of Japanese culture, constitute a collection without parallel in the history of art. Included in this great assortment are sutras, temple and altar appointments, personal ornaments, weapons, musical instruments, masks and costumes used in dances, documents, textiles, and household utensils. The collection is of such great variety and size that it gives a remarkably complete picture of eighth-century Japanese life and art.

Although Buddhism was growing in popularity and prosperity and a remarkable cultural progress was taking place, the Nara period was marred by dynastic intrigues and quarrels of succession causing continuous strife. It was a direct result of one of these conflicts for power that the oldest surviving specimens of the art of printing in the world were produced. In the year 758 the Empress Koken abdicated in favor of the Emperor Jonin; but a few years later, in 764, a revolt occurred. This was successfully suppressed by the former Empress Koken, who banished Jonin to the island of Awaji, deprived him of his title of Emperor, and reascended the throne as the Empress Shotoku. To express her joy and thanks the Empress ordered a million miniature wooden pagodas called *hyakuman-to* (literally, one-million-pagodas) to be made, with the object of dedicating them to Buddhism as a sign of her penitence. These small pagodas were of three, seven, and more stories, each four and a half inches high, with the base three and a half inches in diameter, and a copy of the Dharani sutra was placed in each. A million copies of this sutra were thus printed from either copper or wooden blocks, to save the trouble and time of writing them by hand. The sutras and their pagodas were dedicated to ten large Buddhist temples, a hundred thousand being presented to each of the temples in the year 770. Of the original one hundred thousand presented to the Horyuji temple, more than ten thousand are still preserved there after almost twelve centuries.

THE HEIAN PERIOD

In the closing years of the eighth century the Heian period (794-1185) began with the foundation of a new capital called Heian-kyo, meaning capital of peace and tranquillity, which later became Kyoto. Ten years earlier the capital had moved from Nara to Nagaoka, five miles from Kyoto, where the building of the new city continued until the beginning of 793, when an edict was issued ordering its removal to the present site of Kyoto. The reasons for this sudden change in plans are not officially known but it was probably due to a series of misfortunes within the Imperial household which were attributed to vengeful spirits. After the Emperor had consulted with persons skilled in the art of divination, the new site was selected and the move announced to the local tutelary deity at the Kamo shrine, to the sun goddess at Ise, and to the tombs of the Emperor's ancestors. The new site, nestled picturesquely among surrounding mountains, was remarkable for its natural beauty and an abundance of crystal-clear streams that offered ideal spots for fine mansions with gardens and lakes.

Like Nara, the new capital was laid out on the plan of Ch'ang-an, capital of the Sui and T'ang dynasties in China. Its plan was in the form of a rectangle, crisscrossed by roads with moats of water running alongside. A number of religious houses already existed at or near the new site, the most important being the Kamo shrine, the Gion or Yasaka shrine, and the Koryuji temple, better known as the Uzumasadera. In 805 the celebrated Kiyomizu temple was founded and built on a cliff halfway up the Otowayama, with the materials from the old main hall of the former Imperial palace at Nagaoka constituting the nucleus of the new buildings. One of the most important, from a historical as well as religious standpoint, was the Enryakuji temple, established in 788 by Dengyo-Daishi, the distinguished founder of the Tendai sect. To protect the new capital from evil spirits, which are supposed to come from the northeast, the Emperor Kammu ordered the Enryakuji temple buildings to be located on the summit of Mount Hiei to close the "*kimon*" direction of Kyoto. The *kimon*, literally meaning devil gate, or northeast, is considered by many Japanese to cast an evil spell, so that they will not build a house in that direction, nor sleep in that direction, nor move in that direction, and a gate on the northeast side of a wall around a dwelling must always be securely closed to keep out the Oni or devils. Even as late as the beginning of the seventeenth century the Kanyei-ji temple was built at Uyeno, northeast of Edo, to close the *kimon* gate of the Shogunate capital by order of the Tokugawa regime.

In the opening years of the ninth century Kyoto was one of the largest cities in the world, with a population of over half a million, many fine mansions having handsome gates and beautiful gardens, great tile-roofed temples, and streets that presented a constant pageant of the everyday life of the people. Aristocratic life in Heian times was marked by gaiety and festivities, the nobles residing in palatial residences and enjoying all the privileges and pleasures their birth and wealth could command. In the northern center of the city was the great enclosure with fourteen gates containing the Imperial buildings, the most magnificent of which was the Great Hall of State, resplendent with red-lacquered balustrades and green-blue roof tiles. Here also were the series of enclosures containing the groups of buildings making up the Imperial residence itself. These great houses of the nobility developed the distinctive Japanese style of architecture called *shinden-zukuri*, consisting of a series of large apartments connected by galleries. The wall panels, sliding partitions, and coffered ceilings were decorated by the great secular artists of the time, in splendid works that gave the interiors a native charm and elegance. Landscape painting became very popular and great progress was made in the applied arts such as metalwork, lacquer, and textiles. All the arts began to free themselves from foreign influence and flourished as never before with a truly native vocabulary and a typical Japanese freedom of expression. This was prompted by the suspension of official relations with China, for in the year 894 it was decided to discontinue the missions to the T'ang court. The Heian era abounds in literary masterpieces of great elegance and refinement, and a large number of celebrated works were written in Japanese and were Japanese in subject. An interesting feature of this epoch is the appearance of several women prose writers, among them Lady Murasaki Shikibu, 975-1031, authoress of the famous *Genji Monogatari* or *Tale of Genii*, and Sei Shoangon, circa 1000, authoress of the *Makura-no-Soshi*, or *Miscellany* or

Pillow Book, a charming and lively novel which presents a clear and intimate picture of life at the Heian court.

In this era of luxury and abundance the feudal system began to develop, and the political history of the period is in reality a series of events having drastic effects on the fortunes of three great clans, the Fujiwara, the Taira, and the Minamoto. The struggle to the death between these powerful rival houses created a warrior class which, under the stress of the turbulent times, formulated a code of behavior peculiar to feudal Japan. The stirring events of this period, with the rise and fall of these great clans, its epic stories of courage and loyalty, left a deep impression upon Japanese art and literature. After 1160 the Emperor came under the domination of the house of Taira, which had wrested power by military strength from the Fujiwara clan. The whole of Japan was convulsed with war, famine, and pestilence until 1185, when the Minamoto clan overthrew the Taira clan after protracted warfare, at the great sea battle of Dannoura. From that time onward Japan was governed by successive dynasties of powerful military dictators who wielded Imperial power but never usurped Imperial dignity. The life at court continued to be respected by the military classes for its social and aesthetic traditions, and the throne was always occupied by a direct descendant of the sun goddess.

THE KAMAKURA PERIOD

The Kamakura period (1185-1333) begins with the rise of the Minamoto family to supremacy and the appointment of Yoritomo Minamoto as the first Shogun in 1192. This commission as Sei-i-Taishogun, or Generalissimo for the Subjugation of Eastern Barbarians, gave him complete control over all military forces in the country. The privilege of having his retainers hold the posts of high constables and stewards in charge of the collection of taxes paid in rice, laid the foundations of virtual rule over the entire country. The *bakufu*, or Shogunate government, was originally set up as an organ of control over the warrior groups, with the Shogun to act merely as its commander, and did not mean that the reins of government had been abandoned by the court. Nevertheless, by securing economic and military dominance the Shogunate became politically supreme, although the court still retained certain negative authority as well as its cultural and social prestige. By the end of the twelfth century the feudal system was fully developed, with more than 260 provincial feudal houses hereditarily governed by the daimyo, or local barons, appointed by the Shogun. When Yoritomo died in the last year of the twelfth century, he was succeeded by his two sons, first Yoriie and then Sanetomo, but Sanetomo was assassinated by his nephew, the chief priest of the Hachimangu shrine, in the year 1219, which brought to a close the rule of the Minamoto. A council of regency was formed and presided over by Hojo Tokimasa, the father-in-law of Yoritomo, who was a power behind the Shogun and responsible for many of the Kamakura administrative policies. With the succession of Sanetomo to the office of Shogun, Tokimasa had become the sole regent, and from that time on for over a hundred years the actual power of the Shogunate was controlled by successive regents of the Hojo family.

This was the era of the formation of the samurai caste, and the appearance of a code of ethics for the samurai called *bushido*, or the Way of the Warrior, corresponding to chivalry in medieval Europe. Although *samurai* is usually translated as warrior, it actually means one who serves, in reality the gentleman or knight. But since the samurai was armed with two swords, and guarded, protected, and loyally served his lord, the term eventually came to mean warrior. The unwritten ethical code of the *bushi*—or man of the military caste, as the samurai was often called—with its principles of virtuous conduct, its high sense of obligation, and its tradition of devotion and self-sacrifice, fostered and strengthened the national spirit of the Japanese people and contributed much to their high moral standard. The military families of the Kamakura age constituted a new social class whose strong desire to cultivate the arts and to emulate the cultural life of the aristocracy brought on a period of vigorous artistic development. Paradoxically, the warlike spirit of the Kamakura age had a stimulating effect upon the arts of peace, for not only were works of art demanded by the feudal families as a symbol of culture and success, but also the inherent love of beauty of the Japanese people fostered artistic activity even during times of strife.

Buddhism in this period also played an important role in the development of the arts and provided a place of refuge for scholars and artists. A leading sect was Zen Buddhism, which was introduced into Japan in this epoch. Its monasteries offered a meditative atmosphere and encouraged a type of practical wisdom and subtle simplicity necessary for the pursuit of creative expression. Within the walls of the Zen monasteries many famous landscape gardens were created, and also landscape and figure paintings in harmony with the Japanese temper of mind and love of nature. Zen was founded by two priests: Eisai, 1141-1215, leader of the Rinzai sect, and Dogen, 1200-1250, head of the Soto sect, who had studied in China under noted Zen philosophers. The principles of Zen were enthusiastically practiced by the military caste in the Kamakura era, and found their strongest adherents among the powerful feudal lords and samurai. Zen flourished to such an extent under the patronage of these lords and the Shoguns that it almost ap-

peared as the state religion, and Zen monks were favored guests at the Imperial palace and at the houses of the nobility. Owing to its simple and practical qualities, there was much in Zen to appeal to a warrior, for each believer must work out his own salvation by austere mental discipline, and practice introspection and meditation in order to attain supreme self-realization. In contrast to the difficult terminology of the other Buddhist sects, the teachings of Zen appealed to the temper and ideals of the feudal warrior, since it did not depend upon scriptures, the worship of images, or ceremonies, but entirely upon the effort of the individual to comprehend the meaning of the universe. Zen accepts the world as it is and tries to find beauty in every aspect of it. The belief that the universe is pervaded by one spirit, and many other similar Zen principles, have effected the outlook on life of the Japanese. Their appreciation of art and nature, their refinement, and many of their social conventions as well as spiritual illumination are attributes of Zen.

A characteristic feature of the Kamakura regime of feudal warriors was its simplicity, vigor, and a certain austerity, but the influence of Kyoto, with the glamour of its aristocratic and cultivated society, had a strong and persistent attraction to the simple provincial soldier. At first the manners and behavior of the vassals was rigidly controlled according to the frugal and simple life of Kamakura, but with the increasing attractions of the social life of Kyoto, the power of the regency began to decline. The gradual adoption of metropolitan tastes and manners continued to raise the standard of living of feudal families despite legislative measures taken by the Kamakura rulers to stem what they called a trend toward extravagances.

By the second half of the thirteenth century troubles harassed the Hojo regents from abroad, in relations with China, which was now ruled by Kublai Khan, and internally, from a series of catastrophes. In 1257 a severe earthquake caused wide destruction in the Kamakura region, and in 1259 a serious famine and a great plague spread through the country. In relations with China, although Japanese ships were continuously carrying priests and students to Chinese centers of learning, there had been no official exchange of envoys since the Japanese broke off relations in the year 894. But in 1268 Kublai Khan sent his first envoy to Japan carrying a threatening letter, which was followed by others during the next five years, all of which were refused by the Japanese regents. Then in 1274 a Mongol army of fifteen thousand troops with fifteen thousand Korean sailors and auxiliaries sailed for Japan in 450 ships and landed on the shores of Hakozaki Bay near Hakata in Kyushu, where they were met by soldiers from the local estates. Although the local soldiers were no match for the well-trained Mongol bowmen and the missile machines and firearms of the Chinese, they fought with such fury that the

Mongols were forced to retreat to their ships with high casualties from the fierce Japanese swords. The *bafuku* knew that Kublai Khan would make another attempt at the conquest of Japan, and by the end of 1280 they had learned the Mongols would attack in the following spring. In June of 1281 two great armies sailed for Japan, one from southern China with about a hundred thousand Chinese, and the other from Korea with about fifty thousand Mongols and Koreans. On the 23rd of June the ships began to arrive in separate divisions and put strong forces ashore near Hakata, but the Japanese were prepared, having constructed a stone wall over ten feet high along the coast for several miles. The Japanese fought fiercely, and on the water their small fighting boats inflicted wide and general destruction on the more unwieldy ships of the Mongols. The battles lasted for more than fifty days, when a terrific typhoon arose, with the wind and tide driving the Mongol ships into the narrows, where they were wrecked and their crews became easy prey for the Japanese. Almost the entire fleet of four thousand ships was destroyed, with only two hundred escaping and not more than one-fifth of the invading army surviving the holocaust.

The Kamakura regime had survived each crisis after the intermittent civil wars because it always rewarded its allies with lands taken from the enemy clans. But the Mongol war had so impoverished the whole country that they were unable to compensate the vassals for their war services, and difficulties pressed the Hojo regents from all quarters. Kyoto nobles planned a well-organized campaign against Kamakura with the aid of powerful feudal lords, and by the summer of 1333 Kamakura had been captured and destroyed by fire, while the regent Hojo Takotoki with over two hundred of his family and loyal retainers committed suicide rather than submit to surrender. The throne was then occupied by the Emperor Godaigo, who assumed supreme authority with the assistance of his own ministers. But there remained in the background a number of feudal warriors who had supported him, and among these was Ashikaga Takauji, a powerful Minamoto vassal.

THE MUROMACHI REGIME

The installation of Ashikaga Takauji as Shogun in 1338 inaugurated the Muromachi period, ushering in an age of elegance and profusion in which the arts flourished as never before, even though it was also an era of protracted and destructive warfare. Its name is derived from that quarter of Kyoto in which the Ashikaga Shoguns established their great palatial mansions and gardens and indulged in a luxurious mode of living. Among the many cultural features which distinguish the Muromachi period was the Kinkakuji, or Golden Pavilion, in the Kitano district of Kyoto. It was originally the villa of a court noble but was greatly improved by its second owner, the third Shogun, Ashikaga Yoshimitsu, who spent the latter part of his life there in retirement from the cares of state. Yoshimitsu built the Golden Pavilion and laid out its garden in 1394, and after his death, in obedience to his will, his son turned the villa into a Buddhist temple called Rokuonji. The other outstanding expression of elegant simplicity in architecture in this period is the Ginkakuji, or Silver Pavilion, situated in the section of Kyoto known as Higashiyama. It was originally built by the eighth Shogun, Ashikaga Yoshimasa, in the year 1479, as a country villa for his retirement from the Shogunate. Yoshimasa was addicted to a life of luxury, and although he was a political failure, he was well versed in literature and a patron of the arts, which was a contributing factor in the great cultural accomplishments of the age.

Because so many masterpieces of art appeared in those days, this period of art history has been called the Higashiyama Age. Among the great painters of this age was Sesshu, whose landscapes, executed with a few rapid strokes and washes of ink, reflect the Zen philosophy in terms of the utmost simplicity. There also arose during this period a distinctive Japanese school of painting called Kano, founded by Kano Masanobu and his son Motonobu, after the traditions of Chinese masters, from which they created a style with true native character. It was a time when definite Japanese standards of taste were being formed, particularly under the influence of Zen culture with its principles of simplicity and restraint. And under the patronage of Yoshimasa the cult of the tea ceremony developed into a refined social gathering based upon a prescribed etiquette and conducted for the appreciation of aesthetic pleasures. The prototype of the classic tearoom upon which all later ceremonial tearooms are based is the one in the Togudo, a small building near the Silver Pavilion used by Yoshimasa for his tea ceremonies and incense parties.

While the Ashikaga family were devoting themselves to a life of spendthrift luxury rather than to the duties of government, the provincial domains were turned over to constables who in many cases preferred living at the capital. The constables in turn delegated their duties to local barons, who were able to usurp the rights of office and cause new feudal chieftains to rise to power. One of these, toward the end of the Muromachi period, was Oda Nobunaga in Owari province, who gained power with the help of the neighboring provinces under his control. In 1568 he entered Kyoto intending to restore the powers of the Shogunate, but since the office had become more nominal than real, he overthrew the Ashikaga in 1573 and devoted himself to the task of unifying the country by force of arms.

With the gradual collapse of the Ashikaga Shogunate and its inability to enfore its waning power against the regional lords, the country was plunged into a struggle for the redistribution of feudal power. This was so widespread and protracted that where there had been 260 daimyo or feudal houses about a hundred years earlier, by the year 1600 all but about ten or twelve of these had disappeared and in their place other families had risen to power. The political and social changes were so far-reaching that the entire country was refashioned. With the breakdown of former alliances and groupings, and the elimination of the weaker feudal houses, the conflict turned into a rivalry between a few groups, culminating in the supreme dominance of the Tokugawa Shogunate after 1615. After Nobunaga had banished the Ashikaga from Kyoto in 1573, he was more capable of conquering all the other feudal houses than anyone had been before, and it was possible that he could have unified the country. But his chances suddenly came to an end in 1582 when he was assassinated by one of his generals. The power of leadership now passed to Toyotomi Hideyoshi, one of Nobunaga's illustrious generals, who took up the task where his master had left off, and succeeded in making himself master of the entire country.

THE MOMOYAMA PERIOD

The short period from 1573 to 1615, in which Nobunaga and Hideyoshi flourished, is known as the Momoyama period, after the site in Kyoto where Hideyoshi built a famous castle called Fushimi. Also associated with this period is Azuchi, the place on the shore of Lake Biwa where Nobunaga built another great stone castle in 1576. It was an era of prosperity such as had never before been known and the general taste tended toward grandeur and splendor. Following the example of Azuchi, it became the custom for provincial daimyo to build castles as the center of the local government in their respective fiefs. One of the finest and most beautiful surviving examples is the Himeji castle, also called the Hakurojo or Egret castle. But of all these strongholds the greatest was built by Hideyoshi at Osaka in 1584, more than seven miles in circumference and surrounded by two lines of outer walls each with deep moats. Some idea of the herculean task of building the walls of this colossal structure may be gained from the size of the immense granite blocks, the two largest measuring 98 and 75 square yards respectively. Hideyoshi's Fushimi castle, built at Momoyama in 1594, and many palatial structures said to be related to this castle are still preserved. One is the building which now forms the Shoin, or State Hall, at the Nishi-Honganji temple at Kyoto. Fushimi and many other similar structures are all excellent examples of the architectural beauty of the

Momoyama period; the woodwork is embellished with gold, black, and red lacquer, and the walls, ceilings, and sliding doors are covered with paintings. Great screen painters flourished during the Momoyama era, such as Kano Eitoku, 1543-1590, and Kano Sanraku, 1559-1635, both of whom worked on a large scale with boldness of stroke and brilliance of design in decorative compositions of overwhelming splendor. In the compound of the Nishi-Honganji temple in Kyoto there is a beautiful building called Hiunkaku which was originally a pavilion in the grounds of Hideyoshi's Jurakudai, or Mansion of Pleasures, that illustrates the quiet elegance of some of the palace buildings, in contrast to the gorgeousness of others. It was also during this period that the famous tea master Sen-no-Rikyu further refined the tea ceremony and raised it to the dignity of a national art under the patronage of Hideyoshi.

A series of events occurred at this time which were of major importance to the applied arts, especially in ceramics. Once in 1592 and again in 1597 Hideyoshi dispatched an expeditionary force to Korea. Although the operations of the second were successful, they were terminated in 1598 by the death of Hideyoshi. When the army returned to Japan, its commanders, mostly the local daimyo of the island of Kyushu, brought back hundreds of expert potters and artisans to establish kilns on their domains. The career of Hideyoshi was marked by much fighting and intrigue and upon his death there ensued a furious dispute as to who should be his successor. The political history near the end of the Momoyama era resolves itself into a trial of strength between Tokugawa Ieyasu with his allies on the one side and a group of powerful families on the other. A great and decisive battle was fought at Sekigahara in 1600 in which Ieyasu was victorious. Three years later he was appointed Shogun by the Emperor, but it was not until 1615, with his victory at the seige of Osaka castle, that he subdued his remaining enemies and became supreme ruler of Japan.

THE EDO PERIOD

The Tokugawa or Edo period extends from the year 1615 until 1867 and represents a 250-year rule by the powerful Tokugawa family, who established their military headquarters at Edo, the present Tokyo, making it the *de facto* capital of the country. Tokugawa Ieyasu's policy was not only to make Edo the military and administrative capital, distant from the dangers of court intrigue, but to effect a readjustment of the country's various institutions by making it the economic and cultural center as well. In the social structure of the Edo period the nobles occupied the most exalted social rank but lacked political power and economic influence because the regulations governing the functions of the Emperor and the court had reduced their status to nothing more than an office of Imperial formalities and ceremonials. The warriors, on the other hand, controlled the political and economic affairs, with the *bakufu* as their central authority. The entire country was divided into provincial domains or fiefs, which were governed by about two hundred and seventy daimyo or feudal lords with their families and retainers. The townspeople, or *chonin*, were engaged in trade and industry, while the provincial landowners and peasants followed agricultural pursuits, both groups being subject to the rule of the military. Thus the feudal system of Japan reached its full maturity under the Tokugawa. A steady commerce was carried on from the beginning of the era with Portuguese, Dutch, English and Chinese traders, continuing until the so-called Christian rebellion of Shimabara and Amakusa in Kyushu in 1637 triggered Japan's cessation of intercourse with the outside world in 1639.

During the more than two hundred years that the country was in complete seclusion, all branches of the arts enjoyed a period of striking activity and progress, especially during the Genroku era, from 1688 to 1704. This was the most prosperous era under the Tokugawa, when luxury and extravagance reached a high point and the culture of the townspeople with their growing wealth gravitated around the arts of the Drifting World, or Ukiyo, as it was called. This was a world of theaters, restaurants, and various fugitive pleasures in which the samurai and sons of rich merchants mingled with courtesans, actors, dancers, singers, and jesters. The wood-block prints and popular novels of the time chiefly depicted the life of this Drifting World with its pleasure-hunting citizens who gathered to see the plays and dances and other forms of entertainment in the great district on the outskirts of Edo called Yoshiwara or Reedy Plain. The pleasure quarters of Tokyo were a conspicuous part of this city life and in Kyoto there was the famous district of Shimabara and in Osaka the Shinmachi. This era also witnessed the development of the amazingly accomplished acting of the Kabuki, or popular drama, while the puppet shows succeeded in producing, as they do to the present day, an astonishing illusion of reality. Along with the steadily increasing prosperity of the townspeople and their so-called plebeian culture, the great progress in learning broadened the national spirit. The spread of national consciousness was not limited to domestic affairs; there were more and more discussions and deliberations on pressing questions of relations with the outside world which, together with the many other problems and social changes, began to have their effect on internal conditions.

At the advent of Emperor Meiji, who ascended the throne in the year 1867, the *bakufu* were so exhausted they no longer possessed authority to carry on the administration of the country. In that same year the Shogun Tokugawa Yoshinobu relinquished the reins of government to the Emperor, bringing to a close almost seven hundred years of rule by the military class and marking the end of the feudal system. The Meiji period begins with the Restoration of 1868 when the Emperor issued the administrative principles of sovereignty commonly called the Imperial Oath of Five Articles. In July of that year the Emperor visited Edo and changed the name to Tokyo or Eastern Capital, in contradistinction to Kyoto, known as Saikyo or Western Capital, and in the following year he settled in Tokyo, which became the capital of the country. However, the ancient capital of Kyoto, teeming with the historical and religious traditions of centuries, has remained the cultural center of Japan's arts and crafts, and an Old World atmosphere still lingers there.

II Motifs in Japanese Art

S INCE THE introduction of Chinese art the Japanese have shown a remarkable power of creative assimilation. In all branches of the arts they have expressed a genius for inventiveness, culminating in the Edo period when it reached a truly national character. The Japanese aesthetic sensibility, in particular, rises to such a high level of refinement that their arts are replete with beauties often too subtle for casual Occidental perception. A principal characteristic of Japanese art is that it leaves so much unsaid. A remote allusion or a slight suggestion is often sufficient to satisfy the cultivated Japanese, for it is held that true beauty can be discovered only by mentally completing the incomplete. This quality of æsthetic appreciation owes much to the principles of Zen Buddhism in such cultural pursuits as painting, the tea ceremony, floral arrangement, and the art of garden design. It can be characterized as austere without being rigid, simple without being crude, something subtle and quiet. In Japanese this is called *shibumi* and constitutes the real essence of beauty in everything. One who cannot conceive greatness in the smallest incidents of life is said to be devoid of *shibumi*; a garden rock without moss is considered lacking in *shibumi*; a painting that shows everything instead of leaving something unsaid or possessing a hidden philosophy is without *shibumi*. The artist will often represent the whole sky with one stroke of the brush or a distant mountain with a simple contour line, and sometimes a single flower or tree suffices as a symbol of the inner essence of nature. An expression of the infinite aspects of life and the essential character and emotion of nature is achieved by simplifying its profusion and by an eloquent use of empty space. An appreciation of such æsthetic qualities and symbolism is facilitated by a knowledge of the myths, legends, and meaning of the decorative motifs that inspired Japanese art.

MOTIFS FOR THE DECORATIVE ARTS

The innumerable motifs of Japanese art would fill a voluminous treatise and can only be discussed here in a summary manner. It was not until after the sixteenth century that a prodigious development of the applied arts opened a whole new field which enabled the artist and craftsman to utilize the vast storehouse of Japanese motifs as decorative themes on a great variety of objects. These were small articles of household and personal use, such as netsuke, inro, sword mounts, lacquer boxes, and other small articles, in addition to paintings, color prints, and illustrated books. The miniature sculpture of the netsuke carver is often so full of detail as to present marvels of patience and skill, and under the brush of the lacquer artist the inro was transformed into a thing of astonishing beauty, while *tsuba* and other sword mounts present the most exquisite metalwork ever produced. The introduction of illustrated books early in the seventeenth century provided another fertile field for the imaginative treatment of motifs in ancient lore, the artists frequently writing the texts and illustrating the legends, traditions, and other subjects they recorded. Many illustrated books were intended as models for the use of pupils or craftsmen in the applied arts, and by the end of the eighteenth century books of design were being produced in quantity. With the development of color prints from wood blocks still another avenue was opened for recording not only folklore, legends, and other Chinese and Japanese themes, but an objective study of the people and the customs of the times.

The Japanese have always lived so close to nature that they have developed a profound appreciation of its qualities. Through their belief in Shinto and the teachings of Zen Buddhism, an emblematic association of specific plants and animals often appears in some legendary symbolism handed down from early times. Some of the combinations of plants and animals most frequently associated together in art are deer and maple, boar and lespedeza, plum blossom and dragon, plover and waves, swallow and bamboo, tiger and bamboo, lion and peony, peacock and peony, quail and millet. Another group of emblems, in which the association is more strict, is that of the animal-guardians or messengers with their respective Shinto deities. Among the animals in this category, the deer is the messenger of the Kasuga shrine in Nara, dedicated to Takemikazuchi, a brave general in the legendary age of the gods. The monkey is the messenger of the Sanno-Sama or Hie shrine in Tokyo, which was the most popular shrine in the capital during the Edo period, dedicated to Oyamakui, an ancient Shinto deity. The dove is consecrated to Hachiman, a deity of peace, and every Hachiman shrine throughout the country keeps a large number of them. Hachiman is also considered a god of war because Minamoto Yoritomo, the great feudal lord, was such a devotee of the Hachiman shrine that its deity became erroneously associated with militarism. Of the many Shinto shrines, the Inari are the most popular and most numerous. There is hardly a village or a hamlet that does not have an Inari (rice-bearer) shrine, dedicated to a deified prehistoric princess called Ugatama-no-Mikoto, who is said to have taught the Japanese how to grow rice. Every Inari shrine has a pair of sculptured stone or wood foxes placed in front of it, as the fox is the messenger of Inari. The many red torii often erected in enfilade before the entrance of these picturesque red-colored shrines represent donations from believers. The torii, usually consisting of two wood crossbars resting on a pair of slightly splayed wood posts, is the simple gateway set up at the approach to a Shinto shrine. The ideogram for torii means bird perch, and torii specifically allude to the entrance of the cave on which a rooster perched in the legendary story of Amaterasu. Therefore most Shinto shrines have three torii, to represent the three crowings of the rooster, and thus symbolically purify those who pass through them.

Japanese folklore and legend is extremely rich in stories of animals that possess particular characteristics or are sacred. One of these legendary animals is Tanuki the badger. Gifted with magical and supernatural powers, Tanuki is a peculiarly mischievous creature that takes all manner of disguises to waylay, deceive, or annoy wayfarers. He is often depicted assuming the role of an itinerant monk dressed in a kimono and begging for alms; or causing fishermen to draw up their nets empty and then laughing at their misfortune; or leading people astray in the dark of night as they walk across paddy fields. A popular role of Tanuki is standing by the roadside on his hind legs with a greatly distended belly which he strikes with his forepaws like a drum, or most often a greatly distended scrotum, as depicted in most of the carved wood or sculptured stone images of him. In these carved or sculptured images, Tanuki is most frequently represented wearing a coat of lotus leaves, with a lotus flower on his head that looks like a coolie hat, and carrying in one paw a purse and in the other a sake bottle.

The fox is an animal with a dual character, for with the exception of the Inari fox, a well-disposed and benevolent creature and messenger of the deity of rice, foxes are regarded as evil. They are reputed to have demoniacal powers, such as sorcery and witchcraft—every locality has stories of persons said to have been bewitched by a fox. A particular subject in art is the familiar foxes' wedding, portraying a wedding procession moving when the sun shines amid the rain, with the bride being carried to her husband's house.

MYTHICAL LORE

In the mythical fauna of Japanese lore, none is more commonly represented than the dragon. It is one of the Four Sacred Creatures, which include the ho-o or phoenix, the kirin or pegasus, the kame or tortoise, and the ryu or dragon. Dragons are represented in various forms and shapes, some as huge scaly reptiles with sharp claws, others winged or with horns. The dragon has the miraculous power to live in the heavens, on land, and in the water, and often it is represented calling down the clouds or ascending into the sky; very often it is shown in clouds. Many lakes throughout Japan have their respective stories about dragons that lived in them, and tradition holds that the Imperial sword of Japan was found in the tail of a dragon.

Especially popular is the kame or tortoise, of which there is a proverbial saying that while the tsuru or crane lives for one thousand years, the tortoise lives for ten thousand. The most common presentment of the sacred tortoise, or minogame, is a long, flowing tail, said to grow when it is more than five hundred years old; its origin is probably due to the fact that tortoises kept in ponds become covered with a weed-like growth which resembles the peasant's mino or raincoat made of reeds. A symbol of longevity and good luck, the tortoise plays a conspicuous role in Japanese art and legend. One of the most famous tortoise legends is the story of the young fisherman named Urashima who rode on the back of a tortoise and was taken to Ryugu, or Dragon-Land, the undersea paradise of the Dragon-King, from which he returned after several hundred years, to find everything strange and different. This legend popularized the tortoise motif, which is still much used as a decorative design on the clothes of Japanese children. Thus, since early times an over-all pattern of hexagons derived from tortoise-shell markings has been widely used in textiles and porcelains. The motif evolved from the stylized hexagon formed by the head, tail, and four feet of the tortoise, each projecting from one of the six corners. Frequently the tortoise-shell pattern is worked in a more elaborate manner. For example, the hexagon may display a series of decorative borders or may center a floral motif.

Because of its graceful figure, one of the most popular bird designs in Japan is the crane, and, like the tortoise, it is a symbol of longevity. The combination symbol of *tsurukame*, or crane-and-tortoise, is a popular motif, while the *semba-suru*, literally one thousand cranes, is a symbol of good luck and is a frequent pattern of kimono fabrics. The Japanese carp, or *koi*, is another design motif used in various branches of the applied arts. Its greatest popularity as a symbol is in the *shobu-no-sekku*, or *tango-no-sekku*, the Boys' Festival held on the fifth day of the fifth month each year. At this time, huge carp made of paper or cloth are attached to masts and poles, one carp for each boy in the household, as an emblematic allusion to the perseverance of the *koi* swimming against the current and attempting to leap waterfalls.

RELIGIOUS MOTIFS

In the category of religious subjects that play such an important role in the field of art, the most interesting of all is the assemblage of household divinities called *shichifukujin* or seven gods of good luck. They occupy a prominent place in popular worship and, being endowed with human failings and endless inclinations for enjoyment, they are portrayed by the painter and carver in a pleasantly humorous, if irreverent, way. Of these seven personages, Ebisu is a symbol of fishing, depicted carrying a *tai* fish and a fishing pole. Daikoku is the deity of the kitchen. Standing or sitting on straw-covered bags containing rice, he carries in his right hand a magic mallet that produces everything desired, and holds a large bag over his left shoulder. Images of Daikoku are usually black and placed in the family kitchen to insure a plentiful supply of food. His messengers are said to be mice. Bishamon is the god of dignity who keeps evil and the devil under control. He is represented in full armor carrying a pagoda-shaped shrine in his right hand and a partisan in his left; the latter attribute and his armor are responsible for his being often erroneously included among the gods of war. Benten, the only female member of the group, carries a lute and is regarded as the goddess of music, culture, and beauty, while her attributes are the dragon and the white serpent. Fukurokuji, meaning fortune-fief-longevity, is shown as an old and bearded man with a very high bald head, sometimes unbelievably tall. To his long staff is tied a book which contains the life limits of all persons, and he

is usually accompanied by a crane and tortoise as symbols of longevity, of which he is a god. Jurojin, who also stands for longevity, is depicted as a tall old man in the dress of a scholar, accompanied by a deer. Of the seven gods of good luck, Hotei is probably the most popular. He is a lover of children and symbol of a happy life, portrayed as fat and with a generous allowance of his prominent belly showing, joyously laughing, whether alone or surrounded by children. In one hand he usually holds a Chinese fan and with the other he holds a large bag over his shoulder in which he stows away the Precious Things or *Takaramono*, or which he uses as a receptacle for playful children. The *Takaramono* is a collection of twenty objects, each endowed with emblematic meaning, the representation of which is fairly common, such as an inexhaustible purse of money, the sacred key to the godown of the gods, and so forth. Included in Hotei's bag with the Precious Things is the cargo of the *Takarabune*, the treasure ship of the gods of good luck who are usually represented along with the *Takaramono*.

In religious art the Buddhist pantheon contains a countless host of Buddhas and Bodhisattvas and a bewildering number of other subjects. Of this multitude one of the more popular is Daruma, or Bodhi Dharuma according to his Indian name. He represents a Buddhist monk of the rank of *dharuma*, who went from India to China, where, in the temple of Mien-Pei, he sat in meditation for nine years without moving, finally losing the use of his legs. This long retreat is a perpetual theme for humorous treatment in Japanese art, extending even to the makers of dolls; the *dharuma* doll, without arms or legs and in the form of a roly-poly, is one of the most popular. Other frequent Buddhist subjects include the Niwo or Deva Kings, two wooden guardians standing at the temple gate; Fudo, who is always depicted standing enveloped in flames; and the Shi Tenno, representing the Four Kings of Heaven or Four Guardians, each for a cardinal position of the heavens. Bishamon, for the north, is also seen as the Hindu or Chinese god of wealth, as one of the Twelve Deva Kings, and as one of the gods of good luck. Komoku, for the west, is represented with a book, a brush, and a red fan; Zocho, for the south, in a suit of armor with a spear and a white fan; and Jikoku, for the east, in armor, carrying a sword and a green fan. The wind deity is often depicted carrying on his back a large bag, which he can open to let out wind, and the thunder deity often carries on his back a number of drums, which he can strike to make thunder. According to a legend, little children are told to keep their fronts carefully covered because the thunder deity is always aiming for children's navels. Within the category of malevolent influences is a large group of devils having the generic name of *oni*, the representation of which is common. *Oni* have sharp claws, squarish heads, sharp teeth, and two horns, and on the last day of winter, with the ceremony called *oni tsuina* or *setsubun*, they are expelled from the houses by casting roasted black beans.

The vast field of religious motifs is more clearly comprehended when one realizes that it embraces a very great number of symbolical ornaments having Buddhist, Taoist, and Confucianist significance, such as the eight happy omens, the hundred antiques, the *vajra* or thunderbolt, the Buddhist jewel in a leaf-shaped halo of flames, and the many Taoist and Confucian immortals. In the sacred wheel of Buddha, or Buddhist Wheel of Law, the eight spokes represent the different stages of the Noble Eight-fold Path, which are: right beliefs, right aspirations, right means of livelihood, right acts, right endeavor, right mindfulness, right speech, and right concentration. Seen everywhere are the left-handed swastikas, called *manji*, meaning letter-ten-thousand or creation, which is the symbol of Buddhism, and the *tomoye*, the disc-shaped Shinto symbol of creation consisting of three intertwining forms resembling commas, taken from the Chinese sign around which are arranged the Eight Trigrams or *pa kua*.

NATURE SYMBOLISM

Since practically everything in Japan is given symbolic meaning, it follows that because of the Japanese love of nature, beautiful and thoughtful attributes have been applied to trees, plants, and flowers. A symbol of longevity is the *kiku* or chrysanthemum which, when represented with sixteen petals, is the official emblem of the Imperial family called the *kiku-no-go-mon*. When used as a crest or badge by other families or societies, the number of petals must be greater or less than sixteen. The Empress of Japan has an elegantly designed crest or *mon* consisting of three flowers and three leaves of the *kiri* or paulownia tree. A set of three lucky symbols that occurs prominently in all the arts is the *shochikubai* or pine-bamboo-plum. The pine is a symbol of devotion, because it is evergreen and its needles are usually in pairs, representing conjugal love, and it is also a symbol of longevity; the bamboo stands for devotion and strength, and the plum for perseverance, because its fragrant flowers come out in the early spring after withstanding the cold of winter. Seen often enough to be considered the national flower of Japan is the *sakura* or cherry blossom, which derives its name from Komo-Hana-no-Saku-ya-Hime, a legendary princess to whom Mount Fuji is dedicated; although it has no particular attribute, it expresses the beauty and charm of the Japanese countryside. The lovely flower that is emblematic of purity, wisdom, and Buddhahood is the *hasu* or lotus, invariably seen in its natural or artificial form on the altars of Buddhist temples, as well as in designs for articles used in the Buddhist service. The white lotus is symbolic of death, and since most funerals in Japan are conducted under Buddhist rites, the flower is associated with mournful occasions and therefore is seldom seen as a motif in articles for secular use or decoration.

In the whole realm of Japanese symbolism there is nothing more interesting than the horary and zodiacal characters in the form of animals that are used singly and in combinations. Besides the solar or Gregorian calendar adopted in 1868, there are two ancient calendars still in use in Japan, the lunar calendar which was introduced into Japan along with Chinese learning in the sixth century, and the zodiac calendar, also of Chinese origin. For a variety of reasons the farmers prefer, and still use, the old lunar calendar, which they follow for the sowing of seeds because it tells the climatic changes of the four seasons better than the solar calendar. Since the adoption of the zodiac calendar along with Chinese learning in ancient times, each year in history and each day of the year has had a zodiac sign assigned to it. In accordance with the Chinese custom of dividing the years into cycles of twelve, each year is named after one of the animals of the twelve Oriental signs of the zodiac. These animals are arranged in the cycle in the following order: rat, ox, tiger, hare, dragon, serpent, horse, sheep, monkey, cock, dog, and boar. Correlated with these are the ten trunks, making a reciprocal set of zodiac signs, so that each year in history and each day of the year has one sign of each set. The ten trunks are an arrangement of the years into cycles of ten each, with their names taken from the "five elements" in the following order: wood senior and junior, fire senior and junior, earth senior and junior, metal senior and junior, and water senior and junior.

From ancient China the Japanese adopted many traditions that survive to the present day, one of the more important and meaningful being the "five colors." The proper order of sequence of the five cardinal colors is: yellow, blue, red, white, and black. Each one of the five colors is mutually related in a significant manner to the five directions, the five seasons of time, the five virtues, and the five elements. The proper sequential arrangement of each set to conform to the sequence of the five colors, as well as with one another, is as follows: Direction—center, east, south, west, and north. Seasons of Time—*doyo* (each season has *doyo* consisting of eighteen days at its beginning), spring, summer, autumn, and winter. Virtue—faith, humanity, decorum, justice, and wisdom. Elements—earth, wood, fire, metal, and water. The symbolism attached to these important sets of five Oriental subjects has had a profound effect upon the cultural and legendary tradition of Japan, and their general or abstract principles are found associated in many respects with all phases of Japanese daily life.

III Painting

JAPANESE PAINTING had its beginning in the Asuka period (552-645) with the stimulus provided by the introduction of Chinese learning and the spread of Buddhism. These came by way of the Korean court, the channel through which Japan began to acquire new ideas from the flourishing arts of the Asiatic continent. The basic elements of Chinese art were accepted by the Japanese in principle, and were adapted, modified, and in some cases rejected, in order to conform to their own natural æsthetic expression. Since Buddhism gave the vital incentive to the development of culture by inspiring high ideals and encouraging art and literature, it followed that the earliest paintings had religious subjects. Many of these Buddhist paintings are extant and preserved in ancient temples and monasteries. Among these are the paintings on the doors and panels of the Golden Beetle miniature shrine in the Treasure Depository of the Horyuji temple near Nara. They are among the finest examples of the Asuka period.

THE EARLY CHINESE INFLUENCE

Buddhism continued to provide the principal themes for painting for the next seven hundred years, throughout the Asuka, Nara, Heian, and Kamakura periods. Because the Buddhist monasteries were the centers of culture, it was within their great walled compounds that this religious painting received its inspiration and was produced. The monks derived their creative impulse from great Chinese examples and placed the emphasis on representations of Buddhist divinities and the Buddhist Paradise. The artist-monks of the various monasteries created these paintings for use in their religious services and to spread the faith. Within the monastery buildings were enshrined the images, paintings, and other treasures for the edification of teachers and men of learning who came to these retreats for meditation or to devote themselves to a solitary and contemplative life. Many of these great monasteries were built on the summits or sides of mountains and were designed to conform with the beautiful and impressive natural surroundings. The often remote mountain sites afforded an ideal place for scholars to retire and read the sutras or create works of art. Although Buddhism long remained the chief inspiration in art, traces of secular art began to appear as early as the ninth century.

With the prosperity and luxury which developed in the beginning of the Fujiwara or Late Heian period (897-1185), there occurred a distinct trend away from the assimilation of the T'ang style to one of greater Japanese inspiration. As this movement became more firmly established and more purely Japanese in expression, even Buddhist subjects were frequently painted in a natural landscape setting of trees, rocks, and plants. The great houses of the Fujiwara aristocracy contained spacious apartments whose ceilings, sliding doors, partitions, and wall panels were embellished with beautiful paintings by a new class of secular artists. But Buddhist art did not lose strength or animation, because the great monasteries, with their increasing power and wealth, expended enormous sums to construct fine buildings and decorate their interiors with works of art.

In Buddhist art the iconography of the great divinities was a careful interpretation of the text of the scriptures. From the very beginnings of Buddhism in Japan, images of the *Yakushi Nyorai* or Healing Buddha occupied the central altar in many great temples. Next in importance, the *Bosatsu Kannon* or Compassionate One who alleviates the sufferings of the believer, and Miroku, the Buddha of the next world who brings salvation to the believer, were the most popular among the people at large. Very few examples survive of the numerous paintings and tapestry hangings which decorated the great temples of Nara in the eighth century, when Buddhism

Right: Horokaku mandara: The Buddha and Attendant Divinities. *Color and gold on silk. Fujiwara period, eleventh century. Smithsonian Institution, Freer Gallery of Art, Washington, D.C.*

Below: Nika Byakudo, *or* White Path Crossing Two Rivers, *an allegory of the Jodo sect, showing Amida Buddha about to greet the soul of the true believer if he successfully walks the White Path without falling into the river of fire representing passion or the river with many reptiles representing greed. Color and gold leaf on silk. Kamakura period (1185–1333). Seattle Art Museum.*

was the state religion. One of the few is the exquisite little figure of *Kichijo-ten,* goddess of beauty and fecundity, in the Yakushi-ji, from the end of the Nara period. Still completely imbued with the classic perfection of Chinese prototypes, this is no provincial interpretation but one fully informed with the worldly grace of the T'ang civilization.

At the beginning of the ninth century a new type of religious painting followed the founding of the esoteric Buddhist sects of the Tendai and Shingon, in which their complex symbolism was rigidly represented in pictures and images. The

Nyoirin Kannon. *Ink, color, silver, and gold on silk. Heian period, twelfth century. Smithsonian Institution, Freer Gallery of Art, Washington, D.C.*

Suyamadeva (Emmaten) and Two Attendants, *and (below)* Yamaraya (Emma-o) and Two Attendants. *Color and gold on silk. Early Kamakura period, thirteenth century. Smithsonian Institution, Freer Gallery of Art, Washington, D.C.*

Japanese painter adhered to all the details imposed on him by this mystical iconography of Indian origin, with its pantheon of numerous and varied divinities symbolizing divine power and theological conceptions. To certain divinities he imparted a feeling of tranquil beauty and serenity unruffled by cares, while others appear imposingly powerful and dynamic. Among the esoteric paintings of highest religious importance were the mandara produced under Shingon influence, graphic presentations of the universe in its two aspects, the spiritual cycle and the material cycle, understood by the initiated only.

But with the triumph of the Fujiwara family and suspension of relations with China, there came into being such works as the large eleventh century mandara of the Daigo-ji pagoda, near Kyoto. There, the mandara—a celestial hierarchy of gods portrayed on lotus seats—is treated in so familiar a way that one feels the esoteric iconography had by then become thoroughly assimilated by the Japanese artists.

During the course of the eleventh century the new sect called Jodo, which proclaimed faith in the Buddha Amida, the Merciful One, opened a way of salvation for the common man. The doctrine offered the painters a new iconography of the descent of Amida, who promised to take the faithful believer at the time of his death to Paradise in the Western Heavens. The most complete monument of the cult of Amida is the Phoenix Hall, called Hoodo, in the Byodoin temple at Uji, the central building of which is filled with paintings. It contains nine versions of the descent of Amida, in one of which, instead of the esoteric images of the previous century, the divinity is surrounded by music-making attendants, or *raigo*; below them is a naturalistic landscape suggesting the region of Kyoto. A more personal image is *Amida Welcoming the Faithful to Paradise*, in the central part of an eleventh century triptych in the Hokkeji at Nara. The divinity, seated on a red lotus, is seen in a perfectly symmetrical composition gazing directly at the spectator's eyes: the unmystical face and the delicate drawing of the brilliant red robe create a devotional icon of deeply moving spirituality.

Such paintings, which were intended to establish a spiritual bond between the compassionate divinity and the believer at the hour of his death, played a profound role at the latter's departure from the material world. A later, more humanized conception of the same theme, and one of the largest of such scenes, is the early thirteenth-century *Descent of Amida across the Mountains*, in the Zenrinji at Kyoto. The golden-bodied celestial apparition of Amida emerges, like a moonrise, from behind a mountainous, typically Japanese landscape, in which two small Bodhisattvas and some tiny attendant figures symmetrically arranged combine earthly and heavenly motifs.

In some of these paintings one sees the lovely Japanese landscape at sunset, which suggests Amida's Paradise in the West, the Land of Perfect Bliss; the attendant figure kneeling at Amida's left is the compassionate Kannon. The idea of a spiritual uniting tie is also expressed among pious Buddhists at the moment of death by the custom of holding five strands of colored silk fastened to the joined hands of an image of Amida, in order to be drawn up by the Buddha into the Western Paradise. But in contrast to these enchanting scenes depicting the infinite beauties of a paradise designed to attract people to the faith, the Amidists did not neglect to frighten people with hideous graphic representations of the nether

Above: Toba Sojo, *1053-1140: Detail from the scroll-painting called the* Caricature of Birds and Beasts, *or* Animals at Play, *painted in ink on paper. Kozanji temple, Kyoto.*

Left: A raigo *showing Amida Buddha descending from the Western Paradise to receive the departing soul. The painting was used in the so-called* raigo *ceremonies in Buddhist temples. Gold and color on silk. Fourteenth-fifteenth century. Seattle Art Museum.*

Section from the Jigoku Zoshi, *or* Hell Scroll, *traditionally attributed to Mitsunaga, depicting the fate of various sinners. This detail shows Buddhist priests who disobeyed their vows being driven into the "Shrieking-sound Hell" by horse-headed demons. Color on paper. Kamakura period, about 1200. Seattle Art Museum.*

world, the world of future punishment imagined as below the earth. According to Buddhist teaching, the six realms to which spirits of the dead can transmigrate are those of the infernal hells, of ghosts, of beasts, of demons, of humans, and of deities, all of which are vividly described in the religious paintings of the time.

The painters of the Fujiwara period were men of great learning, equally able to produce masterpieces of religious art for Buddhist monasteries, and secular art for the æsthetic appreciation of the nobility. Closely associated with the art of painting was the practice of calligraphy, which exerted a powerful influence on pictorial art. Calligraphy in Japan, as in China, is one of the great accomplishments, with no counterpart in the West. A skilled calligrapher is essentially an artist who has gone through the most strenuous training in brushwork, design, and composition. Consequently, an appreciation of the written character is essential in order to understand the Japanese philosophy of taste. Each stroke of the character is meticulously placed and must be so drawn as to reflect the beauty of a thought or a stanza of poetry; the abstract patterns of the strokes communicate feeling. The finished expression of line in calligraphy was a fully developed art which, in literary composition, paralleled the pictorial art of narrative scroll-painting toward the end of the Fujiwara period.

Example of fukinuki-yatai *(roofless house); detail from the* Kasuga Gongen Reigenki, *a picture scroll depicting the history of the Kasuga shrine. Kamakura period (1185-1333). Kasuga shrine, Nara.*

Example of the kasumi *technique, from the* Kitano Temman-gu Engi, *by Nobuzane Fujiwara, 1176-1268, a picture scroll illustrating incidents in the life of Tenjin-Sama, to whose spirit the Kitano shrine is dedicated. Kitano shrine. Kyoto.*

NARRATIVE SCROLLS

Scroll-painting, called *e-maki*, or makimono, which received its inspiration from literature, originated in the idea of illustrating historical accounts, stories, poems, and popular narratives. A makimono is a horizontal hand-scroll having pictures of successive scenes arranged in chronological sequence. There are two kinds of makimono, one having continuous or successive illustrations, and the other having individual pictures alternating with portions of a text. The scroll of paper is generally about twelve inches deep and from ten to fifty feet in length. It is affixed to a rod at one end to facilitate rolling and unrolling, and the pictures are viewed from right to left like the text. Ranging in treatment from the poetical to the realistic, many different themes are represented in scroll-paintings: religion, romances, children's stories, historical events, popular customs, famous views, and historic places. A great number of Japanese scroll-paintings are executed in a peculiar perspective called *fukinuki yatai*, or roofless houses. This unique style of illustration gives an oblique view from above with the roof omitted, permitting an unobstructed picture of the interior. The term *monogatari-e*, or story-picture, is given to scroll-paintings of pictures alternating with text, thus serving as a visual realization of the literature. One of the most famous extant examples of this style is the *Genji Monogatari* scroll of the great literary romance of the *Tale of Genji*. The work is attributed to Fujiwara Takayoshi, who was active during the middle of the twelfth century. Actually it consists of two scrolls with excerpts from the fifty-four chapters of this famous novel written by Lady Murasaki in the eleventh century. The story portrays the elegant and romantic atmosphere of the Heian court life and the dramatic passages through the seasons of the year of the courtship and sorrows of Prince Genji, who is deeply in love with Murasaki-No-Ue. All of these scenes are viewed obliquely from above in the usual pictorial device of *fukinuki yatai*.

In contrast to the rich and brilliant colors of the *Genji Monogatari* scroll, which are in perfect harmony with its delicate brushwork, many scroll-paintings are in black and white. An outstanding example of the latter is the *Caricature of Birds and*

Right: A Zen painting by Sesshu, 1420-1506: Daruma (Dharma) and His Disciple Eka (Hui-K'o). *Dharma, an Indian Buddhist priest, is the reputed founder of the Zen sect. Sainenji temple, Aichi prefecture.*

Quail, by Tosa Mitsuoki, 1617-1691. Tokyo National Museum.

Beasts, or *Animals at Play*, a notable achievement in the technique of independent line. It is generally attributed to a nobleman-priest, the abbot Toba Sojo, 1053-1140. In this scroll are depicted animated and spirited rabbits, foxes, monkeys, and frogs frolicking at a picnic. There are four of these amusing and witty scrolls, believed to represent a satire on the behavior of human beings. It is surmised to be a pictorial caricature of the activities of members of the upper classes, who were undoubtedly recognized by the artist's contemporaries.

Although many of the scroll-paintings of the Heian and later periods were religious in subject, the principal usage was for the illustration of literature. Creative writing in Japan was closely associated with scroll literature and much of it was produced solely for that purpose. Picture-scroll art reached its zenith in the Kamakura period (1185-1333), which is noted

Right: Kakemono, in the Suiboku style, attributed to Kitsuzan Mincho, 1352-1431: Hermitage by the Mountain Brook, *ink on paper. Konchi-in monastery, Kyoto.*

Detail from a makimono by Sesshu, 1420–1506: Landscape, *ink and light color on paper. Collection of Motomichi Mori, Yamaguchi.*

for its great number and variety of makimono. These portray a wide range of subjects and present a graphic illustration of feudal life in medieval times. A number of religious scrolls depict the history of famous Buddhist temples and Shinto shrines and the lives of important priests and holy men. Most of the famous temples and shrines have preserved among their treasures a makimono which records its sacred beginning or the religious life of its founder. Other Kamakura scrolls illustrate romantic military stories and battle scenes, and many are beautifully embellished sutras or scriptures. The mode of living and fashions in dress are colorfully depicted in these priceless records, as are the scenes from popular literary works. The technique used in the picture scrolls is a purely Japanese manifestation called Yamato-e, as distinguished from the various styles of Chinese origin.

THE "YAMATO-E" STYLE

Yamato-e, literally Japanese painting, is the most distinctive Japanese style of painting, without counterpart in any other art. The earliest known mention of the word *Yamato-e* is in a text in the fourth year of Chotoku, corresponding to A.D. 999. Almost all scroll-paintings were executed in the Yamato-e style, in which human figures, houses, trees, and other objects are outlined with hair-thin lines and filled in with bright but harmonious colors, in contrast to paintings done with weaker colors or in ink monochrome. In many of the scroll-paintings with illustrated narratives the transitions from one scene to another and the passage of time are described with characters written in a beautiful, often very expressive calligraphy inserted between the pictures. Sometimes the stories which naturally contain the shifting of scenes and the passage of time resort to a device technically called *kasumi*, which is peculiar to the Yamato-e style of painting. The literal meaning of *kasumi* is mist or light fog; but in scroll-painting, *kasumi* means a special treatment of space between pictures to signify a change of location or passage of time. It consists of a pattern of several long streaks, or it may be a well-balanced semi-circular form.

The *kasumi* design is taken from the natural atmospheric formations which are so typical of Japan's moisture-laden climate, with long horizontal sweeps of dense mist cutting across the sky. A beautiful example of *kasumi* in the Japanese countryside occurs at twilight in the springtime, when it is seen in the form of white streaks lying heavily at the foot of a mountain. Scenery of this nature reflects a feeling of solitude and tranquillity. Occasionally the *kasumi* device is seen in other works by the artists of the Yamato-e school, such as on folding screens. The Yamato-e painters received their inspiration from the things closely associated with the everyday lives of the Japanese.

34

Kakemono by Tensho Shubun, c. 1415-1460: Before the House of a Recluse, *ink on paper. Seikado Collection, Tokyo.*

Kakemono by Sesshu, 1420-1506: Winter Landcape, *ink on paper. Tokyo National Museum.*

One of forty-nine kakemono by Kano Motonobu, 1476–1559, that were originally mounted on fusuma depicting landscapes, flowers, and birds; ink and light color on paper. Reiun-in Monastery, Kyoto.

A kakemono by Kano Masanobu, 1434–1530. The subject is Chou Mao-shu, a Chinese Confucian scholar, viewing lotus flowers. Painted in color on paper. Collection of Tomijiro Nakumura, Tokyo.

THE ZEN INFLUENCE

In the Kamakura period the Zen sect of Buddhism arose in Japan, and its prosperity and progress was especially significant among the warrior class. The influence of Zen upon Japan and her people has been so pervasive that it is actually a fundamental part of her culture. The word *Zen* means meditation, and Zen differs from other Buddhist sects in not relying upon formal doctrines or the worship of icons. Instead, followers of Zen are supposed to enlighten themselves by intuitive cognition and meditation in penetrating the meaning of the universe. Because images of Buddhist divinities did not form an all-important part of Zen teaching, their religious art consists chiefly of *chinso*, or portraits of great priests. Another form of Zen painting is the *doshaku-ga*, or a painting illustrating the deeds of famous Zen priests or portraying certain natural scenes or subjects associated with the pursuit of enlightenment. With the spread of Zen in Japan there appeared a demand for Chinese paintings of the Sung and Yuan dynasties, the style of which was adapted by Zen artists to their own particular outlook and taste. These painters usually specialized, some producing only certain kinds of flowers, others devoting themselves to trees, bamboo, and religious or secular subjects. From this dependence on Chinese models, a new style developed in the beginning of the Muromachi period (1338-1573), known as *suiboku*, or black painting.

THE SUIBOKU STYLE

Suiboku painting gives an entirely different value to the meaning of line. In Suiboku painting line is an essential element, marked by great individuality. In contrast to the simple contour lines of the Yamato-e style, which may or may not enclose color, the line in Suiboku varies with the slow or rapid strokes of the brush. The line thus becomes the essential element of expression, with infinite variations in the tone of black taking the place of color. The development of Japanese Suiboku art was due to the Zen artists, who saw a spiritual harmony in black and white and described all colors by black, in accordance with the teachings of Zen Buddhism. Since Suiboku did not follow any prescribed conventions of composition, the artists were able to convey their spiritual thoughts and present a visual conception of the unity of the individual with all nature. The inherent Japanese sensitivity to the beauty of nature, coupled with Zen teachings about the universe and the spirit that permeates everything, heightened æsthetic appreciation as well as spiritual enlightenment. In the latter part of the fourteenth century Suiboku art was greatly stimulated by the work of Kitsuzan Mincho, who was the head priest of the Tofukuji monastery in Kyoto. Landscape became a popular subject, and at about this time poetic inscriptions were beginning to make their appearance on the hanging picture scroll, or kakemono.

Landscape and Flowers, *four of a set of sixteen* fusuma *by Kano Eitoku, 1543-1590; painted in ink on paper.* Tenkyu-in *monastery, Kyoto.*

The traditional Japanese kakemono, or hanging scroll, had its origin in China, where it is mentioned in records as early as the fourth century. It is a painting on silk or paper mounted on a vertical scroll, often with strips of silk brocade around its edges to frame the painting. The whole is in turn backed with heavy paper to stiffen it. The top of the kakemono is folded over to give it strength, and to this fold are attached two narrow strips of silk called *futai*, which hang down several inches. The bottom of the kakemono has a rod, usually tipped with ivory, which serves to roll it up. A particular kind of kakemono called *shi-ga-jiku*, or *shi-jiku*, has a poem or verse inscribed in calligraphic characters on the upper part of the painting proper. The *shi-ga-jiku* was fashionable among Zen priests around the fourteenth and fifteenth centuries. The written characters frequently comprise a poetical description of the painting or complimentary remarks about the artist or his work. Since it was the custom to change the kakemono frequently and replace it with one appropriate to the season or occasion, it was rolled up and placed in a box especially designed to hold it. The box was then stored in the godown, or store house, along with the many other kakemono and household possessions.

The kakemono is hung in a special place in the house, called the tokonoma, where its beauty can be most appreciated and enjoyed. The appropriate times for changing the kakemono are on ceremonial occasions and with the advent of the new seasons of the year. Especially important occasions for the display of symbolic kakemono are the *go-sekku*, or Five Seasons' Offerings. These popular family festival days are the Early Herb Festival in January, the Peach-Blossom Festival in March, the Iris Festival in May, the Star Festival in July, and the Chrysanthemum Festival in September. The most popular are the Peach-Blossom, Iris, and Star festivals, around each of which has grown a wealth of interesting traditions, legends, and stories. The Peach-Blossom is popularly known as Dolls', or Girls', Festival, when ceremonial dolls in traditional and ancient costume are displayed. Since peach blossoms symbolize happiness in marriage, pictures are chosen that are representative of feminine charms and beauty, especially those depicting young girls famed in classical literature.

The Iris Festival, or Boys' Festival, is appropriate for displaying a kakemono depicting the deeds of a traditional Chinese or Japanese hero or other epic subject taken from classical literature or history. The Star Festival, which is more popularly known as Tanabata, was originally fixed for the seventh night of the seventh month by the lunar calendar, but in most places where the Gregorian calendar is used it is celebrated on the night of July 7. It is the most romantic of all the annual occasions and owes its inception to an ancient popular belief that two lovely stars, set far apart on either side of the Milky Way, have a joyous union on that single night of each year. The most important occasion in Japan is the New Year Festival, which is celebrated on the first three days of the year. Special preparations are made in every household, and kakemono having pine trees or other pictures characteristic of this time are hung in the tokonoma. For the many occasions throughout the year which call for a kakemono depicting a symbolic subject, large houses with numerous rooms often have a few hundred hanging scrolls stored in the godown.

SHUBUN, SESSHU

In the early part of the fifteenth century Suiboku landscape painting received a great impetus from the work of Tensho

Shubun. As a priest in the Shokokuji, a Zen temple in Kyoto, Shubun studied painting under Josetsu, another priest in the same temple. He raised the Suiboku style of painting to its highly developed form and was the first of this Chinese school to be appointed as official painter to the Shogun. Active from about 1415 to 1460, he is regarded as founder of this school. Many extant paintings are traditionally attributed to Shubun, as well as some large folding screens. The principles of Zen in painting and a graphic illustration of the Zen vision of the universe are reflected in the great works of Sesshu, who was a pupil of Shubun. Sesshu, 1420-1506, was born in Bitchu province, now Okayama prefecture, and at an early age went to Kyoto, where he became a priest in the Shokokuji temple. He is considered to be the greatest master of the Suiboku school, under whose leadership this black-ink type of painting

was perfected into a truly Japanese style. In 1467 he went to China, where he studied landscape painting, and upon his return about a year later he went to the Unkokuji temple in Yamaguchi prefecture, where he remained most of the rest of his life. While studying in China he achieved great proficiency in landscape painting and was determined to make the natural scenery of China his master. With his ability to understand the elements of this Suiboku style in China, and with his appreciation of nature as seen through the eyes of a Zen priest, he became the foremost artist of the Japanese landscape. The black line in Sesshu's work is the expression of great talent, in which he interpreted both line and color in various tone degrees of black. The works of Sesshu include many subjects and there are numerous extant examples which bear his signature or are attributed to him. His landscapes of the four

Plum Tree and Birds, *set of four* fusuma *by Kano Sanraku, 1559-1635; color on paper. Tenkyu-in monastery, Kyoto.*

Fishing with Cormorants, *one of a pair of six-panel screens by Kano Tan-yu, 1602-1674; color on paper.*
Okura Shuko-kan Museum, Tokyo.

seasons and his folding screens with flowers and birds are exquisite works that reflect his Zen outlook upon the world.

THE TOSA SCHOOL

The prestige of the Chinese style of Suiboku painting continued to exert its force during the opening years of the Muromachi period (1338-1573). For the first sixty years of this period the Ashikaga Shoguns were involved in warfare and in numerous intrigues among the local feudal barons. However, despite a country torn with strife and turmoil, the arts began to flourish in a far greater way than ever before. The new warrior class of feudal lords had risen to power and wealth, creating a demand for works of art that would represent their newly acquired riches with colorful beauty. Two famous schools of painting had their origin in the Muromachi period: one is the Tosa school, and the other the Kano.

The style of painting of the Tosa school is in the manner of the Yamato-e. The leading master of this school during the Muromachi era was Tosa Mitsunobu, 1434-1525, the son of Tosa Mitsuhiro. Tosa-school painters enjoyed innumerable favors and commissions from the nobility, gaining prestige from the fact that many of them belonged to noble families.

Appreciation of art and the other branches of cultural activity had been the chief pastime of the aristocracy since the Heian period and continued on through the Kamakura and Muromachi eras. It is therefore not surprising that Mitsunobu was appointed the chief artist of the Shogun's government and also held the position of head of the official bureau of painting in the Imperial court in 1469. Other members of the Tosa family were also court artists and in turn served as heads of this bureau. A great many of the most famous scroll-paintings depicting the history of certain temples in Kyoto were the work of Mitsunobu. These scrolls were executed in the typical Tosa style of Yamato-e with precise contour lines filled in with serene and subtle colors. Among the treasures of the famous Kitano Tenjin shrine in the weaving quarter of Kyoto are fourteen scrolls of the illustrated history of the shrine. Two of these scrolls were done by Tosa Yukimitsu in the fourteenth century, and three are by Tosa Mitsuoki, 1617-1691. Talented painters of this school created many of the beautiful and rare scrolls depicting the religious and secular history of Japan. The popularity of the Tosa school gradually declined with the diminishing power of the monasteries and the nobles who were its patrons. Its place of prominence gave way to the Kano school, although its style continued to influence subsequent schools. In conformity with the established

Spring and Autumn, *a pair of six-panel folding screens by Kano Hisanobu, active early in the eighteenth century. Color on paper. Author's collection.*

Japanese tradition of inheritance by a chosen member of the family, or by recourse to adoption, the two schools of Tosa and Kano became allied to each other with the marriage of the daughter of Tosa Mitsunobu to Kano Motonobu.

THE GREAT KANO DECORATIONS

The Kano school had its beginnings in the Muromachi period, and in the succeeding Momoyama era attained a pre-eminent position in Japanese painting which continued to the end of the Tokugawa Shogunate. The paintings of the Kano school perfectly reflect an indigenous style which played a decisive role in shaping the typically Japanese æsthetic. The great influence of the Kano school was also due to the fact that many of its painters were officially active either in the service of the Tokugawa government or of feudal lords. These positions, together with the social prestige derived from such service, insured the continuing success of this new hereditary academy of painting. The founder of the school was Kano Masanobu, 1434-1530, who was born in Kyoto of an aristocratic family. He studied painting under Shubun, and while treating the traditional Chinese subjects, gave a purely Japanese inflection to Suiboku art, freeing it from Zen mysticism. His

work appealed to the taste of the military for its beautiful interpretation of nature. The Kano school became firmly established both æsthetically and socially by Masanobu's son Kano Motonobu, 1476-1559, who revived the lyricism inherent in the Japanese tradition. Motonobu lived in Kyoto and served the Ashikaga Shogun as court painter. He was a skilled painter in black and white as well as a superb colorist. He improved the technique of the Kano school by applying to *Suiboku* the traditional elements of the Yamato-e style as interpreted by the Tosa school. Motonobu was a master who excelled in all the categories of painting, including scrolls, landscapes, figures, and flowers-and-birds, which he produced in a charming native manner. The third illustrious member of the Kano family, who also contributed greatly to the art of the Momoyama period, was Kano Eitoku, 1543-1590, a grandson of Motonobu. Although Motonobu had a brother and three sons who preceded Eitoku, they did not achieve the latter's fame. Eitoku was the most distinguished painter of the Momoyama period, serving as painter to the great military feudal lords Oda Nobunaga and Hideyoshi (Plate 1).

The style of the Kano school is a combination of the Yamato-e and the Suiboku styles. Yamato-e with its delicate and precise black brush lines filled in with dense rich colors was the contributing factor which produced the detail and effective color harmony. The Suiboku style embodied the strong black brush strokes of monochrome paintings with their simple forms of Zen expression. In Kano the two styles were skillfully blended to produce impressive compositions of great splendor with high color filling the spaces within heavy black lines. The subjects include landscapes, figures, birds, plants, flowers, and scenes of everyday life. Kano was monumental decoration typifying the Momoyama period, an age of luxury and splendor in which the Zen principles of simplicity gave way to a rich and colorful style of painting. These beautiful and vigorous paintings were produced with gold backgrounds on folding screens and on the wall panels and sliding doors of great houses. The paintings reflected the spirit of the feudal families and their desire for colorful decorative appointments that were inspired by nature. Especially remarkable was the development of domestic interior decoration for the great private military strongholds, the castles built both as fortresses and as residences for the feudal lords. These castles were impressive structures with high and massive stonework, white-walled donjons, and surrounding moats. The first of these great citadels was built by Oda Nobunaga in 1576 at Azuchi on Lake Biwa. All the panel spaces within the many rooms were lavishly decorated with paintings. Within a few years almost every feudal domain had its great castle, which created an urgent demand for paintings to fill the proper interior spaces.

The splendor of the interior decorations of the Azuchi castle as well as of Osaka and Fushimi castles and the Juraku mansion built by Hideyoshi may still be appreciated, as many sections of them today form part of certain famous temples in Kyoto. The magnificent buildings of the Nishi Honganji temple in Kyoto, for instance, were formerly the residence of Fushimi castle and are representative of the taste of this period. Every part of the interior is elaborately decorated with gold or with black or red lacquer, and the ceiling panels, sliding doors, and wall panels were painted by masters of the Kano family or its school. The beautiful Nijo castle in Kyoto, which is a striking example of the splendor of these times, was built by the first Tokugawa Shogun to serve as his residence on the occasion of his visits to Kyoto. Its well-preserved buildings are veritable treasures, with their interiors entirely decorated with some of the greatest works of Kano Tan-yu and other members of the Kano family or Kano-school artists.

From early times Japanese secular painting has been chiefly used for the decoration of interior panel spaces, while the work produced on kakemono has been reserved for the tokonoma. Religious paintings were used for the same purpose in Buddhist monasteries. Therefore it was only natural for the great houses of the nobles and feudal chiefs to have the architectural spaces filled in with paintings. The name *Sho-Heki-Ga* is com-

monly applied as a collective term to include the paintings on wall spaces, sliding doors, and screens. It is because of the peculiar interior appointments of Japanese domestic architecture that the paintings of greatest importance appear in these forms. The sliding doors, called *fusuma* (Plate 3), are movable partitions made of a wooden frame covered on both sides with heavy paper. They are generally in sets of four and serve as partitions between rooms or between a room and a corridor. *Fusuma* are fairly wide, and the obverse and reverse sides form an important part of the interior architectural surfaces for paintings. These *fusuma* are beautiful decorative appointments, especially with the rich and colorful paintings in the style of the Kano school executed in sequential compositions.

The splendor of the Momoyama period can be further witnessed in magnificent paintings on large folding screens. They were just as important to the sumptuous interior decoration

Above: One of a pair of six-panel screens by Tawaraya Sotatsu, 1589-1651, depicting a scene from the Tale of Genji; color on paper. Seikado Foundation, Tokyo.

Right: Pink and White Plum Blossoms, by Ogata Korin, 1658-1716. One of a pair of two-panel screens: color on paper. Collection of Yoshitaka Tsugaru, Tokyo.

Pine Trees in Snow, *a pair of six-panel screens by Maruyama Okyo, 1733-1795; ink and light on paper. Collection of Takakimi Mitsui, Tokyo.*

as the sliding doors and wall panels. The folding screens, or *byobu*, appeared in great numbers during this era and the subsequent Tokugawa period, and their exquisite beauty contributed to the sumptuous surroundings and reflected the affluence of the owner (Plate 4). The dimensions of the usual type of six-paneled screen are about five feet high and twelve feet long, affording a most suitable space for the bold and splendid decorative compositions of the Kano school. Many of the greatest works of the Kano family were executed on screens. On a large scale, boldly depicted, were magnificent landscapes, plum trees with blossoms, ancient pine trees, fantastic rock formations, and an endless variety of brilliantly colored birds. Many majestic Kano compositions on screens are executed without a naturalistic background. This sense of abstraction greatly enhances the principal subject, undisturbed by any unnecessary details. A subject such as a gnarled and ancient pine tree is treated independently of its natural setting, in a portrayal so impressive that it has almost the effect of a physical shock. It causes a natural inward impulse to deep thought since one cannot tell whether the pines are reaching out over the sea or are on a remote mountaintop. The compositions of a pair of screens may be executed either independently or as a sequential subject. In the one form it is represented

by an independent design on each screen, and in the other by a matching or related design, or a continuous design which extends across the full length of both screens of the pair. Many of the most beautiful screens are executed on a gold-leaf background, which produces a rich and elegant contrast with the strong colors. The manner in which the rather large leaves of gold are applied produces a beautiful gradation of tone commonly called *genji-gumo*, or golden clouds. The gradual transition from one hue or shade of gold to another gives a mellowness and a feeling of three-dimensional depth. Kano Eitoku was the fountainhead of this period of Japanese painting, in which nature is interpreted in such a vigorous and elegant manner. Even in his day he was considered the greatest painter of the times, enjoying the patronage of Nobunaga and Hideyoshi, and he and his followers held the highest artistic and social positions.

Among other members of the Kano family who produced great works are Eitoku's oldest son, Kano Mitsunobu, 1565-1608, and his second son, Kano Takanaobu, 1571-1618, who became official painter to the Imperial court. This office had formerly been held by members of the Tosa family when Tosa had been the favored school. When the Tokugawa Shogunate assumed the supreme rule and selected Edo as the seat of government, many Kano-school artists went there to live and work. The city of Kyoto nevertheless remained the seat of the Imperial court and center of traditional culture, and the removal of the centralized government did not hinder the progress of the arts in Kyoto. In this era they flourished and reached greater heights. The two most distinguished members of the Kano family to remain in Kyoto, who produced some of the greatest paintings of the time, were Kano Sanraku, 1559-1635, and his son-in-law Kano Sansetsu, 1589-1651. With the rapid development of the city of Edo, the ever-increasing demand for decorative paintings for the huge new houses of the daimyo afforded ample opportunity for continuance of the Kano school. It was therefore only natural that one member of the family, Kano Tan-yu, 1602-1674, should have become the most famous and most influential artist of the Edo period (Plate 10). Tan-yu studied painting under his father, Takanobu, and after moving to Edo he was honored by an appointment as painter-in-ordinary to the Tokugawa Shogunate.

The year 1615, when Tokugawa Ieyasu was appointed Shogun, marks the beginning of the Edo or Tokugawa regime, which lasted for over two hundred and fifty years under its highly organized feudal system. The new city of Edo grew to tremendous proportions and with it a new order of society and culture was established around the Shogun's court. This new order, which developed with the many changes of the times, had its beginning in the Momoyama period and was fully advanced in these early years of the seventeenth century. Within the framework of this feudal system the new order was established mainly from the shift of provincial powers, the redistribution of many fiefs, and the spread of financial power to the merchants and traders. The rise of the merchant class to a position of wealth provided an ever-expanding demand for works of art, and stimulated a greater appreciation of them. The influence of the Kano school now was as great as it had been in the preceding Momoyama period or possibly greater. With the patronage of the Shogunate, the Kano school was securely established. It is stated that Tan-yu was only sixteen or seventeen years of age when he received his appointment, and when he was twenty he was given a house by the Shogun. The dwelling was located just outside the Kaji-bashi Gate of the great Edo castle.

Other illustrious Kano-school painters of the Edo period were Kano Naonobu, younger brother of Kano Tan-yu; Kano Hisanobu, who flourished in the early years of the eighteenth century and became head of the Kano family in 1743; and Kano Eigaku, who achieved fame in the first half of the nineteenth century (Plate 7).

Landscape with Figures, *by Ike-no-Taiga, 1723-1776, from a set of ten* fusuma; *ink and color on paper. Henjoko-in monastery, Wakayama.*

SOTATSU, KORIN, AND THE NEW REALISM

Painting in the Edo period reached a climax in the early years of the seventeenth century in the work of Tawaraya Sotatsu, 1589-1651, and Ogata Korin, 1658-1716. Sotatsu, who lived in Kyoto, was a high-ranking Buddhist monk who attracted the attention of the emperor Go-mizunoo and thus gained a high reputation at the court. His work is essentially a revival of the old Yamato-e style, strongly influenced by the work of Kano Eitoku. His flowers-and-bird compositions and classical figures, in colors of wonderful brilliance against flat backgrounds of gold, are full of charm and elegance. Ogata Korin, who also worked in Kyoto, rose to fame during the Genroku era (1688-1704), which was the most prosperous period under the Tokugawa Shogunate. Korin first excelled in making spirited designs for pottery, and then turned to painting. His many sketches from nature, especially of birds and flowers, became powerfully stylized in his finished paintings. In bold compositions and rich colors, Korin created some of Japan's most beautiful masterpieces on large screens. The decorative style of Sotatsu and Korin, with its high degree of realism, always based upon subjects from nature, was the foundation of the new art of the Edo period.

Realism in painting was also especially important in the style of the Shijo-Maruyama school. Maruyama Okyo, 1733-1795, was born in Tamba province, the son of a farmer, and moved to Kyoto at an early age. He studied under the master of the Kano school and later studied the realistic paintings of the Sung and Yuan dynasties. His treatment of rocks, trees, plants, flowers, and birds is very true to nature, with almost scientific precision. This school of realistic painting, unconcerned with either metaphysical abstractions or bold stylizations, was enthusiastically appreciated by the people of Kyoto, where it ultimately became the dominant style. This naturalism was further developed by Matsumura Goshun, 1752-1811, founder of the Shijo school. Goshun was born in Kyoto, where he studied poetry and painting under Buson of the Nanga school, and after the death of Buson he became associated with Okyo. He softened the impact of the latter's realism in gentle, intimate landscapes. The style of the Shijo school is thus based on the best elements of the work of Buson and Okyo. Since this is one of the most important schools of painting in the latter part of the Edo and early Meiji periods, it produced many of the most distinguished artists of that time.

After centuries of war and political turmoil, peace finally prevailed under the domination of the Tokugawa regime. This state of quiet and freedom from disturbance enabled men to pursue the enlightenment of spiritual truth and knowledge. It stimulated men's desire to paint for the pleasure of diversion

in an atmosphere of unclouded tranquillity. The intellectual movement which appeared in the Genroku era was in reality a return to Confucianism. During this time the commoners became prosperous and wealthy, and were free to devote leisure hours to cultural pursuits. Great playwrights and novelists were inspired by this Confucian learning, and the ethical teachings of Chinese sages were prevalent in all classes of society. Chinese paintings of the Ming and Ch'ing dynasties were imported into Japan and were greatly admired.

THE NANGA SCHOOL OF LITERATI

Many of these paintings were brought in by Chinese artists, priests, and other learned men when they visited the city of Nagasaki, which was the only port open to foreign intercourse.

Tea and Wine Parties, *a six-panel screen by Yosa-no-Busan,*
1716-1783; color on a satin-weave silk. Collection of Tatsujiro
Hashimoto, Tokyo.

Right: Sketches of Insects and Fishes,
from an album by Watanabe Kazan,
1793-1841; color on silk. Collection of
Junzo Kosaka, Tokyo.

Sketches from the Boat Window, *from an album by Tanomura Chikuden, 1777-1835; in ink and light color on paper. Collection of Komakichi Tamura, Osaka.*

The school of painting which developed from these circumstances is known as Nanga, as it was called in China, or sometimes by its Japanese name of Bunjin-Ga. The Nanga school had its provenance in southern China in the Yuan dynasty and continued through the Ming and early Ch'ing periods. It is actually an art of amateurs, as opposed to the northern Chinese school, which is represented by the works of academic painters. The Nanga school was founded by men of letters who were distinguished in verse and prose, as well as in ethics and the sciences. Each painter worked in his own individual style and pursued this artistic field for his own enjoyment and satisfaction. Many of these literati became masters of the art and attained a certain place in the history of Chinese painting. In Japan the artists who are responsible for the development of this school of painting are Ike-no-Taiga, or Taigado, 1723-1776, and Yosa-no-Buson, 1716-1783. Taiga was chiefly a landscape painter, while Buson, who was a famous poet, portrayed nature so closely in his work that observers were astonished by his realism. There arose a great number of Nanga-school painters in the Edo period, each one creating his own compositions or portrayals to his own taste without regard for any of the conventional or traditional styles. Toward the end of the Edo period many brilliant painters appeared, the most noted among them being Tanomura Chikuden, 1777-1835, and Watanabe Kazan. Chikuden gained great fame as a Nanga landscape painter, while Kazan, who was learned in Confucianism, excelled not only in landscape but also in flower-and-bird compositions and figures.

The Nanga school of painting continued to flourish after the twilight of the Edo period and on through the Meiji era. Among the many artists who distinguished themselves during these times was Tomioka Tessai, 1836-1924. Tessai's life-span covered those eventful and anxious years which witnessed the breakdown of the great feudal system and the restoration of Imperial rule. The new era was ushered in with the recognition of Emperor Meiji as absolute ruler of Japan by virtue of the ordnance of the sun goddess, Amaterasu. Tessai produced a number of superb works in black and white and was a master of calligraphy.

The appreciation of painting was not something enjoyed by the upper classes alone; the common people possessed an inherent liking for it too. But it was not until the beginning of the seventeenth century that genre pictures of a sort appeared at a price they could afford to pay. These were nothing more than swiftly drawn ink-brush sketches daubed with colors and known as Ukiyo-e. Their popularity soon spread throughout the country; particularly appreciated were the ones called *Otsu-e*, produced by many families in the village of Otsu, one of the resting places of the Tokaido Highway on the shore of Lake Biwa, a few miles from Kyoto, where they were sold as cheap souvenirs to the retainers of daimyo and others traveling along the highway. Most of the early *Otsu-e* of the seventeenth century depicted subjects from Buddhist lore and were probably intended for worship by those who could not afford costly images. The popularity of the Buddhist subjects lasted until the end of the seventeenth century, when they were replaced in favor by pictures of an entertaining nature, vigorously drawn ink-brush sketches showing great strength and originality. Most of these sketches were used as talismans and depicted characters from folklore, legends, and mythology. Often they were satirical and had calligraphic inscriptions of humorous poems. The work continued to flourish through the eighteenth and first half of the nineteenth century, when the art of Otsu declined sharply.

MEDIUMS AND MATERIALS OF PAINTING

The essential character of Japanese painting and the manner in which the subject is represented is largely conditioned by the materials and mediums used. These include India ink, watercolor, mineral pigments, paper or silk, and the *fude* or brush. When silk is used, it is usually in strips about twelve inches wide, and when a larger size is required, two or more strips are sewn together. The paper is made from the thin fibrous inner bark of the Asiatic paper-mulberry tree and from other plant substances such as grass, rice straw, or bamboo. The India ink, in the form of a hard oblong inkstick or *sumi*, is made by boiling a type of glue or fish oil and pine soot together. An inkstone or *suzuri* and a water dropper or *mizu sashi* are used to prepare the ink for use. A black oblong inkstone has a flat depressed center portion which slopes gently toward one end to form a well. To make the ink ready for use, drops of water are allowed to run into the well and the inkstick is dipped into the water and rubbed on the stone until the desired blackness is attained. The coloring materials are water colors or mineral pigments, the latter being prepared by

Tomioka Tessai, 1836-1924: The Chinese Poet Su Tung-P'o. *Mushanokoji Collection, Tokyo.*

Tomioka Tessai, 1836-1924: Mountain Villa. *Naito Collection, Tokyo.*

mixing with a kind of glue as a binding medium. The last and most important article, the brush, is used in all branches of Japanese painting and consists of a conical tuft of hair, usually that of the badger, securely fixed in the end of a bamboo tube. Since brush strokes represent the basic principle of Japanese painting, the brush's conical shape is essential to produce certain effects. The black ink lines or strokes clearly reflect the manner in which the artist manipulates his brush. Certain strokes are indicative of the speed or pressure that was used to accentuate a meaning, and the shading of line or the tone gradations denote the angle at which the brush was held. The characteristic expression of line or stroke in Japanese painting achieved with this particular type of brush is a function of the touch and feeling transmitted by the artist.

Left: An Otsu-e, or popular image of the Edo period, late seventeenth or eighteenth century, ink and color on paper, depicting Tametomo, a famous warrior of the Gempei Wars (1180-1185). The image was used as a talisman to scare off the evil spirit of smallpox. Seattle Art Museum.

Right: An Otsu-e of the Edo period, late seventeenth or eighteenth century, depicting Daitoku shaving the head of Fukurokuji, god of longevity; ink and color on paper. It was used as a talisman for a long healthful life. Seattle Art Museum.

IV Color Prints

IN THE early years of the seventeenth century the new style of painting known as Ukiyo-e made its appearance, depicting everyday life, particularly of the lower classes. In contrast to the Yamato-e school with its secular subjects intended for the upper strata of society, the Ukiyo-e was a school of genre painting aimed at providing pictures for the common people. The people of Edo were essentially a prosperous middle class addicted to amusement. Their interests revolved around a certain social or pleasure world called Ukiyo. The term Ukiyo-e is variously translated as "Pictures of the Drifting World," "Pictures of the Floating World," or simply "passing or fleeting world." This is essentially the life of fugitive pleasures of the city, with its theaters, restaurants, puppet shows, wrestling pavilions, and houses of assignation. The indigenous population of the Ukiyo were actors, singers, dancers, prostitutes, courtesans, bath-girls, buffoons, and a various assortment of entertainers. The Ukiyo-e or Pictures of the Drifting World, and the *ukiyo-soshi* or sketchbooks of the Drifting World, chiefly depicted the life of these gay quarters. It was in this environment that the Ukiyo-e artists lived and developed the color prints which originally sold for a few coins on the streets of Edo. The Tosa-school artist Iwasa Matabei, 1578-1650, is popularly regarded as the originator of the Ukiyo-e school, in spite of the fact that his fine genre paintings were executed exclusively for the nobility. Although it is difficult to name any individual as the actual founder of the Ukiyo-e school, the first master to contribute significantly to its development was Hishikawa Moronobu, 1618-1694, one of the most famous book illustrators of that time.

DEVELOPMENT OF THE WOOD-BLOCK PRINT

The Ukiyo-e with its plebeian subjects of everyday pursuits and amusements, its portraits of contemporary actors and favorite beauties, was easily understood and appealed to the taste of the populace. Such a great demand arose for the pictures that the method of rapidly drawing ink sketches daubed with colors was no longer practical. As the demand increased it became necessary to find some means of producing these pictures more easily and at such a low price that they would be available to everyone. The method of reproducing prints from wood blocks was the solution to the problem. Although the art of woodcut in Japan dates from the eighth century, in the Nara period when it was introduced from China, its use had been restricted chiefly to reproductions of Buddhist religious paintings. It is stated that the first book to be illustrated with woodcuts was the *Ise Monogatari*, which is a collection of ancient romances and tales of feudal chivalry published in the tenth century. But Moronobu was the first to realize the unlimited possibilities of the woodcut, and in 1670 he designed the first black-and-white single-sheet print. With an excellent knowledge of the methods of the Tosa and Kano schools, he became a skillful Ukiyo-e artist and created an original style of genre painting especially adapted to the wood block. In the early period of Ukiyo-e the lines were clearly defined in a rather bold manner, without fine detail, in order to facilitate the work of the wood engraver. A short time after the development of the black-and-white print the publishers were pressed by the demand for color pictures. The first step toward satisfying this demand was to color the prints by hand. The process of hand-coloring was very slow; sometimes the work was done by the artist who made the original drawing and sometimes by other artisans. Hand-colored prints became so popular that the method of printing in colors, which was introduced about 1740, was a natural result of the increasing demand. The first of these prints to appear were limited to two colors, green and rose.

In a short time the potentialities of the two-color method were realized, and around 1765 multicolored prints were being produced in Edo. The multicolored print, developed by Harunobu, furnished unlimited possibilities for new styles and designs. The heavy lines, no longer necessary, were replaced by fine and delicate outlines, and figures became slender and graceful. The finished quality of the wood-block print was made possible only by collaboration between the painter, the engraver, and the printer. Although a particular color print is known as the work of the artist who conceived the original composition, he was neither the engraver of the wood block nor its printer. The meticulous cutting of the block by the engraver, and the careful application of colors with precision of registry by the printer, were equally contributing factors to the beauty of the finished print.

To fully appreciate the Japanese color print's essential qualities, it is necessary to understand the unique process by which it was made. A color-print artist first drew the original composition in black outline on a piece of translucent paper. The black-outline drawing, executed with brush and India ink, was complete in every detail and represented the artist's finished work. This foundation picture was then given to the engraver, who pasted it face down upon a block of wood, usually cherry, sawed in the direction of the grain and not across it as in Europe. The paper was carefully rubbed until every detail of the design became clearly visible, and then was oiled. The borders of each black line in the design were incised with a knife by the engraver, and the wood in the spaces between the lines was cut away with tiny chisels so that all the lines of the design on the finished block stood out in relief. On the first proof from this block the artist designated the colors to be used. As a rule the artist did not apply the actual colors on a proof, but left it to the printer to select those most suitable to his process of blending. Separate blocks were cut for each color, engaging the skill of the engraver to make each one in perfect register with the other.

The beauty of the finished color print depended upon the touch of the printer in applying the proper pressure on the paper. In printing, the colors were applied with a brush to the wood block, and each impression was taken by pressing the back of the paper with a kind of pad made of hempen cord. Although a separate block was used for each color, gradations in tone were sometimes produced from an individual color-block by blending different colors or different shades of the same color. Blended color tones, such as those seen in sky and water, were obtained by wiping away the superfluity of color where lighter shades were required. In Japanese wood-block prints no two impressions are exactly alike in color, and sometimes entirely different colors are found on prints of the same design. The quality of the paper with its highly absorbent surface and rich soft creamy tone was of great importance to the final product. It was made from the thin fibrous inner bark of the Asiatic paper-mulberry tree, which produces a tough paper suitable to the wood-block process.

During the early period of wood-block printing an edition was limited to about forty copies, or at the most to about seventy or eighty, but by the early nineteenth century the demand was so great that publishers often ran as many as ten thousand copies from a single set of blocks. In contrast to the painstaking work employed in the earlier periods, the later publishers remained oblivious to the inferior work resulting from the deterioration of the blocks.

The normal size of the Japanese wood-block print is about ten by fifteen inches. Prints consisting of two or three panels placed side by side in series were much in demand in the second half of the eighteenth century, and prints having four or more panels are occasionally found. In these examples, each panel is the same size as the normal print; they were cut on separate blocks and printed on separate sheets. In this same later period a color print called *kakemono-e* made its appearance. It was designed as a vertical panel measuring about ten by thirty inches, made of two separate sheets for a single composition. One of the most interesting and popular types of color print of the mid-eighteenth century was the *hashira-kake*, which was five inches wide by twenty-eight inches long. This became very popular for hanging on the upright wooden posts in the houses of the poorer classes, and was the counterpart of the kakemono or hanging scroll-painting in the houses of the upper classes. It was difficult to lay out a design to conform with the unusual shape of the *hashirakake*, and only painters well versed in the art of proportion could produce one of balanced composition.

UKIYO-E SUBJECTS

The prevailing subjects of Ukiyo-e color prints are actors, scenes from the Kabuki drama, and women. Pictures of actors were in great demand because the lower-class citizens of Edo in those days were fanatic lovers of the popular drama. Color-print portraits of famous actors provided the theatergoer with a vivid mental image of features, costumes, and character parts, as well as the plots and scenes of a particular play. It was not important that these pictures expressed an exact likeness of the actors, so long as the actors were represented dramatically in make-up and costume. There was also a great variety of pictures of women and famous beauties, which were equally as popular as the portraits of actors. The women are depicted engaged in the things associated with their everyday life, their pastimes, their domestic activities. They are seen elegantly dressed in beautiful contemporary fashions, in typical Japanese garden settings and other domestic surroundings peculiar to their manner of living. Charming teahouse girls and geisha are interestingly portrayed at their calling. Each great Ukiyo-e painter represented his female subjects in his own particular way, so that the work of these artists can usually be identified by a certain facial type or other characteristic form. The greatest attention was centered upon the courtesans of the famous Yoshiwara district on the outskirts of Edo, depicted in their magnificent and richly colored dress. The pictures of their beautiful costumes provide a graphic record of the extravagant fashions of the times, when textile design became one of the most important outlets of decorative art.

Collectors and connoisseurs of Japanese prints are well aware of the erotic nature of much Ukiyo-e art. The etymological derivation of Ukiyo-e itself is an indication of this, the original Buddhist connotation being the "transient, unreliable world," which, for the newly liberated townspeople of the seventeenth century, took on hedonistic implications. To them, this transient, fleeting world meant amusements in the courtesan districts and Kabuki theaters of Japanese cities, especially pleasures of the flesh, which constitute the subject of more than half the Ukiyo-e art in the seventeenth and eighteenth centuries. The courtesan, trained and educated in polite accomplishments, was an established personage in the social life of old Japan. So much so that quarters like the Yoshiwara district in the new capital city of Edo easily became accepted centers of refined if *demimondain* entertainment, frequented at first by wealthy samurai, but from the middle of the seventeenth century taken over by the rising merchant class.

Actually, for this lively public, Ukiyo-e began as downright erotica in frank and detailed handbooks such as the *Yoshiwara Pillow*, published in 1660, which was a manual of sex and "courtesan critique." The fact that the first print or two of such books were ordinarily only vaguely erotic, followed by completely unprintable pictures, would seem to indicate an attempt to circumvent the censor. However, the feudal government at this time was little concerned with pornography but rather with sedition and other crimes against the state. This is indicated by the fact that many of the early erotic books bear the names of both the publisher and the artist, whereas decent books are often anonymous. Single prints followed the illustrated books, and the huge contemporary popularity of this art available at nominal prices can to a large extent be attributed to the stimulus provided by the social position of the courtesan plus the traditional Japanese insouciance about "moral problems."

Tokyo, or Edo as it was formerly called, is not an ancient city, since it was merely a village until 1457 when Ota Dokan, a provincial daimyo, chose the site for a castle fortress. In 1590 Tokugawa Ieyasu selected Edo for his provincial military headquarters, and from 1603, when he became the supreme feudal power and was appointed Shogun, he made it his permanent capital. The growth of the city was astonishing in size and splendor. The eighty thousand retainers of the Shogun with their families, and all the feudal lords or daimyo, numbering some two to three hundred, were compelled to spend several months each year at the Edo court and to leave their families in the city as hostages when they returned to their feudal estates. By the year 1787 the population had risen to 1,400,000, in addition to the Shogun's retainers and the families of the daimyo, making Edo one of the largest cities in the world in the eighteenth century. The peace and progressive development of commerce and local industry through the seventeenth century contributed to a substantial rise in the standard of living. As the larger cities prospered, there grew a class of merchants and artisans which was to reach important, and in many ways powerful, dimensions. With the Tokugawa court and administrative government centered in Edo, a great surge of building activity was created by the influx of retainers and daimyo moving in with their soldiers and servants by the thousands. With the construction of the great houses for the daimyo, in addition to buildings for lodging troops, shops and houses for merchants and tradesmen, and dwellings for the workers, the city rapidly reached vast proportions.

From the opening years of the seventeenth century the district called Yoshiwara, or Reedy Plain, on the outskirts of Edo, was a pleasure haunt for people. In this world of lively and fickle pleasures were the Kabuki theaters, puppet theaters, *sumo* bouts, eating places, and licensed houses of entertainment populated with actors, singers, dancers, jesters, storytellers, bath-girls, courtesans, prostitutes, and panders. After a great fire destroyed most of the city in 1657, the Yoshiwara was rebuilt in a different section and its former population of entertainers, pleasure girls, and others plied their trades in the new resorts of gaiety. By the beginning of the eighteenth century it was a thriving and practically self-contained district, complete with tradespeople to provide its needed services. The district was known as the Nightless City, and within its precinct it had its own code or principles of behavior and customs. The beautiful houses of the courtesans reflected a certain elegance and there existed a strict social rank among the courtesans which was observed with a regulated formality. They were attended by personal maids adorned with rich and costly clothing, and were accorded great respect by the inhabitants and patrons of the district. The pleasure quarters were a prominent part of city life not only in Edo, but also in the other larger cities, such as Kyoto, which contained the famous district called Shimabara. These famous pleasure quarters offered a variety of subject material to the Ukiyo-e painter, and wood-block prints of famous women and actors were eagerly purchased.

LANDSCAPE SUBJECTS

Although the pleasure quarter or Ukiyo with its magnificent costumes and women who lived by the allurements of charm and beauty offered the most lucrative subject matter for the color-print artists, new fields began to attract their attention. Many color prints were inspired by legendary and historical stories, by the occupations and customs of the times, and by landscapes. It was in the latter part of the Tokugawa period that the beautiful and interesting scenic color prints by Hokusai and Hiroshige made their appearance, with their innovations in the representation of light and atmospheric conditions. Until this time, with a few exceptions, landscape had been used only as a background or as a scenic setting to complement the depiction of women, who were the principal Ukiyo-e subject. Although these early landscapes showing beautiful views of the country were greatly appreciated, the populace continued a preference for pictures of their favorite actors, beautiful women, and the Yoshiwara courtesans. It was not until an edict was issued in 1842 prohibiting the publication of prints of actors and courtesans that landscape became popular. Around the end of the eighteenth century the principal highways of the country had been greatly improved, which caused commercial traffic to increase and encouraged more people to travel. This in turn created a demand for the scenic color prints of famous views and prominent places. These great highways, especially the Tokaido or Eastern-Sea Way, because it ran eastward along the coast from Kyoto to Edo and was regarded as the most picturesque highway in the world, offered innumerable subjects for the color print, which the traveler appreciated as a memento of the places he had seen. Color prints of these views as well as scenes of Edo were sent or taken home to friends, and this in turn created a desire to travel and see these beautiful scenic spots.

Because the color prints chiefly depicted actors and courtesans, and were made to satisfy the lower classes, they were not considered to have æsthetic qualities. Even the beautiful and exotic scenic views which possess such great artistic merit were not at first appreciated by the Japanese for their intrinsic worth, but were looked upon as a form of cheap commercial handicraft. In the closing years of the Tokugawa period large numbers of color prints were sent to Europe by Dutch traders in Nagasaki, then the only port open to foreign trade, with only Dutch merchants privileged to trade with the Japanese. It was from this medium of trade that European artists and collectors first became acquainted with the Japanese color print, which, dispensed from Holland, found a market in Paris and London. However, it was not until the middle of the nineteenth century that its importance began to be properly evaluated, when a group of French artists were at-

tracted to examples being sold at a shop in Paris. They began to be collected by connoisseurs and a wider knowledge of them was stimulated by Edmond de Goncourt's monographs on Hokusai and Utamaro. Both in Europe and America, and also in Japan, informed appreciation gradually increased until by the turn of the century large sums were paid for rare impressions. The scenic color prints of Hokusai and Hiroshige, which antedate the rise of the Impressionist movement by only a few decades, exerted an important influence on the new trends in painting. Much of the awakened interest in the color print by foreigners and the Japanese themselves was a result of the work and efforts of Professor Ernest F. Fenollosa, who assisted in making collections of Japanese art for the Imperial Museum in Tokyo. He was associated with the University of Tokyo, and was a great admirer and scholar of Japanese painting and sculpture. His writings stimulated considerable interest in Japanese art among connoisseurs in the West. A devout student of Buddhism during his years in Japan, he became a believer, and when he died in London in 1908, his request to have his final resting place in the graveyard of the ancient Miidera temple on the south shore of Lake Biwa was faithfully carried out. The peaceful site of the Miidera temple, long known for the impressive boom of its famous bell in the twilight of early evening, is the subject of Hiroshige's *Eight Famous Views of Lake Biwa*.

The artists of the Ukiyo-e were not aristocrats or learned priests like the painters identified with the Yamato-e, Tosa, and Kano schools. They were commoners with the rank of artisans who frequently executed designs for wood-block prints in addition to their regular occupation as designers of book illustrations or theater posters. Unfortunately, biographical information in many cases is completely lacking, although it is sufficiently complete regarding the outstanding artists of the later period. The following sketches containing important features of the lives of the most prominent color-print painters give some idea of their individual contributions.

THE EARLY PRINT MAKERS

Hishikawa Moronobu, 1625-1695, was born in the province of Chiba and moved to Edo when he was very young. He studied under masters of the Tosa school of painting and was an admirer of the classical genre paintings of Iwasa Matabei. Moronobu became a distinguished painter and, as the leading exponent in the establishment of the wood-block print, was one of the most prolific of Japanese book illustrators. He realized the possibilities of satisfying the demand for the new Ukiyo-e subjects by producing single-sheet prints that could be purchased by the lower classes at a nominal price. Of around a hundred and fifty sets of illustrations by him, perhaps two dozen were erotic, appealing to a wealthy, highly select audience. In such sets the first illustration was apt to be an innocuous, presentable frontispiece. He created an original style of genre painting adaptable to wood blocks with designs of simple lines devoid of detail to enable the still inexperienced engravers of that time to produce the woodcuts more rapidly and more easily. He was a skillful designer and although his drawings of women are lacking in appeal, he had a dynamic style which gave life and animation to the human figure. Moronobu's prints were originally in black and white, and as the demand for color increased, they were painted by hand, some possibly by the artist himself, others by assistants. Still others possibly were colored after his lifetime.

The line of the Torii masters begins with Kiyonobu, 1664-1729, its founder, whose work suggests his early training under his father, an actor as well as a designer of signboards and theater posters. He was the first Ukiyo-e print maker to portray actors as his principal subject, and his sturdy and vigorous style reflects the influence of poster design. The second of the Torii line, Kiyomasu (active from 1696 to the early 1720's), was probably a younger brother of Kiyonobu and a prolific designer of prints of Kabuki actors and Yoshiwara courtesans. Another artist, who produced prints until about 1750, was probably a son of Kiyonobu and adopted his name. When Kiyomasu ceased producing prints around 1730, a designer thought to be a son-in-law of Kiyonobu adopted the name of Kiyomasu and continued in the same style. The

color prints bearing the signature Kiyonobu or Kiyomasu were executed by these two later artists known by those names. Torii Kiyomitsu, 1735-1785, is the third Torii who is credited with the development of the three-color print. Torii Kiyonaga, 1752-1815, who was a leading pupil of Kiyomitsu, and the fourth and last of the Torii masters, developed a style of realism, abandoning the earlier idealism in the depiction of Kabuki actors. His influence on the Ukiyo-e school was as great as was that of Harunobu and was specially marked on the work of his contemporaries. He also developed a new approach in the representation of women, whom he showed as tall, graceful, and beautiful. He developed the landscape background as a beautiful setting for the figures.

Okumura Masanobu, c. 1686-1764, who lived in Edo and studied under Kiyonobu, was a publisher as well as a designer and his name is closely associated with the development of color-printing. His early work is in black and white in the manner of the Torii school but shows great skill in figure subjects, introducing a picturesque style and depicting women at their pastimes and occupations, as well as many scenes of contemporary social life.

Nishikawa Sukenobu, who flourished during the first half of the eighteenth century at Osaka, is noted for his experimental work on printing in six colors. He was a popular book illustrator and his single-sheet prints, which are rare, had a distinctive style. His perpetual theme, whatever the subject, is the grace and beauty of Japanese girlhood. Sukenobu designed erotica on commission from the publishers, but his finest

Hishikawa Moronobu, 1625 to 1695: The Saffron Flower, *a black-and-white book illustration depicting an incident in the eleventh-century novel* The Tale of Genji. *Victoria and Albert Museum.*

55

works are his many volumes of graceful illustrations depicting the daily life of the women of Kyoto.

Utagawa Toyoharu, 1735-1814, founder of the Utagawa line, is said to have been born in Oita prefecture and to have gone to Kyoto when he was a young man to study the painting of the Kano school. He moved to Edo, where he was influenced by Toyonobu, 1711-1785, and created his own characteristic style of Ukiyo-e female figures. He was a skillfull painter and one of the earliest color-print artists to produce pure landscape. He cleverly adapted the European technique of perspective in a particular style of print called *uki-e*. Toyoharu was one of a selected group of painters commissioned in 1796 to repair the Mausoleum of the Shogun at Nikko. Utagawa Toyokuni, 1769-1825, and Utagawa Toyohiro, 1773-1828, both studied under Toyoharu. As a pupil of the latter, Hiroshige acquired great knowledge of landscape painting.

Nishimura Shigenaga, 1697-1756, who was born and lived in Edo, was an amazingly versatile artist. After studying the work of Masanobu and Kiyonobu he developed a style of his own. He was a great innovator of new forms of the Ukiyo-e, especially in landscape-with-figures, but also in the perspective prints and stone-rubbing prints. His work exerted a great influence upon Harunobu and Toyonobu, and the name of Shigenaga ranks high in the history of Ukiyo-e also because of his close connection with the introduction of color-printing.

KORYUSAI, HARUNOBU

Isoda Koryusai, a former samurai who flourished between 1760 and 1780, was a pupil of both Shigenaga and Harunobu, and a friend and favorite of the latter (Plate 6). His earliest work so closely resembles the work of Harunobu that it is difficult to distinguish any difference. After the death of Harunobu, his style assumed a distinctive character with beautiful drawing and rich decorative color schemes. He is noted for his elegant, dramatically designed compositions for the vertically elongated *hashirakake*, or pillar prints. Besides excelling in artistic erotica, Koryusai was also the originator of color-print fashion plates issued in sets for the enjoyment of young women in the provinces, entitled *New Patterns for Young Leaves*.

Suzuki Harunobu, 1725-1770, was the greatest of the Ukiyo-e designers during the latter half of the eighteenth century. He lived in Edo and studied the method of two-color prints under Shigenaga and later the three-color process. It was only during the last five years of his life that he produced the magnificent work for which he is famous. Prior to 1765 Harunobu devoted himself chiefly to the illustrations of books,

Torii Kiyonobu, 1664-1729: A hand-colored wood-block print of a theater scene with the actors Sodezaki Iseno, a female impersonator, and Ogino Isaburo as lovers. Published by Ise-ya Kimbei, about 1726. Victoria and Albert Museum.

Okumura Masanobu, c. 1686 to 1764: A black-and-white wood-block print showing a man and woman with a female attendant. Victoria and Albert Museum.

having until then produced no more than about forty broadsheets. But in 1765, with the aid of certain craftsmen skilled in wood-block cutting and efficient in the method of registration, Harunobu developed and produced the first multicolor prints. With their rich and brilliant colors, these prints became known as *nishiki-e* or brocade prints, because of their resemblance to the beautiful silk fabrics of the time. The few two- and three-color prints that he produced before 1765 included portraits of actors, lovely women, children, and historical and allegorical subjects. His early prints bear a marked resemblance to the work of a contemporary, Kiyomitsu. However, it seems that his great work in the multicolor print originated in the designing of picture-calendars, which are unusual both in composition and in meaning. They became a part of the activities of groups of poets who gathered for the enjoyment and appreciation of the arts. It became a fad for the members to compete among themselves by producing elaborate calendars which they exchanged at New Year gatherings. Harunobu produced a great number of these calendars with intricate designs at the request of the most prominent poets' group. From this experience he began to produce the works for which he is famous, with women and children in domestic settings depicted in a delicate style.

Harunobu expressed the gentle mannerisms, the delicate beauty, and the charm of the feminine world as representative of women in general and not any particular individual. Women are presented with unusually thin necks and tiny hands and feet, like dainty china dolls. They are portrayed in a pure and refreshing fashion in their domestic surroundings, pursuing their customary activities. His graphic delineation is characterized by the sensitive attitudes of his figures, with heads inclined or slightly turned, the lovely curves of their forms and their exquisite costumes gently flowing to complement the posture. When walking or otherwise in motion, their charm is further accentuated by the gently opened fold of the skirt caused by the movement of the legs, and the manner in which the sleeves fall back when carrying an umbrella or holding a book. An important feature of Harunobu's designs is the background setting. He was the first to develop this style of painting, which had only been used in earlier times in a limited manner in religious paintings or depictions of temples. He portrayed his women in an endless variety of settings suitable and proper to the activity or pastime in which they were engaged. Indoors, they are shown occupied with domestic chores, or writing letters by the light of a paper lantern; outdoors, strolling on beautiful spring days against cherry-blossom backgrounds, playing with children in gardens, and walking in gently falling snow. Many of his prints contain a poem from ancient times written across the top in a blank space with a wavy line resembling the line of a cloud.

Two attractive young girls served as models for many of Harunobu's prints; one, the daughter of a toothpick maker, was named Ofuji, and the other, Osen, was a great beauty of about eighteen years of age. Osen was so beautiful that she became a principal topic of conversation in Edo. She was often referred to in the news-sheets and her name was later used for

Above left: Isoda Koryusai, active c. 1760–1780: A hashi-rakake, or pillar print, of a young woman wearing a crest or mon on her kimono of the character ju, which means long life. She is representing the female Sennin of Horaizan, in a garden with a crane, a pine tree, and bamboo, emblems of longevity. It refers to the fabled mountain of Horai on the Island of Everlasting Life, or Paradise. Victoria and Albert Museum.

Above right: Isoda Koryusai: A hashirakake, or pillar print, of the rising sun, a pine tree, and a flight of cranes, all symbols of longevity. Victoria and Albert Museum.

Left: Nishimura Shigenaga, 1697–1756: Hotei, one of the seven gods of good fortune, carrying a lady across a stream. A print in two colors published by Yamashiro-ya. Victoria and Albert Museum.

Suzuki Harunobu, 1725 to 1770: Osen of Kasamori. *Tokyo National Museum.*

characters in plays. She worked in the teahouse at the Kasamori shrine and many Edo people came to see her under the pretense of making a visit to the shrine. Harunobu's pictures of Osen were in great demand. He produced many famous series of prints with delicate brush strokes and tender lines expressing the world of feminine beauty. These include *Manners and Customs, Eight Views of Indoor Life*, and *Six Views of the Tamagawa,* and in his last year he produced a picture book entitled *Beauties of the Yoshiwara Gay Quarters.*

UTAMARO, SHARAKU

Kitagawa Utamaro, 1753-1806, one of the greatest of Ukiyo-e painters, brought the technique of the color print to the highest degree of achievement. At an early age he came to Edo and became a pupil of Toriyama Sekien, a Kano painter and a noted designer of picture books; but he was also greatly influenced by Kiyonaga. Utamaro first produced designs for book illustrations, the earliest being for the text of a play. They were dated 1775 and bore the signature Hosho, which was the name he first used. From biographical sketches it is known that he spent his life in the gay quarters of the Yoshiwara, as had been the custom of the other artists of the Ukiyo-e school. He had many friends among the actors, entertainers, playwrights, bath and teahouse girls, the various frequenters of the district, and the prostitutes. Greatly attracted to the beauty of the women from the famous houses of

entertainment, he portrayed them in much of his best work. And it is this element of "the eternal female" that has made Utamaro the best known in the West of the Ukiyo-e portrayers of sensual feminine beauty. As the artist of the *demimond,* Utamaro was discovered by Edmond de Goncourt in his *Peintre des Maisons Vertes.* Included among his many pictures of pleasure girls and courtesans is a set titled *Women Dressing for a Niwaka Celebration.* The women of the red-light district in Yoshiwara held this celebration annually, and on this occasion they dressed themselves as men and performed various satirical and humorous acts for their own enjoyment. Utamaro was an ugly man and throughout his life this physical handicap seems to have exerted a strong influence on the many things he did and said. In his earliest years in Edo he became acquainted with Tsutaya Juzaburo, poet and an important patron of the theater as well as the foremost publisher of color prints. Tsutaya recognized the work of Utamaro as having great possibilities and furnished him with board and lodging, and later invited him to live in his house. Utamaro was very versatile, excelling in many subjects ranging from animals and insects to landscape and domestic scenes, but his most famous works are his portrayals of women. His pictures were now being signed Utamaro, an adopted name.

Just as Harunobu depicted women as a fixed type, Utamaro gave his beauties the features common to all, representing his ideal of feminine beauty and posture. They all possess the same qualities of sophistication, worldly-wisdom, and coquettishness, whether they are women of the pleasure houses of

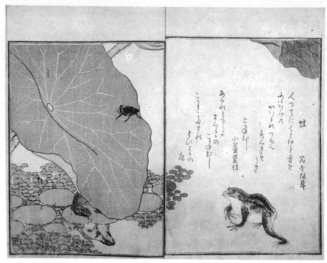

Above: Kitagawa Utamaro, 1753-1806: from A Collection of Insects, *an album published in 1788. Tokyo National Museum.*

Left: Kitagawa Utamaro, 1753-1806: The Middle Class, *from Fuzoku Sandan Musume, or Girls of the Upper, Middle, and Lower Classes. Tokyo National Museum.*

Yoshiwara or girls of genteel and good character (Plate 9). He portrayed them with invariably long faces, and with eyes as narrow as slits, while their bodies are unnaturally tall and voluptuous (Plate 8). The background usually consists of a solid color, and the costumes worn by the women are rather plain when compared to the colorful fabrics painted by other artists. Some of his drawings are executed with very few lines, the contour of his figures being emphasized more by color, with soft warm flesh tones.

Among Utamaro's models was a popular waitress named Okita, who worked in the Naniwaya teahouse, one of the many eating places clustered around the Asakusa Kannon temple. Utamaro's prints of animals, birds, fishes, and insects, which were executed in a most lifelike manner with very accurate detail, were produced for albums, one of which is a famous series titled *A Collection of Insects*, published in 1788.

His designs were in great demand all over Japan and even in China, and this enormous popularity resulted in his inability to maintain his high quality of workmanship. In his later years the demand was so great that many prints attributed to him were the work of pupils. It was also during these last years of his life that rising young color-print artists, particularly Hokusai and Toyokuni, began to gain popularity and overshadow Utamaro. As he could not fail to see his position as foremost print designer being challenged, he became resentful of many of his contemporaries and often resorted to malicious and false accusations against them. In 1804 he painted and had published a set of three conjoined prints which portrayed Hideyoshi, the great military lord of the late sixteenth century, being entertained by his five concubines in a luxurious setting. This was considered an affront to the Tokugawa Shogun and Utamaro was sent to prison, where his hands were bound with chains for fifty days. His early death at the age of fifty-three was probably due to broken pride and dejected spirits following the humiliation of being thrown into prison.

Toshusai Sharaku, active from 1794 to 1795 in Edo, chiefly painted portraits of Kabuki actors, and today, on account of his originality, is regarded as one of the greatest of Ukiyo-e artists, although he was hardly recognized by the public during his lifetime. Sharaku remains an enigma because until the present day the only known facts surrounding his life are his 140 prints executed in a ten-month period from May 1794 to February 1795. Although nothing in the way of essential information has been found about his life, an item appeared in 1868 which sheds some light on him, although its authenticity cannot be proved. Whatever his source, one Tatsuta Shashukin wrote that Sharaku's real name was Saito Jurobei, that he lived in Hatchodori in Edo, and was a No actor in the retinue of the feudal lord of Awa. Sharaku's work was largely disregarded by students of Japanese art until 1910, when Julius Kurth published a book on him in Munich, declaring that he considered Sharaku one of the world's greatest portraitists. Since then he has been a favorite of print collectors. Most of the pictures he produced in that short space of ten months are portraits of actors who were then appearing at the three Kabuki theaters in Edo; a few depict *sumo* wrestlers, and two are historical prints. In studying the style of his work it is interesting to observe that between the earlier and later prints in the series he changed from bust to full-length portrayals and the later ones are smaller in size. His first twenty-eight prints of busts of actors are considered his finest work and the succeeding ones show a gradual decline in quality. The portraits are not attempts at characterizations of the actors themselves, but rather of the expressions of psychological caricature peculiar to the characters they impersonated. The actors' expressions are exaggerated with small eyes, almond-shaped and slanting, large protruding noses, and lips depicting various movements and emotions. In his later prints these bold and interesting facial expressions disappear and are replaced by features more closely resembling the conventional actor prints produced by other artists of the time. A distinctive feature of the earlier prints is that all are signed "Drawn by Toshusai Sharaku," while all those of the later group are signed "Drawn by Sharaku." All the earlier prints have mica backgrounds and were brought out by Tsutaya Juzaburo, the great Ukiyo-e publisher who sponsored Utamaro and others.

HOKUSAI

Katsushika Hokusai, 1760-1849, is one of the few universally known names outside Japan, as well as one of the most distin-

Toshusai Sharaku, active 1794-1795: Matsumoto Koshiro IV as Gorobei, a fishmonger, in A Medley of Tales of Revenge, *Kiri-za theater, May 1794. Tokyo National Museum.*

guished and popular of the Ukiyo-e school. He was born in Katsushika, in Shimafusa province near Edo, was apprenticed to a wood-engraver when about thirteen years old, and then began to study painting under Shunsho at about nineteen. From the latter he took the art name of Shunro, which he used for about fifteen years. During his long lifetime he used about thirty different names to sign his work, which even in Japan at that time was an astonishing number in comparison to the four or five customarily used. He did not adopt the name Hokusai until about 1797. Hokusai's life was most unconventional according to Japanese standards of etiquette and proper behavior. He was restless and forever striving to gain further knowledge of the various schools of painting, such as the Tosa and the Kano. He studied under several masters. At this time European copper-plate engravings made their appearance in Japan, which afforded Hokusai the opportunity to study European perspective and the technique of light and shade. Throughout the earlier part of his life there were many changes in the style of his work and in his subject matter, and it was not until after many years that he finally turned to landscape, a field in which he was a pioneer, and in which he achieved great local popularity and world-wide fame. Pure landscape in its traditional form, used for centuries in Chinese and Japanese painting, had not been introduced in Japanese color prints until Hokusai rediscovered it in his exquisite scenic views. His approach to realism, with distances expressed in three-dimensional perspective, can be seen in his famous *Thirty-six Views of Fuji*. In each of these plates the majestic peak of Fuji is related in scale to its true appearance in the surrounding landscape. Whether the cone is depicted as a magnificent towering peak, or seen from among storm-tossed waves, or glimpsed through a grove of graceful bamboo, his creative genius emerges in the originality of the compositions.

Hokusai introduced effects of light which give a powerful sense of atmospheric conditions: humidity, passing showers, wind, rain, heat, cold. Incorporating these effects of nature in masterfully expressive portrayals of daily life, he was able to produce a beautiful and interesting record of contemporary scenes and activities in Japan. His greatest contributions to the art of the color print are his celebrated landscape series— *Famous Sights of the Eastern Capital*, *Views along the Banks of the Sumida*, *The Fifty-three Stations along the Tokaido*, *Waters in Their Thousand Aspects*, and *Views of Famous Bridges*. His later works include pictures of flowers and birds, and subjects borrowed from the classical literature of Japan and China.

A prolific artist and the most versatile of the color-print painters, Hokusai is best known for his landscapes, but he was equally accomplished in any subject (Plate 2). His *Manga*, a book containing an endless variety of rapid sketches, constitutes a historically priceless encyclopedic work embodying the entire field of Japanese life, legend, historical figures, gods, animals, birds, fishes, flowers, insects, natural flora, and contemporary human figures. The people are depicted in all manner of activities, occupations, and pastimes, with their movements meticulously observed in a powerfully graphic, expressive line (Plate 5). The word *manga* means a cartoon, pictorial caricature, spontaneous drawing, or sketch of daily life. The *Manga* contains fifteen volumes; the first volume was published in 1814 and the last three appeared posthumously. Hokusai continued to work until the last day of his life, and toward the end of his time he produced a three-volume series entitled *A Hundred Views of Fuji*, which bears his final signature, "The Art-Crazy Old Man."

HIROSHIGE

Ando Hiroshige, 1797-1858, with Hokusai and Utamaro, is one of the three artists best known outside Japan. He produced many charming and picturesque color prints which have gained wide popularity for their revelation of the inherent poetry of nature. He depicted the scenic beauty of the Japanese countryside with greater realism than any other artist, and his work was closer to the intimate enchantments of nature than the subtle and exalted rhythms of the earlier Chinese and Japanese landscape masters. He was born in Edo, where his father served as a member of a fire brigade retained by the Tokugawa government. Hiroshige's talent developed at an

Katsushika Hokusai, 1760-1849: A color print of the bridge of boats at Sano, from the set entitled Picturesque Views of Famous Bridges in Several Provinces, *published by Yeijudo (Nishimura-ya) Yohachi, about 1828. Victoria and Albert Museum.*

Katsushika Hokusai, 1760-1849: A color print of the suspension bridge joining the provinces of Hida and Etchu high in the mountains. It is part of a set, Picturesque Views of Famous Bridges in Several Provinces, *published about 1828 by Yeijudo (Nishimura-ya) Yohachi. Victoria and Albert Museum.*

Katsushika Hokusai, 1760–1849: Color print from the series called The Thirty-six Views of Fuji. *It shows the view of Fuji from the village of Sekiya on the banks of the Sumida River. Victoria and Albert Museum.*

early age and his drawings attracted wide attention. In 1812 he entered the studio of Utagawa Toyohiro and progressed so rapidly that he was granted the privilege of taking the name of Utagawa after studying there for only one year. While still with Toyohiro he produced a number of portraits and other subjects in the customary Ukiyo-e style which were published, but after the death of Toyohiro in 1828, Hiroshige developed his own style and around this time produced his first landscapes, which were published in two sets, one entitled *Ten Famous Places in Edo*, and the other *Eight Views of Lake Biwa*. Subsequent albums of sets or series of color prints appeared, such as *Famous Places in Edo*, sets of beautiful bird-and-flower pictures, *Famous Places in Japan*, *Views of Famous Places in Edo in the Four Seasons*, *One Hundred Views of Edo*, *Famous Places in Kyoto*, *Famous Places in Osaka*, and many exquisite single-sheet prints. Hiroshige is best known for his travelogue guidebooks called *The Sixty-nine Stages of the Kiso Kaido*, *The Reisho Tokaido*, and especially *The Fifty-three Stages of the Tokaido*.

Hiroshige's landscapes have a fascinating naturalism and depict the places and things he saw with a remarkable sense of proportion. His mountains, trees, and rocks are related in true perspective, giving a distinctive impression of distances. People, villages, and cityscapes with their everyday life are realistically portrayed in an endless variety of scenes. The vivid manner in which light and atmosphere are expressed in his scenic color prints is a remarkable achievement that few artists have equaled. Hiroshige's masterly portrayal of atmospheric conditions such as snow, driving wind, rainstorms, fleeting clouds, and sudden showers is one of his great contributions. Even the moisture in the air, the feeling of the seasons, and meteorological variations are expressed in a most subtle and sentimental way peculiar to the Japanese. In the series of color prints that Hiroshige produced from the hundreds of sketches made on journeys over the great feudal highways, the well-known scenic spots are observed not only with this feeling of atmospheric realism but also with a sense for the picturesque, depicting chance encounters, peasants, a roadside shrine, and many other incidental features. The human touch in views of this nature appealed especially to travelers as remembrances of their journeys and the life they encountered along the way. Hiroshige undertook his first trip in the year 1832, when he

received the privilege of going along with a courier of the Shogun and his retinue from Edo to Kyoto. It was on this journey that he amassed a wealth of sketches for *The Fifty-three Stages of the Tokaido*, the series of color prints which brought him world fame.

The Tokaido, or Eastern-Sea Way, ran eastward along the coast from Kyoto to Edo, a distance of 345 miles. Of unknown origin, this remarkable highway bears striking testimony to Japan's medieval greatness in the twelfth and thirteenth centuries. Under the Tokugawa regime it received great attention, since it connected the Shogun's seat of government with the Imperial court at Kyoto. It was considered the most picturesque highway in the world, being a wide, well-kept thoroughfare, lined for the greater part of its length with giant pine trees. The Tokaido, like other main highways connecting other parts of Japan with Edo, was thronged with couriers, retainers on official business, and the colorful retinues of daimyo passing to and from their feudal domains, as well as merchants, pilgrims, players, musical performers, itinerant priests, and other travelers. Extended along these principal

Above: Ando Hiroshige, 1797-1858: A White Egret Descending from Flight toward Purple Iris. *Published in the early nineteenth century by Fujioka-ya Keijiro (Shorindo). Victoria and Albert Museum.*

Right: Ando Hiroshige, 1797-1858: The Horikiri Shobuen *or* Iris Gardens of Horikiri, *near Tokyo; dated 1857. Victoria and Albert Museum.*

64

highways was a succession of towns and post stations, in a highly organized system, each containing inns, shops, eating places, houses of entertainment, and a regulated number of horses and carriers for the convenience of travelers. The course of the Tokaido afforded an endless variety of scenes and subjects for Hiroshige to record in his color prints. From Edo, the Tokaido progressed through beautiful mountain country to Hakonemachi, on the eastern shore of Lake Ashi, and continued on in its winding manner, with its sides lined with giant ancient Japanese cedars, to Hakone Barrier. This was formerly one of the largest and most important of the post-stations along the old Tokaido, and one of the principal barriers where travelers had to present their passports to officials in the guardhouses and give their reasons for making the journey. From there it continued on through Mishima to the sea, and all this time the travelers would catch magnificent views of the majestic peak of Fuji. Along the rugged coast route, with mountains rising from the sea, it continued to Nagoya and Kuwana, and then turned inland through impressive mountain passes to Ishiyama, at the south end of Lake Biwa a few miles from Kyoto. Hiroshige's prints of the Tokaido portray with much charm the many people he saw along the way, their mode of travel, their costumes, and in snow or rain pictures the farmers and laborers with straw raincoats, and in others the quaint manner in which his subjects carry their paper umbrellas. At almost every turn on the Tokaido there was an appropriate scenic view or well-known site. One of these, Ishiyama, appears in Hiroshige's *Eight Famous Views of Lake Biwa.* Conforming to the established Japanese manner of depicting certain famous spots in a traditional relationship with the time of day or atmospheric condition, Ishiyama is associated with the autumn moon,

Color print by Ando Hiroshige, 1797-1858: The Treasure Ship with the Seven Gods of Good Fortune, *depicting their emblems, the sacred treasures, and other tokens of good luck for the New Year. The gods in the upper row are: Fukurokuju, with tall head, staff, and scroll, and the robe of a scholar; Benten, the only female, with a stringed instrument called a* biwa; *and Bishamon, in armor and holding a trident. Those in the front row are: Hotei, with his large bag which sometimes contains the sacred treasures; Daikoku, with his mallet and bags of rice; Yebisu, with his fishing rod and a tai fish in a jar; and Jurojin, holding a fan and dressed in the robe of a scholar. The ideogram on the sail is* kotobuki, *which means hope, happiness, long life, good fortune, and so forth. Victoria and Albert Museum.*

65

Ando Hiroshige, 1797-1858: A Snow-covered Street by the Canal *in the Shiba District of Edo, from his series entitled* The Hundred Views of Edo. *Date seal: Snake 12 (A.D. 1857). Victoria and Albert Museum.*

because the Ishiyama temple is at its best when bathed in moonlight at that season.

Another outstanding Hiroshige series is *The Sixty-nine Stages of the Kiso Kaido*. The Kiso Kaido was second only to the Tokaido among the ancient highways and was the mid-mountain way, or Nakasendo as it was sometimes called. From Edo its route went inland to the center of the island of Honshu, through Hachioji, Enzan, and on to Okaya and Shiojiri. Winding over rugged mountains, it passed through Kiso-Fukushima, which stands midway between Tokyo and Kyoto, in the very heart of the beautiful Japanese Alps. During the Tokugawa regime a barrier gate was maintained here by Yamamura, the local daimyo. The road then went to Naka-

tsugawa and terminated at Nagoya, where travelers could continue their journey to Kyoto.

Hiroshige made numerous journeys through various parts of the country, and from the vast material acquired he was able to produce a great variety of color prints and new versions of existing series, as evidenced by the twenty complete or partially finished new or revised versions of the Tokaido set. Around 1850 Hiroshige published a version of the Tokaido series which is called the *Reisho Tokaido*, the name of the subject being written on each print in a formal calligraphic style known as *reisho*. This set consists of the usual number of fifty-five color prints, one for each of the fifty-three post-stations and one each for the terminal points of Edo and Kyoto. In the early period of wood-block prints, an edition was limited to fewer than a hundred copies, and later to around two hundred copies. But the enormous demand for Hiroshige's work caused his publishers to print as many as ten thousand copies of his later sets or series, with consequent deterioration in quality. It is believed that altogether he produced over five thousand drawings for color prints. Two other artists used Hiroshige's name after his death: Shigenobu, who had married Hiroshige's daughter, from whom he was later separated; and Shigemasa her second husband. Two years before his death, Hiroshige retired from his worldly activities to meditate and become enlightened through Zen Buddhism.

Contemporary with Hiroshige during the first half of the nineteenth century was Utagawa Kunisada, 1786-1864, who lived in Edo and at the age of fifteen became a pupil of Utagawa Toyokuni. He was a distinguished and versatile Ukiyo-e artist who specialized in color prints of female figures and Kabuki actors. Another pupil of Toyokuni was Kuniyoshi, 1798-1861, a landscape painter, but best known for striking battle scenes. There was also Keisai Eisen, 1792-1848, a distinguished landscapist, who is said to have begun the famous album called *The Sixty-nine Stages of the Kiso Kaido*, with Hiroshige completing the remaining forty-six.

Wood-block printing declined sharply after Hiroshige, and rapidly lost its popularity as it deteriorated into an endless variety of prints of confused artistic composition, gaudy colors, and tawdry quality. It was not until sometime in the 1880s, after the restoration of Imperial rule by Empress Meiji, and continuing through the turn of the century, that a renascence occurred in the art of wood-block printing in the traditional manner. Among the foremost artists in this period of revival of Ukiyo-e were Kobayashi Kiyochika, 1847-1915; Inoue Yasuji, 1864-1889; Ogura Ryuson, active in the 1880s; Hashiguchi Goyo, 1880-1921, and Ito Shinsui, b. 1896. The finished work of these artists is comparable and in many pieces equal artistically and technically to that done in the classic tradition by the great masters of the past.

V Sculpture

VARIOUS FORMS of primitive sculpture from the very early periods of Japanese history, prior to the introduction of Buddhism, are known to have existed. Of particular importance from the Neolithic age is the earthenware of the Jomon type with intricate sculptural designs, and the sculptured clay figures called *dogu*, which are representations of deities with human attributes. Subsequent to these appeared the earthenware figurines of the Haniwa culture, from the Ancient Burial Mounds period, corresponding in time to the first few centuries of the Christian era. These burial mounds of earth covering the tombs of rulers were of stupendous proportions, often measuring more than seventy acres, and surrounded with moats. For some unknown reason, the Haniwa figurines are not found within the tombs, but instead were placed in groups on top of the mounds. The greater number of Haniwa represent men and women wearing ancient costumes and hairdos, and as a rule the lower part of the figure is cylindrical in shape. Some Haniwa represent domestic animals such as horses, chickens, and dogs, and some are in the form of wild animals such as the boar or monkey. It was undoubtedly the experience of this prehistoric sculpture, reflecting the advanced civilization which produced it, that enabled the Japanese to make such rapid progress in assimilating the techniques of the high culture later brought from the mainland.

THE ASUKA PERIOD

The year 552, when the King of Paikche sent to the Emperor of Japan a gilt bronze image of the Buddha together with a number of volumes of the sutras or scriptures, marks the beginning of the Asuka period (552-645). The name derives from the region called Asuka in Yamato province, now Nara prefecture, where the successive Imperial residences were located. It was a period which witnessed the building of the great temples. A steady stream of scholars, artists, priests, and monks, along with sculptors, bronze workers, painters, and temple carpenters, came from the Asiatic mainland to Japan, and in return Japanese students and missions visited China to gain more knowledge from the learned men at the T'ang capital. With the rapid spread of Buddhism the lords of the noble houses began erecting magnificent Buddhist shrines, and many daughters of noblemen entered monasteries to become nuns. For a century Nara was a hive of building activity, and by the year 624 there were forty-six monasteries and temples housing 816 priests and monks and 569 nuns. Nearly all of the early buildings have long since disappeared because their construction was of wood, which rendered them susceptible to the ravages of fire and gradual deterioration from the elements. Among the few splendid structures of this earliest period of Buddhism that have survived are the famous Golden Hall or Kondo, the five-storied Pagoda, and the Yumedono or Hall of Dreams, which form a part of the many buildings of the Horyuji temple near Nara. The Horyuji, oldest surviving temple in Japan, was founded in 607 by Prince Shotoku Taishi, in obedience to the command of the Empress Suiko. Its architecture is representative of the style that was current in China in the sixth century and was most likely the work of Chinese *émigré* architects and temple craftsmen. Although some of the sculptured images for these early temples were brought over from Korea or China, most of the masterpieces of the Asuka period were created by foreign artists working in Japan with the assistance of native craftsmen. The sculpture of this period was derived from Buddhist art as practiced in China around this time. Its fully developed style in Japan in this period was the result of harmoniously absorbing the finest qualities of the various Chinese dynastic styles into a work of singular beauty.

The Shaka Nyorai Triad, *also called the* Amida Triad *or* Sakyamuni Triad, *executed by Tori Busshi in gilt bronze. Asuka period (552-645). Horyuji temple, Nara.*

The earliest historical reference to sculpture in Japan mentions a Chinese sculptor named Shiba Tatto, who came over from China in the year 522 and is said to have introduced Buddhism among his own circle of friends. His son Tasuna became a master craftsman and is mentioned as having produced a Buddhist image in memory of the Emperor Yomei, who had embraced the new religion. It is also recorded that Tatto's daughter was one of the first three Buddhist nuns received into the new faith in Japan. The outstanding Buddhist sculptor of the Asuka period was Tori Busshi, a son of Tasuna, who received the highest favors from Prince Shotoku for his work and for his devotion to the advancement of Buddhism. In 605 he received an Imperial commission to make two images of the Buddha, one in gilt bronze and the other in embroidery. These images, which were enshrined in the Gangoji monastery, were made in the size called *joroku*, the standard height for a statue of the Buddha. This height, equal to sixteen feet, is said to have been attained by Sakyamuni, the founder of Buddhism. Tori, for his skill in producing these works, was rewarded with the high court rank of *taijin*, and was given an estate in Omi province containing a large

number of rice fields. His most notable work is the famous *Shaka Nyorai Triad*, or *Sakyamuni Triad*, in the Horyuji temple, consisting of a gilt bronze image of the seated Buddha with an attendant Bosatsu standing on either side. An inscription on the halo attached to the Buddha states that the icon was made by Tori in the year 623 at the command of the widow of Prince Shotoku, in memory of her husband, who had died in the preceding year, and was intended to secure his happiness in the Buddhist Paradise. The triad is noted as a representative masterpiece of the Asuka period and as characteristic of Tori-style images, which are magnificently stylized with a realistic portrayal of the features and a peculiar freedom of proportion that is most impressive. A distinctive feature of Asuka-period sculpture is seen in the delicate modeling of the hands and in most cases the gentle features that reflect a sense of kindness and sincerity.

The images most frequently depicted in Buddhist sculpture during the Asuka and Nara periods may be identified by their Japanese names as Butsu or Nyorai, Bosatsu, and Ten. Nyorai means a perfect manifestation of the absolute truth of the universe as attained through Buddhism, and is equivalent to Buddha. Butsu is the Japanese name for Buddha, or one who has attained true enlightenment. Buddha images represent Gautama who, after contemplation under the bo tree, attained Buddhahood and became the Buddha or Sakyamuni. In Japanese the Indian name Sakyamuni is referred to as Shaka Nyorai and Shakamuni Butsu, all names applied to Gautama, the founder of Buddhism. The Buddhist sutras or scriptures state that a Buddha has thirty-two distinguishing physical features, among which is the hair, depicted with many small curls called *rahotsu*, meaning snail hair, because of the resemblance of these evenly spaced conventionalized curls to snail shells. Among other features are a curl of white hair on the forehead that gives off a ray of light, fingers and toes that are slightly webbed, long and slender fingers, and on the soles of the feet the thousand-spoked wheel-marks of Buddha. Another characteristic is that every Buddha has his own symbol, although certain symbols are common to all Buddhas. The Buddhas most frequently found in Japanese art are called Sakyamuni, Dainichi, Amida, and Yakushi. The Japanese name Bosatsu is the equivalent of the Sanskrit name Bodhisattva, meaning enlightened being. Images of Bosatsu, which are believed to represent Gautama, the Buddha Sakyamuni, at the time he was a prince in the Indian kingdom of Kapilavasta, are usually depicted as lovely and graceful, as in the Kannon Bosatsu. The upper part of the body in Bosatsu images is usually naked, and the hair flows down over the shoulders or is arranged in some form of knot. The hands frequently hold such symbols as the lotus flower of Kannon, or the vase and lotus of Juichimen Kannon, the eleven-headed Kannon. The name Ten, often used in Japanese, is the same as Deva, meaning heavenly or divine being. Ten are heavenly gods and goddesses, as distinguished from personages of earth or hell, which are either fierce or benevolent and beautiful.

Among other important images of the Asuka period in the Horyuji temple is the *Yakushi Nyorai* in the Golden Hall. This bronze Buddha is a typical example of the style of Tori, the superb modeling of the face having a strong but tenderly alive expression. An incised inscription on the halo indicates that the image dates from the time of the foundation of the temple. Yakushi Nyorai is the name given to the Buddha who heals physical as well as spiritual ailments that may hinder the faith and enlightenment of a Buddhist devotee. He is usually depicted with a medicine pot in the left hand, while the right forearm is raised with the palm of the hand open toward the front. Within the precinct of the Horyuji is the Yumedono or Hall of Dreams, which is the main hall of the East temple. The most sacred image in this hall is the famous *Nyoirin Kannon*, also known as the *Yumedono Kannon* and *Guze Kannon*. Kannon, whose Chinese name is Kuan-Yin, is the goddess of mercy who in the Buddhist hierarchy of gods appears in a variety of forms, such as in the Six Manifestations of Kannon

and in the Thirty-three Manifestations of Kannon. One of the Six Manifestations is the Nyoirin Kannon, who satisfies human desire by virtue of the wheel and enchanted gem. The famous *Nyoirin Kannon* in the Yumedono had been wrapped in cloth and secretly hidden in this hall for ten centuries until it was rediscovered in the early years of the Meiji period. Carved from a single log of wood, it has a crown of pierced bronze, and the features of the face represent a calm, intellectual, classic beauty. Light falling upon it from certain oblique angles gives a weirdly mysterious dignity to the features. Another very famous and imposing *Nyoirin Kannon* is in the Chuguji nunnery of the Horyuji temple. Carved in camphor wood,

Bronze image of the Yakushi Nyorai, *in the Golden Hall of the Horyuji temple, Nara. Asuka period (552-645).*

also from a single log, the goddess is shown in a sitting position, her right leg resting on her left knee. The statue's originally polychromed and gilded surfaces have long since worn away, and the wood has darkened from centuries of incense smoke to a lustrous purplish-black like ancient bronze. This lovely goddess is portrayed with her elbow resting on her right knee, and the first two fingers of her right hand are lightly touching her cheek. Her eyes are half closed in meditation, and a most tender, compassionate smile animates her lips. Benevolence and salvation to all living things are the attributes of the goddess Kannon. Of all the Buddhist gods, Kannon inspires the widest devotion in Japan, despite the higher rank of Buddha or Nyorai in the Buddhist hierarchy. Another manifestation of the goddess in which she often appears is the Kannon Bosatsu, one of the two attendants in the *Amida Triad*, but in most cases she stands alone as a single object of worship.

From the earliest phases of Buddhism in Japan sculptural images of Kannon were produced in great numbers. In contrast to the serene magnificence and expressive strength which characterize the best images of the Buddha, Kannons have subtle qualities of realism and individual expression often reflecting the feminine beauty of contemporary models. The Asuka period was a high point of Buddhist art and an era in which many great masterpieces were produced. Very soon after the first images were brought over from the mainland, the native genius of the Japanese began to transform the style of sculpture adopted from the Chinese. Aside from certain native innovations expressing a purely Japanese æsthetic taste, the sculptor frequently created in his images a genuine expression of graceful sentiment, tenderness, and warmth.

Flourishing as a living art after a span of fourteen centuries, Japanese sculpture has no counterpart in the cultural history of the world. Sacred images constituted most of the output of Japanese sculpture for the first several centuries, and secular art was largely nonexistent at that time. It is because of their careful preservation as sacred objects, and the fact that many of the temples and monasteries that own them are still standing, that these great works of sculpture have survived so many centuries. The highest expression of the sculptor's art in Japan was reached in Buddhist images, executed in wood, bronze, dry lacquer, or clay. Stone was not used for Buddhist sculpture, as it was in China. The preferred medium was wood, and wood carving was the supreme native endowment peculiar to the Japanese, a genius which persisted for generations. For the first six centuries the statues were carved from a single log, as indicated above for the early Kannons, only the arms and toes usually being cut separately. This method of carving in wood continued to flourish until the Fujiwara period, when the great sculptor Jocho created a new technique which eliminated many of the earlier difficulties.

Nyoirin Kannon, *also called the* Yumedono Kannon *or* Guze Kannon, *carved from a single log of wood.. Asuka period (552-645). Horyuji temple, Nara.*

BUDDHIST BRONZE IMAGES

In contrast to wooden images carved with knife or chisel, those of bronze were the creation of the modeler rather than the sculptor. With the introduction of Buddhism into Japan, Korean bronze casters were among the craftsmen sent over by the King of Paikche, both to make sacred images and to instruct the Japanese in the techniques of the art. The first stage in the process of bronze casting, known as *cire perdue*, or lost wax, was to make a finished wax model of the statue. A thick layer of fine-quality clay was then applied to the wax as a mold and baked, at which stage the wax would run out through apertures in the clay mold. Molten bronze was then poured into the hollow mold. When the bronze had cooled and hardened, the delicate process of cutting away the clay was undertaken as the final stage. Large images were hollow because solid bronze would have been impracticable to move and a useless extravagance. In this process the sculptor modeled the images in wax laid over a rough core of clay. When the wax image was completed in finished detail, more clay was

Nyoirin Kannon, *also called* Miroku Bosatsu *or* Maitreya, *in the Chuguji nunnery of the Horyuji temple at Nara. Carved from a single trunk of the camphor tree. Asuka period (552-645).*

Kannon, Goddess of Mercy, *bearing a lotus, as an attendant of the Amida Buddha, standing with slightly bended knees, welcomes the soul of the deceased. Gold-lacquered wood darkened by incense smoke. Fourteenth century. Seattle Art Museum. Eugene Fuller Memorial Collection.*

in turn laid over the modeled wax. In the heating process the wax ran out through vents and small removal gates, and metal rods secured the space between the inner and outer clay cores. After the molten bronze cast in this mold had cooled, both the inner and outer cores of clay were chipped away. This method of casting was used to make all the large images, except such enormous statues as the Great Buddhas of Nara and Kamakura, which had to be made in cast bronze plates with only the heads and hands cast as single units.

The creative genius of the artists of the Nara period (710-794), and the powerful influence which Buddhism had begun to wield, were major factors contributing to the supreme æsthetic quality of the art of this epoch. With skilled Chinese and Korean sculptors creating masterpieces of sacred images for the new temples and monasteries, the persuasive influence of the T'ang dynasty was strong. Many aspects of Chinese civilization were active in all phases of Japanese court life and scholars were vigorously striving to acquire more and more knowledge from China. This resulted in many reforms and the adoption of T'ang administrative organization

and procedures. With this strong influence of the great culture of China beaming on all phases of Japanese life, the inspiration of T'ang art is also visible in the Buddhist images. A purely native style of sculpture could not be developed in those times because there were certain prescribed canons necessary to follow according to true Buddhist ideals. And since the art of that time was exclusively religious, it followed these fixed forms brought from China, which were in turn adopted from the Buddhist sculptured images of India. But with the rapid development of sculpture in the Nara period, a distinctive native character began to appear and the Japanese craftsmen became masters in their own right.

In the Toin-do, or East Hall, of the Yakushiji temple at Nara one of the famous masterpieces of the Nara period was known as the *Sho Kannon*. This handsome statue exemplifies how far Japanese sculpture was able to assimilate the art of T'ang China and India into a vigorous and noble style of its own. The superb modeling and the beautiful and graceful proportions combine to give the figure a feeling of majestic poise, heightened by the rhythmic folds of the "wet" clinging

Bronze image of the Sho Kannon *in the Toin-do of the Yakushiji temple, Nara. Nara period (710-794).*

drapery revealing the forms of the body. In such examples, the master sculptors of the Nara period reveal a style far more handsome and majestic than the Chinese prototypes. The Japanese sculptor displayed a great talent and taste in proportion and in the manner of handling these loosely hung garments; there is an extraordinary delicacy and refinement of line.

Perhaps the most famous example of this characteristic style of modeling in the Nara period is the small *Amida Triad* in the Tamamushi-no-Zushi, or Golden Beetle Miniature Shrine of Lady Tachibana, in the Kondo of Horyuji temple. Dated about 710, this superb group shows a seated Buddha flanked by standing attendants in small scale, each clothed with clinging garments and each image set upon a lotus calyx. The stems of the flowers are depicted as rising out of a sacred pool which is beautifully represented in the horizontal surface of an oblong bronze base engraved with ripples and lotus leaves. Behind the group, as a backdrop, a bronze screen which is a masterpiece of low-relief sculpture shows heavenly figures seated on lotus blossoms, surrounded by swirling scarves amid gently undulating lotus stems and flowers. These and many other masterpieces of the Nara period were produced when Buddhist art flourished under the patronage of the various Emperors.

During this period Buddhism reached great heights under the sponsorship of the Emperor Shomu and eventually succeeded as the state religion, with the Todaiji temple regarded as the headquarters. The Todaiji was started in 745 on order of Emperor Shomu, and was completed in 752. The most sacred object in the Todaiji is the *Daibutsu* or *Great Buddha*, which is the largest bronze image in the world. Under command of the Emperor, the casting of this great image was begun in 743 at Shigaraki palace near Lake Biwa, but the effort ended in failure for lack of technical skill. The work was resumed at Nara in 745 and successfully completed in 749 after eight different castings. The figure is seated cross-legged on an enormous bronze pedestal composed of fifty-six lotus petals, each ten feet high and alternately turned upward and downward. The work required to execute this colossal image represents a stupendous effort and was a tremendous technical feat for that time. The statue contains over a million pounds of materials, including about 900,000 pounds of bronze, 165 pounds of mercury, and 288 pounds of pure gold. Its immense proportions measure fifty-three feet in height; the head is sixteen feet long and over nine feet wide, while the eyes are almost four feet wide and the hands almost seven feet long. It was necessary to construct the body of this huge work in segments, by applying successive molds one above the other after each preceding segment had cooled. Only the head and the hands were cast as single shells. On three occasions through the centuries the *Great Buddha* has suffered damage necessitating restoration. An earthquake in the year 855 shook off the head; then in 1180 the head and right hand were melted in the fire which destroyed the Great Hall, and in 1567 the head was again knocked off by an earthquake.

CLAY AND DRY-LACQUER SCULPTURE

Among the many treasures lavished upon the Todaiji in the Nara period are a number of clay images in the Hokkedo, or Third Month temple, which are of exquisite workmanship and regarded as representative of the art of that time. Although the method of using clay was abandoned soon after this period, much of the Nara work in this technique reached a height of perfection. In this clay process a frame was made with strips of wood and wound with cords of rice straw or other fibers to provide a ground to hold the clay. A layer of clay containing rice-straw fibers was first applied, then a layer of clay mixed with the fine fibers of the paper-mulberry tree. The final application consisted of a fine clay mixed with either glue or mica dust and laid on with a brush. The finished surface clay either contained the final color pigments or was covered with gold leaf. Although many large images were made of clay,

the method appears to have been used more frequently for smaller works. The clay images of Ni-o which are in the ancient two-storied Chumon or Middle Gate of the Horyuji, are among the earliest specimens of the Nara period, dating from the year 711. Ni-o, or Kongo Rikishi, are a pair of fierce-looking demigods who serve as guardians of a Buddhist precinct, and usually keep watch over the gates.

The main object of worship in the Hokkedo is the celebrated dry-lacquer image of Fuku Kensaku Kannon, which is surrounded by fourteen other images. Of colossal size with its esoteric attributes of three eyes and six arms, it was made in the *dakkatsu kanshitsu* lacquer technique. Clay and dry lacquer were the principal materials used during the late Nara period for images, almost completely replacing wood.

There were two distinct methods of producing dry-lacquer work, namely, *dakkatsu kanshitsu* or hollow dry lacquer, and *mokushin kanshitsu* or wood-core dry lacquer. In the hollow dry-lacquer technique, which was the type used chiefly in the first half of the Nara period, the desired form of the image was first modeled in clay, and several layers of hemp cloth covered with liquid lacquer were applied over this core. After this lacquer shell became perfectly dry and hard, the clay core was carefully chipped away and a wooden framework was con-

Bronze image of Yakushi Nyorai in the Yakushiji temple, Nara. Nara period (710-794).

Bronze image of the Great Buddha *in the Todaiji temple, Nara, completed in 749; Nara period.*

73

structed inside to give additional strength. Such parts as the head and arms were made separately and then stitched to the body and made rigid with coats of lacquer. Various surface details, such as hair and articles of jewelry, were modeled with a mixture of liquid lacquer and sawdust, flour, and powdered incense wood. The finished surface was then lacquered and colored, or covered with gold leaf. In the wood-core dry-lacquer method, which was used chiefly in the latter half of the period, the desired form was first carved of wood, then covered with layers of hemp cloth saturated with liquid lacquer. The entire process was similar to the method of making hollow dry-lacquer work. It is interesting to observe the gradual changes in methods from the hollow dry lacquer of the early eighth century to the wood-core dry lacquer in the second half of the century. Finally the lacquer shell became nothing more than a finishing coat. It was abandoned in the tenth century for wood carving.

One of the many famous dry-lacquer images is the *Hachibu-shu*, or *Eight Supernatural Guardians of Sakyamuni*, in the Kofukuji temple at Nara. A characteristic of the art of the early Nara-period sculptors can be clearly seen in the realistic treatment of the animated and youthful faces. Especially in-

teresting is the distinctive expression and beautiful features of the image of Ashura, one of the *Hachibu-shu*, which are not unlike those of present-day Japanese girls. Images of supernatural beings began to appear in the Nara period, as there were already elements of esoteric Buddhism existing at that time. This form of Buddhism, with its doctrines designed for and understood only by the initiated, introduced a variety of images of supernatural beings, such as an eleven-headed Kannon, an Ashura with three heads and six arms, a so-called thousand-armed Kannon, and many others.

The Heian period (794-1185) begins with the removal of the capital from Nara to Heian, now called Kyoto. It is divided into the Jogan or Konin era (794-897) and the Fujiwara era (897-1185). It was a period in which the arts and culture were stimulated and influenced by the course of political power and religious developments. Thus far Buddhism in Japan had retained all of its principal Chinese features, but with the opening years of the Heian period its doctrines were to be brought to conform more closely with the spiritual needs and temperament of the Japanese.

It was during this time that the work of two great priests, Saicho, founder of the Tendai sect, and Kukai or Kobo Daishi,

Clay image of Ni-o *with mouth open, in the Chumon, or Middle Gate, of the Horyuji temple at Nara, made in 711; Nara period.*

Clay image of Ni-o, *with mouth closed, in the Chumon, or Middle Gate, of the Horyuji temple at Nara, made in 711; Nara period.*

founder of the Shingon sect, gave birth to strong and characteristic forms of Japanese Buddhism. Both of these sects rose to wield considerable influence, and Buddhism now became all powerful, with two rival centers, the monastery on Mount Koya, near Nara, which taught the esoteric philosophy of the Shingon sect with its complex symbolism, and that on Mount Hiei in Kyoto, the seat of the Tendai sect, whose doctrines were based on pantheistic realism. These two monasteries became the fountainheads of Buddhist learning and their teachings greatly influenced the forms of Buddhist art. In contrast to the earlier Buddhist sects called exoteric, meaning easily comprehended, the art of the Heian period was inspired from the theories peculiar to these new esoteric sects, or those having occult or secret philosophies. The earlier Buddhists regarded the Buddha Sakyamuni as a supreme and miraculous personage, while the esoteric Buddhists proclaimed him a god and regarded all phenomena in the universe as manifestations of the power of Dainichi Nyorai, the Supreme Buddha. In the bewildering pantheon of later Buddhism with its immense canon, all Buddhas and Bodhisattvas are representative of individual aspects of Dainichi and have their peculiar functions prescribed by secret canons. Because of these features, a new iconography appeared and the images took strictly prescribed forms of mystery and austerity to represent special attributes, and at times had forbidding expressions. This later Buddhist art sacrificed much of the freedom of expression in the earlier images, whose features radiated grace, kindness, and a tender, warm feeling.

HEIAN CARVED-WOOD IMAGES

With only a few exceptions Japanese temple sculpture from this period onward was entirely executed in wood, and there was a great demand for Buddhist images to furnish the numerous monasteries all over the country. New monasteries were built on the summits and sides of mountains, often in remote regions, as it became the fashion among religious men to indulge in meditation or solitary and contemplative practices in distant retreats. The serene atmosphere within the walls of these monastery compounds inspired artists and sculptors to create beautiful works. The principal reason for the preference for wooden sculpture was the traditional taste for the medium and the traditional skill in the use of the chisel. Much of the wood sculpture of the Heian period was rather simple and tended toward the decorative. A particular feature of this work is the gracefully carved loose hanging garments done in a technique called *homa-shiki*, or rolling-waves style, consisting of beautifully controlled parallel curves resembling sea waves approaching a beach at regular intervals. Heian sculpture of

Dry-lacquer image of Ashura, *one of the eight supernatural guardians of Sakyamuni, in the Kofukuji temple, Nara. Nara period (710-794).*

the Jogan period continued to be carved in the technique called *ichiboku*, in which the head, body, legs, and even the pedestal of a standing figure were carved from a single piece of wood. Any portions that protruded, such as forearms stretched out from the elbows and objects held in the hands, were carved separately. It was also common practice for the protruding knees on a seated image to be carved separately from the rest, which was made from a single piece.

The Late Heian or Fujiwara period (897-1185) covers the three centuries of Japanese history which saw the rise and fall of the Fujiwara family, the warfare of the Taira and Minamoto families, and the final victory of Minamoto Yoritomo, who established the military government at Kamakura. It was an age of luxury and abundance for the upper classes. The beginning of the Fujiwara period preceded by a few years the fall of the T'ang dynasty in China, and the arts of Japan now began to reflect a true native taste and the ancient Japanese love of nature; landscape painting became so popular that it influenced paintings with Buddhist subjects, which frequently have naturalistic backgrounds. Buddhist art continued to flourish under the growing wealth and power of the monasteries. Religious art was greatly stimulated by a new style

Gilt wood image of Amida Nyorai, *by Jocho, in the Hoodo of the Byodoin temple, at Uji. Late Heian period.*

interior is the famous image of *Amida Nyorai*, which is considered to be one of the finest examples of Japanese religious art. This great masterpiece of wood sculpture was executed by Jocho, d. 1057, who was celebrated even during his lifetime. It was Jocho who set the style of Buddhist sculpture during the Fujiwara period, and he was rewarded with many honors in recognition of his great work.

Almost all the sculpture of the Fujiwara period was in wood; however, a new technique appeared called *yosegi*, or assembled wood blocks, in contrast to the single-wood-block method, called *ichiboku*, used during the Early Heian period. In this new technique perfected by Jocho, many small blocks were cut according to geometrical principles and assembled to make a hollow form approximating the shape of the image to be carved. Designating marks were applied to indicate the parts to be cut away and those to be left untouched. The whole was then disassembled and each piece was separately carved by an assistant. After the roughly carved form was set up again and securely reinforced with iron clamps, it represented the true form of the image on which the master sculptor had only to execute the skillful finishing details. With the introduction of this technique a new system originated in the *bussho*, or workshop of a master sculptor and his assistants. These ateliers, or schools of Buddhist sculptors, were founded by great artists and flourished for many generations, often taking their names from the places where they were located. During the preceding Nara period when the great monasteries were built with government funds, each contained an office entrusted with the making of images. The sculptors attached to these administrative offices were usually laymen, but during the second half of the Heian period a great sculptor was often rewarded with a priestly rank. The big monasteries of these times became closely associated with particular great noble and feudal families, and many of the sculptors working exclusively for certain families entered the priesthood and were honored with a high Buddhist rank. Jocho, whose father was a priest working in sculpture, became the first artist in his field to receive such a distinguished honor. Parallel with the system in which sculptors worked exclusively for particular monasteries, there appeared another kind of establishment in the form of private ateliers connected with the houses of master sculptors. Here pupils were trained and sculpture produced in finished form. This custom came in with the introduction of the *yosegi* sculptural technique, providing a more practical method for the employment of many assistants and pupils. With the prosperous conditions existing during the Fujiwara period, these ateliers were able to produce great numbers of images of all kinds to satisfy the demand of this age of luxury.

The years that preceded the close of the Heian period brought with them loss of power of the Fujiwara family and a series

brought about by the rise of the Japanese sect known as Jodo, or Pure Land, under the teachings of Genshin, 942-1017, a very learned man of the Tendai sect. This Buddhist faith teaches the worship of Amida, Buddha of Infinite Qualities, with a doctrine of salvation through absolute faith in the all-saving power of the Buddha Amida, and a promise that the believer will be reborn in Amida's Paradise, the Pure Land of Jodo, by calling upon his name. The influence of Jodo on Buddhist art is clearly seen in the images of Amida with their beautiful expression of tenderness and compassion. All this is in noticeable contrast to the severity and stern expression in the esoteric Buddhist sculpture of the early Heian period. The Jodo faith is characterized in much of the painting, with frequent scenes of Amida and his attendants coming to welcome the dying to Paradise. In architecture, also, it became the fashion among the nobles to build halls dedicated to Amida, such as the famous Phoenix Hall, or Hoodo, of the Byodoin temple at Uji near Kyoto. The original main hall of the Byodoin, known as the Hoodo, was built in 1053 and is representative of the best religious architecture of the period, when the Fujiwara family was in the ascendancy. Among the Buddhist images enshrined in this magnificently decorated of battles fought between the rival clans of the Taira and Minamoto families. The final defeat of the Taira family by Minamoto Yoritomo marks the beginning of the Kamakura period (1185-1333) and the establishment of the seat of government at Kamakura. The center of culture remained in Kyoto, and Kamakura became important for religious activities. This period produced a culture that was vigorous, in which the military families constituted a new class of society and were anxious to cultivate the arts of peace. A strong reaction appeared against the formal Buddhism of the Heian period, expressing itself in the revival of the old Nara sects and in the birth of new sects. Buddhism in the Kamakura period became a popular religion, assuming a truly Japanese character and quality, and Zen Buddhism became particularly popular with the military class. The doctrines of the new sects were practical, simple, and easily understood, and because of this they found their followers among the samurai and commoners. While less emphasis was given to icon worship in the new sects, the art of sculpture attained its highest realistic development in the images of the founders and high priests of the new sects, who were greatly respected for their religious teachings. Icon sculpture retained its traditional form in the images made for the older sects, which included the Shingon and Tendai. Along with the work carried on in the traditional style, a new school made its appearance which was more or less a further development of the realistic trend of the Heian period.

FUJIWARA REALISM

Vivid realism in sculptured wood images, introduced by Kokei, a Nara sculptor, attained its highest development in the Fujiwara period. Among the great number of treasures belonging to the Kofukuji temple at Nara, which is the headquarters of the Hosso sect of Buddhism, are some examples of the work of Kokei. Within the Kofukuji compound is the Nan-endo, a magnificent octagonal hall containing as its principal object of worship the *Fukukenjaku Kannon*, a wooden image made by Kokei in the year 1189, as well as the *Hosso Rokuso*, or *Six Patriarchs of the Hosso Sect*. These works are representative of Kokei's style of realism, which was later perfected by his son Unkei, and his pupil Kaikei. Unkei's work not only achieved perfect realism, as seen in his images of famous priests, but also a dignified strength which harmonized

Wood image of Ni-o, *with mouth open, by Unkei and Kaikei; Kamakura period, thirteenth century. Todaiji temple, Nara.*

Wood image of Ni-o *with mouth closed, by Unkei and Kaikei; Kamakura period, thirteenth century. Todaiji temple, Nara.*

Bronze image of the Great Buddha *at Kamakura, in the precincts of the Kotokuin temple. Kamakura period, cast in 1252.*

by one thousand gilt-bronze images of Kannon, each five feet seven inches in height and arranged in evenly spaced tiers in one enormously long hall which was rebuilt in 1251 after the original temple had been destroyed by fire.

One of the outstanding representative works of this period is the *Kamakura Daibutsu*, or the *Great Buddha of Kamakura*, located in the precincts of the Kotokuin temple. This enormous bronze seated figure of Amida Nyorai is about forty-two feet in height and about ninety-seven feet in circumference at the base. The image was cast in 1252 by an unknown sculptor and is regarded as a much finer work of art than the larger image at the Todaiji temple at Nara. The Kamakura image was originally enshrined in a large building, but this was damaged by a storm in 1369 and the great image has remained in the open since the year 1495, when tidal waves carried away what was left of the old structure.

Besides the sculptured images of Buddhist and Shinto deities, and portraits of contemporary leaders, the Kamakura era produced many other subjects which reflect the great carving of that time. There are, for instance, the *Shi Tenno* or Four Deva Kings, in the form of warrior gods who protect the four directions of the Buddhist universe, and a host of other religious deities as well as imaginary animals. Among the several Shinto animal-guardians or messengers of deities, those most frequently seen are the *Kara-Shishi*, or Chinese Lion, and the *Koma-inu*, or Korean dog, which are placed at the entrance of Shinto shrines as guardians. Although the term *Koma-inu* is applied to this pair of guardians of the sacred precincts, they were originally called by their respective names, *Shishi* being characterized by an open mouth, the *Koma-inu* by a closed one. The Kamakura period is regarded as the apex of Japanese sculpture, when the art reached its culmination in the thirteenth century and then began to decline. The rise in the power and popularity of the Zen sect did not contribute as much to sculpture as it did to the development of painting, because Zen did not attach as much importance to images as the other sects. Religious sculpture declined during the Momoyama and Edo periods, but this was offset by an important development of decorative sculpture for architectural purposes. The earlier type of architectural sculpture is called *kara-yo* or Chinese style, and is also known as temple carving. This was the style of decoration developed in north China and introduced into Japan at the same time as Zen. This style was not only fashionable in buildings associated with Zen Buddhism but also in the buildings of the other sects, in Shinto shrines, and in palaces and mansions. Many of the resplendent examples of the architecture of the Momoyama and Edo periods reflect this exquisite *kara-yo* work with its delicately wrought human figures, animals, birds, and flowers in pictorial compositions.

with the traditional Nara-period work. Kaikei, who had been a pupil of Kokei, was a contemporary of Unkei; but in contrast to the dynamic style of Unkei, his work is characterized by graceful realism with delicate form. Exquisite examples of Kaikei's work include the *Sogyo Hachiman*, which portrays the Shinto god as a Buddhist priest, and the *Jizo Bosatsu*, both of which are in the Todaiji temple. Jizo is a deity of children as well as a guardian of souls, and is one of the most popular Buddhist gods in Japan. He is most commonly seen in the form of a priest, his head shaven, and holding a staff with rings in his right hand and a precious pearl in his left hand. There are many names for Jizo according to his functions, and throughout Japan roadside images of Jizo are numerous. Jizo images either in temples or by the roadside are often seen with cloth bibs around their necks, placed there by parents praying for the recovery of sick children. The work of these two great sculptors of the Kamakura period was carried on by Unkei's sons, Tankei, Koben, and Kosho, and a number of others. Among the few works known to have been executed by Tankei is the *Thousand-handed Kannon* in the Sanju-Sangendo temple at Kyoto. The figure of Kannon is seated and accompanied by twenty-eight followers; they are surrounded

VI Masks

A DISTINCT and often grotesque phase of Japanese wood sculpture had its provenance in ancient religious dances which employed wooden masks. Their use and development corresponds with the unique history of dramatic art in Japan, whose origin can be traced back through the many centuries to the mythological age. Both of the oldest chronicles of Japan, the *Kojiki* and the *Nihonshoki*, written at the beginning of the eighth century, contain interesting legends of the religious dance called *kagura*, or sacred dance with music, from which the Japanese drama developed. They record that when Amaterasu-o-mi-kami, the sun goddess, retired into the Heavenly Cave and the world was thrown into darkness, the heavenly deities were greatly perplexed and in their consternation debated various means to persuade her to come out. At this time the witty and jovial goddess Ameno-uzumeno-mikoto, by performing a comic dance at the entrance of the cave, succeeded in enticing the sun goddess from her hiding place, and light was restored to the universe. The traditional origin of the *kagura* is thus traced to these mythological times, and it is certain that the *kagura* has existed since very ancient times.

In its earliest form it was a pantomime, in which the performers impersonated the deities and imitated their deeds by wearing masks and dancing to the accompaniment of instrumental music and chanting. This simple and primitive sacred *kagura* dance with its crude masks is still practiced in every town and village in Japan. The masks used in the ritual dances in early times were made to suggest supernatural beings and mythical birds and animals, for men imagined the gods and sacred beasts as possessing attributes different from those seen among human beings. With the gradual development of the sacred dance from its primitive beginning to the refined No drama, the carving of the masks improved, many becoming sculptural masterpieces. Certain families specializing in this category of sculpture have been famous, and their original designs have been carefully preserved and imitated down to the present day. The masks used by the Japanese throughout the recorded history of their dance and lyric-drama are not only rich in artistic achievement but cover a wide variety of forms. Masks have been used only in the lyric-dramas and dances; the drama proper is never performed with masks.

It is from the Asiatic mainland that the first ritual and festival masks were introduced into Japan. Although their use in the countries of the mainland gradually declined, their development in Japan continued until it reached the stage of a real art. The earliest factual accounts relating to the history of masks in Japan begin with the seventh century, at which time the dance-drama called *gigaku* was introduced from the continent. Then in the following century the *gigaku* was superseded by another dance-drama brought from the mainland, called *bugaku*, which has been performed until the present time. However, it was not until the eighth and ninth centuries that the use of masks became popular throughout the country, when they were introduced as a part of the Buddhist ceremony known as *gyodo*. The *gigaku* and *bugaku* were principally performed for the aristocracy, and because of this exclusive privilege the commoners were unable to acquire an appreciation of these dance-dramas. However, with the practice of using masks in the Buddhist ceremony of *gyodo*, other plays were developed and the popularity of masks increased until eventually they attained their ultimate refinement as seen in the present-day No and *kyogen* dances. In these dances, acting perfection has reached a high level of accomplishment and the perfected mask serves to create fantastic impressions.

"GIGAKU" DANCE-DRAMA

According to the *Nihonshoki*, *gigaku* was introduced into Japan in the twentieth year of the reign of Empress Suiko, or

Bugaku *mask called Bato. It is used in a vigorous dance with violent movements and said to represent the anger of a son whose father has been killed by wild beasts, or an Empress whose jealousy turned her into a demon. Late Heian period, twelfth century. Itsukushima shrine, Miyajima.*

612, by a Korean named Mimashi from the Kingdom of Paikche. It is said that Mimashi had learned the *gigaku* in the Chinese kingdom of Wu, which was an important country prior to the T'ang dynasty. It is said that the Japanese originally called this dance *gogaku*, or music of *go*, since *go* is their meaning of the Chinese character for *wu*. However, the name *gigaku*, or accomplished music, was later applied to the dance because its music was so much more advanced than the primitive music of Japan. The *gigaku* was but one of many arts being rapidly introduced from the mainland along with Buddhism and Chinese culture. *Gigaku* performances received an enthusiastic reception by the members of the Imperial-court families, who were keenly desirous to acquire as much of the learning and culture of China as possible. It was a time when in every phase of their daily existence the noble families imi-

tated the advanced cultural life of the Chinese. Thus, two able assistants or pupils were quickly appointed to receive complete instruction from Mimashi in the technique of its performance. *Gigaku* dances continued to be the most popular performances for over two centuries, not only at Imperial-court functions but in the Buddhist temples as well, until it was superseded by the *bugaku* dance during the eighth and ninth centuries.

Although the *gigaku* performances no longer exist today, some idea of their colorful display of theatrical pageantry and unrestrained humor is appreciated from the masks that have been preserved since that time. Of the 223 extant *gigaku* masks of the seventh and eighth centuries, 164 are preserved in the Shosoin Treasure Repository at Nara, 28 in the Todaiji temple, and 31 in national museums. The masks in the national museums were originally preserved in the Horyuji temple near

Nara, and are traditionally said to have been brought to Japan by Mimashi. Some of these surviving masks are veritable works of art and possess some characteristics in common with the religious images of the Asuka period. Although a few *gigaku* masks were made of dry lacquer and painted, most of them were carved from wood and painted. In contrast to later types, *gigaku* masks are rather large, as they were designed to cover all or most of the head of the wearer. This large-size mask, with its deep and prominent carving, increased the effectiveness of the portrayal, especially as the performance was held out of doors.

Accounts of the *gigaku* dance recorded in ancient chronicles relate that it was a comic performance. It is also said to have been an elaborate spectacle when it was performed in the courtyards of Buddhist temples or of noble mansions. The colorful costumes and fantastic masks contributed to the gay and festive atmosphere of the open-air performance. Each character was clearly identified by a particular mask. The first to appear was Shishi, a lion, attended by two lion-taming boys called *shishiko*. A king known as Goko and an actor called Chido came next, followed by Kongo, a strong and robust fellow, with Karura, a mythological bird. As the tempo of the dance increased, there appeared a fantastically ugly character called Konron, whose comic gestures stirred the audience to much laughter. When a genteel and beautiful girl called Gojo entered with her escort named Rikishi, Konron began to act a comic love scene in pantomime with crude and unrestrained humor. His actions caused Gojo's escort to become so angry that a humorous fight ensued in which Konron suffered a rather comical but indelicate accident, to the great

Gigaku *mask of Goko, or King of Go. Contemporary records say the actor wearing this mask appeared at the beginning of the* gigaku *performance and played the role of a piper. Asuka period, seventh century. Tokyo National Museum.*

Bugaku ninomai *mask of Ouna, the Old Woman. The* ninomai, *or second dance, is performed by an old man called Jo and his wife Ouna, in which they comically try to imitate the first dance called* amma, *performed by two actors in full court dress. Late Heian period, twelfth century. Itsuku-shima shrine. Miyajima.*

Gigaku *mask of Gojo or Maid of Go. It depicts the purity and beauty of a noble-woman of the ancient Chinese kingdom of Go, where the* gigaku *originated, and is the only female* gigaku *mask. Nara period, eighth century. Shosoin, Nara.*

Left: Gyodo *mask representing Kubanda, one of the Hachibu-shu, or eight bearers of the sacred palanquin in the* gyodo *procession. It was used at the memorial ceremony held at the pagoda of the Toji or Kyo-o Gokokuji temple in 1334. Late Heian period, twelfth century. Kyo-o Gokokuji temple, Kyoto.*

Right: Gyodo *mask of Katen. One of the original masks used by the twelve bearers of the sacred palanquin representing the Twelve Deva Kings, in the* gyodo *procession at the memorial ceremony at the pagoda of the Toji or Kyo-o Gokokuji temple in 1086, and again in 1334. Late Heian period, tenth century. Kyo-o Gokokuji temple, Kyoto.*

delight and laughter of the audience. This scene was quickly followed by more laugh-provoking incidents with the entrance of Taikofu, an old man supported by a boy called Taikoji. The old man's unsteady walk created a comical skit. The next to appear was Baramon, portraying a Brahman of India, who held the attention of the audience with his nimbleness and skill in twirling a long piece of cloth. The final character to come upon the scene is Suiko-o, king of some foreign land, with eight retainers. The names of the latter in Japanese connote that they were all drunkards, and their actions together with their humorous masks provoked great laughter. Judging from these early descriptions of the *gigaku*, the manner in which it was performed resembled a continuous procession, with the actors being introduced one after the other in proper sequence. Small and easily carried musical instruments were used in this dance, which required only three pieces, a *dohatsu* or bronze gong, a *koshi*-tsusumi or hip-drum, and a *fue* or flute.

THE "BUGAKU" DANCE

After more than a century of continuous appreciation by the aristocracy, the *gigaku* finally gave way to the *bugaku* dance, which was also of Chinese origin. In contrast to the rather simple form of the *gigaku*, the *bugaku* is a difficult and complex repertoire of dances given with or without the aid of masks. From the descriptions in ancient chronicles it appears that the *bugaku* in its most finished form was actually a compilation of the traditional music of fourteen countries and the curious dances of eight countries within the structure of the T'ang empire. As these individual dance-dramas were perfected at the T'ang court, they were in turn introduced into Japan. The *bugaku* was thus a highly refined and complicated performance, without the comic vulgarity of the *gigaku*. Various names have been applied by the Japanese to the dances which make up the complete *bugaku* performance. These names are designating titles that also indicate the realm in the T'ang empire from which the dances originated, such as Togaku for China, Bokkaigaku for Manchuria, Koraigaku and Shiragigaku for Korea, Rinyugaku for Indo-China, and so forth. The music and dances of these many regions became the favorite form of entertainment not only at the Imperial-court functions but also in the Buddhist temples. During the succeeding centuries the *bugaku* formed an intricate part of the cultural life of Japan, and the nobles themselves became proficient in the art of rendering its music and performing the dances. The *bugaku* reached its final form during the Heian period (794-1185) and has survived to the present day. Regular performances are given at Imperial-court functions in Tokyo and occasionally at important Buddhist temples and Shinto shrines.

Tsuina *mask of Oni, or Demon, used in the bean-throwing ceremony of the same name on the last day of winter at the Horyuji temple at Nara, in which three demons, a father demon, a mother demon, and a son demon, are driven out by the god Bishamon. Kamakura period, thirteenth century. Horyuji temple, Nara.*

Although *bugaku* reached its highest development during the Heian period, most of the masks preserved in the museums and temples date from the eleventh to fourteenth centuries. Whereas the masks used in the *gigaku* were rather realistic to conform with the character parts of the dance, *bugaku* masks are symbolic. This serves as a subtle accessory to the rhythmic movements expressing human actions and emotions. Since the *bugaku* dance is performed with a fair amount of action, the masks were made very thin and light, with a minimum of weight, and only covered the face. The fine details required to express their symbolic meaning were executed with a delicate touch, and the masks even had various moving parts which were manually manipulated by the wearer. Some *bugaku* masks have eyes that move, and others are made so the mouth will open and close, or the hair move to express certain meanings. A remarkable characteristic of some is the vertical movement of the cheeks, which gives the impression that the eyes and the mouth are being opened and closed. Every detail of these masks could be clearly seen and appreciated by the audience, because the *bugaku* dance was performed on a stage in small quarters, in contrast to the *gigaku* performance, which was given out of doors. The more complex nature of the musical accompaniments for the dance required additional instruments of an advanced type. Since *bugaku* was performed on a stage, the orchestra was placed on either side, and the chief instruments were the *fue* or flute, *biwa* or lute, *koto* or large zither, *sho* or panpipe, *kugo* or harp, *shichiriki* or flageolet, and three kinds of drums, *dadaiko*, *kekko*, and *taiko*. This array of Oriental instruments produced an exotic rhythm which enhanced the beauty of the dance.

"GYODO" MASKS

There is a Buddhist ceremony that still exists in Japan popularly known as *neri-kuyo*, although its correct Buddhist name is *gyodo*. Introduced into Japan from China during the Nara period (710-794), it consists of a procession in which a sacred relic or image, which is normally kept from view in a temple or shrine, is carried through the streets for the people to see. Shortly after its introduction, this ceremony was also practiced at Shinto shrines, and although originally Buddhist, it is now chiefly a Shinto procession. Many *gyodo* masks dating from the tenth century are preserved in the ancient temples at Nara. Since the eighth century the Horyuji temple has celebrated an occasion called the Shoryo ceremony in which the sacred ashes and a small image of Prince Shotoku, the founder of Buddhism in Japan, are carried around the precincts of the temple in a procession. These are borne in an elaborately ornamented palanquin, with the faces of the bearers hidden by *gyodo* masks.

Since it was considered a sacrilege to have the palanquin carried by common coolies, their faces were covered by masks intended to portray the eight attendants of the Buddha, known as the Hachibu-shu. The *gyodo* ceremonial masks include a great variety of grotesque and fantastic representations of many deities. The processions were elaborate and colorful affairs, with brilliant costumes, and the leaders usually wore masks representing such things as lions and goblins. When the famous pagoda of the Kyo-o-Gokokuji temple at Kyoto, popularly known as Toji, was dedicated in the year 1086, the palanquin with its sacred relic was borne by bearers who wore masks representing the Twelve Deva Kings. Some types of *gyodo* dances are still performed in Buddhist temples in various parts of Japan. The *raigo* ceremony is one of these types of *gyodo* which have survived until the present day as religious performances in which the actors wear masks. It originated in the tenth century when the Jodo, or Pure Land, doctrine was being forcibly expounded by Eshin-Sozu. To assist in making this and other Jodo doctrines more easily understood by the commoners, religious pageants were given in the temple precincts. These *raigo* ceremonies became popular in many temples throughout the country. During two of the festival days at the Taimadera temple near the town of Shimoda in the prefecture of Nara, a *raigo* ceremony is enacted each year. It is in honor of Chujo-Hime, daughter of Fujiwara Toyonari, a minister to the Emperor, who according to legend is said to have painted a large picture of the Buddhist Paradise in the year 763. Chujo-Hime became a nun at this temple after assuming the name of Honyo, and, because of her accomplishments, is given this performance in which the Twenty-five Bosatsu welcome her.

SACRED DANCES

Sacred dances and performances as practiced for centuries in the Buddhist temples and Shinto shrines, as well as those

No mask depicting Kagekiyo, a renowned warrior of the Heike family, who fought in their losing conflicts with the Genji family. Early Edo period, seventeenth century. Tokyo National Museum.

performed at the Imperial court, were the sources from which the No drama and the *kyogen* comic interlude developed. Among these early entertainments are the primitive performances called *dengaku*, meaning rustic music, and *sarugaku*. The *dengaku* probably had its origin in a primitive dance held in the fields to pray for divine grace for the crops, while the *sarugaku* probably had its provenance in the ancient *kagura*. Both of these performances developed as incidental entertainments at Shinto festivals. On the picturesque island of Miyajima in the Inland Sea is the famous Itsukushima shrine, which is of very ancient origin. Old records mention its existence as early as the year 811. This beautiful Shinto shrine, with buildings connected by broad galleries, is built out over the sea, and when the tide is coming in the whole structure appears to be floating on the surface of the water. Regular performances of the *kagura* and *bugaku* dances are given as part of the traditional ritual in this impressive and beautiful setting. Along with the masks that were prominent in the history of Japanese dances

and processions is the mask used in the *tsuina* ceremony. This ceremony, also of Chinese origin, was introduced during the Nara period and consists of scattering dried beans to drive out devils or other evil spirits. At first the ceremony was only performed in the Imperial court, but it soon became a regular practice at shrines and temples. In its early prescribed form the principal character was called Hososhi, whose duty it was to exorcise the evil spirits. Hososhi wore an extremely grotesque mask fashioned in the likeness of a most fierce and horrible-looking four-eyed demon. In the original ceremony Hososhi waved a halberd with much ability and nimbleness until he had driven away the invisible enemy.

As time went on and the popularity of the *tsuina* increased, the mask actually became a devil mask and the performance developed a more dramatic and exaggerated form, with the devil being impersonated instead of invisible. During later times the ceremony presented an even more exciting display of action with the introduction of two devils into the cast.

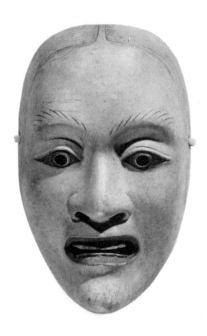

No mask representing Yamauba, a witch residing in the remote mountains. Momoyama period, sixteenth century. Tokyo National Museum.

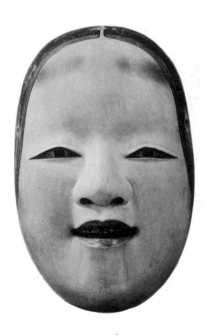

No mask portraying a young girl of the purest of feminine beauty. A masterpiece of the carver's skill, it is known as a ko-omote, *meaning small mask. Muromachi period, fifteenth century. Tokyo National Museum.*

No mask of Uba, or Old Woman. The typical No mask for representing an old woman. Muromachi period, fifteenth century. Hosho No School, Tokyo.

custom also to select famous *sumo* wrestlers, Kabuki actors, or other prominent persons to scatter the beans at these temple functions. Many years ago when the *tsuina* had spread to all parts of Japan and was practiced in temples and shrines, its popularity became so great that the ceremony in its present form, called *setsubun*, was observed, and it is still a custom in Japanese households. On this last night of winter the master of the house scatters a handful of beans at the entrance of the house and in each room, crying loudly, "Devils outside, good luck inside," or "*Oniwa-soto, fukuwa-uchi.*" The prefix *oni* is the Japanese name applied to devils or demons.

THE NO MASK

Of all the masks used by the Japanese in their various dance-dramas since ancient times, the No mask as perfected in the fourteenth century expresses the greatest æsthetic refinement. The best of the No masks are masterpieces of the sculptor's art and developed from the traditional masks used for centuries in *gigaku, bugaku, gyodo,* and other ceremonial performances. The term *no* means performance or accomplishment, and is derived from the word *sarugaku-no-no* or from *dengaku-no-no*, which signifies a performance of *saragaku* or *dengaku*. It therefore came to imply an accomplished performance of a lyric drama. The origin of the No has not been clearly determined, but it is generally believed to have developed from the early *sarugaku* and *dengaku* dances in which masks played an important role. Both of these dances doubtlessly originated from primitive dances held in the fields to pray for divine favor on the crops and were developed during the Heian period (794-1185) by musicians as entertainment for the common people in a form of dramatic dance. The *sarugaku* was performed to the accompaniment of a kind of popular music that originated in China called *sangaku*, which means scattered music. In contrast to the complex dances of the Imperial court and the Buddhist temples, these dances became extremely popular with the commoners, for they were performed in an unrestrained manner, with a quality of seriousness as well as comic interludes.

The majority of the No plays were written during the fourteenth and fifteenth centuries by two famous No actors, Kanami, 1333-1384, and his son Zeami, 1363-1444. Kanami was a Shinto priest attached to the Kasuga shrine at Nara, which is the tutelary shrine of the Fujiwara family, and together with his son, was an accomplished actor. The talent of both Kanami and Zeami came to the attention of the Shogun Yoshimitsu, under whose patronage they were able to develop their earlier performances into more dramatic plays. Through their close association with the Imperial court they achieved

Tsuina masks were then made in pairs, although each one of a pair had its own individual characteristics; the pairs represented a devil-father and devil-son or a devil-husband and devil-wife. Many temples throughout Japan still celebrate elaborate *tsuina* ceremonies, now popularly called *setsubun*. They are observed on the evening of the last day of winter according to the old lunar calendar, which corresponds to the third or fourth day of February in the new solar calendar. The Shinshoji temple at Narita in Chiba prefecture, more popularly known as Narita Fudo, is especially famous for its *mamemaki* or bean-throwing ceremony at the *setsubun* festival. The ceremony is performed here on a much larger scale than in other temples or shrines. This present-day survival of the *tsuina* does not employ the masks as in former days; instead, the head priest, dressed in an elaborate costume, performs the ceremony by tossing blanched beans over the heads of the people gathered around. In more recent years it has been the

No mask of Okina or Hakushi-kijo, the Old Man, used in the No play of the same name. Muromachi period, fifteenth century. Maeda Collection, Tokyo.

great success in creating a new form of lyric drama. Realizing the growing popularity of such dances as the *dengaku* and *sarugaku*, Kanami and Zeami perfected a harmonious blend of their traditional elements of poetry, music, and dancing with the refined melodies and graceful forms of the *shirabyoshi* dances. The *shirabyoshi*, which were then very popular among the nobility, are said to have been introduced by two court ladies at the beginning of the twelfth century. Some early accounts mention the *shirabyoshi* as originally being performed by ladies in long robes with tall headgear and swords sheathed in a white scabbard, impersonating men. *Shirabyoshi* means white-time-beating and in its early form the dance is believed to have been performed to the accompaniment of a *tsusumi* or drum.

Originally the No was a kind of ceremonial performance flourishing at the court of the Ashikaga Shogun Yoshimitsu, and from the Muromachi period (1338-1573) to the beginning of the eighteenth century it continued as a ceremonial function of the military class. About one thousand No plays are said to have been composed, and of the eight hundred that have survived, 242 are still actually performed. Among those currently being performed, more than one hundred were composed by Zeami, including the *Matsukaze* or *The Pine Breeze*, *Hagoromo* or *The Feather Robe*, *Miidera* or *The Mii Temple* among the most celebrated. The No may be described as a solemn lyric performance played by men, consisting of music and dancing accompanied by the recitation of *utai*, with masks being used in the chief roles to indicate the characters portrayed. The No plays are mostly historical romances with a strong influence of Buddhist, especially Zen, views on life. The *utai*, recitative chants which form an essential part of the No, are as old as the original *sarugaku*. *Utai* are of very ancient origin and are archaic in style while rhythmical in tone, usually being composed of alternate lines of five and seven syllables. The orchestral music of the No is produced by hand drums, flutes, and larger drums.

Before the play begins the musicians seat themselves on the floor at the back of the stage, facing the audience. The roof of the stage is the same as that on a Shinto shrine and is supported by four pillars at the corners. After the members of the orchestra have taken their proper positions, the members of the chorus appear and take their places by kneeling in two rows on the right of the stage. The No actors speak their individual parts, while the chorus chants the explanatory portions in *utai* accompanied by the rhythmic beat of the orchestra. The program of the No is arranged according to a traditional convention of prescribed order. This usually consists first of a god-play or *kami-mono*; second, a battle-play in which the ghost of a warrior appears; third, a wig-play consisting chiefly of posturing, with the principal character being a woman; fourth, a lunatic-play and a kind of revenge-play; fifth, an earthly-play. The sixth, in which the program comes to an end, is known as the last-play.

The masks were developed as an integral part of the No and are characterized by skillful carving. Since the No mask was made to cover the face only, and was worn for a considerable time during the enactment of lengthy plots, its lightness was a most important factor. No masks are classified into types, including men, women, deities and sages, insane persons, devils, and mythological creatures. Great care was exerted by the famous mask makers so as to appropriately express the essential quality of each character—beautiful, noble, humble, fierce, tragic, young or old—and also many forms of emotion. With the great acting technique of famous No performers combined with the sculptor's skill in creating a mask that would portray different emotions depending on the way the light struck it, many of these No masks seem to possess the power of changing facial expressions. In contrast to the masks used in the earlier dances such as the *gigaku*, *bugaku*, and *gyodo*, which were produced by the sculptors of Buddhist images in their spare time, the No masks were made by carvers who specialized in such work. The No-mask carvers, or *men-uchi* as they are called, were men who thoroughly understood and had a complete knowledge of the intricate No performance. The masks, carved in wood or made of dry lacquer, are masterpieces of expression conveying feelings of joy, grief, fear, hate, and love.

By about the beginning of the Edo or Tokugawa period (1615-1867) the various character forms of the No masks had become established in all their details and from that time on all No masks were made in exact reproduction. There are many stories attached to certain characteristic No masks which are suggestive of their origin. The *okina* mask which portrays a very old man is said to have had its provenance in the second month of the third year of Daido, 806-810, when a great hole appeared in the earth near the Sarusawa Pond at Nara, which is noted for its sublime beauty on moonlight nights, when the shadow of the Kofukuji five-storied pagoda is reflected in its water. From this opening in the earth there issued forth a dark smoke which spread over the countryside causing illness among the people. The Emperor was greatly concerned about this strange occurrence and summoned a sage of wide renown to make the necessary observations. The sage explained that the negative fire of the earth, which is normally concealed, was escaping through the hole because the ground had caved in, and therefore a positive fire should be applied to restore the equilibrum. Thereupon, a great pyre of wood around the hole was lighted, and after it had burned away, the hole ceased to smoke and the illness abated. To celebrate this strange event the *okina sambasu* dance was performed, and ever since that time it has survived as an ancient tradition. Even to the present day it has been customary to perform the No dance called *takigino*, or full-burning No, on the seventh day of the second month of every year. Traditionally the oldest *okina* mask, bearing the date Genkyu 3, or 1206, is said to be the one preserved in the Asakusa temple in Tokyo, where it is used at the festival held on the fifteenth day of the sixth month every year.

Although many No masks of the earliest period of this lyric dance are preserved in certain temples and shrines, the ones known to have been carved by the famous makers are mostly preserved by descendants of the great No performers. There is no biographical information available about the famous mask makers; only their names are known. The ten master carvers, as they are called, were Koushi Kiyomitsu, Himi Munetada, Tokuwaka Tadamasa, Echi Yoshifune, Akasuru Yoshinari, Fukuhara Bunzo, Ishikawa Tatsuemon,

Nikko, Yasha, and Miroku. These ten are said to have been working about the same time that Kanami and Zeami were developing the No performance into its perfected form.

Like many other traditional things in the history of Japanese culture, there are numerous mask stories which have been handed down through the centuries. Two of these are narratives about the Kwanze family of No actors. One relates to an early member of the Kwanze family who was performing the *No dojoji* in the presence of the Shogun. When he retired under the property bell, being unable to find the proper mask for the next act, he bit his finger and streaked his face with blood, and appeared more horrible than with a mask when the bell was again lifted. The other story is about a Kwanze who requested the elderly carver Gensuke to make him a

Kyogen *mask known as Oto, an abbreviation of Otogozen, meaning Noble Lady. As a popular favorite in the* kyogen *comedy plays, the character is often given other familiar names. Muromachi period, fifteenth century. Kasuga shrine, Nara.*

hannya mask, which belongs to the classification of devil and mythological masks. The old carver sent him a poorly made and ill-fitting one which he could not use. In a fit of rage Kwanze broke it and sent the pieces back by Gensuke's own son and messenger. The disgrace was so great that the old man committed suicide. After many years had passed Kwanze required a certain type of mask to play before the court and a carver was recommended to make it for him. It was the most perfect mask that Kwanze had ever worn and after the performance he found that it could not be removed from his face. The maker was summoned and with much effort he succeeded in pulling it away from Kwanze's face together with a good portion of the actor's skin. This mask had been made by old Gensuke's son and its type has since been called *niku-tsuki-no-men* or face-tearing mask.

THE "KYOGEN" COMIC INTERLUDE

With the development of the No play there appeared a sister performance called *kyogen*, which consisted of one-act comic interludes. *Kyogen* had its origin in the old *sarugaku* dances and, along with the No play, the comic gesturing of *kyogen* was perfected and refined. These one-act interludes are usually performed on the same stage as the No plays and are presented as comic relief to the solemn No performances. Many of them are satires on social evils and human behavior, although the majority are primitive and naïve farces performed to amuse the audience. In contrast to the No plays with their classic and poetic quotations and dialogue in the language of the Kamakura period, the *kyogen* consists entirely of dialogue and monologue in colloquialisms of the Muromachi period, without lyric or epic poetry. Although this language was used a few hundred years ago, the *kyogen* comic interludes with their mimicry and gestures are well understood by the present-day audience. In the same manner as the No and the *kyogen* contrast with each other, their masks also differ. The *kyogen* masks are more simple than the No masks, and as each is intended to portray but a single expression, they are rather naïve, depicting faces of common people, usually in a comic manner. This is in direct contrast to No masks. *Kyogen* masks also are not as numerous in their variety of characters as the No masks, numbering only about twenty that are essential to the portrayal of the parts, including ordinary citizens, smiling gods of good fortune, comical ghosts, and animal and demon masks with whimsical expressions. Just as in the case of the No masks, many of the earliest *kyogen* masks have been preserved, a few in the temples and shrines and the rest chiefly by the descendants of the old *kyogen* families.

The No performance, from the time its perfected form was developed in the Muromachi period, was the dramatic entertainment of the Shoguns and the Imperial court. It was a regular part of the artistic life of the samurai, the military class having been its patrons. During the Edo period some of the earlier Tokugawa Shoguns even went so far as to give certain favorite No actors the rank of samurai, and carried their enthusiasm to further extremes by allowing these actors access to the private apartments of the castles. Shortly after the beginning of the eighteenth century, Arai Hakuseki, who was a distinguished scholar of Confucian learning and an official advisor to the Shogunate, compiled three voluminous reports, presenting in detail the reasons why the No was a danger to the Shogunate and to the state. After considering

The comic kyogen *mask called Nobori-hige, meaning Climbing-whiskers, used for the laughable spirits or ghosts. Edo period, seventeenth century. Tokyo National Museum.*

Kyogen *mask called Kentoku, which is supposed to depict a Buddhist priest named Kentoku, who is said to have made such a face whenever he was exposed to a cold wind. Muromachi period, sixteenth century. Tokyo National Museum.*

this evidence the Shogun, at a court function in the year 1711, agreed to substitute certain pieces of ancient music in place of the No. From this time on the No appears to have lost its official patronage, and it was performed only in certain conservative circles as a cultivated form of entertainment. The No plays and their texts became familiar to many of the better-educated persons in the rich merchant class, and amateurs soon began to take a great interest in learning its dances, dialogue, and chants. The No survives to the present day in all of its ancient beauty, and performances again are provided as part of the official entertainments at the Imperial court.

The cultural history of Japan records an endless repertoire of traditions that survive to the present day. The mask is no exception, as indicated by its popularity in many forms of dances, processions, and festivals in every town and village throughout the country. There is hardly a hamlet that does not have its Inari Shinto shrine dedicated to the prehistoric princess named Ugatama-no-Mikoto, the goddess of rice. At these picturesque little shrines the Hatsuuma Festival is celebrated on the first zodiac horse-day after the cold season according to the old lunar calendar, or about the 12th of February. It is held for the observance of prayers for a good crop of rice and is one of the most popular folk-festivals. Those taking part in the shrine dance wear masks of the fox, who is the messenger of Inari. The masks are sold to the people in open-air stalls set up especially for the festival.

VII Metalwork

THE ART of preparing metals for use from their ores has been practiced by the Japanese from the earliest times. The Neolithic culture of Japan is considered to have been one of the most advanced in the world, because extant metal tools and weapons reveal unusual skills and knowledge. From these early beginnings the Japanese metalworker and artist gradually developed the art to a superlative degree of beauty and perfection. Gold, silver, iron, copper, and tin are the only substances recognized as true metals by early Chinese and Japanese writers. In the Japanese language they are designated collectively by the term *go kin* or the five metals and were believed to have some mystical relationship with the five colors—black, red, blue, white, and yellow—and also with the five planets. According to Chinese philosophy, they were believed to have originated through the sun and the male and female principles of nature, or *yang* and *yin*, acting on the materials of the earth's crust. They were not considered simple elements, but capable under certain conditions and influences of being transmuted one into another. All through the many centuries of Japanese metalwork the master craftsmen did not work solely in precious metals, nor were there any special guilds of goldsmiths or silversmiths. The value of the material was secondary, and metalworkers were content to use any metal, their sole desire being to produce objects which would be valued for beauty of workmanship. So true is this that it is not in gold and silver that most masterpieces are found, but in less costly metals and alloys. In this the Japanese craftsman was a true artist.

THE NOBLE METALS

Gold was regarded by Japanese writers as the king of the five metals. Although never abundant in Japan, it was found in many localities, in the sands of rivers in early times and in mineral veins in later periods. Since its sources of supply were not too plentiful, sumptuary laws limited its use. In the ninth century all officials below sixth rank were forbidden to wear any gold or silver except on their armor and swords and official costume. The effects of these and similar subsequent laws survived until very recent times, so that the only gold ornament permitted a Japanese lady consisted of a simple hairpin; a gentleman might have gold on the mounts on his sword and on his pipe case.

One of the earliest uses of gold was for coating other metals, to protect them from oxidation as well as for display, and in the early centuries it was employed as a coating on bronze and copper objects of personal adornment and on the iron bits and trappings of horses. It is evident that the craftsmen of these ancient periods were highly skilled in the art of metallurgy and the fashioning of metals, as well as in the art of decorating them. Their process of applying thin sheets of copper to iron for protection, and coating it with gold, passed away with them at the end of the period of the Ancient Burial Mounds (c. A.D. 100). Although this method was extensively used during the early centuries, the Japanese also had developed the technique of "onlaying," by which gold was applied directly onto the surface of another metal. In this method the surface of the metal was roughened by crosshatching fine lines into it with a chisel. Then a sheet of gold of the desired thickness was selected and carefully heated, and while still hot was laid on the roughened metal surface. By lightly hammering the gold and rubbing with a smooth stone, it became firmly affixed. Already in the period of the dolmens this method of applying gold was practiced, in the same manner as at the present time.

After the introduction of Buddhism in the sixth century gold was employed more extensively, especially for gilding bronze and wooden images of Buddhist divinities, copper vessels used for ceremonial and ornamental purposes, and copper architectural appliqués for the decoration of temples

Iron kettle for the tea ceremony, with the design of a chrysanthemum and a kiri crest in relief. Attributed to Yojiro, a famous kettle maker of the Momoyama period (1573-1615). It is traditionally said to have belonged to Hideyoshi. Tokyo National Museum.

Ashiya iron kettle, with a design of a deer and maple in relief. Muromachi period, fifteenth century. Collection of Ryoichi Hosomi, Osaka.

and shrines. In somewhat later times the most important use of gold was as a medium of exchange, for which purpose it was in the form of gold dust enclosed in quills or tiny bags, in each case containing a precise weight. Then between the years 1570 and 1580 the first government mint was established for the coinage of gold and silver coins. Only in very rare cases were objects of solid gold ever made, the exception being a few wine cups and very small kettles for heating wine or water which belonged to the houses of certain nobles or daimyo. Since gold was seldom used for any ornamental pieces and sparingly worn as jewelry, its use in the art of the metal craftsman was confined almost exclusively to the decoration on sword mounts and on pipe cases. Even as late as the fifteenth century, solid gold was used sparingly on sword mounts, with the exception of the *menuki* (rivet-heads), its principal use being for inlaid decoration on mounts made of

the beautiful alloy called *shakudo*. During the second quarter of the seventeenth century and again in the Genroku era (1688-1704), which were periods of luxury and abundance, the *tsuba*, *kogai*, and *kozuka* were frequently made of solid gold. Although it was generally used sparingly throughout the many centuries, the use of gold in lacquer work is a technique that is peculiar to Japan and renowned for its exquisite beauty.

Silver, or *gin* as it is called in Japanese, is also sometimes referred to as *shiro-kane*, meaning white metal. The use of silver by the Japanese dates at least as early as the Ancient Burial Mounds period; many objects have been found from that period on which silver has been used for decoration, such as sword scabbards with bands of silver, silver beads for personal ornament, bronze and copper rings coated with silver. Like gold, silver is found in Japan as pure metal but is

Above: Bronze mirror, with a relief design of human figures. Pre-Buddhist period, before A.D. 552. Tokyo National Museum.

Left: Bronze dotaku, *with a relief design representing flowing water. Pre-Buddhist period, before A.D. 552. Tokyo National Museum.*

very limited in its distribution and occurs only in small quantities. Silver plate, in the true meaning of the term, was never used, even in the palaces of the nobles or in the great mansions of the daimyo. It was seldom used even for religious vessels or utensils at Buddhist ceremonies, since due to its cold and somber color it was considered unfit for ornamental objects. With the beginning of the Edo period (1615-1867) and its two hundred and fifty years of peace under the Tokugawa Shogunate, silver came to be extensively used in the decorative arts for inlay, and especially in the form of alloys with copper, used for *tsuba* and other sword mounts. Certain silver alloys peculiar to Japan and bearing the generic name *shibuichi* were widely used by metal craftsmen to provide unusual decorative effects of color, these alloys being made to produce a beautiful gray patina. Along with its use in alloys and as decorative inlay work, silver was also extensively used in lacquer.

COPPER, TIN, AND LEAD

Copper, or *akagane* as it is called, meaning red metal, has played a most important role in the art of Japanese metalwork. In addition to being the principal component of bronze, its uses are far more numerous than in other countries, and many of these applications are without like or equal. In the early centuries of our era the Japanese achieved skill in the arts of preparing copper and employed it in a decorative manner far in advance of any other people. By the end of the period of the dolmens the use of thin sheets of copper coated with gold applied to iron as a protective and decorative feature ceased to exist, as we have seen, but the use of thin copper sheets to protect and ornament surfaces of wood has continued to the present day. The art of gilded copper culminated in the Nara period (710-794), when it was lavishly used to embellish the

Ekagami, mirror with a handle, having the design of a raft under a barren willow. Bronze. By Itani Hoju. Edo period, seventeenth century. Tokyo National Museum.

Bronze mirror with six bells, having a conventionalized geometric design in relief. Pre-Buddhist period, before A.D. 552. Tokyo National Museum.

wooden architecture of temples and shrines with richly worked appliqués. Gilded copper was also extensively used by skilled artisans to make ceremonial vessels, articles for the altar, and metal lanterns for the courtyards and interiors of temples and shrines. Toward the end of the Edo period copper was extensively employed for the decoration of vessels and utensils for domestic use, and for many other articles, including decorative sword mounts. During these later times copper was seldom gilded, as the craftsman preferred to exploit the rich-colored patinas in shades of red and brown to enhance the beauty of his work. The alloy of copper and zinc which produces brass was unknown in Japan before the introduction of Buddhism. Brass, or *shinshu*, never found much favor among Japanese metal craftsmen because its color tone was considered harsh and it does not blend harmoniously with other metals. The use of brass in decorative objects has been almost exclusively restricted to ceremonial vessels and utensils of Buddhist temples and Shinto shrines, especially for the *go-gusoku* or five ornaments of the Buddhist altar.

The principal use of tin and lead in Japan was in the preparation of pewter. Neither of these metals appear to have been used separately, except in rare cases. Tin is found in Japan in many places, although there is only one ancient mine in the country, situated in the old province of Satsuma. Lead was also rarely used, except as an inlay for decorative purposes in early lacquer ware. This lack of interest in the use of tin and lead was not due to the scarcity of either of the ores, for they occur extensively in many districts. But these ores were treated as silver ores, being argentiferous or silver-producing. With primary interest centered in the extraction of silver, the process from early times was practiced in a most wasteful manner, which resulted in the loss of the greater portion of the tin and lead. Pewter, as an alloy of tin and lead, had been used in very ancient times in China, where it seems there was a superstition against its use for domestic vessels owing to a curious belief regarding the origin of tin. This belief prevailed not only in early times but even persisted until recently. Occasionally pewter vessels had been found to communicate poisonous properties to wine kept in them, which the old Chinese philosophers attributed to arsenic. They claimed that tin originates from arsenic by the influence of the female principle of nature called *yin*, acting for a period of two hundred years; therefore, tin used in making pewter must sometimes be a mixture of arsenic and tin if sufficient time has not elapsed for the complete conversion of the arsenic.

According to early records, the use of pewter in Japan was rather common during the Nara period, when vessels and utensils are said to have been made from it. By the Heian period it was used as an inlay decoration in lacquer. It was not until more recent times that pewter became a favorite alloy for keeping tea leaves. The characteristic Japanese tea jar or canister made of pewter is rather ovoid in section with a round lip rim having a tightly fitted cover. These tea jars are usually contained in a silk net of very large mesh which is tied around the neck with a cord so the jar may be hung for safe-keeping. As in the case of silver, pewter was not in favor with the Buddhist priesthood for ritual utensils, which probably further discouraged the Japanese craftsman from applying his skill to its ornamentation except on rare occasions. In rare cases, pewter pieces are found with inlays of copper, bronze, and even gold, but usually its surface is left entirely plain. The beauty and value of old pewter depends entirely on the soft gray mottled patina which its surface acquires after a length of time by constantly being rubbed with a silk cloth.

IRON

According to the old Chinese philosophers, the metallic element iron is a product of the masculine principle of nature called *yang*, and therefore possesses hardness and tenacity. Its use in Japan dates at least from the time of the dolmens, which is around the beginning of our era. From the chambers of these ancient dolmens have come many excellent examples of iron weapons, armor, spearheads and arrowheads, and especially swords that display the splendid workmanship of the early Japanese ironsmith. Of all the articles made of iron and steel since early times the foremost place must be given to the warrior's sword, for in Japan the sword has occupied a pre-eminent position of honor and renown. For more than eighteen centuries the Japanese craftsman has lavished his highest skill to make it perfect not only as a weapon but also as a work of art to be worn in times of peace. Iron swords comprise the articles of greatest importance among the objects found in the burial chambers of the ancient dolmens.

Although the swordmaker and armorer were both smiths, their crafts were entirely distinct. There was an intense jealous rivalry between the two craftsmen and it is rare to find either one encroaching on the rights of the other. In early times the fame of the armorer was measured by the resistance which his masterpieces offered to the cutting blades of his rival, the swordsmith. However, in later times it was the beauty of the ornament with which his armor was adorned that brought him fame. The plates of which the helmet and body armor were constructed were made from both wrought iron and steel, although steel was used less frequently. Great care was used in the selection of the pieces of metal, but the extreme toughness which many possess is imparted by the repeated doubling and welding to which the iron was subjected before it was finally hammered into the finished piece.

Among the famous armor makers, the Myochin family stands out pre-eminently as unequaled. The great fame of this family had its beginning in Kyoto around the middle of the twelfth century when Myochin Munesuke established its name. For more than six centuries the successive generations of Myochin not only continued to be the greatest armor makers but occupied with honor and distinction the position of armorers to the Shogunates. Every piece of hammered ironwork known to have been made by a Myochin, whether plain or ornamental, is a perfect example of the finest workmanship of the ironsmith.

Cast iron does not appear to have been known to the Japanese in prehistoric times, but one of the earliest records to mention it states that in the year 700 an edict was issued restricting the making of cast-iron coins to the government. Cast iron has been principally used by Japanese craftsmen for making small objects, such as kettles and other similar vessels for heating water or wine, and many are masterpieces of modeling and decoration. Iron kettles for cooking purposes were used from very early times but it was not until the end of the Muromachi period (1338-1573) that artistically wrought kettles were made for the ritual of the tea ceremony. These kettles were cast by the lost-wax method, which is explained in the chapter on sculpture. When these castings are removed from the molds, they are, with the exception of the molded ornamental designs, unsuitable to receive any further decoration by inlaying, chasing, or other similar process without additional treatment. At this stage of the process the surface of the casting is hard and brittle and must be softened and decarbonized. The furnace used in this process, which has

Engraved gilt-bronze head of a nyoi, *or priest's scepter. Heian period (794-1185). Tokyo National Museum*

95

remained unchanged for more than four hundred years, consists of a cast-iron pan from which the bottom has been broken away, with a lining of refractory clay. This pan is placed on a fire-clay slab perforated with numerous holes, and these pieces are in turn set upon a few bricks on the floor of the workshop. The cast-iron article is then placed inside the furnace so that it rests directly on the perforated slab, and the space between it and the sides of the pan is filled with lumps of charcoal. The charcoal is ignited and allowed to burn for an hour or more, until nearly consumed; then the object is reversed and the operation is repeated. This heat treatment makes the surface sufficiently soft and malleable for the craftsman to incise clean lines and channels with sharp and unbroken edges for the decoration desired.

After the decorative work has been completed, the unique brown oxidized surface to which these castings owe so much of their beauty has yet to be produced. In the case of the finest objects, the entire surface is worked with a pointed punch to produce an irregular rough effect which is highly esteemed by the Japanese. The casting is then again heated over a charcoal fire, and when it has reached the desired temperature it is rubbed with a liquid composed of plum vinegar containing iron in solution and ferric oxide in suspension. This operation is repeated on each part of the object until the entire surface has been properly treated to the desired amount of rusting. The whole is thoroughly rubbed with a dry cloth, then covered with a thin coat of lacquer and carefully heated over a brazier, with fine particles of water being splashed on it with a brush during this treatment.

The development of the techniques of casting was due to the popularity of the tea ceremony, which was conducted in simple, quiet surroundings, with the refined beauty of the utensils in harmony with Zen principles of restraint and simplicity. The cast-iron objects were chiefly kettles, many being designed by such famous artists as Sesshu, Tosa Mitsunobu, and others of equal fame. The foremost name associated with these kettles is Ashiyagama, which is the generic term applied to kettles made at Ashiya, a coastal village in Fukuoka prefecture. Ashiyagama, or Ashiya kettles, are characterized by the soft effect of the surfaces, so skillfully treated as to produce a natural rustic quality. Together with the kettles of Ashiya, which have been highly prized since the Muromachi period, those made at Temmyo in Sano, north of Tokyo, and called Temmyogama, have also been greatly appreciated by the tea masters. It was not until the Momoyama period (1573-1615) that the kettles made at Kyoto became popular.

In the town of Shiogama on Matsushima Bay in northeastern Japan there is a minor Shinto shrine just a short distance from the main Shiogama shrine, dedicated to four ancient iron kettles which according to tradition were used

by Shiotsuchi-no-Okina in producing salt in prehistoric times. It was he who first taught the Japanese how to make salt. The four kettles are about four feet in diameter and four or five inches deep, with the iron about three inches thick. Early on the morning of the tenth of July each year, the Shinto officials of the iron-kettle shrine will, while they take cold ablutions, observe the ceremony of changing the water of the four kettles, which, it is traditionally said, will change in color when a national calamity is about to take place.

Above: Bronze keman *with chased and openwork designs. Heian period (794–1185). Owned by the Konjiki-do of the Chusonji monastery at Hiraizumi, Iwate prefecture.*

Left: Detail showing one of the finely pierced and line-engraved gilt-bronze plates from a kanchoban *pendant. Asuka period (552–645). Tokyo National Museum.*

BRONZE

The art of casting bronze, which was called *kara-kane* or Chinese metal, has been practiced by the Japanese ever since several centuries before our era, as evidenced by the various examples found in simple burial mounds. They include bronze spears, halberds, and swords, and are another proof of the advanced knowledge of metallurgy and the techniques of founding in prehistoric Japan. The largest cast-bronze objects,

probably of the same period, are *dotaku*, which are curiously bell-shaped. Their exact date is still a subject of dispute among archæologists and their use is not known. It is presumed that *dotaku* were originally used as percussion instruments and possibly, at some later time, as ornamental objects. They are without like or equal and are only found in Japan at certain excavation sites in Honshu and Shikoku. None have ever been found in Kyushu, which is the island nearest to the Asiatic mainland. It appears that they were deliberately buried, but the reason remains unknown. A great number of *dotaku* have been found and their size varies widely from one or two inches in height to three feet, the latter being the most common. These bells are flat in section and usually decorated with an over-all pattern of lattice design or one typically Oriental in feeling called *ryusuimon* or flowing-water pattern. Many are ornamented with interesting primitive pictures depicting such things as fish, deer, turtles, houses, human beings, hunting scenes, and scenes of the everyday life of those ancient times. These castings are thin and are of great importance in the history of bronze founding, for they could only have been produced by the lost-wax process and by the use of a hot mold.

Somewhat later, around the beginning of our era, in the period of Ancient Burial Mounds, the bronze spears, halberds, and swords of the earlier period had disappeared, and in their stead the chief articles of bronze are mirrors, sword pommels, helmets, horse trappings, and small bells. These bells are simple hollow spheres with a slit cut in the lower half, and they contain a loose piece of metal or a small round pebble. They were used as accessories to the warrior's costume, on horse trappings, and for other ornamental purposes. The bronze mirrors found in the ancient burial mounds offer an interesting study of the development of bronze work through many centuries. Metalworkers in China had been casting beautiful bronze mirrors as early as the beginning of the Han dynasty (206 B.C.–A.D. 220). They were introduced into Japan about the end of the Han dynasty. Many of the earliest mirrors cast by the Japanese were exact copies of Chinese prototypes, but there soon appeared a certain native expression which the Japanese always developed immediately after adopting an art from the continent. The characteristic Chinese mirror was decorated with symbolic representations of legendary figures and animals, gods, and mythical characters. For some unknown reason the early Japanese casters merely copied the Chinese mirrors but without reproducing the designs with their original sharp lines, preferring instead to soften them, apparently for æsthetic reasons. The mirror designs gradually assumed a truly indigenous style with hunting scenes, festival dances, scenes with house designs, and conventionalized patterns. A mirror of unusual design that also dates from the time of the Ancient Burial Mounds is the so-called bell mirror.

Gilt-bronze sutra box, with chased and openwork floral designs. Heian period (794-1185). Collection of the Aichi-do of the Chusonji monastery at Hiraizumi, Iwate prefecture.

Bronze sutra box with designs of dragons and clouds; gilt-bronze and silver in relief. Heian period (794 to 1185). Tokyo National Museum.

The bell mirror is found with from four to twelve small round bronze bells attached around its outer edge. Many mirrors of the Nara period are typically Japanese in taste, with shapes that are square, while others are six- and eight-lobed, and eight- and twelve-pointed, generally decorated with birds, flowers, and landscapes.

By the time of the Heian period the mirror had developed a distinctive Japanese style and come to be known as the *wakyo*, or Japanese mirror. The mirrors of Heian times had plain but thinner and higher rims, and the knob or boss in the center for the cord, which was large, plain, and round in the Nara period, became smaller and was usually in the form of a flower. As the mirrors became thinner during the Heian period, the designs were more delicate, with flowers, pine branches, butterflies, leaves of grass, and cranes. During the Kamakura period the *wakyo* was often made with a particular type of design called *e-uta*, or picture poem, combining a piece of poetry along with the pictorial subject. The mirror with a handle most frequently seen in Japan to the present time is called *ekagami*. This type first appeared around the end of the Muromachi period and became popular during the Momoyama period. Since the handle eliminated the need for the cord knob, a greater freedom of design was possible and many beautiful compositions were created. With the beginning of the Edo period the demand for these mirrors grew to such proportions that the quality of workmanship suffered.

The history of the mirror in Japan has its beginning in legendary times. At Uji-Yamada in Ise are the famous Jingu shrines, the Geku dedicated to the goddess of crops, food, and sericulture, and the Kodaijingu, or Naiku, dedicated to the sun goddess, Amaterasu-o-mi-kami. In the Naiku is enshrined the mirror called *Yata-no-Kagami*, which is one of the *Sanshu-no-Shinki* or Three Sacred Treasures—i.e., mirror, sword, and necklace—which constitute the Imperial Regalia of Japan. According to Japanese mythology the mirror was given by Amaterasu-o-mi-kami to Prince Ninigi, her grandson, when the latter came down to earth to reign. Because of this heritage, a mirror is venerated in many Shinto shrines throughout Japan, and in olden times a mirror was offered to a Shinto shrine with a prayer.

TEMPLE BRONZES

Both the Asuka and Nara periods form a brilliant epoch in bronze founding, paralleling the arts of sculpture and painting. Due to the introduction of Buddhism in the sixth century and the establishment of a fixed capital and court at Nara in the year 710, the building of numerous temples proceeded at a rapid pace, and the many skilled artisans brought from China and Korea included workers in bronze and others pro-

Gilt-bronze head of a shakujo, a staff used by Buddhist priests. Nara period (710-794). Tokyo National Museum.

Gilt-bronze reliquary stupa, with openwork and chased designs of flowers, dragons, lions, and flames. Kamakura period (1185-1333). Saidaiji temple, Nara.

ficient in the production of images of Buddhist divinities and vessels for the ceremonies of its rituals. With such a strong emphasis placed on the production of religious art, the development of bronze-founding was largely due to the Buddhist priests, and the chief works in bronze for the succeeding centuries other than Buddhist images were temple lanterns, bells, and other objects for the sacred buildings. Very soon the Japanese craftsmen themselves began to produce in bronze. The most important ancient bronze images and ritual vessels of this period are preserved in the early temples at Nara and Horyuji, in addition to many smaller articles such as bells, gongs, braziers or incense burners, bronze banners, and other objects for ritual purposes. Among the more elaborate

examples of bronze work is the temple ornament called *kanchoban* which is a form of *ban*, literally meaning banner or streamer. *Ban* were commonly made of textiles, although there are a few rare examples fashioned of metal, which were used in the *kancho* ceremony. These bronze *kanchoban* are elaborate pieces consisting of a square top from which hang long pendants of metal plates. In the extremely large *kanchoban* there is a great central baldachin from which are suspended several smaller *ban*, each with its pendants of metal plates. The ornamentation consists of an over-all series of patterns and designs in sharply cut pierced work with the remaining slender surface spaces delicately engraved. Other examples of exquisite openwork with fine engraving are the many halos of

99

Brass censer with a long handle in the shape of a bird's tail. Asuka period (552-645). Tokyo National Museum.

Buddhist icons and the *keman*, or pendant ornament. The *keman* was originally a wreath of flowers used as an ornament in Buddhist temples, but later the real flowers were replaced by leather, wood, and metal substitutes. In the majority of bronze *keman* the openwork design is in the form of conventionalized vines with leaves and flowers, and frequently Buddhist figures are included, beautifully chiseled within the pattern.

From the Heian to the Muromachi period there flourished a curious custom of placing hand-copied sutras in a bronze box or container to be buried in a sutra mound. This practice was influenced by the Buddhist conception of Mappo, or Age of Decadence, which was prevalent at that time, and the sutras or scriptures were buried so that the owner might be prepared for the appearance of the Maitreya Buddha. Buried in the mounds together with these sutra boxes were Buddhist images, mirrors, coins, small containers with lids, and other similar articles. Sutra boxes used for this purpose were made in a wide variety of forms in bronze, and decorated with incised motifs which were sometimes gilded. In the Kimbusanji temple in Nara prefecture there is a sutra box of unusually beautiful form which was excavated from a mound nearby. It consists of a gilt bronze oblong case resting on a support resembling a Chinese table with four legs similar to those of the Ming period. There were also great numbers of sutra boxes for use in the temples and houses of the nobles; they were beautifully decorated and represent the highest skill of the bronze worker. Many of these were of gilt bronze in a delicate openwork of lotus flowers and interlacing vine designs, while others were finely worked with reliefs in gilded bronze and silver. These sutra boxes were usually oblong or cylindrical and some were large enough to contain more than one sutra scroll.

Many of the early pieces of bronze are still being used by the temples that have preserved them for so many centuries. One type is the *shakujo*, a staff used by Buddhist priests. The metal head of the staff is made in a variety of shapes but its principal characteristic is the set of six rings which give off a jangling sound when the staff strikes the ground. It is said that this type of staff originated in India, where it was carried by itinerant monks to frighten away wild animals. Another type of bronze object seen in temples is the *kei* or gong, which is a Buddhist percussion instrument in the form of a flat decorated piece, hung on a rack in front of an image of the Buddha and struck by the priest with a mallet while reciting the sutras. There are also beautifully wrought bronze censers with long handles that are placed before the image of Buddha while the priest is conducting a service. The ends of their long handles curve downward to serve as a support and are usually of an ornamental nature and frequently designed in the shape of a bird's tail or some other similar form. Two of the most interesting articles used in esoteric Buddhism are the *goko-rei* or *vajra* bell, and the *dorje*. They are among the various articles reserved for Buddhist exorcism, the ritual act or process of driving off evil spirits. The *dorje* is the *vajra* or thunderbolt of Jupiter, the symbol of the strong and indestructible, which the priest grasps and manipulates in various ways during prayer. The emblem is a bronze instrument, shaped much like a dumbbell with both ends pointed or having five converging prongs representing the thunderbolt. The *vajra* bell is in the form of a hand-bell and is so named because it has the same five-pointed symbol of the *vajra* or thunderbolt at the end of the handle.

In Buddhist temples are also found ceremonial ornaments placed on the altar known as *san-gusoku*, or the three articles, consisting of a vase, an incense burner, and a candlestick; and also the *go-gusoku*, or the five articles, namely an incense burner, a pair of vases, and a pair of candlesticks. There were also many interesting bronzes made in the form of a tope or stupa to contain sutras or other religious relics, and although they were intended for the temple or house of a nobleman, they were frequently buried in the sutra mounds. The Buddhist stupa is usually in the form of a cylindrical or prismatic tower topped by a cupola erected to contain or form a Buddhist shrine. Aside from the variety of articles of bronze used in the temples for ornamental and ritual purposes, in the courtyard there was frequently a bronze lantern of enormous size. Of particular importance in this category of bronze work is the octagonal lantern that stands in front of the Hall of the Great Buddha in the Todaiji temple at Nara. This great lantern, cast by the lost-wax method, is thirteen feet in height and consists of an octagonal pedestal supporting an octagonal light chamber, in which the panels are alternately one-doored and two-doored. The grilles of the doors portray Bodhisattvas playing the bamboo flute and lions gamboling among clouds. One of the finest works of art of the Nara period, it is said to have been made at the time of the erection of the *Great Buddha* in 749.

The boom of a great Japanese temple bell is a beautiful sound, with a rich tonal vibration which in some bells continues for many minutes. Many bells are famous for this quality; for example, the old bell of the Miidera temple on the shore of Lake Biwa is noted for its melodious tone when heard in the early evening. Among the many great temple bells of Japan, the oldest to bear a date is the one that hangs in the belfry of the Myoshinji temple at Kyoto, with an inscription dated the second year of the Emperor Mommu, or 698. One of the two largest bells is a famous one in the belfry at the Todaiji temple at Nara; it is 13.6 feet in height, 9.2 feet in diameter at its base, and 10 inches thick. This bell was originally cast in 732 but was badly damaged in 989 when the belfry was blown down by a typhoon. It is believed that the present bell was recast in 1239. The other one hangs in the famous belfry of the Chion-in temple at Kyoto; it is the largest bell in Japan, measuring 17.9 feet in height and 8.9 feet in diameter, and weighing seventy-four short tons. At midnight on New Year's Eve, by the light of large bonfires, the bell is struck 108 times according to Buddhist ritual, requiring almost two hours to complete the operation. In section, the Japanese temple bells differ from Western forms in having the rim thickened internally so their mouths are constricted. It is this construction which causes the gentle rising and falling tones characterizing the beautiful boom of Japanese bells. They are neither swung nor furnished with tongues, but are rung by striking the outside with a beam of wood suspended from the bell tower and propelled like a battering ram. At the huge Chion-in belfry, a number of men are needed to propel the wood beam under the direction of a leader. The point on the bell that is struck is a low boss, which is frequently in the form of a lotus flower.

The casting of a large bell in early times in Japan was an important event and was celebrated by religious ceremonies and popular rejoicing. A great festival was held at the temple on the day appointed for running the metal into the mold in the temple grounds. People of all classes came from far and near with contributions, often consisting of bronze mirrors, hairpins, and other ornaments to be added to the bronze in the furnaces, and in succeeding years this occasion was observed by temple festivals.

Bronze kei, *or gong, with relief designs of lotus plants. Heian period (794-1185). Zenrinji temple, Kyoto.*

Gilt-bronze implements for Buddhist exorcism. A goko-rei *or* vajra *bell and a* dorje *or* vajra *(symbolic thunderbolt), resting on a four-footed tray between a pair of flower holders. Kamakura period (1185-1333). Tokyo National Museum.*

101

LATER BRONZE WORK

During the Heian period (794-1185) the art of bronze-founding entered a state of stagnation despite the great richness of this period in other fields of creative activity. But after the protracted warfare and feuds between the Fujiwara, Taira, and Minamoto families, there came a revival of the old art of the Nara period. During the first hundred years of the Kamakura period (1185-1333) there appeared a renaissance in art, and it was during this period that the *Great Buddha* of Kamakura was cast. But from the beginning of the Muromachi period until the end of the Momoyama period only the metal arts contributing to the needs of war flourished, for the country was torn with unrest. It is not until the Edo period, with the Tokugawa Shogunate firmly established and the country again at peace, that the art of bronze again flourished. In the Edo period the foremost examples of the bronze-founder's art are in the mausoleums of the Tokugawa Shoguns at Nikko. The great Toshogu shrine, which is the mausoleum of Tokugawa Ieyasu, 1542-1616, founder of the Tokugawa Shogunate, is the major architectural accomplishment of the Edo period. It required fifteen thousand men for a period of twenty years to complete all of its buildings. This magnificent structure has an infinity of carved detail and gold-leaf decoration and reflects the high level of achievement attained in the decorative arts. Another notable example of this period is the tomb of Ieyasu in the Toshogu shrine, completely cast in bronze, with bronze gates and distinguished by an impressive simplicity of design. Almost the entire surface is covered with a delicate geometric and floral motif, as a ground upon which the bolder ornamentation is molded in relief.

Large standing lanterns of bronze, contributed by the provincial daimyo and nobles, who vied with one another in thus doing honor to their departed chiefs, line the courtyards of the Nikko shrines. Many hundreds of these lanterns, which were given as votive offerings by the wealthy, both to Buddhist temples and to Shinto shrines, were cast during the Edo period. Lanterns of this type adorn the approaches and grounds of every temple of importance in Japan. Each group or pair differs from any other, yet in form and decoration all are in harmony and are characteristic examples of the fine work of the bronze modelers and founders. The extraordinary quality of this bronze work is not due solely to the modeling and casting, but is largely dependent on the physical character of the alloys used. The finest and most perfected alloy is *kara-kane* or Chinese metal, which indicates that it probably originated in China. Distinct from the bronzes of the earlier periods, which were a simple alloy of copper and tin, *kara-kane* contains lead as an essential component. The term *kara-kane* does not signify any specific alloy, since it has a generic rather than

Miniature bronze stupa. Excavated at a sutra mound on Mount Kurama. Heian period (794-1185). Kuramadera temple, Mount Kurama, Kyoto.

Bronze hanging lantern, with a pierced design of bamboo and cherry branches. Muromachi period (1338-1573). Iwayadera temple at Kasama.

Bronze hanging lantern, with an openwork design of plum trees and bamboo. Muromachi period (1338-1573). Tokyo National Museum.

a specific meaning and is applied to a varied group of mixtures of metals of the lead-tin-copper series, in which proportions of copper may range from 71 to 89 per cent, tin 2 to 8 per cent, and lead from 5 to 15 per cent.

BRONZE ALLOYS

As the science and art of preparing metals advanced through the centuries, the Japanese developed and perfected a number of fine and interesting alloys, some of which produced most beautiful color tones. One of these is a bronze called *sentoku*, which is distinctive for its soft golden tones and the satin-like sheen of its surface. It is a yellow bronze composed of copper, tin, and zinc, occupying an intermediate position between *kara-kane* and brass, and was introduced from Ming China in the fifteenth century. According to an old Chinese legend, it was discovered by accident after the destruction of a temple by fire, in which the altar vessels of bronze, gold, and brass melted together in a mass. It is frequently used for vases and similar articles, either with very little ornament in relief or with plain surfaces, to allow full play to its pleasing tones. However, the finest specimens of *sentoku* are found among

beautifully chased *tsuba* and other sword mounts. There is another Japanese alloy called *sawari*, which consists of copper, tin, and lead. This is frequently used for Buddhist ceremonial articles.

Of all the alloys peculiar to Japan the finest and most beautiful are *shakudo* and *shibuichi*. When these are simply cast there is nothing specially attractive in the alloys themselves, their great beauty and decorative value being entirely dependent on the unusual patinas produced by special treatment. *Shakudo* is sometimes called *u-kin*, or cormorant gold, because of the black tone of its patina. But when it is first cast, and before its surface has been suitably treated, it has a dark copper color rather similar to that of ordinary bronze. In order to attain the black surface with a violet sheen of the finest examples, the presence of not less than 4 per cent of gold is mandatory. There are no less than fifteen grades of *shakudo*, the lowest being known as *chusho*, which contains only traces of gold. The *shakudo* produced by the metal craftsmen of Satsuma is generally considered to be the richest in tone and the most valuable. The date of its origin has never been ascertained and it has never been employed for large castings. The finest objects in which *shakudo* was used are sword mounts from the time of Goto Yujo, 1440-1512, the first of a famous

Bronze monastery bell, dated 698. Myoshinji temple, Kyoto.

perfect ground for inlaid designs of gold, silver, and copper. Its physical properties make it an ideal metal for the craftsman and allow him to work and fashion it with complete freedom. It can be hammered into sheets, drawn into wire, or cast into any form. In the process of producing the violet-black patina, the object is first boiled in a solution of lye prepared by leaching wood ashes, and then carefully polished, if necessary, with fine charcoal powder. After this it is immersed in plum vinegar containing salt in solution, then washed with a weak lye, and placed in a tub of water so that all traces of alkali are removed. In the final stage of the process it is placed in a boiling solution of copper sulphate, verdigris, and water, to which is sometimes added potassium nitrate, until the desired tone of patina is produced.

Shibuichi occupies a position of equal importance with *shakudo* in the field of ornamental metalwork. In the main it refers to an alloy consisting of one part silver and three parts copper. But *shibuichi* is a generic name under which must also be included two other alloys, one called *sambo-gin*, which is one part silver and two parts copper, and the other *hoji-gin*, which consists of equal parts of silver and copper. Within the definition of *shibuichi* are also included several lower alloys of the same metals, although the alloy most generally used by the more important metal craftsmen was *sambo-gin* rather than *shibuichi*. As in the case of *shakudo*, the value of this alloy in decorative metalwork is entirely dependent upon its unusual patina. When it is first cast, its color is that of pale gunmetal; it has no particular beauty until given a suitable treatment to produce a patina of tones of gray. The process of producing the beautiful color tones of *shibuichi* is the same as that used for *shakudo*, and the alloy itself has the same ideal physical qualities for inlaid decoration. By using these two remarkable alloys, *shakudo* and *shibuichi*, together with fine inlaid designs in gold, silver, and copper, the Japanese metalworker was able to achieve tonal effects unrivaled by any other metalwork in the world. Ever since the earlier periods, the Japanese metal founder and craftsman has displayed great skill and possessed the quality and versatility of a true artist. Much Japanese metalwork, particularly in sword mounts, is represented by masterpieces of unrivaled beauty.

family of sword-mount artisans. His descendants continued to make sword ornaments and uphold the family name as the greatest in this field for seventeen generations, until the middle of the nineteenth century. Fine *shakudo*, containing 4 or 5 per cent gold, far surpassed any other alloy in the exceptional beauty of its patina. The deep violet-black tones of *shakudo* and the handsome polish it is capable of receiving provide a

VIII Arms and Armor

I**T IS WRITTEN** in the most ancient official chronicle that the Japanese sword had its legendary origin in the cosmogonic Age of the Gods. According to the *Kojiki, or Records of Ancient Matters*, compiled in the year 712, Prince Susano-o-no-Mikoto, brother of the sun goddess, killed an eight-headed dragon in the province of Izumo and found a sword in its tail. This sword, which was originally called *Ame-no-Murakumo-no-Tsurugi*, or Heaven's Cloud-gathering Sword, is one of the three heirlooms of the Imperial family. Legend recounts that when Prince Yamato-Takeru, 82-113, a son of Emperor Keiko, was starting on an expedition against rebel clans in the province of Suruga, he visited the Jingu shrines of Ise and was presented with this sacred sword by Princess Yamato-Hime. While on a moor in the enemy territory, the warrior-prince was surrounded by rebels, who set fire to the grass so that he would be burned to death. He cut the grass around him with his sword, and with flint and tinder from his pouch, he kindled a counterfire against the oncoming flames. The prince was saved through this act and was able to beat off and conquer his enemies. Upon his return the prince left the sword hanging on a mulberry tree, whereupon Princess Iwato secretly carried it away, but it shone so brightly that it set fire to a cedar, which fell into the field burning. Because of this episode in the legendary history of the sword it was renamed the *Kusanagi-no-Tsurugi*, or Grass-mowing Sword, and has been preserved by the Atsuta shrine at Nagoya. The Atsuta shrine, founded in the second century, is said to be the most sacred Shinto shrine next to the great Jingu shrines of Ise. The sacredness attached to the shrine is due to the Grass-mowing Sword which, with the mirror at the Jingu shrines of Ise and the necklace or jewels at the Imperial palace, constitute the Three Sacred Treasures of the Imperial Regalia of Japan. The name Atsuta, meaning Hot Field, is derived by popular etymology from the legend of the sword, and among the many subsidiary shrines within its precincts, the Ya-Tsurugi or Eight Swords shrine is the most important. The fame of the Grass-mowing Sword spread as far as Silla, then one of the three kingdoms of Korea, and at the bidding of the King a priest was ordered to cross over to Japan and steal it. He succeeded in his mission and fled to Hakata in Kyushu, but before he could sail away, the gods of Atsuta discovered the loss and dispatched the god of the Sumiyoshi-Myojin shrine, who overtook the priest and recovered the sword. Having failed in this, the King of Silla sent one of his generals to Japan armed with seven swords, but when he reached the province of Owari the Atsuta gods killed him and captured his seven swords. These swords, together with the *Kusanagi*, constitute the eight swords for which the Ya-Tsurugi shrine was erected.

The oldest form of Japanese sword used during historical times is called the *tsurugi* or *ken*, which has a straight double-edged blade usually wider near the point. However, it was not until the opening years of the eighth century, when the Taiho code instituting the Chinese form of government was being established, that the carefully recorded history of the Japanese blade began. It is generally accepted that Amakuni, the first of some twelve thousand Japanese swordsmiths whose names and dates are known, produced the first single-edged blades. Two or three swords bearing his name are extant. In the second half of the eighth century the Amakuni blade was further developed by Yasutsuna, who worked under the divine inspiration of the gods and established the form of Japanese sword blade that has been retained through the centuries. Japanese scholars divide sword blades into two classes, those produced before 1600 being designated *koto*, or old swords, and those made after that time *shinto*, or new swords, although more recently the term *kinkoto*, or near-old swords, is generally used instead of *shinto*. The superior quality of the *koto* blades was confined to the work of a limited number of famous swordsmiths and their immediate followers, and was due

Tangs and points of koto *blades, with the pattern of watered steel visible on two of the blades. (1) Made by Kunimune (of Bizen and Sagami); c. 1177-1270. (2) Made by Sadamune (Hosho of* Yamato); *early fourteenth century. (3) Made by Kagemitsu (of Osafune, Bizen); fourteenth century. (4) Made by Kanemoto (of Seki, Mino); early sixteenth century. Victoria and Albert Museum.*

principally to the exceptional tempering of the blades. This fine art was perfected only by long experience and observation. The art of blade-making was transmitted exclusively as a professional secret from father to son, and from master to pupil, until it was lost through death or became modified. Many of these traditions were handed down for a considerable length of time through schools or families of swordsmiths, and the blades made by these men are always of great value. Because of their remarkable workmanship and practical value as weapons, the best of the *koto* blades have neither like nor equal, being the finest blades ever produced anywhere.

The word *katana*, which is applied to the single-edged sword, is a rather generic term applied to all such blades, although in the more strict sense it designates the longer of the *dai-sho*, or two swords, carried by the samurai, the shorter one being the *wakizashi*. The elaborate nomenclature used by Japanese sword experts for designating the almost endless types of blades is a science in itself. They are described and distinguished by their relative length, and by the shape of their points and backs. The metal from which these fine blades are made is principally derived from deposits of magnetic iron ore and ferruginous sand, which produced iron and steel of the most excellent quality. It is recorded that the forging of these blades was considered an occupation pleasing to the gods and that as a requisite for success, the swordsmith must lead a more or less religious life according to the Way of the Gods, and abstain from excesses of all kinds. The master swordsmith clad himself in his ceremonial costume and wore

the *yeboshi* or small black-lacquered headpiece, while a *shimenawa*, the sacred rice-straw rope of Shintoism, was stretched across the smithy, with zigzag pieces of paper, called *gohei*, suspended from it to scare away evil spirits and invite good ones. It is said that the famous tenth-century swordsmith Munechika of Satsuma was once performing a critical operation in the forging of the blade known as *Kokitsune-maru* or Little Fox sword when his assistant failed him. But because of his strong belief and adherance to the principles of the Shinto faith, he was assisted at this critical moment by the Fox-Spirit of the Inari shrine, in the form of a woman. This story of the blade is not only a popular historical narrative but is frequently acted on the stage in a No play.

PROCESSES OF SWORD-MAKING

The forging of the Japanese blade required the utmost skill and calculation and the entire process was one of many tedious operations. The method of forging an all-steel blade, and the one preferred by the famous swordsmith Masamune, began with welding a strip of steel to a rod of iron which served as a handle. Other strips of steel were placed upon it and welded into a bar of the required dimensions, usually from six to eight inches in length by one and a quarter to two and a quarter inches in width, the thickness being from one-quarter to three-quarters of an inch, all depending on the final dimensions of the finished blade. This bar was raised to a welding

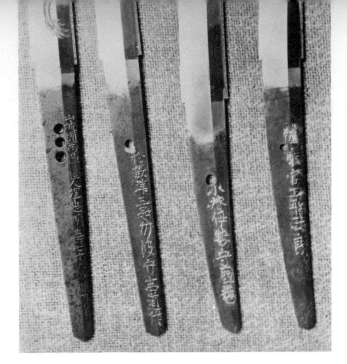

Tangs and points of shinto blades, with the pattern of watered steel visible on three of the blades. (1) Made by Mioju (Umetada, of Kyoto); dated 1632. (2) Made by Yoshimichi (Tamba-no-kami, of Osaka); seventeenth century. (3) Made by Kuniteru (Kobayashi, of Osaka); late seventeenth century. (4) Made by Masayoshi (Taira no, of Satsuma); dated 1784. Victoria and Albert Museum.

heat and notched in the middle with a chisel, then folded upon itself and welded, and then forged into its original dimensions. At the beginning of the forging operation the smith coated the metal with a thin layer of clay containing ashes of burnt straw, before placing it on the fire, and through the entire process of forging great care was used so that no grit or dirt got on the anvil, and the metal was never touched by the hand lest some grease should adhere. All these precautions were of vital importance because of the great risk of slight flaws or specks appearing in welding, which would impair the work. The usual method was to weld four bars together, and then repeat the doubling, welding, and forging nineteen times, so the bar was composed of 4,194,304 layers of metal in its thickness. It is said that between each forging the bar was cooled in oil and water alternately. At this stage of the process the bar was drawn out under the hammer to its required length and shape, and the prescribed curve was given to it. Although whole blades were made of steel as described above, a large proportion of Japanese swords are composite, some being made of steel and iron, or of steel, iron, and a compound of the two metals. There were a number of methods used by the swordsmiths in the process of forging, each having a name by which it is identified. Some of them are extremely complicated, while others are comparatively simple, such as the popular form favored by the Bizen smiths in which a plate of steel is placed between two of iron, with the steel forming the edge. However, it is said that the best examples were produced by welding together plates of iron and steel alter-

nately, folding, welding, and forging them nineteen times, and then hammering them on the narrow edge until that became the broad face of the bar. Sometimes, instead of the bar being hammered on the edge, it was hammered on the angle, which is called hoso-masa, or fine fiber forging.

On many blades, especially those produced by the famous schools of the Senju-in of Yamato and the Awataguchi of Yamashiro, there are beautiful markings. These are the result of peculiar methods of forging and of the juxtaposition of layers of iron and steel of different qualities, which is common in blades of the East. In early times steel was produced in small furnaces much like those of a blacksmith's forge. This resulted in an irregularity of quality and produced a mass having, from the bottom up, cast iron, hard steel, soft steel, wrought iron, and burnt iron. This mass was broken into small pieces and the desired qualities were selected by the experienced eye of the swordsmith, whose knowledge of metals was unequaled. The swordmaker could then produce almost any variety of blade he desired by welding the hard and soft pieces, then doubling, welding, and forging several more times. When the finished product from this process was etched, it was called watered steel. The most common etching substance was a hot solution of an impure native ferric sulphate applied with a rag. As the art of the blade maker developed, he was able to make recognizable patterns by mixing selected qualities of iron and steel plates and welding and doubling the bars in a manner that controlled the watering. In some types of Japanese blades the watering effect was enhanced by gouging out portions of the surface at the later stages of forging and then bringing it to a level with the hammer so the different layers of metal would be visible.

When the forging was completed, the blade was scraped with a *sen*, which is a kind of draw knife, and filed by the smith, who carefully examined its surface in search of defects. The next step was to shape the tang by filing in a particular direction, which produced file marks called *yasuri-me*. These file marks as well as the shape of the tang assist Japanese experts in recognizing the maker of a blade. The ends of some tangs are rounded and called chestnut-shape or *kuri-jiri*, while others are angular and called *ken-kiyo*. After the tang was shaped, the blade was roughly ground, and if the swordsmith was satisfied with it, he placed his name on the tang. Any ornamental work, such as engraving on the blade, was done at that time. It was not the practice for all swordsmiths to sign their blades; Masamune and other famous smiths did not sign their blades because, it is said, these could not be mistaken.

The crucial stage in the process of making a blade is the tempering, for it is there that the skill of the swordsmith is taxed to the utmost to give the blade its real practical value. This tempering produces the *yakiba* or tempered steel edge of the blade, which is a clouded band, usually from one-fourth to one-half inch in width, running along the edge of the sword, sometimes as a simple straight band and sometimes with special outlines. All of the numerous forms of *yakiba* have their special characteristics and are designated by particular names which, together with their exceptions as to special schools of swordsmiths, are almost endless. Although each swordsmith probably had his own secret method, the general process of producing the *yakiba* was to coat the blade to a thickness of about one-eighth inch with a clay having a ferruginous character, made of fine river sand mixed with about one-tenth part of finely powdered charcoal. Before the clay coating on the blade had hardened, a portion was removed by a bamboo stick along the edge on either side to expose the metal. The inner margin of this strip of clay was either made straight, notched, waved, or formed with some peculiar outline. When the clay coating became dry and hard, the blade was securely held and moved backward and forward over a fire of fir charcoal, with the edge downward, until the proper temperature had been reached, which was determined by the color of the exposed part of the metal. The blade was then plunged into a tub of warm water, in a vertical position if it were a straight blade, or in a horizontal position with the point first if it were a curved blade. Among the many stories of swords, there is one about an occasion when Masamune was tempering a blade in the presence of another swordsmith; noticing the latter stealthily put his hand into the water to learn its temperature, Masamune cut the hand off with a quick

stroke of the sword. Since the tempering process is one of the most important stages in blade-making, great skill and experience were required to determine from the color alone when the proper moment had arrived to plunge the blade into the water. Not only the temper of the blade, but also its form, depended upon this decision. The tempering was so highly important that the signature of the swordsmith who tempered the blade was sometimes placed on the tang along with the smith who did the forging, if it was done by a different man. The process of grinding and polishing a Japanese sword is

Complete suit of armor in flame color and gold showing the front and rear views with typical leg covering and shoes; seventeenth century. Metropolitan Museum of Art. Rogers Fund, 1904.

a meticulous operation, and a fine blade sometimes required two months to finish. The work was done on a large fine whetstone that was peculiar to Japan and whose exportation was prohibited by Shogunate decree. Kneeling upon the floor, the sharpener held the blade in his two hands with a rag and moved it backward and forward on the stone. Running lengthwise along the face of the blade are two angles, the *shinogi*, which is along the back part, and the broader plane called the *jigane*, sloping to the edge. The blade, usually measuring from twenty-eight to thirty inches in length, is

slightly curved and a little broader at its base than at the point, but the unusually sharp edge forms a perfect curve from heel to point with no flattening, and always at the same relative distance from the curve of the back. Another amazing detail is that the line which divides the *shinogi* and the *jigane* is an equally true intermediate curve, always at the same relative distance from the other two at the back and edge. It was an achievement of the highest excellence of craftsmanship to produce three such perfect curves. A vertical line cut off the plane of the *shinogi* about one inch from the point, while the line of the edge continued in a curve to the back, and an unparallel inner curve continued the dividing line of the *shinogi* and the *jigane* to the back of the blade. The remarkable strength of the *jigane* is achieved when it is ground by a highly skilled sharpener who will give it a slightly convex shape to lessen the chances of fracture. After the blade is perfectly sharp it is finished with a polishing stone dressed with oil and a fine powder of stone, then finally burnished with a polishing needle. On the finished blade are a number of peculiar markings that become visible only after the work is completed, and among the many special names applied to these appearances are the *nini* and the *niye*. Although these markings do not contribute to the quality of the blade, their existence considerably enhances its value. The *nini* resemble the minute fat globules seen in milk and produce cloudy spots, while the *niye*, which are more rare, are brilliant minute specks.

The practical effectiveness of a sword blade was of the utmost importance to the military man, for his life frequently depended upon its trustworthiness. And as so many essential factors entered into the make-up of a sword, there developed the official sword expert whose knowledge and experience was invaluable to the samurai. It is said the first of these sword experts, or *mekiki*, was appointed by the Ashikaga Shogun Takauji in the fourteenth century. The function of the *mekiki* was to determine the origin and quality of a blade, whether it was signed or unsigned, to estimate its pecuniary value, and to impart this knowledge to the samurai. Even the most outstanding and reputable of the *mekiki* differed at times as to the origin of a given blade. Reading a blade, seeing and knowing the marks that indicated its maker, was an art requiring special faculties and long experience. When a blade had been authenticated, the name of the maker was placed on the tang, usually in gold, and often with the signature of the *mekiki* and his *kakihan* (seal) added in gold.

Among the celebrated *mekiki* were the sword sharpeners of the Honami and Miyoshi families, whose traditions were handed down for many generations. One of the best known is Honami Kosetsu, who was appointed by Hideyoshi in the sixteenth century. It was probably he who introduced the custom of signing unsigned blades in gold, although some attribute it to Honami Kotoku, who wrote a treatise on blades some time earlier. The certificate, or *ori-kami*, of the *mekiki* was written on a sheet of a special kind of thick paper known as *kaga bosho*, made for the Shogun in the province of Kaga, and of which only a hundred sheets were produced each year. The certificate gave the name and residence of the maker of the blade, its dimensions, and any peculiar characteristics by which it could be identified. It further stated the blades' estimated value in gold, and was signed by the *mekiki*, or sometimes by more than one. The seal or seals were impressed on the reverse side. The *mekiki* frequently mentioned, among other things, that he considered the blade worthy of becoming an heirloom, since it was the traditional practice among the aristocracy and noble families to regard fine swords as heirlooms. Prior to the end of the sixteenth century there were a number of famous families of swordsmiths and from time to time the experts prepared lists of blade makers, arranged according to the experts' estimate of their merits, and added to it the average value of their blades. Such a list was compiled for Hideyoshi toward the end of the sixteenth century to enable him to select suitable blades for presentation to his

retainers and military friends. In the year 1702 a list of this nature was compiled in which values were given in mai of gold, a measure of value introduced in the sixteenth century during the time of Nobunaga. It was equivalent to the gold oban, which contained about 4.82 ounces of gold, and its value at that time was equal to about one hundred dollars. In that list no value was given to the blades of six famous swordsmiths, but the highest value of fifty mai was attached to the swords of Sadamune of the Kamakura smiths, an adopted son of Masamune. Other values in the list fall as low as one mai, in which final category there were about twenty names, including Muramasa, whose blades, although unsurpassed for quality, bore a reputation for bloodthirstiness and ill-luck. Blade experts differed widely in their evaluation of the positions of the various swordsmiths, on account of their partiality for certain schools.

SWORDMAKERS AND TRADITIONS

The signatures of the early swordsmiths appearing on the tang are remarkably brief, usually consisting of two characters, and in some cases only one, forming the maker's name, together with the place of residence. Swordsmiths of the twelfth century all had official titles or honorary rank, although this was rarely indicated on the blade until the succeeding century, when it also became the practice to add such names as Fujiwara, Minamoto, and Taira to their own. Honorary titles such as *kami* and *daijo* were in frequent use in the sixteenth century and almost every swordsmith of importance added a title to his signature. Besides the signature of the swordsmith, Japanese blades often carry curious and interesting items engraved on the tang. Occasionally they state that the blade was made especially for a particular person, that it was made by two smiths, or that it was tempered by a certain smith, giving the number of times it had been forged. The names of famous swordmakers are as well known to the Japanese as those of the foremost painters, writers, calligraphers, and historical figures, for the art of the blade maker was looked upon as the most honorable of all crafts. The greatest blade makers appeared in the latter part of the Kamakura period (1185-1333), notably Yoshimitsu of Awataguchi in Kyoto, 1229-1291, Masamune of Sagami, 1264-1343, and his pupil Go Yoshihiro, 1299-1325. The name of Masamune has passed into the Japanese language as a term signifying supreme excellence, for a Masamune blade was unequaled. Masamune operated his forge at the feudal military capital of Kamakura, where blade makers from the provinces came to acquire more knowledge from the great master. In the beginning of the thirteenth century a great impetus to swordmaking was given

Kabuto *or helmet of iron, lacquer, and silk with a wild-boar insigne. Signed Unobouiye; eighteenth century. Metropolitan Museum of Art. Gift of Bashford Dean, 1914.*

by the Emperor Gotoba, who summoned a number of the foremost swordmakers to Kyoto to attend him in rotation. Besides demonstrating their skill in his Imperial presence, they gave him instructions in the art of blade-making. Emperor Gotoba himself produced blades of excellent quality, some of which are extant and marked on the tang with the Imperial sixteen-petal chrysanthemum. These blades are most highly treasured in Japan, and are called *kiku-go-saku*, or make of the august chrysanthemum.

The succeeding centuries were also periods of great activity in swordmaking, not as brilliant as in earlier times, although the names of many great smiths appeared, especially in the seventeenth century. In 1877 the Imperial government under Emperor Meiji issued an edict prohibiting the samurai from wearing the sword, which had been not only his privilege but also the distinctive mark of his traditional military caste. The sword had been the center of the old military life of Japan and it was a part of the education of samurai youths to know its history and its etiquette, for when they reached the age of fifteen they entered man's estate and were honored to wear the coveted weapon. Swords were handed down from father to son as heirlooms and treasured as a most cherished possession. A sword was also traditionally given by a father to his daughter on her wedding day as a symbol of that purity of life which the woman was expected to keep, and it was also the blade with which she might take her own life should it be necessary to do so. In feudal times a samurai's life was pledged to his lord and he was never sure of the fortunes that the following day would bring, for his life might be taken in a fight, or by his own hand under orders of the death penalty for some breach of the rigid code of samurai etiquette. It was therefore of utmost importance that his sword be well selected and properly cared for. Its edge should be so keen that a man's head could be cut off at one blow, and if skillfully done, leave a shred of skin at the throat for the head to hang upon the breast. The Japanese blade is generally regarded as a cutting weapon of the highest order, unsurpassed by even the swords of Damascus, Persia, and India. This was due to the extraordinarily thorough workmanship, the swordsmith's primary desire being to produce a blade that was reliable and a credit to its maker. At times the samurai's blade was tested privately, and sometime officially, by cutting up corpses of persons who had paid the death penalty. The blade's capabilities are occasionally found engraved on the tang, and on some swords a statement is inscribed that it had cut through one, two, or three bodies at a single blow.

Japanese literature contains a wealth of accounts, both historical and legendary, of famous swords connected with the lives of great figures of the past. These include the famous heirloom swords as the *Kogarasu-maru* or the Little Crow, and the *Nuke-maru* or the Springer Out, belonging to the great feudal Taira family. It is said the *Kogarasu-maru* was made during the time of Emperor Kammu in 782 and once was carried away by a crow. The *Nuke-maru* was made in the year 820 and is said to have sprung from its scabbard to destroy a serpent that was about to strike Taira-no-Tadamori while he was asleep. Then there is the famous heirloom sword of the Minamoto family called the *Hize-Kiri* or Beard Cutter, which was made in the tenth century and whose edge was so keen that after cutting off a man's head it passed through his beard before the head fell. Another famous Minamoto heirloom sword is the *Hiza-maru* or Knee Cutter, which was made in the same period and is said to have had such a fine edge that when used to behead a kneeling criminal, it would also cut his knees in its downward stroke. There are also a number of interesting stories regarding certain superstitions associated with particular swords or their makers. Some were considered to bring good fortune, happiness, and longevity to the owner, while others were believed to be unlucky and bring misfortune. The blades of Muramasa of Ise, who flourished in the latter part of the fourteenth century, were considered to be

Kabuto of iron with horn-like ornament and a mask made to resemble a mythical winged being called tengu. *The helmet is of the seventeenth-eighteenth century, while the mask is dated 1713. Metropolitan Museum of Art. Gift of Bashford Dean, 1914.*

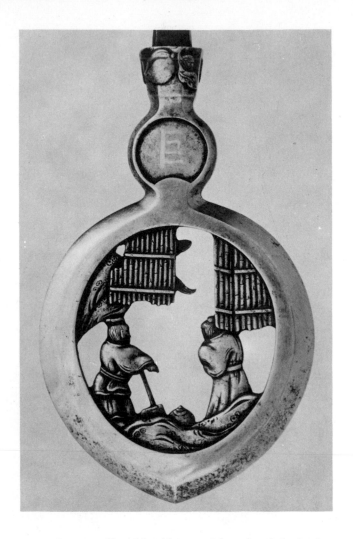

Left above: Willow-leaf-type steel arrowhead depicting herons and reeds; signed Umetada Hikobei no-jo Motoshige, and dated 1645. Metropolitan Museum of Art. Giovanni P. Morosini Collection, 1932.

Right: Bifurcated steel arrowhead with a design of wisteria; eighteenth century. Metropolitan Museum of Art. Giovanni P. Morosini Collection, 1932.

Left: Steel arrowhead in shape of a gem, depicting the story of Kwakkyo; signed Umetada Hikobei no-jo Motoshige, and dated 1645. Metropolitan Museum of Art. Giovanni P. Morosini Collection, 1932.

unworthy as well as bloodthirsty, although of the highest quality. Muramasa, a pupil of Masamune, was a most skillful swordsmith but he possessed a violent mind verging on madness, which was believed to have passed into his blades. Tokugawa Ieyasu, for instance, having been accidentally cut by them, held them to be unlucky. It was a popular belief that the Muramasa blades could induce their owners to commit suicide or even murder and that once a blade had killed a man, the owner would die of starvation unless he appeased the blade with more blood. The lucky and unlucky characteristics attributed to the blades of certain famous swordsmiths have influenced their monetary value through the centuries and at one time the Muramasa blades were even stricken from the blade experts' lists.

ARMOR

With the increase of commercial intercourse between Japan and the Asiatic mainland during the Asuka period

(522-645), armor made of small plates, laced together and overlapping, was introduced for the first time. Portions of these suits of armor are preserved in the Shosoin at Nara together with a large number of arms, all dating from the time of the Emperor Shomu, who reigned from 724 to 749. This variety of armor was adopted by the Japanese and modified according to their own desires and requirements. It was during the Fujiwara era (897-1185), in the latter part of the Heian period, that the two principal types of Japanese armor were developed. The one called *oyoroi* or great harness was used by generals and other warriors of superior rank and consisted of a full suit including the helmet and the large protecting pieces for the arms and shoulders. The other form, known as *hara-maki* or wrapping the belly, was worn by the common soldiers and consisted principally of cuirass and tasses without the shoulder pieces and without the use of a helmet. During the fifteenth century fighting on horseback began to decline and helmets and shoulder pieces were then worn with both types of armor. The Japanese helmet, or *kabuto*, is a most interesting piece of armor and is made in a variety of types. The form

Left. Steel arrowhead with a pierced design of sages playing the game of go; signed Umetada Hikobei no-jo Motoshige, dated 1645. Metropolitan Museum of Art. Giovanni P. Morosini Collection, 1932.

Right: Steel arrowhead with a pierced design of peonies and a Chinese lion or shishi; signed Umetada Hikobei no-jo Motoshige, and dated 1645. Metropolitan Museum of Art. Giovanni P. Morosini Collection, 1932.

most frequently seen has the *hachi* or crown made of a number of gores of iron riveted together with a ridge formed at their joints, which offered powerful resistance to the cut of a sword while keeping the helmet light in weight. To serve as ventilation, there is usually an aperture at the top of the helmet called the *hachimanza*. This is generally in the form of a chrysanthemum with the aperture in the center. There is a *mayezashi* or peak riveted to the lower part of the *hachi*; it was frequently lacquered red on its underside to reflect grotesquely on the face, as well as on the iron mask that served as a visor. These iron masks were tied to the helmet and were made to represent not only terrible-looking faces, but also demons and fantastic animals. Above the peak were fastened the curious ornaments resembling a pair of flat horns which were called *tsunomoto*, while in a socket between the horns was fixed the forecrest or *mayedate*. During the fifteenth and sixteenth centuries the *mon* or family crest came into general use as a motif in the decoration of armor. A *shikoro* or neck protector was attached to the back of the helmet, and was composed of from three to seven rows of metal plates laced to-

gether with silk cords. The whole suit of armor itself was held together in the same manner as the *shikoro*, that is, the many plates of iron were laced together by silk or leather cords, with the cords forming a pattern. It is said that during the latter part of the ninth century the great feudal families adopted particular colors for the cords on their armor, the Fujiwara using light green, the Tachibana yellow, and the Taira purple.

In the thirteenth and fourteenth centuries during the Kamakura period the military class and its feudal system steadily increased its power, and with the growing number of samurai created a golden era for both swordmaker and armorer. Although it was not until the fifteenth and sixteenth centuries that the great families of hereditary armorers rose to their positions of importance, the Myochin family, the greatest of all, trace their origin back several centuries earlier. The family was claimed to descend from the Prime Minister of the Empress Jingo, who invaded Korea at the head of an army in the middle of the third century. However, it was not until the middle of the twelfth century that the recorded history of the family begins with Munesuke, who had at that time been given the family name of Myochin by the Emperor Konoye. The pre-eminent position of the Myochins in the history of Japanese art is not only based upon the superb quality of their armor, but also on their claim to being the founders of ironwork as an art. They were armorers to the court for more than six hundred years, from the twelfth to the end of the eighteenth century, and retained during all that time the foremost position in the armorer's art. The hammer work in iron executed on a piece of armor or on an *okimono* attributed to the Myochin is unexcelled. The practical excellence of their work and their manipulation of the iron is unsurpassed. Although thin and light, their armor is extremely tough, capable of resisting powerful blows from swords and other weapons. The making of *okimono*, which is a generic term applied to decorative ornaments for the tokonoma or alcove, developed into a special art and afforded occasional amusement for the glyptic artists of the older schools. Some of the most exquisite and most ingenious of these earlier *okimono*, such as the wonderfully articulated models of birds, dragons, serpents, and crayfish, came from the studios of the Myochin, and are masterpieces of the metal art.

ARCHERY

The most primitive weapon of sport and warfare is the bow and arrow, and in no other country did it attain greater importance than in Japan. Although firearms were introduced into Japan by the Portuguese in 1543, the bow and arrow, until a very late period, remained the most important of weapons, and the skill of famous archers was celebrated through the centuries. Archery was an essential part of the life of the nobles, and the custom of shooting from horseback so as to send an arrow accurately in any direction while in swift motion was part of their education. Like the other arts of Japan, archery was probably introduced from China. Representations of famous Chinese archers are frequently portrayed on metalwork, the most noted being Yoyuki, who is said to have shot down a goose flying invisible above a cloud, his aim accurately directed by the cry of the bird. Pictures of Japanese military commanders armed with a bow and with a quiver of arrows on the back are frequently seen in old scroll-paintings. The bow and arrow has been traditionally associated with the lives of famous Japanese since ancient times. Thus Jimmu Tenno, the first Emperor of Japan, is often portrayed holding his bow with a giant crow perched upon it. And the Empress Jingo is depicted during her invasion of Korea in the third century riding a horse with her bow in her hand, and in another picture she is seen writing the characters koku-o, or sovereign of the country, upon the face of a rock with her bow at the time of her conquest. A number of fine

examples of bows of the eighth century are preserved in the Shosoin at Nara. These ancient bows range in length from five and a half to seven feet and are made with a variety of deciduous woods, those of azusa or catalpa wood being considered the best.

Japanese archery presents many peculiar features, the first of which is the form of the bow. The usual bow was a long, highly elastic piece, which averaged about six and a half feet in length with a curvature which was reversed when the weapon was strung for use. It was held vertically, and the arrow was discharged at a point nearly two-thirds of the way down the bow, and always on the right side of the bow. The bowstrings were made of hemp fibers twisted together with loops at the ends, and since Japanese arrows were of much greater length than Western ones, the bowstring was drawn well behind the ear. Another peculiar feature of the Japanese bows that are preserved in many of the temples and shrines is their single curve, which is not a true segment of a circle, but a flatter curve at one end than at the other. Therefore the greatest distance between the bow and the string is not in the middle but about two-thirds of the way from the top, where

Left: Steel arrowhead pierced with a cherry blossom design and the characters of the Tenjin shrine; signed Toshiyoshi or Shunkichi; eighteenth century. Metropolitan Museum of Art. Giovanni P. Morosini Collection, 1932.

Center: Willow-leaf-type steel arrowhead pierced with Japanese characters. Eighteenth century. Metropolitan Museum of Art. Giovanni P. Morosini Collection, 1932.

Right: Steel arrowhead with the design of a dragon entwined around a sword; eighteenth century. Metropolitan Museum of Art. Giovanni P. Morosini Collection, 1932.

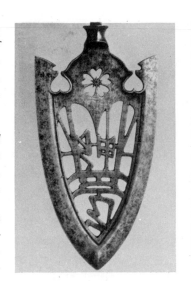  

Right: Steel arrowhead in the shape of a jewel pierced with the design of a dragon; eighteenth century. Metropolitan Museum of Art. Giovanni P. Morosini Collection, 1932.

the grip is placed. The Japanese bow is of excellent composite construction, being built up of two thin strips of bamboo between which are set three somewhat thicker strips of deciduous wood placed edgewise so as to increase its strength. On the outside of these are set two strips of *haze* wood, *Rhus succedanea*, all being secured with fish glue, then lacquered and bound with rattan at various points. In some examples the ends are faced with metal, and since in some bows the string touches these metal facings for some distance from the ends, it produces a sound when striking against them. This sound was frequently used in signaling, and it is said that when the Emperor required water for washing in the morning during ancient times, three of his retainers would signal his desire by twanging their bows.

Preserved in temples and shrines are a number of very long bows that belonged to famous historical figures, and it is easily seen from their form and size that they are very powerful. Two of these are at the great Itsukushima shrine at Miyajima on the Inland Sea. One, eight feet nine inches in length, belonged to Yuasa Matashichiro; the other is eight feet five inches long. The usual length is six feet five inches, as in

the case of the bow of Minamoto Yoritomo, 1147-1199, preserved at the Tsurugaoka Hachimangu shrine at Kamakura, which was founded in 1063 by Minamoto Yorioshi. Many of the great military figures of medieval times are famous for their archery feats. One of these, Minamoto-no-Tametomo, a famous twelfth-century archer whose adventures are told in the literary classic called *Yumiharizuki*, sank a boat with a bow eight feet nine inches in length and an arrow of great weight. On another occasion in the twelfth century during the battle of Yashima, a beautiful island in the Inland Sea renowned for its magnificent views and a place of refuge of the Taira clansmen, the Taira fastened a fan to a bamboo pole in the bow of one of their boats and challenged the Minamoto to exhibit their skill at archery. Yoichi, the best Minamoto bowman, discharged his arrow with such accuracy, from a distance of nearly a hundred yards, that it struck the fan squarely on its rivet and it dropped into the sea.

The arrowhead, called *yano-ne* or *yajiri*, is one of the most interesting products of the Japanese metalworker. Produced by famous swordsmiths, the finest examples display great richness in form and ornament. The earliest mention of an arrow is in accounts of the mythological age shortly after the gods gave birth to the islands of Japan. The sun goddess had sent two deities to earth to prepare the way for her grandson Ninigi-no-Mikoto, upon whom she bestowed the sovereign power of the realm to be handed down to posterity. But one of these divine messengers, having decided to stay on earth and rule himself, was killed by an arrow dropped from the plains of heaven. Among the many great makers of ornamental arrowheads is Umetada Myoju, 1558-1632, swordsmith to Hideyoshi, who is often regarded as the first to raise the craft to an art. The fame of his arrowheads was almost as great as that of his sword blades, and it is among these later arrowheads that the most elaborate examples are found. This beautiful work on *yano-ne* became popular during the Momoyama period (1573-1615) with the developing taste for rich and gorgeous decoration. During the two hundred and fifty years of peace of the Edo period, ornamental ironwork became more elaborate, most of the decorative arrowheads being pierced and saw-cut with a great variety of designs. The *yanagi* or willow-leaf arrowhead, which appears in many shapes and proportions, is the most frequent form, ornamented with an endless variety of openwork designs. Among the designs most often seen are the *sakura* or cherry blossom, the heart-shaped petal of the *sakura*, dragons, family crests, the Imperial *kiri* (paulownia) and the Imperial *kiku* (chrysanthemum), the *yang* and *yin* symbols of creation, the written characters for Hachiman Dai Bosatsu or god of war, and all sorts of typical Japanese motifs, such as the plum and bamboo. These arrowheads are also frequently seen with beautifully

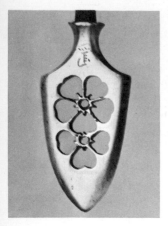  

Left: Willow-leaf-type steel arrowhead with pierced cherry-blossom design; eighteenth century. Metropolitan Museum of Art. Giovanni P. Morosini Collection, 1932.

Center: Willow-leaf steel arrowhead pierced with the Imperial kiri crest; eighteenth century. Metropolitan Museum of Art. Giovanni P. Morosini Collection, 1932.

Right: Whistling arrowhead made of wood; seventeenth century. Metropolitan Museum of Art. Gift of Bashford Dean, 1914.

executed characters in openwork bearing the names of owners, deities, and so forth. Many contain Buddhist prayers written in pierced work so skillfully done that the characters appear to be floating. Many of these Buddhist inscriptions were made for warriors to use as an offering to a temple, others as trophies in honor of victories in war.

There were many types of *yebira* or quivers, some for war, others for hunting, and ornamental ones such as those worn by the palace guards, with the arrows spread out and the feathers protruding behind their backs like the tail of a peacock. The hunting quivers and those used in war were usually little more than a framework of bamboo, while the others were frequently lacquered or otherwise decorated. They are conical or quadrangular in shape, though most of the quivers found in temples are shaped like an armchair with a high back and short legs. The latter are made to hold from twenty to thirty arrows and they were apparently intended to stand on the floor. The common arrows were similar to those used in archery and had conical iron points. For the chase and for war the arrowheads were of steel and appear in a great variety of shapes and sizes. Although there are many subdivisions, the chief categories were the *yanagi-ya* or willow-leaf arrows,

watakusi or flesh tearers or barbed arrows, *kari-mata* or bifurcated or two-pointed arrows, and *togari-ya* or pointed arrows. Each of these types varies greatly in form, some of the willow-leaf arrows being long and sharp, and some of the pointed arrows so wide as to be almost heart-shaped. In the *kari-mata* arrowhead the distance between the points varies from one and a half to six and a half inches, but its principle was always the same. The *kari-mata* was not only used for war but also for big game, and had both the inner curve and the outer edge of equal sharpness. Many of the larger and earlier examples had very long tangs, sometimes measuring fifteen inches or more in length, as a necessary counterpoise, since in some specimens the head weighed as much as eight ounces. Of particular interest is the *kabura-ya* or turnip-headed arrow, which is sometimes called *hiki-me*. This is the sounding or whistling arrow, which is usually made of wood with a pear-shaped contour, with its shoulder or broadest part near the top or foremost portion. Around the shoulder it is pierced with four oblong holes, each hole having its corresponding aperture on the flat top or nose of the arrowhead. The sharp, shrill whistling they produced as they ascended and descended was used as a signal, as well as serving to terrify the enemy.

IX Sword Decoration and Mounts

IN THE early centuries when the sword was in almost constant use as a fighting weapon, its mounts were simple and few in number, being primarily functional accessories to the weapon. But as the feudal system developed and the samurai increased in power and wealth, the art of sword mounts came into being. The Japanese did not wear jewelry, so the art of the metalworker was employed to embellish the sword, and the most eminent artists and chasers contributed their talents to its decoration. In the Edo period the sword was rarely used as a fighting weapon, and it gradually evolved into the most important object of personal adornment, with an increased number of ornamental mounts on its hilt and scabbard being lavishly decorated. The alloys, combinations, unusual patinas, and color treatment of the metals used on sword mounts, combined with exquisite inlaying and chasing, are of remarkable beauty. With this extraordinary range the Japanese metal artist had at disposal a most beautiful and unique palette, unknown in the metalwork of any other country.

Damascening in gold was never practiced on the blade of a Japanese sword as is customary in other Oriental countries, although the swordsmiths occasionally damascened their names on some of the *koto*, or old blades. The earliest method of decorating a blade was by engraving, as seen in examples preserved in temples dating from the Nara and Heian periods. Common on early blades are engraved invocations to Buddhist divinities, such as Fudo, Bishamon, or one of the four Diva Kings. It is said that Prince Shotoku Taishi attributed his victory over Moriya in the year 587 to invocations such as these engraved on his helmet. Bishamon is one of the seven gods of good fortune, and is shown in full armor, with a fierce expression, carrying in his right hand a small pagoda-shaped shrine, and in the left a lance. He is equivalent to the Hindu god of riches, but because he is depicted with armor and lance, he has been erroneously included among the gods of war.

It was not until around the beginning of the thirteenth century that blades were decorated not only with engraving but also with intaglios usually representing Ama-Kurikara —which is the rain dragon entwining a sword—or Fudo, a Buddhist divinity. Fudo corresponds to Achala, a form of the Hindu god Siva, and as such he is one of the supreme trinity, or Dainichi Nyorai in Japanese Buddhism—a perfect manifestation of the absolute truth of the universe, equivalent to Buddha or Dainichi. Of the three divinities forming the trinity, Fudo is known as the destroyer, but since death is a transition to a new form of life, the destroyer is really a re-creator, and thus Fudo is styled the Bright or Happy One. He is represented seated over the brink of a precipice, or standing on a rock, surrounded by flames. In his right hand he carries a *vajra* hilted sword, and in his left is a rope for the binding and chastisement of the powers of evil.

The most usual type of decoration on the blade is in the form of *hi*, or grooves, with the larger grooves serving to render the blade lighter in weight without weakening its strength. In section these grooves are always segments of a circle, those of moderate width being mostly semicircles, while in the wider ones there are frequently motifs worked in relief. These grooves, which were sometimes treated with red lacquer, were called *chi-naga-shi*, or blood channels, by the common people. In another mode of early decoration, chasing was combined with pierced work, the subject usually represented being Ama-Kurikara, the dragon entwining a sword. It is found either in a wide groove or in a panel having a triangular end, with the design cut through the blade.

TYPES AND CHARACTERISTICS

The earliest Japanese sword was the double-edged *ken*, which was succeeded by the first single-edged sword in the

Three beautifully mounted tachi (slung swords) on a sword rack. From top to bottom: (1) Tachi to be worn at court ceremonies, signed on ura (back side of tang) "Etchu-no-Kami Fujiwara-no-Masatoshi, made to order of Lord Tsunemitsu of Shonu rank," and dated 1682. (2) Tachi to be worn with armor, signature only partly legible. (3) Tachi to be worn at court ceremonies, remnants of signature on omote (front face of tang), possibly fifteenth century. Victoria and Albert Museum.

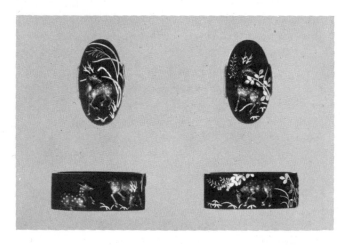

Dai-sho (pair of swords carried by a warrior), the long sword called katana and the short sword called wakizashi. The blades are of the fifteenth century and the mounts are of the eighteenth century. Metropolitan Museum of Art. Gift of Howard Mansfield, 1936.

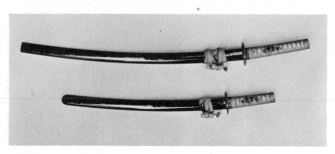

Fuchi and kashira made of shakudo, by Mitsuotomo Kikuoka; eighteenth century. Metropolitan Museum of Art. The Masauji Goda Collection, gift of a trustee, 1917.

eighth century, called the tachi. Many centuries ago the tachi was supplanted as a fighting weapon by the katana, and since then has been used as a state sword. The tachi and katana were similar except for the manner in which they were carried; the tachi was suspended from the sash by two cords with its blade edge downward, and the katana was thrust in the sash with its edge upward. The mounts or fittings on a tachi are also of different shapes from those on the usual swords and are known by different names. The katana is the national sword of Japan and is distinguished by its long, slightly curved, single-edged blade, which averages from twenty-eight to thirty inches in length. A similar sword called the wakizashi was also carried by the samurai, along with the katana, as a supplementary weapon whose blade usually measured about eighteen inches in length. The combination of these swords is called dai-sho, the word dai referring to the katana or longer sword, and sho to the wakizashi or shorter one. Very often the dai-sho pair had identical or similar designs on their mounts. But, since it was the custom to leave the long sword at the door when entering a house and to place the shorter one on the tatami or mat beside its owner, the latter was frequently more elaborately decorated.

It was the tradition for a samurai to give a small sword called mamori katana to his male children under five years of age. This first sword of the military man's son was known as a charm sword and had the hilt and scabbard covered in brocaded silk with a kinchaku, or purse, attached to it. But when the son first started to wear his ceremonial dress, he was presented with a short sword having a plain black-lacquer scabbard and mounted with finely worked fittings. This is the

Left: A tanto *having hilt and sheath of ebony with gold mounts depicting butterflies and flowers, and having a* kozuka *(small knife). Made by Kano Natsuo, and signed and dated 1866. Metropolitan Museum of Art. Bequest of Mrs. H. O. Havemeyer, 1909, The H. O. Havemeyer Collection.*

Right: A nineteenth-century aikuchi *with scabbard and* kozuka *(small knife) with a seventeenth-century blade. The hilt and scabbard are made of steel, silver, and lacquer. Metropolitan Museum of Art. Gift of William B. Osgood Field, 1949.*

sword that was also carried by men when wearing the *kamashimo*, or court dress. Smaller blade weapons, such as daggers, were also beautifully mounted. The *tanto*, whose curved blade is rarely longer than twelve inches, was fitted with a guard and usually had the hilt and scabbard mounted with all the fittings used on the sword, generally elaborately decorated. Also in this category is the *aikuchi*, a knife or dagger without a guard, with a hilt and scabbard which were frequently made of metal and elaborately decorated. During the Tokugawa period the *aikuchi* was carried by persons of rank and by retired soldiers, and was also used in committing hara-kiri, or ceremonial suicide. Another interesting weapon within the category of daggers is the *kwaiken*, which is an early form of either a single-edged or double-edged knife carried by Japanese women and used for ceremonial suicide by severing the veins in the neck.

The hilt of the Japanese sword is usually from eight to ten inches or more in length and generally covered with *same*, which is a rendered sharkskin. It is white in color and is covered with small lumps which are rasped down, partially covered with black lacquer until the hollow centers are filled up, and then ground down to a smooth surface and polished. This is known as *same-nuri*, or sharkskin lacquer, and has the appearance of tiny rounded discs of ivory set in black lacquer. The *tsukaito*, which is placed over the *same*, is a braid wound round the hilt in various patterns, leaving rhomboidal spaces through which the *same* is visible. On the pommel is the protective mount called the *kashira*, while at the lower part of the hilt next to the guard is the *fuchi*, or ring into which the base of the hilt fits. In spite of the small surface at the disposal of the artist,

the *kashira*, which is an oval rarely exceeding one and five-eighths inches in length and five-eighths of an inch in breadth, combines the most beautiful designs with the finest workmanship. With minute chasing of extraordinary skill when done by the foremost masters, the *kashira* and *fuchi* are remarkable also for their combinations of colored metals, the principal part of the design being executed on the *kashira*, and the subordinate part on the *fuchi*. On either side of the hilt is a pair of ornaments called *menuki*, which are held in place by a projecting pin or by braid wound round the hilt. They are usually a matched pair and frequently conform in design to the other fittings. Fine examples of *menuki* worked in gold or other metals are occasionally signed pieces by celebrated artists and are remarkable for their jewel-like quality. They are most often in the form of dragons, flying cranes, rabbits, tigers, Buddhist divinities such as temple guardians, and an endless variety of the most interesting human and animal subjects. Sometimes a broad collar of metal, called the *dogame*, encircles the middle of the hilt and through it the rivet or *mekugi* frequently passes. It is usually decorated with a design of two dragons or a dragon entwining a sword, and is principally found on the hilt of a *tanto*, a variety of dagger.

The decoration of the scabbard of the sword varied both in extent and character depending upon the size and purpose for which the weapon was intended. In the *dai-sho* or pair of swords, mentioned above, the scabbards were almost always made of *hinoki*, the Japanese cypress. They were lacquered in black and frequently decorated with the crest or *mon* of the owner in gold lacquer, and had a finely decorated metal cap at the tip called the *kojiri*. The *wakizashi* was usually fitted with

Left: Pair of menuki *in gold and other metals depicting the famous Chinese warriors Kwanyu and Chorio; eighteenth century. Metropolitan Museum of Art. The Sylmaris Collection, gift of George C. Graves, 1931.*

Below: Pair of gold menuki *representing quail; made by Motonori, nineteenth century. Metropolitan Museum of Art. The Masauji Goda Collection, gift of a trustee, 1917.*

two small sheaths which were hollowed out on either side of the scabbard at the top, and in these were carried two small knives called the *kogai* and the *kozuka*. At the edge of the sheath for the *kogai* is a guard or protective flat piece of ornamental metal called the *kurikata*, while the one for the *kozuka* is called the *uragawara*. Although the *wakizashi* was usually fitted with both the *kogai* and *kozuka*, the *katana* seldom had the *kogai* and frequently had neither. The *kurikata* also served as the fitting through which the *sage-o*, or long flat silken cord, was passed and wound round the scabbard so as to hold the sword securely in place when thrust in the sash. When the feudal swordsman prepared for action, he would draw the *sage-o* from the *kurikata* and throw it with remarkable rapidity over the shoulder and tie it behind the back, catching up the fullness of the wide sleeves and thus baring the forearms. In feudal times the samurai had been trained from boyhood in the art of forming the *sage-o* into many varieties of loops, knots, and nooses which enabled him to use it for binding prisoners.

In the literature of Japanese sword mounts the term *kozuka*—which generally refers to the small knife carried in its sheath in the sword scabbard, including its blade and handle combined—is frequently restricted to the blade only, when detached from the handle, and the term *ko-katana* is applied to the combination of the blade and handle. Its straight single-edged blade is made of *kataha* plates, produced by welding together a plate of steel and one of iron. The steel side of the blade is flat with a high polish, while the iron side tapers to the cutting edge and is unpolished. Frequently the iron side of the blade is beautifully inlaid or engraved with decorative designs and often with engraved graphic symbols or the characters of Japanese writing. The flat metal handle, which is

usually about one-half inch in width and slightly less than four inches in length, is elaborately decorated, and conforms to or matches the *kogai* if they are made to be carried as a pair. The more extended surface of the *kozuka* handle gave the artist greater scope for his design. It is in these mounts that the finest examples of chasing and engraving occur, and they most frequently bear the artist's signature. Among other things, the *kozuka* is said to have been used as a missile, thrown with great accuracy by skillful swordsmen, or sometimes driven into the heart of a fallen foe to deliver the *coup de grâce*. But its principal purpose was to serve the swordsman in every manner in which a knife could be used.

The *kogai*, which like the *kozuka* was carried in a sheath in the scabbard, resembles a head pin or skewer. Its flat, elongated skewer-shape part is made in one piece with the handle. The handle is elaborately decorated and made to conform to the *kozuka*, although its end terminates by curving into and forming a tiny disc-shaped finial. At times the *kogai* was finely split lengthwise, from the center of the end of the handle to the point, forming two equal parts resembling a pair of chopsticks, in which case it was called a *wari-kogai*. Many curious stories have been written about the *kogai* and its uses, and although most of these stories have to be considered as fictional, because no records have been found to establish their validity, they still serve to illustrate how the *kogai* might have been used. It is said that in the days of hereditary feuds and relentless revenge for real or imagined wrong, the avenger, after having slain his enemy, would thrust his *kogai* into the corpse, so that those finding it would recognize the distinguishing mark or badge of the owner of the *kogai*. The identity of the slayer would then be known and suspicion would not fall on an innocent person. Sometimes the slayer even went so far as to write a full statement of the reasons for the deed, bearing his signature and seal, and pinned it to the body of his victim by means of the *kogai*. At times the slayer would surrender to the authorities for trial and punishment; in other instances he would retire to a secluded place and commit *hara-kiri*. But as a rule, having left his *kogai* behind as evidence, he would endeavor to lose his former identity and become a *ronin*, literally meaning wave-man, which was a masterless samurai owing allegiance to no feudal lord. It has also been written that in the old days of continued feudal warfare, it was the custom to decapitate a fallen foe, if he were a warrior of any importance, and to present his head to the feudal lord or general as proof of prowess in battle. Since the samurai could not touch a corpse without being defiled, he would stick the *kogai* into the *mage*, or topknot of hair, thereby forming a handle by which the ghastly trophy could be carried without fear of contamination. Notwithstanding the questionability of these and other stories about the *kogai*, it is established as factual that the *wari-kogai*, or *split kogai*, were used as chopsticks, and the regular *kogai* was used to loosen and dress up the ruffled or matted hair of the warrior when he removed his helmet.

THE "TSUBA"

Of all the fittings on a Japanese sword, the most important, from its size and shape and from the fact that the metal artist lavished his best work on it, is the *tsuba* or guard. It is a flat metal plate, generally elliptical, round, or often resembling a rectangle with gently curving sides and rounded corners, averaging about two and a half inches in diameter. The majority of *tsuba* are made of steel, and the finest are of *shakudo* or *shibuichi* or a combination of both. In the center of the *tsuba* is a specially shaped opening through which the tang passes, and around this opening is a plain narrow space called *seppa dai*. If the *tsuba* bears the signature of the artist, it is found on the *seppa dai*, with his name on the left side of the opening and his residence and date on the right side. The *tsuba* may also have a perforation at either side of the *seppa dai* called *riobitsu*, for the *kogai* and *kozuba* to pass through. Above and below the *tsuba* are two sword fittings resembling washers, which are called *seppa*. Their original use was to support the *tsuba*, which was, in the earlier examples, thinner in the center. *Seppa* are usually ornamented like the other fittings, the larger one, called *o-seppa*, being placed under the *tsuba*. *Tsuba* on the

Left: Kozuka *and* kogai *having a design of lilies by Mitsuyuki Tojo, 1790-1862, of the Goto school; the* kozuka *blade is signed by Sukehiro, 1635-1682. Victoria and Albert Museum.*

Below: A kogai *made of* shakudo *by Rinjo (Mitsuzane) Kanzayemon Goto, with designs of the conventional Chinese lion and bamboo leaves; seventeenth century. Metropolitan Museum of Art. The Masauji Goda Collection, gift of a trustee, 1917.*

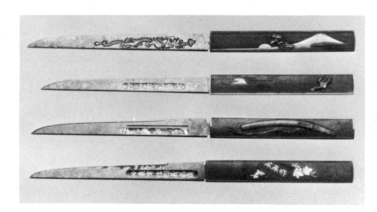

Above: Four kozuka *with handles of* shakudo *and iron with scenes of Mount Fuji, a pine tree, and the moon; the moon and a flying goose; a sword; and a plaque with inscription; seventeenth-eighteenth century. Metropolitan Museum of Art. The Masauji Goda Collection, gift of a trustee, 1917.*

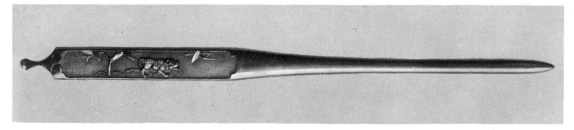

early swords were generally of iron, and they continued to be used almost exclusively during the Muromachi and Momoyama periods. They were still used occasionally in later and more peaceful times when the sword became more of a decorative accessory to the costume.

During the era of peace under the Tokugawa Shogunate, from 1615 to 1867, other metals made their appearance for use on *tsuba* and other sword mounts. The greatest development was made in the alloys of copper, including brass, *sentoku*, *shakudo*, and *shibuichi*. The last three, being peculiar to Japan, are fully described in the chapter on metalwork. Owing to their unusually beautiful patinas of violet-black, ranging to tones of gray and golden bronze, a variety of magnificent combinations were created to produce metalwork never achieved in any other country. The variety of treatment and the ingenuity with which such beautiful effects were created by different groupings of these unusual alloys, and the skillful methods of working them, are a perpetual source of wonder and admiration. *Tsuba* are usually decorated on both faces, the design being either identical or continued from the front on to the back. The designs were executed in every variety of technique, such as inlaying, carving, piercing, and engraving. With an almost endless repertory of subjects and themes, *tsuba* designs present a story of Japan through several centuries, portraying her historical, religious, legendary, mythological, and contemporary customs.

All of the numerous fittings or mounts on a Japanese sword serve a constructive purpose, and all are rather easily removed or attached, making it possible for them to be changed or placed on another hilt or scabbard. There are certain specific Japanese terms used to describe collectively different sets of sword mounts which were made particularly to be used together since they are of conforming decoration. *Mitokoro-mono*, which means objects for three places, is used to describe the *kozuka*, *kogai*, and *menuki* when they comprise a set having conforming or matching decoration. When using the word *soroimono*, meaning a set of conforming objects, the Japanese refer to a set which may consist of any combination of sword mounts, with the exception of the *kogai*, *kozuka*, and *menuki*. A *daisho-no-soroimono* is the complete set of fittings for a pair of swords, which may comprise as many as twenty-four pieces, although such sets are extremely rare. This pair of swords, or *dai-sho*, is the *katana* and *wakizashi*. Then there is the word *kodogu*, which they apply to all mounts collectively on a sword or dagger, with the exception of the *tsuba*. Sword mounts which are not characteristic and are without recognized names are called *kanamono*, which literally means hardware. In the slung sword, or court sword, called the *tachi*, the fittings are of different shapes from those on the usual swords and are known by different names. The lacquering on the scabbard of the *tachi* was regulated by a strict etiquette, with a particular color and style being used on different occasions

Iron tsuba *with a pierced design of rudders. Muromachi period, fifteenth century. Tokyo National Museum.*

Iron tsuba *with a pierced design of sacred fungus and young bracken; fifteenth century. Victoria and Albert Museum.*

Iron tsuba *of the Higo school with openwork design of pine trees; Edo period, seventeenth century. Ishikawa Collection, Tokyo.*

and the number and the position of the crests prescribed. Corresponding to the *kashira*, or pommel, on other Japanese swords, the one on the *tachi* is called the *kabuto gane*, from the word *kabuto*, meaning helmet. These *kabuto gane* cover about one and a half inches of the hilt in depth; the outline of the top is ogee in form, while the broader sides contain a decorative opening. In this open space, reaching from one side of the hilt to the other, is a loop of metal called the *saru-te*, or monkey hand, which is sometimes in the form of two monkey's arms with the hands joined. From this *saru-te* hangs the cord and tassel, usually of leather, having ornamental ends of metal. On the *tachi* scabbard are the *ashi*, or loops, through which cords were passed so that it could be suspended from the sash.

SWORD-MOUNT MAKERS

The principal period of activity in the making of decorative sword mounts may be considered as the 450 years from the middle of the Muromachi period to the year 1877, when the Imperial edict was issued by Emperor Meiji abolishing the wearing of swords. Of the more than three thousand craftsmen of repute recorded as having produced sword mounts during this long period, the greater number belong to distinct and exclusive schools. Such superb skill was expended by great artists in working the metals and in their extraordinary

Iron tsuba *with brass incrustations showing floral ornament in the Onin style. Sixteenth century. Victoria and Albert Museum.*

Iron tsuba *carved with a design of three monkeys. Attributed to Shozui Hamano; Edo period, eighteenth century. Tokyo National Museum.*

manipulation of design, that the Japanese refer to the best work as painting with the chisel. Among the greatest *kinko*, or makers of sword mounts, the most famous is the Goto family, which for generations provided leaders in the classical school of metalwork design, and worked for the daimyo, and for the Shogun and his courts. Starting with its founder, the greatest master in the art of sword mounts, Goto Shirobei, 1439-1512, whose art name was Yujo, the family had an uninterrupted main line of sixteen generations. Yujo came of a samurai family from the province of Mino (now known as Gifu prefecture), and the second master of this family was his son, Sojo, 1460-1538, whose work was in the style of his father but freer and more elaborate. The work of the third master, Joshin, 1511-1562, son of Sojo, is greatly appreciated because of its designs in high relief.

This great family continued as undisputed leader in their field, until finally, the sixteenth and last master, Hojo, died in the year 1856 leaving no son skilled in this work to succeed him. Naturally the position as successor to the Goto Shirobei family was one of great honor, and much coveted. Three years after the death of Hojo, three candidates presented themselves and competed for the position as the seventeenth Goto master. All three were pupils of Goto Ichigo, who gave the honor to his nephew Mitsunori, but unfortunately Mitsunori was never recognized as the seventeenth master because he had not received the personal approval of Hojo during his lifetime. The first eight Goto masters seldom signed their work, although some of it has been identified by the foremost experts, Jujo and Yenjo, who were the twelfth and thirteenth generations of the Goto family and the best qualified for such a task. These experts engraved on the back of the pieces the name of the artist and their own names and wrote out *orikami*, or certificates, giving the name of the masters, a description of the decoration, and the value.

Around the latter part of the eighteenth century, when the thirteenth and fourteenth generations of the Goto masters were flourishing, it was the pride of some of the daimyo to collect complete sets of *mitokoromono* or *kozuka* of the first thirteen or fourteen Goto masters. Some of these sets were completely decorated with the dragon or the Chinese dog of Fo in different forms, or with other popular subjects; other sets had a combination of designs. Although it was always a great satisfaction to be able to collect complete sets of *mitokoromono* of the old Goto masters and to fix them on the new styles of scabbards, it was also the custom to acquire mounts created as new fashions. Around the latter part of the Tokugawa regime there were steadily changing fashions in ornamental mounts made for the *dai-sho*, or two swords. The new style was usually introduced for the time of the New Year, and the daimyo, vassals of high rank, and important

Tsuba *of shibuichi* in the form of a tiger and bamboo. The stripes of the tiger and his eyes are inlaid with gold and metal alloys. Signed Yasuchika Tsuchiya. Edo period, eighteenth century. Tokyo National Museum.

Pierced iron tsuba *in the form of a Chinese fan or hand-screen. Signed Masayoshi (of Satsuma); eighteenth century. Victoria and Albert museum.*

Iron tsuba *having eight openwork designs of family crests in brass and an over-all brass inlaid ground depicting pine needles; eighteenth century. Victoria and Albert Museum.*

officials of the Shogun's court placed their orders for those new swords during the eleventh and twelfth month of the old year, so as to have them for their customary visits of New Year congratulations.

The importance of sword fittings during Tokugawa times is illustrated not only in the rivalry of daimyo in collecting costly sets of the old masters, but also in the practice of giving sets of *mitokoromono* and *soroimono* as presents. It was also customary for princes to include in the dowry of a daughter one or more sets of *mitokoromono* by famous Goto masters. From the time of Hideyoshi in the latter part of the sixteenth century to the end of the Tokugawa period, the daimyo and the highest vassals of the Shogun, when they rode in their palanquins to audiences with the Emperor or the Shogun, usually wore the short sword or *wakizashi*, which they called the *kamashimo-zashi*. The *kamashimo-zashi* derived its name from the court dress of the nobles called *kamashimo*, and it was on these swords that the ornamental mounts of the Goto masters reigned supreme. The elegant ornaments on these *kamashimo-zashi* were almost exclusively made by the Goto family, and the *tsuba*, *fuchi*, and *kashira* were of plain *shakudo* with exquisite *nanako* work, sometimes with the crest of the Tokugawa family or of the daimyo. *Kamashimo-zashi* scab-

bards were always in plain black lacquer, with the matching set of *mitokoromono*, or *kozuka*, *kagai*, and *menuki*, of the finest *nanako* on *shakudo* with gold decoration in relief. The principal designs included dragons, the dog of Fo, scenes from great battles, scenes from the No plays, flowers, and other similar Japanese subjects. At the beginning of the Edo period, in the so-called Kan-ei era (1624-1644), Iemitsu, the third of the Tokugawa Shoguns, and his court adopted a very luxurious mode of living, and during that time sword mounts were often made of solid gold. This period of luxury continued on through the prosperous Genroku era (1688-1704), when daimyo vied with one another in rich and costly sword fittings.

Those of solid gold were mostly used by daimyo, but even some of the more wealthy and important merchants of this era were allowed to wear one sword with pure-gold ornaments. Between 1830 and 1844 the state finances were in such a distressful condition that the so-called Tempo economic reforms were instituted. The people were ordered not to indulge in luxuries, were forbidden to use gold on sword ornaments, and were enjoined to follow a more austere way of life. Luxurious dress was also banished, although ladies of wealth circumvented this by wearing the most costly silks

Tsuba *of shakudo with gold incrustations of peony sprays on a* nanako *(fish-roe) ground in the Goto style; c. 1800. Victoria and Albert Museum.*

Tsuba *of shibuichi inlaid with* shakudo, *depicting the foxes' wedding procession at nighttime and having tiny pierced oblong holes to represent lighted lanterns carried by the foxes; c. 1830. Victoria and Albert Museum.*

under a cheap costume when appearing in public, and the men eluded the law by covering solid-gold sword fittings with black lacquer.

Among the foremost makers of sword mounts, Kane-ie, who flourished around the middle of the Muromachi period, was the first maker of artistically decorated *tsuba*. Many unsigned iron *tsuba* of the fifteenth century are believed to be the work of armorers. While some of these have conventional saw-cut silhouettes of animals, birds, flowers, and leaves, a large number are only ornamented with punch marks or regulated hammer dents. The most perfect examples of iron *tsuba* workmanship are by Umetada Myojo, swordsmith to Hideyoshi, in the latter part of the Momoyama period. Iron *tsuba* decorated with translucent enamel on gold were made in the early seventeenth century by Hirata Donin and came to be known as Hirata enamel. The Hirata family continued his traditions until the first half of the nineteenth century, producing the same style of decoration mostly on *shakudo* instead of iron. In the eighteenth century, or at the earliest in the late seventeenth century, champlevé enamel made its appearance on *tsuba* and *kozuka* executed by Hirada Tokosai and others, and also some beautiful pieces of cloisonné with thin and delicate *cloisons.*

With the continuation of peace under the Tokugawa Shoguns, the sword had, by the Genroku era, become primarily an object of artistic merit and three great schools of chasers were founded, the Yokoya, Nara, and Hamano. All had branched from the Goto school, and they were responsible for the wonderful variety and beauty of workmanship on sword mounts. The Yokoya school was founded by Yokoya Soyo, who formed his own school in about 1640 together with his son, Sochi; the foremost member of this family was Yokoya Somin, c. 1670-1733, whose designs were executed with great freedom. The Nara school was founded by Nara Toshiteru, who also seceded from the Goto. He entered the service of the Tokugawa Shogun Iemitsu in 1624 and worked chiefly in iron. The glory of the Nara school was Nara Yasuchika, a great chaser active between 1670-1744. He worked mostly in *sentoku.*

Around the middle of the eighteenth century Hamano Shozui founded the school known by that name, and produced extraordinary effects on iron *tsuba* that resemble fragments of cast iron and, in strange contrast to these, *tsuba* of bronze often with a very high finish. In the classification of sword mounts it is difficult to distinguish the characteristics of some of these schools, because the style of some of the foremost makers varies so greatly, thus blending into the style of others. Then again, in certain pieces the style of a given master which can be recognized without difficulty has little or no resemblance to the style of another artist in the same school. Because of the manner in which the Japanese connoisseurs break down these principal schools into many sub-schools, it seems that the term *school* in general refers less to artistic style or treatment than to a form of art genealogy. Although the foremost masters in each school have a distinct style of their own, attribution is further complicated by the variations which occur in the work of each master, ranging from engraving in very low relief to very bold relief, while in other work the design is flat with the ground cut away. In the Japanese sword fittings of the eighteenth and nineteenth centuries are found examples of chasing technically unsurpassed anywhere, and it is to the artists of these schools and to their followers that the superb quality of Japan's metal art owes its unchallenged position.

METAL CHASING

The merits of sculpture in metal are evaluated by the Japanese by the quality of the chiseling, rather than by the decorative design itself, which on sword fittings was almost always supplied by painters. Thus the Japanese draw a clear distinction between the decorative design and its technical execution, the degree of excellence residing in the quality of the chisel-work. There are about two hundred and fifty cutting and engraving tools used by the Japanese metal sculptor. In the work of the chaser one feature, scarcely less important than the chiseling of the decoration itself, is the preparation of the ground on which it is applied. In earlier times there was a strict canon with reference to these grounds, the so-called *nanako* style being essential for the mountings of swords for ceremonial occasions, while the *ishime* and *jimigaki* styles were considered less aristocratic. *Nanako*, or fish roe, is a pattern of minute raised dots executed by a sharply struck cupped punch. These microscopic dots covered the whole surface, except the portion carrying the motif itself. In chiseling, the Japanese metalworker always attached great importance to the patina; and *shakudo*, because of its beautiful violet-black color, was the most frequently used for *nanako* work. These minute *nanako* dots are exactly spaced at equal intervals, absolutely uniform in size, and seldom more than one one-hundredth of an inch in diameter, so that, being accurately arranged in either straight or concentric lines, the greatest technical skill was required to execute the patterns. The punching tool was guided solely by the hand and eye, and three or more blows of the mallet were required for each dot.

Daimyo nanako is a pattern of dots arranged in lines separated by spaces of equal width in which the surface is left untouched. This term is also used for an orderly pattern of tiny quadrangular pyramids attained by cutting the surface diagonally with V grooves at right angles to form the pyramids. In the decoration called *gonome nanako* the dots are arranged in perfect diagonal lines forming lozenges, with a dot in the center of each lozenge, making a group of five dots to each lozenge. There is also an intricate *nanako* pattern in which a smaller dot is raised on each of the regular dots, while another type has two smaller dots superimposed on each of the original dots. Still a third variation has separate dots with the ground space stamped with flowers so minute they cannot be seen with the naked eye. There is scarcely any limit to the ingenuity and skill of the Japanese metal artist in producing these fantastic surfaces. The grounds of *ishime* resemble the texture of a stone. There are many varities of *ishime*, although the most characteristic form is a roughened surface produced by a blunt tool. Of these varieties *tatsuta ishime* resembles stone pitting, *nashi-ji* is like the skin of a pear, *hari ishime* appears as though small holes were picked out by a needle, *gozame ishime* resembles Japanese rice-straw mats or *tatami*, and *gama ishime* is like the skin of a toad. *Zaramaki* imitates stone, and in the variety of ground known as *jimigaki* the surface is given the highest possible polish, and is exceptionally beautiful when produced on the violet-black *shakudo*.

126

METAL TREATMENT

The many varieties of carving are classified under the generic name of *bori*, and distinctive appellations are given to them on decorated sword mounts. *Guri bori* is a work in which carving and welding is done on sword fittings in imitation of *guri* lacquer work. It consists of several sheets of metal, usually alternating *shakudo* and copper, welded together. Sometimes as many as fifteen or more of these very thin sheets are found in a *tsuba*, which is slightly more than one-eighth of an inch thick. The carving, which is done in V-shaped channels with sloping sides, cuts through these layers. When fifteen sheets are used, the channels are cut through seven layers on each side, revealing the black and red metals and leaving one layer of *shakudo* in the center. In one form of *guri bori* the channels are rounded at the bottom, which produces a different effect than the form having a sharp bottom. In order to make the black and red colors of the two metals in *guri bori* more effective, the finished piece was subjected to a process of pickling. In the method known as *kata-kiri-bori* the incised chiseling produced decorative effects of unrivaled beauty. This exquisite work was created by the use of the burin or cutting tool to produce lines of varying width and depth of individual value, much as a painter uses his brush. This work is even more astonishing when one realizes that no subsequent retouching or finishing was possible. Another

An iron tsuba with gold and silver inlay in the design of a gourd and vine; signed Sadatsune of Satsuma; nineteenth century. Victoria and Albert Museum.

form of *bori* is the hairline engraving of lines of equal depth and width called *kebori*, which was produced with remarkable fineness. There was also the *sukashi-bori*, a type of perforated or openwork chiseling, which was generally used in conjunction with a variety of metal carving in which the designs appeared on both sides of the piece, approximating carving in the round. When referring to carving in the round, the Japanese also use the term *maru-bori*. In the category of carving in relief or *niku-bori* there is *usu-niku-bori* or low relief, *chiu-niku-bori* or half relief, and *atsu-niku-bori* or high relief, which is also called *taka-bori*.

Although inlaying with gold and silver was among the early forms of decoration in Japan, the metal artist of the feudal periods raised the art to its highest degree of perfection in the execution of elaborate designs on sword fittings. The form of inlay called *hon-zogan* was a process of hammering gold or silver wire into grooves cut in the surface of metal. When this inlay is flat with the surface it is called *hira-zogan*, and when it is projected above the surface it is known as *taka-zogan*. The style known as *togidashi-zogan* or ground-out inlaying is a variety which is distinctive for the exquisite character of its designs. In this process, which is very intricate and difficult, the designs seem to emerge from under the soft metal surface and float in the atmosphere. In another form of decoration called *gomoku-zogan*, used on *tsuba* and other mounts, the surface is covered with tiny pieces of brass and copper wire inlaid in iron, and resembling pine needles floating on a pond or lake. One type of inlay work in which the design appears to have been painted on with India ink is called *sumi-zogan*, or ink inlaying. This is usually a *shibuichi* ground inlaid with *shakudo* in which the design is first cut out of a small block of *shakudo* in relief with all the sides of the cuts sloping so that each cut is wider at its base. A block of *shibuichi* is then cut with channels which correspond perfectly to the parts of the design. The cut design of *shakudo* is laid on and fixed into the grooves of the *shibuichi*, then ground down and polished until the inlaid design and ground are perfectly blended. The method of inlaying gold and silver on an iron surface in delicate and elaborate geometric patterns is called *nunome-zogan*. This process requires the heating of the surface of the iron sufficiently to develop a softness, and then hammering a very thin sheet of gold or silver into the design. Sometimes, when the designs are very intricate, as many as ten processes are used in this technique of inlaying. The decorative process of inserting inlay known as *kiribame-zogan* is a method of chiseling a design in pierced work and outlining the openwork with a veneer of a contrasting metal, such as gold, to emphasize the outline. When the metalworker cuts an openwork floral design or some similar motif in a thin sheet of metal, he fits a delicate banding of a contrasting metal around each petal of the flowers, which produces an effect of transparent flowers outlined in a contrasting metal. A variety of decoration

Pierced iron tsuba *representing five cranes in the Akasaka style; nineteenth century. Victoria and Albert Museum.*

Tsuba *made of shakudo with gold, silver, and copper inlay having a swastika diaper design and heraldic crests in the Kaga style; nineteenth century. Victoria and Albert Museum.*

Pierced iron tsuba *with the design of an egret and a lily pond; nineteenth century. Victoria and Albert Museum.*

127

much practiced by the early metal artists is called *mokume-ji*, or wood-grained ground. In this type, which produces a ground resembling the grain of wood, two thin plates of similar metal of equal size are welded together by hammer. While the mass is still hot, it is coated with a kind of marl and straw ash before being brought to a glowing heat over a charcoal furnace. In this stage the clay or marl is removed and another similar plate is hammered in, and the process is then repeated. A number of plates may be worked together in this manner, depending upon the quality of graining desired, and then the manifold plate is punched from one side so that the opposite side resembles broken blisters. These blisters are hammered down until each produces its own wave effect. Although iron was used exclusively in the earlier *mokume-ji* work on sword mounts, a variety of metals were used in the later periods, with the finest and most beautiful of all having a *shakudo* ground with a gold graining. In all these highly technical processes of decorating fine sword fittings, the exquisite workmanship constitutes a level of art in which Japan has no rival.

X Shinto and Buddhist Architecture

IN THE realm of Japan's artistic heritage, the most profound expression of the country's native charm and beauty resides in the subtle refinements of its Buddhist temples and Shinto shrines. Among the impressive features of Japanese religious architecture is the quality of proportions depending essentially upon mathematical ratios in the dimensions of the building, and harmony in the general balance of the architectonic composition. The disposition and contrasts of light and shade were most skillfully accomplished by the religious architects from early times, color and ornament being subsidiary elements employed in Buddhist architecture. The principal architectural features of Shinto shrines are their elegant simplicity and beauty derived from the relation of contours, surfaces, and intervals.

Japanese architecture originated in the endeavors of the early inhabitants to provide for their physical wants, first with cave dwellings, then with pit houses, ground-level houses and, finally, raised-floor houses. There can be no doubt that climate and the materials at hand affected the forms of the primitive buildings, as indicated in the earliest historical literature, such as the *Kojiki*, or *Records of Ancient Matters*, and the *Nihon Shoki*, or *Chronicles of Japan*, dating from 712 and 720 respectively. Further knowledge of early houses is provided by archæological evidence, in particular the miniature clay Haniwa houses found in the great sepulchral mounds which are the tombs of the rulers, built in the ancient province of Yamato, the present Nara prefecture, and dating from the third and fourth centuries. There are also many bronze mirrors and the *dotaku* or bronze bell-shaped objects on which are depicted houses, thus providing a source of information on Japan's early civilization.

Like the other arts, architecture did not spring into existence in the earliest period, since the ideas of symmetry and proportion could not evolve until at least a moderate degree of civilization had been attained, while the efforts of the primitive people of Japan were directed toward the construction of dwellings which at first were determined solely by their physical needs. The primitive pit house had as a foundation an area of ground dug out to a maximum depth of one meter in an elliptical or rectangular shape with rounded corners, generally with a diameter of from five to six meters. Over this, the superstructure is said to have resembled a tent in shape, erected on an arrangement of four or more posts to support a sloping roof. During the succeeding Neolithic period, which is characterized by more and better implements and the development of agriculture and domestic animals, there evolved alongside of the pit house and the ground-level dwelling, the house with raised floor, a kind of building on piles. The latter was originally used as a storehouse, and its first use as a dwelling was probably only by the ruling class.

The architectural history of Japan is generally conveniently divided into the following six periods: 1. The pre-Buddhist period, extending from the earliest times to the introduction of Buddhism in 552, during which there developed a style of architecture peculiar to Japan. 2. The first period during which Chinese culture was introduced through the medium of Buddhism from 552 to 794, thus including the historical periods of Asuka (552-645) and Nara (710-794). 3. The first period of nationalization of the imported styles, during the Heian period (794-1185), which embraces the Jogan or Early Heian (794-897) and the Fujiwara or Late Heian (897-1185). 4. The second period of Chinese influence, lasting from 1185 until 1573, including the Kamakura (1185-1333) and Muromachi (1338-1573) periods. 5. The second nationalization of the imported styles, which occurred from 1573 until 1867, including the Momoyama (1573-1615) and Edo (1615-1867) periods. 6. The period of European influence, from the Meiji period (1868-1912) onward.

SHINTO ARCHITECTURE

Because of the abundance of trees and other forest growths in Japan, the primitive domestic dwelling houses of the ruling class were built of wood, with pillars thrust into the ground and the whole framework, consisting of posts, beams, rafters, and so forth, tied together with cords made from the twisted fibrous stems of climbing plants. The Japanese propensity for clinging to ancient traditions gives us many insights into her early culture; and because of this a general idea of ancient Japanese architecture before the introduction of Buddhism may be obtained from the Shinto shrines or *jinsha* which have survived. The finest examples are the Daijingu shrines of Ise and the Izumo-Taisha shrine in Izumo province, which, although they have been frequently reconstructed, still preserve their primitive form. In the earliest stages of the ancient cult of Shinto the gods were worshipped at ceremonies conducted in an enclosure made by thrusting branches of evergreen trees into the ground. As Shinto developed into an organized native cult combining nature and ancestor worship, with its enormous pantheon embracing many nature gods and goddesses, it became the custom to use such objects as mirrors or jewels to symbolize the presence of a god, and therefore a dwelling in which to enshrine them was provided. The Japanese word *miya*, meaning honorable house, is used for both a shrine and the house of a chieftain, since for many centuries there was no distinction between a domestic dwelling and a shrine.

The earliest and most primitive form of Shinto architecture is called the *tenchi kongen* style, and consists of two posts set in the ground supporting a ridge pole, to each end of which were fastened two rafters sloping to the ground. A number of horizontal beams were tied to these rafters to support a thatch which served as roof as well as walls. Subsequently this whole structure of the *tenchi kongen* house was elevated by introducing walls on four sides and a raised floor, thus producing a simple house with gabled roof. This is the form of the original Shinto-shrine style called *yuiitsu shimmei*, as represented by the shrines at Ise. A Shinto shrine contains no image or idol except for a symbol, and has no provision for joint worship by a congregation, so that only enough space is actually needed to accommodate an altar and the priests or other officiating persons. The individual worshipper does not enter the shrine, but will first stop at the *mitarashi* or sacred water cistern, which is in front of every Shinto shrine, and wash his mouth and hands symbolically for the purification of his body and soul. He will stand outside and ring the gong or round bell by pulling or shaking the long rope or drapes that hang from it and clap his hands, usually twice, before worshipping the deity of the shrine.

The Shinto shrine has none of the magnificence of the Buddhist temple and from remote antiquity has represented the purest type of Japanese architecture. The Jingu shrines of Ise consist of Kodaijingu or the Naiku (Inner shrine) dedicated to the sun goddess, Amaterasu-o-mi-kami, and the Toyouke-daijingu or the Geku (Outer shrine) dedicated to Toyouke-

The Naiku (or Inner shrine) of the Jingu shrines of Ise, dedicated to the sun goddess, Amaterasu-o-mi-Kami.

Izumo Taisha, or Great Shrine of Izumo, at Taisha, Shimane prefecture.

130

o-mi-kami, the goddess of farms, crops, food, and sericulture. They are believed to possess today precisely the appearance they presented in the year 478 when they were moved thither in obedience to a revelation from the sun goddess. During the reign of the Emperor Temmu, 672-686, it was decreed that the Ise shrines should be rebuilt every twentieth year, alternately on each of two sites set apart for the purpose, the features of the old edifice being reproduced in the new with scrupulous accuracy. With few exceptions, the Imperial rebuilding decree has been observed, and the shrines have actually been reconstructed fifty-nine times during these thirteen hundred years. The Ise shrines are constructed of *hinoki* wood or Japanese cypress, *Chamaecyparis obtusa*, from the state forests in the Kiso mountains. In form they represent the ancient Japanese style, built with thick pillars to hold the framework, with a great pillar at either end to support the ridge pole. A peculiar feature of their construction is the extended projection of the two rafters called *chigi* at each end of the roof, which provides additional support for the ridge pole and resembles an animal's horn at each gable end. The roof is thatched, and in order to bind the ridge and rafters firmly together and to keep the thatch in position, two boards are laid lengthwise at the apex of the roof with a wider board lying along the apex and extending beyond the ends of the roof. To keep this topmost ridge board in place with its two subsidiary boards, heavy logs called *katsuogi* are laid upon it at right angles. At a later date, due to improved methods of construction, the *chigi* or crosspieces of the ancient style came to be regarded merely as ornaments placed upon the ridge board, often having their ends embellished with carvings.

The center of the cult of Shinto is the great shrines at Ise, where only Imperial personages and Imperial envoys are permitted beyond a certain fence, and the sacred mirror or *Yata-no-kagami*—which is one of the Three Sacred Treasures—is enshrined in the Naiku shrine, dedicated to the sun goddess. But the oldest shrine in Japan is the Izumo-Taisha, or Oyashiro or Great Shrine of Izumo, which is dedicated to the god Onamuchi-no-Mikoto. He is the strongest and bravest of the sons of Susano-o, brother of the sun goddess, who is said to have founded a state in the province of Izumo and later retired to Taisha, where a large palace was built to receive him. This is said to be the origin of the shrine, which seems to have been on a large scale at first and then been gradually reduced. It is recorded that the Emperor Suinin rebuilt this shrine sometime around the first century "in the same manner as the Emperor's palace," and it is thereby proved that the shrine building possesses the original architectural form of a dwelling house of ancient times. It is further recorded that before the shrine was reduced in scale when rebuilt, its height was about 160 feet, and although this figure should not neces-

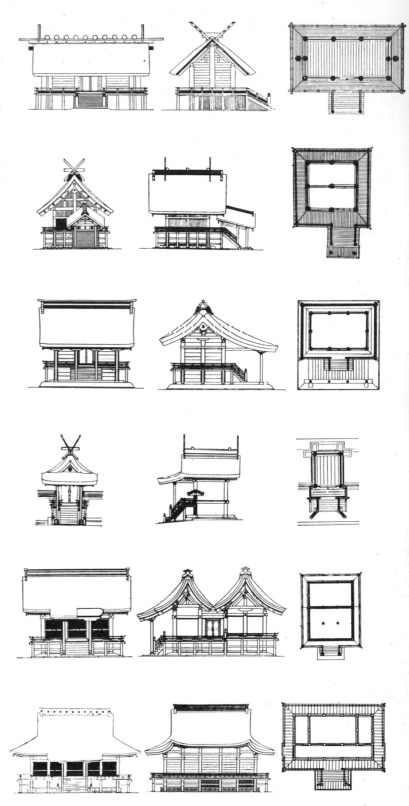

The principal types of Shinto shrines, showing the front view, the side view, and the plan. From top to bottom: Shimmei, Taisha, Nagare, Kasuga, Hachiman, and Hie types. Tokyo National Museum.

Main sanctuary of the Kamogamo shrine at Kyoto, an example of the Nagare type of Shinto architecture. Founded in the Nara period, eighth century.

Main sanctuary of the Usa shrine in Oita prefecture, founded in 725 in the Nara period, an example of the Hachiman type of Shinto architecture.

sarily be taken literally, it appears that the structure was of a remarkably large size. Its architectural type is known as *taisha* or *oyashiro* and differs somewhat from the shrines of Ise, for it has undergone certain changes and departed more from its original form than the Ise shrines.

Throughout the country nearly every ancient grove of dense trees harbors a Shinto shrine, each with one or more gateways called torii, a kind of beamed propylon. The avenue of approach to a Shinto shrine passes under at least one torii, which usually consists of two thick logs placed upright and slightly splayed, their upper ends mortised into a horizontal log that projects beyond them at either side, with another horizontal log slightly below it. The extreme simplicity and graceful proportion of this symbol of Shinto, which has become a symbol of Japan herself, presents a refined and noble appearance. Originally designed as a perch for fowls that sing to the deities at daybreak, the torii subsequently came to be regarded as a gateway characteristic of Shinto. An ancient custom of offering live cocks to a shrine undoubtedly had some connection with the legendary rooster that perched upon the entrance of the Cave of Heaven, where the sun goddess hid herself and caused darkness to cover the earth. And since the sun goddess is the supreme divinity of Shinto, it was natural for believers to make offerings of cocks to herald the rising sun. These cocks were originally placed on a bird perch made of two wooden posts and a crossbar erected in front of the shrine, and even after the perch evolved into the symbolical Shinto gateway, it still retained the original name of torii and its ideogram meaning bird perch.

The shrine buildings of Ise and Izumo, known as the *yuiitsu shimmei* and *taisha* forms respectively, represent the primitive types of the ancient Imperial palace and the dwelling houses of the ruling class, in addition to being beautiful symbols of the sacred ideals of the people. The extreme simplicity and refined architectural form of these shrines instill a profound impression of their role as the houses of the gods. Because they are situated in groves of ancient trees or in the depths of a forest, a beautiful feeling of closeness to nature emanates from them. The Japan of ancient times seems to dwell there and pervades the whole of the atmosphere with a silent message from the past. It is this charm of old Japan that still lingers in the sacred precincts of Shinto shrines.

The invasion of Korea by a strong expeditionary force under the Empress Jingo in the third century marked the first time Japan was brought into intimate communication with the Asiatic mainland. This prepared the way for the flow of continental culture and the gradual introduction of Chinese civilization and Buddhism in the sixth century. As in the other arts, Buddhism exerted a strong influence on Shinto architecture, as did the harmonizing of the two faiths in the middle of the eighth century, resulting in a certain elaboration of style with the introduction of a particular curvature of the roof. While the great shrines of Ise and Izumo continued to preserve their original ancient form, possibly because of their role as the most important and oldest shrines of Shinto, it was inevitable that Shinto architecture in general should gradually be influenced by Buddhist styles. Shinto shrines were always built of wood, principally *hinoki* or cypress, which acquires a beautiful sheen with age. The tendency to introduce certain Buddhist architectural features in Shinto buildings began in the Heian period (794-1185), when shrines were often painted in colors, usually a rich vermilion, and were designed with curving roofs supported by a system of brackets called *to-kyo*. It was also during the Heian period that great two-storied gates appeared at the entrances of shrines, and the covered corridors resembling colonnades.

From the introduction of these features of continental origin there developed four principal types of Shinto shrine in addition to the earlier forms of *shimmei* and *taisha* as seen at Ise and Izumo. They include the Nagare, Kasuga, Hachiman, and Hie types. The best examples of the Nagare type are represented by the main sanctuary of the famous Kamogamo shrine in the city of Kyoto near the banks of the Kamogawa

River, and the fine two-storied gate and corridor of the Shimogamo shrine nearby. The Kamogamo, founded in the Nara period (710-794), became the most important shrine and the house of the tutelary deity of Kyoto, this being the deity to whom the Emperor sent his message concerning the decision to remove the capital from the ill-fated site at Nagaoka to Kyoto. The main shrine building at the Kamogamo is three bays in width and two in length, with its entrance on the long side parallel with the ridge of the roof. In Japanese architecture the term *bay* is used to denote a span or distance in a building between two adjacent pillars; thus if a building contains five pillars on one of its sides, it is said to have four bays. Ever since the introduction of the Nagare type of shrine, its form has been extremely popular, particularly because of its beautifully proportioned roof. Its gabled

Main sanctuary of the Hie shrine on Lake Biwa near Otsu, an example of the Hie style of Shinto architecture, founded in the ninth century and rebuilt according to the original plan in the Momoyama period (1573-1615).

roof is greatly extended in a graceful curve over the front side of the building to provide a sort of shelter for the worshippers and bears the name of *gohai* or *kohai*, a term applied to a space for worshippers in front of a religious building where the staircase is located and sheltered by extended eaves. Every year on the fifteenth day of May a great festival is held jointly by the Shimogamo and Kamogamo shrines. It is known as the Aoi Matsuri, or Hollyhock Festival, and consists of a procession reminiscent of ancient times with retainers, pages, halberd bearers, and an Imperial ox carriage. Representing the Imperial procession which formerly used to pay homage at the shrines, it starts early in the morning at the Imperial palace nearby and proceeds with an Imperial messenger and his suite in full court costume, to both shrines. The origin of this festival, at which leaves of hollyhock are offered to the gods and goddesses enshrined in both the shrines, is traced back to the sixth century, when it was performed to propitiate the deities of the shrines, whose anger was indicated by great storms throughout the country.

The Kasuga type receives its name from the Kasuga shrine, situated in the midst of verdant woods at Nara, where an atmosphere of peace and sanctity is imparted within its precincts. The shrine was founded in 768 as the tutelary shrine of the Fujiwara family and a sanctuary for their ancestral deities, and it used to be regularly reconstructed every twenty years. Its present form is considered to have developed at the beginning of the Heian period. It actually consists of four small shrines painted in rich vermilion, reached by passing along a beautiful avenue lined with numerous rows of stone lanterns on both sides, some three thousand in all, which are lighted twice each year, on the night of the Setsubun Festival in Feb-

ruary and on the night of August 15. The main sanctuary is one bay square and has a gabled roof; its entrance is on the gabled side, and an impressive gallery surrounds all four of the shrine buildings. An extremely large Japanese cedar stands at the left corner of the main shrine, behind which is the Utsushidono, a hall where the divine spirits are temporarily transferred when repairs are being made to the main shrine. The roof of the main shrine is made of thin narrow strips of cypress and is curved in the manner of the Nagare type; its ridge is surmounted by two sets of crossed poles called *oki-chigi*, which are the type of *chigi* used for ornamental purposes. The Kasuga-type shrine was one of the two most common forms of Shinto architecture, and it was chiefly used in Nara and surrounding districts. It has not been as popular as the Nagare type of shrine, which can be found in all parts of the country.

The Hachiman type is best illustrated by the main sanctuary of the Usa shrine near the coast of the Inland Sea in the northern part of Kyushu. It is one of the three most noted Hachiman shrines in Japan, the other two being Iwashimizu near Kyoto and the Hakozaki shrine near Hakata, where the great Mongol invasion occurred in the latter part of the thirteenth century. The Usa shrine, which was founded in 725 and is dedicated to the Emperor Ojin, Hime-Okami, and the Empress Jingo, is a beautiful example of this particular style of Shinto architecture with its bright-red color and elaborate carving. The shrine is embowered in a grove of ancient trees. Its main building consists of two rooms, each with a gabled roof, and connected to each other along their eave sides. It somewhat resembles two buildings joined together with the entrance on the side parallel to the ridge of the roof, which is

Main sanctuary of the Osaki Hachiman shrine at Sendai, one of the outstanding examples of the Gongen style of Shinto architecture, built in 1606. Momoyama period.

Main sanctuary of the Kibitsu shrine in Okayama prefecture, built during the Oei era (1394–1428). Muromachi period.

134

Main sanctuary of the Toshogu shrine at Nikko, showing the Kara-mon, or Chinese Gate; to the left and right of the gate is the Sacred Fence. Edo period, seventeenth century.

curved at the eaves and extended in front to form a *gohai* or shelter for the worshippers.

The Hie style is typified by the main sanctuary of the Hie shrine at the foot of Mount Hiei on the shore of Lake Biwa near Otsu. It is said to have been founded in the closing years of the ninth century and rebuilt according to its original plan during the Momoyama period (1573-1615). This building is particularly noted for its fine example of *irimoya* or hipped and gabled roof with a *hisashi*, which is an extension of the eaves of the main roof or additional eaves under it to provide a shelter for a corridor or open veranda. During the Late Heian period (897-1185) the architectural style of Shinto shrines very often closely resembled the form of palaces and mansions of the nobles, and an excellent example is the main building of the Yasaka shrine, commonly called the Gion shrine, in Kyoto, which is said to have originally been the principal hall or *shinden* of the house of Fujiwara Mototsune with its *hisashi* and half hipped and half gabled roof.

In the Momoyama period a new style of shrine architecture called Gongen was developed in which the roofs of two separate buildings were connected with an *ai-no-ma* or span roof covering a corridor. The principal examples of the Gongen style are the Kitano shrine in Kyoto and the Osaki Hachiman shrine in Sendai, whose main building, noted for its architectural beauty, was built in 1606. Inside and outside, these structures are embellished with colored wood carvings of great richness and beauty; the Kitano shrine, with a number of supplementary halls, is on a much larger scale than the Osaki shrine. The Kitano shrine is better known as the Kitano Tenjin, for it was established in 947 and dedicated to Sugawara Michizane, who is deified under the name of Tenjin. His death in 903, after he had been exiled to Kyushu, was followed by such severe earthquakes and thunderstorms in the city that it was thought advisable to appease his spirit by erecting a building in which he could be enshrined. The present buildings were erected in 1607 by Toyotami Hideyoshi and include two gates, a main hall, and an oratory, with a complicated plan of roof ridges and carefully laid cypress shingles which give a most interesting and beautiful variety to the buildings.

Among the important changes that took place in Shinto architecture during the Kamakura period and the following periods of Muromachi, Momoyama, and Edo, were increasing influences of Buddhist architecture, the larger-scale construction of the buildings, and the adoption of the Gongen style after the Momoyama period. During the first half of the Heian period about the only feature of Buddhist architecture that was introduced into the design of Shinto buildings was the *funa-hijiki* or peculiar boat-shaped arm extending horizontally to support the eaves or some other part of a building. After the middle of the Heian period a more complicated bracket system was adopted from Buddhist design with the use of the *de-mitsuto*, which consists of an arm having three wooden cubes to form the lowest support bracket on a pillar. More complex arrangements of brackets and other forms of Buddhist architecture strongly influenced Shinto buildings through the following periods, in particular the great curved roofs and gables.

From around the end of the Kamakura or the beginning of the Muromachi period there appeared many charming small shrines in local districts, called *ko-miya* or little shrines, which measure less than six feet wide. In contrast, the increasing scale of the important shrines followed the trend in Buddhist temples. Many fine examples noted for their relatively free qualities of design were inspired by Buddhist forms, such as the Kibitsu, which is the largest shrine in Okayama prefecture, whose reputation ranks next to the Itsukushima shrine at Miyajima on the Inland Sea. The Itsukushima shrine, situated at one of the three most beautiful scenic spots in Japan, consists of the main shrine and several subsidiary shrines and buildings, all connected by broad corridors or galleries which stretch over the sea on both sides of the shrine, so that when the tide is coming in the whole edifice seems to be floating on the surface of the sea. The huge camphor-wood torii rising out of the water about five hundred feet from the shore is fifty-three feet in height and presents an unforgettable picture, especially when the rays of the sun cause its reflection to be seen in the placid waters of the Inland Sea.

The Japanese have a saying, "Never say *kekko* (magnificent) until you have seen Nikko." Situated near the banks of the Daiya river on a hillside in the midst of a forest of ancient Japanese cedars, Nikko is one of the most beautiful places in Japan, and the site of the elaborate and colorful Toshogu shrine, dedicated to Tokugawa Ieyasu, 1542-1616, founder of the Tokugawa Shogunate. Its Yomeimon or Gate of Sunlight is the most elaborate and magnificent gate in Japan, a perfect expression of the art of the Edo period. Only of small dimensions, twenty-two feet wide, fifteen feet deep, and thirty-seven feet high, it is a twelve-columned, two-storied structure having hipped-gable ends with cusped gables on four sides. Its extremely rich carved decoration on the ends of rafters consists of dragons' heads or dragons and clouds, all in gold foil, while other beam-ends are carved with lions' heads and dragons' heads painted white. The elaborate brackets supporting the balcony are designed in the form of peonies and lions, with carvings of a Chinese prince, sages, and some immortals between them. The railing of the balcony depicts a group of Chinese children at play. On the ceiling of the porticoes are two beautiful paintings of dragons; the one nearer the entrance, known as the *nobori-ryu* or ascending dragon, is the work of Kano Tan-yu, 1602-1674; the inner one, the *kudari-ryu* or descending dragon, was executed by

The great camphor-wood torii of the Itsukushima shrine at Miyajima; it differs from the usual torii in the form of its pillars, and bears a tablet with the autograph of Prince Arisugawa.

Itsukushima shrine at Miyajima; view from the Inland Sea of the low stage and the high stage where the sacred Shinto dances are performed.

136

Yomeimon or Gate of Sunlight of the Toshogu shrine at Nikko, Tochigi prefecture. Edo period, early seventeenth century.

Kano Eishin, 1613-1685. With every pillar, beam, bracket, ceiling, and wall embellished, the endless carvings and paintings of the many Nikko shrines, while lacking the pure spirit of Japanese art, represent the highest possible achievement in the elaboration of Shinto shrines.

BUDDHIST ARCHITECTURE

Although there had been a gradual flow of Chinese culture from about the third century, it was not until the introduction of Buddhism into Japan in the year 552 that native architecture began to be materially changed under its influence. During the reign of the Empress Suiko, temples were built on a grand scale one after another, including such great edifices and their monasteries as the Hokoji, the Shitennoji, and the Horyuji. With one exception, all these great temples have long since been destroyed by fire, and in many cases rebuilt. The Horyuji alone has miraculously survived for more than thirteen hundred years and it has the distinction of being the oldest wooden structure in the world. As one of the seven great temples of Nara, it is regarded as the fountainhead of Japanese art and culture. These famous structures are built of a fine quality of *hinoki*, the Japanese cypress, and those which are still preserved within the precincts of the Horyuji in their original form are the Kondo or main building, the Chumon or middle gate, the Goju-no-to or five-storied pagoda, and part of the corridor or colonnade. Dating from the year 607, their architecture follows Chinese prototypes prevalent during the period of the Six Dynasties in China. The distinctive features of religious architecture of the Asuka period are the pronounced entasis in the slight convexity of the pillars, the peculiar and interesting system of brackets called *to-kyo*, and the beam supports called *kaeru-mata*. *To-kyo* is a device which supports the eaves or some other part of a building, consisting of an arm or arms called *hijiki* extending horizontally with a square wooden block or blocks called *to* or *masu* placed on top. In the large buildings with their huge and greatly extended

137

roofs the arrangement of *to-kyo* becomes very intricate, with series of *to* placed upon *hijiki* and repeated in an expanding manner until their projection creates sufficient support for the eaves. The *kaeru-mata*, or frog's legs, are the ornamented triangular-shaped supports placed in the centers of tie-beams.

By the beginning of the eighth century the Japanese had begun to acquire a vast knowledge of government and to adopt the arts and culture of China through constant intercourse between the two countries. Official envoys and students were able to learn much from their observances and studies of Chinese civilization, which during the centuries of the Sui and T'ang dynasties reached the highest degree of cultural attainment in the world. The ancient custom for the Japanese Emperors to move their palaces and capital to a new site at the time of accession because of the belief that a house in which a death took place was unclean, was abandoned, with the establishment of the permanent capital in the province of Yamato, at Heijo-kyo, which later became Nara. This was in 710 during the reign of the Empress-Regnant Gemmyo, at a time when T'ang culture was dominant in all phases of Japanese life, and the new capital was laid out on a magnificent scale after the T'ang capital of Ch'ang-an. This gave an important stimulus to architectural development. The Imperial inner city of resplendent palace buildings with red-colored pillars and great roofs of green glazed tiles, and the mansions of the nobles nearby, reflected the splendor of the Nara period.

Great monasteries were erected one after the other at an almost frantic pace during the time that Nara remained the

To-To, or East Pagoda, of the Yakushiji temple at Nara, a three-storied structure showing the use of intermediate projections called mokoshi. *Built in 680. Yakushiji temple, Nara.*

Right: To-kyo *(brackets) of the south portal of the Todaiji temple at Nara, showing the elaborate use of such brackets in the Tenjiku-yo style of Buddhist architecture. Built in 1199. Kamakura period.*

138

capital from 710 until 794, culminating with the construction of the Hall of the Great Buddha at the Todaiji temple. The exterior portions of temples were painted with a red oxide of lead, and the interiors were decorated in a peculiar method known as *ungen* in which different shades of colors were carefully graduated. Among the main temple buildings that have survived, now preserved as National Treasures, is the To-To or East Pagoda of the Yakushiji temple erected in 680 near the city of Nara. It is remarkable for its beautiful proportions. It is a three-storied pagoda measuring 115 feet in height and thirty feet square at its base, and is supported by seventeen pillars. But it appears to be six-storied since each story has an intermediate projection between the floors as an additional wooden roof. These projections, which are called *mokoshi*, literally meaning lean-tos, are frequently found on either three or four sides of buildings in the form of projecting eaves or roofs under the main roof as an additional protection against the weather. Hanging from the corners of these mokoshi, and also from the roof corners, are bronze *futaku*, or wind-bells, which resemble the great temple bells in miniature form. They are often more elongated and have a thin, flat piece of bronze cut in the shape of the Chinese cloud motif which is hung from the tongue of the bell and cause the bell to ring when the wind blows. An interesting feature of the Japanese pagoda is the exceptionally tall *sorin*, an ornament, usually of bronze, surmounting the roof. The principal parts of the *sorin*, from the base upward, are the *roban* or dew basin, the *fukubachi* or inverted bowl, the *ukebana* or everted flower,

the *kurin* or nine rings, the *suien* or water flame, the *ryusha* or dragon vehicle, and the *hoshu* or sacred gem. The Kondo of the Toshodaiji, the Hokke-do of the Todaiji, and the Yume-dono of the Horyuji are among other surviving temple buildings of the Nara period. The Kondo or main hall of the Toshodaiji is celebrated for its elegant form and for the fine proportions of its colonnade on the front side. The Yumedono or Hall of Dreams of the Horyuji temple is the main hall of the east temple and is considered the most beautiful octagonal building in Japan. It is called Hall of Dreams because Prince Shotoku was known to sit there in deep meditation while pondering a passage in the three sutras. The Hokke-do or Third Month temple, founded in 733 and the oldest extant structure of the Todaiji, is named from the custom of holding a yearly service for the Hokke scripture in the month of March.

The succeeding Heian period, from 794 to 1185, marks the first period of nationalization of the architectural styles brought from the mainland. Around the closing years of the Nara period many difficulties had arisen that tended to retard the cultural and economic advancement of the country, brought about by a variety of circumstances including the too-excessive influence wielded by Buddhism. A marked deterioration in the relations of Buddhism and the state prompted the court to move the seat of government to Heian-kyo, or Kyoto, in the year 794 in order to break up certain destructive social and economic practices and begin a new life in the capital of peace and tranquillity, as it was called. The architectural changes that took place in the Heian period were principally in the arrangement of the temple buildings brought about by new practices and ideals with the establishment of the Tendai sect and the Shingon sect. Buddhism again became extremely powerful and its popularity was widespread among the people. There were two great rival centers: the monastery on Mount Koya, south of Nara, where the esoteric philosophy of the Shingon sect, with its complex symbolism, was taught; and that on Mount Hiei, northeast of Kyoto, the seat of the Tendai sect, whose doctrines were based upon pantheistic realism. These two fountainheads of Buddhist learning were built in the isolation of rugged mountainsides in the hope of avoiding excessive involvement in political matters; as a result the architectural arrangement had to conform with the natural surroundings, and instead of the regular pattern when laid out on level ground, there was greater freedom in the location of the individual buildings. At the same time the advancement in temple design is seen in the extreme beauty of proportion of the five-storied pagoda of the Daigoji temple in Kyoto built in 951. In the early part of the Heian period there appeared a peculiar variety of pagoda called *taho-to*, or treasure tope, which became an essential element in Shingon monasteries. This form derived from the Indian stupa or tope,

Chumon, or Middle Gate, of the Horyuji temple at Nara, built in 607. Asuka period.

which was usually in the shape of a cylindrical or prismatic low tower topped by a cupola, erected to house relics of Buddha or contain a Buddhist shrine. Under Japanese influence the *taho-to* came to resemble a two-storied pagoda with a square lower story covered with a roof or *mokoshi*, and a more narrow circular upper story covered with a great roof having deep projecting eaves. Early Heian architecture is beautifully represented by the invaluable examples of the main hall of the Muroji temple south of Nara as well as its very small five-storied pagoda, both of which were built in 824.

One of the finest examples of late Heian temple architecture is the Hoodo, or Phoenix Hall, of the Byodoin at Uji in the suburb of Kyoto. Originally a villa of Fujiwara-no-Michinaga, it was converted into a monastery in 1052, and the original main hall, known as the Phoenix Hall, has been carefully preserved since its construction in 1053. Its elegant proportions typify the best religious architectural accomplishments of the time. The temple was designed to represent the mythical phoenix of Chinese legend in the act of descending to the ground. The main hall is supposed to represent its body, the lateral corridors its wings, and the rear corridor its tail. Toward the end of the Heian period the great popularity of the new Jodo or Pure Land sect, based upon the belief that the only way to salvation lay in absolute trust in the all-saving power of Amitabha Buddha, or the Buddha Amida, influenced architecture. The large monasteries built during this time were erected principally by various members of the Fujiwara clan, and although lacking the appearance of strength and grandeur of the older temples, they reflected a quality of dignity and elegance and the native freedom of expression

that typifies purely Japanese art. The most important building in the monasteries of the Jodo sect was the Amida-do, or Hall of Amida. In plan, the Amida-do was almost always square, with an image of the Buddha in the *Nai-jin* or inner sanctuary, which is in the center of the interior in an area one bay square surrounded by an open space or corridor for people to walk around while reciting the *Nembutsu* or Invocation to Buddha. The simplest form of the Amida-do is three bays square, but the larger buildings often are five bays square, while the elaborate Phoenix Hall of the Byodoin temple is nothing more than an Amida-do with a sanctuary of one bay square in the center building.

The second period of Chinese influence was during the Kamakura and Muromachi periods, when a further development in religious architecture took place through the introduction of the new styles from the mainland. Two important architectural influences that inspired many of the buildings of this period were the Tenjiku-yo or "Indian style" and the Kara-yo or "Chinese style," as opposed to the Wa-yo or "Japanese style" which finally merged with the Chinese style to form a mixed style. The most striking feature of the so-called Indian style is the use of an elaborate system of brackets, often with as many as seven arms projecting to the front of the pillars, A reflection of the Tenjiku-yo style appeared in Japan around the beginning of the Kamakura period in the reconstruction of the great monastery of the Todaiji, which had seen unsurpassed prosperity and power during the Nara period but had been reduced to ashes by a general of the Taira clan in 1180 during a civil war. The Todaiji had been conceived on a grand scale and its restoration, which was directed

The Hokke-do, or Third Month temple, of the Todaiji temple at Nara, founded in 733. Nara period.

The Hoodo, or Phoenix Hall, of the Byodoin monastery at Uji, Kyoto prefecture, built in 1053. Early Heian period.

by the priest Shunjobo Chogen, was an enormous under-taking requiring vast knowledge and experience in religious architecture. The Tenjiku-yo style of the restored buildings is actually a modification of a style of temple architecture of the Sung dynasty in China. The fact that it was called "Indian style" arose from a misunderstanding of the term used. Chogen, a great architect, was able to accomplish the work of restoration of the Todaiji because he had studied architecture in China and supervised the construction of many monasteries in that country during three long visits there. He employed the same principles of Sung architecture in the construction of other temples in Japan, although the only one to survive is the Jodo-do Hall of the Jodoji monastery at Harima on the Inland Sea.

The Kara-yo or "Chinese style" was introduced into Japan along with Zen Buddhism to become the typical style of the Zen monasteries. Among the characteristic features of the Chinese style are the tiled floor, a roof having a steep slope, and vigorous upturned curves at the corners of the eaves with the rafters arranged in a radiating manner at the corners, called

ogi-daruki or fan rafters. Another architectural feature of the Kara-yo style was the *Tsume-Gumi*, or compact system, in which the *to-kyo* or brackets were used not only on the tops of pillars but on the intercolumnar spaces as well. The plan that is almost universal in the Kara-yo style has a main hall of three bays square, and in the larger structures the hall is pro-vided with the *mokoshi*, or additional roof. In the center of the interior there is a Nai-jin or inner sanctuary of one bay square, in the rear portion of which is placed the dais to hold the principal image of the temple. Carved decoration came to be used on the rafters at the gable ends and also on the ends of heading beams, which later led to the development of sculp-tured ornamentation. Fine examples of the Kara-yo style include the Shariden or Relic Hall of the Engakuji temple at Kamakura, the Kaisando or Founder's Hall of the Eihoji temple at Tajimi in Gifu prefecture, and the Hondo of the Shuonan monastery at Tanabemachi in Kyoto prefecture.

The Wa-yo or Japanese style may be regarded as a revival of the Nara-period architecture from five hundred years earlier, which did not adhere to the rigid Chinese method of planning but allowed a greater freedom in the arrangement of the different buildings of a temple. There was a strong preference for this traditional style in the Nara district itself, where great numbers of Buddhist monasteries were restored and reconstructed during the Kamakura period under the pressure of the newly risen sects. The restored buildings within the precinct of the Kofukuji monastery at Nara, which was one of the seven great temples of Nara and at the height of its prosperity had as many as 175 buildings, are considered to be the best examples of the Wa-yo style. The To-Kondo or East Main Hall and the five-storied pagoda of the Kofukuji are fine extant examples of the Nara period, while the Hokuendo or North Octagonal Hall and the three-storied pagoda represent the late Heian period. Many outstanding examples of the Japanese style were built during the Kamakura period in various provinces, for example the main hall of the Saimyoji temple at Kamomachi, Soraku-gun in Kyoto prefecture, and the Renge-o-in monastery in Kyoto, which is also called the Sanju-Sangen-do because of the *sanju-san* or thirty-three spaces between the pillars in the structure. The unique feature of this temple is its principal image, the *Thousand-handed Goddess Kannon*, carved by the famous sculptor Tankei in his eighty-second year. One of the oldest examples of the Wa-yo style is the charming *taho-to* or stupa of the Ishiyamadera. The subject of one of Hiroshige's *Eight Views of Lake Biwa* is the Ishiyama temple, from whose grounds the view over the lake is so beautiful on a moonlit night in autumn. The temple is also noted for its Genji-no-ma or Hall of Genji, the building in which Lady Murasaki Shikibu, 975-1031, wrote her famous classic romance, the *Genji Monogatari*.

South portal of the Todaiji temple at Nara, built in 1199, in the Tenjiku-yo style of Buddhist architecture. Kamakura period.

Belfry of the Todaiji temple at Nara, with its great bronze bell originally cast in 732. Nara period.

The second epoch of nationalization of Buddhist architectural styles adopted from the Chinese spans the three centuries from 1573 to 1867, covering the Momoyama and Edo periods. Buddhist temples of the Momoyama period began to acquire the native style of architecture that was prevalent before the Kamakura period. As has already been noted, the arts of Japan then became almost entirely free of foreign influences and the large-scale decorative compositions that covered the great panels on the walls of castles and mansions were being created. Buddhist architecture of the Momoyama era is also distinguished for its resplendent coloring and elaborate sculptured ornament. The restoration of Buddhist monasteries during the Momoyama period was carried on at a great pace under the leadership of Toyotomi Hideyoshi and later by his son Hideyori. Typical of the Momoyama style are several

buildings of the Zuiganji temple at Matsushima, founded in 828 and reconstructed in 1609 by order of Date Masamune, one of the most powerful feudal lords of Japan. An avenue of ancient Japanese cedars leads to the temple, past many rock-cut caves, some two stories high and all begrimed with the smoke of incense. These caves are said to have been used in earlier times by traveling priests for religious meditation. Other examples of Momoyama religious architecture are the main hall of the Toji in Kyoto; the Kara-mon or Chinese gateway of the Daitokuji, which was formerly a gateway in the Juraku-dai mansion of Hideyoshi; the Chokushimon or Gate for Imperial Messengers at the Diatokuji in Kyoto; the Samboin temple in Kyoto, containing several chambers decorated by Kano Sanraku; and the Ohiroma or Stork Chambers of the Nishi Honganji temple in Kyoto, which is gorgeously

The Shariden, or Relic Hall, of the Engakuji temple at Kamakura, a fine example of the Kara-yo style of Buddhist architecture. Built during the Einin era (1293-1299). Kamakura period.

143

The taho-to (stupa) of the Ishiyamadera, built in 1194 in the Wa-yo style of Buddhist architecture. Kamakura period. Ishiyama temple, Otsu, Shiga prefecture.

Left: Main Hall of the Saimyoji temple at Kamomachi, Soraku-gun, in Kyoto prefecture, an example of Wa-yo style of Buddhist architecture. Kamakura period.

Right: Main Hall of the Toji temple at Kyoto, rebuilt sometime between 1599–1606. Momoyama period.

decorated with paintings by Kano Tan-yu, Kano Ryokei, and Maruyama Okyo.

In the Edo period the primary emphasis was on decorative detail, with the general form and proportions being overlooked and the different styles losing their distinctive characteristics. Of particular interest are the buildings of the Mampukuji temple at Uji, the headquarters of the Obaku sect of Buddhism established in 1659 by Ingen, a famous Chinese priest. These temple structures follow the style of the later Ming period and are in sharp contrast to other Buddhist temples in Japan. Two of the most representative examples of the Edo period are the Hall of the Great Buddha at the Todaiji in Nara, and the main hall of the Seisuiji temple, more commonly known as the Kiyomizu temple, which stands on a great wooden platform on a cliff offering a panoramic view of Kyoto and its neighboring districts. The famous two-storied gate of the Nanzenji in Kyoto, called the Sammon, was erected in 1628 and is widely known for a legend relating to the notorious robber Ishikawa Goemon. During the earlier part of the Edo period many of the temples in Kyoto that had fallen into a state of disrepair were restored by the successive Tokugawa Shoguns in a series of magnificent reconstruction projects. The great five-storied pagoda of the Toji temple in Kyoto, rebuilt by Iemitsu, the third Tokugawa Shogun, is the highest pagoda in Japan, measuring 182 feet. It stands near the southwest entrance to the city as a noble and beautiful symbol of the Old World atmosphere which still lingers over this center of Buddhism.

Among the distinctive features in the architecture of Japanese Buddhist temples is a raised gallery, reached by a flight of steps in the center of the approach front, with a balustrade continuing as the gallery railing. A system of deep bracketing corbeled out from the main pillars sometimes supports this gallery, which is sheltered by the great projecting eaves. In the larger temples there is a columned loggia within this raised gallery which passes usually around the two sides and the front of the building. The main façade contains one, two, or three sections provided with folding doors which open outward, sometimes in double folds; these are generally left open, as this provides the principal light in the interior. The harmonious arrangement of the pillars, posts, brackets, and beams, which follow a particular standard of measurement, is a principal feature of both the interior and exterior architecture, and an elaborate cornice of wooden bracketing on the walls forms the major ornamental detail. The ceiling is usually paneled and subdivided by ribs into small rectangular coffers sometimes filled with paintings, and the ribs are lacquered and ornamented with metal clasps at their intersections. The floor is partly bare and partly covered with *tatami* or mats, but in many of the fine temples the floors of the gallery and of the central part of the main hall from the entrance to the altar are richly lacquered. In temples of huge dimensions an interior peristyle, or system of roof-supporting columns, is used, each column carrying a profuse system of bracketing to harmonize with that of the cornice. Due to the peculiar construction of the framework of the Japanese roof with its immense weight and heavy projections, there is no thrust on the outer walls because all the weight acts vertically on the interior points of support.

Although the forms of roof are varied, their principal feature is a steep slope at the top, gradually flattening toward the eaves to produce a somewhat concave appearance which is often accentuated by the tilt given to the eaves at the four corners. They are extremely picturesque with their large pantiles, their heavy ribs of tile cresting with large terminals carried along the ridge, and their sloping gables. There are four fundamental forms of roof design: the gabled roof, the pyramidal roof, the hipped-ridge roof, and the hipped-and-

gabled roof. The gabled roof, or *kirizuma* type, consists of two slopes with a heavy rib of tiles along the ridge and along the gable ends. In the pyramidal roof, or *hogyo* type, the ridges that divide the several segments are heavily ribbed with tiles, and at the top where they meet, the intersection is surmounted with a bronze *roban* or dew basin to support certain rooftop ornaments. The hipped-ridge roof, called the *yosemune* or *shichu* type, consists of four sloping sides, those parallel to the ridge having four angles, while those on the opposite sides are triangular in form. The hipped-and-gabled roof, or *irimoya* type, could be described as a gabled roof with the addition of eaves projecting along all four sides. Much of the beauty and charm of Japanese architecture is expressed in the interesting variety of its roofs, from the grand and imposing

dhist building is generally constructed in the *hongawara* manner, which consists of vertical rows of semi-cylindrical tiles alternating with rows of slightly concave flat tiles. The tiles at the lower ends of the rows of semi-cylindrical tiles along the end of the eaves, which are rounded in section, are called *tomoye-gawara* and usually are decorated with designs of lotus flowers, the *tomoye* or circle of three intertwining comma-shaped objects representing the symbol of creation, or some other appropriate subject. The flat tiles at the end of the eaves are called *kakakusa-gawara* and their ends are generally decorated with a flower, leaf, or scroll design. The pleasing proportions and perfectly designed curves of Japanese roofs add much to their beauty, as do the graceful projecting eaves supported on an interesting system of bracketing. Throughout the cen-

   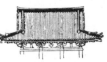

The four fundamental forms of temple roofs: 1. Gable roof, or kirizuma. 2. Pyramidal roo), or hogyo. 3. Hipped-ridge roof, or yosemune or shichu. 4. Hipped-and-gabled roof, or irimoya. Tokyo National Museum.

tiled roofs of Buddhist temples, to the unusually lovely roof of a Shinto shrine covered with thin narrow pieces of *hinoki* the picturesque thatched roofs of farmhouses, and the dwelling houses with roofs of gray-colored tiles that blend so perfectly with the frequent haze of the atmosphere. The roof of a Bud-

turies of Japan's cultural history, religious ideals have been the principal factor influencing the style of architecture, with Shinto exerting its inherent simplicity and Buddhism leaning toward the ornate, while the traditional Japanese dwelling retained an air of elegant simplicity and subtle refinement.

XI Domestic Architecture

JAPANESE domestic architecture, which first developed as a purely native style during the Heian period, has always aimed at a perfect harmony with nature between the house and the garden. This intrinsic relationship is so strong that the two seem to merge with a feeling of complete unity. Nature endowed Japan with beautiful features, and the architectural composition of the domestic dwelling house has been designed to conform with the landscape. The deeply ingrained Japanese appreciation of natural beauty was also greatly stimulated by the teachings of Zen, which developed during the Kamakura period. The Zen belief that the universe is pervaded by one spirit, and that the individual is one with all nature, has for centuries played an important role in Japanese culture. Actually, Zen gave direction to an ingrained love of nature inherent in the Japanese character from earliest times. The original Japanese religion was an unorganized worship of nature and the spirits of the dead, which, through the centuries, developed into the native Shinto cult. The pantheon of this beautiful native religion embraces many nature gods and goddesses, including those of the sea, rivers, mountains, fire, and winds, and many deified persons. In addition, there are those things to which the ancients ascribed divinity, such as the sun and the moon, the flowers, rocks, and trees. The worship of such things is an expression of the belief that natural objects are endowed with indwelling souls, and this is the reason that certain trees and rocks are frequently seen along the wayside adorned with the *shimenawa* or Sacred Rope of Shinto, in the conviction that they are inhabited by a divine spirit.

THE "SHINDEN-ZUKURI" MANSION STYLE

The intimate relationship of the house with its landscape setting, which developed between the tenth and twelfth centuries in the latter part of the Heian period, is the essence of a form of domestic architecture called *shinden-zukuri*. Representing the first truly Japanese domestic style, these imposing dwellings were built for court nobles in beautiful locations within the city of Kyoto, with picturesque mountains as a background. The mansion consisted of a number of buildings, or halls, arranged symmetrically around a main hall, called *shinden*, and connected to each other by galleries. The establishment was located in the middle of the estate and faced south, toward the principal garden and a large pond or lake. The *shinden*, with this southern outlook, was reserved as the reception and living room of the master of the house. The term *living room* in Japanese domestic architecture refers to the room used not only for reading, studying, and dressing, but also for sleeping. The subsidiary buildings with their apartments were called *tainoya* (literally, matching houses), and contained living rooms for various members of the family, that of the mistress being the northern hall. Connected to each of the *tainoya* on either side of the master's hall were two very long galleries that extended in a southerly direction, with pavilions at the ends extending slightly beyond the bank of the lake and over the water. The *shinden* was usually about seventy feet long by fifty feet wide, surrounded on all four sides by a closed veranda which was in turn surrounded by a more narrow open veranda. The floor of the entire mansion was of wood, raised above the ground on heavy supporting posts, and the walls consisted of a series of wooden shutters which swung outward vertically, and could be held open during the day with iron hooks as fasteners, while a fabric or bamboo curtain hung on the inner side. It was not possible for rain to come in the open windows or even onto the veranda because the roof, which was built up with thin strips of cypress in a thatchlike manner, projected well beyond the building line. Each subsidiary hall was laid out exactly like the main hall, the interior consisting of a single, large, open space divided into sections by a variety of movable partitions, such as sectional folding screens called *byobu*, single or double-section screens called *tsuitate*, and large portable framework stands called *kicho*, which were hung with silks. At this time the T'ang dynasty in China was on the decline and the Chinese influence was beginning to wane in Japan, with the result that the native Japanese character was becoming more accentuated. A new class of secular artists was commissioned to embellish some of the mansions with elaborate paintings on ceilings and colorful screen compositions. In this period, mats were not used to cover the floors but served merely for reclining and sitting, and were moved about at will. In time the symmetrical plan of the various buildings of the *shinden-sukuri* style gave way to the typical Japanese arrangement of joining the buildings one to the other in a meandering manner which no longer required connecting galleries.

Toward the end of the twelfth century, with the rise of feudalism, the seat of administrative government of the military caste was established at Kamakura in eastern Japan, for

The Shomeimon Gate of the Imperial palace at Kyoto. Reconstructed after repeated fires in the style of the Late Heian period, eleventh to twelfth century.

The Shishinden or Ceremonial Hall of the Imperial palace at Kyoto. Rebuilt after the fire of 1854 as a reproduction of the original palace building of the early part of the Heian period (794-1185).

Guest hall of the Kojo-in monastery at Otsu, Shiga prefecture, built in 1601 in the style of the dwelling houses universally used since the end of the Muromachi period (1338-1573). Momoyama period (1573-1615).

which this period is named. The residences of the newly risen upper-class warriors, though influenced by the *shinden-sukuri* of the aristocracy at Kyoto, lacked their distinction and were basically simple and practical. By the first half of the fourteenth century, with the fall of the Kamakura regime and rise of the Ashikaga, the administrative headquarters were moved back to Kyoto and established in a section of the city called Muromachi. On account of this the Ashikaga period is also known as the Muromachi period. The military caste adopted more and more the mode of living of the aristocracy and planned their dwellings in conformity with the style of the *shinden-zukuri*. But out of it developed a new style of building called the *shoin-zukuri*, in which the symmetrical arrangement of the *shinden-zukuri* gave way to a free plan, with the various subsidiary buildings grouped in a functional and informal manner about the main structure. To meet the necessities of the time and to conform to the mode of living, the large interiors were now partitioned by means of sliding doors

Ninomaru palace in the Nijo castle at Nijo Horikawa in Kyoto. Edo period, first half of the seventeenth century.

General view of part of the main group of shoin-zukuri-*style buildings of the Katsura Detached Palace at Kyoto. Edo period, early seventeenth century.*

Interior view of the corridor along the front of the Shishinden or Ceremonial Hall of the Imperial palace at Kyoto. A representation of the style of the Late Heian period, eleventh to twelfth century.

149

Arrangement of part of the main group of shoin-zukuri-*style buildings of the Katsura Detached Palace at Kyoto. Edo period, early seventeenth century.*

called *fusuma*, and translucent paper began to be used for windows and for the outside sliding doors called *shoji*, which also had appeared. The characteristic *shoin-zukuri* interior architecture included the recess in the wall called the tokonoma, the recess of shelves called the *tana* or *chigai-dana*, and the bay window near the tokonoma for reading and writing called the *shoin*. The entire floor surface was now covered with mats called *tatami*. The last important addition to appear were sliding wooden shutters called *amado*. In substance, the domestic architecture of the Muromachi period contained all the principal elements of and closely resembled the fine dwellings of today.

During the Momoyama period the palatial mansions in the *shoin-zukuri* style reflected the vigorous growth and flourishing activity of all the arts. The magnificence of the interior decoration of the feudal lords' dwellings is beyond conception. There were finely chased and gilded metalwork appointments, elaborate wood carvings, especially in the *ramma* or horizontal opening above the lintel which partitions off the rooms, and magnificent paintings on screens, wall panels, coffered ceiling panels, and on the *fusuma* or interior sliding doors. It was the era of the great screen painters such as Kano Eitoko and Kano Sanraku with their large-scale decorative compositions covering huge panels of paper or silk. The mastery with which these painters embellished suite after suite in the apartments with a profusion of resplendent color and fine detail has no counterpart. On surfaces of gold leaf were depicted gorgeous landscapes with ancient pine trees, plum trees with their white blossoms, gardens and groves rich with brilliant leaves, birds with bright plumage, wild geese in the moonlight, fantastic rocks, and an endless variety of other subjects. The splendor of these interiors can best be exemplified by the buildings forming a part of the Nishi Honganji temple in Kyoto, which

were moved from the site of Hideyoshi's famous Jurakudai mansion at Momoyama, and the Ninomaru palace in the Nijo castle. Within the vast walled compound of Nijo castle this magnificent mansion was originally built by Ieyasu, the first Tokugawa Shogun, to serve as his residence on the occasion of his visits to Kyoto. In plan it is typical of the palatial houses of the feudal lords of the Edo period, which consisted of several main buildings joined together at their corners like a series of steps. With the increase in the financial power of the commoners during the Edo period, the *shoin-zukuri* in a more simplified form became, as it has remained until the present time, the style of residence for the merchant class and wealthy farmers in the provincial districts.

THE JAPANESE HOUSE

The traditional Japanese dwelling as it is today, even in the urban districts, developed during the Edo period. The planning and layout were largely influenced by the climate and the manner in which the Japanese sit and recline. According to custom, the Japanese always remove their shoes when entering the house and sit on their knees and heels on the mats or *tatami* that cover the floor surface or on a cushion placed upon the floor. Since no seat furniture is necessary because of this mode of sitting, the rooms are small and the ceilings low, and with the rooms free of furniture they need not be reserved for any one specific purpose. The design and construction is not only architecturally beautiful but practical as well, and with the climate as a major factor in the layout and general planning, an unusually charming effect is the result. The climate of the main islands of Japan is about the same all over, with the four seasons of about equal duration and clearly divided one from the other. The summer months are very oppressive, less because of the heat, which is not excessive, than on account of the extreme humidity. This is the opposite of the winter, with its low humidity and moderate temperatures. The high rainfall is another factor that has influenced the planning of the house, because, although the rain falls throughout the year, there is a particular rainy season from about the middle of June, lasting for a month or more. This season is called *nyubai*, or *baiu* or *tsuyu*, and is characterized by cloudy and sultry days mostly accompanied by rain, with some periods of about three days each having torrential downpours. The Japanese rainy season has always been officially designated in the old lunar calendar by the ideograms for *nyubai*, meaning "entry to the plum season," and the ideograms used for *baiu*, meaning "plum-rain," which suggests that the rainy season begins when the plums are ripe. Because of these climatic features, a primary consideration in the planning and building of the Japanese house is aimed at meeting the conditions of the summer months. Not only is the climate unpleasant during the rainy season but it is a time when mildew is a serious factor unless there is free circulation of air. Therefore the house has only a few permanent walls, and the external and internal divisions are formed with sliding and removable doors which permit the air to move freely throughout the entire house. To protect these sliding exterior walls from the summer sun and rain, the roof must project as far as possible and a veranda should extend at least along the south side of the house to provide sufficient shade. And lastly, as a protection against dampness, the ground floor of the house has traditionally been built one and a half to two and a half feet above the ground on posts.

The extensive apertures consisting of sliding doors make the Japanese house more pleasant for summer living, and they also make the house and the garden flow one into the other. The house is always constructed of unpainted wood, while the fixed walls are made of a bamboo latticework covered with a kind of mud plaster mixed with chopped straw, and the roof is of pantiles. There is a pleasing harmony between the silvery-gray of the heavy roof tiles and the haze of the prevalent atmosphere. A characteristic feature of the hipped-and-gabled roofs is the ridges built up of many layers of tiles, with a tile representing water at the end of each ridge. Originally this tile was made to represent the face of a devil and was called *oni-gawara*, meaning devil tile, to protect the house against evil. Most of these end tiles at the present time repre-

The Ohiroma, or Stork Chamber, of the shoin *in the Nishi Honganji temple compound at Kyoto, formerly the residence of Hideyoshi at Fushimi castle, and now the audience chamber of the abbot. It is gorgeously decorated with paintings by the foremost members of the Kano family and noted for the exquisite carvings of storks in the* ramma *(opening above lintel). Momoyama period.*

The main chamber in the living quarters of the Ninomaru palace in the Nijo castle at Kyoto, with paintings attributed to Kano Tan-yu, 1602–1674, and his school on the walls and sliding screens, and the highly decorated coffered ceiling with paintings on a gold-leaf ground. Edo period, first half of the seventeenth century.

Interior of the living quarters of Nagoya castle, showing one of the wall panels and some of the fusuma, *the large* ramma *above the* fusuma, *and corner of the coffered ceiling. The castle was completed in 1612 by order of Ieyasu, founder of the Tokugawa Shogunate, as a fortified residence for his son Yoshinao, whose descendants resided there until 1868. It was completely destroyed in an air raid in 1945. Momoyama period (1573-1615).*

Interior of the living quarters of Nagoya castle showing the chigai-dana *and the use of beautifully painted* fusuma *between the rooms. Built in 1612 and destroyed in an air raid in 1945. Momoyama period (1573-1615).*

sent waves or a waterfall as a charm against fire; some have an ornament of lotus flowers called *tomoye-gawara*, others the *tomoye* or circle composed of three intertwining commas, which is the symbol of Shinto, still others simply the ideogram for water. The layout of the typical Japanese house comprises three distinct parts: the area raised above the ground and covered with mats or *tatami* which includes all the living quarters; the raised part with wooden floor which includes the corridors, veranda, and usually the kitchen; and a small lower portion of almost ground level which includes the bathroom, a section of the kitchen, and the entrance hall. The measurement of a room or any other part of a house spread with mats, as well as those parts having wooden or ground-level floors, is based on the size of a mat as the unit of measurement. A mat is three feet by six feet. The over-all area of a house is always given in terms of *tsubo*, which is six by six feet. The *tatami* are made of a fine woven rush with a narrow border of black fabric on the long side, mounted on a rice-straw body about two inches thick, which makes the *tatami* soft and pleasant to walk on.

The rather primitive simplicity that characterizes the Japanese dwelling does not imply that it is built with primitive methods and archaic design, but actually represents a purity of style developed by a refinement of taste through several centuries. The fact that the floor level is raised from one and

a half to two and a half feet above the ground on posts, that the floors are of *tatami*, that the wooden construction and the movable walls and partitions appear primitive, is actually the result of a particular mode of living and is especially adapted to conform with the climate. The intimate relationship of Japanese life with nature manifests itself also in the beauty of the wood surfaces and the skill with which they are treated. Unfinished and unpainted wood is usually employed for both the inside and outside of the house, and the meticulous selection and the combinations of different kinds of wood create a particularly pleasing effect. One of the principal woods used in the finer houses is the *hinoki* cypress, *Chamaecyparis obtusa*, which is smooth and dense, with very fine grain, a pleasing odor, and a light color that attains a silvery-gray sheen with the passage of time. Also frequently used is another cypress, *Thujopsis dolabrata*, called *hiba*, which closely resembles *hinoki*. Hardwoods are likewise employed, such as a maple, *Acer palmatum*, called *momiji* or *kaede*, with bright-yellow color; a kind of sandalwood, *Zelkova serrata*, with a grain of vigorous curves; and *Morus alba*, a mulberry wood light-yellow in color, called *kuwa*. A beautiful decorative wood is the *kiri* or paulownia, *Paulownia tomentosa*, with a light, silvery-violet color and fine grain. There is also *Cryptomeria japonica*, called *sugi*, which is a species of cedar with a reddish-brown color in the center that becomes lighter toward the outside. *Sugi* has both a wavy and a very fine straight grain, and is extensively used for uprights and ceiling panels; slender young trunks of *sugi* are often used in their natural form, with the bark peeled off and polished, for the posts of tokonoma. Bamboo is extensively used as a building material in addition to wood, and produces a soft and charming effect, especially the beautiful native varieties whose trunks attain a height of as much as sixty-five feet with a proportionately large diameter.

The planning and layout of the Japanese house has produced not only a work of architectural beauty but one that is flexible for the practical, utilitarian usage of the various rooms. As none of the rooms with matted floors are actually reserved for any exclusive purpose, and the partitions are so easily rearranged, each room can be used for any purpose desired. The custom of sitting on the matted floor and the absence of furniture and bedsteads gives the rooms a more spacious appearance, while the white of the *shoji* doors, the fresh pale-green of the *tatami*, and the beautiful tones of the natural wood create a feeling of great elegance and utmost refinement of taste. There is also a minimum of interior decoration, and the arrangement of the rooms is determined by the size of the house. The sliding partitions between the rooms, called *fusuma*, are also removable when the full space of two or more rooms is desired for some particular purpose. There is usually a set of four *fusuma* separating the average-size rooms, and *fusuma* also serve as doors on wall cupboards and as entrance doors into living rooms. A *fusuma* is five feet ten inches in height, with a normal width of about three feet, and is composed of a wooden frame with several layers of heavy paper glued to it on both sides, and a piece of decorative paper or a painting laid on to cover the whole surface, with a narrow frame of wood, usually lacquered in black, bordering the entire parti-

Himeji castle at Himeji-shi, Hyogo prefecture, showing the main buildings originally built by Hideyoshi, and enlarged by Tokugawa Ieyasu. Momoyama period (1573–1615).

153

tion. The *fusuma* slides between an upper and lower beam in which there are usually two grooves. Between the upper beam or lintel and the ceiling beam there is an open space called *ramma*. *Ramma* are never fully closed, since their purpose is to permit a free circulation of air between the rooms; they are ornamented with a delicate wooden latticework or a wooden panel carved with openwork designs, in the large mansions often with very elaborate compositions.

Since there are only a few fixed walls in a Japanese house and the greater part of the outside wall space is provided with many wide window openings, principally in the form of sliding doors, there is a freer circulation of air throughout the house. There is also a wide outlook on the beauties of the garden, especially because of the manner in which the Japanese sit upon the floor. On the sides of the house where there is no veranda, the openings are in the form of paper windows called elbow-rest windows, because they slide on a low sill about twelve inches high to offer an unobstructed view from a squatting position. Almost every small house has a veranda facing the south that also serves as a corridor, instead of an inside corridor, and the design of large houses often includes two or more verandas in addition to one or more inside corridors, because of the more complex arrangement of the rooms. In the larger houses these verandas, which are three and a half feet in width, often extend the full length of the side of the house and are usually enclosed on the outer side with sliding glass doors, while the floors are generally of highly polished *hinoki*. The sides of the rooms that open on the veranda are provided with sliding paper doors called *shoji*, which are the same height as the *fusuma* and slide in grooves between the floor beam and the lintel. Both the paper windows and the *shoji* consist of frames with a latticework of thin strips of wood. To the side of the *shoji* that faces the outside of the house is applied the plain white translucent paper that produces a soft light, giving the room a warm and peaceful feel-

ing. Above the lintel of the *shoji* doors are *ramma* openings the same as above the *fusuma*, but instead of having openwork carvings or latticework the openings are fitted with little *shoji* windows that can be opened and closed to control ventilation.

For protection against the rain as well as to keep out possible intruders at night, *shoji* doors and windows that open directly to the outside where there is no closed veranda have a particular kind of sliding wooden shutter called *amado*, or rain door. The sides of the *amado* are provided with either overlapping pieces or grooves so that each section can fit securely into the next with the aid of a bolt, the end ones being bolted to the beams at both the top and the bottom. During the day, when the *amado* are not in use they are slid into compartments placed at the ends of the door and window openings. An important type of annex building that forms part of the larger houses is the *dozo* or *kura*, which is a fireproof godown or storehouse. Since the wooden construction of the Japanese house presents an ever-present fire hazard, the better dwelling houses often have one or more of these godowns in which most of their valuable possessions are stored. Godowns are either attached to the house or separated from it, and are usually two-storied with exceptionally thick walls of concrete that are painted either black or white. The very thick roof is concrete, as well as the windows and door, which are also of exceptionally thick concrete and swing on hinges. The earlier godowns were made of clay, and when fire threatened the house, the godown windows were immediately closed and their joints or seams filled with clay that was always kept nearby for that purpose.

In the Japanese house, customary usage of particular rooms rather than any special furnishings distinguishes one from another. Living rooms, guest rooms, reception rooms, and so forth are thus easily interchangeable because of the flexible plan of the house. The principal room is the reception room,

House of a feudal vassal, an old samurai mansion, at Tsuyama, Okayama, showing servants' quarters along the wall. Edo period, seventeenth century.

Left: Interior of a living room in the Kangaku-in monastery of the Miidera temple (also called Onjoji temple), near Otsu on Lake Biwa, Shiga prefecture. Built in 1600. Momoyama period.

Center: Guest room in the main house of the Koho-an, a minor monastery of the Daitokuji temple at Kyoto, showing the arrangement of shoji, a bell-shaped window, the tokonoma, and the fusuma. Edo period, early seventeenth century.

Right: Interior view of a room in the Kujo-kan, a building formerly on the premises of Prince Kujo's residence in Kyoto, showing the chigai-dana and the tokonoma with a painting by an artist of the Kano school. Edo period, seventeenth century. Tokyo National Museum.

with an anteroom of almost equal size connected to it by sliding doors or *fusuma*. The average size of the reception room is from eight to ten mats, and together with its anteroom often serves as a guest chamber. When greater space is required, as for a large gathering, its size can be considerably increased by removing the four *fusuma* doors separating the reception room and the anteroom. These rooms always open up to face the garden and generally have a veranda extending the full length of one, two, or three sides, thus bringing house and garden in closer proximity and heightening the feeling of harmony with nature. Among the most important features of the reception room are: the tokonoma, an alcove which constitutes a kind of shrine dedicated to the exercise of æsthetic pleasures; a *tana* or *chigai-dana*, a recess with a specially composed arrangement of shelves and wall cupboards; and a *shoin*, which is a particular variety of bay window. The only appointments in the anteroom are one or more built-in wall cupboards.

The tokonoma constitutes the most important feature of a Japanese room. It is always found in the reception room and frequently in the living room of the larger houses as well; there is also always one in the principal room of the houses of the less affluent. A tokonoma is a recessed portion of the room, the place of honor where a hanging scroll-painting and flowers are placed so that their æsthetic qualities may be appreciated. It is said that the tokonoma had its origin during medieval times in the Zen monasteries when the priests hung Buddhist pictures on the wall behind a low stand on which was placed a vase of flowers, a candlestick, and an incense burner. From this arrangement there developed an alcove in the wall with a built-in altar which became the prototype of the secular tokonoma. The earliest tokonoma in domestic dwellings was actually a family altar on which was placed an image of the Buddha together with an offering of incense and flowers, before which all members of the family would gather to worship each morning and evening. The religious significance of the tokonoma gradually disappeared, but although it later came only to have æsthetic meaning, the Japanese have always retained a feeling of sacredness for it. The earlier religious pictures have been replaced by secular ones in the form of kakemono, the vertical hanging scrolls, of which some are rare and beautiful poetical works of calligraphy, while others are ink paintings of landscapes, figure subjects, and other characteristic themes of Japanese art. Like the floral arrangements and ornaments that are placed one at a time in the tokonoma, the kakemono is changed at frequent intervals for the enjoyment of another, for the observance of certain holidays and festival days, or to conform with the season of the year. The larger mansions often possess a few hundred or more kakemono that have been acquired through many generations of art collecting. The kakemono which are not in use are rolled up, placed in boxes especially made for each individual one, and kept in the fireproof godown within the precincts of the property. Tokonoma vary in form or in the arrangement of their details. The form most commonly used consists of a platform, three by six feet, raised a few inches above the floor level, faced on the front with a sill that is almost always black-lacquered, and having its own floor surface, of either a *tatami* or polished boards, which is level with the sill. Across the upper portion, and somewhat higher than the lintels over doors, is a crossbeam between the posts at either side, with the space from the beam to the ceiling filled in with wall plaster to produce a frame for the tokonoma. The tokonoma is seldom if ever placed in the center of the wall, because the rooms are designed asymmetrically. In the Japanese room the place of honor is in front of the tokonoma, and the principal guest sits there with his back toward it. For centuries the tokonoma has had the unique distinction of being considered a sacred place in the home, and in view of its moral and spiritual significance, one never enters within its recess.

Next in importance in the reception room are the *tana* and *shoin*, which give the room a variety of interesting arrangements. The *tana*, or *chigai-dana*, is a recess with artistically designed shelves and wall cupboards. It is often called a *tokowaki*, meaning side of the tokonoma. Its principal purpose is to provide variation in the architectural design of the room, but it also serves to display one or a few objects of art. Although its form is at times very complex, its most characteristic arrangement consists of small cupboards with sliding doors placed above and below wall shelves. These wall shelves usually consist of two boards that do not extend the full width of the recess and are joined one above the other by a short wooden rod. A most unusual and interesting asymmetrical arrangement of shelves is seen in the design of some *tana*, but

the most refined compositions are those having only two or three shelves between the cupboards. The *shoin* came in as part of the architectural development of residences. Originally the term *shoin* was applied to a bay window with a wide sill used for reading and writing in the dwelling houses of Zen priests, and it also designated the study itself. When the *shoin* developed as a part of domestic architecture, the term was applied indifferently to any room in the house having such a bay window or to a suite of rooms having such a bay in its principal room. Although the *shoin* now acts as a decorative feature of the reception room in the larger houses, its original purpose was to serve as a reading bay, and it consisted of a wide bay window with delicately latticed sliding *shoji* windows above a deep sill which was raised several inches above the floor and had a cupboard with sliding doors beneath. This original type of *shoin* is called a *tsukejoin* or projecting *shoin*, while a more simplified type that is frequently used is called a *hirajoin* or flat *shoin*. The *hirajoin* is identical to the *tsukejoin* except that it is flush with the wall and the lower portion consists of a flat wall space below the sliding windows instead of the raised and deep sill. The *shoin* constitutes a beautiful decorative feature of interior architecture and is always placed next to, and at right angles to, the tokonoma, with the windows opening directly onto the veranda.

House of a feudal vassal, at Tsuyama, Okayama, showing part of the main house within the compound wall. Edo period, seventeenth century.

The Kara-mon of the Daitokuji temple at Kyoto, originally the gateway to the Juraku-dai mansion of Hideyoshi. Momoyama period (1573-1615).

The Ginkakuji, or Silver Pavilion, of the Jishoji Kyoto. Originally built by Yoshimasa, the eigh Ashikaga Shogun, in 1479 as a country vil Muromachi period.

The dining room in a Japanese house is called *chanoma*, which, when literally translated, means the room of the tea. Essentially the dining room for the family, it is a small room measuring from four and a half to eight mats, depending upon the size of the house. It serves a variety of other purposes—for example, as a family sitting room and as a sewing room or workroom for the mistress of the house—but traditionally it is never used as a bedroom. The rooms reserved for sleeping are the living rooms, which average from six to ten mats in size and are always provided with wall cupboards having sliding doors. There are many living rooms in the larger houses, as it is the custom for each member of the family to have his own room. Some of these living rooms have anterooms, while they frequently have a tokonoma and generally have a veranda which faces a garden. There are sometimes a few movable chests-of-drawers and cupboards in the living rooms, but their use is somewhat restricted due to the many built-in cupboards and drawers. A low table is the most common piece of movable furniture found in the Japanese room. It serves many purposes, especially as a dining table when the traditional individual trays or *ozen* are not used. When the living room is used for sleeping, a *toko* or *futon*, which is the Japanese bed, is brought out from the wall cupboard and spread upon the *tatami* floor. The *futon* is a

mattress of wadded cotton about an inch or so in thickness on which is placed a pillow and the quilted bed coverlet. In the morning when the bed is no longer in use, it is folded and stored in a wall cupboard, thereby leaving the living room free to be used for other purposes.

The refined elegance in the appearance of a Japanese room emanates from its design, the beauty and native charm of the natural wood surfaces, the soft light transmitted through the paper doors, and the lovely tone of the pale-green *tatami*. The only article that frequently serves to embellish the room is a characteristic Japanese folding floor screen called a *byobu* or an ordinary single-panel screen called a *tsuitate*. Still preserved in most Japanese homes is the ancient tradition of having both Shinto and Buddhist deities venerated in miniature family altars, which are usually placed in two of the principal rooms. The Shinto altar, called *kamidana*, is often a small shrine placed upon a board shelf high up in the corner of the room near the ceiling. In many of the large homes of the old families, especially in the provincial districts, the *kamidana* are frequently handsome architectural reproductions of the characteristic styles of Shinto shrines and measure as much as six feet in height. The *kami* or deity is represented by a small sacred tablet bearing its name and placed in the miniature shrine or directly upon the wooden shelf. Besides the tutelary *kami*

The Hiunkaku in the compound of the Nishi Honganji temple at Kyoto, originally a pavilion in the grounds of Hideyoshi's Jurakudai mansion. Momoyama period (1573-1615).

from that locality, the most important *kami* venerated is Amaterasu, the sun goddess, who is the ancestress of the Imperial family. A candle is lighted every morning and every member of the family pays homage according to the Shinto custom of bowing before the shrine, clapping their hands, usually twice, and offering a prayer. On the first and fifteenth day of each month miniature sake bottles and fresh branches of the camellia-like *sakaki* tree, *Eurya ochnacea*, the sacred tree of Shinto, are offered.

Since the worship of Amaterasu and the local deities does not conflict with faith in Buddha, the Buddhist family altar, called *Butsudan*, is also found in most homes. In contrast to the Shinto altar, which is plain and bare of ornament, the *Butsudan* is usually much decorated with fine lacquer work and elaborate carvings. It contains an image representing Buddha or some other Buddhist deity, together with small tablets that are venerated and inscribed with the posthumous Buddhist names of the deceased members of the family, who in old families with a long history sometimes span several centuries. A small bowl of boiled rice is offered every morning to the deceased members, together with fruits, sweets, or vegetables; and any gift received by the family, except fish or fowl, is first offered to the Buddhist altar before it is used or eaten. These offerings to the Buddhist family altar signify that the deceased members are treated as though they were alive, and every morning every member of the family addresses the shrine by saying a reverent "good morning" to show respect to the departed ones.

The Japanese house is still heated in the traditional manner with a charcoal burner or brazier called a *hibachi*. Although the average climate during the winter months is not as uncomfortable as the humid climate of summer, it is moderately cold, and is especially unpleasant because the construction of the Japanese house offers very little protection against it. The Japanese have to be warmly dressed during the cold months,

since they are able to warm only their hands over the charcoal burner. The *hibachi* or portable brazier may be made of wood, porcelain, or metal, and its shape varies from square or oblong to round. It contains a metal container in which fine ashes are allowed to accumulate and on which glowing charcoal is burned. In the big farmhouses in the rural districts a large fireplace is still used for burning wood, while in the very cold parts of Japan a kind of fire pan of stone sunk in the floor is used. A low table-like framework is placed above the fire-pan opening with a cloth spread over it, and the family can sit around the hearth with the lower part of their bodies covered with the cloth for additional warmth.

In earlier times the Japanese lighted their homes by means of *ando* or *andon*, square-shaped paper lanterns having a rigid wooden frame, open at the top, and resting on a flat base or supported on four short legs, or held within a stand with four delicate supports. These lanterns, which rested upon the floor and were formerly lighted with candles or with lamps that burned rapeseed oil, are still used for decorative as well as utilitarian lighting in the principal rooms. There is also a variety of folding paper lantern used for both indoor and outdoor purposes. This type of lantern first appeared around the beginning of the seventeenth century during the Tokugawa period. They immediately became popular and were extensively used for all forms of lighting, especially because they could be carried around easily. The typical Japanese paper lantern, called *chochin* or carrying lantern, is made of numerous pliant splittings of bamboo that are bent into circles and placed one above the other with paper pasted over them. To the bottom is affixed a collar of thin wood with a solid piece having a pricket for the candle, while the top piece is just a collar of wood. Since most *chochin* are made for outside use, the paper is treated with a heavy coating of fish oil as a protection against the weather. The streets were not lighted during earlier days except at festival times, and paper lanterns

Left: The *Shokin-tei* pavilion of the Katsura Detached Palace at Kyoto, in which are included a tea-ceremony room and a moon-viewing veranda overlooking the pond. Edo period, early seventeenth century.

Center: A bench under the roof of the *Shokin-tei* pavilion showing the rural cottage style of architecture. Edo period, early seventeenth century. Katsura Detached Palace at Kyoto.

Right: A room in a dwelling house with the sliding shoji removed to bring it into closer harmony with its garden and pond. Jiro Harada, Tokyo National Museum.

View from the room of a dwelling house arranged around an interior garden. Jiro Harada, Tokyo National Museum.

Interior of a main room in a dwelling house showing the tokonoma with a kakemono hanging in it, and a bell-shaped window. Jiro Harada, Tokyo National Museum.

were carried by those going out at night. Although this practice is no longer necessary in the cities, lanterns are still widely used in rural districts, where they are still marked with the family crest to identify the person carrying one on dark nights. The Japanese will not use a lantern that is plain white, because a purely white lantern is used at the time of a Buddhist funeral. Therefore, every *chochin* has something painted or written on it, such as the family crest of its owner, a picture, or ideograms meaning "good night" or "beware of fire." Among the popular types of *chochin* are the *odawara-chochin*, a cylindrical lantern named after the town of Odawara, and the *gifu-chochin*, named for the city of Gifu and noted for its delicate oval shape and beautiful designs of flowers, birds, and insects painted on its thin paper covering. Originally Gifu lanterns were principally used throughout the house at the time of the Buddhist Obon Festival, which lasts for three days beginning July 13, during which time the departed members of the family return from the spirit world for a brief visit. Other lanterns are: the *yumihari-chochin* with its bow-shaped handle connected to its base so it can stand; the *takahari-chochin*, a cylindrical lantern, usually with the family crest, which is placed under a little protecting roof on a high post at the door or gate of the house; and the *hozuki-chochin* or red-berry lantern, which is rather small and round and of bright-red color, used in lantern processions and at festivals. It has been a Japanese custom to hang beautifully decorated paper lanterns in the house and in the garden on summer evenings, their soft light giving off a feeling of freshness much like the *furin*, or little wind bells, that are hung on the verandas.

XII Landscape Gardening

THE JAPANESE love of nature finds its most articulate expression in the art of landscape gardening. In order to fully appreciate the profound beauty of this art, with its unique and varied composition, it is necessary to penetrate into the symbolism which animates its design. Without this deeper meaning imparted to the most rudimentary methods of Japanese landscape gardening, it would possess merely the empty charm of novelty or fanciful conceit. It is generally accepted that the rules and theories underlying the art of landscape gardening in Japan have been handed down in a continuous tradition from early to modern times and are still evident in the present-day examples.

The aim of a Japanese garden is to make a "landscape-picture" of the countryside, with its many famous views and favorite rural spots. The most striking features of the varied landscape of Japan are depicted in a composition of hills, stones, cascades, streams, and lakes. Nature's peculiar characteristics indigenous to Japanese scenery, with its strange and fantastic exaggerations of form, are carefully studied and interpreted in the landscape garden. In these artistic productions, as in Japanese painting, the landscape designer follows the traditional canons which prescribe an essence of reality rather than naturalistic appearance. The principles of Japanese art require a careful selection and modification of the constituent parts of a scene rather than a completely realistic reproduction of nature, and most often tend to accentuate certain characteristics. The Japanese love of nature is an inherited and educated taste acquired from traditional customs, arts, and culture. The transmutation of nature into conventionalized motifs and decorative designs, as seen in many branches of art, is familiar to all Japanese, and these have become the accepted traditional forms derived from natural life. It is from these conventional conceptions that the Japanese have formulated an interpretation of nature peculiar to themselves. Thus, landscape gardening is a representation of the natural scenery of their country as reflected in their art. The garden designer uses the scenery of Japan as his model, selecting the natural features and plant life for his composition, as well as certain characteristic structures, such as bridges, pagodas, and shrines, which are seen as a part of every rural view.

The only deviation from the strict adherence to nature is in the artificial contours imparted to certain trees and shrubs by pruning and shaping to produce conventional representations of favorite forms seen in nature. It is not the ordinary pine tree that is used as a model, but one that has been molded into strange and unusual shapes by age and tempests. The expression of nature as represented in the landscape garden is executed with careful consideration for æsthetic principles of balance, unity, scale, proportion, and harmony. Japanese landscape gardens are not only representations of natural scenes, but often are expressions of an abstract sentiment or symbolical meaning. Since the Japanese garden is essentially a retreat for the enjoyment of peaceful seclusion and meditation, it should reflect the temperament and sentiments of the master of the house. The garden attached to the dwelling house of a priest is designed to express the qualities of virtue and dignified solitude; other gardens may suggest the attributes of Buddhist divinities or depict philosophic traditions.

THE FIRST LANDSCAPE GARDENS

The introduction of Buddhism and its attendant culture from Korea in the sixth century was the channel for the earliest landscape gardens in Japan and these were principally laid out in connection with the ancient monasteries and temples. In 710, when the Empress-Regnant Gemmyo established the city of Nara as the first permanent seat of court and government in the province of Yamato, the art of landscape gardening entered a phase of rapid development along with the

Garden of the Saihoji temple at Kyoto, designed by Muso Kokushi, 1275-1351. Muromachi period.

progress of architecture. The influence which Chinese culture exerted was manifest in the construction of the palaces, villas, and mansions of the wealthy nobles, and beautiful landscape gardens contributed to the magnificence of these buildings, providing their owners with picturesque settings in which to enjoy leisure moments and to entertain their guests. By the time of the luxurious Fujiwara period (897-1185) the aristocratic society had developed a standard of living that was distinctly metropolitan in its manners and cultural activities. In 794 the capital had been transferred from Nara to Kyoto, which was surrounded on three sides by beautiful mountains and traversed by rivers of crystal-clear water, providing an ideal setting for landscape gardens. The temples, palaces, and mansions of the new capital were erected on a grand scale, and since there were many natural hills, woods, springs, and ponds within the city limits, their gardens were enriched with these natural creations. Gardens of huge proportions were the fashion, and many were intended to resemble particular places noted for scenic beauty. For example, the garden at the mansion of Fujiwara Sukechika symbolized the bay at Ama-no-hashidate on the Sea of Japan. Ama-no-hashidate literally means Bridge of Heaven and since ancient times has been famous for its beautiful view from the mountains looking down upon a long and extremely narrow sand bar that traverses the bay. Pine trees bent into fantastic shapes by the wintry storms are seen in great numbers along the entire length of the sand bar and enhance its unique beauty. During this second half of the Heian period, or Fujiwara era, when the new *shinden-zukuri* style of architecture was perfected with its spacious and luxurious apartments connected by galleries, the gardens were made to conform with this arrangement. The focus of the garden was the main house, or *shinden*, which looked out on a court having at its farther end a large pond containing three islets. The islet nearest to the *shinden*, which was called *naka-jima*, was approached by way of an arched bridge that spanned the water obliquely. Bridges spanned the water between the remaining islets, and the final bridge to the other side of the pond had a removable section to allow boats to pass. On the banks of the pond, and along the stream that flowed into it, were great boulders, trees, and all manner of vegetation skillfully arranged in a naturalistic setting, sometimes with rocky beaches and sand bars. Although these fabulous gardens of the Fujiwara period long ago disappeared, many great temples and monasteries have preserved certain aspects of them which conform to the detailed descriptions contained in old record books of gardens.

ZEN GARDENS

With the introduction of the Zen sect of Buddhism in the Kamakura period (1185-1333) the symbolical representation of nature in the arrangement of gardens and the *kara-yo* style of architecture became popular forms for monasteries and dwelling houses. The philosophical spirit of Zen, with its speculations reaching beyond the limits of human knowledge, tended to make these gardens symbolic, and although many were designed after those of the earlier Heian style, there developed a garden of smaller proportions in which the reproduction of nature was the principal aim. The most prominent features of the Zen-inspired gardens were rocks, water, evergreen trees and plants, and the skillful use of the natural characteristics of the site to produce picturesque effects. The most famous designer of Zen gardens, and the one who contributed the most to their development, was Muso Kokushi, 1275-1351, a Zen priest of noble birth also known as Soseki. He spent the later years of his life in Kyoto, where he created a number of superb gardens of rare beauty within the precincts of many temples. Among these is the landscape garden in front of the abbot's apartment at the Tenryuji temple, and the famous garden of the Saihoji temple. In the latter the natural configuration of the site was most skillfully used: around a large pond of irregular shape, fine rock settings are profusely overgrown with many species of beautiful moss of unusual thickness. A supreme work of genius, it has become better known as the Kokedera, or Moss temple.

The *shinden*-style houses with their vast gardens prevailed during the early part of the Muromachi period (1338-1573), and the first families of the Ashikaga Shoguns found great delight in emulating the aristocratic culture of the Fujiwara nobility. Later in the Muromachi period when the *shoin* style of architecture reached its fully developed form, the landscape gardens that symbolically represented Zen ideals were also adopted. Perhaps the garden that most perfectly exemplifies this Zen inspiration is at the Jishoji temple, popularly called Ginkakuji or Silver Pavilion, originally built in 1479 by the Ashikaga Shogun Yoshimasa as a country villa, at Higashiyama in Kyoto. While the gardens of the rich mansions followed the style of the famous moss garden of the Saihoji, and also the style of gardens attached to the smaller monasteries situated within the compounds of large monasteries, a more abridged form with symbolic interpretations began to find favor. This school of landscape gardening is often suggestive of the ink landscape painting of Chinese origin, usually being composed of stones, sand, and small evergreens to symbolize a pond, a stream, the ocean, or mountains and hills with waterfalls. The two most famous gardens of this style, one at the Ryoanji temple and the other at the Daitokuji temple, both at Kyoto,

are said to have been made by Soami, who designed the garden of the Silver Pavilion. The Ryoanji, at Kyoto, was originally the Kitayama villa of the military lord Hosokawa Katsumoto, and was converted into a Zen monastery in the latter part of the fifteenth century. The small south garden of the *hojo*, or dwelling of the head priest, occupies a space within the walls of about 130 *tsubo* or approximately 4680 square feet. This garden, which is regarded as one of the masterpieces of Soami, who was greatly influenced by Zen philosophy, is composed exclusively of stones and white sand, and its simplicity is so extreme that it can be appreciated only by those who understand.

The technique of gardening to represent mountains and water by various combinations of stones and sand or earth, is called *kare sansui*, or dry landscape, and is seen in many excellent examples of the Muromachi period when Zen philosophy was popular. The Ryoanji garden is one of the finest examples of the dry-landscape style; the masterful use of space has never been expressed so purely and symbolically. Its fifteen stones are grouped into five sets of two, three, or five and arranged with perfect proportion on the level white-sand ground, which has a meticulously worked pattern of straight parallel ridges made with a bamboo rake. Zen Buddhism relies upon the individual to grasp the meaning of hidden essentials concealed behind outward appearances and to mentally interpret their significance. Therefore, to some these rocks suggest the legend of *tora-no-ko watashi*, in which tigers lead their cubs across a mountain stream; to others they resemble high mountain peaks soaring above an expanse of clouds, or islands in an ocean. The best time to see them is on a clear moonlight night when they appear as living things of nature. The other famous garden created by Soami is that of the Daisen-in, one of the smaller monasteries within the compound of the Daitokuji temple at Kyoto. Like the garden of the Ryoanji, it is in the dry-landscape style with a miniature reproduction of nature confined to a small space of about eleven hundred square feet, alongside the dwelling house of a priest. In the background is a group of carefully trained trees to represent distant mountains. Vertical rocks symbolize cliffs and a waterfall, and horizontal stones represent objects such as embankments, bridges, and a boat. The level ground symbolizes a river and is covered with pine needles. In this garden, designed under the spiritual philosophy of Zen, all these stones exist in the world of symbolic expression transcending the actual world. The Zen priests gave names to the stones as suggested by their shapes: "tiger's head" stone, "genius' hat" stone, "lying-ox" stone, "clear-mirror" stone, "tortoise-shell" stone, "long ship" stone, Fudo stone, Kannon stone, Daruma stone (so named after the first patriarch of Buddhism), "saddle-shaped" stone, Buddhist paten stone, "faint-smell" stone.

Garden of the Nanzenji temple at Kyoto, next to the living quarters of the abbot. Attributed to Kobori Enshu, 1579-1647, it is in the dry-landscape style, with rocks, trees, and white sand.

Garden of the Ryoanji temple at Kyoto, in the kare sansui *or dry-landscape style. Attributed to Soami. Muromachi period, early sixteenth century.*

THE STROLL GARDEN

Japanese landscape gardening thus developed from the earlier *shinden*-style garden, which frequently served as a place of outdoor entertainment, to the garden based on Zen principles to be enjoyed for its æsthetic quality. It was this latter type with its symbolic representations that developed into the *roji* style of small garden attached to the teahouse, which is fully described in the chapter on the tea ceremony. Along with the *roji* type that appeared in the Momoyama period (1573-1615) and was further developed in the Edo period (1615-1867), another style was created which is called the stroll garden. This type of garden appeared because of the increase in the area of gardens that adorned the great mansions of the daimyo and feudal lords. In these great stroll gardens there were also the various structures that form a part of the tea ceremony, with interesting paths leading to them. Landscape designers endeavored to create these stroll gardens so as to have scenic views in harmony with the desire to enjoy the pleasures of meditation. One of the foremost examples of the stroll style of garden is that of the Katsura Detached Palace in the western outskirts of Kyoto. The grounds contain numerous buildings and have quiet beautiful surroundings and views of the mountains in the background. A peculiarity of this garden is the manner in which it is planned, for wherever one stands the scene always appears to be the front view and one never feels as though standing in the wrong position to enjoy the beauties of the landscape.

Unnatural regularity is carefully avoided in Japanese landscape gardening, and the variety obtained is the result of resourceful manipulation of design. Of primary importance are contour, form, and proportion, with the combination of colors being a natural result rather than one of particular arrangement. In contrast to the Occidental method of making bouquets of flowers, in which a variety of color is crushed together and individual form and beauty are all but lost, the Japanese prefer to display the natural lines of branches and stems so as to exhibit the subtle shapes and colors of each bud and blossom in an open and well-balanced composition. This same subordination of color to form, and the same simple naturalness as opposed to ostentatious artificiality, are evident in even the most minute details of Japanese gardening.

In theory Japanese landscape gardening falls into three styles of composition. These divisions are the *shin*, or finished or elaborate style, the *gio* or intermediate style, and the *so*, which is the abbreviated or free style of flat garden. This classification pertains to the manner, free or refined, as seen in the composition, and to some extent to the nature of the materials used. The garden is regarded as a poem or picture intended to inspire some worthy sentiment or to suggest some natural scene that is particularly favored by the owner. At times a purely abstract sentiment is conveyed by the composition of the garden, such as contemplation or peaceful retirement from the cares of the world, solitude or dignified seclusion. Garden record books of early times show that the Japanese have always frowned upon making a garden an ornamental appendage to the house or making any ostentatious display. Gardens should be pleasant retreats for hours of leisure and should be created from a genuine love of nature, and they should be so arranged that each of the four seasons contributes to their artistic beauty. Since it is the intention of Japanese gardens to provide a place for unrestrained ease and meditation, there are various sentiments that landscape gardeners are said to have expressed in their works, such as long life and

Garden of the Daisen-in monastery in the compound of the Daitokuji temple at Kyoto, built by Soami at the beginning of the sixteenth century.

happiness, gentleness, the pleasure of retirement, and many others. These fanciful conceptions are inspired by the emotion aroused by natural scenery, whether it be awe-inspiring, solitary, gay, or placid. Their value is largely dependent upon occult meanings, historical or philosophical, which are associated with many of the compositions of gardens, in particular those gardens attached to religious houses.

Designers of Japanese landscape gardens visit appropriate scenery, draw sketches, and make notes of their observations. It is from these sketches and notes that suggestions are supplied which contribute to originality of composition. An extensive and complicated scene is never attempted in its entirety; instead, the contours and peculiarities of portions of it are studied separately. The immediate view in front that can be fully observed from one point of sight, with its most striking contours of mountain, valley, rock formations, stream, and most prominent trees, both in the foreground and in the distance, is sketched first. Then sketches are made of the other parts of the scene by turning a little to the right and then to the left. Although these sketches depict all of the principal details, they can only be useful as a general guide for the subsequent execution of the garden, as variations from them are governed by the actual site. A reproduction of the real scene is never followed too closely, for the garden must conform to the nature of its surroundings, and to the size, form, and character of the trees, rocks, and lanterns to be used.

Through the centuries there have been many theories as to the procedure of laying out the garden; some say the foreground should be finished first, others that it should be the background, while all agree the middle distance should be finished last. The renowned tea master Sen-no-Rikyu taught the "distance-lowering" method, in his system of composition,

in which distant mountains should be lower than the near ones, with larger trees planted in the front and smaller ones in the back, and distant water placed higher in the background. An opposite method was taught by the famous tea master Furuta Oribe, called "distance-raising" method, in which he favored placing the larger hills and trees in the background and the lower ones in the foreground. The theories of Rikyu's method become more acceptable when it is understood that the mountains are of similar magnitude, or that the view is from a mountain looking toward the distant plain. The scale of a garden must be carefully considered, and since the principal purpose of a garden is summer enjoyment, foliage should be arranged sparingly to produce a cool and refreshing appearance. The presence of water, preferably that which is clear, shallow, and running, produces the most refreshing effect. However, if the character of the garden requires water and it is not obtainable, the designer then arranges the hills, rocks, and trees to produce a composition suggesting water. Although the distribution of the many features of a garden is not confined to any particular set of rules, there are certain principles which serve the designer as a guide in his arrangements within the composition. It must always be remembered that the garden is more than an artistic arrangement of trees and rocks; it is a real picture composition to the Japanese, intended to represent some imaginary or true landscape.

THE HILL-GARDEN STYLE

The *tsukiyama-niwa*, or hill garden, is the most complete landscape garden, and since an ideal Japanese landscape scene must contain mountains and water scenery, the term *sansui*, which is used to denote such a view, is also given to the best of these artificial landscapes. In the hill-garden style, hills are the most prominent feature, and from their form, character, and distribution are meant to represent actual mountain scenery, with the distant peak, the sweeping contours of the nearer mountains, and the low rounded hills in the foreground all ideally arranged. Of great importance is the principle of suggesting to the imagination the impression of space by the use of obliterations and blank spaces, which is a common feature of Japanese painting. In the finished garden there are five principal hills, with hill number one forming the main feature of the nearer distance. It should have broad sweeping sides. Adjacent to hill number one should be placed hill number two, which is somewhat smaller and different in character, with the space between the two usually having rock formations and a cascade. Upon the opposite side of hill number one is placed hill number three, slightly more to the foreground so as to suggest a lower hill divided from the principal mountain by a valley. In the near foreground is hill number four, which is smaller and with none of the characteristics of the larger mountains, since it should be low and rounded and contain a fair amount of detail in the form of rocks and plants. In the remotest part of the garden is hill number five, which is steep and has very little detail because it represents a mountain of great distance with a feeling of mystery.

In contrast to the hill garden is the *hira-niwa*, or flat garden, in which rocks, and shrubs of rounded form, are sometimes grouped so as to suggest mountain scenery. *Hira-niwa* gardens are supposed to represent either a mountain valley or a sea-coast scene, sometimes with groups of rocks arranged to suggest islands in the sea. The level portions of Japanese gardens have frequently made use of turf in more recent times; however, these portions were formerly finished with hard-packed earth or covered with white sand or finely broken shells, while the hills were partly covered with different varieties of moss. Each of the component parts of the garden is carefully placed to suggest the desired natural scene or the sentiment to be expressed in the composition in keeping with the desired religious or secular thought. Most of the delicate sensibility expressed by certain features of a garden derives from the thoughts and works of sages, poets, and philosophers, who not only practiced the accomplished arts, but were the

Garden of the Samboin monastery at Kyoto, showing a part of the pond containing several islands connected by bridges in a variety of designs. Momoyama period (1573-1615).

chief patrons. Just as the traditional beliefs possess ideal moral qualities, the æsthetic principles governing the art of Japanese gardens are hardly separable from the ethics which inspire them.

A finished hill garden is not complete nor is it considered perfect unless it contains a real or suggested waterfall or cascade which occupies the most important position in the background between hills number one and two. An especially favored cascade is the one called Rozan by the Japanese; often referred to in Chinese poetry, it is near the high mountain called Riumon, in the province of Chiang-so in southern China. According to the principles of garden design, a tree should be placed so that its branches may hide the outlet of the cascade, and heavy foliage should surround it to give it an appearance of depth and remoteness. Such a scenic composition in temple gardens is often said to impart a suggestion of a famous scene at the foot of the Himalayas, renowned in Buddhist teachings for its cascade and its lake from which four rivers issue. A favorite classical model for garden lakes, often represented in the lotus ponds of temples and monasteries, is taken from a famous Chinese lake which the Japanese call Seiko. Such lakes are frequently spanned by an arched stone bridge of Chinese design called the Full Moon Bridge. According to the theory of landscape design, the Japanese skillfully arrange the composition of a garden to compensate for the limited area of the lake by hiding and intercepting parts of the contour with plants and shrubbery. By this careful planning the conception of a large lake is suggested to the imagination, as it is never completely visible in its entirety from any one point. This suggestion of limitless space by partial deletion of contour lines, which is an important principle in Japanese painting, is equally important in the art of landscape gardens. Varieties of islands are often introduced into the water scenery, bearing descriptive names according to their form and character; however, strictly considered there are only four important ones in the rules for gardens. The first is known as *horaijima*, or island of the blessed, and since it is supposed to be an island in the sea, it is placed in the center of the lake. The placing of the six rocks around it symbolizes a tortoise, with the stones representing the head, legs, and tail. Usually a pine tree is placed in the center of the *horaijima*, both the pine and tortoise being symbolic of longevity. The second island is called *fukiagejima*, or wind-swept isle, and, being a sea island like the first, it is not connected with a bridge. The two other islands are called *shujinto*, or master's isle, and *kiakujinto*, or guest's isle. The master's isle is placed in the foreground, often with a small summerhouse or shelter on it, and approached by a bridge. The guest's isle is placed in the background of the landscape and approached by bridges and stepping stones. Many motifs of Japanese

decoration have become intrinsically expressive of moral virtues. The lotus-covered lake, the blessed isle, the pine tree, the plum tree, the bamboo, and the suggested shape of the tortoise all have a symbolical meaning and convey some familiar sentiment in the art of landscape gardening.

GARDEN STONES AND TREES

In all forms of Japanese gardens the proper selection and arrangement of stones is one of the most important principles. To constitute a harmonious composition with the trees and shrubs, the stones must be of proper size and proportion to conform with the scale of the garden. Great care and unusually sharp observation are necessary to arrange garden stones so they will appear to have been placed there by nature. There are certain superstitions attached to the particular arrangements and forms of stones; tradition has sanctioned some forms as being of good omen, and others are condemned as of evil omen. Certain stones having propitious qualities consecrate the garden and are considered of the utmost importance to a complete arrangement. From very early times it has been the custom of priests to attach some religious meaning to the principal stones in the gardens of temples and monasteries, by giving them names according to certain holy functions or names of Buddhist divinities.

The nomenclature applied to the vast numbers of garden stones is of great length and of considerable complexity. Some names merely apply to the place of origin of a specific type of stone, or to its geological nature, while other names refer to the position or function of stones in a garden, such as "wayside" stone or "torrent-breaking" stone, and even in domestic gardens some stones bear the names of Buddhist deities. The names reserved for certain stones depending upon their purpose or position have not only been most interesting but also most helpful to a better understanding and appreciation of this beautiful and ancient art of the Japanese. Among the stones seen on hills are the "mountain-summit" stone, "mist-enveloping" stone and "propitious-cloud" stone, while those of a cascade include Fudo, the Buddhist divinity to whom cascades are especially dedicated, and who is always represented by a vertical stone. Then there are often eight smaller stones called "children's" stones that surround Fudo and represent the children who are his attendants. Also in the category of cascade stones are the "water-dividing" stone, "cascade-basin" stone, and "water-receiving" stone. Others used to adorn the water scenery are the "falling-water" stone, which is at the base of the cascade and breaks the torrent into a spray, and the "water-tray" stone, which is large and flat and placed in a lake so that its surface is slightly above the water level but slightly covered when the water rises. Upon the bank of the lake there is a pair of stones that suggests in form sleeping male and female mandarin ducks, which according to the Chinese classics represent conjugal fidelity. On the master's island there are the stone of easy rest and the stone of amusement, while on the guest's island are three stones whose names refer to the functions of hospitality, "guest-honoring" stone, "shoe-removing" stone, and "obeisance" stone. Certain ideas derived from ancient axioms were applied to the composition of landscape gardens, for according to the early philosophy of Japan, inanimate things of the universe possess male or female attributes, and the beauties of the natural physical features of the world are created by a blending of the sexual essences. Trees and stones were endowed with imaginary sex, determined by their relative æsthetic value in a garden composition, with the strong and stately forms classified as male and others as female.

Trees and shrubs are planted only after all the principal stones have been properly placed. The suitable arrangement of the trees, shrubs, and varieties of grasses must be carefully considered because the garden stones can serve their proper purpose only when this arrangement is completed. When a number of trees are grouped together, different species are usually selected to contrast one with another, with form and contour receiving special attention. The garden designer is always careful to place trees and shrubs in characteristic places to conform with their natural habits of growth; thus, a mountain plant or tree is not planted in a valley, or vice versa. Then again, with the exception of the plum tree, which blooms early in the year, trees that shed their leaves are not placed in the foreground. The art of pruning trees and shrubs is highly developed in Japan, and it is done in a manner consistent with the character of the particular trees thus treated. The Japanese possess a remarkable sense of the fundamental characteristics of nature's forms and have applied this natural instinct to their art of horticulture. The *matsu*, or native pine, is a tree of rugged irregularity, but the Japanese gardener will skillfully group its needle foliage into clumps having a flat and somewhat rounded form. Since the clumps of needles on the Japanese pine are inclined to become large and full, the gardener will often pluck the needles by hand, leaving only about a dozen or so in each clump. Such pine trees or branches of pine trees, having so few needles, are often depicted in Japanese paintings and also used as motifs in the decorative arts.

The formal pruning, trimming, and other treatments practiced on trees exaggerate some of the natural characteristic forms, but at the same time keep the form in the closest harmony with nature. In the nursery, the garden pine receives an extensive and thorough surgical treatment by having its branches bent or broken, then bound with cords and splints to produce a form of unusual beauty, as seen in many of the finest natural examples in Japan. Many of the favorite surgical methods practiced on the native pine produce the peculiar shapes often portrayed in Japanese scroll-paintings, such as the irregularly shaped branches with their clumps of needles in the form of discs or balls. The training of branches on horizontal bamboo poles so that they grow into an arrangement of lines and ridges is another favorite method that has been practiced from ancient times and carried to perfection in so many of the gardens in Zen monasteries. The representation of mountain scenery is often achieved by pruning low shrubs, especially those of the juniper variety, into rounded or hemispherical forms to be placed in clumps on the sides of hills. In dry or waterless gardens the branches are trained to resemble weeping trees, which suggests a waterfall, with sand on the ground to represent a lake or stream. The immense importance given by the Japanese to form and line in their horticultural art is essential to the finished composition, which relies upon the imagination of the observer to interpret its meaning and understand its beauty. Japanese gardens are so arranged that the changing seasons may contribute in rotation to their artistic quality. Nature in her changing moods, gay, colorful, placid, solitary, friendly, or tempestuous, arouses in the soul certain sentiments and feelings according to one's culture and character. By a strict obedience to the laws of nature the garden designer is able to produce an impression of some famous scenic spot, such as Arashiyama on the Oi River near Kyoto, which is believed to contain all the beauties of nature within its limited area, and whose depiction in the garden is conveyed by the cherry trees and maples planted on mountain hills.

According to the rules of Japanese gardening, there are certain positions that are considered best for the planting of trees. The mouth of a cascade is one of these choice positions, for here the tree would produce an effect of gloom and remoteness. Other trees should be planted by wells and water-basins to provide shade, and still others should be placed near a lake so as to cast their shadows on the water. Many names applied to the trees in a garden indicate their importance and function. The "principal" tree is a large pine or oak tree of beautiful proportions that should occupy the most prominent position. Second to this is the "view-perfecting" tree, then the tree of "setting sun," which is often a maple that reddens in the autumn, placed so that the rays of the setting sun pass through it. There is the tree of "solitude" to suggest a feeling of meditation, and the "distancing pine" placed with indistinct outlines partially behind the intermediate hills. A pine tree of bended form is often placed at the edge of a lake; its long branches are trained to stretch out over the water and frequently supported upon props protruding from the lake.

View of the Samboin monastery garden from the adjoining buildings. Momoyama period (1573–1615).

Ever-changing rich color effects are acquired from the many flowering trees and shrubs as well as those of brilliant foliage that are so abundant in Japan: the cherry, plum, peach, wisteria, camellia, azalea, and a variety of others, in successive order from the early spring to autumn. With the exception of lotus plants placed in lakes and iris planted at the edge of a stream, flowering plants are seldom if ever used. However, flowering shrubs and grasses are important to the composition of a garden, for their colors enhance the view during the autumn. Flower beds are considered to be effeminate in taste and are placed in another part of the grounds independent of the garden, usually in a flat area near the ladies' apartments.

Since the level portions of Japanese gardens are generally covered with sand or gravel, or in many cases a well-swept hard surface of earth, a pathway is frequently made of *tsutai-ishi*, or stepping stones. These stones serve to protect the sanded or bare-earth areas and provide comfort when strolling in wet weather, and they also form an important feature of the garden. There are certain rules applying to the arrangement of stepping stones to give variety to the composition as well as convenience in walking. A stone of much broader and higher proportions than the others is placed in front of the house to serve as a convenient step from the veranda. Sufficient space between this stone and the veranda must be allowed so that the clogs or sandals may be hidden from view when

removed before entering the house. Although a variety of stones are used in their natural shapes and arranged in an irregular formation in a curving line, cut stones of rectangular form and others which are hewn but retain natural contours are also used. The name *tobi-ishi*, or flying stones is often applied to these pathways, since their formation is supposed to resemble a flight of birds, and some arrangements are called sea-gull style and wild-goose style. A long rectangular strip of hewn stone is occasionally placed in front of the veranda, or irregular pieces of hewn stone in various sizes are formed into a long oblong strip. Sometimes the spaces separating these irregular stones are filled with mortar, or frequently with large pebbles laid in mortar.

LANTERNS AND OTHER ORNAMENTS

Another important feature in Japanese gardens is the stone lantern, which, aside from its utilitarian purpose, adds a touch of elegance. The stone lantern is of Japanese origin and was once used as a dedication object in the courtyards and along the approaches of Buddhist temples and Shinto shrines. It is said its first use was secular, by tea masters during the Momoyama period for ornamenting their *roji*, or tea gardens. The usual material used for lanterns is granite or syenite.

The stroll garden of the Katsura Detached Palace at Kyoto, attributed to Kobori Enshu. A great number of stone lanterns are used to light the paths and stepping stones connecting the teahouses. Edo period, early seventeenth century.

There are a number of different types or styles of stone lanterns, and they take their names from temples or shrines, their places of origin, or the individuals who designed them. The size and proportion of lanterns, or *toro*, is of great importance and must conform to the general character of the garden. According to the general rules of gardening, a lantern should be placed near a lake or at a boat landing, in such a way that its light may be reflected in the water. The usual height of a stone lantern is from five to six feet; however, since lanterns were originally used for practical purposes, some are from one to three feet in height when used to light such places as a footpath. A lantern should always be harmoniously blended into the garden composition by a proper placing of stones, shrubs, or trees near it. The calm and serene appearance which the light produces comes from an oil lamp placed in the light chamber of the lantern. Stone lanterns are not only admired for their beauty of form but also for their age, and since special emphasis is placed on this, various methods are used to produce an aged appearance, such as making white lichen or green moss grow on them.

Of the great variety of lanterns, one of the most frequent is the *kasuga*, which has a long cylindrical standard with a hexagonal lamp chamber and base, and a rounded hexagonal roof tilted at the eaves and surmounted by a flame-shaped finial. Two faces of the hexagonal lamp chamber are open to receive the oil lamp, while the stone surfaces of the remaining four sides are carved with a buck, a doe, the sun, and the moon respectively. There are four other lanterns of similar shape to the *kasuga*, but each bears a different name. The name *kasuga* probably originated from the carved representation of a buck and a doe, deer being the divine messenger of the Shinto Kasuga shrine at Nara, which is famous for the great number of stone lanterns within its precincts. Along both sides of the approach to the main shrine are some three thousand stone lanterns of various shapes which are lighted twice each year, once on the night of the Setsubun festival in February, and again on a night in the middle of August. When these stone lanterns are lighted along with the great numbers of hanging metal lanterns around the shrine buildings, they present a fascinating spectacle like some fairyland scene.

Among the most charming lanterns are the type called *yukimi-doro*, or snow-scene lanterns, because of their picturesque aspect when snow is falling. *Yukimi* average from two to three feet in height and consist of a round, square, or hexagonal lamp chamber supported directly on three, four, or six curved legs, surmounted by a circular roof of extremely broad proportions, somewhat resembling a coolie hat. Since the broad surface of the roof is particularly designed to receive the snow, these lanterns produce a most picturesque effect when the garden is clad with a placid mantle of snow. Among the many other types of lanterns is the *rankei-gata*, or valley lantern, whose lamp chamber rests on either one or two long curving supports placed on the edge of a lake, and the *miyagata*, or shrine-shaped lantern, having a square lamp chamber on a square-shaped standard, and surmounted with a roof resembling that of a temple. Wooden lanterns are principally used near resting shelters and summerhouses on a garden path. They are of rustic form and have a square lamp chamber with paper doors which is supported on a wooden post, and a roof made either of wood or rushes. Bronze hanging lanterns are frequently suspended from the eaves of the veranda of a house or teahouse, and frequently over the garden water basin.

Another favorite garden ornament is the stone pagoda, which usually consists of three or five stories and is similar in form to the wooden pagodas attached to Buddhist temples. Stone pagodas are often supported upon splayed legs, and with their lack of intricate detail are elegant and classic in form. A stone pagoda contributes much to the picturesque appearance of the garden, especially when placed in a secluded position on the side of a mountain. Of particular importance also are the many kinds of garden bridges used for reaching the islands in the lake or for spanning streams. Constructed either of stone, or wood, or earth and logs, they comprise a variety of styles ranging from the most elaborate to simple and rustic ones. In important gardens, arched bridges of cut stone are often used, while other bridges are simply made of a long slab of rough stone. Some of the more elaborate stone bridges consist of several spans and are adorned with beautifully carved rail-posts. Of complex construction are the wooden bridges built in a horizontal manner with a typical Japanese architectural railing and posts, with each end supported by an arrangement of superimposed beams protruding one row above the other, resembling a great bracket. Called *rankan-bashi*, or bracket bridges, they are most picturesque and typical throughout Japan. A more simple but charming form of wooden bridge is constructed with planks laid crosswise on arched beams, which are in turn given intermediate support by a trestle-like part fixed in the bed of the stream. Then there are the interesting *do-bashi*, or earth bridges, consisting of bundles of fagots or small logs laid crosswise on a framework of timber.

This is then covered with about six inches of earth and gravel, while the edges or sides of the bridge are planted with a strip of turf secured with bamboo and bound with cord, to hold the earth in place. An old form of wooden bridge, called *yatsuhashi*, is frequently seen across the swampy beds of iris. They consist of long, wide planks placed one after the other in a zigzag arrangement and supported on wooden poles fixed in the mud. When the crossing of a lake or stream is planned by using a combination of bridge and stepping stones, an interesting type of bridge called the *nozoki-bashi*, or peeping bridge, is frequently used. This consists of a gentle half-curve constructed so that the outer end, which is higher than the shore end, terminates at a point just beyond the rise of the curve, with stepping stones, high above the surface of the water, continuing from this point onward.

WALLS AND HEDGES

A variety of styles of walls, fences, and hedges comprise the enclosures of Japanese gardens. Although walls are generally the means by which the entire property is enclosed, they often serve as the boundaries of gardens. The typical Japanese wall surrounding the older properties is of great thickness, constructed of clay in a framework of heavy timber, with an elaborate wooden bracketed cornice surmounted with a slanting roof of ornamental tiles. To enhance the grandeur of these walls, huge roofed gateways of striking design are provided for the entrances. Many of these walls and gateways are extant in the city of Kyoto, among the most beautiful of which are those around the Imperial palace and around the Nishi Honganji and Higashi Honganji temples. The enclosures of gardens proper usually consist of fences, not only for the whole of the garden, but also in short lengths to be used as screens to divide a part of the garden, or to hide something considered unsightly. When a fence is erected as a screen it often consists of two portions built parallel to each other with a four- or six-foot space between, and overlapping at the point where they meet. Garden fences have been considered to be important ornamental pieces ever since they were first used extensively during the Kamakura period. The many kinds of Japanese fences are unique and most interesting, being made in a variety of materials, such as bamboo, wooden boards, plaited bamboo, rushes, reeds, and twigs. All these materials are used not only alone but in a great variety of combinations and designs, for fences and also for gateways and gates, with a never-ending diversity of design, contributing a great deal of interest to the picturesque architectural arrangement of the house and its garden. Most of the fence gates are made of bamboo or a combination of bamboo and rushes and reeds. Some very in-

Earthen wall and entrance to a garden in the Katsura Detached Palace at Kyoto. Edo period, early seventeenth century.

teresting fences are also made from these materials, and are used as screens. They are called *sode-gaki*, literally sleeve fences, and consist of a single unit of gate-like form supposedly intended to conceal some object in the garden, but actually chiefly ornamental in purpose. Usually about three or four feet wide, and from five to seven feet high, they are used principally at the side of the water basin, or arranged near the veranda. Their designs and forms are endless, and often appear in irregular and unusual shapes, with each having its particular characteristics and being known by a certain name. The water basins found in all Japanese gardens are provided for the purpose of rinsing the hands, and are therefore placed near the veranda so as to be conveniently reached with a ladle. Water basins are made in a variety of materials including stone, wood, and pottery, and their forms depend principally upon the taste of the individual.

All these important accessories of a Japanese garden, with their historical and romantic connections, contribute to the æsthetic value of the perfected composition in which the rocks, the trees, and even the waterfalls appear to be endowed with imaginary as well as real symbols expressive of moral virtues. The Japanese landscape garden is more than a mere representation of natural scenes; it expresses the philosophy, the cultural refinement, and the character and temperament of the Japanese. Domestic architecture in Japan has two important features that are by no means disregarded in the arrangement of a garden, namely the absence of symmetry and the lack of compactness, which render it consistent with freedom of design. It is important that a harmonious relationship be preserved between the garden and the adjacent buildings, and that the principal rooms be provided with a desirable view. There is no discernible division or variance of character between the grounds of the property and the surrounding landscape. Artistic taste is distinctly manifest in the manner of scattering throughout the composition such architectural objects as stone lanterns, pagodas, bridges, and rustic resting houses, for though placed with great care and design, they are disposed so as to appear as natural as the landscape itself. The natural beauty of the landscape garden, with its symbolical qualities, forms an essential part of true Japanese architecture and portrays the sentimental appreciation of nature inherent in the Japanese.

XIII Floral Art

THE ART of arranging flowers known as Ikebana or Living Flowers is an æsthetic achievement peculiar to the Japanese. The appreciation of beauty
in nature is universal but the symbolic beauty the Japanese
find in nature is unique. This concept of symbolism, applied
to their own plant material and spiritual requirements, is the
essence of Japanese floral art. By retaining a suggestion of the
natural growth of flowers and of the landscape to which they
belong, the Japanese have found a way of arranging flowers
that enables man to grasp nature in her loveliest aspect and
to elevate his mind to spiritual beauty and perfection. The
æsthetic rules on which the floral art of Japan is based derive
from a profound knowledge of plant life acquired by close
and constant observation of nature itself. The masters of the
Ikenobo school who originally formulated these precepts were
men of deep æsthetic sensibility. This beautiful art, cherished
and developed through the centuries by priests, poets, æsthetes,
and philosophers, still exercises a strong influence on the lives
of all the Japanese, and at the present time there are more
than three hundred different schools of flower arrangement.

The main principles are essentially the same in all schools,
as they derive to a greater or less extent from the Ikenobo
school. The differences are slight and of little importance. An
understanding of these fundamental principles is necessary for
an appreciation of the symbolism and beauty of the art as it
evolved in the hands of this cultivated people. It is indeed a
well-known fact that a Japanese flower arrangement following
these classical rules surpasses in beauty and in depth of meaning
any other known arrangement or method of grouping.

BUDDHIST ORIGINS AND IKENOBO

Although there are many conflicting records concerning the
origin of the art of arranging flowers, it is always attributed
to Buddhist teachings. It seems that it was received from China
together with so many of the other forms of art associated with
the introduction of Buddhism into Japan around the middle
of the sixth century. However, the practice of arranging
flowers as it developed in Japan is without prototype and is
a purely Japanese cultural achievement.

The earliest school of flower arrangement in Japan has an
authentic age of thirteen hundred years. Ono-no-Imoko,
a member of the Imperial court, is regarded as the founder
of this school. His patron, Prince Shotoku Taishi, who was
regent to the great Empress-Regnant Suiko, was a fervent
Buddhist, under whose leadership Japanese civilization made
notable progress. Ono-no-Imoko was the first official envoy
to the Chinese court representing all of Japan. He visited
China in 607 and again in 608, accompanied by a number of
scholars chosen by Prince Shotoku to study abroad. When
Prince Shotoku died in 621, Ono-no-Imoko decided to
devote the remainder of his life to prayer for the repose
of his patron's soul. He spent his days in meditation at a
hermitage with a lovely garden and lake which Shotoku
Taishi had planned from Chinese models, situated behind
the main hall of the Rokkakudo or six-sided temple at
Kyoto, founded by Shotoku in 587. Here, according to tradition, Ono-no-Imoko conceived the idea that floral offerings
to Buddha should express or symbolize the part that the love
of flowers plays in harmonizing man and nature. Within his
lifetime his method of arranging flowers was followed by
other priests, and such arrangements were called "in the style
of the floral offerings in the hermitage by the lake," or Ikenobo.
This school, still bearing the same name, continues to be the
most popular school of flower arrangement in Japan. By 1935
the nominal head of the school was the forty-third in line from
the founder. Followers still live and practice the art on the
spot where the seeds were first planted thirteen hundred years
ago. Although the art has been modified and refined by successive masters, the underlying principles have remained the
same. Each arrangement must express the nature of the plant

173

and branches of flowerless trees and plants. In fact, the branches of certain evergreens and other flowerless trees and plants, such as the pine, maple, and bamboo, are given the highest rank among *hana*. Thus the blossom itself is regarded as only one detail of the composition, possessing little artistic value if it is separated from those lines of growth which give it its character. For example, the roughness of the trunk of the plum tree is to the Japanese inseparably connected with any beauty which the blossoms themselves possess. A floral arrangement in Japan is a sincere attempt to bring a small part of nature into the house, an expression of nature's grandeur and power. One of the earliest forms of arranging flowers was called *shin-no-hana*. These floral compositions, which were of an extravagant character, were arranged formally around a stiff and vertical central or *shin* branch and were more in the form of a Western bouquet. It seems that even these earliest arrangements were triangular in general outline and comprised three main branches, as in arrangements of today.

THE RIKKA STYLE

Floral compositions, which developed under the influence of Buddhism, were at first restricted to religious purposes. Later they were also employed as secular decorations at the Imperial court. A very ornate and complicated style of formal composition consisting of pine and other evergreens together with colored blossoms deriving from *shin-no-hana* was soon developed and still survives under the name of Rikka or Rikkwa, meaning Standing or Erect Flowers. The first known treatise giving definite rules and nomenclature to the different members of a Rikka composition was written by Sen-ke, the twelfth master of the Ikenobo teachers, who died around the middle of the eleventh century. Through his teachings Rikka arrangements were brought to a high degree of excellence and in many instances became an exposition of skill. During the luxurious and elegant Heian period (794-1185) the making of these arrangements became a polite accomplishment of the court nobles. Rikka arrangements, which are six or more feet in height and require days to complete, are intended to symbolize a segment of natural scenery. Various plant materials are employed to represent different objects in nature, such as white chrysanthemums for a small stream and pine branches for rocks and stones. These handsome, artfully-arranged Rikka compositions remained in favor until the Kamakura era at the end of the twelfth century.

The Rikka style has a definite form controlled by a theoretical distribution of seven governing lines. The principal line or branch is the *shin*, meaning core or heart, and it is the first member of a Rikka composition to be fixed. Theo-

Ikenobo Rikka flower arrangement and diagrammatic drawing showing the main lines. The accessory branches are arranged around them, building up a complex composition. Ikenobo Floral Art Institute, Kyoto.

material and the individuality of the arranger, and must symbolize some philosophical thought.

In Japan the expression "flower arrangement" is used in a rather extended sense. To those acquainted only with Western flower arrangement, the word *flower* suggests blossoms only or blossoms with only so much of their stems as is necessary to make an attractive bouquet, with perhaps additional greenery to display the flowers most effectively. In Japan, on the other hand, the word *hana*, the closest English equivalent for which is *flower*, refers not only to the blossom but also to the stem, as well as to branches of flowering plants and trees retically it should be central and perfectly vertical. The *shin* should possess straightness, height, and lightness. In ancient times the pine was always selected because of its erect character. Considerable care is given to the posing of the central branch to make it appear powerful and vigorous and never weak or unstable. The other governing lines are essentially auxiliary lines contributing principally to the *shin* but necessary to the balance and completeness of the composition. In order to give body and beauty to the entire composition, additional foliage and flowers are added after the seven lines have been placed. In addition to the lines and masses, the forms of the spaces and hollows in a composition are of primary importance. Perhaps the most striking characteristic of a Rikka composition is the bunch-like nature of the design as compared to some of the later schools, such as the Enshu, in which the designs possess a more austere refinement and the open lineal character is pronounced. In the Rikka style the lineal character is absent to a great extent, although a suggestion of the governing lines is evident in the outline of a Rikka arrangement and the triangular contour predominates. The method employed in the later formal styles of flower arrangement can be traced directly to a simplification or modification of the original Rikka style, with all the superfluous branches being omitted.

The abundance of different materials which is a marked feature of a Rikka composition is noticeably reduced in the later schools of formal arrangements. Rikka arrangements are divided into *shin*, *gyo*, and *so*, referring to the different degrees of elaboration or sketchiness. The *shin* style, which represents the finished and formal floral composition, derives its beauty from its approach to symmetry or regularity in respect to perfection in balance and proportion. The *so* style is the opposite to this kind of beauty, and the *gyo* is intermediary between the two. These three general styles of composition apply not only to the Rikka arrangement, but to all floral arrangements, since they constitute the fundamental forms of floral art in Japan. A special branch of the Rikka style which is sometimes referred to as a sand-bowl arrangement was the decorative use of thick stubs and branches of trees and water plants arranged in a broad shallow basin or bowl. This arrangement, which suggests a garden in miniature, was held together by a wooden framework placed in the bottom of the basin and afterward concealed by sand, pebbles, and water. The composition of these arrangements was also controlled by the theory of the seven governing lines. The tendency in the sand-bowl arrangement was to emphasize the horizontal, while in the standing vase arrangement the vertical was emphasized.

Pre-eminent in the history of æsthetics is the spread of culture and refinement emanating from the elegant court

Ikenobo Shoka flower arrangement, which is a simplification of the formal Rikka arrangement. The triangular composition made up of three main lines is the fundamental composition of Ikebana. Ikenobo Floral Art Institute, Kyoto.

society of Kyoto in the Heian period. The ceremonial code of the T'ang court was adopted and carefully followed. Unfortunately, the constant preoccupation with details of court etiquette and dress, with elaborate rites and æsthetic pastimes, made it difficult if not impossible to cope with the urgent affairs of government. Incursions by barbarians, rivalries of great families, and plots centered around the throne were only a few of the troubles resulting from the continuously diminishing powers of the sovereigns. Gradually the administrative power came into the hands of the military clans, culminating with the establishment of the supreme power in

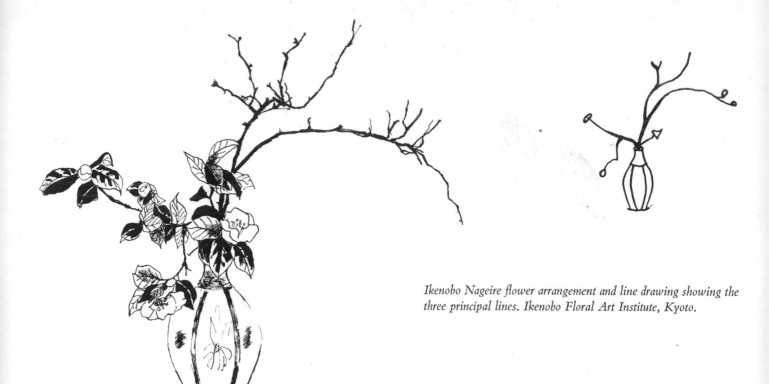

Ikenobo Nageire flower arrangement and line drawing showing the three principal lines. Ikenobo Floral Art Institute, Kyoto.

the hands of the Minamoto clan at Kamakura in 1185. The meditative Zen sect, probably the most notable development of Buddhism in Japan, had its beginnings in this age, and because the self-discipline of Zen Buddhism was especially suitable to the ethical code of the military class, this sect found strong adherents among the powerful leaders at Kamakura. According to Zen teachings moral life is associated with a certain æsthetic sensibility, and this combination of moral life with a sense of beauty makes it easy to understand how the practice of flower arrangement became an æsthetic refinement among the military class.

Because of the great emphasis placed by Zen on the affinity of man's soul with nature, a floral arrangement was regarded as a natural expression of the unity of all life. So it is no paradox that the ethical code of the warrior, described in more recent times as *bushido*, a term analogous to the English word *chivalry* and translated as the Way of the Warrior, includes in its creed the practice of flower arrangement as a means for composure of the mind.

ZEN INFLUENCE AND THE DIFFERENT SCHOOLS

The ideas of naturalism and simplicity, frugality and restraint found in Zen teachings were mirrored in the later styles of flower arrangement, which adopted to some extent terms and theories similar to those of the Rikka style but in a simplified form. The more modern development of floral art is inseparably connected with the tea ceremony. It was chiefly with the object of adaptation to the tea ceremony that the first modification in floral art took place, and the principal floral designers who inaugurated these modifications were to a great extent famous tea masters. Under the influence of the frugality and almost rustic simplicity that governed the tea-room, a floral composition often took the form of a simple arrangement of a single flower and its leaves or a spray of flowering shrub. But this affected simplicity did not permit sufficient scope for the practice of elaboration in flower arrangement, and other forms of arrangement were developed appropriate to the large rooms of the aristocracy but based upon principles which had thus been inaugurated.

It is popularly accepted that the Ginkakuji or Silver Pavilion in Kyoto built by the famous Shogun Yoshimasa in 1479 is the birthplace of the more modern floral art in Japan. Ad-

1 (Facing) Two-panel detail o, a pair of six-panel screens depicting birds in a landscape with willow trees, peonies, etc. Painting on paper. Attributed to Eitoku Kano. Late Momoyama period. Courtesy, Smithsonian Institution, Freer Gallery of Art, Washington, D.C.

2 Hokusai. *Breaking Waves. Painting; ukiyo-e school. Edo period, nineteenth century. Courtesy, Smithsonian Institution, Freer Gallery of Art, Washington, D.C.*

3 Set of four fusuma; gold-leaf ground on paper. Snow-covered willow tree depicting the beginning of spring, according to the old calendar, with camellias which bloom while snow still covers the ground. Black lacquer frames and circular bronze hikite, or inset finger pulls, with cherry blossom motif. Kano school, Edo period, second half of the seventeenth century. Author's collection.

4 Sotatsu, Nomura. Six-panel screen depicting waves at Matsushima. Painting on paper. Momoyama period. Courtesy, Smithsonian Institution, Freer Gallery of Art, Washington, D.C.

5 (Left) Hokusai. Portrait of a courtesan walking. Painting; ukiyo-school. Edo period, nineteenth century. Courtesy, Smithsonian Institution, Freer Gallery of Art, Washington, D.C.

6 (Below) Koriusai. Winter: a young woman walking in the snow. Painting; ukiyo-e school. Edo period, c. 1760-1780. Courtesy, Smithsonian Institution, Freer Gallery of Art, Washington, D.C.

7 (Right) Two-panel screen; gold-leaf ground on paper with design of peonies blooming among golden clouds. Kano school, Edo period, early eighteenth century. Author's collection.

8 (Below) Utamaro. Moonlight Revelry at the Dozo Sagami. Detail of painting; ukiyo-e school. Edo period, eighteenth century. Courtesy, Smithsonian Institution, Freer Gallery of Art, Washington, D.C.

9 (Left) Utamaro. The Niwaka Performers. Depicting a courtesan carrying a wheat pestle and two geisha masquerading as fan peddlers taking part in a Niwaka celebration in the Yoshiwara. Wood-block print, mica ground. Signed Utamaro ga. Early 1790's. Collection Charles A. Greenfield, New York.

10 (Below) Ceremonial Reception Hall of the Ninomaru Palace in the Nijo Castle at Kyoto. Paintings on the wall panels and on the coffered ceiling on a gold-leaf ground attributed to Kano Tan-yu, 1602–1674, and his school. Edo period, first half of the seventeenth century. Courtesy, Japan National Tourist Association.

Facing 11 and 12: (Above) Ko-Kutani plate with quail on a rock and peonies. Edo period, probably fourth quarter of the seventeenth century. Courtesy, Seattle Art Museum. (Below) Nabeshima dish with cockscomb design; made at the Okochi kiln of Lord Nabeshima of Saga province. Edo period, eighteenth century. Courtesy, Seattle Art Museum.

14 (Above) Imari plate decorated with peony basket and floral motif in over-glaze enamels. Edo period, 1700. Courtesy, Smithsonian Institution, Freer Gallery of Art, Washington, D.C.

13 (Left) Kakiemon jar decorated with floral medallions and arabesques in over-glaze enamels. Edo period, seventeenth century. Courtesy, Smithsonian Institution, Freer Gallery of Art, Washington, D.C.

16 Lid of Suzuri-bako depicting a rabbit in tall grass in gold lacquer on a brown lacquer ground. Unsigned. Momoyama period, sixteenth century. Collection Charles A. Greenfield, New York.

17 (Below) Lid of lacquer Suzuri-bako. Natural wood edged in black lacquer with gold designs; depicting quail in pottery, with millet, stalks, and twisted leaves in pottery, mother-of-pearl, pewter, and gold lacquer. Signed with pottery seal, Hanzan. Edo period, eighteenth century. Collection Charles A. Greenfield, New York.

(Facing) Lid of roiro lacquer Suzuri-bako. ...picting a woman with girl attendant writing characters which mean "perseverance in love" ...a roofed wall by ejecting liquid black tooth-...n from her mouth. Signed Kinyosai, Shotoku ..., 1715, Edo period. Collection Charles A. Green-...d, New York.

19 (Left) Inro. Edo period. Left: roiro lacquer inro of two cases with porcelain owl perched on gold lacquer branch with hanging rattle-board, and mother-of-pearl tree stump; signed Ritsuo and green seal Kwan, early eighteenth century. Wood and ivory netsuke of owl with young on a tree stump; signed Ikkyu, eighteenth century. Umimatsu wood ojime of cicada on a tree stump; signed Rensai, nineteenth century. Right: four-case inro of hirame-nashi-ji lacquer depicting three children fixing their hair. Signed Koami Nagataka, kakihan, seventeenth century. Carved ivory netsuke of children playing with a mask; signed Tomonobu, eighteenth century. Carved coral ojime. Collection Charles A. Greenfield, New York.

(Right) Sumo player's inro. Roiro ground decorated with elephant caparison in lacquer with pottery, ivory, and other inlays. Signed 'tsuo and seal Kwan. Edo period, early eighteenth century. Oni mask 'suke in red lacquer and carved wood dragon ojime. These huge inro mplemented the size of the sumo players who wore them. Collection arles A. Greenfield, New York.

(Facing) Lid of lacquer Tebako. Natural unpolished kiri wood with 'en "hanging objects" in bas-relief. Signed, with gold lacquer signature d green pottery seal, Ritsuo Ukanshi. Edo period, early eighteenth century. llection Charles A. Greenfield, New York.

23 (Below) Netsuke. Edo period. Carved wood and ivory netsuke of Onna Daruma; signed Minko and seal, eighteenth century. Collection Charles A. Greenfield, New York.

21 (Above) Carved ivory netsuke. Edo period. Upper left: man with a shovel; unsigned. Upper right: a yakko or samurai's servant; unsigned. Lower left: Oishi, seventh act of Chushingura; signed Rantei, early nineteenth century. Lower right: a rakan using the burning o-kyu or moxa treatment; signed Shuzan, eighteenth century. Collection Charles A. Greenfield, New York.

22 (Right) Netsuke. Edo period. Carved and colored wood netsuke of a sennin carrying a smiling child on his back; by Yoshimura Shuzan, eighteenth century.

24 (Facing) Carved wood netsuke. Edo period. Upper left: kuzunoha and abe no seimai or Fox-Mother; signed Kakuho. Upper right: laughing boy holding a jar with tortoise-shell, mother-of-pearl, and jade inlay; signed Hojitsu, nineteenth century. Center: rat cleaning his face with his paw; signed Masakatsu, early nineteenth century. Lower left: frog on a pumpkin stem; signed Matsushita Sukenaga, early nineteenth century. Lower right: gama sennin and the toad; signed Toyomasa, early nineteenth century. Collection Charles A. Greenfield, New York.

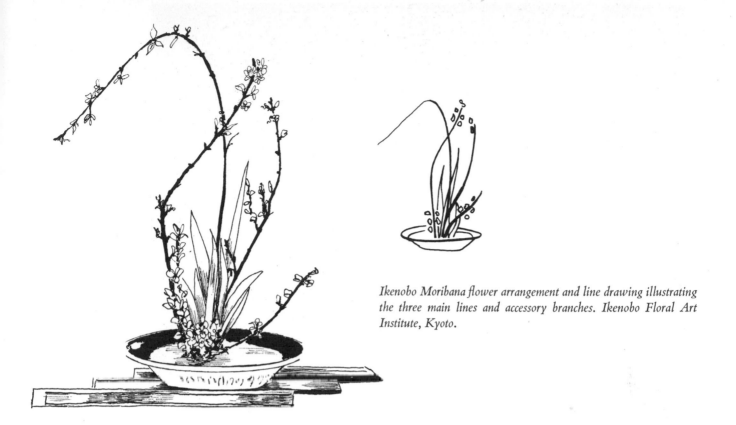

Ikenobo Moribana flower arrangement and line drawing illustrating the three main lines and accessory branches. Ikenobo Floral Art Institute, Kyoto.

jacent to the Silver Pavilion, Yoshimasa built a devotional hall containing a small room that is the prototype of the classic tearoom of four and a half *tatami* (nine square feet). It is generally believed that this was the first tearoom in Japan. Under the patronage of Yoshimasa, a man of remarkable æsthetic sensibility, the tea ceremony and the art of flower arrangement were greatly stimulated. Among the attendants at the Ginkakuji was Soami, 1472-1523, who, together with his father, Geiami, 1431-1485, and his grandfather Noami, 1397-1476, was an important figure in the history of Japanese æsthetics. Noami, a monk who was a favorite of Yoshimasa, was skilled in the arts of the tea ceremony, flower arrangement, incense judging, verse-linking, and landscape gardening. His æsthetic influence was great and his standards were

Facing 25 and 26: (Above) Kosode with Kambun design of waterwheels and waterfalls in block printing, tying and dyeing, and painting on satin damask. Edo period, Kambun era, 1661–1673. Courtesy, Life Magazine. All rights reserved. Collection Mr. and Mrs. Shizuo Nomura, Kyoto. (Below) Kosode of satin damask with tied-and-dyed and embroidered Kambun design depicting the eight bridges over flowing water from the Ise Monogatari, a tenth-century tale. Edo period, Kambun era, 1661–1673. Courtesy, Life Magazine. All rights reserved. Collection Mr. and Mrs. Shizuo Nomura, Kyoto.

carried on by Geiami and Soami. It is generally believed that the beautiful garden at the Silver Pavilion was designed by Soami. There is also a book on flower arrangement attributed to him.

As a result of the impetus given to culture by Yoshimasa, different schools of flower arrangement came into existence. But the differences between these schools lie principally in the nomenclature applied to the branches or lines; for example, a five-lined arrangement may be earth, fire, water, metal, and wood, and the teaching symbolized by them. The chief object of the nomenclature is to impart an appearance of originality and mystery to the various versions of what is essentially one and the same art. A considerable amount of Chinese philosophy, together with many traditional superstitions, such as ideas of good and evil luck, are mixed with the theory of the art and contribute to the mystery. Modifications in the arrangements made by these schools were slight and none departed very much in actual form. The main principles of the art are the same throughout, and floral designs regarded as works of art today depend as they did three or more hundred years ago on the same old canons.

For example, a style of floral arrangement known as Nageire or Thrown-in style came into use about this time and was brought into fashion by the tea masters. Japanese floral art is usually divided into two main branches, namely the formal, deriving from Rikka, and the natural, deriving from

193

Enshu school. An arrangement of orchid leaves. The center leaf curves gracefully and shows chiefly its front surface. The other leaves are kept firmly together at their base and are arranged to show portions of their front and back surfaces in such a manner that the male and female elements are properly balanced. Essentially the general form of the composition assumes a trilineal arrangement. Asiatic Society of Japan.

Nageire. However, it is of first importance to remember that although Nageire is a free and natural arrangement of flowers apparently carelessly placed in a container, it also conforms to the old art canons. To the unpracticed eye the difference in arrangement between these two schools will appear very slight, almost negligible. In fact, the more nearly a Nageire composition approximates a formal arrangement, the more highly it is regarded. One of the principal characteristics of a Nageire arrangement lies in the small quantity of plant material used. Generally the arrangement consists of no more than one well-shaped branch and a few sprays of flowers at its base.

Some of the literature on Japanese floral art gives three divisions or forms of flower arrangement, the third being Moribana, literally meaning to heap or pile up. Moribana, a much later style, is an informal arrangement and lays stress on naturalness. Very little bending of the branches is permitted. As in both the formal and natural styles, Moribana conforms to the age-old standards. Although there are various kinds of Moribana arrangements, determined by the shape of the container and the plant material used, they are usually made in flat dish-like or bowl-like receptacles, which may be round, oval, or irregular in shape, with the arrangement suggesting natural landscape scenery. The amount of water visible in such arrangements is dependent on the season.

During the peaceful era of the Tokugawa Shogunate flower arrangement continued to flourish. New schools came into existence but there was considerable similarity in their results. The polite pastime of Ikebana was no longer confined to priests and court nobles, but became an accomplishment of all classes of people. By the time of the Meiji Restoration in 1868, almost every household had at least one member adept in making a flower arrangement. The best compositions display a bold and vigorous quality essentially identifiable with a masculine touch. Both in flower arrangement and in the tea ceremony men have always played the leading role. However, with the Meiji Restoration and the partial emancipation of women, many new schools were founded by women, although men continue to be the leading practitioners of this art. As a result of the influence of the West, which has swept over Japan since the end of the nineteenth century, new schools are always coming into existence to meet the new requirements for Western-style rooms where a tokonoma is not available. Some of these ultramodern schools have entirely disregarded the traditional principles, and they use the square or the circle for the general outline instead of the triangle, and delight in using even numbers. But even these very advanced schools almost unconsciously follow the laws of natural growth and emphasize beauty of line.

PRINCIPLES OF COMPOSITION

The balance and beauty of lines in the open lineal character given to a Japanese floral design is the distinguishing feature of Japanese flower arrangement. Far greater stress is placed on beauty of line than on harmony of color. Various plant materials are used to produce a linear composition which in the language of line conveys an unmistakable impression of the natural process of growth and the life-rhythm of the plants. This appreciation for lines of motion imbues Japanese floral designs with a living quality, so they are not simply groups of flowers detached from their parent stems, soon to fade. An analysis of Japanese flower arrangement reveals that the directions taken by the governing lines of each group of stems or branches, which are founded on principles of proportion and harmony displayed by nature in many creations, form the basis of all flower compositions. Technically the surface of the water in which the flowers are placed is regarded as the soil from which the plant material is to spring, and it is therefore necessary for the arranger to convey the impression of a strong and vigorous origin in accordance with the law of natural growth. Any feeling of weakness must be carefully avoided in the springing lines, which must leave the mouth of the container as a growing single unit, like the trunk of a tree. In the arrangement of the principal lines of a composition from the point of their separation, the designer carefully avoids a symmetrical distribution and aims rather to obtain a more subtle balance through a pleasing variety of forms. To achieve harmony and balance without resorting to symmetry requires a special genius, and the Japanese happily possessed the imagination to develop this peculiar but very characteristic type of asymmetrical design. In a flower composition care should be taken to use an odd number of branches or flowers, of which no two should ever be the same height. In addition to the lines of the branches and stems, the form and different surfaces of the leaves and the distribution of the buds and blossoms receive an equal share of attention and play their allotted parts in each floral design.

The lines of each stem, or more correctly the governing lines of each group of stems, are given primary attention. There are usually from three to seven governing lines, although compositions of one or two lines as well as of more than seven are sometimes made. The triple or three-lined arrangement is much favored and may be taken as the original model for all arrangements. Although various names, such as heaven-earth-man or spiritual truth-harmonizer-material substance, are applied to these three cardinal lines, they may be simply called principal, secondary, and tertiary. These three lines may contain only one branch or many. The principal, which is the longest and most central line, determines

Enshu school. An arrangement of bamboo combined with Nuphar japonicum *in a bronze sand-bowl. The arrangement is a double one, which sometimes occurs in such a broad flat vessel. The materials are placed side by side and are detached at the base. Because of the character of the thick-stemmed bamboo, the vertical tubes are cut off with a splice cut. The leaf branches which are attached are distributed to suggest a trilineal composition. The other arrangement of* Nuphar japonicum *reveals seven leaves and two flowers, with the longest leaf taking the position of the principal line and showing mainly its front surface. The remaining leaves are carefully distributed as supports, their front and back surfaces being judiciously balanced. Asiatic Society of Japan.*

195

Enshu school. An arrangement of a white plum branch in a broad flat bronze basin. The composition is trilineal. The secondary or soe branch is treated as a streamer and dips into the water of the vessel. Such an arrangement is called the "water-diving plum." Asiatic Society of Japan.

Enshu school. An arrangement in a bamboo vase with three openings. At the top is a trilineal composition of flowering narcissus. The middle arrangement is a trilineal composition of flowering narcissus. Beneath is a three-stemmed arrangement of chrysanthemum having five flowers. The plants represented are tree, water, and land plants respectively. Asiatic Society of Japan.

the shape and size of the arrangement, with all other lines being in fixed proportion to it. Regardless of the general shape of the principal branch, to achieve proper balance the tip of the main branch should be directly above the point where that branch springs from the container. The secondary is the intermediate or harmonizing line and the tertiary is the shortest line. Theoretically, the secondary is one-half and the tertiary is one-fourth the length of the principal. Although the curves of these lines vary in the different designs, as a general rule the secondary has a more vertical tendency and the tertiary a more lateral one. By changing the direction and giving a different character to the curves of these three main branches, an almost endless variety of designs may be created. In a five-line arrangement two additional lines are used, namely the support placed between the principal and secondary and the sub-principal placed between the principal and

tertiary. In a seven-line arrangement the two extra members are the sidepiece placed between the support and the secondary, and the trunk piece placed between the sub-principal and the tertiary.

The general form of these three-, five-, or seven-line compositions depends chiefly on the amount of curvature given to the principal. In schools displaying little affectation this curvature is slight, but in a school such as the Enshu, which is characterized by a high degree of artificiality, the principal or central stem is given a bold lateral curvature from a point about three inches above the "springing" and then a reverse curve so that the upper extremity is vertically above the base, thus maintaining its center of gravity. In a broad sense the general form of the curvature may be compared to a bow when it is strung. When it is necessary to lower the height of a composition, the lateral curvature of the principal is made

Enshu school. An arrangement o, shochikubai or the favorite combination of pine, bamboo, and plum treated in a fanciful manner. The pine and plum branches are arranged in a cylinder-shaped vase of natural bamboo with a small sprout attached to it. In this composition the pine forms the principal and tertiary lines and the plum forms the secondary line and augments the principal. Asiatic Society of Japan.

more pronounced and the directions of the other governing lines are correspondingly changed to obtain proper lineal balance and harmony. Regardless of the amount of the curvature, the general direction of the principal line is vertical, and if the three governing lines in such a style of composition were enclosed in a triangle, the hypotenuse would be vertical.

There is, however, another style of composition used in a large class of flower arrangements in which the three governing lines are enclosed in a triangle whose hypotenuse is horizontal, giving a horizontal or almost horizontal direction to the principal line. This style is mainly employed for compositions arranged in either hanging vessels or standing vessels on high shelves, the idea being to suggest floral growth projecting laterally on the edge of a cliff. It often happens in this style of composition that one of the two auxiliary lines

on the side toward which the principal bends is given a noticeable droop and is lengthened proportionately to accentuate the droop. This droop is known as a streamer and only one occurs in a composition, as similarity is at all times avoided. When five- or seven-line compositions are desired, the extra auxiliary lines are added. Although flower compositions are designed to be seen principally from one point of view, namely, in front of the tokonoma, all the governing lines of a composition have directions of varying degrees forward and backward in addition to the vertical and lateral directions already mentioned. This avoids any tendency to flatness and gives some consideration to the over-all effect from points to the right and left.

In arranging the lines of a composition there are certain errors which are to be avoided. One of these is referred to as cross-cutting, which occurs when two different lines intersect one another. Window-cutting and lattice-cutting are other errors; in the former the branches cross in curves to form looped openings, while in the latter the crossings suggest latticework. Correctly arranged, a floral composition is not only a thing of beauty but an expression of living flowers. Although some highly artificial compositions in which the material has been much bent and twisted may exaggerate the features peculiar to a plant and almost caricature it, they do suggest most vividly the feeling of natural growth. It is this portrayal of natural growth suggesting the life rhythm of the plant that the Japanese endeavor to present in their floral compositions, rather than a faithful copy of nature.

No flower or plant is too humble to be used, a thing of beauty being possible with the most commonplace materials. In choosing the plant material the seasonal factor is an important consideration. Flowers forced to blossom out of season are in most instances not used. Each flower has its proper season and month. Many flowers are common to several months or seasons, and certain distinctive characteristics occur during the various seasons of their growth, such as an unusual bend or vitality to the leaves. When making a composition of such flowers, it is necessary to keep these distinctions in mind and express them in the arrangement. Then, too, the character of the season must be represented as much as possible in a floral composition. For example, a spring arrangement should be simple and vigorous, suggesting the growth of young plant life, while a summer arrangement should be profuse and luxuriant. A fall arrangement sometimes includes a broken branch or a dried seed pod to suggest the coming cold season. Evergreen branches are much favored for a winter arrangement, which should be relatively sparse. In all Japanese flower arrangements the number of flowers are relatively few, but each flower is shown to its best advantage.

The idea of applying sex to plants and trees and to inanimate stones and rocks in a Japanese garden is a rather common fancy and it is also applied in several ways to leaves and flowers in a floral composition. This distinction is not so much one of individual form as of forms in contrast or in combination, regarded as male and female with respect to each other. For example, rocks of a different character placed side by side in a garden become male and female, but if used individually they have no sex. The observance of such capricious fancies is not without value in the arts of design because they help to create a harmony of well-balanced contrasts. In a floral arrangement the front and back of leaves, which are male and female respectively, are given careful consideration, especially when the leaves are large and important, the purpose being to achieve well-balanced masses by twisting and turning the leaves so that both surfaces are alternately displayed. In flowers the buds are regarded as female and the flower in full bloom as male. Colors of flowers also have sex; red is a favorite masculine color and white a favorite female color.

THE MATERIALS AND VESSELS USED

Flower arrangements are made with one species of tree or plant alone or by combining two or more species. Although in the early Rikka style many kinds of flowers were combined in one composition, in the succeeding styles the number was considerably reduced. Combinations of two or three species are still rather common, particularly in those vessels having two or three openings, such as certain bamboo vessels with a top and two side openings. In all compositions, either single or combined, the special nature and character of the materials used are carefully observed and followed. The rules governing any Japanese flower arrangement presume that the arranger possesses an intimate knowledge of plant growth. The distinction between trees and plants and between land and water plants is scrupulously observed. The locality of growth,

Above: Enshu school. An arrangement of Nuphar japonicum comprising seven leaves and two flowers in a fancy bronze vase with a fish-shaped base. The principal leaf reveals its front surface and the remaining leaves reveal both their front and back surfaces in a carefully balanced composition. Asiatic Society of Japan.

Below: Enshu Nageire. An informal hanging arrangement of clematis with two flowers placed in an iron gourd-shaped vase hooked to the pillar of the tokonoma. The simplicity of the arrangement is especially suitable for a small tea room. Asiatic Society of Japan.

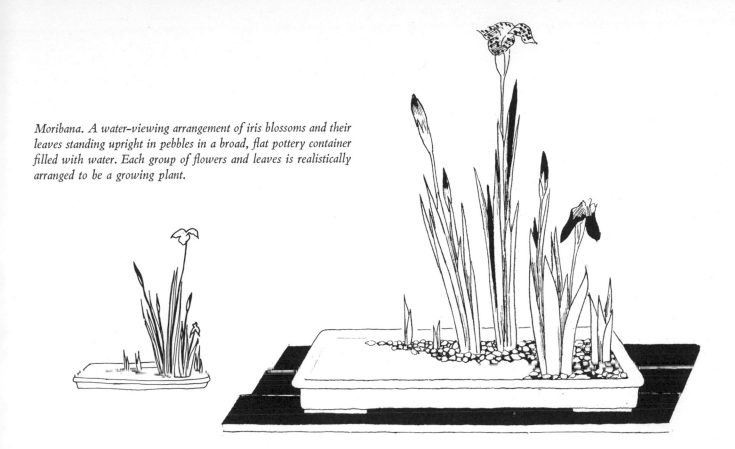

Moribana. A water-viewing arrangement of iris blossoms and their leaves standing upright in pebbles in a broad, flat pottery container filled with water. Each group of flowers and leaves is realistically arranged to be a growing plant.

whether mountain, plain, or water, has considerable influence on the arrangement and the character of the design employed. For example, water plants are never combined with land plants, and they are arranged in a different manner and with different surroundings than land plants. To arrange flowers that grow on mountains with those that grow on the plains would be considered inappropriate. A plant growing at the foot of a tree must be given a position in a floral composition lower than a tree branch. Blossom-bearing trees and flowering plants are treated as quite distinct in character. Thus one can readily understand the need on the part of the arranger for a proper knowledge and familiarity with the natural characteristics of plant material, and why exotic plants about which little is known are carefully avoided by the Japanese.

Closely associated with the nature of a floral arrangement is the form of vessel used. A flower composition must always be in harmony with the vase in which it is contained. The vase should be less conspicuous than its contents, both in color and design. In a general sense Japanese flower vessels may be divided into three types: the standing type placed on a dais, table, or shelf; the hanging variety, familiarly known as hooked vessels, fastened either to a wall or pillar; and those suspended by chains or cords from a ceiling or beam. These vessels vary greatly in size, shape, and material. The ordinary wide-mouth standing vase, generally made of bronze and in

almost endless number of shapes, varies from a shallow saucer-like vessel to one of trumpet shape, usually supported on short legs or sometimes on a decorative base in the form of rocks, waves, or an animal grouping. Occasionally these bronze vessels are of considerable height and have a long and wide neck with a round or oval-shaped body. Broad and shallow flower tubs and bowls furnish another related category of standing vessels, and were used from relatively early times for arranging plants and trees associated with water. Properly they were used for the arrangement of water plants and grasses, although very often plants and trees growing on the banks of streams and lakes were permitted, suggesting a scene along the edge of the water. There are two principal types: the sand bowl and the horse tub. The latter is correctly made of lacquered wood and is circular in plan, while the sand bowl is usually of bronze or porcelain and is commonly oblong or polygonal and sometimes oval in plan. Each type contains a layer of pebbles or sand covered with water. In these arrangements water is regarded as a part of the composition and is plainly visible. Sand-bowl and tub arrangements are much favored in the warm months when the sight of water has a cooling or refreshing effect.

Baskets of woven bamboo or reed are another popular type of standing receptacle for flowers. Of Chinese provenance, they are generally believed to have been first used by Yoshimasa. Essentially there are two principal shapes: the basket with a bail handle and the basket with a straight neck and no handle. In addition to these two classic models, there are other decorative standing forms, as well as certain shapes designed particularly for hanging, such as a gourd shape. With the exception of the woven flower baskets, all standing vessels are properly placed on a thin flat tray made of polished or lacquered wood. Sometimes a decorative stand or very low table is substituted for the tray. According to tradition, the custom of dispensing with trays for flower baskets is due to Yoshimasa, who was so pleased with the elegant simplicity of the woven basket presented to him by a Chinese craftsman that he ordered it to be placed on the dais without any tray because he did not wish to detract from the character of the basket.

Also attributed to Yoshimasa's patronage is the use of bamboo vessels for flower receptacles. It appears that the earliest form was simply a bamboo cylinder with the bottom closed by a bamboo node. There are more than forty principal shapes of bamboo standing and hanging vases, which are largely made possible by the facility with which bamboo can be cut into different shapes. Side openings, sometimes at different levels, and portions of the side cut out from the top are especially typical. The invention of the majority of these different shapes is usually attributed to different tea masters.

According to tradition, Sen-no-Rikyu, a celebrated tea master, was the first man to use a bamboo vase for flower arrangement. A striking and highly decorative form of standing vessel is the flower chariot, which often figures prominently in paintings on screens and other decorative objects. It appears that the idea for these chariots was inspired by the large tubs profusely filled with flowers drawn upon richly decorated wheeled chariots used in certain festivals. Especially typical are the black-lacquered flower chariots enriched with silver fittings.

Floral compositions in the hanging or so-called hooked vessels are arranged in a horizontal direction, suggesting flowers over a cliff. In most instances the shape of the bottom conveys the method of use. The hanging bamboo variety is most frequently characterized by narrow side openings. Other hanging bamboo vessels are often made from the irregular root of the bamboo, and their name is derived from their supposed resemblance to certain natural forms, such as a conch shell or gourd. These curious and irregular forms are greatly favored for the tearoom, where rustic simplicity both in floral composition and vessel is highly esteemed. To provide a decorative background for the hooked variety, pillar tablets about three or four feet in length and four inches in width are very often hung between the vase and the pillar. As a rule these tablets

Moribana. A water-viewing arrangement of lotus blossoms in a broad shallow white pottery vessel. Water-viewing arrangements are much favored as summer compositions. In this particular composition the seed pod, flower, and bud are employed, representing the past, present, and future, the three phases of human life.

are oblong, taper toward the top, or have slightly curving sides extending from the top to the bottom. The early tablets, which were lacquered black, were inscribed with a poem in gold characters.

The third class of vessel is the suspended vessel. Belonging to this category is the popular crescent-shaped vessel, made of pottery or bronze, and suspended by a single chain. Most suspended vessels, however, are of a horizontal character and require additional supporting chains. Especially characteristic of these elongated vessels are some resembling a boat, of which the early ones are generally believed to have been made of bronze. Some of the more ambitious ones were copied from the elaborate pleasure boats. Boat-shaped vessels are always hung above eye level so that the water is not visible, which would suggest a leaking boat and therefore be unlucky. The most familiar boat-shaped vessels are those made of a tube of bamboo with the ends splayed to resemble a simple boat or punt. In these vessels the tips of the main part of the floral arrangement are well within the triangle formed by the supporting chains, and the tip of the central stem is directly under the apex. Only the streamer, if used, is outside the triangle, sweeping over the side to represent the single long oar which the Japanese use to propel boats. Floral arrangements of a nautical character, such as a becalmed or swiftly moving sailing ship, are particularly interesting. Certain rules are employed to convey by the lines of the flowers and stems the mast, oar, and general motion of a ship. The central flower stem represents the mast; the other lines suggest the sails, and the streamer suggests the single oar. In a "homeward-bound" or *iri-fune* boat arrangement, which expresses the wish for the return of a friend, the prow of the vessel may point either toward the right or left, and each school of flower arrangement decides which one it prefers. The "outward-bound" or *de-fune* boat arrangement, which expresses farewell, is the reverse of the *iri-fune*. For a "homeward-bound" arrangement, the masters of the Ikenobo school point the prow to the right and the streamer sweeps to the left toward the stern, and this is reversed for the "outward-bound" arrangement. The plant material in the "in-port" or *tomari-fune* arrangement is of a rather straight nature, conveying the idea of no wind or motion. Well buckets, either circular or square, are still another form of hanging vessel. There are also some hanging vessels of a more novel nature, such as inverted bronze parasols and bells and sea shells.

The proper place for displaying a floral composition is the tokonoma, which, as we have seen, is found in all important rooms of the Japanese house and is the center of interest. It owes its æsthetic significance chiefly to the habit of Zen priests and tea masters of placing in it a picture or vase of flowers. In the tokonoma the host exhibits his choicest treasures, which are shown for a short time and then replaced by others. As a rule the seasonal factor influences the selection of objects displayed. On the back wall of the tokonoma is hung the kakemono. The flower arrangement is placed on the dais or floor of the tokonoma toward the front and side of the kakemono. When a hanging arrangement is used, it is either suspended by chains from the ceiling or is hooked to the pillar of the alcove. General rules are established for the size and position of the flower arrangement in relation to the kakemono, and for the methods of harmoniously combining these two kinds of decoration. When a long kakemono is exhibited, the floral composition is kept low, so as not to obscure any part of the picture. In all cases the signature of the artist, any calligraphy, and the faces of figures must be visible. When the kakemono is the work of a celebrated poet or painter, a flower arrangement is generally omitted, to allow undivided attention to the work of art.

It is important that the floral design should harmonize with the character of the picture. When it is necessary to use the same flowers in a composition that appear in the kakemono, the floral design should be subordinated, so as not to detract from the work of the artist. If a poem is inscribed on the kakemono, the floral design should, if possible, correspond to the subject of the poem. A marked feature is the supposed association always existing between the picture and the floral composition. For example, if a painting depicts a landscape with mountains and a lake, an arrangement of a water plant is most suitable, for it may be supposed to exist in the foreground of such a landscape. Popular traditions based on associations are also observed. For example, if the artist whose work appears on the kakemono is known to admire cherry blossoms, an arrangement of them is most appropriate. The many double associations appearing in Japanese art motifs deriving from the animal and vegetable kingdom, such as the lion and the peony, are also faithfully kept in mind.

Occasionally small floral arrangements are placed on the tier of shelves called *tana*, in the recess adjoining the tokonoma. Properly, if three arrangements are used they should follow the natural distribution of growth found in real scenery. The so-called hill, plain, and water style, a triple arrangement representing natural scenery, is most characteristic and is also used for the bamboo vase with a mouth and two side openings. Thick tree branches representing a mountain are used for the top, land plants for the middle, and water plants for the bottom. In addition to the flower arrangements placed in the tokonoma and on the *tana* shelves, other novel arrangements having no association with the permanent alcoves are also occasionally made and placed on a flower stand or hung on a flower horse, the latter comprising two side posts and a top crosspiece. The typical flower stand has two small shelves connected by vertical and horizontal framing that is lacquered black and enriched with metal mounts.

PREPARATION OF PLANT MATERIAL

The lineal character required for the various flowers and branches of trees is first based upon a careful selection of suitable material. In the formal schools, such as the Ikenobo, where skill of arrangement and beauty of line are of first importance, the next step comprises the bending, twisting, and binding together of the material selected into the desired shape. In Moribana and Nageire very little binding of branches is allowed, since naturalness is a feature of both styles. Regardless of the curve of the branch, all tips should point upward. The final step is to eliminate, by trimming or cutting, any material which does not directly contribute to the beauty of the finished composition. Before wedging the manipulated plant material into the container, certain steps are taken to prolong its life. Naturally, fresh clean water and careful handling both in cutting and arranging are the best preservatives. Cuttings are always made early in the morning or early in the evening, except in very cold weather. If the cuttings are not used immediately, some teachers recommend that all plant material except the blossoms should be submerged in water for several hours. Other teachers find that immediate immersion, except in very warm weather, is harmful to long vitality and produces brittleness in the stems, which are subjected to considerable bending. These teachers recommend only a short immersion just before use, except in the winter months when the stems and branches are very brittle. At this season it is customary to thaw the branches over a charcoal brazier in order to make them softer and more flexible. Large delicate blossoms are wrapped separately in soft paper and if very fragile they are kept wrapped until the arrangement is finished. There are two essential factors to be considered with the cuttings; namely, how to preserve the succulence of the stem extremities so that water continues to rise in the tissues, and how to obtain softness and flexibility in the stems, permitting them to yield to the necessary twisting and bending until the desired curves are obtained.

There are three principal methods of treating the stem extremities, that is, by crushing, charring, or plunging in boiling water. After crushing, some require an artificial preservative, often a simple household commodity rubbed into the crushed ends. For example, sugar is recommended for asters, powdered aspirin tablets for chrysanthemums, salt for columbine and morning glories, an equal mixture of salt and alum for poppies, boric acid for carnations, and powdered alum for flowers secreting a milky fluid. Sugar water forced in with a syringe

Ikenobo school. An arrangement of flowering magnolia branches in a trilineal composition placed in a woven reed basket of traditional shape.

is suggested for all hollow-stemmed flowers such as water lilies or calla lilies. Branches of evergreen and fruit-bearing trees require no artificial preservative; their stem ends are split for a couple of inches, or if the stems are small enough, they are crushed. To keep pine needles green and shiny, they are frequently washed with a mixture of sulfur or gamboge and size. The stem ends of certain plants characterized by woody and sturdy stems may be treated either by charring or plunging in boiling water. Included among the plants especially suitable for these two methods are the aster, azalea, chrysanthemum, hydrangea, and peony. When either of these methods is used, the entire branch is wrapped in cloth or paper, exposing only the stem end. About one-half inch of the stem end is plunged into boiling water for about two minutes. Afterward, the branch is unwrapped and held upside-down, and cold clean water is poured over the entire branch for several minutes.

Considerable care and skill are required to make the artificial curves especially associated with the formal floral composition. Some stems are more flexible and will bend without snapping, while the more brittle and harder stems require special treatment. In most instances a cloth is wrapped around the stem at the point of bending to prevent splintering. Sometimes the stem at the point of bending is either softened with boiling water or gradually warmed over a low fire. Occasionally it is carefully shaved with a knife. In order to avoid unsightly angles, the stem is generally bent at several points, which produces a smooth and shapely curve. After any forcible bending, it is recommended to dip that part of the stem in cold water, which destroys the elasticity and makes the curve permanent.

One of the most difficult steps relating to the manipulation of plant material is the fixing of the stems in the container, for which many kinds of fasteners or plant holders are used. The stems must leave the mouth of the container as a growing unit, which requires firm and skillful fixing. An early type of fastener used for a vase with a cylindrical mouth was in the form of a cylindrical piece of wood with a wedge-shaped slit wide enough to hold the stems. Perhaps the most common types are simply the fork of a branch or two twigs forming an X-shape, with other twigs pressed in at right angles to hold the stems and branches upright. All of these fasteners are fixed just beneath the surface of the water and should not be visible. A characteristic form for sand bowls and other flat-shaped receptacles is made of a sheet of metal with rows of upright nails or holes of different diameter. These are concealed beneath the sand or pebbles. There are also the many decorative metal plant holders, in the form of crabs, tortoises, or dragons, which are intended to be visible and are used in shallow receptacles.

SYMBOLIC MEANINGS AND ATTRIBUTES

An instinctive love of symbolism is a fundamental Japanese characteristic. It seems to be practically impossible for them to admire flowers simply as flowers. Instead, they regard them as a medium for expressing some mental concept. The Japanese are always searching for the hidden meaning behind the

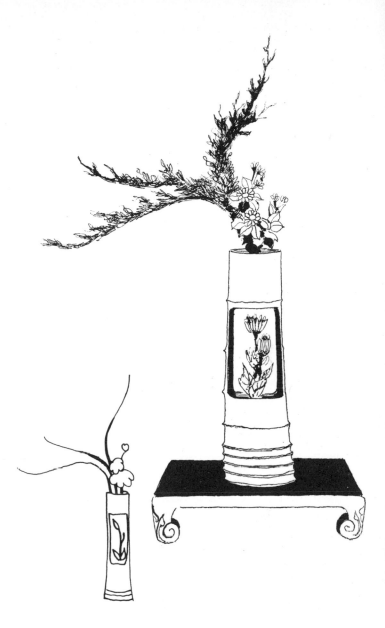

Ikenobo school. An arrangement in a bamboo vase with two openings. At the top is a trilineal composition of cypress and small pink chrysanthemums. The lower composition comprises three small yellow chrysanthemums assuming the general form of a trilineal group.

external beauty of nature, and great importance is attached to the expression of this meaning. Philosophical interpretations suggesting permanent eternal ideas, historical associations, a legion of traditional fancies, and the double combinations of flowers with certain bird and animal attributes are among the flower subjects or themes which have become a permanent part of the Japanese cultural heritage and hold an important position in art and literature. The months of the year and the various deities and pleasures which custom has associated

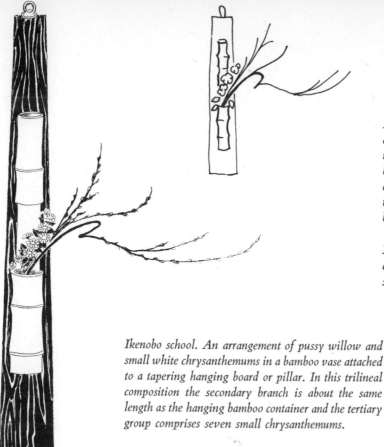

Right: Ikenobo school. De-fume *or outgoing-boat arrangement made of iris. The tips of the main part of the composition are kept well within the triangle formed by the chains, and the tip of the principal line is directly. beneath the apex. The long leaves sweeping to the right suggest the single oar employed to propel boats. In this composition they become the streamer.*

Far right: Ikenobo school. An arrangement of bush clover in a suspended moon-shaped bronze vase. The secondary line is treated as a streamer.

Ikenobo school. An arrangement of pussy willow and small white chrysanthemums in a bamboo vase attached to a tapering hanging board or pillar. In this trilineal composition the secondary branch is about the same length as the hanging bamboo container and the tertiary group comprises seven small chrysanthemums.

with them through the centuries form an endless source of material for the artist in every kind of art. Japan is rich in seasonal flowers, and almost every month is known by its special blossoms. Ordinary and familiar flowers growing in the garden and in the field have been given a conspicuous place in the numerous festivals celebrated in Japan throughout the calendar year. The flowers most esteemed are those endeared by custom and tradition and cherished as harbingers of the season rather than those known for their rarity or spectacular bloom. Flower viewing is one of the favorite pursuits of outdoor life. By a fanciful conceit a snow-covered landscape is considered to be winter's floral display and thus is one of the flower festivals of the year.

The Chinese lunar calendar formerly used by the Japanese was especially adaptable to the seasonal succession of flowers. The Japanese spring, which started with the Chinese New Year and began about February, was heralded by the appearance of the plum blossom, which opened even while the snow was still on the ground. The plum blossom, because of its duration and sweet scent and the classical simplicity and beauty of its form, is much more favored for floral compositions than its flashy rival the cherry blossom. Silhouetted against gray skies in a bare winter landscape, the delicate blossom, fresh, undaunted, and leafless, presents an un-forgettable picture. In selecting plum blossoms for a floral arrangement the rugged and angular nature of the plum tree, its straight stiff shoots, and the sparse distribution of its buds and blossoms are carefully kept in mind. An unusual plum-blossom arrangement made in an oblong flat-shaped receptacle filled with water shows the principal branch bending into and disappearing under the water and the blossom-covered extremity reappearing. According to one story, this floral design was inspired by real scenery and for that reason the composition is sometimes called water-diving plum or plum of the mountain stream. For the New Year's floral arrangement as well as for the first of the Five Seasons festivals, called the Early Herb Festival, the plum is combined with the pine and bamboo. This traditional triad known as *Shochikubai* suggests enduring happiness and is used on many felicitous occasions, especially at wedding ceremonies, if the plum blossom is in season. The so-called Japanese nightingale is also associated with the plum tree.

Although the peach blossom which follows shortly after the plum is notable for its size, color, and beauty, it by no means attains the traditional esteem and admiration given to its predecessor. The peach blossom is chiefly used in floral compositions during the Peach Blossom Festival, popularly known as the Girls' Festival or Dolls' Festival, which occurs

on the third day of the third month and is the second of the Five Seasons festivals. Many weddings take place during this month, when the peach blossoms are an attractive feature of the spring landscape. The associated idea of the peach as the symbol of life makes its use most suitable. As a rule the cuttings are considerably thinned out, because the blossoming peach branches are inclined to be too exuberant to please the taste of the flower artist.

The cherry tree, with its gay and showy blossoms, is never used in combination with any other plant material and its blossom has the place of honor on the tokonoma because it is the national flower of Japan. Patronized by Emperors and extolled by poets, the cherry blossom vies with the chrysanthemum in the affection of the Japanese. However, probably because of the transitory nature of its beauty, lasting as it does for a short space of only three to four days, it has not attained a prominent place in floral compositions as compared to the chrysanthemum or the plum. The latter retains its beauty for an entire month. Because of the ephemeral character of the cherry blossom, its use is avoided for weddings or other felicitous occasions. The falling petals of full-blown cherry blossoms have their own distinctive charm and they have been compared in poetry, where they have become a favorite theme, to tears shed by a saddened sky. In an arrange-

ment of cherry blossoms several petals are often placed in the water of the vase, and it is recommended that the petals falling on the floor of the tokonoma should not be swept away. Singly, the cherry blossom possesses no great attraction and has no particular distinction of form, but in a mass on a tree it has a floral richness of unsurpassed beauty. The wild cherry, although indigenous to Japan, is nowhere mentioned in early records before the fifth century. It did not achieve the position of a national flower until the eighth century, when the Emperor Shomu, attracted by the beauty of the blossoms, ordered cherry trees to be planted in the gardens near the Imperial palace at Nara. Up to that time the plum tree had held the interest of the Emperor and his court. From the ninth century onward Imperial garden parties to view the cherry blossoms became customary and cherry trees were planted near the palace at each succeeding capital.

The celebration of the Boys' Festival or Iris Festival occurs on the fifth day of the fifth month and coincides with the blooming of a form of iris called *shobu-no-hana*. The leaf —which in almost all water plants receives the major share of attention—resembles a sword and therefore harmonizes most appropriately with the dolls or figures representing ancient warriors in full armor displayed in Japanese houses on that day. Boys also carry the sword-like leaf, which for them symbolizes success. On the festival day, iris leaves are soaked in the hot bath, because of the traditional belief that the so-called iris bath provides miraculous protection against disease. For the festival also, finely chopped iris leaves are mixed with sake, a drink which was especially enjoyed by the samurai. Several species of iris are common to Japan; one kind, lasting through three seasons into the fall, has characteristics peculiar to each season which are carefully distinguished in floral design. For example, the early leaves are stiff and straight, while in the fall the leaves are curled and bent. Associated in art with the iris are the kingfisher, mandarin ducks, and other water birds. Sometimes, particularly in hot weather, various kinds of small water plants are arranged at the base of a large irregularly shaped stone, which is supposed to suggest a mountain and is used as the main part of a floral design arranged in a shallow flat receptacle.

The wistaria, which blooms in May, is usually regarded as the most important of blossoming vines. However, since purple is associated with mourning and since the Japanese word for droop, *sagaru*, means to decline or retrograde, wistaria is avoided on weddings and other felicitous occasions. The nature of the plant is especially adaptable to suspended arrangements, with the streamer being stressed. Since it usually grows in gardens on trellises overhanging a lake or stream, it is also used in shallow flat receptacles filled with water suggesting such real scenery. To convey the impression of landscape in miniature, stones are sometimes introduced in the floral design to simulate the edge of a large lake. The pheasant is associated with the wistaria.

The peony, queen of Chinese flowers, was introduced into Japan in the eighth century. Although essentially a favorite of the upper classes, it is a persuasive motif in Japanese decoration. It is used in combination with the peacock, the golden pheasant, and the lion, and with such companions it constantly appears in the decoration of temples and palace walls. Traditionally it is one of the three flowers to which royal rank has been attributed, the other two being the cherry blossom and the lotus. With its exuberant curly petals, the peony is sometimes known as the flower of prosperity, because it retains its beauty so long, sometimes lasting for twenty days. The leaves are occasionally closely grouped around one of the governing lines in a floral design, which is supposed to suggest the lion hiding in thick foliage.

The lotus, a water plant blossoming in the middle of summer, is regarded as the national flower of India. It is closely associated with the Buddhist religion, and orthodox Buddhists avoid its use except for sacred purposes. In sculpture and painting the image of Buddha is always seen seated on a lotus flower. Because of its association with life hereafter, its use is considered appropriate for funeral ceremonies. A symbol of

the three Buddhist divisions of time—past, present, and future—it is regarded as an appropriate theme for religious contemplation and is therefore a favorite flower of monastic retreats. Large perfect leaves with their broad surfaces of deep green and emerald and full-blown blossoms represent the present. Curled leaves not entirely open and buds suggest the future, while withered and partly decayed leaves and seed pods suggest the past. Combined with the lotus in decorative design are the mandarin duck and other waterfowl.

On the seventh day of the seventh month the Star Festival, more popularly known as *Tanabata*, is held and is the fourth of the Five Seasons festivals. In honor of the legendary union of two stars on this date, it is customary for young people to celebrate by making offerings of peaches, melons, pears, and cake. These, generally made of paper, are hung on the many bamboo branches set up in the garden for the occasion. Long narrow strips of variously colored paper on which are written poems associated with romantic legends are also hung on the branches of bamboo. Although scarcely to be considered as a floral composition, this motif is frequently used in the decorative arts.

The chrysanthemum, the principal flower of fall, is probably the best loved of all flowers and is by far the popular choice for a floral composition. A triumph of Japanese horticultural skill, the chrysanthemum is available throughout the year and is considered appropriate for all occasions, including the most formal. Although some scholars claim that the small wild chrysanthemum is indigenous to Japan, historical records indicate that it was imported from China and first cultivated during the Nara period. Recognized as the symbol of the sun, the chrysanthemum was used as a crest as early as the ninth century, but it was not until a thousand years later that it became the exclusive privilege of the Emperor. It appears often in the decorative arts, though never with sixteen petals, this form being the special mark of the Emperor. The chrysanthemum was always held in high esteem by the court, and as early as the ninth century garden parties were given at the Imperial palace to celebrate its blossoming time. The Chrysanthemum Festival, which is the last of the Five Seasons festivals, takes place on the ninth day of the ninth month. On this day a floral composition of chrysanthemums is displayed in the tokonoma of practically every Japanese household together with an appropriate kakemono. Since the chrysanthemum lasts longer than the majority of flowers, it has come to be associated with longevity. In design it is represented with the crane, also emblematic of longevity.

Undoubtedly the pine, foremost of all evergreens, is the most important of all flowerless trees in Japan, and its use in flower arrangement is surpassed only by the chrysanthemum, with which it is frequently combined. The pine, a constant

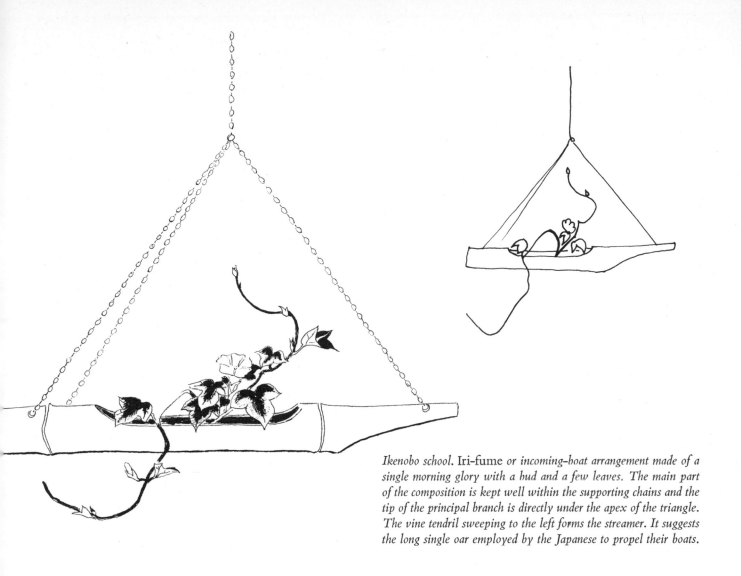

Ikenobo school. Iri-fume *or incoming-boat arrangement made of a single morning glory with a bud and a few leaves. The main part of the composition is kept well within the supporting chains and the tip of the principal branch is directly under the apex of the triangle. The vine tendril sweeping to the left forms the streamer. It suggests the long single oar employed by the Japanese to propel their boats.*

feature of the Japanese landscape, is symbolical of strength and endurance and therefore suggests the idea of a long and hardy life. Its use in floral art is considered a very good omen and thus plays an important role in floral compositions on all congratulatory occasions. Combined with the plum and bamboo, it forms the traditional triad for a New Year's arrangement. In the arts of decoration it is associated with the crane and tortoise, both being emblems of longevity. A miniature representation of these three is especially favored for a wedding celebration. The pine also symbolizes loyalty and faithfulness. A characteristic arrangement combining the pine and white chrysanthemum stands for landscape in floral design. This derives from a well-known poem in which the white chrysanthemum seen beneath the pine branches is likened to the moon between black clouds.

The bamboo, because of its peculiar character, is regarded in a strict sense as neither plant nor tree, but may be used in place of either. Properly it is never arranged in a vessel made

of bamboo. Although thin sprays or branches of bamboo are often combined with other trees or plants, for simple compositions a portion of the stalk is selected with a few leaf-clad twigs attached. The number of nodes or joints in the stem should be uneven and the top is cut either horizontally or obliquely. The bamboo remains green the entire year, and typifies the virtue of straightforwardness or uprightness of character. In the arts of decoration the bamboo is represented together with the tiger and the sparrow, but never with both at the same time. The dual association of the sparrow and bamboo is said to represent loyalty to the throne. These dual associations, which are of Chinese provenance, are so carefully observed by the Japanese that it would be deemed most inappropriate to display a painting of sparrows and an arrangement of ordinary garden flowers at the same time. It would be essential to use some form of bamboo in the floral composition. In addition to the double combinations already mentioned, some popular associations appearing in the arts of design are the maple with the deer, autumn grasses with the wild boar, and the willow with the frog.

Among many other familiar flowers and plants well known to the flower artist is the *omoto* plant, esteemed for its hardy and shiny-green sword-like leaves which retain their color throughout the year and for its berries that turn red in winter. Because the characters used for writing the name *omoto* can also be read "ten thousand years green," this plant makes a popular subject for celebrating a new undertaking, such as a house-warming. The Chinese orchid, or wood orchid, with its small almost colorless flowers is prized for the soft lines of its leaves and is found in many floral compositions. Similar to the European crocus, it has a small yellow flower which appears even before the plum blossom. Pushing its way up through the snow, it suggests the idea of the fertility of life hidden in the earth. Both this blossom and the narcissus, or Chinese lily, are prized by floral artists because they are available at a season when flowering plants are scarce. Their blade-shaped leaves receive most of the attention in a floral design. There are also the creeping plants characterized by limp and delicate stems, such as the morning-glory, which are difficult to arrange according to the lineal rules of floral art. A simple and modest arrangement of one flower and one leaf or perhaps a few leaves is especially characteristic and was much favored for the tearoom where simplicity and natural-ness were stressed. Certain flowers are avoided for festive occasions because of associations that may be interpreted as unlucky. Included in this group are flowers of a poisonous nature or evil smell or ones that change color. A prejudice exists against the camellia because the petals do not fall off one by one, but drop off suddenly, all at one time, like a head struck off by a sword. Nevertheless, the camellia is still held in considerable esteem because it is indigenous to Japan and has been used since early times, and it is also an evergreen symbolizing unchangeableness. In floral design the arrange-ment of its glossy oval leaves receives the most attention. Although space will not permit any further elaboration of the character and habits of the different flowers employed in floral art, it can be readily appreciated that the floral artist must always possess a sympathetic feeling for the virtues and weak-nesses of each member of the floral kingdom from which he selects his material.

XIV Tea Ceremony

THE TEA CULT or tea ceremony, called *cha-no-yu*, is a secular ritual indigenous to Japan, where it is regarded as a cultural institution of æsthetic appreciation and philosophical enlightenment. The tea plant, however, was known from very early times to Chinese botanists and was highly prized for medicinal purposes. It was considered to possess the virtues of relieving fatigue and strengthening the will, and to have the quality of pleasing the soul with its delicate bitterness and flower-like aroma. Chinese Taoists believed it to be an elixir of immortality, while the Buddhists used it to prevent drowsiness during their long hours of meditation. The latter custom was practiced in Japan among the Buddhists of the southern Zen sect, who established an elaborate ritual of tea as a part of their religious ceremonies. The Zen monks would gather before the image of Bodhidharma and drink tea from a single bowl with the profound formality of a holy sacrament. It is from this Zen ritual that the tea ceremony of Japan was finally developed into a secular accomplishment in the fifteenth century.

The earliest records in which tea drinking is mentioned relate that in the year 729 the Emperor Shomu invited one hundred Buddhist monks to the Imperial palace in Nara to take tea. The tea leaves used at this early date in Japan were probably brought from China by missions to the T'ang court, for it was not until the year 805 that the Buddhist priest Saicho, founder of the Tendai sect, is said to have brought seeds from China and planted them at Mount Hiei, near Kyoto. The introduction of the tea plant into Japan is also ascribed to the famous priest Kobo Daishi, founder of the Shingon sect, who had gone to China on the same mission with Saicho. He is said to have planted the seeds at Mount Koya, near Osaka. However, it was not until around 816 that the regular planting of tea gardens was begun on any considerable scale, and from that time onward many tea gardens are mentioned in the succeeding centuries. It is recorded that in the year 816 a Buddhist priest presented a cup of tea to the Emperor Saga at his palace at Karasaki on the shore of Lake Biwa during a poetry tournament that was being held there, and the Emperor was so delighted with its fragrance and taste that he ordered tea plants to be grown in the vicinity.

BEGINNINGS OF THE TEA CULT

Because of the close association of tea with Buddhism and its use at certain rituals, it seems reasonable to suppose that the tea ceremony had its origin in religious or semireligious practices. Although it is not clear whether any formalized tea ceremony was established during these early times, it appears that the enjoyment of tea drinking was often made an ostensible motive for indulging in conversations of a religious and poetical nature. Even in these early times it is evident that the Japanese attached great importance and some ceremonial significance to the drinking of tea, which undoubtedly contributed much to the literary spirit that centuries later produced beautiful court compositions during the brilliant days of the Heian period. Very little is mentioned about tea after the early ninth-century record of the planting of a tea garden by the Emperor Saga, and it is not until the twelfth century that it again becomes an important subject. In the year 1191 it appears that the planting of tea was reintroduced into Japan by Eisai, a famous Buddhist priest who had gone to China to study Zen doctrines. It was Eisai who founded the Zen sect in Japan and also founded the Kenninji temple in Kyoto, where his tomb is located. Some of the seeds of the tea shrub brought from China by Eisai were planted at Hakata in Kyushu, and the others were given to a priest named Myo-e-Shonin, who grew tea at Uji near Kyoto, which is still renowned for producing the finest tea in the world. Thus, the tea plant was introduced into Japan for the second time by Buddhist priests and

The Togudo in the Ginka-kuji or Silver Pavilion at Kyoto, which contains the historic tearoom called Dojinsai, built by Shuko, in the late fifteenth century.

tea drinking became popular among the Zen sectarians as an aid in keeping them awake during their long meditations and vigils. Eisai made tea drinking a kind of Zen ritual, and as Zen prospered among the warrior class and spread throughout the country, the ritual constituted the foundation on which the later tea ceremony developed. The Japanese also considered tea to have great healing powers, for according to tradition when a fatal epidemic spread through Kyoto during the reign of Emperor Murakami, a son of the former Emperor Daigo carved a wooden image of Kannon, the goddess of mercy, and drew it about the city on a cart. He offered prayers for the sick and made them drink of the tea which had been offered to the divine image and thus caused many to become well again.

By the Muromachi period (1338-1573) Zen ideals became more widespread and Chinese culture exerted its influence on the arts. Under the patronage of Yoshimasa, the Ashikaga Shogun, the cult of the tea ceremony developed into a social gathering conducted according to a prescribed etiquette, with which the art of incense burning and floral arranging was closely connected. Yoshimasa, 1435-1490, was well versed in literature and the arts, and on his retirement from the Shogunate he caused a beautiful villa to be built at Higashi-yama in Kyoto in the year 1479, with the Ginkakuji, or Silver Pavilion, as the main structure, where he indulged in æsthetic and epicurean pursuits. It was during this era that an æsthetic evolution occurred based upon truly Japanese tastes, and because so many masterpieces of fine art and exquisite

examples of the applied arts were produced at this time, it is frequently referred to in art history as the Higashiyama period. Although it is difficult to determine the exact date when the first rules for the tea ceremony were drawn up, the Zen monk Shuko, 1422-1502, is regarded as the founder of the cult in its regulated form. After Yoshimasa had retired to enjoy a life of ease and luxury at his villa Ginkakuji, he appointed Shuko to the position of Sosho, or master of polite ceremonies. Yoshimasa learned the art of drinking tea from Shuko and he became so fascinated with it that he made a huge collection of tea utensils and curios. Most of these treasures collected by Yoshimasa survive under the name of Higashiyama pieces and are included in many noted private collections, some being of incalculable worth. Besides entertaining his friends and retainers at tea, Yoshimasa used to reward his warriors with gifts of valuable tea utensils, instead of fine weapons, as had been the custom among feudal lords.

The tea ceremony that Yoshimasa enjoyed so much and found so favorable for strengthening his ties among his retainers through friendly intercourse, is said to have been given its first code of regulation by Shuko, based upon the information given to him by persons who understood the formalities of the early ceremony. At Yoshimasa's villa, Shuko supervised the building of the Togudo, a devotional hall near the Silver Pavilion, which contains the historic tearoom called Dojinsai. This small tearoom, measuring four and a half mats, or about nine feet square, is the prototype of the classic tearoom upon which all later ceremonial tearooms are based. A

210

Stone lantern and koshikake *(waiting bench) in the tea garden of the Rokusoan teahouse in the garden of the Tokyo National Museum.*

corridor from this tearoom to two small rooms called the *roseitei*, which were reproductions of those used by Yoshimasa for his incense parties. The tea-ceremony code as drawn up by Shuko, with its refined and elegant simplicity, was more specifically set forth in regulated form by Jo-o, 1503-1555, a tea master who possessed a strong feeling for the Zen principles of frugality and restraint.

THE TEA MASTER RIKYU

The fashion of giving tea parties, conducted according to prescribed principles of etiquette in simple and quiet surroundings, became an æsthetic pastime for the feudal lords and others of the warrior class as well as for the literati. The tea ceremony offered a calm withdrawal from worldly cares and a serene atmosphere to discuss and enjoy the cultural refinements of life. Toward the end of the Muromachi period, Oda Nobunaga, one of the greatest military figures of Japan, became the *de facto* ruler of the country, and being a devotee of the tea ceremony, made Sen-no-Soeki, 1521-1591, who is better known by his court name Rikyu, his master of polite ceremonies. Rikyu had been a pupil of two noted *cha-jin*, or tea masters, and after the death of Nobunaga, he became tea master to Hideyoshi, 1536-1598. Rikyu is considered one of the most important figures of the Momoyama period. He was chosen by Hideyoshi to remodel the rules of *cha-na-yu* and purge it of all extravagances and excesses which had

entered the ceremony after the time of Shuko. The strict rules and etiquette prescribed by Rikyu still constitute the basic principles as taught by the various schools that came after him. Hideyoshi had a penchant for giving huge entertainments both for an ostentatious display of his wealth and power and as a means of encouraging his powerful vassals to vie with one another on a grand scale of luxury so as to render them more weak financially and less formidable as rivals. One of Hideyoshi's most celebrated entertainments was the famous Kitano tea party, which was given in November of 1587. In the preceding month he had proclaimed publicly in Kyoto, Osaka, and other cities and towns that he was giving this great tea party and that all citizens were invited to attend, from the wealthiest daimyo to the most humble peasant. The announcement said they were only required to bring a kettle, a tea bowl, and a mat upon which to sit, which was a rather generous request, for the feast lasted ten days and was provided with music, dancing, and plays. It was due to the ostentatious activities of Nobunaga, Hideyoshi, and their wealthy vassals that the tea ceremony suffered a gradual decline from the lofty æsthetic standards originally laid down by Shuko during the time of the first Ashikaga Shoguns in the Muromachi period. This deviation from the high principles of the æsthetic qualities of the tea ceremony was only temporary. Under the influence of Rikyu, styles having elegant and severe beauty were encouraged in the arts, for Rikyu was then famous as a tea master, noted for his art of floral arrangement, and as an arbiter of social etiquette and taste.

211

At the time Rikyu assumed the task of formulating severe canons for the conduct of the tea ceremony, the country was suffering from a long period of protracted warfare. Despite this, the temper of the Japanese in the Momoyama period (1573-1615) was such that they loved grandeur and splendor, and both the fine and applied arts were extremely rich in form and color.

The principles laid down by Rikyu called for utter simplicity in all matters connected with *cha-no-yu* and for the tearoom to be decorated according to the severest style. After Rikyu, his favorite pupil, Furuta Oribe, 1543-1615, became one of the most distinguished tea masters of all time, serving under three famous leaders, Nobunaga, Hideyoshi, and Tokugawa Ieyasu, and further improving the established principles by returning more to the older custom. In contrast to Oribe, Kabori Masakazu, 1579-1647, Lord of Enshu province, a noted tea master and connoisseur whose school is known as Enshu Ryu, introduced a profusion of rich and beautiful objects of various kinds into the ceremony, thereby departing from the severe style of Rikyu. Besides these men, who were the most outstanding, there were many other noted tea masters, including several feudal lords who distinguished themselves as expert in the art of the tea ceremony.

Because there is a close relationship between Zen Buddhism and tea, and the tea ceremony evolved from the Zen ritual, it is only natural that its true principles and ideals are in harmony with the philosophy of Zen. The ideals of Zen regarding life and art are embodied in the underlying sentiment of the tea ceremony, especially its principles of frugality and restraint, which have influenced prescribed etiquette. Together with its religious teachings, the chief contribution of Zen to Japanese life has been in the realm of æsthetics. Zen, following the concepts of Taoism, accepts the mundane as it is and, unlike the Confucians and other Buddhists sects, tries to find beauty in our world of woe and worry. This is admirably expressed in the famous Sung allegory of the three vinegar tasters, in which Sakyamuni, Confucius, and Lao-tzu, the founder of Taoism, once stood before a jar of vinegar, the emblem of life, and each dipped in his finger to taste the liquid. Confucius found it sour, the Buddha called it bitter, and Lao-tzu pronounced it sweet. Zen philosophy teaches that the value of suggestion is of utmost importance in art, for in leaving something untouched the beholder is thereby allowed to complete the scene with his thoughts, and thus a great masterpiece irresistibly holds his attention until he feels a part of it. The æsthetic ideals furnished by Zen philosophy, such as its recognition of the worldly as of equal importance with the spiritual, have permeated all phases of Japanese life and have contributed much to her art and culture over the centuries.

THE TEAHOUSE

The underlying sentiment of the tea ceremony is a result of the Zen conception of greatness in the smallest incidents of life and the æsthetic ideals derived from its teachings. Not only did the ritual of drinking tea out of a bowl before the image of Bodhidharma lay the foundations of the tea ceremony, but the simplicity and purism of the tearoom was derived from the Zen monastery. Even the architecture of the teahouse and the arrangement of the tea garden reflect the philosophies of Zen that are forever present in all phases of Japanese culture. The traditional arrangement of a formal tea garden with its teahouse and other appointments follows certain prescribed rules for the proper conduct of a tea ceremony. The garden, or *roji*, is usually partitioned by a low hedge which divides it into the outer garden, or *soto-roji*, and the inner garden, or *uchi-roji*. Within the garden gate, a very short walk paved with stones leads to a small cottage containing the *yoritsuki*, or waiting room, usually of three *tatami* or mats in size, where the guests convene and prepare for the tea ceremony. Close to the *yoritsuki* is the *koshikake*, or waiting bench, in the form of a roofed arbor, where the guests wait until their host appears to greet them. From the arbor, a winding path of irregularly laid stepping stones,

The mizuya *(water room) next to the tea-ceremony room in Mr. Yagi's house at Kyoto.*

212

which also bears the name of *roji*, leads through the *chumon*, or middle gate, to the teahouse, or *sukiya*, in the inner garden. The small rustic middle gate is usually in the form of a framework having a thatched roof, or occasionally is just a low swinging gate made of bamboo. Along the *roji*, between the middle gate and the teahouse, is the *tsukubai*, or stone water basin, where the guests observe the formality of washing before entering the tearoom. A stone lantern stands close by the water basin, and if the tea ceremony is given in the evening, a lighted candle is placed in its light-chamber. There is another small roofed arbor with a bench near the teahouse, but not on the principal path, provided as a place for the guests to rest during the short intermission between the first and second sessions of the formal tea ceremony.

Many of these small teahouses or *sukiya* were built after the favorite styles of famous tea masters such as Kobori Enshu and Sen-no-Rikyu. Of simple and rustic architecture, with a framework of roughly prepared wood and bamboo, plaster walls, and a thatched roof, the teahouse represents a poetic impulse in harmony with the calm atmosphere of the garden and the reverence and purity of the tea ceremony. The architecture of the teahouse follows the plain and simple forms of the Japanese farmhouse with its thatched roof, and the carefully planned asymmetrical composition is skillfully

A tsukubai *(stone water basin) and stone lantern in the garden of the* Kankyu-an *teahouse at Kyoto. Japan Travel Bureau.*

The Jo-an tea-ceremony house with open skylight, built by Oda Urakusai during the Tensho era (1573-1592); Momoyama period. In the villa of Mr. Mitsui at Oiso, Kanagawa prefecture.

handled by a particular branch of builders and carpenters especially trained in the minutest details of construction. The interior of the teahouse consists of the tearoom proper, designed to accommodate not more than five guests, and a *mizuya*, or water-room, which is a pantry adjoining the tearoom where the tea utensils are washed and arranged. The area of the conventional tearoom is four and a half *tatami* or mats, the half mat filling the space in the center of the room. At one corner of this half mat a square hearth is sunk into the floor, to form a brazier on which is placed an iron kettle. The mat used in tearooms is slightly larger than the standard size used in the ordinary dwelling house, being six feet four inches by three feet two inches according to Kyoto standards. The only entrance to the tearoom from the outside is through an opening usually measuring about two feet by two and a half

feet—so small that the guests have to creep through. Although the tearoom is unimpressive in appearance, its design and materials are intended to suggest what the Japanese call *wabi* or *sabi*, which is the true spirit of the tea ceremony as established by Sen-no-Rikyu and may be translated as gracefulness, tranquillity, and rusticity. The principal features of the interior architecture of the tearoom are a small tokonoma, slender pillars made from natural logs, small windows with grilles of bamboo, and the *shoji* or sliding doors covered with paper. The low ceiling is of irregular height, with its different portions varying in design and made of such materials as rice straw, rushes, bark of Japanese cedar, narrow strips of wood, and bamboo. Despite the appearance of refined poverty, these tearooms are made of the choicest of materials and are frequently more costly per square foot then a fine dwelling.

Left: View of the nijiriguchi *(small entrance) to the Yuin tearoom at Kyoto. Japan Travel Bureau.*

Below: Tearoom in the tea-ceremony house at the Ryuko-in, showing the view toward the veranda or corridor which overlooks the garden. Daitokuji temple, Kyoto.*

Below center: The tearoom in the tea-ceremony house known as Jo-an, built by Oda Urakusai during the Tensho era (1573-1592); Momoyama period. In Mr. Mitsui's villa at Oiso, Kanagawa prefecture.*

Below right: The tea-ceremony room in the teahouse at the Ryuko-in, a minor monastery in the Daitokuji temple at Kyoto, showing the* chigai-dana *and the* tokonoma.

The tearoom is absolutely empty, except for the few things that may be placed there temporarily for æsthetic appreciation.

THE TEA CEREMONY

There are a number of ways of conducting the tea ceremony, depending on the seasons of the year and the occasions, as well as according to the precepts of different schools. Not all tearooms are built as a separate structure, some being attached to the main dwelling. The early tearoom, in fact, consisted merely of a portion of a large room partitioned off by screens for the purpose of the tea gathering. The name *kakoi* was applied to this partitioned area and the term is still used for those tearooms which are built into the main house. As distinguished from tea served informally without invitation, the formal tea ceremony, called *cha-no-yu*, is an entertainment that the host has prepared with great care. It consists of a light repast called *kaiseki*, followed by a thick pasty tea called *koicha*, and lastly a foaming tea brew known as *usucha*. A regular formal tea ceremony lasts about four hours, but only about one hour is required for an informal *cha-no-yu* where only powdered tea is served. There are various hours during the day that are considered proper for holding a tea ceremony. One is the *yogomi*, literally meaning overnight, which is held at 5 A.M. in the summertime, when the morning glory and other similar flowers of convolvulaceous vines, which quickly fade, are used to decorate the tokonoma. The *asa-cha*, or morning tea, is served at 7 A.M. in the wintertime because this is the time when the beauty of the snow which

has fallen during the night can be enjoyed with all its freshness. The other proper hours are *hango*, or after breakfast, at 8 A.M.; *shojo*, or midday, at noon; *ya-wa*, or night conversation, at 6 P.M.; and *fuji*, which is conducted at any other time than the preceding hours.

When a formal *cha-no-yu* is given, invitations are sent out a week in advance or earlier if desired, either in writing or in person, usually to the prescribed number of five guests. It is the duty of the guests to reply promptly in writing or by some other proper means, and, according to polite etiquette, those accepting will call on the host the day before the party to express their thanks. The many details incident to this elaborate preparation are attended to by the host, who gives special thought to the selection of the kakemono or hanging scroll to be placed in the tokonoma, to the floral arrangement, and to the food to be prepared. Just before the time set for the party the host sweeps the garden and its path, sprinkles it with water, sees that the tearoom and its surroundings are thoroughly clean, and arranges the tea utensils in proper order. There are certain prescribed duties expected of the guests, such as those pertaining to their costume, which for men on formal occasions should be a black silk kimono with three or five family crests on it, a divided skirt or *hakama*, and white *tabi* or socks; for women, a kimono with crests and white *tabi*. Among other things, the guests are supposed to take along a small folding fan, one or two *fukusa*, or square pieces of silk, and a pad of *kaishi*, or small pieces of white paper on which the guests place their cakes during the *cha-no-yu*.

The guests arrive about a quarter of an hour before the time appointed and assemble in a small waiting room called

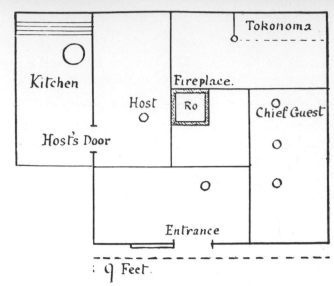

Above: Floor plan of a four-and-a-half-mat tearoom showing the proper sitting arrangement of the host and guests, the position of the tokonoma, the fireplace, and the kitchen or water room. Japan Society of London.

Left: Interior of a tea-ceremony room showing the sunken hearth with iron kettle, and a tana or stand for holding the utensils. Tokyo National Museum.

the *yoritsuki*, where they may prepare for the party. While the guests are waiting in the *yoritsuki*, an assistant to the host usually appears at the entrance and bows, then prepares a cup of hot water for each guest to drink and invites them to sit on the *koshikake*, a waiting bench outside the waiting room, where a tobacco tray and cushions are provided. The order of seating in the tearoom is frequently decided upon by the host and the guests in advance; however, the guests sometimes arrange that matter between themselves while waiting in the *yoritsuki*. In any event, the principal guest or *shokyaku* is generally chosen on account of his experience and skill in *cha-no-yu*, and as guest of honor he acts as spokesman for the others, heads the procession to the tearoom, and keeps his responsible position until the entertainment is over. Sometimes, according to sixteenth-century custom, as soon as the guests are assembled on the waiting bench they announce themselves by knocking on the *bangi*, or wooden gong, provided by the host. After the host has made a final examination of the tearoom and pantry and is satisfied that all is in proper order, he comes into the garden as far as the middle gate or sometimes to the waiting bench, where he bows and promptly retraces his steps to the tearoom. The guests in turn bow to the host and understand this polite salutation to mean that the host is prepared to receive them. As the host proceeds toward the tearoom his guests follow him slowly in single file with the principal guest leading.

It is along this garden path, or *roji*, that the landscape architect has expended his talent to create a scene of nature in miniature form which in the finest tea garden is a work of rare beauty. The garden path, which is often only a short distance from the waiting room to the tearoom, is intended to instill a feeling of calm and peace in accordance with the spirit of the tea ceremony. The carefully laid stepping stones meander along the way amid the shade of evergreen trees, carefully trained shrubs, stately clumps of bamboo, grasses, ferns and moss, and dry pine needles. Weathered rocks skillfully placed as though nature herself had arranged them in the depths of a forest or as part of a mountain cataract contribute to the atmosphere of the tea garden. Near the tearoom the guests come upon the *tsukubai*, a stone water basin near a lichen-covered stone lantern. Here at the water basin, which contains clear cool water and may be kept constantly filled to overflowing with water running through a stem of bamboo, the guests perform a ceremonial washing of hands and rinsing of mouths before entering the tearoom. This formality probably had its origin in the purification ritual performed by worshippers before the larger Shinto shrines, where ladles were provided at a large cistern which was constantly kept filled by running water. The slow walk along the *roji* and this purification formality are intended to put the guests in a frame of mind conducive to a full appreciation of the æsthetic qualities found in the tearoom and in the ceremony. In feudal times if a guest were a samurai he would leave his sword or swords on a rack provided for that purpose beneath the eaves, a reminder that the tearoom was a house of peace.

On arrival, the guests leave their sandals near the stone step, and then enter the tearoom by creeping through the *nijiriguchi*, or small entrance, and in their proper order show their respect by kneeling before the tokonoma. Proper etiquette requires the guest to hold his folding fan before him while admiring the kakemono hanging in the tokonoma, and then with the same poise and bearing admire the portable brazier or the sunken hearth holding the kettle. After showing their respect and admiration, the guests take their proper places according to the rules of the tea ceremony, with the principal guest being seated before the tokonoma. The pantry adjoining the tearoom is called a *mizuya*, or water-room, and is used for washing and arranging the utensils for the tea ceremony. It is from this pantry that the host makes his appearance into the tearoom, where the principal guest greets him and expresses his thanks for having been invited. The other guests also greet the host in the same manner and in the proper order. As their spokesman, the principal guest inquires about the garden and about the kakemono that hangs in the tokonoma.

At the first session of a formal tea ceremony an especially prepared light repast called *kaiseki* is served after the guests and the host have exchanged greetings and the guests are properly seated. The *kaiseki* consists of a few dishes prepared with the greatest care and served according to a fixed order. It has always been the custom for the host to bring in and serve these dishes himself, although he does not eat with his guests. The first dish to be brought in is a soup made of soybean paste served in a covered lacquer bowl. Then rice is served in a covered lacquer bowl. Raw fish or shellfish or hors d'oeuvres called *mukozuke* are offered next and served in a porcelain dish. These three dishes are brought into the tearoom on typical square-shaped Japanese lacquer dinner trays called *ozen*. Following the lead of the principal guest, the others simultaneously uncover each bowl by using both hands and place the covers beside the trays; then after having eaten the soup and rice, they replace the covers. A metal sake pot called a *kannabe* and shallow sake cups are brought in and sake is poured for each guest, to be drunk while they eat the *mukozuke* dish. A large wooden vessel of rice is brought in so each guest may help himself, along with another bowl of bean-paste soup. The next course consists of *imono*, vegetables and boiled fish, served in a covered lacquer bowl, and another serving of sake. Next a large porcelain plate or a set of two lacquered boxes is brought in containing *yakimono*, which is broiled fish with vegetables, and the guests each take their proper portions and place them on the inverted cover of one of the lacquer bowls or in the empty *mukozuke* dish. Another

serving of rice accompanies the *yakimono*, and then a small bowl of clear soup is also served.

At this point in the *kaiseki* the host takes away the two lacquer boxes or the large porcelain plate and the wooden rice vessel as he retires to the pantry. The next course is called *hassun*, which consists of two delicacies, one from the sea and one from the soil, the portion for each guest being placed upon the inverted cover of a lacquer bowl. Along with the *hassun* the host brings in a sake pot and asks that he may have the honor of drinking from the cup of his guests. The host first serves the *hassun* to the principal guest and fills his cup with sake. After emptying the cup, the principal guest gives it to the host to hold, so it may be filled by the guest. When the eating and drinking are over, the host brings in a large lacquer vessel with a spout containing hot salted water and boiled rice, along with some pickled delicacies in a porcelain

Tea-ceremony utensils: described as follows with the century date given: Lacquered utensil stand (eighteenth); on the top is a lacquered tea caddy for powdered green tea (eighteenth); a Hagi-ware pottery tea bowl (eighteenth) on which is a seventeenth-century bamboo teaspoon by Rikyu, while inside the bowl is a modern tea whisk. On the lower part of the stand is an iron fire pot by Shobei (eighteenth) with ashes inside ready to receive the charcoal. In the middle is the fire iron on which the kettle rests, and in front a Raku-pottery shallow bowl (nineteenth). An iron kettle by Kojomi (eighteenth) with a nineteenth-century cover. Next there is the iron stand (eighteenth) to rest the cover of the kettle on, and a modern Raku-pottery vase to hold the bamboo ladle (modern), and a pair of iron chopsticks for charcoal (eighteenth), and a Bizen stoneware water pot (seventeenth). Behind the stand is a seventeenth-century two-panel low screen used in the tea ceremony around the brazier in a large room in a house. To the right is a Chinese Ming lacquer incense box, a silk napkin or fukusa, a Sung lacquer cake dish, a seventeenth-century coal basket, an eighteenth-century cane mat, a modern feather brush for ashes, and a pair of iron rings to lift the kettle. Metropolitan Museum of Art.

plate. The watered rice is poured into the rice bowl of each guest, and is now eaten along with the pickled delicacies. This hot water is also poured into the empty soup bowl in order to wash off the chopsticks. On each guest's dinner tray are still left the two lacquer bowls with covers and the *mukozuke* porcelain dish, which are now wiped clean with the pieces of white paper from the pad called *kaishi* brought by the guests. The chopsticks, which are rested on and protrude over the rim of the dinner tray, are now pushed into the tray, signifying that the repast has ended. Then sweets are served, and the host carries the trays to the pantry one at a time.

When this first part of the formal tea ceremony has ended, the guests retire, to the waiting room if the tearoom is connected with the main dwelling house, or to a small roofed arbor with waiting bench called the *koshikake*, which is near the teahouse. Here they sit and relax between the first and second sessions in a kind of intermediate retirement called the *nakadachi*. In the second session the true ceremony of tea takes place. The host summons the guests by softly striking a gong or thick tonal board hung near the teahouse. Either five or seven strokes are given as the signal for the guests to return to the tearoom, and now the host is prepared to serve the *koicha*, or thick green tea. The guests repeat the purification formality at the stone water basin and then enter the tearoom in the same manner as before, led by the principal guest. After entering, they inspect and admire the floral arrangement which has replaced the kakemono in the tokonoma, and the kettle on the portable brazier or hearth, depending upon the season of the year. Both the hearth and kettle are particularly important articles of the tea ceremony and the host is very proud to have his guests examine them and appreciate their æsthetic qualities. The hearth is a deep, square fire-holder which is inset in the corner of the half-size *tatami* in the center of the tearoom, where stands the brazier. When not in use, from early summer until late autumn, the hearth opening is covered by a full piece of the small-size *tatami* mat. The wooden framework of the hearth is often particularly interesting, being carefully designed with simple details worked out in a charming rustic manner. The kettle is also an article of special attention, often an art object of great age, perhaps a signed piece by one of the famous early kettle makers. Fixed ceremonial rules are followed when making the fire, and after it has been properly arranged and is burning well, a piece of incense is carefully dropped onto the red-hot charcoal. In the calm and peaceful atmosphere of the tearoom the hollow singing tones produced by a careful arrangement of pieces of iron in the bottom of the kettle are poetically likened to the sound of distant surf breaking on a rock-bound coast, the rustling sound of wind in far-away pines, or the echoes of a mountain cataract.

The host now sits by the hearth with all the utensils for making the tea at his side. These articles, which are usually prized collectors' pieces, include: the *chawan* or tea bowl; the *chaire* or tea caddy; the *mizusashi* or water jar; the *chasen* or bamboo tea whisk used to beat the powdered green tea in hot water; the *chashaku* or very thin bamboo spoon used to con-

The principal utensils for the tea ceremony, comprising: 1. tea mill; 2. tongs; 3. charcoal basket; 4. furnace; 5. kettle; 6. water vessel; 7. tea bowl; 8. bamboo whisk; 9. incense box; 10. handles for kettle; 11. bamboo mat; 12. three feather dusters; 13. slop bowl; 14. bamboo teaspoon; 15. tea jar; 16. silk bag for tea jar; 17. bamboo water ladle; 18. stand for water ladle. Japan Society of London.

Utensils for the tea ceremony, including portable fire braziers, a feather to brush ashes, charcoal baskets, and ash containers. Japan Travel Bureau.

vey the portions of powdered tea from the caddy to the tea bowl; the *chakin* or tea cloth, a small oblong piece of white linen used to wipe the tea bowl; the *koboshi* or *kensui* or receptacle for waste water; the *hishaku* or bamboo ladle used for the water in the kettle; a *futa-oki* or small article of porcelain, metal, or bamboo on which to place the cover of the kettle or the ladle; and the *fukusa* or small piece of silk, two of which are used by the host, one suspended from his obi and the other thrust in the bosom of the kimono. When all these utensils for the tea ceremony have been arranged in their proper places, the host is then ready to prepare a cup of tea.

This second session of a formal *cha-no-yu* party begins with *koicha*, a thick pasty green tea which is regarded as the most important part of the ceremony. The host first brings in a receptacle containing cakes, and places it before the principal guest. He then lightly wipes the teaspoon and tea caddy with the *fukusa* he carries in his obi. He next puts hot water from the kettle into the tea bowl, using the bamboo ladle to wash the tea whisk, then empties the tea bowl by pouring the water into the waste-water bowl and wipes the tea bowl dry with his tea cloth. Two or three spoonfuls of this powdered tea for the *koicha* service, which is made from the leaves of the older tea plants, and enough hot water to make three and a half mouthfuls for one person, are whipped to a creamy froth with the split-bamboo whisk. When the host considers the tea to be ready to serve, he places the bowl before the head guest, who then makes a bow to the other guests and, holding the tea bowl on a *fukusa* in the palm of his left hand and support-

ing one side with his right hand, takes one sip and compliments the host on its fine preparation. The etiquette of the tea ceremony prescribes that he then take two or more sips, wipe the edge of the bowl where his lips touched with a piece of paper, or with his fingers, which are in turn wiped with a piece of paper, and pass the bowl to the second guest, who passes it to the third, and so on until all guests have sipped its contents. After all guests have partaken of the tea, the host washes both the teaspoon and the tea whisk. Then, in proper observance of the ceremonial, he tucks an end of his *fukusa* into his obi, pours a ladleful of water into the kettle, and replaces its cover.

The succeeding and final part of the formal *cha-no-yu* party is the serving of *usucha*, the complete service of which, with all of its formalities, forms the only course in the shorter informal *cha-no-yu* party. The difference between *koicha*, a thick pasty green tea, and *usucha*, a thin foamy green tea, is that the powdered tea for *koicha* is made from the young leaves of tea shrubs that are from twenty to seventy years old, while tea powder for *usucha* is made from the young leaves of tea shrubs that are from three to fifteen years old. The serving of *usucha* is conducted in the same manner as the *koicha* service, with all of its progressive formalities. When the *usucha* part of the second session has ended, the principal guest requests the host to allow him the privilege of examining and admiring the tea bowl, for these tea bowls are a proud possession of the host because of their rarity, some having been made by one of the great potters or artists of earlier times or having been

Tea-ceremony articles. A row of chaire *(lacquered tea caddies), two of which are wrapped in silk containers, and four* chashaku *(bamboo teaspoons). Japan Travel Bureau.*

Tea-ceremony articles. First row: hishaku, *bamboo ladle to dip water from a kettle. Second row:* futa-oki, *rests for the kettle lid or ladle. Third row:* kensui, *bowls for waste water. Fourth and fifth rows:* mizasashi, *water jars. Japan Travel Bureau.*

Tea bowls and bamboo tea whisks for the tea ceremony. Japan Travel Bureau.

in the possession of one of the famous tea masters such as Rikyu, Oribe, or Enshu. Of equal importance is the tea caddy, not only prized for age and workmanship, but also because more than a few extant ones were once in the collections of great historical figures such as Hideyoshi and Nobunaga. These articles and others are carefully studied and passed on by the principal guest and the other guests in the proper order.

After the *usucha* course and the formalities of the tea ceremony are over, the guests take their leave of the host by departing through the *nijiriguchi* or small door and return to the *yoritsuki* or waiting room, where they originally assembled. On the day following the party, *cha-no-yu* etiquette prescribes that each guest thank the host for his hospitality by sending him a letter or by calling at his home in person.

This secular ceremony of tea, with its severe canons of simplicity and its many beautiful associations derived from Zen philosophy, is reflected in the art, architecture, and everyday life of the Japanese. The *cha-no-yu* is also closely related to literary accomplishments and to many branches of the lesser arts. It exerted a powerful influence on the arts of pottery-making, landscape gardening, and floral arrangement. Its influence in the field of ceramics was so great that the majority of early kilns and famous potters produced articles exclusively for the tea ceremony. The devotees of the tea cult are not only well versed in the art and culture of Japan but also in those of Korea and China, and take pleasure in exchanging critical opinions on philosophy and æsthetics with carefully selected friends in the pure and peaceful atmosphere of the tearoom.

The six positions of drinking tea 1. Takes bowl; 2. raises it to level of forehead; 3. lowers it; 4. drinks; 5. lowers it again, and 6. returns it to same position as at first. During the last four positions the bowl is given half a turn toward the right, gradually bringing the side which was facing the drinker round to the opposite position. Japan Society of London.

XV Incense Ceremony

THE EXQUISITE pastime of the burning of incense known as *kodo* is regarded by the Japanese as an æsthetic accomplishment which creates mental tranquillity by developing a refined sense of smell. *Kodo* was a favorite pursuit of the aristocracy in earlier times and has continued to be enjoyed by devotees among the upper classes in Japan. Incense burning in Japan is generally accepted as having been introduced by Buddhist priests in the sixth century at the time Buddhism was brought to Japan from Korea. The Indian *Ramayana* and *Mahabharata* mention the employment of incense by the Hindus from remotest antiquity, in the worship of the gods and the burning of the dead. Its use was obviously continued by Buddhists as part of their religious ceremonies, and it is still used in Tibet, Burma, Ceylon, China, and Japan. It is recorded in the early chronicles that a piece of incense wood was washed ashore on the island of Awaji, where the Inland Sea begins, and presented to the Empress-Regnant Suiko. Incense said to have been sent to the Emperor Shomu in the eighth century, from central Asia, is listed among the treasures of the Shosoin Repository at Nara. The original inventory of the Shosoin lists two pieces of incense wood, one under the name of Zensenko, a log of large size, measuring over three feet in length by more than a foot in diameter, the other under the name of *O-Jukko*, a big hollow log, to which are attached old labels indicating that pieces were cut off from it and given to the Shogun Ashikaga Yoshimasa in the fifteenth century, and to Oda Nobunaga in the sixteenth century, and that the Emperor Meiji had a piece cut off on the occasion of his visit to Nara on the ninth of February, 1877.

USE AND SPREAD OF INCENSE

After these early years of the Nara period various kinds of incense were brought from Korea, China, and Central Asia; but it is the mixed incense known as *awase-ko*, introduced from China in the tenth century, that constitutes the foundation of the incense used until the present time. The numerous substances used for incense in the Eastern countries are obtained from certain resins and gum resins, barks, woods, dried flowers, fruits, and seeds. Included among some of the more common aromatic substances used in the East are gum benjamin, camphor laurel, gum dragon or dragon's blood, rose mallow, star anise, sweet flag, and several others. The burning of incense has been associated with Buddhism for centuries, and incense is used by priests for ceremonies of purification before coming into contact with a sacred image or officiating at an altar. But in the fifteenth century it also came into favor for secular purposes, such as for scenting the air of a room when a guest was expected and perfuming clothing by spreading the various articles across a rack in the center of which an incense brazier was placed. In feudal times warriors often burned incense in their helmets before entering the field of battle, as it was considered proper etiquette to maintain the manners and customs of polite society even on the field of combat.

With the increased popularity of the use of incense, there was much competition among the growing number of furnishers of the fragrant compounds. Each maker claimed such high merit for his particular products that the individual buyer learned to sample and place his own valuation on the different kinds to get the type he preferred. It is said that this custom of selecting one's particular brand is the origin of meetings between friends to test their olfactory powers, which in time developed into organized competitions for discerning different combinations of incense materials. The incense ceremony, like the tea ceremony, is a social gathering conducted according to a prescribed etiquette in quiet surroundings, and a highly moral and æsthetic form of entertainment requiring a maximum of concentration.

It is difficult to fix a date for the final evolution of the incense ceremony as a fully constituted secular ritual, but by the fifteenth century it appears to have acquired some formulas and etiquette under the patronage of the Shogun Ashikaga Yoshimasa (1435-1490). In the Togudo, the small and beautiful building adjacent to Yoshimasa's Ginkakuji or Silver Pavilion, which contains the famous tearoom designed by the Zen monk Shuko, there are two rooms called the *roseitei*, which are reproductions of those used by Yoshimasa for his incense parties. These parties seem to have enjoyed the same widespread vogue as the tea ceremony. The famous tea master Shino Soshin is regarded as having founded the incense ceremony in its regulated form at the close of the fifteenth century. It remained almost exclusively a pastime of the aristocracy until the end of the seventeenth century during the Edo period, when many cultivated members of the wealthy merchant class became devotees of the ceremony. It continued to enjoy much favor through the remainder of the Edo period, but after the Meiji Restoration in 1868 its popularity lessened. With the tea ceremony and the art of floral arrangement, the incense ceremony was an æsthetic pastime in vogue among polite circles, where this ancient triad was regarded as an institution of cultural enlightenment and mental composure. All three were characteristically Japanese and became an intrinsic part of the education of noble men and women. Each contributed to a strict observance of ceremony and a highly developed sense of courtesy and behavior in keeping with Japan's ancient philosophies and traditions.

THE INCENSE CEREMONY

The fundamental principle of the incense ceremony consists in guessing the nature and name of some incense from the perfume of its smoke. A system of strict conventions and intricate rules laid down for the proper conduct of the incense ceremony is closely observed by those who participate in the entertainment. The room used for the ceremony is usually of eight mats, occasionally of ten, and always has a tokonoma. In the eight-mat room, two mats form the center portion, with one placed across each end and two on each side parallel to the center ones, which makes the dimensions of the room twelve feet by twelve feet, since each mat is three feet wide by six feet in length. It was the custom for the game to be played with more than five contestants, and sometimes those taking part were divided into two sides. Since the game requires strict mental concentration on one's sense of smell, the host must take every precaution to keep the air free from a possible conflicting odor, and even the floral arrangement in the tokonoma must not contain any flowers with scent. To

greet the guests as they enter the room, the host takes his place in the corner opposite the tokonoma, and then the guests take their places along the side of the room adjacent to the tokonoma. In addition to the playing guests, three others take their places along the side opposite the tokonoma, as follows: the *metsuke* or umpire, the *fudamoto*, who is in charge of the counters and performs other duties, and the scorekeeper. According to the prescribed etiquette, the host retires to the small room called *mizuya* or water-room to get the various utensils for the game, and then takes his place on the side of the room opposite to and facing the guests. He first brings in the *kobon*, a special tray on which the utensils of the ceremony are placed, with the *kogutate* or stand to hold the utensils placed in the center. At the left is the *kogu* or *kobako*, a cabinet with three compartments, one each for the incense, the *ginyo* or talc squares, and the charred residue of the incense. To the right

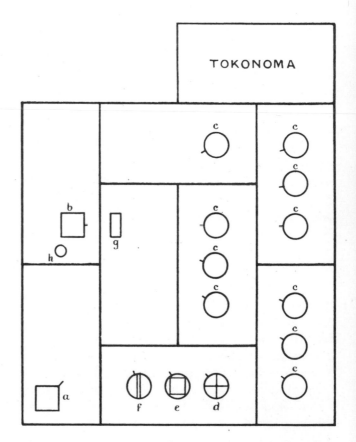

Floor plan and arrangement of an eight-mat room for the incense ceremony. a. position of host when receiving guests; b. position of host when conducting the ceremony; c. guests; d. metsuke (umpire); e. scorekeeper; f. fudamoto (in charge of the counters); g. kogu (cabinet for utensils), and h. hitori-koro, with supply of red-hot charcoal. Japan Society of London.

of the *kogutate*, on the tray, is the celadon *koro* or incense burner with three feet, placed so that two of its feet are facing toward the guests.

The next item to be brought in by the host is the *hitori-koro*, the vessel to hold the red-hot charcoal made of a fine powder of pine cones and *kurumi* nuts blended into a thin paste and formed into small cakes. After placing this upon the floor the host will then dust all the utensils with the *fukusa* or small piece of silk, which he carries in his obi. The next step is the preparation of the fire in the incense burner, a performance requiring particular skill and done according to fixed ceremonial rules. The host will then remove the cover of the *hitori-koro* with a pair of *hibashi* or metal chopsticks and take out one cake of red-hot charcoal to be placed in the *koro* or incense burner. The *koro* is partially filled with fine oyster-shell ashes that he carefully arranges to completely cover the red-

hot charcoal and form a cone. These ashes are delicately shaped with an *osaye* or silver spatula especially made for that purpose, while the tip of the cone is just slightly flattened. After this delicate and skillful molding of the cone is completed, a hole is carefully made with a utensil called the *kiri* or pointer, to provide a tiny chimney from the top of the cone to the charcoal in the center, for the heat to rise. With a pair of *ginyo-basami* or silver tweezers to hold the *ginyo* or talc squares, he places the talc over the chimney hole in the cone and, with a pair of wooden chopsticks called *kobashi*, removes a piece of incense from the *kobako* and sets it on the talc. The *koro*, with its thin vapor of perfume rising gently in the air, is now ready to be passed among the guests. Even the passing of the *koro* is performed according to the rules of the ceremony: it is held in the left hand, with three fingers grasping the base, the index finger at the side, and the two feet or tiny legs of the *koro*

Lacquered cabinet with utensils for the incense ceremony decorated throughout with views of the cherry blossoms on Mount Yoshino, with rafts and fallen petals on the river, a bridge, etc., in gold and silver takamakie, *gold and silver* kirikane, hirame nashi-ji, *and gold and silver foil on black* ro-iro. *Interior and base of* nashi-ji. *Silver mounts. The cabinet is in three stages with cupboard, four drawers, tray, and writing box with tray fitting in lower stage. Late eighteenth century. Victoria and Albert Museum.*

Kodogu *(utensils) for the incense ceremony. From left to right, upper grouping: 1.* koban *(scoreboard); next group, 2. upper, ginyo, koshiki or hishiki (talc square); 3. middle; three fuda (counters); 4. lower, kozutsumi (folded paper for incense); 5. top: kizami-ban (paperweight or chopping block for incense); 6. ginyo-basami (silver tweezers to hold ginyo); 7. pair of hibashi (metal-tipped chopsticks for hot charcoal); 8. silver extinguisher; 9. kisi (pointer); 10. osaye (metal-tipped spatula to arrange ashes);* 11. hane *(feather brush); 12. knife to cut incense; 13. saw to cut incense; 14. asaye (silver spatula); 15. top right: mallet and chisel to cut incense. Bottom row left to right: 1. celadon koro (incense burner); 2. kobako (case for mica squares, incense, and* takigara *(incense disk); 3. kogu-tate (silver stand to hold the silver utensils); 4. fudazutsu (box for receiving counters or written guesses); and 5. hitori-koro (box for hot charcoal). Victoria and Albert Museum.*

turned toward the one who is passing it. When the *koro* has been received by each guest and the round is completed, the charred residue of incense is taken from the talc with the *nata*, a wooden utensil having a sharp point, and with the *hane* or tiny brush of feathers, and then placed in the metal-lined lower compartment of the *kobako*. The talc is also removed from the cone, and a fresh piece is used for each round of the competition.

Sticks of incense vary considerably both in quality and in cost, and the perceptible differences between the best blends are very subtle, so that the players must be endowed with very acute and cultivated senses to guess the correct names at the end of a long game. There are a number of varieties of the game, each with its own formula or conventional method. Of these various types the one called *jisshu-ko* or ten incenses, played with four different kinds of incense, is described as follows. Three of the four samples are given a name such as that of a flower or something fanciful, while the fourth sample is called the "guest." Three sets are made up with each set containing a specimen of each one of the named samples. These, together with the sample called "guest," are placed in small individual boxes that are closed except for a narrow slit on the top, making a total of ten boxes in all. Then an additional set of the three named samples only is made up, with each specimen placed in its own incense box to be passed around with the smoke from the incense rising through the narrow slit, as a preliminary trial only, while its name is being announced. According to the rules no trial is made of the "guest" incense. The next step in the game consists of passing the ten boxes with their burning incense, to test the skill of each contestant. At the beginning of the game each of the players has been given the appropriate *fuda* or counters by the *fudamoto*, one for each of the three named incenses and one for the "guest" incense. The players record their guesses by placing the counters on the *koban* or scoreboards, which in turn are handed in at the end of the game according to certain intricate rules and counted up by the *fudamoto*, who then returns them to the *fudazutsu* or counters box.

In addition to the *jisshu-ko* variety of incense game, there are nine other principal varieties, such as the *meisho-ko* or famous places, and the *yeto-ko* or twelve animals of the zodiac, each one with its own characteristics and rules. Prizes were often given to the winners of these contests, and in ancient times, swords and armor were bestowed as prizes when such incense parties were held by nobles and feudal lords. Since the incense ceremony was one of the principal cultural pastimes of the upper classes, the players not only contented themselves with the identification of the various kinds of incense, but often competed with verses of poetry to supplement their score. There was a close affinity between the incense ceremony

with its poetical symbolism and the infinite number of famous works of Japanese literature, for many of the favorite varieties of incense were not only named after flowers and plants but bore names taken from the classics. Among those named after stories and legends of old Japan were the *hana-chiru-sato* or village of falling flowers; *hannia*, after a character in a No dance; *tanka*, meaning banks of mist in the springtime; *shagetsu* or slanting moon; and *hoke-kyo*, the Scripture of the Lotus of Truth, the sutra on which the teachings of the Nichiren sect of Buddhism are based. In submitting a poetical verse along with their guesses as to the kind of incense, the players competed either with stanzas of famous poems or with appropriate verses of their own composition. In this highly developed form of intellectual entertainment, the competition of verses beautifully complemented the elegant ritual of the incense ceremony.

The exquisite *ko-awase*, or incense-ceremony sets of lacquer utensils called *kodogu*, used in this accomplished pastime have long been treasured by collectors. A complete set of *kodogu*

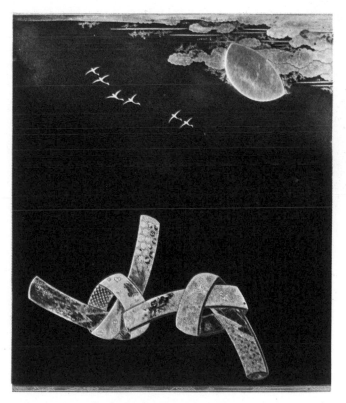

Lacquer cover of cabinet for incense-ceremony utensils. Ro-iro *lacquer decoration with a true lovers knot with brocade pattern and clouds enriched with* kirikane, *and geese flying home in gold* takamakie; *half-moon in silver inlay. Mid-eighteenth century. Victoria and Albert Museum.*

Small lacquer boxes and tray for incense. Upper left: circular box in form of a drum with silver bands enclosing three tiny boxes in form of the Shinto tomoye. The interior is of nashi-ji and the base of fundame, while the tiny inner boxes are decorated with waves in hiramakie on fundame with their interior in nashi-ji. Late eighteenth century. Upper right: cover for the box, decorated with herons in a stream in gold and silver takamakie enriched with kirikane on fundame ground. Upper center: tiny tray depicting men working, with salt pans, fish nets drying, etc., in gold and black takamakie *enriched with gold and silver foil and* kirikane *and* fundame *ground. Mid-eighteenth century. Lower left: base of round box of carved red lacquer with chrysanthemums and butterflies on waves, with the cover for same (lower right) decorated with lotus and other plants with a praying mantis. Late eighteenth century. Lower center: cover for a six-lobed box, decorated with herons in a stream in gold and silver* takamakie *enriched with* kirikane *on* fundame *ground. Early eighteenth century. Victoria and Albert Museum.*

contains the following articles: the *koban* or scoreboard; *ginyo, koshiki,* or *hishiki,* the talc square to burn incense on; *fuda* or counters; *kobashi* or wooden chopsticks to pick up incense; *kozutsumi* or folded paper for incense; *kizami-ban,* or chopping block for incense; *ginyo-basami* or silver tweezers to hold *ginyo; hibashi,* the metal chopsticks to hold hot charcoal; *kiri* or pointer; *osaye* or metal spatula to arrange the ashes; *hane* or feather brush; *koro* or incense burner; *kobako* or cabinet for the talc squares, incense, and charred incense ashes; the *kogutate* or stand to hold the seven utensils, the *fudazutsu* or box for counters; and the *hitori-koro,* which is the box for hot charcoal.

XVI Pottery and Porcelain

CERAMIC ART in Japan had its origin in the Neolithic age, when the Jomon type of earthenware was produced. The name *jomon*, meaning rope-pattern, was given to this type of earthenware because the surfaces reveal the marks of a coiled rope used to secure its form before it was placed in the kiln. As the skill of the potter improved during the later period of Jomon pottery, a wide variety of shapes and designs appeared, many of complicated ornament with a feeling of primitive freedom of expression. In these later Jomon types, the elaborate sculptured motifs and the relief designs produced by applying thin cords of clay clearly reflect the highly developed pottery of the Japanese stone age. The era of Jomon culture lasted for several thousand years, until a new people migrated from the Asiatic mainland around the first or second century B. C. and brought with them a culture based on agriculture. This new culture is called Yayoi after the distinctive type of earthenware first found in a Neolithic site at a place in Tokyo known by that name.

EARLY POTTERY TYPES

In contrast to the earlier Jomon type, Yayoi earthenware is usually undecorated and of simple form with an elegant contour, the body being shaped on the throwing-wheel. Japanese civilization advanced rapidly during the era of Yayoi culture, for it was during this period that simple communities of kinsmen developed into strong patriarchal families with subordinate families subject to them. As time went on these patriarchal families began to form stronger political communities called *uji*, from which a group of small domains was created. From this system of family domains arose several powerful states, among which was the region known as Yamato, controlled by the Imperial Yamato clan.

This era, which extends from the third or fourth century until about the seventh century, is called the period of Ancient Burial Mounds, from the great sepulchral mounds erected by these clans. It was during this age of dolmens that the small clay figures called Haniwa appeared for the first time. Haniwa are usually cylindrical in the lower portions with the upper part in the form of human or animal figures. For some curious reason Haniwa were not included with the tomb objects, but are found instead grouped in a circle on the mound about the tomb. The type of earthenware that came into existence in this era is called Sue-type pottery, or *sue yaki*, the word *yaki* being frequently used in Japanese ceramics to signify ware or baked ware. Sue ware appears to be a generic name applied to all unglazed pottery and includes those early types used especially for religious offerings and rituals, such as *iwaibe yaki* and *imbe yaki*. With the introduction of a new type of kiln called "cellar kiln," which was set up on the slope of a hill, in contrast to the earlier type erected on level ground, Sue-ware vessels were fired at a much higher temperature and were consequently very hard. The advent of this so-called cellar kiln was of great significance in the history of Japanese pottery and contributed to its rapid advancement. Vessels of Sue ware continued to be produced in a number of districts throughout the country until after the thirteenth century, when they began to acquire local characteristics.

The introduction of Buddhism in the sixth century and the influences from China which followed gave a great stimulus to all the arts. But it was not until the Nara period (710-794) that glazed pottery made its appearance, many examples of which have been preserved since the eighth century in the

Yayoi earthenware jar of yellow clay slightly tinged with pink, and a smooth surface. Late Neolithic Age. Tokyo National Museum.

Shosoin Repository at Nara. Until recent years these pieces were believed to be of Chinese origin, but it has now been ascertained from careful study of their shape, material, style, and glaze that they were almost certainly produced in Japan in the Nara period. These specimens closely resemble T'ang three-color ware, but in each of their properties and specific characteristics they differ from true Chinese pieces known to have been produced during the T'ang dynasty. Glazing was an important stage in the development of the potter's art because it enabled vessels to hold water, making them suitable for domestic uses. When articles of glazed pottery become everyday household and dining accessories, the natural tendency is for them to acquire æsthetical and ornamental qualities. Although glazed pottery was produced by the kilns at Seto from as early as the ninth century, it was not until the first half of the thirteenth century, during the Kamakura period, that the first major development of ceramic art took place. This forward move was influenced by Chinese wares, when Kato Shirozaemon, generally known as Toshiro of Owari, returned from China in the year 1227 and began to produce famous wares in imitation of Sung and Yuan ceramics. He was followed by a long line of descendants, all of whom produced excellent native Japanese examples after the glazes of Chinese prototypes. Many of the early pottery vessels of Seto with their thick glazes have always been highly prized by the tea masters, especially the exceedingly rare specimens made by Toshiro and his immediate descendants.

POTTERY FOR THE TEA CEREMONY

The cult of tea was still another important influence that stimulated the art of pottery-making in Japan. Although it is recorded in ancient chronicles that tea drinking was already known to the Imperial household in the early part of the eighth century, it was not until the Kamakura period (1185-1333) that as a ritual of the Zen sect it became better known. From this Zen ritual, which had its origin among the Taoists in China, the tea ceremony reached its final development in Japan in the fifteenth century, as we have seen, under the patronage of Yoshimasa, the Ashikaga Shogun. The principles of utter simplicity laid down by the celebrated tea master Shuko and further developed by the tea master Sen-no-Rikyu, under the patronage of Toyotomi Hideyoshi, had a direct bearing on the æsthetics of Japanese pottery.

There was very little progress in the art of pottery-making in the sixteenth century until the last decade, when Hideyoshi dispatched an army to Korea, first in 1592 and again in 1597. These military operations came to an end in 1598 with the death of Hideyoshi, but when the army returned, its com-

Jomon earthenware jar. Neolithic Age. Tokyo National Museum.

manders brought many Korean artisans back to Japan with them. Since the main forces of this army belonged to various daimyo of the island of Kyushu, it was here that these Koreans settled and set up kilns in the feudal domains. This was an important event in the cultural history of Japan, responsible for great advancement in the art of the potter. Among the feudal lords who brought back these potters and ceramic artists was Shimazu Yoshihiro, at whose castle town of Chosa in Satsuma the Koreans set up a number of kilns. It is recorded that the feudal lord of Nabeshima returned from the expedition with a few hundred potters, and that the Daimyo Terumoto brought with him the Korean potter later known as Koraizayemon, whose decoration on *hagi yaki* has always been favored by the Japanese and whose family continued the kiln for eleven generations. Many other potteries were either founded or assisted by these Korean artisans in such places as Karatsu, Yatsushiro, Takatori, and Kyoto.

The wares produced at these kilns were in the manner of their Korean prototypes, with grayish-white and cream glazes, plain or painted in blue or brown; and also greenish-gray celadon with or without the inlaid decoration called *mishima*. The great tea masters such as Shino Soshin, Furuta Oribe, and Sen-no-Rikyu had much to do with furthering this development. Not only were regular potters encouraged by the devotees of the tea ceremony, but painters and "gentlemen potters" also turned to making vessels by hand in a simple, unassuming manner.

The tea masters favored an extremely austere, sober utensil in a soft monochrome, and they were chiefly responsible for the popularity and appreciation of the type of ware known as Raku. This is a soft, low-temperature, hand-modeled pottery with a thick rich glaze, in a variety of subdued colors, first made by Chojiro, under the guidance of Sen-no-Rikyu, grand arbiter of the tea cult in Kyoto during the second half of the sixteenth century. Its development and characteristics are purely Japanese and it has no exact counterpart outside of Japan. No other pottery better exemplifies the fastidious taste of the tea masters than an original Raku tea bowl with its primitive simplicity of form, its crude uneven modeling, and its thick glaze which is pleasant to the lips. Painted design was superfluous and when it occurred was only faintly sketched with swift brush strokes. Among the many amateur potters who produced Raku tea bowls the most famous was Hon-ami Koetsu, 1568-1637, a celebrated painter, calligrapher, lacquer artist, and tea master. Extant pieces of Raku-type pottery made by Koetsu are very rare and, as masterpieces of great skill and sensitivity of taste, are valued as priceless possessions by tea masters. The æsthetic qualities of the tea bowl lie in perfectly fulfilling its function. Its soft, coarse clay is a non-conductor of heat, so that although filled with hot tea, it may

Haniwa clay image of an armored man. Ancient Burial Mound Age, c. third to seventh century A.D. Tokyo National Museum.

be grasped with comfort by the fingers. Its shape allows it to be passed from one person to another without fear of spilling, and its slightly rolled-in rim with thick glaze enhances the pleasure of tea drinking.

The art that lies in the tea bowl is further displayed in the soft-textured body and the quality and execution of the thick glaze. Many tea bowls are appreciated for the skill and care with which the potter reserved some portion of the clay free of glaze for examination, and for unusual tinges of color at the edge of the thick glaze. There is a marked absence of painted decoration on a great majority of tea bowls, this being considered unessential and distracting.

After Raku ware, the kinds of pottery most highly prized among tea masters are Hagi, Karatsu, Old Seto, Tamba, Iga, and Shiragaki. Tea utensils of Bizen ware are greatly enjoyed by tea devotees for the exquisite charm of the faint wet color displayed by a water jar or flower holder when sprinkled with

Seto pottery jar with four ears, engraved with a design of lotus. Kamakura period (1185-1333). Tokyo National Museum.

water. The real appreciation of tea-ceremony pottery requires a knowledge of its characteristics, the varieties of clay, the shapes and the glazes peculiar to certain wares or kilns. The æsthetic qualities of these old wares are deeply appreciated for the many distinctive features found in various types, such as the very hard and fine stonewares of Bizen, the yellowish glazes of some Old Seto ware, the thick uneven glazes of Shino ware. The potter's individuality also emerges in the varied methods by which the vessels are shaped, sometimes on the throwing wheel, other times with a spatula or by hand. The pottery of the tea ceremony affords supreme evidence that the pure spirit of art may enter into and ennoble the most humble of man's creations.

As the demand for various kinds of pottery for domestic use increased, there developed a taste for a less austere type among the new merchant class of townspeople. Because of this, and with the increasing ability of the potters, a rapid development took place in the seventeenth century in many parts of Japan, principally in the Seto district and in Kyoto. Around this time the typical pottery ware of Kyoto was made of a hard white clay with a deep cream color, or sometimes a light buff glaze, covered with a network of fine crackles. Much of this ware was made in the Awata and Omuro districts of the city and has continued to be produced until the present time. The first Kyoto potter to use enamel colors on these wares was Ninsei, who learned the secret from a porcelain maker in Hizen after the middle of the seventeenth century. It is partly the style of painting and partly the choice of colors which makes Ninsei's work æsthetically distinctive, and which provided Japanese potters with a truly indigenous style of enameling. Another famous Kyoto artist who contributed much to the history of Japanese pottery is Ogata Kenzan, 1662-1743, with his distinctive Chinese ink-style painted decoration executed with graceful freedom of expression. His calligraphic designs and stylized sketches—of flowers and trees, a flight of geese, or a glimpse of landscape—are remarkable for their firmness of stroke and economy of line. The slight but suggestive decoration which was applied by Ninsei and Kenzan, although contrary to the principles of the more severe masters of the tea cult, was accepted and even favored by others for the tea ceremony. It may be that to such severe tea masters as Rikyu, some of the productions of these potters would be unacceptable, and yet both potters were capable of enjoying the pure spirit of the tea ceremony and creating wares pleasing to its votaries when called upon to do so. The importance of Ninsei and Kenzan to the pottery art of Japan lies not only in their artistic achievements, but in the fact that they nurtured a national style of pottery decoration. This native style was further developed in Kyoto by many distinguished potters in the eighteenth century whose descendants still operate some of the hereditary kilns.

BEGINNINGS OF JAPANESE PORCELAIN

The beautiful Chinese porcelains of the Ming dynasty were always highly prized by the Japanese, and it was hoped that the Korean potters who were brought along by the various daimyo on their return from the invasion of Korea would produce such work. These artisans, who were skilled in making porcelain in their native land, at first made only pottery wares, since proper materials for porcelain had not yet been discovered in Japan. Among the artisans brought from Korea in 1598 was a potter called Ri Sampei, whose Japanese name is Kanae Sampei. Around the year 1616 Sampei discovered china clay of fine quality at Izumiyama in Arita in Hizen province, and succeeded in making porcelain. Sampei was one of the many potters who came to Japan with Nabeshima, the daimyo of Hizen, and set up kilns; but it was not until about forty years later that any real progress was made in developing true porcelain.

This early period of the Tokugawa Shogunate now witnessed rapid advances in the production of fine porcelain, especially such famous wares as Kakiemon, Imari, Nabeshima, and Kutani. These four wares exemplify the apex of Japanese colored porcelains with white grounds. They seldom bear the seal or mark of a potter or kiln. With the exception of Nabeshima, whose wares were made for presentation purposes and use in feudal houses, the kilns were producing articles chiefly on a commercial basis for daily use and export, and their productions were the work of many contributing workers and potters. In contrast to this, it was the traditional practice of the potters of Kyoto almost always to place the seal of the kiln or their personal seal on all pieces they considered as having artistic merit. The Kyoto potters, and those working at similar small kilns at other locations, usually used a pseudonym, as was the practice in other forms of Japanese art. There were many inconsistencies in this practice, since some artisans placed their personal seal on all pieces made at their kiln, while the successors of a famous potter or artist continued to use his original seal, and still others used many pseudonyms. In addition, the practice of legal adoption further complicates matters and makes it difficult and in many cases impossible to accurately record the various generations of a family of potters. The seals of famous tea masters, or *cha jin*, were placed upon specific types of wares they preferred, with the result that these wares produced by small kilns are known

Tea bowl of yellow Seto ware having a brownish-colored body covered with a yellow glaze in which are spots of copper-green. Momoyama period (1573-1615). Collection of Issei Hatakeyama, Tokyo.

Karatsu-ware pottery jar having a brown-colored clay body covered with a greenish-brown glaze and decorated with a design of flowering grasses. Edo period, seventeenth century. Collection of Sukezo Idemitsu, Tokyo.

231

Square pottery dish of Oribe ware with a design of stripes. Momoyama period (1573-1615). Tokyo National Museum.

by the name of the tea master, although he was neither potter nor artist. Included among these famous tea masters whose designs or names are closely associated with many kilns are Rikyu, Oribe, and Enshu, who appear most often.

From the Middle Ages, when the Seto wares were produced, the ceramic art has manifested a feeling which is purely Japanese. The taste and temperament of the Japanese is reflected and expressed in the pottery and porcelain which they prefer for their own use and enjoyment. An appreciation of Japanese ceramics, with their immense variety and complexity, is best acquired through a knowledge and understanding of the most important types, both of pottery and of such colored porcelains as Nabeshima, Kakiemon, Imari, and Kutani. Imari and Kakeimon are both familiar names in Europe, as this ware was exported in fairly large quantities from Arita during the first half of the eighteenth century. The earliest examples were taken to Europe by Dutch traders in the latter part of the seventeenth century, before the discovery of porcelain in Europe, and consequently were highly prized in the West. The English East India Company and the French Compagnie des Indes began shipping these wares around the end of the seventeenth century. The earlier Kakiemon designs were profusely copied in the eighteenth century at Meissen, Chantilly, Worcester, Chelsea, Bow, Derby, and other places. The brocaded Imari designs in blue, red, and gold were also the inspiration for many patterns produced at these European manufactories. Descriptions of the most important pottery

and porcelain ware of Japan, including their historical background and distinctive characteristics, are given in the following sections.

SETO

The town of Seto in the former province of Owari is perhaps the oldest pottery center in Japan. Although its kilns are referred to in ninth-century Imperial records, it was not until the first half of the thirteenth century, during the Kamakura period, that the first step was taken in the development of Seto ware. This period marks the actual beginning of the growth and advancement of Japanese ceramic art, in which Seto ware was to achieve the foremost position for many centuries. In fact, from early times in Japan the word *setomono* has been commonly applied to ceramic wares, and the word *setomonoya* means a pottery shop. One of the most famous names among Japanese potters is Kato Shirozaemon, 1169 to 1249, usually called Toshiro of Owari, who is generally regarded as the founder of ceramic art in Japan. He first established a kiln at Seto in the early part of the thirteenth century, where he produced a primitive unglazed pottery ware. In the year 1223, in the company of a Buddhist priest named Dogen, he visited China, where he studied the art of porcelain-making for a period of four years. Upon his return to Japan he traveled to many parts of the country in search of a clay of the finest quality to produce porcelain, but as this venture was without reward, he returned to Seto and resumed his work there. Some of his earliest pieces, called Toshiro-Karamono, are highly prized in Japan. They were made from clay that he had brought from China. The first Seto wares believed to have been produced by Toshiro have a brownish glaze streaked with black, and a rich reddish-brown glaze with splotches of golden brown. The work of Toshiro was carried on by a long line of descendants, all endeavoring to produce wares similar to the beautiful Sung celadons, called *seiji* in Japan, which were highly valued by the court nobles and feudal lords.

The term Yellow Seto or *ki seto* is generally applied to all varieties of Old Seto or *ko seto* pottery having a yellowish or amber-colored glaze. This glaze, which is greatly admired by the devotees of the tea ceremony, is the result of incorrect firing in an attempt to imitate celadon, and its production was continued until modern times. The amber-colored glaze, which followed the yellowish one, contained a large quantity of iron which caused its color to be slightly muddy in tone. Toward the end of the Middle Ages the Old Seto glaze became brownish and dark brown in color and was chiefly applied to such articles as tea jars and similar vessels. The potters made remarkable progress in their technique of deco-

rating these Seto wares with impressed patterns and incised designs which were used singly or combined one with the other. A variety of motifs were used, such as plum blossoms, chrysanthemums, peonies, willows, pine needles, foliage, and bands of circles in an over-all pattern or as a single decoration. The style of decoration as well as the selection of motifs strongly resembles the technique and design found on Sung and Yuan celadons from China and the inlaid celadons of the Korai period of Korea, since these were the prototypes that influenced the Seto wares. The shapes and forms of the Seto wares were also taken from these Chinese and Korean types, such as the bottle-shaped vases, jars with narrow necks, incense burners, and *temmoku*-type tea bowls copied after the *Chien yao* tea bowls of China.

As the tea ceremony grew in popularity the Seto potters began to produce imitations of the small tea jars of the Ming dynasty imported from China. These jars, having four small loops close to the neck to secure a cord, are covered with an uneven dark-brown or dark-amber glaze, and those of superior quality are known as Shunkei tea jars after a Seto potter of that time. From the end of the sixteenth century through the early part of the seventeenth century Seto wares were produced with crudely painted designs in a purely Japanese taste which developed from the orders for tea jars given to some Seto

Tea bowl of ash-gray Shino ware known as "unohana-gaki," meaning a fence along which bloom the tiny white blossoms of the utsugi (Japanese snowflower). End of fifteenth century. Tokyo National Museum.

Shino-ware pottery jar with a crude brush design of landscape. Momoyama period (1573-1615). Collection of Nisaburo Taka-mitsu, Tokyo.

233

potters by Oribe, the famous tea master. This type of ware, with its sketchily draw designs, is known as *e-seto*, or painted or picture *seto*. With the beginning of the nineteenth century the Seto kilns began to produce porcelain wares, the introduction and development of which was due to the work of Kato Tamikichi, who studied the technique at various kilns in Arita. Most of this porcelain was made in underglaze blue-and-white. The town of Seto is still one of the busiest porcelain centers in Japan with over five hundred producing kilns, and in the town park stands a great porcelain plaque in memory of the famous potter Toshiro. Also in the town is the Kama Shinto shrine, dedicated to Kato Tamikichi, who introduced the Arita method of making porcelain in 1807.

KARATSU

The principal port of communication with Korea during early times was the city of Karatsu in the northern part of Kyushu, which was one of the leading pottery centers where the ancient Sue earthenware had been produced. However, it was not until the end of the sixteenth century, when great numbers of Korean potters were brought over with the returning army of Hideyoshi, that the advanced ceramic technique was introduced from northern Korea and glazed pottery was first produced. The Karatsu kilns began to make a high-fired, hard pottery with a thick opaque glaze and a transparent loquat-colored glaze. Later productions, called *e-karatsu*, or Karatsu with designs, were painted in brown or blackish-brown with iron oxide under the glaze and had scant designs that were crudely executed. The glazes on *e-karatsu* comprise a translucent white feldspathic glaze and a transparent ash-colored glaze, while wares such as tea bowls and jars of crude and uneven form have milk-white and dark-brown glazes in monochrome.

Many Karatsu vessels are most highly prized by devotees of the tea ceremony as having been made by a special process. Inside the vessel can be seen many small, round marks, or a wavy pattern, caused by beating during the process of formation in order to harden the clay. The ware known as brush-marked Karatsu is a type of Korean decoration of the Yi dynasty which was produced by dipping the brush in a colored oxide or slip and drawing the design with a continuous stroke until the brush was dry or free of its content. The seventeenth-century wares of the Karatsu kilns included a type of decoration known as *mishima*, which is purely Korean in its origin, and was first made only at those Kyushu locations where Korean potters had settled. It consists of small repetitive and radiating designs in the form of stars, circles, semicircles, conventionalized flowers, and lines. The designs, which are

usually impressed and only rarely incised, are filled with a white slip, frequently on a gray glaze. The name is derived from the supposed resemblance of these rows of repeat-designs to the rows of characters in the yearly Mishima calendar, for which the town of Mishima in Japan was famous. The Japanese term *mishima* is also used to describe all wares having incised or impressed designs and filled with slip, whether they are of Japanese or Korean origin.

SHINO

Toward the end of the fifteenth century, potters of the Seto district in the province of Owari were commissioned to make certain tea bowls and other articles for use in the tea ceremony conducted by a distinguished tea master called Shino Soshin. The most notable productions were the powdered-tea bowls which have a thick opaque white glaze and those having an iron-oxide black glaze. These wares, which were crudely formed with a rough and uneven glaze, have continued to be favored for use in the tea ceremony. The uneven white glazed wares often have a reddish tinge where the glaze is thinnest, which is called fire color by the tea masters, and considered to be one of its most charming characteristics. The *e-shino*, or painted Shino ware, is decorated in brown iron oxide under the white glaze and is distinguished by its simplicity and thickness of line. An unusual feature of some Shino ware is that the glaze was wiped off part of the piece, leaving the body and its brown design exposed. The body of Shino ware is heavy and coarse, reflecting a crude peasant technique, and its thick glaze is heavily crackled or covered with tiny holes where bubbles have formed. The gray Shino ware, popularly

called *nezumi-shino*, has a white body covered with an engobe of dark-brown slip having designs executed in graffito under a white glaze.

ORIBE

Famous in the history of Japanese ceramics is *oribe yaki*, or Oribe ware. It is named for Furuta Oribe, 1543-1615, one of the most distinguished tea masters of all time. He served under three celebrated leaders, Oda Nobunaga, builder of the great Azuchi castle on the shore of Lake Biwa, Hideyoshi, and Tokugawa Ieyasu. Oribe, whose father had been a Buddhist priest and later a retainer of Hideyoshi, was born in Mino not far from the pottery district of Seto. Under Nobunaga, Oribe served as a samurai, and under Hideyoshi he was made a daimyo and placed in charge of a castle in Kyoto. While there he became the pupil of Sen-no-Rikyu, the great master of the tea ceremony, and later served as a teacher of this ceremony to Ieyasu's son, the Tokugawa Shogun. In 1615, after the siege of Osaka castle which made Ieyasu supreme ruler of Japan, one of Oribe's retainers was discovered to be chief of a group of conspirators who tried to set fire to the city of Kyoto. According to Japanese custom, Oribe was held responsible for the act and ordered to commit suicide. Oribe's life span covered some of the most exciting and eventful years in Japanese history, and although his career was with the great war lords, he was basically concerned with the more beautiful and peaceful aspects of life. The designs and shapes of his pottery articles have been greatly admired by the Japanese for over three hundred years and have strongly influenced the ceramic art of Japan until the present day.

Oribe wares are divided into three categories, each according to its characteristics: Green, or *ao oribe*; Red, or *aka oribe*; and Black, or *kuro oribe*. All three of these Oribe types have a portion of the surface covered with a beautiful sea-green glaze which blends into a bluish and purple-red tone at the thin edges. On the Green and Black types the balance of the surface is covered with a thick gray glaze and on the Red type with a reddish-brown glaze. Beneath the reddish-brown and the gray glazes is a design drawn with brown iron oxide and executed with swift, sure strokes of the brush. When Oribe ware is completely covered with the sea-green glaze, it is referred to as *ao oribe*. The Oribe wares were produced by kilns in both the Mino and Seto districts. The designs and shapes of Oribe ware are distinctive and charming with purely Japanese characteristics and taste, and were created in an asymmetrical manner with the component parts harmoniously related one to the other. The sketchy designs of rustic simplicity include such motifs as leaves of grass, a few rice stalks, a spider's web, pine needles, and conventionalized patterns. The forms found in these wares connected with Oribe's name include such popular ones as rectangular trays with vertical sides, either singly or connected together irregularly, fan-shaped dishes with vertical sides, square dishes, and square and round jars, all ingeniously executed with slightly dented or bent shapes in a free and unreserved technique.

RAKU

The pottery called Raku was created in Kyoto sometime during the second half of the sixteenth century when there

Left: Tea bowl of white Raku ware of a type called "Fuji-san" because the hazy grayish-white glaze on the upper half suggests the snow-capped Mount Fuji, and the lower half, the misty scenery at the foot of Mount Fuji at daybreak. Made by Hon-ami Koetsu, 1558-1637. Collection of Tadamasa Sakai, Tokyo.

Right: Black Raku tea bowl known as "Shunkan." Attributed to Chojiro, 1515-1592. Mitsui Collection, Tokyo.

235

was a great demand for articles for the tea ceremony. This famous ware was first produced by a potter called Sasaki Chojiro, 1515-1592, and his son, Jokei. The father of Chojiro was a potter named Ameya, who had emigrated from Korea, settled in Kyoto, and set up a kiln for the production of roof tiles. After his death Chojiro and his son continued to operate the kiln. They were commissioned to make the roof tiles for the beautiful pleasure pavilion called Jurakudai which Hideyoshi was having built in the year 1587. It was at this time that the tea ceremony, which had become an institution in the previous Muromachi period, was raised to the dignity of a national art by Hideyoshi's tea master, Sen-no-Rikyu. Under Rikyu's guidance Chojiro and Jokei soon began

Small Satsuma vase for holding a single flower; drum-shaped body with design of dragon, phoenix, and floral sprays in colored enamels on a cream-colored ground and crackled glaze. Edo period, c. 1780. Collection of K. Imai, Kyoto.

making wares exclusively for use in the tea ceremony, and in recognition of this work and because of a close friendship, Rikyu gave to Chojiro his family name of Tanaka. Then shortly after the death of Chojiro, Hideyoshi presented a gold seal to Jokei in memory of Chojiro, which bore the character *raku*, meaning enjoyment of freedom, to be used to impress every piece of pottery he produced. Later generations of the Raku family preferred to use their own seals of *raku*, which they impressed on their respective pieces. The family of Raku-ware makers has continued for fourteen generations until the present day, each successive generation being appointed by the master of the house. The most distinguished members were Chojiro, and Nonko, 1599-1658, who was the son of Jokei and became a Buddhist monk, at which time he assumed the name of Donyu. Raku ware was also produced in the kilns at Seto and Mino.

Raku yaki is a low-fired soft pottery having a thick heavy glaze. The ware has been a favorite with the tea masters for centuries and comprises all the pottery articles for use in the tea ceremony, such as tea bowls, small jars, flower holders, incense burners, and incense boxes. Raku tea bowls are more highly valued by devotees of the tea cult than any other ware. This preference is due to the fact that the bowls are most suitable for powdered tea, and also because of the tradition that they were the favorite tea bowls of the great tea master Rikyu. There are three types: Black Raku or *kuro raku*, Red Raku or *aka raku*, and White Raku or *shiro raku*. The thick glaze has a soft appearance and a pleasant soft feel to the touch. The glazes are always monochrome and comprise black, various tones of brown, shades of gray, yellowish white, a soft yellow, and red. Designs are rarely painted on the glaze, although occasionally a faint sketch of a pine tree, a heron, or Fujiyama is done by lightly scraping away the glaze. The Japanese greatly admire the natural design resulting from the uneven flow of the glaze while firing, and to these they have applied specific terms, such as *maku* for the wavy welt lines caused by the flow of the glaze, and *nagare* for the lines ending in a teardrop.

A unique feature of Raku ware is that it is occasionally shaped by hand without the use of the potter's wheel. One method is to shape the bowl from a lump of clay with the fingers and a bamboo spatula, leaving the base very thick. Then, by turning the bowl upside-down, the foot rim is cut to its proper shape. The other method is to roll the clay into rope-like pieces about one-half inch in diameter, coil it upon itself to form the bowl, and then pat it to the desired shape with the fingers. The foot rim is then shaped separately and fluted when the bowl is finished. In this process the outline of the coils is not entirely erased. The crudely formed tea bowls with their lip rims bent slightly inward are always made in an

Satsuma sake bottle with design of seasonal flowers in colored enamels and gold, on cream-colored ground, with crackled glaze. Made originally to fit in a gold-lacquered luncheon box. Edo period, end of eighteenth century. Collection of K. Imai, Kyoto.

Teapot of Satsuma ware with loops for overarching handle which was usually made of rattan or bamboo. The glaze is rather drab, while the clouds and flying storks are painted in greenish-gray. c. 1840. Victoria and Albert Museum.

unrestrained manner with a gentle unevenness that makes them pleasant to hold and to drink from.

SATSUMA

The pottery produced in the kilns at Chosa, Ryumonji, Nayeshirogawa, and Tateno, located in the former domain of the House of Shimazu, which ruled over the provinces of Satsuma and Osumi, is generally called Satsuma. These kilns were set up and operated by Korean potters brought back to Japan by Shimazu Yoshihiro in 1598 after the military expedition to Korea. The early Satsuma wares copied the potteries of the Yi dynasty of Korea, with monochrome glazes laid thickly upon a crudely formed body of high-fired, hard and coarse pottery. All these early Satsuma wares are highly valued for use in the tea ceremony, for which purpose most of the original productions were made. The wares of these kilns are designated as Old Satsuma or *ko satsuma* and comprise *jakatsu* or serpent and scorpion glaze, being a milk-white glaze laid over a thick black glaze that produced a beautiful and unusual color tone reflecting tiny spots of white. The Black Satsuma or *kuro satsuma* and White Satsuma or *shiro satsuma* are terms applied to a coarse and heavy pottery having a thick black glaze covered with either a milk-white or a brownish glaze, depending upon the degree of dark or white glaze most prominent or conspicuous. Later Satsuma wares

included an over-all impressed design or pattern inlaid with white slip called *mishima satsuma*, copied from Korean prototypes, while others had delicate sketches done with a greenish-brown glaze on a brownish crackled glaze. There are also some with splashes of greenish-brown on a heavy tea-colored glaze, others with a dark-green or brown glaze spattered with golden brown tea-dust, and some with black glazes. All of the wares described above are recognized and classified by the Japanese as Satsuma. The name Satsuma has been associated, by the average foreigner and those not familiar with Japanese ceramics, with entirely different wares generally made for the export and tourist trade which are not typically Japanese and do not reflect Japanese taste. One of these, an attempt to copy the late eighteenth- and early nineteenth-century wares, is a cream-colored, high-fired type of pottery with a crackled glaze having an over-all elaborate and gaudy decoration in enamel colors. The other ware covers a wide variety of ornamental pieces and small figures executed in a gaudy manner for this trade. Most of the export and tourist wares called Satsuma have been produced at various kilns in Tokyo, Kobe, and Kyoto for the past seventy-five years.

HAGI

The port town of Hagi on the Sea of Japan was formerly the castle headquarters of the Mori family in the province

237

of Nagato. The seventeenth-century Hagi pottery wares were copied exactly from the Yi-dynasty wares of Korea, especially those called *ido yaki*. The principal potter of Hagi ware was a Korean named Rikei, who came to Japan with the feudal lord Mori Terumoto when he returned after the Hideyoshi expedition to Korea in 1598. Rikei became a naturalized citizen and took the Japanese name of Koraizayemon, under which name the family has continued to produce pottery wares for eleven generations. *Hagi yaki*, or Hagi ware, were mostly tea utensils and have been greatly admired by devotees of the tea ceremony, who place Raku pottery first, Hagi second, and Karatsu third. Hagi tea bowls are considered to have a most delicate feel in the hands, second only to Raku ware. The body of Hagi ware is a thick crudely formed fine-grain pottery usually with monochrome glazes. The early productions were generally covered with a milk-white glaze and a transparent yellow-green glaze. From this milk-white glaze a later and rather beautiful glaze called White Hagi, or *shiro hagi*, developed, and also another glaze of loquat color resembling that found on the original Korean *ido* bowls. Other glazes were later developed in imitation of Korean wares, such as the brush-marked ware with its wide brush strokes done in a swift manner, also scantily drawn designs that were executed in iron oxide under the glaze, and *mishima* decoration, as well as various glazes having light-green and gray colors.

AWAJI

The pottery wares of Awaji are synonymous with and also referred to as Mimpei ware. The picturesque island of Awaji is only a few miles distant from the city of Kobe at the eastern end of the Inland Sea and, according to Japanese mythology, was one of the first islands created by the ancestral deities of Japan. The ware was first produced around 1831 by Kashu Mimpei, who was greatly interested in ceramic art. This ware has a smooth brownish-white body covered with a creamy-colored glaze that varies occasionally to a light buff. Awaji-ware glazes are sometimes finely crackled. Many Awaji productions are characterized by beautiful monochrome glazes, such as Chinese Imperial yellow, turquoise blue, apple green, and a blackish brown. Of special interest is the Awaji or Mimpei glaze, which is beautifully mottled to resemble tortoise shell. The articles made particularly for the tea ceremony have a soft body, while the wares for domestic use have a dense hard body of fine texture. The designs on some pieces were executed in various colors, occasionally with gold, and some Awaji pieces contain a molded decoration done in low relief.

Tea bowl of Hagi ware with chocolate-colored pottery body covered with a pale greenish glaze. c. 1640. Victoria and Albert Museum.

AWATA

In the Awataguchi district of Kyoto, which in ancient times was noted for its swordsmiths, are many kilns still producing ceramic wares in much the same manner as their predecessors did in the seventeenth century. The early kilns at Awataguchi produced pottery articles for the tea ceremony. *Awata yaki*, or Awata ware, has a white clay body and the glaze is generally a deep cream color or occasionally a light buff covered with a network of very fine crackle. The decoration is in rich enamel colors comprising red, green, and light blue, sometimes with gold. An interesting distinction in this ware is the use of underglaze iron-brown and underglaze blue. Ninsei, having worked at Awataguchi for a short time, exerted great influence on the pottery of Awata. The most prominent ceramic artists of Awata are members of the Kinkozan family and the Taizan family; the latter produced wares for the Imperial family.

BANKO

In the second half of the eighteenth century a wealthy merchant and amateur ceramist named Numanami Gozayemon began to make pottery wares after the manner of Ninsei and Kenzan. He lived at Kuwana, where travelers embarked on a boat to cross Ise Bay to visit the famous shrines rather than risk the several dangerous rivers on the way. Kuwana was also one of the fifty-three stages on the Tokaido highway depicted by Hiroshige in his famous series of wood-block prints of that title. Most of the earliest productions of Gozayemon's kiln were Raku-type wares for the tea ceremony. His work was greatly admired by the Tokugawa Shogun, who requested him to move to Edo, now Tokyo, where he was appointed official potter in 1785. Gozayemon died around 1800, and about thirty years later a potter named Mori Yusetsu is said to have found his formula for making enamel colors. Yusetsu purchased the seal of the Banko kiln from a grandson of Gozayemon, as there had not been any successor to carry on the pottery. The Gozayemon wares included fine imitations of Delft faïence of Holland and Chinese *famille verte* and *famille rose*. There were other Banko productions such as brownish-glazed wares, underglaze blue ware, and a soft pottery ware having a cream-colored crackled glaze with designs executed in red. The Banko kiln in Tokyo is still in existence.

BIZEN

Bizen ware, made in Okayama prefecture, was one of the first of the early Sue wares to acquire individual characteristics. Bizen is distinctive for its very high-fired clay body which closely resembles bronze, both to the eye and to the touch. The wares which date from the thirteenth century were originally produced for household and ritual use and include such articles as jugs and seed jars that are highly prized by the tea masters, who use them for holding water or flowers. Some Bizen wares produced for the tea ceremony are frequently called Imbe, which is a more thin and delicate ware first made about the end of the sixteenth century by members of the clan or family of that name. In addition to the unglazed bronze-colored *bizen yaki*, there is an unusual type called *ao bizen* made from a grayish-green clay which was greatly

Above: Banko-ware candlestick with a design of chrysanthemums in overglaze colored enamels. Edo period, early nineteenth century. Private collection, Tokyo.

Below: Flower holder of Awaji ware having a flat extended mouth in a separate piece and two small handles in the form of elephants' heads. Cream-colored body with crackled glaze, painted in enamel colors with gilding. Made by Kashin Sanpei in Awaji, late nineteenth century. Victoria and Albert Museum.

prized during the Edo period. All the wares made during the seventeenth and eighteenth centuries are known as Old Bizen or *ko bizen*. In the seventeenth century the *hidasuki* type of Bizen appeared with the beautiful scarlet marks which are so highly valued for use as tea utensils. In the firing of *hidasuki* ware each piece is partly wrapped in straw dampened with salt water from the sea and placed in the kiln. In the firing, the parts of the body touched by the wet straw develop scarlet streaks and markings. In the seventeenth century the productions of the bronze-colored Bizen ware included numerous figure subjects executed in a most pleasing manner, including mythological personages, gods, animals, birds, and fishes. Old

Bizen stoneware figure of Hotei, one of the shichifukujin or seven gods of good fortune. He is a lover of children and a symbol of a happy life. He is seen here in his happy role with a child at his side, the sacred gem in his right hand and his bag in which he puts playful children or the sacred treasures. About 1800. British Museum.

Bizen wares have always been highly valued by the Japanese, especially by the tea devotees who enjoy the moist color effect produced on an unglazed Bizen vessel when lightly splashed with drops of water.

EIRAKU AND KAIRAKU-EN

Around the middle of the sixteenth century Nishimura Soin, the son of a samurai called Zengoro, was the official potter at the Kasuga shrine at Nara. He produced the various unglazed articles used at the shrine for ritual offerings as well as a type of earthenware charcoal brazier called a *furo*. Under the direction of a famous tea master who was a pupil of Rikyu he made a particular type of *furo* having a deep black sheen or luster which was used especially for the tea ceremony. To each generation of Zengoro descendants was transmitted the secret of making this type of *furo*. One of the most noted of this line was Zengoro Hozen, 1795-1855, who became famous for his imitations of Ming porcelains. In the beginning of the second quarter of the nineteenth century, while working at his kiln in Kyoto, he was invited to go to the Tokugawa castle at Mito, the seat of the Lord of Kishu, where he set up a kiln in the famous garden known as Kairaku-en. Hozen is celebrated for his remarkably beautiful wares in imitation of Ming three-color wares, underglaze blue-and-white ware after Shonzui, and *kinran-de* porcelain having a red ground with gold brocade designs after the Chinese manner. Hozen's productions commonly referred to by the Japanese as Kairaku-en ware comprise colored glazes which completely cover the ware in green, yellow, and purple, and occasionally white. Sometimes turquoise blue is used in place of one of the three colors. In this ware a slight ridge outlines the designs and separates one glaze from the other, and all these colors are skillfully blended on each piece. He also produced many pieces after the style of Ninsei's enameled pottery. The name Eiraku, which is the Japanese name for the Ming Emperor Yung Lo, was given to Hozen, written on a silver seal by the Tokugawa Lord of Kishu in appreciation of his work in the style of Ming porcelain. After that all the successive potters of this Zengoro line have used the name of Eiraku along with their artist pseudonyms on their individual pieces. Hozen's son, Wazen, born in 1824 in the twelfth generation of the Zengoro line, succeeded to his father's work and excelled in making gilded porcelain having a rich coral-red ground with finely executed decoration in gold. He is also famous for his finely executed porcelain tea bowls, rice bowls, and dishes having this rich red ground with exquisite designs in gold or silver, frequently combined with underglaze blue-and-white decoration. The ceramic wares bearing the Eiraku seal through

Kairaku-en-ware pottery tea bowl with a design of flowering grasses. Edo period, first half nineteenth century. Tokyo National Museum.

Tea bowl made by Ninsei in the middle of the seventeenth century. Pottery body covered with a black overglaze and a design of round fans in red and light-green overglaze enamel colors with silver and gold. Tokusawa Collection, Tokyo.

these many generations are numerous and of great variety, and at the present time the artist potter known as Eiraku, Hozen, or Nishimura Zengoro, the sixteenth generation of the line, is producing wares of the finest quality both in the traditional style of the family as well as in a modern Japanese style of his own creation.

NINSEI

One of the most celebrated names associated with the ceramic history of Japan is Ninsei, a painter and potter of Kyoto active around the middle of the seventeenth century. The dates of his birth and death are usually given as 1596-1666, but these have not been confirmed. Ninsei's work had a significant influence upon the wares of Kyoto, with their characteristic style reflecting his achievements as an artist-potter. His real name was Nonomura Seiyemon and his artist name of Ninsei was derived from the seal with which his work is impressed, bearing the characters *nin* and *sei*, the latter taken from his own name. The character *nin* was bestowed upon him by Prince Ninnaji, who was the traditional superior of the Ninnaji temple in Kyoto, formerly known as Omuro palace, near which Ninsei had set up a kiln. Ninsei was an accomplished artist who had studied under masters of both the Tosa and Kano schools. His pieces were principally

utensils for use in the tea ceremony, including finely shaped and delicately worked tea jars, tea bowls, and water jars, and beautifully modeled incense burners in the form of birds and sea shells. Ninsei's first wares were made at the kilns in the Omuro district of Kyoto, where he produced articles similar to those of other kiln centers, such as the primitive types so much in demand. He learned the secret of enamel colors and to him is usually credited the creation of a school of beautifully executed overglaze pottery. The influence of Ninsei's work was firmly infused in the qualities of Kyoto ware, for which the term *Kyo* is often used as a broad description. The body of Ninsei's ware is fine and hard, and said to have been made from a paste called *shigaraki* clay. His glazes usually show a very fine network of crackle and have a soft warm effect. The glazes preferred by Ninsei were a lustrous black, a translucent milk-white, a pearl gray, and especially one of raven-black produced by laying green glaze over a black glaze which was sometimes sprinkled with tiny flecks of gold, a technique inspired by Japanese gold-lacquer ware. His designs are characterized by richness of effect, with minute detail and exquisite enamel colors, especially in the depiction of plants and flowers. In Ninsei ware the traditional Japanese characteristic of balancing motifs against bare, undecorated areas is beautifully exemplified. In later life Ninsei traveled throughout Japan visiting innumerable kilns and devoting much time to teaching other potters. Often while visiting a kiln he would practice his own art, which accounts for Ninsei ware being considered characteristic of so many locations about the country. Because of his widespread fame during his lifetime, his work was imitated by potters almost everywhere, sometimes badly.

KENZAN

A predominating trait of Japanese pottery, in particular that of Kyoto, is its remarkable freedom of shape and decoration. Typical of this freedom, which is especially appealing to Japanese taste, is the work of Ogata Shinsho, 1662-1743, usually known as Ogata Kenzan, a poet and potter of Kyoto. He was a younger brother of the famous painter Ogata Korin, who was also celebrated for exquisite lacquer work. Kenzan worked at various kilns in Kyoto, where he produced articles mostly for the tea ceremony in an entirely new style of ceramic decoration. His designs are applied in quick strokes of the brush directly on the soft clay body of Raku-type ware and other similar pottery. Both bold and sketchy in a most unconventional manner, Kenzan's designs are more easily appreciated as painting than as ceramic decoration. Sometimes as an additional touch he would include a piece of poetry with the design. Kenzan's designs have continued to exert a strong influence on Kyoto wares as well as on wares in other parts of the country until the present day. The color technique, with its superb combinations, is one of the unusual features of Kenzan's work. The designs most frequently found include autumn flowers, a few cherry blossoms, bamboo leaves gently touched with snow, three blades of grass, a branch with plum blossoms, a stalk or two of rice, and water plants. In his later years he retired to a small village near Tokyo called Iriya, where he produced some of his best work. Kenzan was a disciple of Ninsei, and because he did not have an immediate successor, a son of Ninsei continued the name of Kenzan. Kenzan's free and distinctive style is still being copied by local potters.

KYOTO WARE

The ancient capital city of Kyoto, which has been the center of Japanese civilization and culture from its founding in the year 794, is picturesquely nestled among surrounding mountains. Teeming with historical and religious traditions, this great center of Buddhism is a unique city in which the spirit of old Japan lingers. Though often the scene of fighting and conspiracies of powerful feudal houses, the city has always preserved its ancient prestige and cultural elegance emanating from the Imperial court. It has also played an important role in art and literature and for a long time has been a center famous for ceramic artists and potters. The terms Kyoto ware, *kyoto yaki*, and *kyo yaki* are synonymous, and are applied to a great variety of wares produced in private kilns in and around the capital. In particular they refer to those pottery

Kyoto-ware porcelain bowl by Dohachi, 1783-1855. Design of cherry trees and maple trees. Edo period. Tokyo National Museum.

Pottery writing screen depicting a mountain, pine tree, and house roughly sketched with quick brush strokes by Kenzan. c. 1740. Metropolitan Museum of Art. Gift of Howard Mansfield, 1936.

242

wares decorated with overglaze enamel colors as developed by Ninsei in the seventeenth century, and the glazed Raku- and Seto-type wares. Kyoto wares are made of a variety of different kinds and blends of clay because the local deposits were exhausted at an early date and it had to be brought from many distant places. The characteristic wares of Kyoto are classified according to the style or design of certain individual artists or potters. Among the outstanding ceramic artists of Kyoto, besides Ninsei and Kenzan, previously discussed, are many who flourished from the late eighteenth century through the nineteenth century, including Okuda-Eisen, Aoki-Mokubei, Takahashi-Dohachi, Nin'ami-Dohachi, Eiraku-Hozen, Eiraku-Wazen, and Makuzu-Chozo. Several small private kilns have been continuously producing the same wares since the sixteenth and seventeenth centuries and are still being operated by family descendants. Included among the old family potters working at their private kilns are Rokubei, Chikusen, Eiraku, Kawai, and Seifu.

KIYOMIZU

On a cliff near the summit of Mount Otowayama, in the eastern part of the city of Kyoto, stands the famous Kiyomizu temple, and preserved in the many buildings within its precincts are a number of Buddhist masterpieces. Around this mountain, which is popularly called Kiyomizu, and in the district below known as Kiyomizu-zaka, are kiln sites whose products bear the name *kiyomizu yaki*. The wares called Old Kiyomizu or *ko kiyomizu* are chiefly imitations and adaptations of Chinese enameled porcelains: the underglaze blue-and-white, celadon, and three-color ware of the Ming and Ch'ing dynasties. This early Kiyomizu was a pottery having a creamy-white clay body and a cream-colored glaze which might or might not be crackled. There were probably more than ten kilns located in this area in the latter half of the seventeenth century, making articles for the tea ceremony. In the eighteenth century, when there was a rage for Chinese ware, these kilns began to produce enameled pottery, and in the beginning of the nineteenth century porcelain was added. At the present time Kiyomizu ware includes both pottery and porcelain. Among the outstanding artist-potters of Kyoto still operating private family kilns in the Kiyomizu district are Rokubei and Chikusen. Rokubei, who is the fifth generation, is the descendant of Shimizu Rokubei, 1740-1799, a potter who came to Kyoto from Settsu. Miura Chikusen, the fourth generation to operate the family kiln, is noted for his exquisite imitations of Ming and Ch'ing underglaze blue-and-white, which are considered the finest of this type of work produced anywhere at the present time. The style of wares produced in this district underwent changes with the passing of time, from the very earliest tea-ceremony utensils to enameled pottery as introduced by Ninsei and the imitations of Chinese wares known as *ko kiyomizu*. The later Kiyomizu wares reflect the artistic ceramic traditions of Kyoto and are essentially Japanese in their color decoration.

Shonzui-style octagonal bowl with cover, in underglaze blue-and-white, by Kawamoto Hansuke: Edo period, early nineteenth century. Tokyo National Museum.

SHONZUI

Shonzui ware is named after Gorodayu Go Shonzui, a potter who traveled to China in the year 1513 to study the art of making and decorating porcelain. Upon his return to Japan he settled at Arita in Hizen province, where he produced porcelain wares of underglaze blue-and-white. He is said to have brought back quantities of china clay. Shonzui design, known as *kara-kusa*, is characterized by oblique wavy bands of underglaze blue alternating with white bands. The designs on the blue bands are in reserve and consist chiefly of brocade and imbricated patterns. These bands are generally used in combination with landscapes, and also with flower and plant designs in the Chinese manner. A favorite style of Shonzui decoration consists of geometrical patterns, especially in the form of linked circles or disks. Many extant examples ascribed to Shonzui and bearing his seal are of excellent form and beautifully decorated with such patterns, borrowed from Chinese designs of the late Ming period. These Shonzui designs with various pattern combinations are purely Japanese in feeling and have a unique charm when applied to such articles as rice bowls and water jars.

IMARI

The ceramic wares produced in the northern part of the island of Kyushu, principally in Hizen province, which is now Saga prefecture, bear the generic name of Imari ware or *imari yaki*. The many kilns in this area include Hirado, Okochi, Nabeshima, Kakiemon, and those located in Arita. Collectively these ceramics are called Arita ware, but during the Tokugawa Shogunate the wares produced commercially in the city of Arita were exported to other parts of Japan from the port town of Imari and have been popularly called Imari ware. The English term Old Imari, which is well known in Europe, refers to the ware dating from the early eighteenth century on and does not signify the early ware of Arita. At the beginning of the seventeenth century, when china clay of fine quality was discovered in Izumiyama, the Korean potters who settled in Hizen province were able to make porcelain for the first time after the aforementioned Shonzui. These porcelain wares have a fine hard white body decorated in underglaze blue-and-white. The style and technique of decoration was naturally influenced by the blue-and-white porcelains of the Yi dynasty of Korea, for these potters were skilled in making

Imari dish having a design of horse-chestnuts in overglaze colored enamels. Edo period, eighteenth century. Takasu Collection, Tokyo.

Imari dish. Design of conventionalized birds and flowers copied from silk brocade patterns. Edo period, eighteenth century. Tokyo National Museum.

244

Imari dish. Design of Dutch ships and Dutch-men in eighteenth-century costume. Edo period, eighteenth century. Kato Collection, Tokyo.

such porcelain in their native country. After a short time the Chinese blue-and-white porcelain of the Ming dynasty began to exert its influence and finally replaced the original productions of the Yi-dynasty style. In Japanese the term *sometsuke* is applied to blue-and-white wares, while *gosu* is applied to the Ming blue-and-white wares of China or imitations. Most of the blue-and-white wares were for daily use and included rice bowls, plates, sake bottles, candlesticks, *shoyu* oil pots, chopstick holders, and flower holders. The designs were numerous and included all kinds of Chinese and Japanese subjects such as flowers, plants, grasses, trees, birds, animals, fishes, celestial subjects, landscapes, and seascapes (Plate 14). Blue-and-white wares have always appealed to the Japanese æsthetic sense of purity and elegance, and they have always been favored for daily use.

ARITA PORCELAIN

In the middle of the seventeenth century the art of making porcelain with overglaze enamel decoration was developed

at Arita by Kakiemon and Tokuemon. The early Arita porcelain decorated in overglaze colors was influenced by late Ming wares, but it soon developed into a purely Japanese style inspired by the designs and colors of the prevailing fashion in brocade textiles. The fully developed expression of this characteristic style became known as *imari nishiki-de*, or Imari Brocade, and all through the Tokugawa period these Arita wares remained in great favor and typified the Japanese taste for enameled porcelains, particularly among the rich merchant class, which leaned toward elaborate designs and richness of color. The designs on Imari ware cover the entire surface, leaving almost no ground. They are composed in a pleasing and ingenious manner upon the surface of plates and bowls in a symmetrical and well-balanced pattern. Imari ware was exported by Dutch and English traders to Europe, where it was greatly admired and imitated at such places as Meissen, Worcester, Chelsea, and Delft. Its colored enamels include semi-opaque purple, transparent sapphire blue, dull yellow, bluish-green, underglaze blue and, in the older pieces, a rather dull rich vermilion. Many pieces of early Imari have designs depicting the manners and customs of the times, showing

Imari wine bottle with a design in overglaze enamels of the seven sages in a bamboo grove. Edo period, seventeenth century. Amamiya Collection, Tokyo.

Kakiemon bottle vase in overglaze colored enamels with a design of flowers and birds. Edo period, seventeenth century. Nakajima Collection, Tokyo.

figures of Japanese men and women similar to those in genre wood-block prints.

One of the most attractive designs found on early Imari bowls is the *yoraku* or necklace motif. This usually consists of six large round medallions of a beautiful warm, dull red or vermilion connected with delicate conventionalized pendant flowers or arabesque designs in enamel colors. Appearing on the inner side wall of the bowl, the design is repeated in the same elaborate manner on the outside. The *imari yoraku* design as produced on the early wares with its elegant composition and rich colors has always been greatly favored in Japan. The Dutch traders, on the other hand, were particularly attracted by the beautifully decorated *imari nishiki-de* porcelains, and many pieces of this ware were made with elaborate designs of eighteenth-century Dutch ships and figures in Dutch costume. The *nishiki-de* became overelaborate and gaudy,

with an abundance of colors lavishly emphasized by too much gold, resulting in a complete loss of its original refined elegance. As the domestic and export demand increased, even during the early part of the eighteenth century, *imari nishiki-de* became a standardized style and potters of the Arita district not only produced their wares in their homes and fired them at a large community kiln, but there also sprang up in Arita a place called Akae-machi, or town of color painters, where workers specialized in overglaze enamel decoration. There were also ceramic artists who specialized only in painting figure subjects, while common workers were employed to draw and paint designs allotted to them on a production basis. Many of the later Imari wares were especially made for the export market and, as such, lost the original beautiful quality of the early Imari and also lost the warm rich elegance which had appealed to the Japanese taste.

246

KAKIEMON

The beautifully decorated porcelain ware made at the Nangawara kiln known as Kakiemon received its name from the famous Japanese potter who was most prominent in the early history of Arita ware, Sakaida Kizoemon. The exact dates of his birth and death are unknown but usually are given as 1596-1666. He was the pupil of a famous Arita potter called Takahara Goroshichi, who had retired to a Buddhist monastery because of the turbulent times. They worked together during the early years of the Kan-ei era (1624-1644) producing blue-and-white porcelain of superb quality, but little is known of their later association. Sometime during this same period Sakaida Kizoemon began experimenting in the technique of making colored enamel glazes, a secret that was given to him by a rich Arita merchant named Tokuemon. While Tokuemon was visiting Nagasaki, the only port open to foreign ships, he met a Chinese potter from whom he purchased this secret process, which was then unknown in Japan. Success did not come easily, since the early experiments failed to produce the desired result, and Kizoemon was to try many different methods before he finally perfected the proper formulas. He finally succeeded in producing a porcelain ornament in the form of persimmon with such perfect color that it resembled the real fruit. He presented it to the feudal lord of the Nabeshima family, who was so amazed with its beauty that he bestowed upon Kizoemon the name of Kakiemon, from the Japanese word *kaki*, meaning persimmon.

Kakiemon ware of the earlier period, from about 1640 to 1680, was made from a clay of high quality and purity which is said to have been from Izumiyama, thus belonging to Nabeshima, the feudal lord of Hizen province. The white glaze has a warmth and richness and is pleasing to the touch. The colored enamels are lustrous and exquisitely combined (Plate 13). The hues occurring most frequently are an iron red, a pure and transparent blue-green, *aubergine*, light blue, grayish yellow, and black. The iron red is rather light in tone, with an unusual richness which is complemented by the beautiful glaze on the body. Many of the motifs were of Chinese origin, such as the phoenix, the dragon, and the *fu* lion. But Kakiemon's designs represent true Japanese elegance in their simplicity, with motifs delicately balanced against large areas of bare space. His designs of flowers, plants, rocks, grasses, plum branches, and trees were ingeniously drawn in a naturalistic manner with a distinctive combination of colors, and most of the warm opaque body glaze of the background was left free to enhance the exquisite composition. It was the early Kakiemon ware that was taken by Dutch and English traders to Europe, where it was greatly admired and collected, and much copied in the eighteenth century at Meissen, Chelsea, Bow, Worcester, and Chantilly.

The second period of Kakiemon, from 1680 to 1720, is represented by a complete change in style. This transparent-glaze ware is characterized by *nishiki-de* decoration in the Imari style; but although this is the principal feature of the second period, much was still produced in the original

Above: Kakiemon bowl in the shape of an open flower. Decorated in overglaze enamels with a design of flowers and birds. Edo period, eighteenth century. Nakao Collection, Tokyo.

Right: Kakiemon wine ewer. Design of plum trees and bamboo in overglaze enamels. Edo period, eighteenth century. Takasu Collection, Tokyo.

Kakiemon dish, with plum tree and deer design. Edo period, eighteenth century. Tokyo National Museum.

Nabeshima dish. Design of wisteria branches in underglaze blue-and-white. Edo period, eighteenth century. Tokyo National Museum.

Kakiemon style. The demands of the rich merchant class and the popular taste of the time were responsible for this departure from the earlier charming and elegant work in favor of the intricate designs and striking colors of Imari. The designs included all of the typical Imari work, with a limited use of figure subjects forming part of the decoration. A characteristic feature of this *kakiemon nishiki-de* decoration is that the center portion was usually plain, or contained beautiful and picturesque figure subjects, while the outside surface had a design in the original Kakiemon style. This is a distinguishing quality of *kakiemon nishiki-de* as compared to Imari, in which the whole surface of the ware was covered both inside and outside with textile patterns and colorful design combinations. The Kakiemon kilns have operated continuously for three hundred years and are at present under the direction of the twelfth generation.

NABESHIMA

A distinctive porcelain included in the classification of Arita ware is known as Nabeshima. It was produced in the private kilns of the feudal lord of Saga, head of the House of Nabeshima, whose castle was at the town of Saga in Hizen province in the northern part of the island of Kyushu. The powerful Nabeshima family ruled the northern part of Kyushu for several hundred years and produced many great daimyo. In the closing years of the sixteenth century Lord Nabeshima, Daimyo of Saga, returned from the expedition to Korea with a great number of potters who set up kilns in his domains. At the end of the first quarter of the eighteenth century the Daimyo of Saga, who was interested in ceramic art, appointed his most able potters to produce porcelain wares of the highest quality and elegance for his personal use and for gifts. These wares, which are commonly known as Nabeshima, were made at the Okochi kiln, or Okawachi kiln as it is sometimes called (Plate 12). The kilns of Nabeshima produced underglaze blue-and-white and celadons of great refinement, but it is the *iro nabeshima*, or enameled Nabeshima, of the Okochi kiln that is especially noted for its elegance. These wares were produced under the patronage of the Nabeshima lords without interruption until the Meiji Restoration, after which time they were made commercially. The Nabeshima wares were made of high-quality, pure-white clay and most of the

Nabeshima plate with design of a camellia in full bloom by a bamboo fence, in colored enamels. Edo period mid-eighteenth century. Yamanaka and Company, New York and Osaka.

Nabeshima dish with design of peonies and waves of overglaze enamels. Edo period, eighteenth century. Tokyo National Museum.

articles were plates for daily use of the feudal lords and for presentation purposes. Only the finest pieces were selected for these uses, while those that were not entirely perfect were destroyed.

The potting is remarkable for its elegance and exactness, and the plates, which can be described as very shallow bowls or deep plates, have a high and prominent foot rim. Nabeshima designs possess great elegance, usually in a distinctive asymmetrical composition in subtle balance. These beautiful and graceful designs of flowers, plants, trees and, occasionally, birds were inspired by nature and depicted in a distinctive Nabeshima manner. Their elegance is due to the precision with which the design has been adapted to the curved sides of the dishes and to the avoidance of anything not absolutely essential to the composition. Much of the surface space was left undecorated. Occasionally landscapes were designed in the manner of the Kano school of painting, and sometimes designs of fences were used and executed in a zigzag manner. Many asymmetrical but well-balanced designs were inspired by the beautiful silk fabrics called *yuzen*.

Nabeshima is noted for its brilliant enamel colors, usually limited to a rich iron red, a soft fresh green, and a light yellow.

The designs were most carefully drawn with an outline of underglaze blue; then the glaze was applied and fired in a high-temperature kiln. Colored enamels were applied over the glaze and fired in a low-temperature kiln. In the earlier Nabeshima pieces this technique of color application was executed with great care and skill so that the enamel colors were laid on so exactly that the underglaze blue outline is unnoticed. A characteristic feature of Nabeshima plates is the very high foot rim with a "comb" pattern, which was not allowed to be imitated by other kilns. The comb pattern was in underglaze blue, the row of teeth being drawn in perfect regularity with very fine brush outlines and filled in with cobalt blue. On the underside or outside of the deep plates appears the characteristic Nabeshima arrangement of the Chinese money or coin motif, or other traditional Chinese motifs, although occasionally the peach and peony designs are seen. These carefully drawn designs in underglaze blue divide the space on the outside methodically into three equal sections. The Nabeshima wares with their essentially Japanese designs executed with such elegance exemplify the exquisite aristocratic taste of the Nabeshima lords and are prized for their richly enameled beauty.

249

HIRADO

The small island of Hirado, located a few miles off the coast of the old Hizen province, has been an active ceramic center since the beginning of the seventeenth century. In the year 1598 when the feudal lord of Hirado returned from the Korean expedition, he brought back many Korean potters who set up kilns in his island possession; but the production of porcelain wares did not start until around the middle of the eighteenth century, when china clay of the finest quality was found at Amakusa. These wares were made at the Mikawachi kilns and are characterized by a hard pure-white body with underglaze-blue decoration. The blue is rather weak and its outlines and edges are inclined to be fuzzy. Like Nabeshima ware, the Hirado pieces were made only for the use of the feudal lords until the Meiji Restoration in 1868, when the kilns began to operate for the public market. The principal forms of Hirado porcelains were plates, tea bowls, sake cups, sake bottles, and beautifully modeled small figures of animals, human subjects, birds, and flowers, all skillfully executed, with many examples of special elegance and elaborate workmanship.

KUTANI

Near the Yamashiro Spa not far from the coast of the Sea of Japan in the remote mountain village of Kutani, or Nine Valleys, are the old Kutani kiln sites which date from around the middle of the seventeenth century. It was here that the

Kutani bottle in the shape of a double gourd decorated with design of lions and peonies in overglaze enamels. Edo period, seventeenth century. Tokyo National Museum.

250

Hirado plate made at the Mikawachi kiln. Underglaze-blue decoration of the Buddhist emblem within a circle of ju-i motifs, and orchids in a soft blue on white ground. Edo period about 1750. Author's collection.

Kutani wine ewer. Design of plum tree. Edo period, seventeenth century. Tokyo National Museum.

ko kutani, or Old Kutani, enameled porcelain wares were produced. Although practically unknown outside of Japan, these wares have always been most highly prized by the Japanese for their magnificence of decoration, which is thoroughly Japanese (Plate 11). In comparison with the refinement and elegance of the enameled porcelains of Nabeshima and Kakiemon, *ko kutani* ware possesses an unusual quality of freshness, intensity of color, and vigor of design which gives a great warmth of feeling.

With the discovery of china clay for making porcelain in this vicinity in the middle of the seventeenth century, the Daimyo of Kaga province, Maeda Toshiharu, head of the feudal house of Maeda, established kilns at Kutani. The earliest wares being unsatisfactory, he sent Goto Saijiro, one of his best potters, to visit the kilns in Kyushu to study the technique of making and decorating porcelain. Ten years passed before Saijiro returned to Kutani, around 1660. It is not certain whether he visited the Arita kilns or traveled to China to study the Imperial kilns in Ching-te-Chen, but the knowledge that Saijiro acquired, together with the enthusiasm and financial aid of this powerful feudal lord, resulted in the perfection of the enameled porcelain ware known as *ko kutani*. Its production continued until Saijiro's death a few years after 1700, and the making of this original *kutani yaki* came to an end. For the next hundred years or so the kilns produced a poor-quality ware which satisfied the local needs for daily use. The kilns were re-established in the early years of the nineteenth century, and their later wares copied from *ko kutani* are known as *shin kutani* (New Kutani) or simply as Kutani.

The relatively short period of production of *ko kutani*, from about 1660 to 1700, is remarkable for an endless variety of articles. This extensive production was made possible by a highly organized system and efficiency comparable to the Imperial kilns of China, and an assemblage of good artists and potters from the various kiln sites in Japan as well as Korean and Chinese artisans. The body of *ko kutani* is coarse and the glaze impure, covering the vessel in a thick and uneven manner. The enamel colors are rich and thick, the red being dark and the green resembling the deep blue-green of sea water. The term *akae kutani* refers to those pieces in which the red and green are supplemented by purple, yellow, overglaze blue, and occasionally gold and silver. *Ao kutani*, or Green Kutani, which has no red enamel, has yellow, green, and purple enamels. Some of the designs were inspired by the Chinese late Ming and early Ch'ing enameled porcelains; others are of purely Japanese origin. The Japanese examples range in style from Imari and Kakiemon to the style of Kyoto pottery painting and the Kano school of painting. *Ko kutani* designs are bold and free, executed with a quick and sure brush stroke. The colors are harmoniously combined and the

Kutani plate o, enneagonal shape with landscape and flower-and-bird panels in colored enamels. Signed. Edo period, late seventeenth century. Yamanaka and Company, New York and Osaka.

designs create an over-all effect of colorful rustic charm. A typical *ko kutani* composition consisted of dividing the plate rim into symmetrically arranged compartments of geometric shapes or diaper patterns, with the principal design in the center of the plate. The style executed in the manner of the Kano school of painting is especially beautiful, with its purely Japanese subjects taken from nature and from the everyday life of the country, including human figures, birds, flowers, plants, trees, landscapes, and seascapes. Around the middle of this phase of *ko kutani* the use of cobalt blue came to an end and the red enamel color disappeared, which seems to indicate that these materials had originally been brought from China and were now exhausted. Due to this shortage of pigments, Green Kutani, or *ao kutani*, was developed with over-all designs in three colors, purple, green, and yellow, outlined with black. *Ko kutani* and *ao kutani* wares, with their native charm of color and design, have the richness of unaffected rusticity.

XVII Lacquer

THE DEVELOPMENT of the art of lacquer in Japan begins with the introduction of Buddhism, which as in all the other arts was the great force that stimulated the progress of culture. Preserved in the Treasure Hall or Kondo at Horyuji is the Tamamushi-no-zushi, or Golden Beetle Miniature Shrine, the earliest extant example of Japanese lacquer work. It was originally a precious sanctuary belonging to the Empress Suiko, whose son, Prince Shotoku Taishi, was the actual founder of Buddhism in Japan. Dating from the Asuka period (552-645), it is square and in the form of a shrine, complete with roof and doors, and mounted on a pedestal. Its name originated from the fact that the crossbeams, corners, and edges were originally profusely inlaid with the multicolored wings of the insect *tamamushi* or jewel beetle, set in an exquisite metal edging of honeysuckle design. The jewel-beetle wings have long since disappeared, leaving only the metal appliqués. The shrine and its pedestal are black lacquered and covered with Buddhist narrative scenes painted in *mitsudaso*, a kind of oil pigment used chiefly in the Asuka and Nara periods. The yellow, vermilion, and green used in the paintings were applied as part of the lacquer process.

BEGINNINGS OF JAPANESE LACQUER

The early lacquer art of Japan was based upon methods learned from the Chinese. The first official envoy to the court of the Sui dynasty in China left Japan in the year 607, and with the accession of the T'ang dynasty in 618, Japanese missions increased in number. These missions included specialists in many fields, such as carpenters, founders, craftsmen, and artists, who studied the culture and arts as practiced by the Chinese in those times. In the year 645 the Emperor issued an edict known as the Taika Reform, which was based on the land-ownership laws of the Sui and T'ang dynasties and had

a far-reaching effect on the lacquer art of Japan. The Code of Taiho, or Great Treasure, was promulgated in 701, with the Great Council of State as the supreme organ of government, and the Department of Religion holding equal rank. Various ministries were established and within the Ministry of the Treasury was organized among others an Office of the Guild of Lacquer Workers. Included in the terms of this code were the introduction of a new system of land tenure, and a new system of taxation by which textiles, silk, rice, or other commodities locally produced were payable in fixed amounts in lieu of labor.

The Taika Reform declared that under the new system of land allotment the arable fields, principally the wet rice fields, were to be distributed among the cultivators, with the size determined by the number of members in a household. In addition to the grants of land, each household was given a plot of ground on which it was mandatory to cultivate both lacquer trees and mulberry trees (the latter for silkworms). It was necessary for the government to provide for an ample supply of lacquer, to meet the demand due to the growing popularity and prosperity of Buddhism. The Nara period (710-794) is characterized by the pervading influence of Buddhism, which caused such rapid progress in all fields of art and stimulated the building of great temples and monasteries. The interior architecture and furnishings of these great Buddhist buildings required large quantities of lacquer for the embellishment of altars, shrines, pillars, and various religious accessories.

Although the principal method for making lacquer ware from early times had been to apply the lacquer on an article of wood or bamboo, a new process was introduced from China. This was known as the dry-lacquer technique and was a favorite method for making various utensils as well as Buddhist images. The process consisted of covering a model form with hempen cloth, to which coats of lacquer were applied, and when the lacquer dried, the form was removed. Another technique introduced from China during the Nara period was called *hyomon*, or sheet design. This consisted of cutting thin sheets of gold or silver into designs and laying them on a lacquered surface, and then applying additional coats of lacquer.

As the Japanese artists and craftsmen gained more knowledge of lacquer processes, they far surpassed the Chinese work and developed its æsthetic qualities to such a degree that it actually became a fine art in the truest sense of the word. During the Heian period (794-1185) lacquer not only reached a high level of technical proficiency and artistic skill, but also acquired a truly Japanese character. This development was due both to the taste of the nobility and to the continual progress of Buddhism, which created a great demand for fine articles for personal use and for the adornment of religious property. Around the time of Emperor Ichijo, who reigned from 980 to 1011, the brilliant society at the Imperial court included a group of talented women, among whom was Lady Murasaki Shikibu, who wrote the famous novel *Genji Monogatari*, or *Tale of Genji*. The scroll-paintings illustrating this great story of Genji, with the beautiful interior furnishings of the houses vividly portrayed, also record the lacquer cosmetic kits, inkstone boxes, fan boxes, and other de luxe articles used by courtiers and their ladies. These lacquer objects for personal use were exquisite works of art, usually of black or red lacquer, though green or gold was sometimes used. The designs painted with gold lacquer were representative of the finest artistic accomplishment. The Japanese inkstone box or *suzuri-bako* was one of the articles on which the artist expended his best work. It is a flat box to hold the writer's equipment, comprising an inkstone or *suzuri*, a water dropper or *mizu-sashi*, and compartments for holding the brushes and the inkstick or *sumi*. Cosmetic kits were made in various forms containing tiny drawers and compartments decorated with the most exquisite lacquer work. These magnificent boxes were equipped with various toilet articles beautifully decorated with lacquer. They contained such articles as a mirror together with its container, boxes for tooth black, a box for powder, boxes for incense, a silver bowl, a comb, a rouge brush, a mascara brush, silver scissors, and tweezers. There also were handsome lacquer boxes for holding the Buddhist sutras or scriptures, and many other articles for household use.

Lacquer was lavishly used for the decoration of the many Buddhist temples that were being built at that time. The most famous of these edifices of the Heian period is the Hoodo or Phoenix Hall, attached to the Byodoin temple at Uji, near Kyoto, on the bank of the Uji River in the mountains. Originally a villa of the Prince Minister Fujiwara-no-Michinaga, 966-1024, it was converted into a monastery in 1052. Built in 1053, the Phoenix Hall is one of the finest examples of religious architecture of the late Heian or Fujiwara period. It was designed to represent the mythological phoenix, or *ho-o*, of Chinese origin, in the act of alighting on the ground. Its magnificent interior is noted for sumptuous lacquer decorations with inlays of mother-of-pearl. Many other fine examples of this great period of lacquer work are extant in the famous buildings of Kyoto, the center of culture and the seat of the Imperial court from the year 794. The closing years of the Heian period, which brought with them the decline of the Fujiwara family and strife between various clans, saw the fall and final defeat of the great

Sutra box in gold lacquer showing a design of clouds, falling rain, and vegetation. Late Heian period, eleventh century. Tokyo National Museum.

Gold-lacquer cosmetic box with nacre inlay having a design of shallow water flowing through submerged wheels (detail). Late Heian period, eleventh or twelfth century. Tokyo National Museum.

254

Lacquer sake bottles: Left: Carved wood figure of Hotei in a drunken condition, lacquered red, green, and black; thirteenth century. Right: A carved wood figure of Kosho, a page of honor in the house of a daimyo, wearing ceremonial dress and holding a gourd bottle, decorated in colored lacquers with gold hiramakie; late eighteenth century. Victoria and Albert Museum.

Taira family by Minamoto Yoritomo, who rose to the supreme power in 1185.

Despite the establishment of his headquarters at Kamakura, Kyoto remained the capital and retained its cultural and artistic ascendency. Yoritomo showed a keen interest in religion and respected cultural learning; and although he had limited cultivation, he spent large sums on the restoration of temples, monasteries, and shrines. The Kamakura period, during which the feudal system reached great heights, produced luxurious residences and a profusion of fine works of art. The technical processes of lacquer work were greatly developed, especially in the inlaying of lacquer with gold, silver, and mother-of-pearl. A particular variety of Kamakura lacquer ware is known as *negoro-nuri* or *negoro* lacquer. It first appeared at the end of the thirteenth century, at which time priests from the great Shingon-sect monastery on Koyasan in the Kii Peninsula

moved to the Negoro-Dera, a monastery in the same province. Here they began the production of black-and-red lacquer vessels for domestic use, and the name *negoro* has become a general term applied to plain black-and-red lacquer utensils. Another name connected with lacquer work of this period is *kamakura-bori*, which is a rustic style of carving and lacquering in which rough designs were first carved in high relief and then lacquered in black and red. The early designs for *kamakuri-bori* lacquer consisted chiefly of plum blossoms, peonies, diaper patterns, and a cloud pattern.

LACQUER IN THE MUROMACHI PERIOD

Through the beginning of the Muromachi period (1338–1573) lacquer continued to flourish along with the other arts

Gold-lacquered sutra box with lotus-flower design (detail). Late Heian period, twelfth century. Tokyo National Museum.

Cosmetic box in gold lacquer and mother-of-pearl inlay with a design of deer in an autumn field (detail). Kamakura period, twelfth or thirteenth century. Tokyo National Museum.

255

Left: Lacquered cabinet (kodansu) fitted with a hinged door enclosing five drawers. The front is decorated with deer, birds, and maple trees; on one side are cherry trees in blossom and orange trees with fruit; on the other, cherry trees in blossom and maple; on the end, morning-glories. In silver and gold lacquer on black and shell inlay touched with gold lacquer; each panel is framed by a border of conventional ornament of gold and inlaid shell. Metal fittings. Sixteenth century. Victoria and Albert Museum.

Right: Inkstone box in gold lacquer showing a full moon rising from behind a mountain. Muromachi period, sixteenth century. Tokyo National Museum.

despite the strife and intrigue of the age. The Shogun Ashikaga Yoshimasa, who was addicted to a life of luxury, was largely responsible for the great developments in art, and especially in lacquer. Well versed in literature and art, Yoshimasa gave serious attention to the tea and the incense ceremonies, as previously noted, and as a patron of the arts maintained many artists of distinction. Because so many masterpieces of art appeared in those days, art historians call this era the Higashi-yama Age. Among the foremost lacquer artists employed by the Shogun Yoshimasa was Michinaga Koami, who distinguished himself in the lacquer technique called *taka-makie*, or relief lacquer. According to records of the Koami family, he created a new approach to lacquer decoration by employing the works of famous painters, such as Soami, Noami, Kano Motonobu, and Tosa Mitsunobu, as designs. Another famous lacquer artist in the service of Yoshimasa in the latter part of the Muromachi period was Igarashi Shinsai. These and several other artists were responsible for the perfection of the *taka-makie* decoration and the beautiful *nashi-ji*, which consists of several coats of lacquer at various depths sprinkled with gold or silver, resembling the skin of a pear.

Many designs used on the lacquer ware of this period were of a most refined and delicate nature after the style adapted from paintings of the Sung and Yuan dynasties of China (Plate 16). The passion for things Chinese was great in the intellectual circles of Muromachi and, among the tea masters, for objects of use in the tea ceremony. Due in part to the then current mode of elegance that found enjoyment in exotic

things, the art and literature of the Sung and Yuan dynasties were also greatly appreciated. Trade with China grew in volume and travelers made more frequent trips, both countries being eager to exchange their products. Chinese lacquer ware was highly prized and among the imported articles could be found all the various techniques and forms made in China. The type of Chinese lacquer most highly favored by the Japanese was the *tsui-shiu*, in which several layers of colored lacquer are revealed by carving. In Japan this work is called *guri*, which is the Japanese word for carving. It is claimed that copies of this famous Chinese carved lacquer ware were first made at Murakami, a city at the foot of the mountains in a magnificent section of the rock-bound coast on the Japan Sea, and to the present day, Murakami is noted for its carved lacquer ware. While the Japanese were importing Chinese lacquer wares, they were in turn sending their own lacquer articles to China, where they were highly treasured. It was the Japanese gold lacquer decoration that was most favored by the Chinese, and it is recorded that China sent lacquer artists to Japan to study the various techniques. Although Japan learned about lacquering from China, she developed magnificent work far beyond the Chinese conception.

MOMOYAMA LACQUER

In the opening years of the Momoyama period (1573-1615) the delicate and rather complicated designs of Chinese inspira-

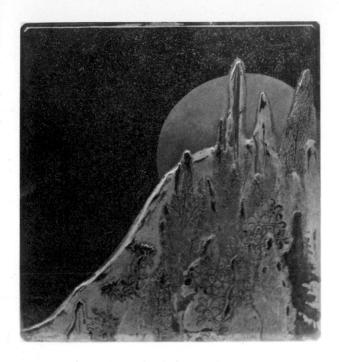

Lacquer writing box in the form of a koto. *The cover has a dragon and brocade pattern in gold and silver* takamakie *and* hiramakie. *The tray, which fits inside, shows a landscape with moon in pewter, and the clouds, rice paddies, stream, and maple tree in the wind are in gold* takamakie *on* nashi-ji *ground. The frame is in* nashi-ji *with inkstone and brass water dropper in shape of a fan. Late seventeenth century. Victoria and Albert Museum.*

tion began to lose their appeal, the rising warrior class of this time favoring the more simplified and striking designs purely Japanese in treatment. After the gradual collapse of Ashikaga rule and the short career of Nobunaga as supreme war lord, the rule of the entire country was assumed by Hideyoshi. The age in which Nobunaga and Hideyoshi flourished is characterized by, among other things, great progress in the realm of art. Hideyoshi's residences were profusely decorated by the foremost artists of the time. The famous Kodaiji temple in Kyoto was built in 1606 by Hideyoshi's widow in memory of her late husband, and although it has been ravaged by repeated fires, the mortuary chapel has survived in a splendid state of preservation with its beautiful decorations of *taka-makie* or raised lacquer.

A characteristic feature of the Momoyama period, which is named after Hideyoshi's palace, was the diminishing interest in the austere principles of Zen Buddhism. A new warrior class appeared with the redistribution of feudal manors, and the temper of the Japanese was such that they enjoyed grandeur and splendor. Both in the fine and applied arts the delicate forms and rich colors reflected a feeling of vigor. Skilled artisans and artists were retained by the new daimyo as part of their households, for the decoration of their great residences and castles with works of art in this age of gold and color. Even the lacquer art of the preceding period with its fine lines and sensitive brush strokes was replaced by brilliance of color and striking designs. The precise and complicated designs of the Muromachi became clear and simplified and extremely elegant in manner. Favorite motifs included chrysanthemums and paulownia leaves and flowers strewn about or incorporated in the principal pictorial composition. Frequent use of both gold and silver lacquer in the same work was a common practice. A great exponent of the gold lacquer work which so forcefully expressed the dynamic quality of Momoyama art was Hon-ami Koetsu, 1558-1637, the foremost artist of this era. His simple yet forceful designs in *taka-makie* reflect his great ability as a painter, lacquer artist, ceramic designer, and skilled calligrapher. Koetsu and his contemporaries contributed a great many pieces of lacquer which compare favorably with the finest æsthetic accomplishments in any field of art. During the time of Hideyoshi, Japan reached a high level of prosperity which created a favorable climate for flourishing activity in the world of art. Upon the death of Hideyoshi in 1598 the country was again thrown into a state of warfare, which lasted for the next several years, until Tokugawa Ieyasu succeeded in subduing the rival families and became supreme ruler of Japan.

DEVELOPMENT OF LACQUER IN THE EDO PERIOD

The siege and fall of Osaka castle in the year 1615, which as we have seen marks the beginning of the Edo or Tokugawa period, brought no cessation of artistic creativity. The dominance of the Tokugawa family over Japan, which lasted until

257

1867, is the period in which the feudal system reached its full maturity. As a result of the so-called Christian Rebellion of Shimabara in 1637, the cessation of intercourse with the outside world closed the ports to foreign ships. A few Dutch and Chinese were allowed to remain in Nagasaki and a limited number of trading ships annually called at the port to exchange goods. From a cultural standpoint the stoppage of overseas travel and trade was a serious handicap, but as the country progressed under the policy of isolation, the Japanese raised their artistic resources to still greater heights. There was a strong revival of Confucianism, and the ruling class promoted and patronized Chinese learning. The study of this philosophy with its practical wisdom, and the teachings of the sages, was responsible for the Chinese influence in the designs on lacquer ware. There was a large demand for lacquer in the Chinese style, in particular the carved red-and-black lacquer called *chinkinbori*, and the *somada* technique, which is a delicate inlay of shell in black lacquer.

Around the early part of the eighteenth century the decorative work in lacquer began to assume an indigenous style. The painter Ogata Korin, 1658-1716, a follower of Hon-ami Koetsu, produced some of the most original lacquer work of the Tokugawa period, typically Japanese in design, color, and expression. He rose to fame in the Genroku era (1688-1704), the most prosperous time under the Tokugawa rule, when luxury and extravagance reached a climax. Korin was one of Japan's greatest painters, and in his lacquer work he combined a sculptural treatment and a sparing use of gold to produce sober effects quite in keeping with his style of painting. There were many great lacquer artists of the Edo period whose names are well known, such as Hanzan, Ritsuo, Kyui, and the distinguished members of the families of Koma and Koami (Plates 17 and 18). Of great importance to the art of Japan was the establishment, in the beginning of the Tokugawa period, of a famous school of lacquer artists in Edo, which flourished for more than three hundred years. The Koami of the eighth generation and Koma Kito-ye were the respective heads of this school at its inception. In 1636 Iemitsu, the third of the Tokugawa Shoguns, appointed Koma as Court Lacquerer, a post which was held by the Koma family of lacquerers for eleven generations.

One of the most celebrated lacquer artists of the Tokugawa period was Yamamoto Shunsho, who was active in Kyoto during the latter part of the seventeenth century, and whose work was carried on by selected descendants for ten generations. There was also the famed Kagikawa school founded by Kagikawa Kujiro, who inaugurated traditions handed down by its members continuously for over two hundred years. Their work was signed with the name of the school together with a seal of jar-shaped contour, which varied widely in its

form. A particular lacquer technique called *togidashi* is one of the distinguishing features of the work of Shiomi Masanari, who flourished at Kyoto from about 1716 to 1736. *Togidashi* consists of building up a design with many coats of lacquer in gold or silver and colors, which is then finally rubbed down to reveal them on a smooth polished surface. This magnificent lacquer work was developed to its finished quality of excellence in the eighteenth century, and the name of Masanari was inherited by many generations of distinguished followers.

The development of the art of lacquer was greatly stimulated by the devotees of the tea and incense ceremonies. As noted in previous chapters, many utensils for use in these ceremonies were of lacquer. The exquisite workmanship and mastery of the various lacquer techniques stamp the finished elegance of the Tokugawa work. The designs, executed with beautiful colors in a purely Japanese manner, include wistaria, blades of grass, bamboo, folding fans, sheaves of grain, and chrysanthemums. Especially beautiful is the work on the charming small lacquer medicine boxes called inro, which were popular among the samurai and merchant class of this period of feudal rule.

When the Meiji period was ushered in, the ancient art of lacquer in its traditional form went into a temporary decline, but with the new government firmly established and an upsurge of prosperity, the art was revived by a number of outstanding lacquerists. Among them may be cited Shirayama Shosai, Ikeda Taishin, Ogawa Shomin, Kawanobe Itcho, and Shibata Zeshin. Zeshin, 1807-1891, was apprenticed to Koma Kwansei when he was only eleven years of age, and is famed as one of the greatest masters of inro lacquer. The inro is probably the best known and most widely collected article of Japanese lacquer work. The decorative lacquer work on inro reached its height in the seventeenth and eighteenth centuries with the great demand by the merchants for ornaments which would vie with the ornamental sword-guards or *tsuba* of the daimyo and samurai.

THE USES OF LACQUER

Many distinctive Japanese articles and utensils were traditionally made in lacquer. Typical is the Japanese lacquered soup bowl with its cover, which is said to improve the taste of the soup, and the lacquered sake cups. Used at weddings, these sake cups or *sakazuki* were in sets of three, and are in the form of extremely shallow bowls graduating in diameter from two to three inches from the smallest one to the largest of the set. They are placed one on top of the other upon a square lacquered stand specially made to hold them. At a wedding the bride and bridegroom observe the ceremony of *san-san-kudo*,

A set of lacquer boxes having a cover showing a river landscape with trees, mountains, a mill, a country house, boats, a cottage, temples, etc., in takamakie *enriched with* kirikane *on a ground of* nashi-ji. *The three Tokugawa crests are inlaid in gold. Early eighteenth century. Victoria and Albert Museum.*

Lacquer writing box. Early eighteenth century. The cover on the right has a design of rocks, rushes, and a stream in gold takamakie, *enriched with* kirikane *with two mandarin ducks of various colors on a black ground. The frame on the left is decorated with a motif of waves and clouds in gold* togidashi, *containing an oval inkstone and silver crane-shaped water dropper enriched with gold. Victoria and Albert Museum.*

259

meaning three threes are nine, when they sip three times out of three different sake cups, by which they pledge their marriage vows. According to Japanese belief three means good luck, and *san-san-kudo* therefore signifies the wish for a happy union. An attractive article for personal use is the *kodansu*, the name given to a lacquered rectangular cabinet with two small cupboard doors enclosing a nest of drawers. Its average height is about thirteen inches, its width about fifteen inches, and its depth about twelve inches. The *kodansu*, with its finely lacquered interior portions and its chased brass hasps and lock plate, is not only a beautiful decorative object but also serves as a dressing case for jewelry, handkerchiefs, and other small articles of personal use. Another object reserved for feminine use is the kimono tray or *midaro kago*. It is a very large lacquered tray characterized by deep sides, generally made of the finest quality black lacquer with the family crest or *mon* executed in gold in the center. The kimono tray is placed on the *tatami* or matted floor, and a tall two-panel screen is generally placed in front of it. The tray was a dressing-room accessory for a Japanese lady to drop her kimono and other clothing into, which could then be removed by a servant.

An important article for use in the home and in the tea and incense ceremonies was the lacquered incense box called a *kobako* or *kogu*, which was one of the choice pieces on which the artist lavished his finest work. Due to the Japanese way of

living, lacquer trays of various types are important household accessories. *Kasane*, meaning one over the other, is the name given to a tier of lacquered trays so designed that one is stacked upon the other to form a block-like or box-like arrangement. The *kasane* generally comprises three and occasionally five trays and is furnished with a lid. It is made in various sizes and serves many purposes, one of which is a tray or *ozen*. Traditionally the Japanese used individual dining trays rather than a large dining table. The trays are either flat or mounted on very short straight legs, at a convenient height for the diner as he sits on the *tatami* floor, Japanese fashion. This custom of individual trays is still observed in some Japanese homes and inns. *Ozen* are made in various sizes for the different courses, the *ozen* most commonly used being about one square foot in size. A very small *ozen* is used for tea and cake and also for sake. Essentially the *ozen* is a very plain tray and is generally lacquered black, deep red, or dull orange monochrome. At a regular Japanese dinner, a guest is frequently provided with two side trays besides the main one. When these lacquer trays are placed upon the *tatami* floor before each guest with the various small porcelain dishes and bowls, they present an attractive and colorful effect in the elegant simplicity of the Japanese room.

Among the many other articles traditionally made in lacquer were the *shikishi bako*, a box for small square pieces of paper called *shikishi*, which were used for writing poems; the

Lacquered cabinet consisting of one large and six small drawers within two folding doors. In carved wood, lacquered black, green, red, and yellow. Details finished in guri (carved lacquer). The front is decorated with dragons, birds, and clouds in panels with borders of peaches; the lower drawer, with peaches on geometric ground, framed by key-pattern black border. The inside of doors carved in intaglio with flowers in vases and other motifs on black ground; gourd plants on fronts of drawers. Gilt metal fittings. Late eighteenth century. Victoria and Albert Museum.

Left: Tray for smoking set. Black-lacquer ground with a design in gold hiramakie *depicting men towing a boat upstream and pine trees in the distance. Edo period, early nineteenth century. Tokyo National Museum.*

Below: Lacquer document box showing the exquisite work of one of its sides of pavilions with court nobles, a lake and garden, etc. Border of conventional flowers and scrolls in gold and silver hiramakie *enriched with gold and silver foil on black ground. Mid-eighteenth century. Victoria and Albert Museum.*

bento bako, a picnic box in which to carry food and drink; the *tabako bon* or smoking box for the ash tray and charcoal; the *tebako* or large deep box for holding paper; the *fubako*, a letter box or dispatch box used for the delivery of letters by hand; the *hasami bako*, a lacquered traveling box or chest for clothes, which was carried at the end of a pole resting over the shoulder of a carrier; the *cha bako* or box for tea-ceremony utensils; the *natsume* or lacquer box for holding powdered tea, the *cha-ire* or tea jar; and the *katana kake*, or rack for holding either three or five swords.

With the exception of some of the interior appointments that were decorated with red-and-black lacquer in the palaces and great mansions of the nobles and feudal lords in early times, almost all articles of lacquer ware were small in size. However, some of the vehicles employed from ancient times until the Meiji Restoration are magnificent examples of the art of lacquer. These conveyances were ox-drawn carriages used only by people of the highest rank, and the *norimono* (palanquin) which served to carry aristocrats and officers of high position. The ox-carriages were of great size with two huge wooden wheels; they were adorned with curtains of the finest bamboo craftsmanship suspended in front, and thick cords and tassels of plaited silk. The whole of these great ox-

carriages was embellished with rich and elaborate lacquer work of superb quality, and the draft animal, an ox of handsome proportions, was covered with a caparison of brilliantly colored silks. Great care and expense was lavished upon these highly ornate vehicles, as they were for the special use of the Emperor, the Shogun, and their immediate families. The palanquin or *norimono* was usually very ornate, often being made of fine lacquer work. It resembled a miniature Japanese house slung by its roof-ridge from a massive pole which projected sufficiently at either end to allow it to rest on the shoulders of carriers. The only other form of conveyance was the *kago*, an open palanquin, of V-shaped construction in cross-section, which was slung from a pole that rested on the shoulders of two porters. The *kago*, which was the humblest of the vehicles considered appropriate for the upper classes, is occasionally depicted in Japanese color prints. These three vehicles represented the manner of travel until the year 1870, when a Japanese invented the *jinrikisha*, the use of which eventually spread through the whole of the Far East. Nevertheless, the magnificence of the lacquered ox-carriages can still be appreciated when these pieces are used to represent the Shogun's retinue in the procession of the Jidai Matsuri, the annual festival of the Heian shrine at Kyoto. During the Edo

Left: Lacquer picnic set consisting of four boxes and a large tray showing over-all geometric patterns and sprays of cherry blossom, in shell inlay on ro-iro. Also included in the set are one sake cup and two sake bottles in bronze with flower-shaped crests applied and silver stoppers and mount-piece. Early nineteenth century. Victoria and Albert Museum.

Right: Enlarged detail of lacquer decoration on a writing-box table. The shells with their interiors depicting flowers, and the one shell with a design of an Imperial ox-carriage, are in takamakie enriched with shell and kirikane on coarse hirame ground. Early nineteenth century. Victoria and Albert Museum.

period when the Hina Matsuri, or Doll's Festival, was celebrated, it became the fashion in Kyoto to ornament the doll stand with miniature reproductions of a bride's outfit of the kind used by an aristocratic family. Included among the various articles was a miniature ox-carriage with an exquisite over-all decoration with delicate gold and colored lacquer work. These beautiful pieces have continued to be used until the present time during the Dolls' Festival.

TECHNIQUES OF LACQUER

The technique and practice of Far Eastern lacquer, its methods and its materials, are different from any other type of lacquer work. In contrast to the European so-called lacquer, which is nothing more than a varnish consisting of a solution of shellac in alcohol, Chinese and Japanese lacquer work is produced from true lacquer. This is the sap of a tree, the *Rhus vernicifera*, which in the best work is used in its natural state, and only processed for the removal of excess water and impurities. The tree was indigenous to China, and was cultivated in Japan from at least the sixth century. As previously mentioned, its cultivation in this early period was constantly encouraged by Imperial decree. The lacquer is obtained by tapping trees when they are about ten years old, this being done during the season from June to September. The trees are tapped with groups of horizontal incisions starting from the foot of the tree and continuing upward in alternating series from left to right. Branches of one-inch diameter and more are also tapped after the bark has been removed, while the smaller branches, which yield a particular quality of sap for special uses, called *seshime*, are cut off and their sap collected

by steeping in water. Although this tapping process is responsible for killing the tree, several new shoots grow again from the roots. Within six or seven years the tree is again mature enough for tapping, and these cycles of growth and tapping continue for an extended length of time before the tree becomes completely drained of its strength. The crude lacquer thus obtained is a gray liquid which turns yellow-brown and then black when exposed to the air. This sap is placed in wooden tubs to be stirred and pounded so as to produce a uniform consistency, and then the impurities are removed by straining through pieces of cloth. The fluid is then heated by the rays of the sun or over a very low fire to evaporate the excess water content.

The peculiar qualities and characteristics of Chinese and Japanese lacquer account for its superiority over any other kind, and for its distinctive beauty. Far Eastern lacquer attains its extreme hardness by being subjected to moisture during the drying process. Actually a lacquered article is placed in a "damp box" many times, this procedure being repeated after each coat is applied during the course of work. As a result of this drying method, the lacquer becomes so hard that for its final treatment it can be ground down with a whetstone to the utmost degree of smoothness. It can be given the richest and most brilliant polish by rubbing with deer-horn ashes, fine burnt clay, or other similar materials. Lacquer treated through these processes is remarkable for its resistance to acid and heat. It is owing to the extreme durability of lacquer ware that the Japanese have been able to use it for many centuries for their household utensils.

The principal method of making lacquer ware has remained the same for centuries. The article to be lacquered is generally made of a variety of white pine with a soft and even grain.

Lacquer smoking cabinet in shape of a six-panel screen with three drawers, the upper part fitted with lacquer tobacco box with inro-shaped cover, silver box for ashes, and silver stove with pouch-shaped cover; gilt and chased with conventional floral scrolls. Cabinet decorated on front with various flowers and the back with Chinese sages engaged in various amusements; in gold and silver togidashi on polished black ground in panels on gold fundame. Early nineteenth century. Victoria and Albert Museum.

After the article has been shaped by the woodworker, its surface is made smooth and prepared with a coat of *seshime* lacquer to provide an even base to receive the successive series of layers. A coat of lacquer composition is then laid on and smoothed with a whetstone. The next coat is a more refined composition made of lacquer and burnt clay, which is ground down and then laid away to dry for no less than twelve hours. Then a mixture of rice paste and lacquer is applied as an adhesive, over which is affixed a layer of flax cloth or Japanese paper, and the article is again put away to dry for about twenty-four hours. Over this coating of cloth is applied a coat of fine lacquer composition and the article is again dried and this process is repeated many times. After these several repeated coatings an application of very hard lacquer is given, and after an extended drying period the surface is finely ground. Following this, ten or more coats of lacquer are applied, each requiring time to dry and each being rubbed down and polished until the object so treated is then ready for the artist to begin his work of decorating.

The artist generally executes his design in outline with a thin paste of white lead and then fills in the details of the design with colors of metal dust or foil. This is covered with transparent lacquer and polished. When relief work is desired the designs are built up with a heavy paste of white lead, lampblack, camphor, and black lacquer. When gold or silver dust is applied on the painted decoration, it is done with the aid of a tiny bamboo tube or with a quill. After applying gold, silver, and other metallic filings or powders, several polishing processes are necessary to produce the proper luster. In the decorative processes using fragments of gold or silver foil, such as in *hirame* or *kiribame* work, a pointed wooden tool is employed to apply each minute piece individually. Some-

times more than five hundred separate pieces of foil fragments are required to fill in a square inch of design in these two processes. It can be seen that the many processes necessary to make the finest lacquer ware required laborious and painstaking work. Through the ingenuity and remarkable skill of the artisan and the artist, Japanese lacquer ware of the great periods represents some of the finest pieces of craftsmanship ever executed anywhere in the world.

The different techniques employed by the Japanese lacquer artist to create these masterpieces have special designations. The following concise descriptions or definitions cover all the important Japanese lacquer methods. *Hira-makie* is decoration in low relief, being built up with lacquer in its pure state. *Taka-makie* refers to decoration in relief of varying depth, built up with a lacquer composition consisting of white lead, a lacquer putty, lampblack, powder, and camphor, and frequently enriched with gold or silver foil. *Hirame* is made with minute, irregularly shaped pieces of gold or silver foil placed separately on the surface. *Hakeme* is applied to a surface of lacquer which shows the brush marks. *Nashi-ji* is work resembling the skin of a pear. Minute flakes of gold or silver are sprinkled on the surface and covered with a coat of lacquer. Many successive layers of this process are applied, each being hardened before applying the next. After the desired number of coats are applied, the surface is rubbed to a high polish which produces color tones ranging from a golden to a deep red or brown, depending upon the depth or number of coats used. This technique reached its highest degree of perfection during the fifteenth century. *Hirame-nashi-ji* refers to the *hirame* method when applied in many coats of varying depth. *Mura-nashi-ji* applies to *nashi-ji* when it is marred by an uneven distribution of the gold and silver. *Giobu-nashi-ji* means

Lacquered box with tray decorated with conventional chrysanthe-mums and stream pattern in bands of gold hirame *and* nashi-ji *on black ground. Copper mounts in form of* kiri *crests. Late nineteenth century. Victoria and Albert Museum.*

nashi-ji work having particles of gold foil intermixed on the topmost coat. *Negoro-nuri* is mottled red-and-black lacquer on carved wood. *Guri* refers to the process of applying several layers of colored lacquer and carving the design with deeply cut V-shaped channels to reveal the edges of the various colored layers. This process originated in China, where it is called *tsui-shiu*. *Kamakura-bori* lacquer decoration is said to have been first made at the end of the twelfth century. It consists of wood carved in relief, originally coated with red or black lacquer, and later with other colors. The designs were usually plum blossoms and peonies against rather bold diaper backgrounds. *Chinkinbori* represents lacquer traced with shallow engraving and filled in with gold lacquer. *Fundame* refers to fine gold and silver powder worked in the lacquer and rubbed to produce a flat, dull finish on the surface. *Urushi-e,* or lacquer picture, has the decoration painted in black or colored lacquers. *Mokume* represents the imitation of the grain of wood. *Kiribame* is a variety of work having minute sheets of gold or silver inlaid separately in the surface of lacquer as a mosaic; this method was introduced in the fifteenth century. *Kin-makie* is the term used to describe a ground covered with gold lacquer. *Makie* literally means sprinkled picture, and the term is now used in a general way to describe any kind of gold or silver picture done on lacquer ware. *Kingin-e* refers to a lacquer process of the Nara period prior to the development of *makie*, in which the design is drawn with a compound of gold or silver powder and glue. *Shu-nuri* means cinnabar or red lacquer.

An early lacquer process that had its origin in the Heian period and became very popular during Kamakura times was *ikaki-ji*, in which the entire surface, or a portion of it, is covered with sprinkled gold or silver filings. In *sabi-ji*, the lacquering is done to imitate the surface of rusty iron. *Togidashi* is an unusually beautiful form of lacquer work in which the design is built up with many coats of lacquer in gold or silver and colors and then rubbed down to reveal them. The term is also applied to black-and-gold lacquer work. *Zokoku-nuri* has the design carved out and filled in with colored lacquer and then rubbed down. The name is derived from Tamakaji Zokoku, a lacquer artist working in the late eighteenth century, who is said to have invented this process. *Wakasa-nuri* consists of various mottled lacquer colors, such as black, white, silver, and gold, overlaid upon each other so as to produce cloud motifs or similar effects. The *zonsei-nuri* technique is rather similar to *zokoku-nuri*, except that its designs are conventionalized with mottled and irregular patterns. *Zogan-nuri* represents a lacquer technique which imitates cloisonné enamel, in which the design is outlined with gold or silver wire with lacquer inlaid in the spaces between. A technique in which only colored lacquers are intermingled and then ground down to a smooth finish is called *tsugaru-nuri*. The name is derived from the Daimyo of Tsugaru, on whose feudal estate this type of lacquer was made. *Tame-nuri* is the name given to a transparent dark brownish-red lacquer which is used as a finishing coat over a colored lacquer ground. *Shunkei-nuri* is said to have been invented by Shunkei, a lacquer artist of Sakai, in the latter part of the fourteenth century. It was originally used as a polish for natural wood, and later as a finishing coat of lacquer having a transparent reddish-brown color.

Roiro is the name given by the Japanese to the finest quality of polished black lacquer (Plate 15). To produce a piece of *roiro* lacquer with its perfect black, no less than twenty to thirty processes are required, each involving the most careful and exacting work when rubbing. The taste for *roiro* lacquer began in the Momoyama period when the famous tea master Sen-no-Rikyu set the fashion of using black utensils at the tea ceremony. The name *raden* is given to a decoration of shell, pewter, and gold or silver foil. The shells used in this work, which is also called *kanagai*, are sea ear, nautilus, and similar nacreous shells. Lacquer ware having *raden* decoration was made as early as the eighth century in Japan, and articles made with this kind of work have been preserved in the Shosoin Treasure Repository of the Todaiji temple at Nara ever since they were donated by the Empress-Regnant Koken in 765. Many famous temples of the early periods contained *raden* decoration on altars, pillars, and on other interior parts. A great number of sword scabbards were decorated with *raden*, which was very fashionable with the warrior class.

XVIII Inro, Netsuke, Yatate, Tobacco Pouch and Pipe Case, and Hiuchi-Bukuro

I N NO BRANCH of the applied arts is Japanese decorative genius more in evidence than in inro, and in none has more exquisite lacquer work been lavished, often with designs by the foremost artists of the time. This small and beautiful object has no counterpart in any other country, and is probably the favorite and most widely collected article of Japanese lacquer work. For several centuries the term *inro* has been applied to the miniature medicine case carried by the Japanese gentleman, hanging from his girdle or obi. The word originally signified a vessel or basket (*ro*) to hold seals (*in*), and although the name is something of a misnomer, it is an aid in determining the origin of the inro. Since the name literally means seal basket, it therefore suggests that originally the inro had no connection with medicine.

ORIGINS OF THE INRO

The inro in its present form was first made around the middle of the sixteenth century, but its true origin is shrouded in mystery. It has been suggested that it was derived from the seal case, as the name implies, and there is even the erroneous inference that its origin may be traced back to the *hiuchi-bukuro*, a receptacle for holding flint, steel, and tinder, which was carried suspended from the girdle in ancient times. It is most likely that many of the earlier inro, in the form by which they are presently known, were used to hold a seal or chop for making one's impression, and that they soon evolved into portable medicine cases. From ancient times, and long before the Christian era, the seal was regarded as a most important article among the Chinese, and when Chinese culture exerted its influence upon the Japanese in the seventh century, the seal attained a relatively high position in the life of those times.

Though the science of written characters is of ancient origin in Asia, until recent times it was reserved to the small group of the leisured class, the masses using crosses, circles, or the imprint of the finger or hand when affixing a sign on a document. In Japan various official seals were used by the Emperor, the ministers, and others as early as the Nara period, and although their use was rather general among leading persons, it was not until around the sixteenth century that the practice became common among people of all classes. The seal is usually made of hardwood or ivory and bears the name of the person in raised or incised characters; it is inked with cinnabar or lampblack mixed with oil so that the impression can be made. Since relatively few persons were able to sign with their *kakihan*, or written seal, an edict was issued early in the seventeenth century which permitted the lower classes to use a legal seal, while at the same time forbidding the use of a seal to the nobility and to all grades of the military class except by special permission. At that time it was considered a breach of etiquette and a lack of respect to use anything other than the *kakihan*, but as time went on the use of the seal became general among all people and it even became a legal rule that no official document or other writing would be valid without the personal seal, a practice which exists to the present day.

A number of passages in sixteenth-century Japanese records refer to inro or seal boxes of Chinese style made of carved red or black lacquer, generally about four inches in diameter, round or square, and consisting of a series of from three to five shallow boxes fitting into each other. An inro of this type is illustrated in a Japanese book published in 1523, and shows the four round cases secured together with a cord which passes up through apertures on either side. The cord is tied with a bow at the bottom and has a netsuke and *ojime* at the top so the inro could be carried about by hand. Because of the great importance attached to individuals' seals, they soon became valuable objects on which the artist worked beautiful ornamental designs, and the seal boxes also became fine works of

Inro of red kamakura-bori *lacquer showing a Chinese sage with an attendant on one side and a ho-o bird on the other, with top carved in openwork design of conventional flowers and leaves. It is composed of two cases. Early eighteenth century. The* ojime *is of green glass, and the netsuke is of carved wood depicting Hotei in red, blue, and white lacquer. Victoria and Albert Museum.*

Guri (carved-lacquer) inro with Chinese sages and their attendants in a grove of bamboo and pines, with an over-all geometric ground. Four cases. Seventeenth century. The ojime *(bead) is of* guri *lacquer and depicts Chinese boys at play. The netsuke is in the form of a Manju cake, in* guri *lacquer, and shows Chinese boys at play and an over-all geometric ground. Both date from the late seventeenth century. Victoria and Albert Museum.*

art so they could be placed upon a shelf in the *chigai-dana* or shelved alcove.

The original inro seal boxes from China were protected from damage by a brocade or leather bag, which in turn was enclosed by a sheathing cover having a cord so it could be carried by hand, hung by a neck chain, or attached to the girdle. From presumptive evidence these outer containers are believed to have been made of plaited work, because the Chinese often used finely woven bags and baskets made of reeds or thread-like splits of bamboo. Receptacles of this kind were frequently lacquered to make them more durable, and were used for a great many purposes in Japan. The more practical inro of Chinese origin had two compartments, one on each side, to hold the seal and the oily substance. The science of preparing medicines was introduced into Japan from China around the first century of our era, and the chief ingredients used were herbs, roots, flowers, parts of animals, and minerals. From very early times the Japanese were seasoned travellers, and as drugs were apt to spoil during a long trip from the heat or the moisture, they were carried in small bags or receptacles of wood, bamboo, bone, or horn and suspended from the girdle. Preserved among the treasures in the Shosoin are a number of small receptacles of Chinese origin that were probably used as medicine boxes when enclosed in silk net bags and attached to the girdle. Special containers used in ancient times for keeping drugs in houses are mentioned in writings of the Kamakura period, where they are called *kusuri-bako*, or medicine boxes. The records say these *kusuri-bako* were used during the Early Heian period (794-897) and describe them as lacquered boxes measuring over one foot square and containing several vessels for medicines. At some later date the *kusuri-bako* was made into a small portable container tied with cords in which to carry drugs. This was called a *yakuro*, and came into the category of *sagemono*, or hanging things. Lacquer was the preferred material for these boxes or containers because it was believed to preserve the drugs and keep them fresh. It seems that until the late Middle Ages the average Japanese carried only one pouch, which was made of leather or basketwork, and was used to keep his amulet, seal, medicines, and flint, steel, and tinder. Feudal lords and court nobles often carried receptacles which were indiscriminately called inro. They consisted of several superimposed cases similar to the Chinese seal box and were beautifully lacquered or carved.

THE TYPES OF INRO

In the latter part of the seventeenth century the inro with its netsuke, or toggle, became a veritable work of art. The inro in its fully developed form is composed of a nest of superimposed tiny cases or boxes, fitting tightly into each other, and held in position by a silk cord which passes across the bottom and to the top through channels on the sides. Above the top of the inro the cord passes through a sliding bead called *ojime*, which keeps the cases tightly secured together, and is attached to the netsuke at the end. Although single-case inro are sometimes found, they generally consist of from two to seven cases, with the interiors of the two-case inro occasionally subdivided to form double compartments, each furnished with a tiny tray. The majority of inro are elliptical in section, and are composed of from three to five cases, with the usual dimensions being from three to four inches in height, and from two to two and a half inches in width, with their depth about three-quarters of an inch. Other forms in which inro were made range from rectangular, cylindrical, and hexagonal to octagonal in section. Some examples of inro are in the form of a miniature cabinet having small drawers and even a space for a tiny spoon. Particularly interesting is a device to enclose and protect the inro, consisting of a kind of sheath, frequently of openwork to permit a portion of the inro decoration to be seen. Although the beauty and fineness of an inro is determined by its artistic workmanship and design, the extraordinary accuracy with which the small cases are fitted to each other is worthy of consideration. These small articles, with their difficult curves in related succession, are skillfully and delicately made, the wood or leather core being worked to an extreme thinness. The exactness to which this core has been carved and the perfection with which the cases fit into one another represents the finest quality of woodworking and craftmanship known. The majority of inro are lacquered, but they are also made of plain and polished wood, of wood inlaid with various metals, ivory, or shell, and occasionally of carved wood.

In æsthetic quality inro reached their apex during the Tokugawa period. During the second half of the Tokugawa period a large number of schools of inro became famous for particular designs, shapes, and colors. However, due to the lack of descriptive detail in existing records, it is not possible to ascertain the development of subsequent shapes of the inro as they became fashionable. Although their shapes vary considerably, one particular feature separates the majority of inro into two categories, depending upon the disposition of the cord. In some inro the cord channels are inside the body, and on others the channels protrude along either side in the form of tubes. In the former type with invisible channels the inro tends to be elliptical in section, while in the latter type with external channels the shape is flatter in section and tapers toward the sides. Occasionally inro are found having a rectangular or hexagonal cross-section with wider central sections;

Ro-iro *lacquer inro with two* bugaku *masks in* takamakie *of gold and colors, enriched with inlay of gold and shell. Composed of five cases, with two cases having double compartments. Late eighteenth century. The* ojime *is a carved wood mask and the netsuke is of gold* takamakie *in the form of a box for masks. Victoria and Albert Museum.*

Ro-iro *lacquer inro having the design of a cottage, a pine tree, and a charm under the eave of the roof to exorcise demons and evil spirits. The decoration is in* takamakie *of gold, silver, red, and brown. Early nineteenth century. Signed Tatsuke Kukio. The cylindrical-shaped* ojime *is ornamented with twisted bands of gold, silver, bronze, and* shibuichi, *while the netsuke is in the form of a carved-wood goat. Victoria and Albert Museum.*

267

these were popular during the second half of the eighteenth century. The top and bottom surfaces may be either flat, slightly convex with a gentle curve at the edges, or flat with a slight step around the edge.

These variations are not restricted to any one type of inro but are used interchangeably in an endless variety of different combinations according to the individual taste of the artist. In the sheath inro mentioned above, the superimposed cases are slipped into a closely fitting sheath. The sheath, which is open at the top, contains the cord channels and has an aperture on the bottom surface so that the series of cases can be pushed upward with the finger. The drawer inro, instead of being composed of the usual cases or compartments, opens on one side by a panel that slides within grooves, or by a panel hinged at the bottom. When open, the interior reveals a series of tiny drawers, each having a minute knob and fitted within the body with utmost precision. The cord channels are delicately worked so as to pass through the length of the sliding panel and behind the drawers on the other side of the body. Apart from the characteristic inro with its distinctive form, a small percentage of examples dating from the middle of the nineteenth century onward were made as novelties in a wide variety of shapes.

INRO TECHNIQUES

The case or body of the earliest inro were made of leather, and the finest examples continued to be made in the same material. The core usually consisted of *hinoki* cypress covered with a strong and finely cured ox-leather. Occasionally inro were produced by a very delicate method in which the body was mostly composed of lacquer. The craftsman would use as his core a very thin skin from a dog or cat, which was saturated with lacquer, then covered with a piece of fine cloth or mulberry paper and, when sufficiently dry, shaped to its final form and given many coats of lacquer. A simpler process used in a great number of inro consisted of a *hinoki* core which required fewer coatings of lacquer, but at the same time made it more susceptible to damage.

From the closing years of the Tokugawa period and throughout the Meiji period there persisted a great demand for inro, which in turn encouraged the artisans to resort to easier and quicker methods of production. These inferior inro were made by fashioning and gluing together thin pliable sheets of *hinoki* wood to form the core, which was saturated with the juice of unripened persimmons, called *shibu*, to close the pores and harden the wood. This was followed by several coats of *sabi*, a paste consisting of raw lacquer and clay, which prepared the surface for the final decoration and lacquering.

Reddish-brown lacquer inro shaded with fundame, *representing Daruma in a sack; he has glass eyes and at his feet is a whisk. It consists of a single case. Early nineteenth century. The* ojime *is a silver bead inlaid with gold. The netsuke is of carved wood and represents Fukurokuju, one of the seven gods of good fortune. Victoria and Albert Museum.*

This method at times resulted in minute shrinkage, causing the cases of these inro to lose their precision-like fit. The traditional techniques used in making the finer examples were intricate, painstaking, and time-consuming, the artisan not only applying his skill to the exterior but making the interior surfaces equally fine. There existed a branch of inro artisans who specialized in making the core, those of Kyoto being particularly noted for this work. The greatest precision was required, as the sections had to be so constructed that sufficient tolerance was allowed to compensate for the many layers of lacquer to be applied by the artist. This calculated allowance was necessary to make these sections fit so perfectly that they would form an airtight union, but at the same time be able to slide open without strain. Innumerable layers of *sabi* were built up on all the raw bodies of inro, each coat being allowed to dry and then rubbed down to a smooth surface. This process created a hard surface on which to apply the layers of lacquer to produce the finished work. It was so important for the raw core of the inro to be perfectly seasoned to avoid any shrinkage or distortion, that the lacquer artist would keep it hanging from the ceiling for several years to acclimate it to the variations of the weather.

The remarkable precision with which the sectional cases and cover of a fine inro fit into one another is an amazing accomplishment and a tribute to the ingenuity and skill of the Japanese craftsman. The designs executed on the exterior of inro are so perfectly carried through in the different sections that the joints are almost invisible. The method of decorating inro requires that the interior surfaces be finished before any work is commenced on the exterior. These interior surfaces are often finished in a red or black lacquer monochrome, particularly in the older examples, while the later ones were

Fundame *lacquer inro deco-rated with a representation of the ceremony of the last day of winter. Daruma, in metal-work enriched with gold, is looking through a window lined with shell and throwing out oni—also in metalwork —by scattering beans in the traditional manner. It is com-posed of five cases. Early nineteenth century and signed Kajikawa. The* kagamibuta *netsuke is ornamented with the heads of two manju danc-ers in gold and metal in a* fundame *frame. Victoria and Albert Museum.*

Carved-wood inro in the form of a cicada, consisting of three cases. Late nineteenth century. The ojime *is of carved wood in the form of two monkeys and the netsuke, also of carved wood, repre-sents a cicada chrysalis. Vic-toria and Albert Museum.*

frequently finished with a dull gold-colored lacquer. Oc-casionally the outer surface of the tiny recessed portion of the rims, which form the ridge joining one case to the other, is decorated with fine gold lines or a delicately engraved scroll pattern. Finishing the interior surfaces is a most important stage in the whole process of making a fine inro, especially because of the extreme care required to see that the tolerance allowed in the undecorated body is fully adjusted by successive layers of lacquer to make the joint neither too loose nor too tight.

Of the two methods practiced in the subsequent work of decorating the external surface, the one more generally used consisted of first clamping the cases or sections tightly to-gether by applying to the point of contact between the cases a waxy substance called *bintsuke*. With all the cases thus tightly fixed together, the artist then had an unbroken surface on which to apply the several coats of colored lacquer required for the ground of the finished decoration. The final stage in this process is the delicate work of cutting through the lacquer with an extremely fine, sharp knife to separate the sections. To ascertain the proper line of cutting, the inro is very slightly warmed over a slow fire, which causes the waxy substance to melt on the inside of the body and make the cleft lines slightly visible. This cutting must be done with the greatest care and exactness, as an error would necessitate retouching the lacquer before the final polishing operation and could easily result in certain discolorations. The alternate method is finer but more tedious, the sections being pasted together and cut apart after each layer of lacquer. When each coat of lacquer has been thoroughly dried and polished, it can be very skillfully cracked along the cleft line by warming the fixing paste. In this painstaking method the film of fixing wax must be completely

removed between each operation, and any excess lacquer particles must be closely ground away each time. This is especially tedious when practiced for high-relief lacquer.

The technique of inro decoration involved principally the various processes that were developed and applied in the art of lacquer. Since the inro was considered the most important accessory to costume, it became an article of luxury com-manding high prices. The finest inro were usually executed by such artists as Ogata Korin, Hon-ami Koetsu, or Koami Michinaga, or adapted from the works of the great painters such as the masters of the Tosa and Kano schools. Many of the designs were taken directly from or based upon kakemono paintings, floor screens, or sliding doors by famous artists. In the traditional taste of the Japanese nobility of ancient times the designs included scenes of court life, majestic landscapes, the beautiful Japanese interpretation of waves, snow scenes, ancient trees, exquisite flowers, and conventionalized motifs of fans, plants, and native architecture. With the growing wealth and cultural development of the *chonin*, or towns-people, in the large urban areas, new decorative motifs ap-peared, inspired by the Kabuki actors and other inhabitants of the Ukiyo, or Drifting World, of the Tokugawa period. However, the new modes created by the demand of this new class of society did not displace the traditional modes preferred by the upper classes. With the increase in wealth among a large segment of the citizens the demand for inro continued to increase, as it was usually the only article of personal adorn-ment (Plate 20). The pictorial designs were taken from legend, mythology, scenes from the No drama and Kabuki theater, famous views of Japan as depicted in color prints, stylized motifs, representations of the gods of good fortune, and other subjects. Although the majority of inro were of lacquer, many beautiful inro were made of metal, cloisonné, carved ivory, coral, tortoise shell, carved wood, finely woven basketwork hardened with lacquer, and other materials. Many examples of metal inro bear the signature of famous sword-mount artists.

USES OF INRO

The inro gradually evolved from being an article primarily worn for utilitarian purposes to one having great æsthetic value, an object of virtu. To the daimyo and wealthy merchants they not only became costly objects purchased in great numbers to be worn; they were also collected as art objects (Plate 19). It became the fashion to form collections of sets of inro executed by famous artists, and these were often arranged on sliding frames in beautiful lacquered cabinets. When extremely fine examples of inro were worn or carried about, they were often enclosed in beautiful containers of fine brocades for protection against damage. But, although the inro gradually developed into an extremely beautiful object as an accessory to the costume, and the best were exquisite works of art, it was not worn by women. For that matter the feminine dress of the Tokugawa period did not permit sagemono, or hanging things, or any kind of girdle pendant, because the obi was very wide and wound around the body several times, making a tight, hard, corset-like girdle, so that it was difficult for the netsuke and cord to be passed beneath it. There was,

however, a miniature inro called kwaichu, which could be attached to the broacaded silk hanagami-bukuro, a sort of flat folded pocketbook carried by women. The hanagami-bukuro was used to contain such things as paper handkerchiefs and rouge, and was carried in the breastfold of the kimono with one corner slightly protruding.

The inro was a recognized accessory of the costume of a gentleman, and it was worn by the nobles and those of the feudal military class. Because Buddhism does not allow its disciples to wear articles of personal adornment, the inro was not carried by priests or monks, and therefore religious subjects were not depicted on inro until the Meiji period, when some were made for the export market. The exception to this rule is that the inro still forms a part of the prescribed costume of the komuso, a street-musician, who, with his head hidden deep in a huge rush basket-like headpiece, plays a vertical bamboo flute called shakuhachi. Theoretically komuso belonged to a Buddhist sect called Fukeshu, which in early times had many temples throughout the country, but they were actually itinerant priests unaffiliated with any particular sect. In feudal times komuso were often samurai in disguise, traveling about the country in search of an enemy, but today they are still seen playing their bamboo flutes and begging for alms from house to house. Until rather recent times elderly Japanese men were often seen carrying an inro at the girdle of the kimono, together with the pipe case and tobacco pouch, and the kinchaku or money pouch.

Amber netsuke of a chrysanthemum. Signed Kaigyoku, 1813-1892. Edo period. Collection Charles A. Greenfield, New York.

Netsuke of wood and various materials in form of an alms-bowl containing a Buddhist bell, a worn ink stick, a magatama, and a Buddhist rosary; cord-hole edged with stained ivory. Signed Tokoku and seal. Edo period, late nineteenth century. Collection Charles A. Greenfield, New York

NETSUKE

One of the most interesting and remarkable objects of creative art is the Japanese netsuke or carved toggle attached to the cord of all kinds of *sagemono*, such as the inro, money pouch, pipe case and tobacco pouch, and the yatate or brush case, to keep them securely suspended from the girdle. As the Japanese native costume, the kimono, was not provided with either pockets or pouches, it was necessary for the gentleman to carry his inro and other small objects slung by a cord to his obi or girdle like a chatelaine. The netsuke is believed to date from the fifteenth century, but it did not attain its greatest artistic development until the introduction of the beautiful examples of inro. With the great demand for fine inro during the Tokugawa period, the finest specimens of netsuke appeared and this art of miniature sculpture then reached its apex. Although the netsuke is not restricted to use with the inro, the best examples were made for this, an inro being incomplete without its cord, *ojime*, and netsuke. The *himo* or cord of an inro, which calls for the finest plaited silk, is passed up through the channels on each side of the inro, and then passed through the *ojime*, a sliding bead, to hold the cords tightly together where they cross the top of the inro. The ends are finally knotted into the netsuke in such a manner that the knot is concealed. The length of the cord is usually about three feet, and about one-third of its length is used on the underside of the inro to tie an elaborate bow having many

Stained ivory netsuke of a cicada. Signed Masatsugu, 1813-1892. Edo period. Collection Charles A. Greenfield, New York.

Lacquer netsuke of a deer in colored takamakie. Edo period, signed Kajikawa and red seal, early nineteenth century. Collection Charles A. Greenfield, New York.

Ivory and lacquer netsuke of Kikujido in gold takamakie with ivory face and black lacquer hair. Signed Jokasai, c. 1800. Edo period. Collection Charles A. Greenfield, New York.

271

loops. Sufficient length of cord was left between the netsuke and the inro to allow for the width of the obi, with about three or four inches to spare so that the inro could hang gracefully below the obi. The color of the cord was not selected particularly to harmonize with the color of the inro, but to satisfy a personal preference, or was determined by the traditional colors of a family. The choice of color was frequently a matter of superstition, some individuals having lucky and unlucky colors depending on the nature of the year of their birth. Sometimes the selection was determined according to the ancient Chinese traditions regarding the five colors linked to the five elements—water, fire, earth, wood, and metal.

A variety of materials were used for netsuke, including wood, ivory, horn, metal, ceramics, and lacquer, the two principal ones being wood and ivory. To the connoisseur, netsuke in wood are generally considered to have the most value, not only because of the traditional Japanese mastery in wood carving, but also because the texture of wood lends itself to greater freedom of style than the harder, colder material of ivory. However, even in ivory the Japanese artist produced work unsurpassed for a remarkable quality of freshness and freedom of expression. Of the various kinds of wood, *hinoki* was highly favored, not only because of its beautiful and immaculate texture, but also as having been traditionally used from ancient times for building Shinto shrines and carving Buddhist images. However, the wood most widely used for netsuke was *tsuge* or boxwood, on account of its hard, tenacious, and fine-grained character, and because its luster increased with use. Among other woods used were ebony, cherry, yew, tea, persimmon, camphor, sandalwood, and camellia (Plate 24). Pieces of bamboo from the stem or the root were frequently used, as were extremely thin splits of bamboo woven into various shapes. Ivory was as widely used as boxwood for making netsuke, this material having been imported from China since ancient times. The Japanese carver is famous for his extraordinary skill in achieving incredible minute detail and delicacy of form in this material (Plate 21). Many fine netsuke were made in the various lacquer processes, and also of ceramic, but these lack the fine workmanship and detail of those in wood or ivory. When metal was used for netsuke it was often in the form of brass or copper wires woven into various shapes, as well as the alloys called *shakudo* and *shibuichi* used in sword mounts, which were used for the lids on the so-called *kagamibuta*-type netsuke.

The size and shape of the netsuke conform to the purpose for which it is intended, generally averaging about one and a half inches in length. The holes through which the cord passes are often ingeniously made as a functional part of the design, so as not to mar the general effect. Netsuke are some-times classified according to their designs, which are of almost endless variety—legendary characters, contemporary life, mythological subjects, animals, masks—or sometimes simply by the material out of which they are made. However, they are more usually classified according to their form and designated as *katabori*, *kagamibuta*, *manju*, *ryusa*, *sashi*, and *ichiraku*. *Katabori*, or figure-carved netsuke, are of immense variety, ranging from human figures to animals, birds, insects, and other creatures depicted realistically. In the *kagamibuta* category the netsuke are in the form of a tiny bowl made of ivory or horn and provided with a metal lid most frequently of the *shakudo* or *shibuichi* alloy. The artistic value of *kagamibuta* netsuke resides in the beautiful work executed on the metal cover rather than to that on the bowl portion, which is of secondary importance. In this type the cord is fastened to the underside of the lid and passed through a hole in the bottom of the bowl. *Manju* netsuke are flat and either round or oval in shape, or occasionally squarish with rounded corners. The name of this category of netsuke comes from its resemblance to the shape of a *manju*, a kind of Japanese cake. *Manju* netsuke occur either as a single piece or in a double form consisting of two *manju*, one over the other. Netsuke of the *ryusa* category have the same form as *manju* except that they are hollowed out and carved in an openwork design. *Sashi* netsuke are made in a long and slender form at times measuring as much as five inches. This type is often found in the shape of a beautifully proportioned elongated gourd or stick of wood with a realistically carved insect upon it. *Ichiraku* netsuke are made of slender pieces of metal, rattan, or bambo woven into various forms.

The creative imagination of the Japanese is perhaps best exemplified by the great variety and ingenuity of netsuke design. Unlike much of the art of Japan, which continued within the bounds of a well-defined æsthetic tradition, the art of netsuke-carving developed in a completely free and unrestrained manner. Its designs and subject matter cover the whole field of Japanese mythology, literature, history, folklore, and everyday life, and constitute a complete index of Japanese decorative motifs (Plates 22 and 23). In the category of natural history many of them are remarkably accurate representations of insects, reptiles, fish, tortoises, birds, mice, rabbits, and all manner of animal life. An absorbing subject in the miniature carving of netsuke is the many kinds of No masks, skillfully portraying facial expression. The netsuke used on the cord of an inro was carefully selected so as to harmonize in some way with the design on the inro. If the inro depicted a moonlight scene, the netsuke might be in the form of a crane; a tortoise netsuke would go well with a design of pine trees, and a netsuke in the form of a sage would complement the design of a remote mountain scene on an

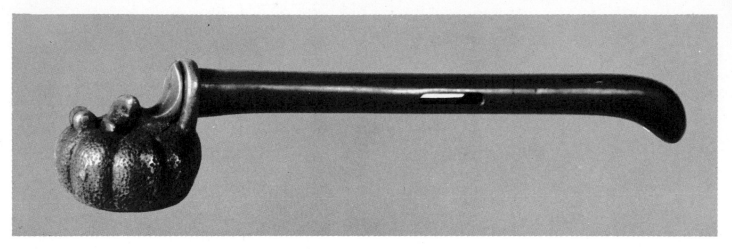

Wrought-iron yatate with the inkwell in the form of a fruit. Edo period, eighteenth century. Tokyo National Museum.

inro. The fascination of netsuke carving lies not only in the infinite variety of forms and designs, but also in the fantastic workmanship found in the finest examples, which are often masterpieces of miniature sculpture.

YATATE

Among the articles included in the category of *sagemono*, or hanging things, which were carried by men in earlier times, was the yatate, a container for writing equipment. When it originated is not known, but it became popular during the Tokugawa period and continued to be an indispensable article for almost all classes of people through the early part of the Meiji period. The yatate consists essentially of two sections, a small round shallow bowl-shaped inkwell with a hinged lid, and a long hollow stem or tube in which the *fude*, or writing brush, is carried. Most yatate were made with these two sections conjoined, with the inkwell fixed to the end of the brush tube and carried at the girdle by means of a netsuke and cord, like the inro; in others two sections were separate units, the inkwell serving as a netsuke and thrust up through the obi. The writing ink was first ground and diluted and then soaked into an absorbent substance, such as cotton or *moxa*, to prevent spilling. *Moxa*, which is a corruption of the Japanese word *mogusa*, is produced from the fibers of an Oriental wormwood identified as *Artemisia moxa*. It was considered to be the better substance for the yatate, but because it was rather costly, only the wealthy could afford it. The greater number of yatate were made of bamboo, wood, brass, iron, or silver, some of the more elaborate ones being decorated with carving, metal inlays, engraving, or chasing. In contrast to the inro,

which was a most important accessory to the costume of the daimyo, samurai, and merchant classes, and an elaborate and costly object of virtu, the yatate very seldom received the same artistic treatment. Yatate were principally considered utilitarian pieces, and although the majority were fine articles of wood or bamboo, they were usually left in the natural wood finish or lacquered.

The reason for calling this writing-equipment container a yatate has not been clearly determined, as the word literally means arrow stand. A late eighteenth-century record states that the writing case usually carried instead of the *suzuri*, or inkstone, was called a yatate. It further states that in ancient times the *suzuri* was carried in the *yebira*, or quiver, and the word may derive from this custom. The same record suggests that it may have been called a yatate because one of the forms in which it appears is known as *dohio-utsubo* and resembles a quiver in shape, or because the brush is carried in the manner of an arrow in a quiver. The nobles of the court and many of the warrior class were able scholars proficient in the art of composing poems. These poetical compositions were the written medium in which people of cultivation expressed to one another their feelings of love, friendship, joy, sorrow, happiness, loneliness, and like sentiments and thoughts. Because it was necessary to have one's own writing equipment when traveling away from home, it was the custom in early times to carry a *suzuri*, or inkstone, a *sumi*, or inkstick, and a writing brush in the quiver. According to twelfth-century records the name *yatate-no-suzuri* was given to the inkstone because it was carried in the quiver; however, the same name is used in other contemporary records and refers to the inkstone carried in the bosom of the costume or in the pouch on the sleeve of armor. It is therefore difficult to ascertain with certainty whether the portable writing case as we know it was called yatate because the earlier examples resembled the shape of a quiver, or because the name was an abbreviation of *yatate-no-suzuri*.

It is believed that the first portable yatate appeared during the Kambun era (1661-1673), at which time a feud existed between the Machi-yakko and the retainers of the Hatamoto or banner knights in the city of Edo. The Machi-yakko were workers employed by the labor contractors, and as they were not of samurai rank and not allowed to carry a sword, it is said they adopted as their defensive weapon a huge tobacco pipe made entirely of iron. These measured about fifteen to sixteen inches in length and were called *kenkwa-kiseru* or fighting pipes. When their use or possession was finally forbidden by the Shogunate government, they were replaced by the *shakuhachi* or bamboo flute, and by the yatate. These huge yatate, measuring fifteen to eighteen inches in length, proved to be formidable weapons and seem to be the first yatate in portable form. Around this time yatate were carried by persons when traveling around the country and especially by Kiso lumber merchants when buying lumber in the vast mountains of the Kiso region. The early examples were made of iron and brass, while later specimens were often made of alloys, such as *shakudo* and *shibuichi*.

Toward the latter part of the Tokugawa period yatate were worn as an essential article by men of all classes—the carpenter, the merchant, the blacksmith, and others, as well as the daimyo and scholar. When the warriors were in camp, or *jinchu*, they carried with them a *jinchu-yatate* which was usually made of wood in the form of a lacquered folding fan. The interior was provided with hollowed-out spaces to contain the inkwell and writing brush, while the cover was fixed by a rivet at the lower end in the same manner as a fan. There were variations in the style and shape of yatate depending upon the place of origin. A style particularly favored by men of the literary world was called a *kwaichu-yatate*, a small metal container made to carry inside a purse, which was in turn carried in the *kwaichu*, or bosom of the costume. This form of yatate was made of silver, copper, or an alloy of pleasing color, decorated or left in the plain metal finish, and equipped with the articles for writing, with the brush usually having a telescoping shaft. Toward the latter part of the Tokugawa period yatate in a wide variety of shapes appeared, mostly from the workshops of the Osaka craftsmen. In these Osaka examples the inkwell portion of the yatate was made to resemble an endless variety of subjects, such as baskets, lanterns, kitchen utensils, musical instruments, and so forth. The Kyoto craftsmen produced yatate in the form of a quiver made of *shibuichi* having a warm, beautiful gray patina and inlaid with simple designs of silver.

TOBACCO POUCH AND PIPE CASE

Around the middle of the eighteenth century it became the fashion among Japanese men to carry a tobacco pouch with a sheath for the pipe, which was suspended from the obi by a cord and netsuke, in the same manner as an inro. Smoking began during the early part of the Tensho era (1573-1592), when tobacco was first brought to Japan by Portuguese traders, whose ships made frequent calls at the port of Nagasaki. However, it was not until the year 1605 that tobacco was actually cultivated in Japan, at a place called Sakura-no-baba on the island of Kyushu near Nagasaki. When it was first introduced it was smoked wrapped, either in paper or in a particular type of leaf, but this method soon gave way to a kind of bamboo pipe, and later to a metal pipe which was introduced from Korea or China at the end of the sixteenth century. The smoking habit was enthusiastically taken up by people all over the country, but soon became the subject of condemnation by certain moralists, including the famous Confucian scholar Hayashi Razan, who at the same time conceded that he could not break himself of the habit. In fact, smoking became so popular that its use was forbidden by an edict in the year 1609, which proved ineffective and was followed by three or four similar edicts during the ensuing years. Tobacco importation was then carried on by smuggling, and it is said that tobacco was at one time sold under the fictitious name of Life-prolonging Tea.

In these early times tobacco was very expensive, which made smoking a luxury reserved only for the wealthy. Thus it was restricted to the pleasure of the feudal lords, and then only in the privacy of the home. In time, as the smoking habit became more general and tobacco more plentiful, it was considered proper etiquette to offer it to guests to be smoked in pipes provided by the host. During the second quarter of the seventeenth century it became the fashion to carry pipes measuring more than three feet in length which were lavishly decorated and intended more for show than for use. It is recorded that in the early years of the eighteenth century the bamboo stems of pipes were decorated with fine lacquer work; but later, toward the middle of the century, beautifully decorated pipes were being made of iron and brass, without a bamboo stem. Strict regulations were also enforced during the Meiwa era (1764-1772), prescribing the styles of pipe that could be carried by the various classes. Different shapes and styles of decoration were designated for pipes carried by the members of the military class, the townspeople, actors and other entertainers, artisans, and so on. The custom of carrying a tobacco pouch with a netsuke and *ojime* attached to it became popular during this period. Except for the samurai class, the custom of wearing a tobacco pouch became widespread

Tobacco pouch, pipe case, and pipe. Top: bamboo smoking pipe with chased and inlaid metalwork mounts. Middle: carved ivory pipe case. Bottom: tobacco pouch of leather with gold-foil imprint and finely chased metal mounts of dragons and waves. Edo period, early nineteenth century. Tokyo National Museum.

among all classes, especially the merchants, whose taste created a demand for fine and costly examples.

Both the tobacco pouch and the sheath-like container for the pipe were made of leather and worn together with a cord and netsuke suspended from the girdle. The beautiful colored designs worked on the surfaces of the fine specimens exemplify the superb talent of the Japanese leather craftsman. Toward the middle of the nineteenth century, with the changes in fashion, the sheath of leather was replaced by a pipe case made of wood, horn, ivory, or other rigid material, usually having carved decoration covering the entire surface. Although a cord with netsuke and *ojime* was sometimes used to suspend this new-style tobacco pouch and pipe case from the girdle, it soon became the fashion to wear the pipe case thrust through the girdle with the pouch tied to it. The tobacco pouch was a flat, rectangular-shaped container with a cover-flap secured with a clasp, measuring about three inches in length. The pipe case was elliptical in section and averaged about eight inches long by about one inch wide, with a telescoping cap having the same contour as the body. The *kiseru*, or tobacco pipe, which the case was made to hold, is unique for its bamboo stem of narrow diameter, and its metal mouthpiece and bowl. The tiny bowl, no larger than

the diameter of a pea, served to hold only a small pinch of fine-cut tobacco, enough for only two or three whiffs. The custom of smoking the *kiseru*, generally with several pipefuls in succession, has remained widespread to the present day. For the convenience of *kiseru* smokers a *tabako-bon*, literally meaning tobacco box, is provided. This is a square, box-like container, made of wood, bamboo, porcelain, or metal, with a metal or porcelain container to hold pieces of live charcoal for lighting the *kiseru*, and a bamboo tube into which the ashes can be knocked from the pipe. Since the custom of smoking a *kiseru* is still widely practiced in Japan, the pipe case and tobacco pouch are frequently seen worn in the obi of the native costume in many provincial places.

HIUCHI-BUKURO

Of all the *sagemono*, or receptacles suspended from the girdle, the earliest is the hiuchi-bukuro, or tinder pouch. It was used to contain flint, steel, and tinder for the convenience of travelers and warriors when camping and hunting. Although frequently mentioned in ancient records in connection with certain well-known figures in Japanese mythology, its

275

usual shape is not described. The earliest known references appear in the *Kojiki*, or *Records of Ancient Matters*, written in the year 712, which relate how Prince Yamato-Takeru, in the first century a. d., surrounded by a band of rebels on a moor, saved himself by kindling a fire against the oncoming flames with the flint and tinder from his pouch. Scroll-paintings of the thirteenth century depict tinder pouches of oval shape, attached to the swords of warriors. There seems to have been an opening at each end of the pouch, with a cord passed through a fold to form a noose so the opening could be tightly closed. The lengths of cord were held together with an *ojime*, or sliding bead, and attached to the sword.

Toward the end of the thirteenth century the tinder pouch began to be used as a container for such things as medicine and money as well as for flint and steel. This custom prevailed until the latter part of the sixteenth century, when the wearing of an inro and a *kinchaku* or money pouch suspended from the obi displaced the custom of carrying the hiuchi-bukuro attached to the sword. Instead, the samurai of the Tokugawa period carried fire-striking paraphernalia in the *kinchaku* worn at the girdle. Later, when it became fashionable to carry the tobacco pouch and pipe, different kinds of elaborately designed hiuchi-bukuro of brocade or leather were introduced. These were carried by men of all classes, with the exception of farmers and laborers, who could afford only a common variety. As in other customs of Japanese life, a code of etiquette was observed in the wearing of the hiuchi-bukuro. For instance, it was considered improper and a violation of good taste to carry a hiuchi-bukuro on ceremonial occasions. An exception to this rule of etiquette was extended to lay priests, elders, and persons over forty years of age, who were exempt at all times from this restriction.

While most of the hiuchi-bukuro were actually decorative containers in which the fire-striking articles were carried, some of those made during the latter part of the Tokugawa period were taken from Chinese prototypes having the piece of steel exposed at the bottom. Since the hiuchi-bukuro was essential to pipe smokers, the netsuke was often made to serve as a *suigara-uke*, or ash bowl. This form of netsuke was most frequently used by peasants because of the practice of knocking the ashes into a holder and lighting the next pipeful with the still burning tobacco. The piece of steel carried in the hiuchi-bukuro is known as *hiuchi-kama* or *hiuchi-kane*, and is said to have been triangular in form during ancient times. This was because fire, as one of the five elements, was believed to have a southern position and a triangular shape, while the flint was supposed to be rectangular, being a product of the earth. The flint of fire-striking stone, called *hiuchi-ishi*, is a very hard kind of quartz which readily strikes sparks with the steel and causes the tinder to ignite. The tinder was usually made from charred linen or a mixture of kapok and natural bamboo powder.

In many domestic households the Japanese have preserved from ancient times a simple Shinto ritual in which the family will purify all the rooms by the sparks from flint and steel. It is performed early in the morning preparatory to offering prayers before the Shinto family shrine in the house. This practice is based upon the purification ritual of Shinto, which is of great antiquity and consists of an invocation to the gods to cleanse the people of their transgressions. There is also the custom, still in practice, of using flint and steel to produce sparks to ignite the fires that burn at the altars of Shinto shrines and Buddhist temples. Traditionally, a piece of heavy cord called *hinawa*, or fire-rope, was often carried in the hiuchi-bukuro to be used as a fuse for igniting purposes. It was made of cotton, cypress-wood bark, or the fibers of bamboo, mixed with saltpeter. A rope of this material is still used in the ancient Shinto Okera-Mairi ceremony at the Yasaka shrine at Kyoto, more commonly known as the Gion shrine. The Okera-Mairi is the first worship at the Gion shrine at daybreak on New Year's Day, although it actually starts at midnight on December 31, when the sacred fire is kindled by the sparks from flint and steel. At this time every year the precincts of the great shrine present one of the most impressive scenes, reminiscent of ancient times in Japan, when each of the many thousands of worshippers at the shrine takes a piece of the rope provided by the shrine and ignites the end of it from the sacred fire. The smoldering end is kept alive by twirling the rope, so that it can be taken home to light the fire on which is cooked the first meal of the New Year, in keeping with the belief that this will ward off pestilence and evil spirits.

XIX Textiles

THE ART of the weaver has been practiced in Japan from early times and, like other crafts and vocations, it is frequently mentioned in legends and tales of old Japan. One of the most popular celebrations in Japan is the ancient Star Festival or Tanabata, which means weaving loom. On the seventh night of the seventh month two lovely stars, the Cowherd star or Altair, and the Weaver star or Vega, which are far apart on either side of the Milky Way, are said to have a joyous reunion each year. The popular custom of praying to the Cowherd star for a good harvest and to the Weaver star for skill in weaving, has been observed in Japan for centuries. The Empress-Regnant Koken is said to have had the festival officially celebrated for the first time in the seventh year of Tempyo-Shoho, 755.

Because the earliest fabrics have long since disappeared or rotted away, our only information on the textiles and costume of the ancient periods comes from a few early records. The *Nihon-Shoki*, one of the two oldest chronicles of Japan, written in the year 720, states that a skilled seamstress and a weaver were specially sent by the King of Paikche to the Japanese court in the third century A. D. It is further recorded that during the fourth and fifth centuries a large number of Chinese and Korean weavers had come to Japan and been naturalized. These skilled artisans were greatly appreciated by the noble families and in consideration of their importance were given land grants and clan surnames. These *émigré* craftsmen, together with many others who followed during these early times, were responsible for the rapid development of the weaving and dyeing industry in Japan. As in the other arts, the spectacular progress of the textile craft was stimulated by the introduction of Buddhism and Chinese learning in the sixth century.

JAPAN'S FIRST TEXTILES

Not far from the city of Nara the famous nunnery known as Chuguji, within the precinct of the ancient Horyuji temple founded in 607, has among its relics the oldest surviving embroidery in Japan. Listed as a National Treasure, this is a fragment of a large mandara showing a scene of the Tenjukoku or the land of Heavenly Longevity. A mandara is a type of picture graphically depicting the Buddhist pantheon. During these early periods, inspired by the mystical doctrines of Buddhism, the artists sought to express difficult cosmological ideas in their paintings. Of the embroidered mandara in the Chuguji, which was originally sixteen feet long, there remains only a small fragment measuring three and a half feet by three feet. Many years ago the fragments of the original embroidery were gathered, patched together, and made into the frame-like screen which can be seen today. Although it may not give a full idea of the original, it serves as a priceless example of the kind of work done over thirteen centuries ago. According to tradition, it dates from the year 622, when the Princess Tachibana-no-Oiratsume, widow of Prince Shotoku, was granted permission by the Empress Suiko to have this embroidered hanging made by the young ladies of the Imperial court. The mandara is a tribute to Prince Shotoku for the great progress he brought to Japanese civilization in making Buddhism the religion of the court, and building great temples and monasteries, including the Horyuji. In threads of many colors the hanging portrayed the Prince's rebirth in the Buddhist Paradise with its many human figures, pavilions, phoenixes, and other symbolic things to secure his eternal happiness. Within the Kondo or main hall of the Horyuji temple other examples of rare textiles of the Asuka period are also preserved, including religious embroideries and brocades.

Many fine examples of Japan's early embroidered works are found among the treasured collections of famous temples and monasteries. A number of the earliest forms of extant Japanese embroideries are hangings containing images of the Buddha and pictures of a religious nature. Many embroidered pieces were worked with silk and gold threads in conjunction with resist dyeing. The finest embroidery work in Japan has been produced in Kyoto ever since the city was founded in

794. Just as in China, Japanese embroidery has traditionally been the occupation of men specially trained for this work. The Kyoto embroiderers lavished their greatest skill on costume, since this category comprised the largest and most important use of Japan's exquisite fabrics. Magnificent also was the work on *fukusa*, the richly woven square pieces used for covering beautiful lacquer boxes containing ceremonial presents. It was the custom of the receiver of the gift to return the box and its *fukusa* to the donor. Along with the advancement of the other arts, it was only natural that during the Tokugawa period celebrated artists such as Kano Tan-yu, 1602-1674, and Ogata Korin, 1658-1716, designed elaborate textiles for Japanese costumes and *fukusa*.

Characteristic of the fine and meticulous Japanese embroidery are the different kinds of stitches that are used. Some embroidery is done in long, even stitches which generally run diagonally in an almost parallel manner so as to provide an effect of satin. In this method the embroiderers used both floss silk thread, which is a lustrous untwisted thread, and twisted silk thread. Another method consists of long and short stitches alternating between each other to produce an overlapping effect. This type of work is usually sewn only with floss silk and is called laid work or "couching." It is done by laying gold and silk threads side by side and stitching them down with fine threads of silk. The gold is usually made of fine strips of gold foil wound around a core of silk or cotton. Beautiful work is also produced with a knotted stitch. In this method the needle is partially drawn up from the underside, and thread is wound around it several times; then the needle is passed through the base fabric and returned to the underside close to where it was originally pushed upward, to secure the knot in position. This very fine and delicate work of knotted stitches covers the entire surface of a piece of embroidery, whereas in European work it is used in a limited fashion, as for the centers of flowers.

NARA AND HEIAN TEXTILES

In the Nara period (710-794) the weaving and dyeing crafts developed rapidly, owing to the continued immigration of Chinese artisans and the knowledge of the techniques of T'ang-dynasty textiles acquired by Japanese travelers to China. A further stimulus was provided by the Taika Reform of 645 and the Code of Taiho in 701, in which the highly developed Chinese administrative system was adopted under a centralized organ of government. Within this elaborate framework of administration many offices were established for the advancement of various arts and crafts. Under the great Council of State were placed eight ministries, of which the Ministry of

Civil Affairs had a Bureau of the Palace Wardrobe. There was also set up within the Ministry of the Treasury an Office of the Guild of Weavers and an Office of the Guild of Needle-workers. A Palace Dyeing Office was set up in the Ministry of the Imperial Household. The Office of the Guild of Weavers and the Office of the Guild of Needleworkers were responsible for the supervision and advancement of the textile crafts, while the Bureau of the Palace Wardrobe and the Palace Dyeing Office directed the activities of sewing and dyeing for the use of the Imperial family and the court nobles.

Under this official direction many techniques of weaving and dyeing were developed in the Nara period, especially of luxurious brocade fabrics and figured silks. One of these beautiful brocades which is still being made is called *tsuzure-ori* or linked-weaving. It is a technique in which the warp threads are stretched on a loom and the weft threads are put in only where desired with the fingers, and then pushed into place with a comb, rather than thrown across the loom by means of one or more shuttles. A favorite design in brocades from the Nara period onward is the lion-hunt pattern, which is composed of a series of circular motifs, each enclosing a scene of horsemen capturing a lion. The lion-hunt motif originated in Persia around the time of the Sassanian dynasty (227-641) and was introduced into Japan via China.

A beautiful figured silk material of the Nara period known as *aya*, distinctive for its delicacy, is made with a twill weave which causes an interesting formation of diagonal lines in the cloth. A variety of fabrics made during the early periods of Japanese history were used particularly for priestly robes and wearing apparel. It is said that a very thin material called *usumono* and three fine silk gauzes called *ra, sha,* and *ro* were introduced into Japan from Korea around the third century. Of these silk gauzes, *ra* is distinguished by its stiff-textured open weave, *sha* by its soft-textured weave, and *ro* by its vertical or horizontal stripes of open weave. A large number of brocades were also produced during this early period.

In addition to silk, many other materials were used for weaving into a fiber cloth called *nuno*. One type of *nuno*, used from ancient times and called *taye* or *shirotaye*, is woven with threads made from the fibers of the inner bark of the Asiatic paper-mulberry tree, which is similar to a material still used in Polynesia for making tapa cloth. Another variety is *asa-nuno*, woven with threads made from the fiber of hemp. There was also a very early fabric known as *shizuri*, said to be the first figured cloth made in Japan; the warp threads were made of hemp and other bark fibers dyed with various colors to produce striped patterns when woven with the weft threads. It is recorded that a woolen garment sent to the Japanese Emperor in the sixth century by the King of Paikche, from Korea, marked the introduction of weaving wool. This fabric called *kamo* or *origamo*, was first woven from goats' hair and later from rabbits' hair. Early records also mention a coarse material known as *tsumugi* or *momen-tsumugi*, which was originally made of cotton and later woven with silk. It is known that in the eighth century a robe of *tsumugi* belonged to the Emperor Shomu, the most devout Buddhist of the Emperors of the Nara period, who was responsible for the casting of the famous *Daibutsu* or *Great Buddha* of Nara. There were various methods of dyeing employed during the Nara period, such as *kyokechi*, a kind of stencil dyeing, *rokechi* or resist dyeing, and *kokechi*, also known as *shibori*, or tying and dyeing. The magnificent fabrics of the weavers and dyers of the Nara period established the foundation of Japanese textiles and still exert a strong influence on present-day materials in Japan.

During the succeeding Heian and Kamakura periods, the dyeing and weaving crafts continued to flourish and new techniques were developed to meet the requirements of gradual changes in the style of costume. In particular, the creation of a fashionable dress for the ladies of the nobility, called *juni-hitoe*, affected the craft of dyeing. The *juni-hitoe*, which was characterized by many layers of kimono, was more adaptable to small designs worked in repeat patterns in solid colors. Since each under-kimono was slightly visible at the neck, sleeves, and hem, it was necessary to achieve a harmony of graduated color, with each kimono a slightly different shade of the same color. The new style caused a great increase in the demand for dyed fabrics because large amounts were needed for each costume. Also, different colors were required for the many social events throughout the year, and particular colors were prescribed to be worn for each of the seasons as well. Among many other new developments introduced in the making of fabrics were raised and double weaves, especially a corded silk cloth called *seigo*, which was used until the end of the Tokugawa period for summer court robes. While the extravagant use of rich fabrics for ceremonial robes and court dress constituted the demand of the noble families, there was evident an increasing popularity among the commoners for dress of more casual and picturesque designs and patterns. It was this indigenous æsthetic taste and temperament of the Japanese that now began to affect the designing and dyeing of textiles and laid the foundation for the beautiful purely Japanese fabrics.

MUROMACHI INNOVATIONS AND IMPORTATIONS

Despite the constant political disturbances and military strife of the Muromachi period (1338-1573), continuous prog-

ress was made in the textile arts. The demands of the great daimyo furthered the development of all the arts and crafts, and the increasing feudal power in the provinces spread culture and learning throughout the country. These influences created and developed local industries and crafts in the feudal domains of the provincial barons, and these prospered with the rising standards of living of the commoners. In the mode of dress there was a gradual change in the style of the *kosode* or kimono, with a shorter sleeve and an over-all simplification of design. The natural result of this change in dress style to one of elegant simplicity was the development of beautiful hand-painted designs in a true and restrained Japanese taste. An outstanding design technique developed in the Muromachi and Momoyama periods is the style known as *tsuji-ga-hana* dyeing. This technique consists of tying and dyeing, combined with a hand-painted design executed with a certain freedom of expression. *Tsuji-ga-hana* fabrics have an elegant and intimate beauty found only in the work of Japanese designers and craftsmen. The Muromachi period also saw the introduction of certain new silk textiles from Ming China, cotton fabrics from India, and velvets and woolens from Europe. These imported fabrics, brought to the seaports of Sakai and Hakata, introduced many new techniques in the weaving and design-

A fragment of aya *material made in the eighth century. The well-preserved design represents the Wheel of Buddha. Victoria and Albert Museum.*

279

Detail of a heavy silk brocade woven with a design of ox-carriages and books on an over-all geometric-pattern ground. Momoyama period (1573-1615). Tokyo National Museum.

ing of Japanese textiles which have continued to exert their influence until the present time. The city of Hakata, which was formerly called Na-no-Otsu, was well known in the Middle Ages as one of the most important trading ports, and was the scene of many fierce combats at the time of the Mongol invasions when Kublai Khan made his attempts to invade Japan during the Kamakura period, in 1274 and 1281. Hakata, which now forms part of Fukuoka on the island of Kyushu, has been noted for its silk industry ever since the Kamakura period, at which time it was producing fabrics in the style of the Chinese Sung-dynasty prototypes. Of particular interest is the silk known as the Hakata weave, which was originated by a weaver named Takawaka Iemon, in the Tensho era (1573-1591).

The China trade was a lucrative source of income, and after the fall of the Mongol dynasty the Shogun sent envoys to the Ming court to prepare for the resumption of trade between the two countries. This trade provided a strong impetus to the growth of a number of seaports, of which

Sakai was the most important. The city of Sakai, located on Osaka Bay a short distance from the city of Osaka, is an ancient trading port where ships from China and other foreign countries called from early in the fifteenth century. This traffic stimulated a great development in the industry and commerce of Sakai and it soon became a doorway to Kyoto, as well as to the home provinces of warriors coming up the Inland Sea and from Shikoku. Its unique position encouraged a class of military contractors and moneylenders, and its prosperity was also vastly increased by its thriving industry. As the fortunes of the Shoguns declined, the feudal lords came to the Sakai merchants to borrow money on the security of taxes from the Ashikaga domains. This further strengthened the position of the merchant group and the city enjoyed many privileges similar to the free cities of medieval Europe. In the sixteenth century Sakai was noted for its silk-weaving industry, which continued to prosper until the ports of Japan were closed to foreign intercourse in 1639. With the stoppage of imports of Chinese silk the industry began to decline. Among the silk fabrics which were imported from China and later produced at Sakai was a crepe material called *chirimen*, and a taffeta called *kaiki*. These and other imported fabrics were extensively reproduced in the Sakai textile houses during the sixteenth century by Chinese weavers. Sakai was also noted for its *kinran*, or gold brocade, which was woven with narrow strips of gold foil. In the seventeenth century *kinran* was produced in Kyoto and has continued as one of its principal silk fabrics until the present day. Another beautiful brocade called *ginran* is similar to *kinran*, except that it is made with silver-foil threads instead of gold. The weavers of Sakai also introduced an exquisite damask known as *donsu*, which later became famous as a Kyoto fabric when a weaver in that city began producing a particular type called *shukin-donsu*, which is characterized by a design of floral medallions.

The foreign ships that called at Japanese ports during this period brought a variety of fabrics with figured and striped weaves. These products of Europe, the Near East, and China were in great demand and highly prized, not only for costume material but by collectors as well. It is stated that many of these fabrics became popular for use as mountings for kakemono and also for making small individual pouches in which utensils for the tea ceremony were kept. These exotic textiles from other lands were known as *meibutsu-kire*, or "celebrated" fabrics. Although some of the Chinese textiles were of early origin, most were produced during the Ming dynasty and there was keen competition among collectors for the finest materials and those having unusual qualities. These so-called celebrated fabrics included gold brocades, damask, and many other types, affording the weavers of Sakai a valuable opportunity to imitate them.

Velvet was another Japanese textile of the late sixteenth century, introduced by a mission that had gone to China to represent the Emperor. Among the many beautiful presents brought back were fine velvets called *birodo*. This encouraged the production of velvets in Japan, and from these early examples there developed the beautiful *birodo-yuzen*. In *birodo-yuzen* the velvet provides the ground on which beautiful pictures in soft color tones are produced partly by cutting and partly by dyeing. The method of producing *birodo-yuzen* is unique, the only tool used by the artisan-cutter being a small sharp chisel having a V-shaped point. This tiny chisel is placed in a small iron holder resembling a pencil, with diminutive guards at the tip. These guards, between which the chisel projects, serve as guides, making it possible for the artisan to control the depth of the cuts. The velvet, when given to the cutter, already contains a colored picture permanently fixed by the *yuzen* process, wherein the velvet has been completely finished in all of its manufacturing stages except for the cutting of looped threads.

The cutting artist lays the velvet on his bench and carves into the design with his chisel in the same manner as an artist would shade the lines of a design with a pencil. In his fingers the tiny chisel becomes a painter's brush with which he delicately cuts the fine filaments of silk at varying depths with great precision. Great skill is required, for example, in cutting the design of a leaf or a cherry-blossom petal in low relief with such care that the serration on the edge of the leaf and the delicate veining on the petal remain clearly indicated. Among the many subjects of *birodo-yuzen* velvets are evocations of famous scenic places in Japan, which with their serene colors are works of art of great charm.

THE MOMOYAMA AND EDO PERIODS

The Momoyama period (1573-1615) was so filled with medieval warfare that it is difficult to believe that it was an age of expanding culture and productive developments. By the end of this period Japan had reached a stage of abundance and prosperity such as had never been known before. The closing years of the Momoyama era brought with them decisive conflicts from which the House of Tokugawa emerged as the supreme power and established the Shogunate of that name to rule Japan for more than 250 years. The long era of peace of the Edo period witnessed many developments in the art of weaving and dyeing, and also the perfection of the elegant style of the Japanese kimono. The rise of the merchant class to a position of power and wealth created a new aristocracy, and the extravagance of textiles and costume reflected the general prosperity of the *bourgeoisie*. The weaving

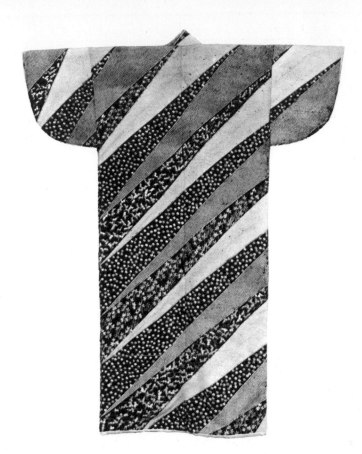

Kosode *of plain-weave silk with diagonal stripes of embroidered flowers and leaves on a black ground, alternating with and fitting into tied-and-dyed stripes of blue and black. Momoyama period, sixteenth century. Tokyo National Museum.*

and dyeing crafts were no longer reserved for the privileged upper class, for during this period people of all classes adopted the elegant perfected style of *kosode* or kimono.

Throughout the tumultuous Momoyama period the trend in textiles had been from small woven designs and patterns to hand-painted decoration executed with great freedom and inventiveness. The era excelled in designs expensively worked with gold and silver leaf and embroidery, as well as elegant gold brocades and tied-and-dyed fabrics. In the early part of the Edo period costume design displayed a freedom of expression which eventually developed into ample-scaled designs known as *kambun*. This large and striking type of design is characterized by colorful asymmetrical motifs splashed across the shoulder of a *kosode* or in a diagonal manner down the back. The name is derived from the Kambun era (1661-1673), during which time it became popular. The middle of the Edo period saw the perfection of the *yuzen* dye technique, in which magnificent designs were produced by using a resist rice-paste applied by hand. Many of the foremost artists of the time created elaborate kimono designs in a distinctly Japanese style to be dyed and further enhanced with exquisite embroidery. In this great age of kimono textiles Kyoto was the center of the weaving and dyeing arts, and a number of specialty fabrics were produced in the local domains of feudal daimyo.

KYOTO AND ITS INFLUENCE

From its founding in the year 794 the city of Kyoto has remained famous for its weaving and dyeing industries, particularly because of the continued demands made by the Imperial court for elaborate ceremonial fabrics. At first, Chinese artisans were brought in, and their methods were quickly learned by the local Kyoto weavers, who in turn began to produce fine silk gauze, damask, brocade, satin, and crepe. The civil strife during the turbulent fifteenth century prevented the development of the industry for a while, but it was restored during the peace of the Tokugawa regime. An important impetus to the textile industry came when the

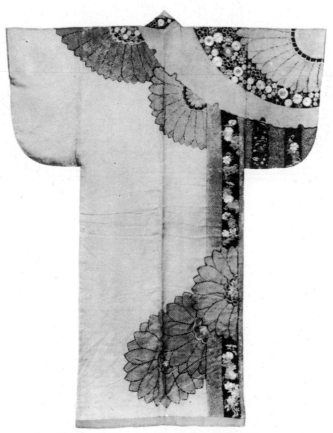

Kosode of white silk damask with a design of huge chrysanthemums in the tied-and-dyed method. Large shoulder designs such as this were popular in the Kambun era (1661-1673). Edo period. Nagao Museum, Kamakura.

Tokugawa Shogunate decreed that all silk fabrics used by the Imperial court and by the nobles should be made at Nishijin. This famous silk-weaving district is in the northwest part of the city of Kyoto; its name, signifying Western Camp, is reminiscent of the fierce internecine strife that raged through the city during the fifteenth century. Even today the sound of hand looms is heard coming from nearly every house in the Nishijin district, where silk weaving is still carried on as a home industry.

A certain kind of silk weaving called *ori-iro*, meaning woven in color, was invented by a Kyoto weaver sometime before the end of the fifteenth century. It is produced by a combination of two differently colored threads, which gives the effect of a monochrome. Also associated with Kyoto weaving is a satin fabric known as *shusu*, which was copied after the Chinese style. Sometime during the Keicho era (1596-1615), Kyoto weavers began to make an extremely fine satin damask that was also inspired by Chinese prototypes, with geometrical woven designs called *rinzu*. During this same era there appeared the *higaki-rinzu*, which owes its name to a popular design common at that time showing a *higaki* or wooden fence with *kiku* or chrysanthemums. Another beautiful silk fabric, first made in Kyoto in the latter part of the seventeenth century, is *kohaku*, which is a kind of taffeta. Along with the many beautiful silk fabrics produced on the looms in the Nishijin district of Kyoto were exquisite brocades, or *nishiki*. The Japanese term *nishiki* was applied to any fabric with a design woven of several colors, while *yoko nishiki* is applied when the design was woven in the woof, and *tate nishiki* is used when the design is in the warp. Brocades in which the design was made by linked-weaving are known as *tsuzure-ori*—or just *tsuzure*, as they are called today. In the linked-weaving method, which is done on a hand loom, the cross threads are laid in with the fingers and pushed into their places with a comb by hand. These woof threads extend only as far as the outlines of each figure in the design, and every section of the design has a rim of minute holes, which makes the design appear suspended in the ground, or linked into it. There was also a particular kind of brocade known as *karaori*, or Chinese weave, composed of gold and silver threads, as well as threads of various colors. The technique for making *karaori* was introduced from Ming China during the Tensho era (1573-1591) and some of the finest examples were produced for the upper garment worn by No actors in female roles. These fabrics still bear the name *karaori*. Two other beautiful brocades or *nishiki* are the *kambata*, which is similar to the *karaori*, and the *yori-ito-ori*, which has corded threads in the weft.

Kyoto being the creative center of Japan's art and culture, the work of the Nishijin weavers and dyers extended its influence into the provinces. One of the most flourishing provincial towns was Kiryu, whose weaving industry is one of the oldest in the Kanto district, with records of silk fabrics being woven there as early as the eighth century. In the Keicho era (1596-1615) the Kiryu silks were used to make warriors' banners, and the fabrics of Chinese-style weaves were also famous. The Edo period saw many other provincial weaving centers prosper and produce the particular fabrics for which they became noted. In the same Kanto district on the old feudal highway called Oshu-Kaido is the town of Isezaki, a famous weaving center which was noted for its *meisen* fabric, woven with threads of floss silk. In the same general direction from the city of Tokyo along the ancient highway called the Mikuni-Kaido, in the rugged mountainous region facing the Sea of Japan, is the town of Ojiya, formerly in Echigo province, which is especially noted today for its *oji-ya-chijimi*, a kind of hemp cloth. During the Edo period its weavers produced a beautiful silk fabric called *ojiya* crepe or *echigo* crepe. Another early weaving center was Hachijo-jima, an island of two extinct volcanoes which lies about 260 miles south of Tokyo. This island has been noted until the present day for its fabrics called *ki-hachijo*, made from the silk of wild silkworms, with designs dyed in brown, black, and yellow stripes. The earliest record of the island's production of this fabric dates from the Edo period, when it was made for the use of the Tokugawa family. Near the city of Matsuyama, in Shikoku, the weavers made a cotton cloth with a splashed design produced by pre-dyed threads woven in the material called *iyo-kasuri*. A cloth having the same weave as *iyo-kasuri* but characterized by a deep-blue dye was made in Satsuma. Kagoshima, the ancient castle town of the Shimazu family, later became the most famous center for this fabric. Absorbing evidence of the long history of Japanese textiles and costume is provided by their vivid portrayal in an endless variety of scroll-paintings since early times. They are also beautifully depicted in colorful Ukiyo-e and other paintings, not to speak of the great numbers of Ukiyo-e color prints. These sources constitute a most valuable record of Japanese textile designs and styles of dress and afford a fascinating study of the mode of living during many centuries.

DYED AND PRINTED TEXTILES

Dyeing in Japan has a long history of development beginning many centuries ago. A number of early examples of dyed silks are preserved in the Shosoin Treasure Repository at the Todaiji temple in Nara, including some materials produced by block-printing. These precious fabrics of the Nara period (710-794) are among the art treasures which once belonged to the Emperor Shomu; upon his death they were donated to the Todaiji temple by his consort Komyo-Kogo and their daughter, the Empress-Regnant Koken. In this category of textiles there are four principal methods or processes of dyeing: *rokechi* or resist dyeing; *kokechi* or tying and dyeing, which is also called *shibori*: *kyokechi* or stencil dyeing; and *itazome* or block-printing. All of these methods were already fairly well advanced during the Nara period, and in succeeding periods were progressively developed into veritable works of art. Two kinds of block-printing methods are practiced in Japan, positive and negative. In positive block-printing the design is in color, whereas in negative block-printing the ground is in color and the design in reserve. In both processes the block of wood is prepared by incising or engraving the design on the flat smooth surface of the block so that the lines of the design stand out in relief and the spaces between are hollowed out. When printing with the positive method, the relief portions of the block are covered with color; then the cloth is pressed against the block and rubbed with a device resembling a padded mallet. In the negative method, the relief design on the block is left free of color and the printing is

Detail of a design in the kyokechi *(stencil-dyeing) method. Edo period, eighteenth century. Victoria and Albert Museum.*

effected by the hollow portions. A woodworker bores small funnel-shaped openings from the reserve side of the block into the hollow spaces of the incised design and the block is then lacquered or varnished to make it waterproof. The printer stretches the cloth over another block of wood having a smooth and even surface, and places the incised block face down on the cloth. The two blocks are clamped securely together, and the dye color is poured through the funnel-shaped holes until the hollows are filled. In this manner the ground portions represented by the hollows receive the color while the design is left in reserve.

In *kyokechi* or stencil dyeing the cloth is folded once and securely clamped between two thin boards in which the design to be colored has been cut out. The dye color is then applied to these cut-out spaces but prevented from spreading between the tightly fixed boards. This method produces a symmetrical design, the cloth being folded double. Examples of stencil dyeing are distinguishable from any other process by the fuzzy outlines of the design and the line of dye color visible where the cloth has been folded. For several centuries Kyoto has been the great center for beautiful fabrics produced by the various techniques of dyeing. A particular process of dyeing characteristic of Kyoto is the *rokechi* or resist method, which is produced by drawing the design and covering the portions of the cloth with a resist where the color is not wanted. A resist of beeswax was used in earlier times, but the later method was to use rice paste, or sometimes a paste of alum and buckwheat. The cloth so prepared is then dipped in a dye vat, which allows the color to become fixed only on the exposed portions. The resist is then removed by washing and the process is repeated as many times as desired depending upon the number of different colors required in the design.

The traditional methods still used by the dye workers of Kyoto contribute much to the picturesque and colorful everyday life of this ancient city. The wide and very shallow Kamogawa flows through the center of Kyoto, and is crossed by many bridges of historical importance. The city is also intersected by a network of narrow and very shallow canals which are crossed by hundreds of small bridges, many of ancient Japanese architecture. The water, which flows rather

Above: Detail of a kosode of plain-weave silk with a design of a house on the shore of a lake and poetical ideograms in the yuzen *dyeing method. Edo period, eighteenth century. Tokyo National Museum.*

Below: Silk fukusa with a design of a cock and a hen with two chicks, and kiri *crests along the border, in the* yuzen *dyeing method. Edo period, eighteenth century. Victoria and Albert Museum.*

Furisode *of crimson silk damask with a bold design of a sheaf of* noshi, *a ceremonial decoration used on gift packages. The exquisite silks comprising the design were executed in the* yuzen, *tie-and-dye, embroidery, and gold-leaf appliqué techniques. Middle Edo period, seventeenth century. Yuzenshikai Collection, Kyoto.*

swiftly, is crystal clear, and to this water Kyoto owes some of its importance, for nowhere else in Japan can fabrics be bleached so white and dyed in such beautiful and brilliant colors. In the canals and in the broad Kamogawa with its clean pebble bottom, the workers can always be seen washing out the resist paste and allowing the dyes to set. Owing to the many brilliant colors of the long and narrow kimono fabrics, this presents a picturesque scene with hundreds of pieces of cloth rippling with the flow of the water.

It is believed that the method of tying and dyeing known as *kokechi*, or *shibori*, is the oldest of the various techniques of dyeing patterns. In this method, usually small portions of the fabric are gathered and tied with thread according to the design, and then only these parts are dipped into the dye vat. If the thread is wound tightly, the color cannot penetrate beyond it and therefore leaves only the gathered part with the color applied. Many colors can be introduced into a pattern with this process and very interesting results can be obtained. A characteristic Japanese pattern done with the tying-and-dyeing method is called *kanoko*, or young deer. This pattern was popular during the Edo period and consists of pressing tiny pointed sticks from the underside of the fabric to form little cone-shaped protrusions about half an inch apart over the entire cloth. Each little cone-shaped portion is tightly wound with waxed silk thread, and the entire fabric is dipped into the dye vat. The waxed silk thread serves as a resist and prevents that minute portion of the fabric from receiving any color. Except when the cloth is stretched afterward, this dyeing method produces a shrinkage which leaves the cloth permanently covered with tiny raised points where each stick was tied. This unique eye-pattern, or *meyui*, is said to resemble the eye-like spots of color on the coat of a fawn.

285

Kosode *of plain-weave silk with a burnt-orange ground, and a scene of the Yoshiwara district dyed by the* yuzen *method. Edo period, eighteenth century. Nagao Museum, Kamakura.*

The dyed fabrics known as *yuzen* are a particularly famous specialty of Kyoto. The *yuzen* process first appeared in the Genroku era (1688-1704). Although factual information is lacking as to the inventor of the method, it has been attributed to a painter named Miyazaki Yuzensai and to a priest named Fukae Yuzen. This new process became the most important and popular dyeing art of the Edo period, affording an unlimited freedom of design and colors. The multicolored pictorial designs and patterns printed on the silk enlisted skills which the designer shared with the dyer. The *yuzen* method consists of drawing detailed designs on the fabric with a small stick and rice-paste resist. The exquisite designs and the gorgeous colors that were achieved in *yuzen* dyeing made it the most famous fabric of the Edo period and its popularity has continued until the present day.

Designs for fabrics in the extravagant Genroku era were frequently created by the greatest painters of the day. The fascinating patterns of bold stripes or checks known today as *genroku* are modern revivals of the gay and showy costumes of the theaters and the pleasure quarters of the Yoshiwara in those times.

Besides the *yuzen* dyes developed in Kyoto, which are also called *kyo-yuzen*, as well as *kamogawa*, after the river of that name in Kyoto, there is another popular one called *kaga yuzen*. This name is derived from the old province of Kaga, a mountainous district on the coast of the Japan Sea now called Ishikawa prefecture. Kaga province was the vast domain of the powerful Maeda family, whose lords encouraged many local industries, including pottery, lacquer, and textiles. The Kaga variety of *yuzen* does not differ in process from the Kyoto variety, but it is noted for its beautiful color effects. It combines within a single pattern striking tones of vermilion. red, and purple with a generous amount of green and light green. The Edo period produced another type of dye process called *chaya-tsuji*, which like *yuzen* was also made with a stick and rice-paste resist. It originally consisted of dyeing a fine quality of hemp fabric with indigo. Much of this *chaya-tsuji* was made with handsome designs of landscapes in an indigo monochrome on a white ground, and was considered the most refined summer-kimono fabric of that time. The *chaya-tsuji* was so highly regarded that its production was exclusively controlled and reserved by the Shogun, the three great Tokugawa houses, and thet hree great Tokugawa princes.

A popular process of dyeing widely practiced since Tokugawa times is called *fuki-ye* or blown picture. It consists of drawing an outline design and applying a resist of rice paste to the portion to be left in reserve, or over an already dyed section to be protected from another dyeing of color. Sometimes pieces of paper are cut according to the design and securely laid on the cloth. The dye is then placed in a funnel-like metal device and sprayed on by blowing through a tube. This *fuki-ye* method is still practiced as a household pastime in many parts of Japan. There was also a painted cotton fabric of great beauty made during the seventeenth century and known as *kakisarasa*. The name *kakisarasa*, or painted cotton, is derived from two words, the Japanese *kaki*, which when written with a particular designating character means a painting, and the Hindu *sarasa*, meaning calico. According to an early record, it was produced by laying a piece of fine cotton cloth on a smooth board, and with a brush applying a liquid preparation of the distilled juice of unripe persimmons. When this was dry, the designs were painted on by hand in as many colors as desired.

The colorful and beautiful Japanese garments of the present day are made from fabrics that are still being produced in the traditional processes, especially in Kyoto, which remains the center of the art industries of Japan.

ALTHOUGH the culture of Korea and China provided fundamental principles for the development of Japan's social order, it never became an overwhelming influence. The Japanese temperament and æsthetic taste resisted a complete acceptance of this foreign culture, adopting its best qualities and transforming them into a distinctive native style. The history of Japanese costume reveals the inspiration which came from China in the early periods, but it also makes clear the distinctively Japanese element, which has survived to the present day in the beautiful native kimono. This purely indigenous dress is one of the most colorful and most beautiful in the world and its historical development over hundreds of years presents a fascinating story.

HANIWA AND ASUKA COSTUME

Our knowledge of costume styles during the earlier periods is based on the chronicles of those times, as well as on portrayals of dress in paintings. The first period of costume style dates from very ancient times until the beginning of the third century A. D., during which time a strict caste system developed. The costume of the upper classes toward the end of this period was similar to the Chinese dress of the Han dynasty, and was most likely introduced into Japan by way of Korea.

The study of this early costume is made possible by the small clay figures of the Haniwa culture, found in the sepulchral mounds which form the principal repositories of the third century. Besides the mounds of simple form covering sarcophagi of earthenware or stone, there are the great tombs of the rulers consisting of a stone chamber covered by a large mound. The latter are of stupendous dimensions, some being ninety feet high and covering an area of eighty acres complete with moats. Within their stone chambers are found pottery vases, jewelry, metal mirrors, weapons, and other articles of iron or bronze. The clay Haniwa figurines, which are found outside the tomb, sometimes represent animals, but usually men and women with regular features, wearing clothes of the Han dynasty, including earrings and necklaces. The principal garments worn by the men appear to have been a coat and *hakama*, or loose trousers; by the women, a coat and skirt, the latter called *mo* or *kinumo*. The sleeves are close-fitting and the legs of the *hakama* appear tied just above the knees with a cord. The outer garments seen in these Haniwa figures show that the hair was elaborately dressed, while others have the head covered with a kind of cap or other form of headwear. The dress of the women included a scarf called *hire*, which hung over the shoulders and served both as a piece of personal adornment and to provide warmth. It also was used to wrap and carry things, much in the manner that the *furoshiki* is used today. The most prominent objects of personal adornment found in the tombs are a type of curved ornament called *magatama*. These usually occur in the form of a necklace, and the comma-shaped pieces evidently originally derived from the teeth or claws of animals. The *magatama* found in the great tombs of rulers are often of very fine workmanship, and are made of a variety of materials including jade, nephrite, quartz, glass, jasper, serpentine, and agate. That certain magic properties were ascribed to these *magatama* is indicated by the fact that until very recent times people in Asiatic Siberia and Korea regarded the claw of the tiger as an amulet of great power. This earliest period of Japanese costume comes to a close during the first years of the third century, which corresponds to the time when the Empress Jingo led a great army to the conquest of Silla in Korea. The seacoast near Kashii in Kyushu, where the Shinto shrine of Kashii-no-Miya is located, is believed to be the place where the Empress Jingo embarked on her expedition. This beautiful shrine, surrounded with great ancient trees, is dedicated to the Empress Jingo and is a symbol of the adventurous spirit which was responsible for the closer contacts of Japan with Korea and China, which in turn contributed so much to the development of Japanese art and culture.

The second period in the history of Japanese costume is marked by the introduction of Chinese culture and religion. The invasion of the kingdom of Silla by the Empress Jingo, about A. D. 220, was the beginning of Korean influence in Japan, and resulted in the introduction of Buddhism in the sixth century. During these four centuries, ending with the closing years of the Asuka period (552-645), Japanese costume reflected the influence of the mainland. The Japanese eagerly adopted the Asiatic upper-class dress and with it new fashions of hairdress. The new costumes were made of fine silk in twill and brocade weaves with beautiful designs, and were of great length with very large sleeves. As the needs of society advanced and the demand for fine fabrics increased, guilds were formed, such as the Oribe guild of weavers and the Ayabe guild of workers skilled in brocade. During the preceding centuries there had been a constant immigration of Koreans, who were probably of Chinese origin, as they claimed descent from Chinese families, and also of Chinese who were refugees from the dynastic wars in their own country. Many of these artisans were not only weavers and brocade workers but also farmers familiar with the culture of silkworms. The brocade-makers' guild or Ayabe was formed by artisans known as the men of Han, and it is recorded that the chief of this guild was granted a title of nobility by the Japanese court.

T'ANG INFLUENCE

The third period of costume extends from about 607 until 897, and includes the Nara period (710-794) and the first part of the Heian period, known as Jogan or Early Heian (794-897). These years coincide with the T'ang dynasty in China, and until the end of the Nara period it was the fashion in Japan to imitate all things Chinese. The first official mission to represent Japan at the Chinese court left in the year 607 and though it was ostensibly a good-will mission, the most important object was to obtain new knowledge. Each mission included a number of scholars who stayed for long periods to pursue their special studies, as well as skilled artisans who studied Chinese methods. The Japanese modified their administrative system along Chinese lines, and one of the first measures was the formation of a court hierarchy based on official ranks, which were distinguished by titles and costumes according to Chinese custom. Under the regency of Prince Shotoku Taishi, 573-621, far-reaching reforms were adopted which greatly changed and stimulated the advancement of culture, the political system, and religion, and even prescribed the color of the caps and robes to distinguish the many subdivisions of the grades of rank. From the time of Prince Shotoku direct intercourse with China increased rapidly, opening up the great T'ang civilization and culture to the Japanese. As a result, Japanese culture and manners changed greatly and the city of Nara was modeled after the Chinese capital at Ch'ang-an. The Code of Taiho, which was promulgated in 701 and revised in 718, prescribed the official dress of the Nara period according to Chinese style. In the system enacted by the code there were three types of official apparel. The most lavish and formal dress was for ceremonial occasions and worn by the Emperor, the princes and princesses, and the noble ladies and gentlemen of the court. It was reserved for the most important functions or occasions, such as the Ceremony of Imperial Accession, the Great Thanksgiving Service when prayers are offered to Toyouke-Omikami, the goddess of farms, crops, food, and sericulture, and the Ceremony of New Year's Reverence to the Emperor. A less formal costume was the court dress worn by nobles when attending ordinary court activities. The official dress worn by lower-rank officials and commoners who were charged with administrative activities constitutes the third type.

The court dress was of the greatest importance. The material differed according to the seasons and the colors were prescribed according to rank. There were many rules and regulations that determined the dress of the various classes, and these differences were strictly observed, especially as to color. The Nara court dress for men consisted of an upper garment called a *ho*, a *hakama* resembling loose trousers, and a braided sash. The court dress of the ladies of the Nara period consisted of a short upper garment and a long skirt called a *mo*. Both the men and the women of this era dressed their hair and also used powder and rouge. The custom of blackening the teeth was introduced at this time and the ladies adopted the practice of using beauty patches or spots, called *kashi*, of crimson color which were applied to the forehead and cheeks. While the noble and upper classes followed the dictates of Chinese manners and dress, the commoners clung to the traditional native customs, so that there were two distinctive modes of dress and living in the Nara period. The various forms of annual festivals, dances, music, and amusements of the court were of Chinese origin and blended with those of Japan.

During the Early Heian period, the ceremonial dress of the Nara period became more restricted in use, while the court dress was employed more widely. The latter finally developed into the *sokutai*, which is still used for great formal occasions. At the end of the Early Heian period in 897, official relations with China ceased because a very influential official in the Imperial court did not see fit to accept an appointment as ambassador to the T'ang court. He petitioned the Emperor to stop sending missions to China and quoted reports from Japanese monks studying there that conditions were bad and travel dangerous. The T'ang dynasty was on the wane and the Japanese had reached a stage where they preferred a life free from foreign influence. This enabled them to assimilate and adapt to their own taste those aspects of Chinese culture which could be harmoniously blended with their traditional manners and customs. Intellectual pursuits and art turned to native sources of inspiration, and fashion in dress gave way to Japanese style.

THE MEDIEVAL PERIOD

The fourth period of costume embraces almost five centuries of Japan's medieval history, from 897 until about 1477. Beginning with the Late Heian or Fujiwara period (897-1185) and including the Kamakura (1185-1333), it ends in the middle of the Muromachi period, at the close of the Onin Civil War in 1477. When this great struggle for feudal power ended, fighting continued in most provinces and the Ashikaga Shoguns were powerless. Even the Imperial house was almost penniless and anarchy prevailed in a great number of the provinces until about 1500. The Fujiwara period, as previously noted, was an age of luxury and profusion. The palatial architecture of the nobility, called *shinden-zukuri*, was embellished with magnificent paintings by the new class of secular artists. From this time also dates Lady Murasaki's literary masterpiece, *Genji Monogatari*, and other works, such as the *Miscellany of Sei Shonagon*, or *Pillow Book*, which provide an enduring picture of the elegant society and life at court and the colorful atmosphere created by the rich and gorgeous costume. In the beautiful picture scrolls of makimono, the Fujiwara court painters and calligraphers have left a priceless pictorial record of costume and manners of living. The court dress and the ornaments for personal attire were colorful and elaborate. The formal court dress of the nobles called the *i-kan*, which was used for ceremonial occasions, was complemented by a high crowned headpiece without a brim called the *kammuri*. For less formal occasions new forms appeared such as the *noshi* and the *karaginu*. Both were outer garments, the *noshi* becoming the most widely used dress for the men of the Fujiwara period; the *karaginu* was reserved for outdoor wear.

The fashionable dress of the ladies of the nobility, called *juni-hitoe*, also had the short loose overgarment or *karaginu*. The *juni-hitoe*, or twelve-layer dress, is more properly called court-ladies attire or *nyobo shozoku*. This dress, made of the most beautiful silks and brocades, consisted of many layers of undergarments of various colors, and a very long pleated skirt. The skirt was tied around the waist over the outer garment or robe, and spread out voluminously in the back. The outer robe was made of a brocaded silk fabric, and the skirt was of silk with designs which were embroidered, printed, tied-and-dyed, or painted. The skirt was often further enriched with decoration of mother-of-pearl, semiprecious jewels, tiny mirrors, and gold or silver foil. A more simplified form of this twelve-layer dress, widely used by the ladies of the court for everyday wear, was an extremely elegant and graceful gar-

ment called *ko-uchigi*, after the name of the outermost robe worn with it. The many so-called layers of these dresses were of solid colors, and it was the practice to give careful thought and consideration to the harmonious combination of the various colors. This skillfull selection of colors was most important because a slight portion of each garment was visible, one beneath the other. A line of color represented by each layer or undergarment was arranged to show at the neckline, at the sleeves, and at the hem of the skirt. The dictates of fashion prescribed certain color arrangements known as *kasane-no-irome*, or color composition of dress-layers, and each set of blended colors was given the name of a flower or a plant. It was the custom to wear each set of colors at a particular time in conformity with the social seasons and the seasons of the year. Such names as wistaria, azalea, pine, and hibiscus were applied to these sets, and the gradation of carefully selected color tones produced a chromatic effect punctuated by the vermilion of the undermost garment.

The many social institutions of the Fujiwara were highly developed, and in the elaborate ceremonials, festivals, music, and other cultural activities there existed the highest degree of refinement and elegance. Social ethics, manners, and rituals followed the strictest rules. Great beauty of thought and delicacy of sentiment were expressed in the literature of this period, with subtle forms of poetry written on beautiful paper

Juni-hitoe, *or twelve-layer dress, worn by the ladies of the court during the Fujiwara period (897-1185). This illustration is of a juni-hitoe worn at the enthronement ceremony of the late Emperor Taisho in 1915. Tokyo National Museum.*

scented with incense. Elegant calligraphy was practiced in the writing of letters, which were very properly hung on a branch of willow, flowering cherry, or plum and delivered by a personal servant. The magnificent costume constituted an intrinsic part of this colorful and elegant manner of living. The dress of both the men and the women increased in length and fullness, and pleats and folds became deeper. Conventionalized designs and geometrical patterns became a prominent feature in the *noshi* or outer-garment. Closely graded shades of color were popular and the dyed pictorial designs on fabrics almost entirely disappeared. The most fashionable dyed fabrics were the *susogo*, in which the color tone grew darker toward the lower part of the garment, and the *murago*, which had cloud-like effects of light and dark. In contrast to the extremely rich and voluminous dress of the nobility, with its strict code of color combinations and many-layered under-garments, the commoners at the end of the Fujiwara period began using fabrics with large-scale designs and figures. They used these strikingly colorful fabrics for their relatively simple kimono or *kosode*, with its short and narrow sleeves. This more simplified dress reflected a strong trend toward the restraint and purity which have always characterized the Japanese refinement of taste.

Throughout the remainder of the fourth period of costume, from the beginning of the Kamakura period (1185-1333) to about the middle of the Muromachi period (c. 1477), the outstanding characteristic in the changing fashions of dress was a trend toward simplification. The style of apparel previously used by the commoners now became popular among the upper classes. The more simplified standards of the new ruling military caste, which had their effect upon architecture and decoration, in turn influenced certain changes in costume. It was the age of the samurai, with the warrior in the supremacy, and manners and customs were influenced by this new feudal regime. Nevertheless, after the early years of warfare the new ruling class turned to the cultivation of the arts and soon adopted the fashions of Kyoto, which, despite the establishment of the Shogun's headquarters at Kamakura, remained the center of culture. The samurai penchant for elaboration was tempered by the simplicity of Zen taste. The simple, practical code of social ethics of Zen, with its severe spiritual training through meditation and self-denial, accorded well with the temper and ideals of the feudal warrior and in turn affected fashions in dress.

The Kamakura period is especially rich in picture scrolls, or makimono, which most vividly illustrate the manner of living and the beautiful costumes of the time. The *karaginu*, or outer-garment originally used for outdoor wear, became the ceremonial attire of the new warrior class, while the *sokutai* costume of the men of the Heian period, and the

ko-uchigi and Chinese robe and long skirt of the ladies became the most formal dress, worn only on rare occasions. The decorative designs of these ceremonial costumes were strictly regulated according to prescribed forms: the *ho* costume of the Emperor was decorated with phoenixes, paulownia, and bamboo; the robe of an abdicated Emperor had bamboo and paulownia within circles. The dress of the nobles and feudal lords varied according to the status of the wearer, with the clan crests accompanied by geometrical or floral motifs. As an accessory to the furnishings of a wardrobe, the dress-scenting rack was an important item. It was made of a number of lacquered rods tied together in such a manner as to allow it to be folded up when not in use. Garments were draped over the rack and scented by the burning of incense placed under them. Court maidens wore a most becoming headpiece which consisted of a shallow, broad-brimmed hat called *ichime-gasa*, from which hung a very long white silk mantle known as a *mushi-no-tareginu*.

Contemporary costumes called *hitatare* and *suikan*, previously worn by the commoners, became popular attire for the every-day use of the samurai caste and later came to typify their most usual dress. These two costumes became so closely associated with the samurai class that the *suikan* had to be made of a plain silk fabric, while the fabric for the *hitatare* was determined by the rank and importance of the person. The attire called *yoroi-hitatare* was reserved for the use of the samurai, as it was especially designed to conform with and be worn under armor, while the *jimbaori* was a coat worn over the armor. Beautiful and rich fabrics were used for the *yoroi-hitatare*, such as tied-and-dyed cloth, figured silks, and fine brocades. The samurai and their colorful costumes formed a most picturesque part of the everyday life of Kamakura times. The great war romances such as the *Heike Monogatari* and the *Hogen Monogatari* belong to this colorful period and are not only inspiring stories of a feudal time, but also beautiful literary works. The *Heike Monogatari*, written in poetical prose to be chanted to the accompaniment of a lute, reflects the pure Japanese æsthetic taste. The war narratives, which dealt with the changing fortunes of military leaders and were often reproduced in makimono, made illustrated stories of great graphic power. The making of weapons and armor became a great art, on which the decorative work is comparable to any other form of art at its best, and this was also the period of the celebrated swordsmiths such as Okazaki Masamune. Because the military families constituted the highest stratum of society, all things peculiar to the life of the samurai had an impressive influence on the everyday life and art of Japan.

The manner of living, the pursuit of amusement, and the collecting of objects of art were most expensive pleasures, which caused many vassals to become involved in financial difficulties. Although some were under economic pressure through expenditure on war services against the Mongols, who unsuccessfully attempted to invade Japan, it was mainly the attempts to keep up with the rising standard of living that brought about many of their difficulties. The inevitable economic breakdown, together with the conspiracies of various nobles of Kyoto and feudal barons, were contributing factors which eventually culminated in an armed attack on Kamakura and its capture in the summer of 1333. The Hojo regent Takotoki and more than two hundred of his family and faithful retainers took their own lives rather than suffer the abasement of pride. After the fall of the Kamakura Shogunate the country was torn by wars due to the rivalry between the great feudal lords.

In 1338 Ashikaga Takauji established the Shogunate government which ruled until 1573. This era of the Ashikaga Shoguns is called the Muromachi period, after the name of the section of Kyoto in which they lived and enjoyed a life of ease amid magnificent gardens. The new group of provincial daimyo were quickly influenced by the ancient culture of the Imperial court, and while they looked upon the nobles with disdain, they sought to emulate their manners and refinement. The third Ashikaga Shogun, Yoshimitsu, retired from the Shogunate in 1395 to his villa at Kitayama in Kyoto, where he built the three-storied structure called Kinkaku, or Golden Pavilion, with a picturesque garden around it. There he lived a life of extreme luxury.

The feudal warriors of this new aristocracy were not content at first with the prevailing elegance of the court nobles. Although they ultimately were completely subjugated by the traditional Kyoto culture, in the early part of the Muromachi period they were more inclined to look upon it as decadent. The natural reaction was a strong taste for something new and different, which led to a resumption of intercourse with China and to a period of Chinese modes, just as the desire for novelty in the Nara period had been responsible for the adoption of T'ang fashions. Envoys were sent by the Shogunate to the Ming court, and Zen priests are known to have directed commercial activities with China in their capacity as advisers to the Shogun. The power of Zen increased greatly during the Muromachi period because it encouraged a type of practical wisdom which appealed to the warrior class, and Zen monasteries were the center of Chinese learning. The mania for things Chinese was a characteristic feature of the intellectual circles of the Muromachi period, and the great feudal barons liked to wear Chinese dress. Yoshimitsu even adopted the custom of being carried about in a Chinese enclosed palanquin. As the years passed during the Muromachi period, the Japanese developed a sense of antiquarian sentiment, and the charm of traditional things began to exert its influence.

The parvenu fashions adopted by the feudal newcomers at the beginning of this period were eventually cast aside in favor of the cultural institutions of aristocratic Japanese elegance.

A new style of costume appeared called the daimon, meaning great crest, which was distinctive for its design of large family crests or *mon*. The daimon, together with an almost identical dress known as the *suo*, became the typical costume of the samurai and replaced the earlier *hitatare*. There also appeared a style of dress for men consisting of the former undergarment or *kosode* worn with the *hakama* or loose trousers. The costume for women also started a period of transition, which was eventually to carry it through various stages of simplification until it achieved its present form of colorful elegance. Various layers were gradually eliminated from the voluminous twelve-layer dress, until the *kosode* or innermost kimono finally became the outside garment. However, at court functions and on formal occasions it was the custom for women to wear an *uchikake*, or court lady's ceremonial outer garment or cloak, over the *kosode*, frequently tied about the waist and draped loosely over the shoulders. With the elimination of the former layers of harmoniously blended solid colors, a new treatment of design was adopted for the outer fabrics. By about the middle of the Muromachi period beautiful and colorful pictorial designs of rather large size appeared on the *kosode* fabrics. The trend in fashion favored the *shibori* or tied-and-dyed method for dyed patterns, the most popular style being the *tsuji-ga-hana*, or flowers in crisscross, which was a combination of *shibori* dyeing and hand-painted designs. It was at this time that silk fabrics were introduced from Ming China, including gold brocade or *kinran*, silk damask or *donsu*, and fine crepe or *chirimen*. These imports stimulated the weaving of magnificent Japanese prototypes at Sakai, the foremost port of that time. From here these beautiful weaving techniques spread to Kyoto, along with methods of producing certain woolen fabrics and velvets brought to Japan by Spanish and Portuguese ships. All these fabrics added to the colorful and magnificent life at Kyoto in the setting of the luxurious mansions and exquisite gardens of the Ashikaga. The area was known as Higashiyama, or East Mountain, after the section of Kyoto where the eighth Ashikaga Shogun, Yoshimasa, built his fabulous Ginkaku villa on Higashiyama. Here, toward the end of the fifteenth century, the æsthetic life of the Muromachi period reached its peak. During the closing years of the fifteenth century the country was once again plunged into a prolonged civil war.

MOMOYAMA SPLENDOR

The fifth period of Japanese costume starts around 1477. The Ashikaga Shoguns were powerless, the Imperial house was

Nuihaku-*type No costume of plain-weave silk, with one half having an over-all embroidered conventional design of flowering vines on a black ground and the other half large dew-laden leaves of grass in gold foil appliqué and large fans. Momoyama period (1573-1615). Tokyo National Museum.*

almost bankrupt, and continuous warfare prevailed in most of the provinces. This period of dress extended through the Momoyama period (1573-1615) and lasted to the end of the Edo or Tokugawa period (1615-1867). The first part of this era of costume is known as *Sengoku Jidai*, meaning the Age of the Country at War. The Momoyama period, associated with the two great men responsible for bringing order and unity out of this chaos, Oda Nobunaga and Toyotomi Hideyoshi, was an era of great splendor, of magnificent mansions and enormous castles decorated with great works of art. The tea ceremony, or *cha-no-yu*, which had already become an institution in the preceding Muromachi period, was now practiced with religious zeal. Both Nobunaga and Hideyoshi had a passion for it, and the great tea master Rikyu, who flourished at this time, raised it to the dignity of a veritable cult. All the arts reached a climax and were full of vigor and rich in delicate forms and colors. Costume at the beginning of the Momoyama period had become rather simplified and both men and women were wearing the same basic type of apparel consisting simply of the *kosode* or kimono, and the obi. The crafts of weaving and dyeing were, however, highly developed, and exquisite and brilliant fabrics were being produced, the fixed mode of attire opening up a new field for

these artisans. The magnificent brocades of the Nishijin weavers in Kyoto came into existence, especially the now famous *nishijin-obi*. Costumes became purely Japanese in taste and gorgeous creations of the art of elegant fashion. A particular kind of leather *tabi* called *murasakigawa* came into style, and there also appeared the *nagoya-obi*, which is a narrow rope-like girdle named after its place of origin near Karatsu in Kyushu.

It was during the Momoyama period that the Japanese costume finally developed into the elegant kimono and obi. The gradual discarding of successive layers resulted in the innermost garment or *kosode* finally becoming the simplified kimono. This evolution is particularly interesting when it is realized that until then this was the only garment worn by the lower classes. It now became the common attire of the Japanese regardless of sex or social position.

Although the kimono with its elegantly proportioned lines afforded a broad field for the creation of decorative designs, the technical processes available in the Momoyama period were comparatively limited in scope. The greatest development was in embroidery and in a continuation of the *tsuji-ga-hana* or tie-and-dye with hand-painted designs, as it was not until the middle of the Edo period that the beautiful *yuzen* process of dyeing was perfected. From very early times the art of embroidery had been practiced in Japan for the ornamentation of sumptuous fabrics, especially for the intricate work of portraying Buddhist subjects and making mandara hangings for temples and monasteries, as well as for decorating the Chinese robe and long skirt. With the introduction of the colorful and finely woven fabrics, embroidery was confined to articles of costume for ceremonial occasions. Through the Middle Ages its use was more or less restricted, but in the Momoyama era the elegant and simplified style of the *kosode* or kimono opened up unlimited possibilities. During this period embroidery became a veritable art form, with its magnificent pictorial designs in brilliantly colored silk threads. Many of the embroidered fabrics were enriched with designs worked with gold or silver foil in imitation of the beautiful *inkin* fabrics imported from Ming China. This type of work, known as *surihaku* in Japan, is produced by drawing the design on the fabric with a glue and then applying tiny pieces of gold or silver leaf to the prepared lines. When *kosode* are made with the *surihaku*, or "rubbed-on metal-leaf process," they are called *nuihaku*, or embroidery and foil, and although the effect is one of brilliance, the designs with their beautiful detail show great refinement. The Momoyama designs executed in *nuihaku*, as well as the tied-and-dyed process, gained in individuality in contrast to the earlier designs, which were for the most part repeated motifs. Many *kosode* were designed by famous artists to be executed on the fabric by the dyer or needleworker. The increasingly indigenous character of *kosode* fabrics is exemplified by an unusual type of design which appeared in the Momoyama period consisting of divisions into clearly prescribed sections. There are three particular types of these sectional designs, known as *katami-gawari*, *dan-gawari*, and *katasuso*, each name applying to both the kind of design and the garment on which it is applied. The type called *katami-gawari*, meaning "two different sides," is characterized by being divided vertically at the middle of the garment both in the front and in the back, with each side composed of a different fabric. Already in the Kamakura period some of the garments were made in this manner, chiefly with the purpose of creating a distinct color contrast, but in the Momoyama period a contrast both in design and color was sought. The type of design called *dan-gawari* consists of partitioned squares, while the *katasuso* is comprised of design spaces separated by line motifs resembling clouds. This form of design continued to be extremely popular until around the Kambun era (1661-1673) in the Edo period, when the style began to change to large designs of a rather bold nature covering the entire *kosode* (Plates 25 and 26). All through the Momoyama period and into the early part of the Edo period the *dofuku*, a kind of cloak which derived from a form of robe used by Buddhist monks, continued to be worn by men. The *uchikake*, or ceremonial outer garment of court ladies, also continued to be worn throughout the Momoyama period and into the Edo era.

EDO COSTUMES AND FASHIONS

For the next two hundred and fifty years, from 1615 to 1867, during the span of Tokugawa dominance known as the Edo or Tokugawa period, Japanese society experienced the fully developed feudal system, in which the classes were clearly demarcated. They were divided between the court nobles, who occupied the most exalted rank, the warriors, who wielded all the power and influence in political and economic affairs, and the farmers and townspeople. During this time, in the early years of the seventeenth century, all foreign traders were forbidden entrance to Japanese ports, with the exception of a few Dutch, Chinese and Koreans. These European traders, because they came to Japan by way of the southern seas, were called Southern Foreigners or Southern Barbarians. Their style of dress nevertheless influenced some fashions in fabrics as well as costume. As the Edo period progressed, the rich and colorful fabrics of the Momoyama era soon developed into a costly and luxurious art for those who could afford such fine pieces. The men of this period began to use over the kimono a form of loose cloak

No costume of the nuihaku *type. The material is a flat-weave brown silk, with a design of court carriages in the most delicate and fine needlework. The heavily laden stems of lilies are in embroidery, and the flowing vertical lines are appliqués in gold leaf. Momoyama period, sixteenth century. Tokyo National Museum.*

called *haori*, which is still worn, and the *furisode*, a kimono similar to the *kosode* but having longer sleeves.

Costume fabrics reached their greatest richness in the Genroku era (1688-1704), which was the most prosperous time in the Edo period. It was an epoch marked by luxury and extravagance, when the whole of Japan enjoyed the blessings of abundance. At this time there were two separate, parallel cultures, the old culture which adhered to the traditional classic æsthetics, and the new, which was represented by the popular tastes of the era. The culture of the majority of the townspeople of Edo was centered on the Ukiyo or Drifting World—a world of pleasures, restaurants, theaters, tea pavilions, and houses of assignation, whose citizens included dancers, singers, actors, bath-house girls, and courtesans. The great pleasure haunt of Edo was the Yoshiwara district, where the citizens gathered to enjoy the dances and plays, and indulge in frivolous and dissipating amusements. The people and the gay quarters of Yoshiwara were skillfully depicted in the endless variety of color-prints called Ukiyo-e, which afford a graphic record of the magnificent costumes worn during the Edo period. The Ukiyo-e portray in excellent detail the dress of the famous courtesans and popular actors, while other color prints present a historical record of the costume worn during Tokugawa times. Throughout the early part of the Edo period until the end of the Genroku era, No performances were patronized by the Shoguns and became a regular part of the feudal ceremonial on most important occasions. The No costume became incredibly beautiful, and was often made of silk fabrics with designs woven in dazzling colors, or of gorgeous embroidery with exquisite designs. A particular type of No costume which combined elegance and splendor was the *karaori*. Originally the name *karaori* was applied to all silk fabrics from China, since *kara* means China. In the Heian period the name was given to brocades having gold and floss-silk threads. When the term *karaori* is used to describe a No costume, it refers to a short-sleeved kimono worn by actors when impersonating female roles. The costume worn by No actors portraying male characters is called an *atsuita*, or *atsuita karaori* when unusually beautiful.

Not long after the Genroku era the No appears to have lost its official patronage, but it survived in the more conservative circles because of the appreciation of its traditional qualities by educated commoners, the nobles, and the upper classes. The No drama developed under the patronage of the feudal daimyo, and the general public of the Edo period found it much too solemn. In the opening years of the seventeenth century there appeared in Kyoto a new type of performance which soon developed into the popular drama called Kabuki. This form of drama, which evolved from the original performance of a talented young actress named Okuni, was enthusiastically received by the people of Kyoto, and her fame quickly spread to Edo. In 1607 Okuni and her troupe of performers, dancers, and musicians went to Edo, where they achieved great success. The Kabuki drama became an elaborate and brilliant affair, with magnificent and costly costumes which reflected the lavish taste of the actors. The theater exerted a strong influence upon the life of the Japanese during the Edo period, as it was the most popular form of entertainment. The Ukiyo-e color prints of famous actors of the day were eagerly purchased by theatergoers for their vivid portrayal of the characters and the beautiful costumes worn in certain roles. The entire repertory of the styles of costume that had been fashionable during the many centuries of Japanese history is represented on the Kabuki stage. The theater had a noticeable effect upon contemporary conduct, both the behavior and the dress of the actors being followed with such keen interest that they influenced fashions. The Yoshiwara courtesans so profusely depicted in the Ukiyo-e color prints were equally responsible for setting fashions in dress, modes of hairdressing, and fabric design which were extensively copied and popularized by the common people. The lavish and costly costumes worn by the famous Yoshiwara courtesans, together with the dress of the upper classes, actu-

ally reached the level of a fine art in the Genroku era, and great artists often were commissioned to execute the designs. In fact, the art of costume reached such a height of magnificence that a peculiar form of fashion display appeared in the custom called *kosode-maku*. This unexampled form of human vanity consisted of hanging a beautiful kimono on a cord stretched between two trees, in order to reflect the affluence of the family. The prevailing manner of living and the fashions of the Edo period were actually the creation of the people themselves rather than, as formerly, dictated by the nobility or the aristocratic military class. Having the wealth to satisfy their tastes, the cultivated townspeople tended toward costumes that were extravagant and luxurious, while the upper classes preferred the elegant simplicity of traditional modes.

During Tokugawa times the hairdress of women differed according to their social rank and profession. The style of hairdress in which the front portion of the hair was elaborately puffed out was called *maegami*, while the style with the sides spread out was called *bin*, and the *tsuto* consisted of gracefully draping

Above: Kosode *with a* dan-gawari *design dyed in the* tsuji-ga-hana *method. Momoyama period (1573-1615). Akashi Collection, Tokyo.*

Right: Uchikake *of white silk damask, embroidered with flowing diagonal designs and flowers. This formal gown was worn by a mistress of Iesada, the thirteenth Tokugawa Shogun. Edo period, first half nineteenth century. Tokyo National Museum.*

the hair in the back. In this period the use of false hair came into vogue and the elaborate coiffure was adorned with long hairpins, combs, and ornaments. It was also the fashion for the ladies of the court and the women court attendants to paint their eyebrows and blacken their teeth. Married women of the common classes also blackened their teeth and at the same time shaved off their eyebrows, while women of all classes used powder and rouge. Women's dress became highly extravagant both in materials and in design during the early part of the Edo period.

By the year 1700 the townspeople had reached a high point of affluence and culture, which gave them a position of real importance. Although the military class still maintained their dignity and high social standing, the commoners now had most of the money, enabling them to enjoy the many pleasures of life. As the citizens developed a strong class character that competed with the military caste, it was inevitable that the interests of the two classes should clash. After the Kyoho era (1716–1736) the ruling military clique issued various procla-

mations in an attempt to regulate the lives of the townspeople, in a desperate effort to stop extravagance and pleasures. Many stern edicts were issued against townspeople living extravagantly and giving lavish entertainments, and against townspeople and servants wearing silks or cloth mantles. But the people, having acquired wealth and cultivation, intended to enjoy the pleasures they could afford. Many richly dressed shopkeepers were arrested, and on occasion a rich merchant would have his wealth confiscated for a too ostentatious manner of living. The edicts of the Shogunate had little effect and did little to stop the townspeople from indulging in expensive pleasures; having become inured to luxury, they simply spent their money on more costly things that were also less obvious. During these times men would wear an unpretentious outer-garment lined with some rich fabric, and women would often be seen dressed outwardly as a maidservant while underneath they would be wearing the most beautiful and costly silk fabrics. As the Edo period progressed, the continuous conflict between the interests of the military and the merchant classes gradually moderated with the declining economic power of the samurai. Finally they intermingled, and the Edo period with its 250 years of peaceful seclusion came to an end with the restoration of Imperial government. In 1868 the Emperor Meiji issued the administrative rules for the sovereign, commonly called the Imperial Oath of Five Articles, and set the course for a new order.

THE KIMONO AND OTHER TRADITIONAL DRESS

The Edo period exerted a strong native æsthetic influence on the arts and manners of the country, and was responsible for developing a truly Japanese taste in dress which laid the foundations for the present-day styles. The development of the kimono, which has undergone a most unusual course through the centuries, has no parallel in the history of costume. After the Restoration of 1868 the picturesque garments of the nobility were no longer seen on ordinary occasions, and the Emperor Meiji himself, as well as the Empress, appeared in European dress. However, the traditional Japanese kimono, in the simplified and elegant style it reached in the Edo period, has survived as a national dress to the present day. Although Western clothes are used for everyday wear in urban and metropolitan centers, the native dress is usually worn at home, being loose, more comfortable, and more suitable for Japanese domestic life. Compared to the national dress of other countries, there is far less distinction between male and female attire, nor do the garments of Japanese children essentially differ from those of their elders. The wide-sleeved kimono

No costume of the atsuita *type. The material on one side is crimson satin and on the other side it is of gold thread. The design of calligraphy from an anthology of Japanese-Chinese poetry is woven so finely it seems hand-written. Early Edo period, seventeenth century. Tokyo National Museum.*

with its obi or sash is common for both sexes of all ages. Another characteristic feature is the absence of headwear and gloves, as well as a complete absence of jewelry or costume ornament.

The outer garments worn by men include the kimono, the *haori*, and the *hakama*. The kimono is rectangular in shape with short, deep, square-cut sleeves and a stand-up roll-collar of even width throughout. In the front the lapel folds left over right, forming a V-shaped opening at the neck, and the kimono is secured about the waist with the narrow sash called an obi. The kimono reaches to the ankles, where it is the same width as at the shoulders, and is not gathered up over the girdle. Like most Japanese garments, the kimono is usually made at home, as it requires only the simplest tailoring. It is made from a complete dress-length piece of fabric woven especially for kimono and generally measuring about ten yards in length by eighteen inches in width, and is of cotton, hemp-cloth, or silk. None of the material is wasted, because triangular pieces are folded to shape rather than cut, and any differences of length or width are adjusted by tucks. Since the

ordinary unlined kimono does not afford the proper protection against the cold, one, two, and sometimes three robes of identical cut are worn. These are lined with floss, or with a layer of cotton covered with a thin layer of floss.

A lined kimono made of silk is called a *kosode*; if it is made of hemp-cloth it is called a *nunoko*; and if more than one is worn the outer kimono is called an *uwagi* or upper dress and the other one or two are known as *shitagi* or lower dress. Under the kimono is worn a cotton shirt called a *juban*, which is cut exactly like the kimono. It is made of cotton but the sleeves are white or blue-and-white silk. A small portion of the *juban* shows at the neck opening and also extends slightly beyond the sleeves of the kimono. The *yukata* is a cool, comfortable kimono for summer, worn at home, or after bathing, or for evening walks. It is made of cotton and is usually white with simple designs in blue. Also for summer wear is a thin hempen kimono called a *katabira*. If these are used for formal summer wear they are black, the only ornament being the wearer's family crest or *mon* painted in colors and placed in prescribed positions. There are two kinds of obi for men, the

296

kaku-obi for formal occasions and the ordinary *heko-obi* for informal wear. The *kaku-obi* is made of a stiff silk or cotton in dark colors with a wide center stripe in various colors. The obi is about four inches wide, and is wound three times around the waist and tied behind with a double knot having the short ends turned upward.

An outer garment called the *haori* is worn over the kimono in the manner of a coat or jacket. It reaches to slightly above the knees and is fuller around the body, being provided with gores or triangular pieces of cloth set in the sides. It is open in front and only loosely fastened across the chest by two silk cords or *himo*. The *haori* has a turned-down roll-collar and the inside of the body part is lined, generally with colorful and beautiful fabrics with elaborate designs sometimes enhanced with embroidery. The outside fabric is black or other dark-color silk usually having a striped pattern. The *haori* for formal occasions is always of black silk with one, three, five, or sometimes seven reproductions of the wearer's family crest or *mon* painted on white circles. The circles are from one to two inches in diameter and were left in reserve at the time the fabric was dyed. In the clearly prescribed manner of wearing the family emblem, a single *mon* is placed high between the shoulders. If three are used, the additional two are placed at the back of each elbow; if five, the additional two are put on the breast of each lapel; and if all seven, the final pair are placed inside each elbow.

For very formal occasions the proper garment is the *hakama*, a sort of loose trousers or divided skirt. The sides are open halfway to the bottom, with further play provided by six deep tapering pleats. The *hakama* is fastened by two long bands wound twice around the waist and is generally made of a fine-quality hard silk of dark tones with vertical stripes. The Japanese wear a special kind of sock called *tabi* with every kind of dress except the informal summer kimono or *yukata*. The *tabi* is a combination sock and slipper, and is the only article of footwear permitted to be worn inside the Japanese house. *Tabi* are about ankle high, made of cotton or silk with a slightly stiffened sole, and provided with a separate space for the big toe, to allow the cord on the footwear to pass between it and the second toe. The *tabi* is fastened at the back with an overlap having metal or horn hook tabs with thread loops on the inner side. White *tabi* are reserved for formal occasions, while dark-blue *tabi* with white soles are always used for ordinary wear. For normal everyday footwear there is a particular kind of sandal called a *zori*, which is usually made of fine rice-straw matting and has a sole of coiled hemp-rope or some similar material. One of better quality having a rawhide sole is called a *setta*. Zori are kept on the foot by two thick cords or *hanao* attached on each side near the front and connected with a short piece of cord which is gripped between the first and second toes. When walking in the rain or snow, or on ground that is dusty or wet, a kind of patten

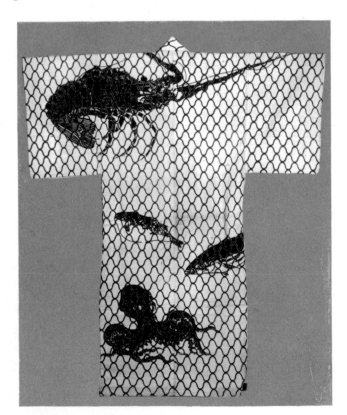

Yukata *of white cotton with a dark-blue stenciled design of a fishnet in which have been caught lobsters, crabs, globefish, and octopus. Edo period, eighteenth century. Matsuzakaya Collection, Kyoto.*

Yukata *of white cotton with a sharp and clear dark-blue stencil design depicting three famous scenes of Japan, from top to bottom, Miyajima, Ama-no-Hashidate, and Matsushima. Edo period, eighteenth century. Matsuzakaya Collection. Kyoto.*

called a *geta* is employed. It consists of a wooden sole with square ends made of a lightweight wood such as paulownia, and raised on two oak or beech blocks set across the underside. The *geta* is attached to the foot in the same manner as the *zori*.

The kimono worn by women has a somewhat different cut and design from the men's kimono. It has no sewn tucks at the waist, which allows a woman of average height to wear it full length and slightly sweeping the floor or to tuck it up to a desired height with two cords wound about the waist. The *eri*, or roll-collar, is slightly wider and longer than the man's, and the sleeves are a little longer but with a greater depth and smaller openings for the hands. Because the wide obi rises so high, the sleeves are joined to the body of the kimono for only ten inches, the rest of their depth being left open on the inner side, thus allowing a greater display of the undergarments. For formal occasions three kimono are worn with the inner two having plain white *eri*, but in warm weather only two are worn. On especially formal occasions the outer kimono is plain black with the wearer's family *mon* displayed in the same manner as prescribed for the men's *haori*. The correct color for kimono worn by young unmarried women is gray, pale blue, or mauve, with modest designs either embroidered, painted, or woven around the lower portion of the skirt and sleeves, and having the *mon* blazoned in their proper places. *Mon* are not displayed on kimono for daily use. The underwear worn by ladies beneath the kimono consists of a short white cotton petticoat or *futano* reaching to the knees; a short chemise or *shita-juban*, and a long petticoat or *koshimaki* which reaches to the feet. During Edo times the name *koshimaki* was applied to a ceremonial summer robe worn by court ladies at the palace. A kimono of hempen cloth and tied with a narrow sash was worn underneath, while the *koshimaki* was merely wrapped around the body. The material was always black or dark brown and the lining was crimson. The present *koshimaki*, which is of a plain white for matrons, of colorful and beautiful designs for young ladies, and plain red for little girls, offers a pleasing color contrast with the kimono. The silk or cotton *shita-juban* is either plain white or some light color with a detachable collar-lapel or *han-eri* of embroidered designs. The cool summer kimono or *yukata* for women is essentially the same as the men's.

The obi or sash worn by the Japanese woman is the most beautiful and most costly article of her costume, and women of all ages are permitted by traditional fashion to wear obi of colorful and elaborate designs. The most gorgeous figured silks and brocades that the wearer can afford are acquired for making an obi, which measures about four or five yards in length by about fourteen inches in width. The two principal varieties of obi are the *chuya-obi* for informal wear, and the *maru-obi* for formal dress. The *chuya-obi*, which is slightly stiffened with canvas, has a facing material of a dark-color silk, with the lining material of a lighter ground and different design. The *maru-obi* is of a heavier material and both sides are alike, because it is of double width and folded lengthwise with the selvages sewn together. The obi is wound twice around the waist, leaving in the back a short end of about two feet and a longer end of about five feet. In recent times the obi most frequently has been worn by folding it in two to reduce its width around the body, with the lining inwards, and with the ends opened out to their full width. It is tied in the back with a large, square-shaped, flat knot which permits the material to be displayed to its fullest advantage. Although the knot holds firmly, it occasionally requires tightening, which is remedied, if the wearer so wishes, by tying a very narrow silk band, or *obijima*, around the center portion. Ukiyo-e color prints of famous courtesans frequently show them with the obi tied in front in accordance with an edict of the Shogunate issued around the year 1780 and applying specifically to courtesans; however, obi were often also worn by others tied in the front during those times.

The *haori* has only been adopted by women since about the middle of the seventeenth century and is reserved for purely informal wear. The footwear for women is essentially the same as for the men, consisting of the *tabi*, the *zori*, and the *geta*. However, in more recent times a *zori* for women has appeared which consists of a shaped sole rising to a high platform heel and made in colorful materials. Because it had been the tradition of Japanese women to have elaborate coiffures, headwear was necessarily not used except for a hood in extremely cold weather. It has never been the custom for women to wear inro or other such articles hanging from the obi as in the case of men. In their stead the women carry an oblong wallet, or *hakoseko*, made of magnificently woven silk, in which to carry small articles for personal use. The *hakoseko* is worn partly thrust into the left side of the opening at the neck, with a portion of it showing.

The colorful kimono patterns and designs, so intimately associated with the daily life of the Japanese, have frequently been taken from the various decorative paintings of famous artists of earlier times. These designs often ornament the beautiful native costume of young Japanese women with large conventionalized flowers, charming little birds, trees, or waves. Such designs and patterns are not just reserved for young ladies, but are also used on the kimono of matrons, although smaller in scale and in more subdued colors. In the present-day Japanese costume, the beauty and elegance of its historical background is reflected in exquisite materials and designs. It reflects the manners and customs that contributed to its development and the whole concept of social life during the great periods when feudalism was at its height.

XXI Dolls

THERE ARE only a few days in the year on which there is not a festival being celebrated somewhere in Japan. Though almost all are of a religious nature, there are certain popular family festival days called the Five Seasons festivals or *go-sekku* which are celebrated throughout the country. Among them are the Dolls' Festival and the Boys' Festival, which had their origin in ancient Japanese beliefs that the people could purify themselves through certain rituals and acquire protection from misfortune by driving evil spirits from their bodies. This popular belief was partly adopted from an ancient Chinese custom and partly from the native Japanese Shinto ceremony of purification.

Of all the *go-sekku* days the Dolls' Festival was the one that aroused the greatest fervor. Small figures or images were used as talismans against evil, and it was the custom to cast them into the river after the purification rite had been performed. With the passage of time these talisman figures became increasingly elaborate and, instead of being cast into the waters after the ceremony, they were kept as ornamental objects and displayed in a ceremonial manner. The figures soon became veritable works of art, representing nobles, court ladies, court attendants, ladies-in-waiting, and many other personages. Usually they were clothed in rich silk garments. These figures, and many others made from various materials and in many different techniques, are commonly referred to as "Japanese dolls" and are intended as ornamental objects to be appreciated for their beauty in workmanship and costume. Although it has been the general practice to apply the term *Japanese doll* to these figures, the English word *doll* correctly means a child's plaything in the shape of a human figure, and should not be applied to magical figures, idols, votive offerings, and costume figures. In Japanese, however, the word *ningyo* refers both to a doll used as a child's plaything and to small ornamental human figures. The Chinese character in the Japanese language representing *ningyo* means human shape or a figure of human shape.

It is recorded in early chronicles that there was a custom during the Heian period (794-1185) of making dolls known as *hina*. They were made to represent girls and boys, and were used as playthings by the children of noble families. The accounts further relate that along with the *hina* a variety of toys were made during this period, such as miniature palaces, feudal carriages, tiny chests, and dining trays and utensils. For boys, there were also dolls representing warriors and men on horseback. But aside from a few of these references in old records, there is no evidence pertaining to dolls in medieval times and none are known to be extant. For the Edo period (1615-1867) the historical record becomes clearer, as much was written about dolls in those times and many are preserved in fine collections. In this period of two and a half centuries of peace under the rule of the Tokugawa Shogunate the art of dollmaking reached its culmination. Whereas in earlier times all forms of culture were restricted to the noble and military classes, the rise of the merchant class during the Edo period brought about many changes in the life of the townspeople. As this new urban class acquired more and more wealth, it was only natural that their cultural aspirations increased. Among their many desires was the wish to have dolls of fine workmanship, dressed in beautiful costumes. A further impetus was given to the art of dollmaking by the great interest in collecting them for display and by the popularity of the Dolls' Festival. The Edo period is noted for the wide variety of beautiful dolls made for the affluent townspeople, as well as for examples of a more rustic nature made in the provincial villages. It was also in this period that the doll play or *bunraku* puppet show was developed to a fine art.

GIRLS' AND BOYS' FESTIVALS

The custom of celebrating the Dolls' Festival specially for girls originated around the middle of the Edo period. The

299

Above: Dairi-sama *dolls which represent the Emperor and* Empress, *used for display in the Girls' Festival. Edo period, nineteenth century. Tokyo National Museum.*

Hina-ningyo, *or display dolls for the Girls' Festival, representing the Emperor and the Empress, with paper clothing. Edo period, eighteenth century. Tokyo National Museum.*

proper name for this day is Peach-Blossom Festival, but it is popularly called *hina matsuri*, meaning Dolls' Festival, or Girls' Festival, and is held every year on the third day of the third month. Originally its date of celebration was fixed in the third month according to the old lunar calendar, to coincide with the blooming of the peach trees. The dolls displayed on this occasion are not the everyday playthings of children. They are ceremonial dolls which in many families have been handed down from generation to generation as treasured heirlooms. These dolls are displayed in a prescribed ceremonial arrangement in the principal room of the house for the duration of the festival. Then, when the display is dismantled, the dolls and other pieces used in the ceremony are carefully placed in boxes and stored away in the family godown. Generally a set of festival dolls consists of at least fifteen, in ancient costume and arranged on a stand having five or seven step-like tiers covered with red fabric. In addition to the festival dolls the display includes many other appropriate objects, such as miniature household accessories and other articles of fine workmanship. These accessories include such things as a cabinet fitted with tiny drawers, a brazier or *hibachi*, dining trays set with porcelain utensils and chopsticks, a toilet stand with mirror, musical instruments, and an ancient two-wheeled court carriage. The dolls most highly valued for

the festival are known as *dairi-sama*, representing the Emperor and Empress dressed in court costumes of costly silks. The *dairi-sama* occupy the highest tier, and behind them are miniature gold-leaf folding screens that also serve as a background for two tiny paper lanterns mounted on stands and two vases containing sprigs of miniature peach blossoms. On the second tier are placed three court ladies and tiny dining trays with bowls and dishes, while court attendants and musicians are placed on the third and possibly fourth tiers. As a rule the lower tiers are reserved for the many other objects connected with the festival.

The other popular festival in which dolls play a prominent part is the Iris Festival or Boys' Festival celebrated on the fifth day of the fifth month. In Japanese it is called *shobu-no-sekku*, *shobu* being the word for iris, which has been closely associated with this festival for centuries. From early times the iris has been regarded as possessing miraculous powers against misfortune and illness, and the ancient custom of steeping its leaves in the very hot water of the Japanese bath is still practiced. On this festival day little boys used the long blade-shaped leaves of iris to play soldiers, and these leaves were also placed on the eaves of houses to keep away the evil spirits. Just as the Peach-Blossom Festival gradually developed into a festival for girls around the middle of the Edo period, the evolution of the Boys' Festival appears to have followed the same pattern. Around the beginning of the Edo period it was the custom for samurai on this day to set up a kind of semi-enclosure outside the entrance gate to the house to contain a display. Within this enclosure were arranged articles in imitation of helmets, spears, halberds, battle streamers, and banners. Later, the display was set up inside the gate, and in the cities the merchants arranged similar displays inside the doorways of their shops. Craftsmen soon began to make fine miniature reproductions of arms, armor, and other articles of war, as well as dolls representing samurai and warriors on horseback. In the latter part of the Edo period it became the custom to display these warrior dolls and their miniature accessories in an arrangement similar to that of the Girls' Festival. On the tiers of the stand were displayed dolls representing famous feudal generals such as Toyotomi Hideyoshi and Minamoto Yoshitsune, and legendary figures like Kintoki, whose exploits are familiar to all Japanese boys. In many large houses a few articles are often placed on display along with the miniature pieces, such as a long lacquered bow with a quiver of arrows and a beautifully decorated Japanese sword. A rack is sometimes placed near the display to hold spears, various long weapons, and handsome silk banners bearing the family crest.

A picturesque old custom observed during the season of the Boys' Festival is the erection of a tall bamboo or wooden pole in the garden or on the rooftop, to which is fastened the symbol of a carp and a long streamer. The streamer, called *fukinagashi*, is made of several very narrow strips of silk cloth fastened to a ring at the top of the pole. The carp symbol, or *koi nobori*, which is fastened to the pole under the streamer, is made of two pieces of paper, muslin, or silk joined together in such a way as to fill out in the wind and resemble a fish swimming in the air. Traditionally one carp symbol is hoisted for each son in the family, starting with a large one, perhaps measuring fifteen feet or more for the oldest son, and progressing to smaller ones for the younger sons. A diminutive one is always used for babies. The carp has been a symbol of strength and perseverance because of its ability to fight its way up swift streams and jump waterfalls, and these attributes of determination are accordingly regarded as a proper example for young boys.

CLAY AND PORCELAIN DOLLS

The full range of Japanese dolls covers a wide variety of types classified according to the material of which they are made, the manner in which they are dressed, and the purpose for which they are used. Many dolls were made to serve as children's playthings and are now valued for their antiquarian interest. Others are prized for their fine craftsmanship and magnificent costumes. In the Edo period dolls made of clay were popular playthings for children, and they were produced in many parts of the country. In the urban areas as well as in the country districts these clay dolls were often used as charms against misfortune and sometimes were placed on altars to bring the favor of the gods on the crops. Made of fine ceramic clay, they were formed in a mold, fired in a kiln, and painted with gay colors. They depict a wide variety of subjects mostly taken from the everyday life of the Japanese. Certain places were noted for particular types of clay dolls; for example, the

Isho-ningyo, *a naked doll with changeable clothes in the form of a boy. Edo period, early nineteenth century. Tokyo National Museum.*

Obunko-ningyo *(receptacle doll) representing Urashima, a legendary fisherman. The Shogun's gifts to his retainers were often these papier-mâché bowls with lids in the form of dolls. Edo period, early nineteenth century. Tokyo National Museum.*

Ukiyo-ningyo, *or genre doll of the Ukiyo or Drifting World of Edo, representing a woman serving at a brothel as maid to a courtesan. Edo period, early eighteenth century. Tokyo National Museum.*

so-called *fushimi-ningyo* came from the district in Kyoto called Fushimi, where the magnificent castle of Hideyoshi had stood. *Fushimi-ningyo* dolls are known to have been extremely popular throughout the provinces and in the large cities since the early part of the Edo period. Their production was carried on as a home industry much the same as the weaving and dyeing trades in the Nishijin district. Among more than three hundred different subjects of *fushimi-ningyo*, the most common were the seven gods of good fortune, mythological, legendary, and historical personages, and genre figures of the contemporary everyday life of the Edo period.

From very early times the approaches to Shinto shrines and Buddhist temples provided an ideal location for shops and stalls, and dolls were sold along with other objects to attract visitors. One of the most picturesque of these approaches is the long, narrow, winding, and steep road up the Otowayama in Kyoto, where the famous Kiyomizu temple has stood since its founding in the year 805. The colorful shops that line both sides of this road are filled with all sorts of Japanese wares for the thousands who visit the temple precincts.

The making of clay dolls was also carried on as a household industry in many other parts of the country, often as a spare-time occupation of farmers in provincial villages. Most of these provincial examples were copies of the various types of *fushimi-ningyo*, as the local dollmakers in general were not sufficiently skilled to create new or different types. One of the few places where indigenous types were created was the town of Koga in Kyushu, not far from Nagasaki, which was noted for a doll called *oranda*, meaning Holland, since it portrayed a Dutch sea captain holding a gun in his hand. Because foreign sailing ships frequently called at the port of Nagasaki, many of the Koga dolls depict foreigners — for example, the one called *acha-san*, which represents a Chinese holding a chicken. Another provincial doll famous since early times is the *ejiko*, which admirably expresses the colorful charm of Japanese folk art. The *ejiko* doll is the product of local craftsmen in the prefectures of the most northeastern regions of the main island of Honshu. Dressed in picturesque clothing and sitting in a round straw basket, it shows how a tiny Japanese baby is left at home while the parents are at work in the fields.

Another place noted for its clay dolls is Hakata, where *hakata-ningyo* developed from a rather crude product in the early years of the Edo period to an artistic genre doll, notably those representing actors and dancers. In most of the places throughout the country where clay dolls have continued to be produced since the Edo period, neither the method of making them nor the model has changed during the past two or three hundred years.

There also appeared during the Edo period beautiful figurines made of porcelain that were used as ornamental pieces

Saga-ningyo *representing a standing woman. Edo period, first half of the eighteenth century. Tokyo National Museum.*

to be placed in the tokonoma in the houses of affluent merchants. They represented legendary figures, gods of good fortune, little children, and many other favorite subjects. The craftsmanship found in many of these porcelain dolls possesses the same kind of naïve native character as found in Old Kutani ware. The dollmakers also produced a great variety of ornamental figures clothed in different costumes to represent people in all walks of life. Within the category of costume dolls are included *ukiyo-ningyo*, *mitsuore-ningyo*, and *kimekomi-ningyo*. The type known as *ukiyo-ningyo* derives its name from the word *Ukiyo*, meaning the Drifting World or Floating World, as it was called in the current language of the day. *Ukiyo-ningyo* realistically portrayed the people and their costume as seen in the everyday life of Edo, especially Kabuki actors, courtesans, No performers, and others of the pleasure district of Yoshiwara. There is a variety of *ukiyo-ningyo* called *oyama-ningyo* which represents women in contemporary costume and coiffure. They were called *oyama-ningyo* because *oyama* is the name applied to Kabuki actors who take the roles of female characters, and these dolls were said to represent them in these parts.

The head and hands of *ukiyo-ningyo* were made of wood, while the body was of either rice straw or wood. The crepe or brocade costume was made in the same manner as a real garment, or by pasting tiny pieces of fabric to the wooden body. The name generally applied to this category of costume doll is *kimekomi-ningyo*, which is derived from the word *kimekomu*, meaning to insert in a groove. It is so called because the pieces of fabric simulating the costume are fixed with glue at the ends and inserted into grooves provided for that purpose

Left: Ukiyo-ningyo *representing a young Kabuki actor impersonating a warrior. Edo period, early eighteenth century. Tokyo National Museum.*

Below: Ukiyo-ningyo, *or genre dolls of the Ukiyo or Drifting World. A* daijin *or rich merchant (left) and his* yakko *or servant (right). Edo period, early eighteenth century. Tokyo National Museum.*

The name *kamo-ningyo* is frequently given to these *kimekomi-ningyo* in keeping with a legend that a Shinto priest made the first doll of this type from the wood of a willow tree that grew on the bank of the Kamogawa in Kyoto. Also included within this same classification of costume dolls are the so-called *mitsuore-ningyo*, which actually are intended to be playthings for children, in contrast to the others which are ornamental figures. The *mitsuore-ningyu* were made with movable joints, and this name, which literally means three-bend doll, was given to them because their characteristic poses are standing, bowing, and squatting in typical Japanese manner. Occasionally *mitsuore-ningyo* were made as ornamental figures in the form of lovely women and Kabuki actors, but the majority represented little children and were used as playthings. In their principal form they portrayed little Japanese children, from babies to six-year-olds, with captivating expressions of tender happiness.

WOODEN DOLLS

Wooden dolls are divided into three principal types: the *saga-ningyo*, the *nara-ningyo*, and the *gosho-ningyo*. *Saga-ningyo* were intended as ornamental figures and include a wide variety of subjects taken from the everyday life of the Edo period, as well as popular gods and legendary persons. The name is said to derive from a district in the western part of Kyoto called Saga, where an unknown dollmaker is believed to have made the first doll of this type. *Saga-ningyo* were skillfully carved in wood and the parts that represent the costume were painted with rich colors, frequently with portions of gold leaf to resemble costly brocades. After these dolls had received the finishing touches by the carver, they were coated with a thick application of *gofun*, a fine oyster-shell powder, and *nikawa*, a kind of glue. The thick layer of this mixture provided an ideal surface for the meticulously painted costume portion with beautiful designs copied from fine silks.

The type of wooden doll called *gosho-ningyo* was a product of Kyoto, where they were made during the Edo period. The word *gosho* means palace, and according to stories handed down from those times, this type of doll was used for gifts by the members of the Imperial household and the nobles. As a rule *gosho-ningyo* represent boys, from tiny babies to about six years of age, and they are usually clothed only in a *haragake*, which is a piece of cloth covering the front of the body and tied behind the neck and waist. These dolls were made in a variety of poses, such as standing, crawling, and sitting, sometimes with a musical instrument or other object in their hands. Their form is rather plump with an unusually large round head, and the white body is characterized by a high glossy finish. The finest quality *gosho-ningyo* were carved from *kiri* wood, which is also known as the paulownia or Empress tree. The limbs and the body were carved separately and then fixed together with glue. Many coats of *gofun* and *nikawa* were applied to the surface, and polished to produce a very high gloss. The eyes, nose, mouth, and a few strokes of paint to simulate hair on the forehead were the only added finishing touches. Many later examples of *gosho-ningyo* were made of *neri-mono*, a composition of sawdust and grain flour, which was molded to form the doll. Another later method was called *hariko*, or papier-mâché, whereby the doll was molded from a layer of papier-mâché that was applied to a model. When this layer had dried, it was cut from the model in two parts and fixed together to make a hollow doll. *Gosho-ningyo* were not only popular as dolls from the early part of

Mitsuore-ningyo, or three-bend doll, in the form of a little boy. By Shugetsu. Edo period, early nineteenth century. Tokyo National Museum.

304

the Edo period but were widely used as talismans and kept in houses to ward off evil spirits and taken on journeys for protection against accidents.

In contrast to both the *saga-ningyo* and *gosho-ningyo*, the wooden doll called *nara-ningyo* is a vigorously carved piece with very little color applied. The carving is sharp and deep and is executed with the skilful touch of a sculptor. According to tradition, the *nara-ningyo* were first made during the early years of the Edo period by a craftsman of the Kasuga shrine at Nara. The figures portray No actors in various characteristic roles taken from the more popular performances. The original models or prototypes from which the *nara-ningyo* were evolved were tiny wooden figures of No actors used as netsuke. Many dolls having unique characteristics were made in the provinces and display the typical naïve folk art of the regional craftsmen.

The vast territory covering the northeastern portion of Honshu is called the Tohoku region. Most of it, with its picturesque villages lying among beautiful mountains and along the rugged seacoast, is reminiscent of feudal days. In this region are made the famous *kokeshi* dolls, which were originally intended as playthings for children in that part of Japan. It is probably the most popular object of folk art that has continued until the present day. It is believed that during the Edo period the local craftsmen made these *kokeshi* as a side line to their regular trade of turning wooden bowls, dishes, and other household utensils. Although the *kokeshi* is made in a most primitive manner by turning on a lathe, its plain cylindrical body, rounded shoulder line, and loose-jointed head produce a unique and charming form. The eyes, nose, and hair, each painted with thin delicate strokes, portray a

fascinating expression that is not found in any other type of doll. Typical of much of the work in this mountainous region are the peculiar local designs painted on the body in only two or three primary colors.

PUPPETS

Another form of the art of the doll craftsman is found in the small figures used in the famous Japanese puppet show called *bunraku*. The puppet drama was originally introduced from China in the eighth century, and for a long time the performances were confined to religious functions. As the centuries passed, it gradually became a popular entertainment of the people, and in the seventeenth century it took the form that is known at the present time. In the Keicho era (1596-1615) there was a noted player of the *samisen* named Menukiya Chozaburo, who perfected the art by working with a puppet showman of Nishinomiya, near the city of Kobe. He coordinated the art of manipulating the puppets to the accompaniment of the chanting of *joruri* and to the music of the *samisen*. *Joruri* can be described as dramatic ballads usually written with alternating lines of five and seven syllables, and sung or chanted to the music of the *samisen*. The puppet show grew rapidly in popularity and became a favorite entertainment among the people, with many theaters being established in Kyoto, Osaka, and Edo. Toward the close of the seventeenth century a great *joruri* chanter named Takemoto Gidayu, 1651-1714, rose to fame in Osaka as the creator of a new style of *joruri* chanting. He became so famous throughout Japan, and his school attracted so many disciples, that almost all

Gosho-ningyo *wearing the traditional* haragake *which covers only the front of the body above the waist. Edo period, early nineteenth century. Tokyo National Museum.*

Nara-ningyo, *made by Morikawa Toen, depicting a scene in a No drama in which Ushiwaka (right), a celebrated twelfth-century warrior, engages in a duel with Benkei. Edo period, early nineteenth century. Tokyo National Museum.*

Kokeshi dolls from the Tohoku region in northeastern Japan. Japan Travel Bureau.

joruri chanters adopted his style, until finally *joruri* itself was often called *gidayu*.

The rapid rise of the Gidayu school was largely due to the fine works of *joruri* written by Chikamatsu Monzaemon, 1653-1724, a famous writer for the Kabuki theater and Japan's foremost literary genius. Among more than a hundred dra-

mas by him, the most noted are *The Love Suicide at Amijima* or *Ten-no-Amijima*, *The Courier of Hates* or *Meido-no-Hikyaku*, *The Hell of Oil* or *Abura-Jigoku*, and *The Battle of Kokusen-ya* or *Kokusen-ya-Kassen*. Innumerable characters are portrayed in a *joruri* drama, but the number of puppet heads used for a performance is limited, with many different costumes employed for each head. The heads of *bunraku* puppets are realistically carved with fine representations of human features. Many are constructed so that the mouth, eyelids, eyebrows, eyeballs, and ears can be moved to produce a more effective expression.

There are two kinds of puppets, namely small and large, the small ones being not more than twelve inches tall and operated from above with presumably invisible strings. The large ones are at least two-thirds life-size, and when worked by skillful manipulators appear to have all the characteristics of human beings. Each of these large puppets requires one master operator and two skilled assistants. The master operator is usually clad in a gaily colored costume, while his assistants are garbed in black hoods and robes. These black robes make them less conspicuous, and their presence on the stage is overlooked, in keeping with the traditional Japanese practice of mentally separating them from the play as abstract conceptions. Performances of *bunraku* are produced in a most realistic fashion when conducted by a master of the art, and the puppets become real persons whose lives of adventure, romance, sorrow, and tragedy inspire deep response in the onlookers.

THE ORIGIN of the fan in Oriental countries is difficult to surmise, but in one form or another it is undoubtedly of great antiquity. Its provenance is traditionally attributed to China, whose early fans consisted of dried and stiffened leaves, an arrangement of feathers fixed into a handle, or a frame of wood with some sort of fabric stretched upon it. The fan passed from China by way of Korea to Japan in the earliest centuries of our era. The evolution of the fan in Japan followed the same course of development as other branches of the arts introduced from the mainland, and the natural aptitude of the Japanese craftsman, with his creative genius, expressed itself in a great variety of fans for every purpose. Through every period from the seventh century to the end of feudal times in the nineteenth century, the fan flourished in Japan to such an extent that it became a practically indispensable part of the national costume for both men and women of all classes. The ingenuity of the Japanese craftsman and the creative imagination of the Japanese artist in adapting beautifully expressive designs to the shape of the fan contributed to its popularity as an article of use and of æsthetic elegance. The invention of the folding fan is indeed credited to Japan, where it was first made in the seventh century, although the flat or Chinese fan, called *uchiwa* by the Japanese, which was introduced centuries earlier, has remained in general use up to the present time. And it was also the Japanese who originated and introduced the particular kind of fan or hand-screen, also called *uchiwa*, which is made by splitting one end of a piece of bamboo into a form of rays on which ornamental silk or paper is stretched, while the other end of the bamboo stick serves as a handle.

INVENTION AND STRUCTURE OF THE FAN

According to accounts in ancient chronicles the invention of the *ogi* or folding fan is attributed to a fanmaker of the Tenji era (668-672) who lived in Tamba province near Kyoto, and whose name has been lost. The old records relate that this fanmaker was married to a shrew, and one night when a bat flew into their house, she began to revile her husband for not being quick enough to catch it and put it outside. Finally the bat came too close to the flame of a lamp and scorched its wings. As the man picked it up from the floor to put it out in the garden, one of its wings opened, and this gave him the idea of a fan that could be folded and carried in the sleeve of one's dress. It is said that the first folding fan he made was composed of twenty-one ribs of *hinoki* cypress. The name *ogi* applied to all folding fans had its origin in the word *owogu*, meaning to fan or fanning. But as the emblem of life, the symbolical name for the folding fan in Japan is *suyehiro*, which is derived from *suye*, meaning end (in the sense of future), and *hiro*, meaning wide-spreading, or, by extension, prosperous. The fan is a symbol of good luck, and especially of future prosperity, because it grows larger as it opens, the starting point being the rivet end from which the frame expands, just as the road of life widens out toward eternity. The folding fan is also said to be the analogue of the imposing and majestic Fujiyama, the one being the emblem of the other reversed.

The functions of the fan in the everyday life of the Japanese are very comprehensive, as it is an accessory of both sexes and of all ages, besides having been put to every possible use. These uses and applications have ranged over a wide variety of purposes: as an insignia of office, as an accessory of ceremonial costume, as an art object embellished with a beautiful painting, as a medium for writing poetical verse or for fine calligraphy, as a weapon of offense and defense in battle, as a fire bellows, as a salver. It is carried by professional people when they appear before the public; in polite society it is supposed to be carried when visiting friends. Fans of great beauty often are presented as gifts on felicitous occasions, and always are exchanged by a betrothed couple, as well as carried by the bride at her wedding ceremony as a traditional custom.

Folding iron war fan or gun sen *mounted with paper and painted with a characteristic red sun. Eighteenth century. Metropolitan Museum of Art. Gift of George M. Lefferts, 1910.*

Court fan having thirty-two ribs of hinoki *cypress joined with strings. Both sides with paintings in color. Heian period, eleventh century. Itsukushima shrine, Miyajima.*

The *ogi* consists of a framework of wood or bamboo ribs radiating from a single pivot. The thin and narrow sticks that form the segmental division when open are fixed between two *oya-bone* or parent sticks, which curve slightly inward to keep the fan compact when closed, and the whole is riveted at the pivot by means of a bit of tube and two washers, called the *kaname* or crab's eye. To this framework a sheet of paper is pasted on one side and a corresponding second sheet is fixed on the opposite side in the same manner. The fan must then be opened and closed many times, to make the folds in the paper fall easily and spread out again when opened. Depending upon the variety of fan, the number of ribs in the frame varies from three to thirty-eight, and although each side is usually covered with paper, fans are sometimes made by fixing the two pieces of paper together and covering one side only, with the ribs visible on the other side.

The *uchiwa* or flat, stiff fan is constructed on a framework made of a piece of bamboo split into several segments up to a certain point, the rest of the stick constituting the handle. Each of the split segments is secured in its proper place by fine string that is skillfully interwoven. Upon this delicate framework are fixed the paper faces of the fan, which have been previously decorated with designs. The entire fan with its frame and handle is thus formed of a single piece, which is prevented from splitting beyond the prescribed point for the handle by a well-marked joint or node on the bamboo stem, where the cavity is closed by a strong diaphragm. The node also provides a structural point for the bow-shaped spread of the fan. The two decorative faces of the fan, which may be either block-printed or hand-painted, are pasted on either side of the frame with a mixture of boiled rice and seaweed or

the roots of various plants, and then firmly secured around the outside circumference of the frame with a narrow strip of gilded or colored paper. There are a number of different types of *uchiwa*, which literally means beating-feather, indicating its origin as a fan of feathers, but they vary only slightly one from the other and always retain the rounded contour of the frame.

TYPES AND USES OF THE FAN

Among the many uses to which Japanese fans are put, one of the most curious and interesting is in war. There are two types of war fan, the *gumbai uchiwa* and the *gun-sen* or *tetsu-sen*, which were used by warriors on the field of battle as offensive and defensive weapons, and for signaling. The *gumbai uchiwa* is a flat portable hand-screen made of iron or wood heavily lacquered in black, or occasionally of two pieces of hardened leather fastened together, on a straight iron handle. *Gumbai uchiwa* were usually decorated with an emblematic design such as the sun, the moon, the north star, the *tomoye* sign of Shinto, the Buddhist swastika, or perhaps a family crest. The *gun-sen* is a folding fan in which the outside or parent ribs are of finely wrought iron inlaid with precious metal; the inside ribs are usually of iron, although sometimes of bamboo. The faces of the *gun-sen* were of a very strong paper, usually painted black with a red sun in the center; sometimes the motif was the moon or dragon and groups of stars. Throughout the various periods of Japan's military history these war fans remained a prominent feature of the soldier's equipment. They appear in almost every painting depicting military exploits, especially in the detailed representations of battle scenes in scroll-paintings of the late Heian and Kamakura periods. The banners of nobles, feudal lords, and commanders, which were actually standards in a variety of shapes and materials, very often had a fan fixed on top of the pole above the ensign. Many of these standards were huge affairs, such as the military fan banner of the Tokugawa family, called the *uma jirushi* or horse ensign, which was borne before them as a symbol of their presence. The *uma jirushi* was larger than the fan banners borne by princes and feudal lords, and had ribs five feet long and faces composed of eighteen thicknesses of heavy paper glued together and covered with silk and gold leaf; it was attached to the top of a fifteen-foot pole by a swivel so as to rotate in the wind. Another fan frequently seen being held by warriors in scroll-paintings was the *jin-sen*, a camp fan resembling an *uchiwa* in shape and made of pheasant or peacock feathers affixed separately.

From very early times strictly prescribed rules of etiquette governed the ceremonial use of the fan at the Imperial court, and they are still observed at all court functions requiring the ancient style of costume. Before the fan took its place as an accessory at court, it was customary for the nobles and court ladies to carry a short tapered flat staff of wood or ivory called a *shaku*, which had to be held upright against the lower part of the chest, at a certain angle, to give its holder a dignified bearing when appearing before the Imperial family. Flexible court fans first made their appearance in the seventh century, supplanting the *shaku*, and were carried as prescribed accessories to court dress by all who were in attendance, from fifteen years of age upward, including the Emperor. One of the ceremonial court fans used from early times is the *chukei*, dating from the seventh century, which is carried by priests and nobles. The *chukei* is similar to the original folding fan, and its fifteen bamboo ribs have a divergence from the handle that keeps the fan end slightly open when the handle end is closed. The fans adopted by the Emperor and the Shōgun were of this same construction that gave the appearance of being partially open when folded up. Similar fans, differing slightly in detail, were carried by the courtiers. The *komori* is one of these open court fans with fourteen bamboo ribs, upon which is pasted colored paper usually having a beautiful painted design. The *komori* fan is said to signify the bat because it suggests the manner in which a bat closes its wings.

The *hi-ogi*, a court fan dating from the eleventh century, has twenty-four ribs and is often carried by the Emperor and nobles at the Imperial court, held vertically in the right hand. It is also carried by the Empress and called *akoya-ogi*; on these occasions it is fastened with ribbons of white silk, and to each of the two outside parent ribs is fastened a fine tassel four feet long, consisting of seven silk cords of seven colors, a symbol

Lacquered war fan known as a gumbai uchiwa. *Eighteenth century. Metropolitan Museum of Art. Rogers Fund, 1925.*

of the seven colors of the Orient with their correlated virtues and elements. The type of knot with which the ribbon is tied varies according to the design motifs, which may depict a pine tree, a plum blossom, or some other floral symbol. These fans are called *hi-ogi* from the *hinoki* cypress of which they are made. *Hinoki* is a choice wood for fans with its soft velvety touch, its lustrous golden-brown color and pleasant odor. The fan carried by court ladies from the seventh century until 1868, called *akome-ogi*, is a folding fan composed of thirty-eight *hinoki* ribs lacquered white, and fan faces decorated with the emblems of longevity, such as the pine tree, chrysanthemum, or plum blossom. The *akome-ogi* was further decorated with twelve long streamers of various-colored silks.

ATTRIBUTES AND APPLICATIONS

Since the fan is regarded by the Japanese as a symbol of life and enters into almost every phase of human activity, it is used on nearly every occasion and event of the year. The fan is used as a symbolic insignia in dances, on ceremonial holidays, and on festive occasions; it is bestowed as a parting gift between friends and lovers to insure reunions, and it has a host of other uses. The *suye-hiro-ogi*, which was introduced in the seventh century, is a folding fan used in the No dances, and is composed of from fifteen to twenty-four ribs. The *Rikiu* or *Rikyu ogi* was introduced by the famous tea master Sen-no-Rikyu in the seventeenth century and used at the tea ceremony to hold little cakes, especially on the first day of the New Year. The fan is composed of three ribs—two parent ribs and one in the middle—and it is said to commemorate the curing of

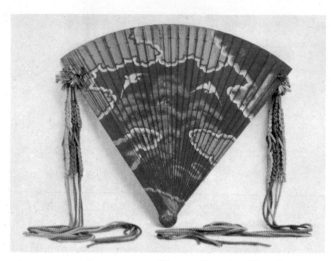

Hi-ogi or court fan consisting of twenty-four ribs of hinoki *cypress joined with strings. Paintings in gold and silver are on both sides; the illustrated side has a design of clouds, cranes, pine trees, and bamboo. Edo period, early nineteenth century. Tokyo National Museum.*

the illness of Emperor Murakami by tea given to him by the goddess Kannon. The fans used by dancing girls and geisha are known as *mai ogi*, and are weighted with a leaden rivet to give a graceful undulating movement as they wave them to and fro. These fans, which have been in use since the seventeenth century, are made with ten ribs only and are covered with thick monochrome paper having a *mon* or crest painted on it. For the sacred dances performed by priestesses and children at certain religious services at the famous Shinto shrines at Nara, Ise, and Itsukushima, there are also fans of particular form reserved for this purpose. There are also fans of huge proportions carried in the religious processions at the Ise shrine in honor of the sun goddess; these are never used for any other purpose.

The fan is often used as a conventionalized motif for family crests, or its shape is used as a model for kites, while charming little fans are made for children. There are even miniature fans for dolls. The fan is also seen at all Japanese wrestling or sumo bouts as the insignia of the umpire. The umpire's fan is in the form of a round black-lacquered *uchiwa*, called a *gioji-no-uchiwa* (*gioji* means umpire). It is said that the first umpire to be appointed was named Kiyobayashi. Upon this appointment by the Emperor Shomu in the eighth century, Kiyobayashi was presented with a badge of office in the form of an *uchiwa*, upon which were inscribed characters signifying The Prince of Lions. There are also a number of other sports and pastimes in which the fan occupies an important place.

Many fans are intended for purely practical and useful purposes. One of these is the *shibu uchiwa*, used chiefly in the kitchen in the capacity of bellows; for protection it is liberally coated with mucilage made from the astringent juice of unripened persimmons. Even farmers use a special type of fan called an *aori*, from the word meaning to flap, which is a winnowing fan for separating the chaff from the grain as it falls to the ground from a curiously shaped basket. There is also the *mita ogi*, a huge fan measuring seven feet in height and composed of six blades of *hinoki*, which is carried by firemen in processions and at festivals. A fan of curious form is the *maki uchiwa*, which is circular when opened, and is so built as to allow each of the half-segments of the circle to fold up against the central stick or handle when closed. Then there are the peculiar bamboo fans made in the city of Fukui and called *mizu uchiwa*. They are constructed with waterproof paper that contains a light coating of lacquer to make it impervious to dampness. The *mizu uchiwa* was invented around the end of the seventeenth century as a special type of refrigerant fan; it is dipped in water to increase the cooling effect by evaporation. For centuries fans were used as albums for calligraphic autographs of famous artists or literary men. In the first part of the fourteenth century Kusunoki Masashige, one of the noblest characters in Japanese history, inscribed his poems on fans.

On the first day of the New Year, particularly in the provincial towns and cities, wandering street-singers visit houses, door after door, to drive away evil by chanting some words of exorcism. They are called *manzai* strollers and always perform in pairs. One is dressed to represent Daikoku and beats a *tsuzumi* drum; the other impersonates Ebisu carrying a fan. While chanting exorcisms they repeat the word *manzai*, meaning "ten thousand years of life to you." At the great procession of the Gion Festival in Kyoto a number of *hoko*, the beautifully decorated ornamental towers placed on four massive wooden wheels, are seen being pulled by hundreds of coolies directed by men on the *hoko* making certain motions or signs with fans. As a departure from the regular uses of the fan, the Japanese have an interesting game called *ogi otoshi*, in which a target somewhat resembling the shape of a butterfly is placed on a low stand on the floor. The game is played by two people, each facing the target on either side and sitting on the floor at a given distance. They endeavor to hit the *cho* or target with a fan thrown with a quick and peculiar turn of the wrist which causes the fan to reverse itself in the air and strike the target with the rivet end. Very often tiny bells were attached to the edge of the *cho* to sound when a successful hit had been made. All of these uses and many more contribute to the highly important and vital part the fan plays in the everyday life of the Japanese.

XXIII Cloisonné Enamel

ALTHOUGH the art of enameling on metal is not one of the old traditional branches of Japanese art, it was known in Japan as early as the eighth century. Preserved in the Shosoin at Nara there is a beautiful twelve-pointed silver mirror of Chinese origin among the many objects of art and personal use there that once belonged to the Emperor Shomu, who died in the year 756. The back of this silver mirror is made of cloisonné enamel, with thin gold partitions separating green, brown, and purple-hued enamels set in a gold base. The mirror is kept in a case of lacquered hide lined with white *ashiginu*, which is a silk of plain weave. From ancient times the art of enameling had been practiced in China, especially for religious articles used in Buddhist ceremonies and later for objects of secular use. But it was not until the closing years of the sixteenth century that the art of working with enamels was actually introduced into Japan from China, and because it resembled the seven precious things mentioned in Buddhist sutras, it was called *shippo*, literally meaning seven-treasures, namely gold, silver, agate, amber, emerald, coral, and tortoise shell.

The earliest enamel work in Japan consisted principally of subsidiary ornament on small objects, and was first practiced by Hirata Donin and the members of his family from about the last decade of the sixteenth century onward. It is said that Hirata was born at Mino-o, a beautiful place not far from Osaka, and that later he began working in metals at Kyoto. He undoubtedly produced the cloisonné enamel fittings called *kugikakushi* that were in the Fushimi castle at Momoyama in Kyoto, and in Tokugawa Ieyasu's castle at Nagoya. These *kugikakushi* are ornamental metal pieces used in classical buildings to cover the wooden pegs where the lintel and upright cross. Hirata's enamels were greatly admired by Ieyasu, who commissioned Hirata as metal chaser and maker of cloisonné in the year 1611. The earliest Hirata enamels are in a clear, dark green for the decoration of small objects; later members of the Hirata house developed a metallic ground of gilt bronze enriched with splotches of various colors, as well as a white enamel celebrated for its purity of tone and substance. However, it is for their fine enameling on sword mounts that the various members of the Hirata family are especially noted.

DEVELOPMENT OF JAPANESE ENAMELS

All through the seventeenth and eighteenth centuries, enameling on metal in Japan continued to be applied chiefly as a subsidiary decoration, and it was not until the second quarter of the nineteenth century that independent art objects were made which can correctly be called enamels. Their surfaces were covered with vitrified pastes applied either in the champlevé or the cloisonné technique. This work, in which Japan excels above all other Far Eastern countries, was originated by Kaji Tsunekichi of Nagoya about 1838. Tsunekichi was born in Nagoya in 1802, became a samurai, and later studied the art of enameling, which up to that time had been limited to decorating the surfaces of objects with small ornamental pieces that were soldered on or inlaid. Tsunekichi's work consisted of covering the entire surface of the metal object with colored enamels separated by thin metallic fillets, just as in the medieval European cloisonné enamels. As the demand for this kind of work increased, other craftsmen were encouraged to follow the art, until finally several highly skilled practitioners of cloisonné enamel were active at Nagoya in the method introduced by Tsunekichi. Until 1858, when Japan abolished her policy of isolation, cloisonné enamel was used exclusively for small objects that were traditionally Japanese. But, with the opening of certain Japanese ports of call and the establishment of intercourse with foreign countries, an overseas demand developed which called for enamels of large dimensions. As a result, by about 1865 a large export trade

Left: Mirror. Cloisonné on copper. By Hirata Hikoichi. Design of tomoye, *or Shinto symbol of creation, and two flying birds. Edo period, early nineteenth century. Tokyo National Museum.*

Right: Mirror. Cloisonné on copper. By Ito Katsumi. Design of flowers and birds. Edo period, early nineteenth century. Tokyo National Museum.

had developed with the countries of Europe and America, in enamels which had no prototype in Japan, such as vases, lamp bases, bowls, censers, boxes, and so forth. The majority of these objects are without æsthetic merit, clumsy, and artistically unpleasing, especially because many are copied from bronzes whose massive forms are incongruous for thin enameled vessels.

The earliest examples of Japanese cloisonné enamel were executed with extraordinary technical skill; the base metal, usually of copper, is extremely thin; the thin and delicate fillets are laid on with great care and accuracy; the colors are even, and the designs have an authentic quality. Although the colors in these early enamels are rather somber and somewhat impure, being of a dull green, a cloudy white, and a blue lacking in lucidity, their depth and waxy softness radiate a certain mellowness and charm. The fillets are of exquisite fineness, producing designs of extraordinary delicacy and elaboration. In the execution of floral motifs, even the edges of tiny leaves are carefully notched to conform to recognizable species, and the stems of plants flow gracefully through the design, usually in a conventionalized manner. There is infinite variety as well as singular beauty in the designs, whose grounds were almost always covered with a delicate scrollwork of tiny leaves. Stylized birds, flowers, trees, and fishes were freely used as the principal theme, usually in a kind of medallion, against grounds with over-all diaper designs of natural or conventionalized motifs. Very often the decorative ground contained such diminutive and delicately worked motifs that it is difficult for the eye to follow the intricate network of vines and branches. Despite the gradual decline in quality to meet the demands of the export market, a few energetic artists around 1875 succeeded in producing works in cloisonné of extreme beauty that established new standards for excellence. In this art the compound of enamel is a clear, colorless,

transparent vitreous mixture called flux, composed of silica, minium, and potash. This base or flux is colored by the addition of metal oxides, and its hardness depends upon the proportion of silica to the other substances in the composition. It is essential for the enamels to be hard and the metal base pure, and the two must be fused at very high temperatures, to make them impervious to corrosion from atmospheric agencies. Fine gold or pure copper, as thin as possible, are the best metals for a base upon which to enamel. The method known as champlevé enamel is produced by cutting away portions of the base plate to make cells or troughs, leaving a metal dividing line which forms the outline of the design. Pulverized enamel is laid into these cells and then fused; after cooling it is filed and finally made smooth with a pumice stone and polished with rouge and crocus powder. In cloisonné enamel the metal cells are formed by delicate ribbon-like strips of metal, bent and laid on according to the outline of the design, then fixed to the metal base with silver solder or by the enamel itself. The rest of the process is similar to the champlevé method.

SCHOOLS OF ENAMELING

Of the three schools of enameling that appeared toward the end of the nineteenth century the one founded by Namikawa Yasuyuki of Kyoto possessed the greatest æsthetic quality. In contrast to the uninspired export ware, the work of Namikawa is characterized by graceful, technically flawless examples with purity of designs and richness of decoration attained in soft, harmonious colors. The enamel artists active at this time in Nagoya, Tokyo, and Yokohama are generally considered as a branch of the Kyoto school of Namikawa. But the distinguishing feature of the Kyoto school is its elegantly balanced

Left: Cloisonné tea kettle with a conventionalized Chinese peony motif in dull red, light blue, dark yellow, and white on deep-green ground. Kaji Tsunekichi school. Edo period, second quarter of the nineteenth century. Author's collection.

Right: Small wine pot of cloisonné on copper, the delicate fillets making an overall design of geometrical motifs. Edo period, early nineteenth century. Victoria and Albert Museum.

and delicate decoration which generally spreads across the entire surface, whereas the work from the other localities shows a tendency toward pictorial effect, placing the design on a monochrome ground of subdued tone. The great command of color pastes achieved by the artists of the Kyoto school in compounding and firing vitrifiable enamels enabled them to produce exquisite examples of cloisonné technically unequaled in any other country.

The second of the three schools of enameling was founded by Namikawa Sosuke of Tokyo, as an outgrowth of the branch of the Kyoto school. It developed a method of concealing the metal partitions in order to enhance the pictorial qualities of the design. These works are therefore commonly called cloisonless enamels, although they are not always without cloisons, or partitions, because the design is usually made at the beginning with a thin ribbon of metal, in the same manner as regular cloisonné enamel. However, as the work progresses these delicate cloisons are covered over and hidden, unless they are needed to emphasize the design, and the finished piece reveals only a picture or design motif in beautiful vitrified enamels.

The work of the third school, whose artists were active in Tokyo and Nagoya, is chiefly characterized by monochromatic and translucid enamels. The inspiration for this work came from the exquisite monochrome porcelains of China, whose beauty and depth of tone resides in the colored glazes which are typically associated with hard-paste porcelain. These glazes consist of fusible feldspathic rock or *petuntse*, which is powdered and mixed with lime, sand, potash or quartz, and other ingredients. They require a high temperature to fuse them and normally they are translucent and perfectly united with the hard paste material, being fired simultaneously. Acting upon the theory that a vitrified enamel may be made to perform, at least partially, the function of a porcelain glaze, these artists

Bottle-shaped flower holder. Cloisonné on copper, showing a design of flowers and butterflies. By Namikawa Yasuyuki of Kyoto. Nineteenth century. Tokyo National Museum.

Tablet of cloisonné on copper, showing a design of Mount Fuji with clouds. By Namikawa Sosuke of Tokyo. Nineteenth century. Tokyo National Museum.

of Tokyo and Nagoya produced a variety of beautiful examples of monochrome enamel. Included in the range of colors are rich canary and straw yellows, red, rose pompadour, *aubergine*, lapis lazuli, leaf and grass green, and dove gray. In the finest examples, exceptional skill was required to spread and fix the enamel so that neither the rim nor the interior of a vase would show any break in the continuity of the color, or reveal that the base was made of copper instead of porcelain. The other accomplishment of this school was in translucid enamels, usually applied over a base having a decorative theme. This was a process of chiseling a design in the metal base so that it was visible through the translucent enamel, which produced beautiful effects of broken and softened lights.

Admirable results were produced by first applying colored enamels to the designs chiseled in the base and then covering the whole with a clear translucent enamel. A distinctive design, for instance, was created by deeply chiseling a repeated wave motif on a base of gold and applying an over-all glaze of translucent *aubergine*. Another example of the achievements of this method is the depiction, through a medium of azure blue, of brilliant goldfish and gaily colored carp swimming in silvery waves, or birds with bright-colored plumage soaring among fleecy clouds. Although the decorative designs that lend themselves to the process of translucid enamels are not numerous, the artists of this school were able to produce works of art of delicate beauty.

Left: Incense burner. Cloisonné on copper. Design of landscape and temple. By Namikawa Yasuyuki of Kyoto. Nineteenth century. Tokyo National Museum.

Right: Flower vase. Cloisonné on copper, showing a design of chrysanthemums. By Namikawa Yasuyuki of Kyoto. Nineteenth century. Tokyo National Museum.

XXIV Shosoin, the Imperial Repository

IN THE early days in Japan every important temple had within its compound several storehouses called godowns for storing the objects used in religious ceremonies. The name *Sho-so*, meaning Chief Repository, was given to the principal one or pair of these storehouses, and its premises, usually surrounded by a wall and including the repository itself, were called Shosoin. Thus in the history of Japan there have been many Shosoin connected with the various temples. But at the present time the name Shosoin refers only to the renowned Imperial Repository, a wooden treasure house standing a short distance directly back of the Hall of the Great Buddha of the Todaiji monastery at Nara, the resplendent capital and cultural center of Japan from 710 to 794. This repository was originally the Shosoin of the Todaiji monastery, probably built about the same time as the Hall of the Great Buddha, which was finished in 751 or 752. This wooden treasure house, serving to preserve a unique collection of eighth-century art, is without parallel. That such a wooden structure has stood for more than a thousand years against the destructive forces of nature and human turmoil is sufficient cause for wonder, but that its thousands of precious relics have survived virtually intact is miraculous. The exotic contents of the famous Imperial Repository serve as a remarkable testimony to the many high achievements of the eighth century, the classical epoch in Japanese culture. Like a magic mirror they reflect and record the brilliant life of that time. These treasures, divided into some twenty-five different categories, comprise documents, household furniture, kitchen utensils, writing equipage, musical instruments, masks and costumes used in dances, personal ornaments, weapons (swords, bows, arrows, and spears), armor, horse-trappings, medicines, Buddhist images, temple and altar utensils, sutras and their accessories, belongings of the priests, objects used in ceremonies, carpenters' tools, incense wood, textiles, glass beads, implements used in games, and miscellaneous things. There are no less than 240 kinds of objects included in the different categories. But even this does not begin to convey the enormous size of the collection. For example, flower baskets, which are treated as a single item, number 565; pewter dishes number 697; and arrows number 3703. Of the fragments of textile fabrics, more than 66,812 have been mounted for better preservation, and a few ancient chests filled with more textiles still remain untouched. By keeping these facts and figures in mind one can form some idea of the size and variety of the collection and begin to appreciate the remarkably complete and clear picture the Shosoin treasures give of eighth-century Japan. In this respect the Shosoin remains unrivaled and alone in the annals of art history.

CEREMONIAL OPENING AND CLOSING

The Shosoin is closed throughout the year, except for the short period of its annual airing, which occurs in the autumn and never extends beyond twenty-six days. Even during that period, short as it is, the Shosoin is closed on wet or rainy days. Until the Meiji period, the treasures sometimes remained untouched for years. A record of 1666 states that the Shosoin was opened that year for inspection as "it had not been opened for a long time." The preceding date of inspection was 1613. The next opening and closing following the inspection of 1666 was in 1693. Then the Shosoin remained sealed until 1833, when the building was reroofed, at which time urgent repairs were made on some of the treasures and the documents were classified. In 1883 a petition to open the Repository every year for the purpose of airing the treasures received Imperial sanction and, at the same time, the Imperial household granted to a certain number of persons the privilege of viewing the treasures. Now in the autumn of each year scholars of Oriental culture from all parts of the world converge upon the little town of Nara for the purpose of studying the remarkable examples of the arts and crafts of a glorious, long-vanished civilization. Visitors are admitted during two weeks of its annual airing period. Due to the limited space, the number of visitors is necessarily restricted. Admission is by card only, preference being given to those having academic qualifications. Unfortunately, the view the privileged visitors get of these treasures is tantalizingly inadequate, as the only lighting in the building is through the three doors and it is necessary to depend upon an electric flashlight. Then, too, the objects are viewed at a distance, as they are kept in glass cases. It is only when the relics are taken out of the cases to be photographed, examined, and measured for the *Shosoin Gomotsu Zuroku*, or the *Catalogue of the Imperial Treasures in the Shosoin*, of which eighteen folio volumes are available at the present time, that these precious heirlooms can be examined more closely. Then, much too soon, comes a period of eleven months before the treasures can again be seen.

The formal opening and closing of the historic Shosoin is deeply impressive. It is performed in conformity with ancient custom, though the great formality followed in feudal days has been dispensed with in more recent times. In normal years the three doors of the Shosoin are opened around the 21st of October by Imperial command, in order to air the treasures. The remaining days in October are generally given to the photographing, cataloguing, and other work connected with the preservation of the collection. The first two weeks in November are reserved for visitors. On the day of opening and at the appointed hour, which is usually ten o'clock in the morning, the Imperial messenger accompanied by the president of the Imperial Household Museums, the director of the Imperial Household Museum of Nara, and a few members of the Museum staff proceed to the door of the north section by ascending a temporary staircase, but not before each has removed his shoes. First a wooden box covering the lock and fastenings is removed, disclosing a big padlock tied with rope—of which about thirty-five feet, doubled, is used for each lock—and a paper bearing the seal of the Imperial messenger who was present at the closing of the previous year. This seal is fastened to the ends of string wrapped around a bamboo sheath covering the Emperor's signature. Finally, when several more steps in the procedure have been duly observed, the paper with the Emperor's signature is revealed, at the sight of which all persons present bow in reverence. The Imperial signature is put in a lacquered box and later returned to Tokyo. Then, after the rest of the rope is unwound, the lock is opened with a key and removed from the doors. But since the doors are bolted from the inside, they also must be unlocked. Finally the massive double doors, each one of which is more than four feet wide and eleven feet high,

swing slowly inward on wooden pivots, and the officials step into the dim and silent room to see whether everything is in order. Then the Middle and finally the South sections are opened in exactly the same manner. Once the formal opening is completed, the Imperial messenger returns immediately to Tokyo to report the proceeding to the Emperor.

When the time arrives to close the Repository, which usually happens on the 16th of November, the proceedings are reversed. A new signature of His Majesty is brought from Tokyo in a lacquered box, and the Imperial messenger, after seeing that the three locks are properly placed and that each is bound with a new rope tied in special knots, winds a piece of paper around the ropes and encloses them in a bamboo sheath. Another paper bearing his own seal is placed around this and finally the locks and fastenings are once again covered with a wooden box, not to be disturbed for another eleven months.

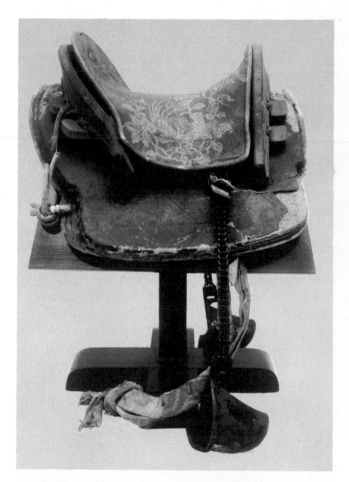

Saddle of mulberry wood covered with smoked leather and having a design of birds and flowers in brown. Iron box-stirrups lacquered black attached by iron chains. The girth has the date inscribed as follows: Tempyo Shoho fourth year, tenth month (i.e., A.D. 752). Shosoin, Nara.

CONSTRUCTION AND PRESERVATION OF THE SHOSOIN

This historic treasure house, surrounded by trees, is a rectangular wooden structure made of *hinoki* and *asunaro* wood. It has a massive, heavily tiled, upward-curving roof resting upon short columns. It faces east and is some 109 feet in length and some thirty feet in width. The height from the ground to the projecting eaves is twenty-seven feet, and to the ridge of the roof, forty-five feet. The entire structure is almost nine feet above the ground, and is supported by forty massive pillars arranged in four rows of ten each. The interior of the building comprises three sections, namely the North, Middle, and South. The Middle section is about four feet longer than the other two, which are almost equal in size. Each section has an upper and lower floor with its own staircase. There is also an attic extending the entire length of the building, connected by a staircase in the Middle section.

Crowded in glass showcases placed against the walls and standing in the center of each room are thousands of priceless objects, many of which were deposited in the Shosoin twelve hundred years ago. These objects are chiefly for domestic and ritual use and are made of metal, glass, pottery, wood, horn, or other materials. Prior to 1880-1882, when the present arrangement of showcases fitted with shelves was installed, most of the treasures were kept in chests which were carried out of the building when their contents were aired. Each section is provided with a massive double door that opens inward. There are no windows, in fact no apertures of any kind except for the three doors. Then, too, there are no steps leading up to the three entrances. During the short period each year when the Repository is open in order to air its treasures, a temporary balcony, extending the length of the building, with a staircase in the middle, is placed against the building.

Except for the Middle section, which is made of thick flat boards, the Repository is constructed in the *aze-kura* style of architecture. This style is typical of the ancient Japanese storehouses and can best be described as log-cabin construction. The section of each log used in the construction was originally cut as an almost equilateral triangle, and then by chamfering the apexes a hexagon was obtained, with three long sides of about ten to twelve inches and three short sides of about three inches. These roughly hewn timbers are laid lengthwise and crossed at the four corners in the manner of a log cabin. No nails were used in the joining. As a result of this type of construction the exterior of the North and South sections is deeply corrugated in appearance, while the interior reveals a plain surface. The "party walls" of the Middle section are corrugated, however, since they are the exterior of the North and South sections. This type of building, whether intentionally or not, solved the vital problem of ventilation necessary for the preservation of the treasures contained inside. In dry weather the timbers contract, permitting air to enter and circulate, and in rainy weather the timbers expand, thereby keeping out the dampness. It still remains a matter of conjecture whether the Shosoin was originally constructed in its present form as one building, or as two buildings, with the space between being at some later date boarded in to form the Middle section to provide additional storage space for the increasing number of treasures. Excellent reasons have been advanced in support of each theory, so the matter will probably remain an open question.

The sanctity of the seals of the Emperors who have reigned over Japan in an unbroken lineage through twenty-six centuries has provided the primary protection for these magnificent treasures stored in the Shosoin. This respect for the Imperial seal is due to the reverence and loyalty the people of Japan have at all times given to their Emperor. Wars and fires have surged to the very doors of this Repository. Once in 1180 and again in 1567 the Hall of the Great Buddha was burned by warriors and other fires consumed the nearby Kofukuji temple, which consisted of one hundred and seventy-five buildings at its most flourishing period. Yet no soldiers have ever been assigned to guard or protect the Shosoin. It has stood safe, protected solely by the Imperial seal, for more than twelve hundred years. Only three times in its long history has the sanctity of the Imperial seal been violated. In 1040 a thief burned a hole through the floor of the Shosoin and stole some treasures. Again in 1230 a thief broke through the floor and stole eight bronze mirrors. The last recorded theft was in 1612, when it was discovered that some treasures had been stolen.

A peculiarly characteristic Japanese trait which also has served to protect and preserve these treasures is the abiding sentiment of reverence and esteem with which the Japanese have always regarded hereditary treasures. Heirlooms handed down from father to son have always been cherished and stored with loving care. The successive Emperors who have cared for the treasures in the Imperial Repository from the day of dedication in 756 to the present time exemplify this tradition. As previously mentioned, it is indeed miraculous that an inflammable wooden structure exposed to storms, fires, and all kinds of dangers should have remained intact for twelve centuries. Once in 1254 the North section was struck by lightning. Fortunately the damage was very slight, but the scar can still be seen on the wall on the North section. As an offering of gratitude to the dragon god for extinguishing the fire, the Sugimoto shrine was built very near to the Repository. After each period for airing the treasures, directly after the sealing of the Repository, a religious ceremony is performed

The Shosoin (treasure house) of the Todaiji monastery, Nara. Front façade facing east. Eighth century.

at the Sugimoto shrine to entreat protection until the treasures are again to be aired. According to the records, lightning rods were erected, apparently for the first time, in 1877.

HISTORICAL BACKGROUND OF THE CONTENTS

For a more perfect understanding and appreciation of the Shosoin, it is necessary to refer to the origin of its establishment. Shomu, 701-756, who was the forty-fifth Emperor of Japan, ascended the throne in 724. He was married to the Princess Asuka, a daughter of the great Fujiwara-no-Fubito. In 729, when she was created an Empress with the title of Komyo-Kogo, she became the first Fujiwara Empress of Japan. From that time, for twelve centuries, the Emperor always selected his consort from the House of Fujiwara, until 1924 when the Crown Prince chose for his wife someone who was not a descendant of Fujiwara-no-Kamatari. (Fujiwara-no-Fubito was a son of the great Fujiwara-no-Kamatari; thus they were of the same family.)

After the Imperial installation of the Empress Komyo, an epidemic of smallpox broke out in Japan and spread until it reached the patrician circles of Nara. Frantic efforts were made by the Emperor and his court to stem the tide of this dread disease. Buddhist priests used the occasion to entreat the Emperor to turn to Buddhism for help. Inspired by their religious exhortations and encouraged by his pious consort, Shomu conceived the idea of erecting a large image of Buddha in the middle of Nara and making it, together with its counterparts in the provincial temples, an object of national worship. But the erection of this huge image of the Buddha brought to an acute form the vexing problem of assimilating Buddhism and the ancient Japanese religion of Shintoism. The Emperor remembered only too well that his title to the throne

Detail of the Shosoin, showing the aze-kura *method of construction. Todaiji monastery, Nara. Eighth century.*

depended upon the Shinto doctrine of his divine descent from Amaterasu. We have seen that an answer to this problem was found by the famous monk Gyogi, who was deeply interested in the advancement of the material as well as the religious welfare of Japan. According to the tradition, Gyogi journeyed to the Grand Shrine of Ise in order to learn the wishes of the sun goddess, and spent seven days and seven nights in prayer and fasting at the threshold of her shrine. At the end of this time a divine voice uttered an oracle which was interpreted as propitious to the reconciliation of the two faiths. Another happy omen occurring shortly afterward, which further substantiated this interpretation, was the dream in which the sun goddess appeared to the Emperor and announced that the sun and the Buddha were one and the same.

Satisfied with these auspicious revelations, several Imperial edicts were issued in the years 741, 742, and 743 ordering a temple with a seven-storied pagoda to be built in every province throughout the realm. A copy in gold letters of the Konkomyo sutra was to be placed in each temple, together with an announcement of the Emperor's intention to start the construction of the great image of Buddha in Nara. An inscribed copper plaque and a sutra cover with woven characters

Arm-rest (end view) of tzu-t'an *wood decorated with a marquetry of ivory and gold. Eighth century. Shosoin, Nara.*

which record some of these edicts are contained among the treasures in the Shosoin.

The *Great Buddha* or *Daibutsu*, the casting of which was a herculean achievement, is the holiest object of the Todaiji. The bronze figure is seated cross-legged on a tremendous pedestal composed of fifty-six lotus petals, and the hands are in the traditional posture of preaching, the right hand giving ease of mind, the left granting wishes. Mercury and a considerable quantity of gold were required for gilding the image, and because gold was scarce in Japan, the gilding presented a difficult problem. But by a miraculous chance a provincial governor discovered a gold mine in his territory in 749, and he sent several hundred pounds of gold to Nara. This discovery was regarded as an event of such magnitude that nationwide rejoicings were decreed. The Emperor Shomu sent messengers to proclaim the good news to shrines throughout the realm, and a ceremony was held in the Hall of the Great Buddha, as recorded in the *Nihon-shoki*, or *Chronicles of Japan*, compiled in the eighth century. According to this record, the Emperor, Empress, Princess Imperial, ministers of state, and members of the Imperial court proceeded to the Todaiji to worship and give thanks to the *Great Buddha*. In the name of the Emperor, one of the ministers addressed the *Buddha:*

"This is the word of the Sovereign who is a servant of the Three Treasures (the Three Treasures form the Sacred Trinity of the Buddhist belief and are the Buddha, Dharma or the Law, and Sangha or the Congregation of Believers), which he himself speaks before the image of Roshana. In this land of Yamato, since the beginning of Heaven and Earth, gold, though it has been brought as an offering from other countries, was thought not to exist. But in the east of the land which we rule . . . gold has been found. Hearing this we were astonished and rejoiced, feeling that this was a gift bestowed upon us by the love and blessing of Roshana Buddha. We have received it with reverence and humbly accepted it, and have brought with us all our officials to worship and give thanks . . ."

Swept along by the religious fervor accompanying the completion of the great image, the devout Emperor Shomu abdicated his throne in favor of his daughter in order that he might renounce temporal affairs and devote his life to spiritual contemplation and prayer. Accordingly his daughter, the Princess Abe, ascended the throne in August 749 as Empress Takano, although she is generally known in history under the more familiar title of Empress Koken.

The final ceremony at which the eyes of the gigantic image were touched to imbue it with the spirit of Buddha, known as the "eye-opening" ceremony, occurred on May 26, 752, which was the traditional anniversary of the birth of Buddha and also the bicentenary of the introduction of Buddhism into Japan. On that particular day the Great Hall, filled with flow-

ers and incense, and lighted with candles, presented a spectacle
of untold Oriental splendor. Magnificent offerings were
heaped on the altar before the immense bronze image and the
ancient musical performance known as *gigaku* was given on
platforms especially erected for the occasion outside the temple.
Among the treasures in the Shosoin are 164 *gigaku* masks believed to have been used in connection with the religious
services observed at the Todaiji, especially this "eye-opening"
ceremony. Then, before the great idol and in the presence of
the Imperial family, the musicians, the dancers, and the ten
thousand attending priests, the eyes of the *Great Buddha* were
"opened" by the priest Bodhisena. This was done, it is believed, by painting in the pupils of the eyes with ink and a
very large writing brush to symbolize bringing the statue to
life, the final touch in the creation. To the brush were tied
long cords, each several hundred yards long, which were held
in the hands of the thousands of people assembled for the
occasion, thus permitting them to participate in the "eye-
opening" ceremony. One of the treasures in the Shosoin is a
big ball of light-blue silk cord, with a paper tag attached to it
on which is written that it was used in the "eye-opening"
ceremony, May 26, 752.

Hundreds of other relics belonging to the original "eye-
opening" ceremony are preserved in the Shosoin, and more
than a hundred of these are dated. Pieces of the Imperial
jeweled headdresses worn by Shomu and Komyo, and the two
original chests which contained them, still exist. Notations on
paper tags attached to them, dated May 26, 752, state that one
belonged to Shomu and the other to Komyo. The fragments
comprise pearls, rock crystal, coral, colored glass beads, gold
and silver settings, and parts of the lacquered silk gauze covering the framework. It is believed that the crowns were
fashioned in the style of T'ang ceremonial headdresses. According to a later record, the Emperor Shomu's jeweled head-
dress, as well as three others and a number of ceremonial robes,
were taken out of the Repository in the chests containing
them on April 14, 1242, to be used at the coronation of the
Emperor Gosaga on April 18. When the headdresses were
returned to the Repository after the enthronement, the contents of the chests were examined and found to be broken
into many pieces. Apparently the men carrying the chests had
been unaware of their precious contents. Of interest is an
unusually large writing brush, with an imitation mottled
bamboo stem, measuring more than two feet in length. It has
an engraved inscription stating that it was used for the "eye-
opening" ceremony of September 22, 1185. The inscription
calls it the Tempyo Brush, thus suggesting that it was the one
used at the original "eye-opening" of the *Great Buddha* in 752,
as well as at the subsequent one in 1185, when the ceremony
was repeated for the new head of the *Great Buddha*, the original

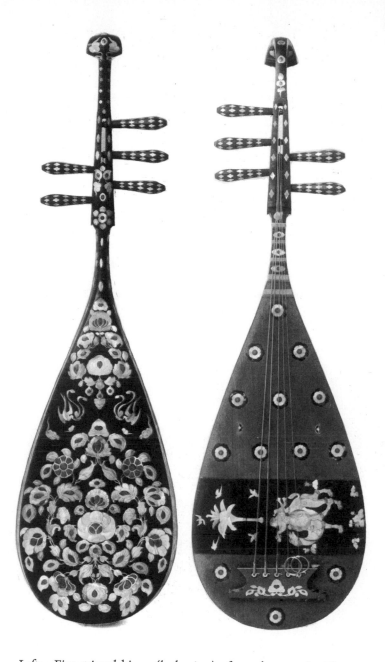

Left: Five-stringed biwa *(back view) of* tzu-t'an *wood with
designs of flowers and birds inlaid with mother-of-pearl, tortoise
shell, and amber. The amber for the centers of flowers and leaves is
used in such a manner that the colors applied on the ground beneath
may be seen. Eighth century. Shosoin, Nara.*

Right: Five-stringed biwa *(front view) of* tzu-t'an *wood inlaid
with mother-of-pearl, amber, and tortoise shell, having a plectrum
guard of a band of tortoise shell inlaid with mother-of-pearl,
depicting a man riding on a camel and playing on an instrument
with a plectrum. Eighth century. Shosoin, Nara.*

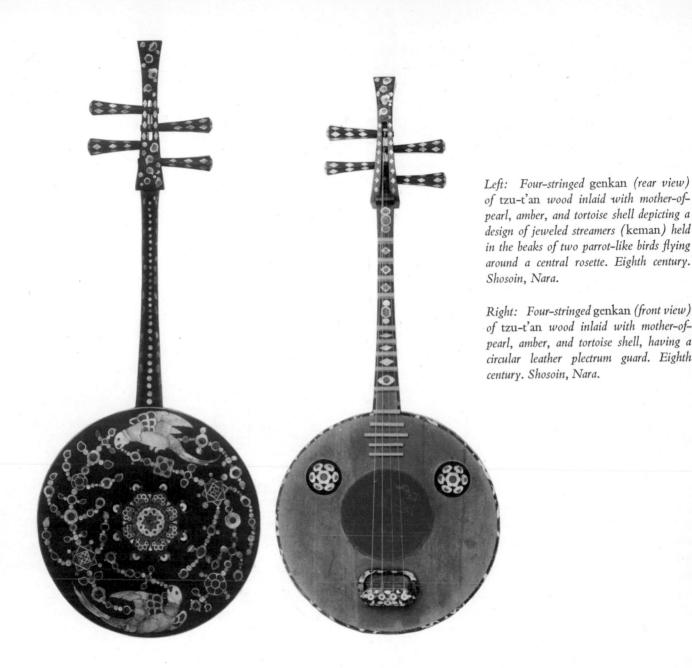

Left: Four-stringed genkan *(rear view) of tzu-t'an wood inlaid with mother-of-pearl, amber, and tortoise shell depicting a design of jeweled streamers (keman) held in the beaks of two parrot-like birds flying around a central rosette. Eighth century. Shosoin, Nara.*

Right: Four-stringed genkan *(front view) of tzu-t'an wood inlaid with mother-of-pearl, amber, and tortoise shell, having a circular leather plectrum guard. Eighth century. Shosoin, Nara.*

head having been destroyed in the fire that consumed the Great Hall in 1180. There is also an inkstick, broken into three pieces and mended, with an attached paper tag, calling the stick a "Tempyo Treasure" and recording that it was used in 1185 at the "eye-opening" ceremony, thereby indicating the same history for the inkstick as for the writing brush.

The next important dates in the history of the Shosoin are two religious ceremonies held before the *Great Buddha*, from both of which a number of dated relics survive. The first was a great gathering of the Ninno-ye, a religious service held in adoration of the Ninno sutra, on May 6, 753. The second occurred on August 30, 755, when a commemorative religious ceremony was held on the first anniversary of the death of the

mother of the Emperor-Abdicant Shomu. Seventeen flower baskets used to hold flowers during Buddhist ceremonies bear this date. From the earlier ceremony are three bags for screens made of hemp cloth, printed or stamped with a design of flowers and birds. Written on each one is a description of the screen it contained, the date May 6, 753, and the name Todaiji. The description on one bag relates that the hemp cloth was made in 749 in the province of Kozuke and was sent as a *corvée* cloth. The next date is June 3, 756, the day on which the Emperor-Abdicant Shomu died. In appraising the Emperor Shomu's contribution to the development of Japanese culture, it must be remembered that Buddhism gave new direction to it, and that Shomu, through his devout faith and his interest

EMPRESS KOMYO'S DEEDS OF GIFT

Unquestionably the most important treasures preserved in the Shosoin are those which belonged to the Emperor Shomu, and so the most important date in the history of the Shosoin is July 22, 756, marking the forty-ninth day after the death of Shomu, when an elaborate religious ceremony was performed and prayers were offered for the repose of his soul, as is still the custom to the present time. On that day his grief-stricken widow, the Empress Dowager Komyo, dedicated all Shomu's personal belongings to the *Great Buddha*, the image the Emperor had ordered to be cast little more than a decade earlier. These included arms and armor, musical instruments, manuscripts, mirrors, screens, ceremonial robes, and objects of virtu, numbering more than 650 items. These offerings form the nucleus of the collection, and make the Repository a veritable shrine of ancient art. Accompanying these rare treasures are five *Kenmotsucho* or Deeds of Gift, each in the form of a long scroll of white hemp paper, wound around a stick of *tzu-t'an* wood. The first and most important of these *Kenmotsucho* bears a detailed description of each article dedicated; at the end of the long inventory is a passage to the effect that all these articles are either treasures that the late Emperor had handled or utensils that he had used in the palace. This historic document begins with a prayer by the Empress Dowager to the *Great Buddha* for the repose of the late Emperor's soul and a supplication that he may finally be admitted to the Sacred Hall of the Buddha of Light. With touching eloquence she recalls her late husband's wisdom and saintly life and resolves by the performance of good deeds to help her husband's spirit. To this end she donates these relics to the Todaiji by way of offering to the Buddha. The scroll, which is dated July 22, 756, concludes with the signatures of five court dignitaries, and is stamped with 489 Imperial seals, which almost cover its entire surface. A large number of the sacred relics described in the Deed of Gift are still extant in the Repository.

Many of the Imperial relics, the provenance of which will be considered later, are of surpassing beauty and craftsmanship. A fine example of finished workmanship is a sword embellished with gold and silver and described in the *Kenmotsucho* as *kara tachi*, or Chinese slung sword, because of its style. The sword, with a shagreen-covered hilt and lacquered scabbard, has a rich mount of silver gilt floral designs, and is jeweled with colored glass balls and crystals set over vermilion pigment. Of the arm-rests described in the *Kenmotsucho*, one type is

Lacquered ewer of bamboo basketwork covered with cloth and lacquered with an over-all decoration of flowers, birds, and animals in a silver heidatsu. *The lid and the mouth form the shape of a bird's head. Eighth century. Shosoin, Nara.*

bolster- or pillow-shaped, entirely covered with brocade. Another type of arm-rest is of the same shape as those used today in a Japanese home when sitting on the matted floor. It is made of wood, and the oblong top, provided with a pad, rests on end-supports mounted on a shaped base. The example in the Repository is of *tzu-t'an* wood and is richly decorated with floral designs inlaid in ivory and gold. Screens are an important item among the many treasures dedicated to the Great Buddha. One hundred screens, each comprising six panels, except for a pair with four panels, are mentioned in the *Kenmotsucho* of National Treasures. On August 26, 756, an additional two pair of screens were dedicated and this dedication was followed on November 6, 758, by two single screens. Of these 106 screens described in the *Kenmotsucho*, the records show that two screens were withdrawn between the years 787 and 793 and thirty-six were taken out in 814. This tallies exactly with the official record of 856, which lists sixty-eight screens. At the present time some forty panels remain, twelve of which are in two six-paneled screens. One of the latter is especially noteworthy, being executed in the T'ang style of secular painting. Each of the panels depicts a young lady standing under a pine tree, wearing a dress decorated with birds' feathers. Most of the feathers have fallen off, showing only the outline drawing done in ink. Her face and hands are delicately tinted and she has light-blue beauty spots on her forehead and on either side of her mouth.

Musical instruments are an entrancing category of the collection, charmingly evoking the gay and elegant court life of the Nara period (710-794). Some of the stringed instruments, in particular, are remarkable for their rarity and superb craftsmanship. The *biwa*, which belongs to the lute class and has a pear-shaped body continuing into a fretted neck, is represented

in the collection by a beautiful five-stringed example made of *tzu-t'an* wood. The back and sides are richly inlaid with mother-of-pearl, amber, and tortoise shell, worked in designs of flowers and birds. The amber is used for the center of the flowers and leaves in such a manner that the colors applied on the ground underneath are visible. The plectrum guard, which is a wide horizontal band under the strings where the plectrum strikes, consists of a solid band of tortoise shell with an inlay of mother-of-pearl depicting a palm tree and a man playing a musical instrument while riding on a camel. The ivory plectrum is dyed crimson and is minutely carved on both sides with designs of flowers, birds, and animals. Some of the carved designs are in color, the color being added where the carving cut through the surface stain of the ivory. Both the *biwa* and the plectrum are identified with the ones described in the *Kenmotsucho*. A magnificent *genkan*, a four-stringed musical instrument which also belongs to the lute class and resembles a banjo with its long fretted neck and tambourine-shaped body, is also in the collection and is identified with one mentioned in the *Kenmotsucho*. It is made of *tzu-t'an* wood and the circular back is elaborately decorated with a central rosette around which are flying two exotic birds holding long streamers in their beaks, the design being executed in an inlay of mother-of-pearl, amber, and tortoise shell. One of the most remarkable of the stringed musical instruments is a lacquered Chinese kin profusely inlaid with gold and silver, regarded as one of the most beautiful known examples of ancient decorated lacquer. In this style of decoration, known as *hyomon* in Japanese documents, thin sheets of gold and silver are cut into various motifs in the form of men, animals, birds, flowers, and similar subjects, and inlaid or embedded in the lacquer surface. Then the entire surface is covered with additional

Box for go game board of transparent horse-hoof or buffalo horn inlaid with lines of deer horn to form an over-all hexagonal pattern. Under the transparent pieces a floral design in gold and silver leaf is laid alternately on the green ground. Eighth century. Shosoin, Nara.

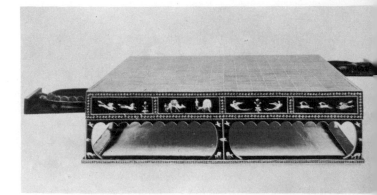

Go game board veneered with tzu-t'an wood inlaid with deer horn and various colored woods. The sides are decorated with a carved and colored horn inlay of men and beasts, flowers and birds. Each drawer contains a receptacle, one in the form of a tortoise, and the other in the form of a terrapin; their backs hollowed out to receive go pieces. Eighth century. Shosoin, Nara.

layers of lacquer that are later ground or rubbed down to reveal the inlay, and finally polished. It is interesting to note that the Chinese kin is not the original kin mentioned in the *Kenmotsucho* as being decorated in *hyomon*, but rather a substitute for it also decorated in *hyomon*. According to the Shosoin archives the original kin was withdrawn on December 4, 814, and the present one was substituted on July 14, 817. The present kin bears the inscription that it was made in 795.

The Chinese kin is the only object in the Repository described as being in *hyomon*. Apparently the term is not found in Chinese records. A similar style of decoration is known as *heidatsu*, and sometimes the two terms are regarded as being interchangeable. The making of *heidatsu* was prohibited in China during the reign of Su Tsung (756-762) as being too costly. A splendid example of silver *heidatsu*, which is also minutely described in the *Kenmotsucho*, is a gracefully proportioned lacquered wine ewer made of bamboo basketwork covered with cloth and lacquered. It is exquisitely decorated with flowers, birds, and animals in silver *heidatsu*. The inside is finished in plain lacquer. The lid and the pouring spout form the shape of a bird's head and a silver chain is attached to the lid and handle.

Games are another interesting category of the Imperial treasures preserved in the Shosoin. A board for the game of *go*, which is the Eastern equivalent of checkers, and the box in which it was kept are recorded in the *Kenmotsucho*. The *go* board, in the form of a low square stand, is about twenty inches square and four inches high, and the top is inlaid with stringing lines of ivory to form squares for playing the game. Beneath the top is a narrow frieze which rests on an open box-like construction. This type of decorative openwork, which originated in a very ancient Chinese platform, is called *kazama* in Japan. The narrow frieze is fitted with two drawers, one diagonally across from the other, each having a loose-ring handle. The drawers are so constructed that if one is pulled out, the other comes out automatically, and the closing operates in a similar manner. One drawer is provided with a receptacle in the form of a tortoise and the other drawer has a receptacle in the form of a terrapin, the backs of both being hollowed out to contain the *go* pieces. Each side of the frieze is divided into four panels banded with a geometrical repeat design, inlaid with ivory, deer horn, and various colored woods. The panels are decorated with a carved and colored deer-horn inlay of men and animals in hunting scenes and flowers and birds. The box, which is provided with a lid, is covered entirely with buffalo horn inlaid with stringing lines of deer horn to form a parquetry of hexagons. The box is further enriched with a floral motif in gold and silver leaf laid alternately on a green ground and centered in each hexagon under the transparent surface of horn.

Silver incense burner decorated with an engraved openwork design of flower and leaf scrolls containing a lion and a phoenix. Eighth century. Shosoin, Nara.

Displaying a similar quality of finished craftsmanship and also mentioned in the *Kenmotsucho* is a board for the game of *sugoroku*, which is the Eastern equivalent of backgammon. The size and construction of the *sugoroku* gaming board is essentially the same as the *go* board. It is made of *tzu-t'an* and richly inlaid with various other kinds of wood, colored deer horn, bamboo, and ivory, in an over-all design of flowers, birds, and similar motifs. The box for the *sugoroku* board is made of braided bamboo strips worked in an over-all lozenge pattern, each lozenge enclosing a floral motif. The *Kenmotsucho* also mentions *sugoroku* dice. Of these only six remain, three having rounded corners and three being perfect cubes.

A second *Kenmotsucho*—bearing the same date as the *Kenmotsucho* of National Treasures, July 22, 756, and the same five signatures, and stamped with forty-three Imperial seals—is a Deed of Gift of Medicines, offering to the *Great Buddha* twenty-one chests filled with sixty different kinds of medicines. Also written on a scroll of white hemp paper, a long inventory lists the name of each medicine, its weight, and a description of its container. At the conclusion of the list is a prayer which, in part, says in effect that any person suffering from illness should apply to the High Priests of the Temple; that those persons partaking of these medicines may be either cured or spared from all ailments; that they may enjoy a long life and after death may live in eternal Paradise with the Buddha. At least twenty-six of the sixty different kinds of medicines described in the Deed of Gift still remain in the Repository.

In addition to the medicines there are also still in existence at least thirty-five accessories, such as the original bags bearing the names of the medicines.

The three remaining *Kenmotsucho* preserved in the Repository cite additional important offerings made to the Todaiji by the Empress Dowager Komyo. One of these, dated August 26, 756, offers folding screens, patterned rugs, etc., of which a few of the original items mentioned remain. Among the articles still extant are four pairs of slippers made of hemp cloth, covered with brocade and enriched with embroidered flowers; and a spherical silver incense burner decorated with over-all pierced floral scrolls. Another *Kenmotsucho*, dated July 10, 758, offers scrolls of writings by Wang Hsi-chih, the renowned fourth-century calligrapher, and by his son, Wang Hsien-chih, who, like his more illustrious father, also excelled in calligraphy. Of the twenty rolls or volumes of Wang Hsi-chih's calligraphy recorded, none remain. According to documents preserved in the Shosoin, all the rolls were taken out on September 4, 781. Twelve were returned later in the same month, and the remaining eight volumes in 784. However, they were again taken out in 820 and never returned. The last of the *Kenmotsucho*, dated November 6, 758, offers folding screens bearing the handwritings of Prince Fujiwara-no-Fubito, the father of Komyo, who in the dedication refers to this gift as her rarest treasure. None of these screens remain.

Several items of unusual interest are in the form of manuscripts. One manuscript, listed as *Zasshu* or *A Miscellany*, is described in the *Kenmotsucho* of National Treasures as being written by the Emperor Shomu. It consists of more than 140 stanzas selected from Chinese poems written during the Six Dynasties (265-589), and the Sui (589-618) and T'ang (618-906) dynasties. At the end of the scroll is a notation that the copying was completed on October 13, 731. Another manuscript, titled *Toka Rissei* or *A Model Letter Writer*, is described in the *Kenmotsucho* as having been written by the Empress Komyo. The scroll, which is written on white hemp paper, comprises thirty-six model letters and a corresponding number of replies. A third manuscript, titled *Gakki-ron* or *An Essay*, is described in the *Kenmotsucho* as being in the hand of the Empress Komyo. The essay is a famous Chinese one written in the third century. The scroll bears the date November 11, 744, and the signature "third daughter of Fujiwara."

According to the *Kenmotsucho* of National Treasures, these three scrolls, as well as a number of other objects belonging to the Emperor Shomu, were kept in a red lacquered cabinet. The reverence with which the Japanese have always regarded their hereditary treasures is aptly revealed in a statement made in the *Kenmotsucho* regarding the history of this cabinet. It states that the cabinet was bequeathed by the Emperor Temmu, reigned 673-686, to the Empress Jito, reigned 690-696, to the Emperor Mommu, reigned 697-707, to the Empress Gensho, reigned 715-723, to the Emperor Shomu, reigned 724-748 and to the Empress Koken, reigned 749-758, before it was offered to the *Great Buddha*. The cabinet, which is covered with transparent lacquer permitting the grain of the wood to show through, is forty inches high, thirty-four inches wide, and seventeen inches deep. It rests on a base of decorative openwork called *kazama*, and has two long doors enriched with gilt copper mounts. Of particular interest among the many personal belongings of the Emperor Shomu kept in this cabinet are six ivory foot-rules. None are exactly equal in size. They average around thirty centimeters in length, three centimeters in width, and one centimeter in thickness. Two are stained red and carved on both sides with continuous designs of animals, birds, and flowers. Two are stained blue and carved on both sides. The carving on one side of one of these blue-stained foot-rules is divided into ten equal parts. It is thought that these carved ivories probably served as paperweights rather than as standard measures. The remaining two foot-rules are white and plain. Each is divided by finely carved lines into ten equal sections, and each section is subdivided again into ten equal parts. One foot-rule is only seven milli-

Red lacquered cabinet or bookcase coated with a transparent lacquer permitting the grain of the wood to show through and decorated with gilt copper mounts. Eighth century. Shosoin, Nara.

meters shorter than the standard foot measure of the present time.

THE SHOSOIN RECORDS THROUGH THE CENTURIES

In addition to the five *Kenmotsucho* preserved in the Shosoin, there are also twelve important ancient scrolls, each bearing a title and each consisting of a number of sheets of documents mounted into a scroll. These documents relate chiefly to the withdrawal, return, or substitution of objects stored in the Repository, to Imperial gifts, and to the airing and inspection of the treasures. Mention has already been made of the document dated April 28, 784, concerning the return of Wang Hsi-chih's calligraphies, and also the removal of the lacquered Chinese kin and its subsequent replacement, which became the occasion of one of the notable substitutions entered in the Shosoin records. A scroll of marked interest because of the humane and religious purposes prompting it bears the title *Petitions for Gold Dust and Cassia*. The scroll comprises two sheets of paper, each with a separate petition and each having a character "*gi*" or "*yoroshi*," the sign of the Imperial sanction, acknowledging that the request is approved. One document, dated February 11, 757, is from the Department of Temple-building, asking for 2016 ryo of gold dust. Another scroll, bearing the title *Shutsunyucho* or *A Memorandum of Articles Withdrawn or Entered* and comprising twelve sheets of documents dealing with articles put in or taken out of the Repository from October 30, 756, to September 10, 781, refers to the gold dust, saying that 2016 ryo of gold dust was given on February 14, 757, to the Department of Temple-building for gilding the image of the *Great Buddha*. The other document in the *Petitions for Gold Dust and Cassia*, dated April 20, 759, is from the Charitable Medical Institution and asks for one hundred kin of cassia (cinnamon). There is also another entry in the Shosoin records referring to one hundred and fifty kin of cassia taken out August 28, 764, for the Seyaku-in, a charity institution for the distribution of medicines. These examples serve to illustrate the methodical recording of each detail concerning these Imperial relics.

It is interesting to note that the *Kenmotsucho* of Medicines records, "*keishin* (cassia) 560 kin and bags; these kept in the third, fourth, and fifth chests." One of the scrolls consists of fourteen sheets of documents bearing dates from 757 to 1231, concerning articles of Imperial dedication. It includes lists of the Imperial gifts stored in the chests in the Shosoin, and descriptive accounts of other Imperial objects dedicated. Two scrolls, one titled *Memorandum of Rare Treasures*, dated August 13, 787, and the other titled *Inventory at the Airing*, dated

Left: Ivory foot-rule (front view) dyed scarlet, with the carved designs of animals, birds, and flowers in other colors. Length 11 3/4 inches, width 1 1/8 inches, thickness 3/8 inch. Eighth century. Shosoin, Nara.

Right: Ivory foot-rule (rear view). Shosoin, Nara.

Gilt-bronze chintaku *of cylindrical form with a tongue suspended by a decorative metal piece. Eighth century. Shosoin, Nara.*

five *Kenmotsucho*, gives them great historic value. They are in truth treasures in themselves—perhaps the rarest of all those preserved within the walls of the Shosoin.

An elaborate and impressive commemorative service, marking the first anniversary of the abdicated Emperor Shomu's death, was held at the Todaiji on May 24, 757. In the Shosoin there are one hundred and three flower baskets bearing the same date, which were used to hold flowers during the Buddhist ceremonies at the Todaiji. There are also ten gilt-bronze cylindrical bells called *chintaku*, each having a tongue with a decorative metal pendant. Nine of these bells bear the engraved inscription "Todaiji Maeban Chintaku, May 24, 757." It is presumed from the inscription that they were used on some kind of banner or *mai*, probably as an ornament. Eight other similar bells show some variation in shape. There is also a fragment of a white silk bag on which is written, "Bag for Todaiji Maeban Chintaku, May 24, 757." Of interest are a pair of ceremonial plows and brooms dedicated by the Empress Koken on February 15, 758, which according to the lunar calendar then in use was the *ne-no-hi*, or first Day of the Rat in the first month of the year. On this day it was customary in ancient China to observe a ceremony in which the Emperor tilled the field and the Empress swept the room in which the silkworms were raised. Later, the custom came to be observed in Japan, and the Empress Koken probably used the plow and the broom on the first Rat Day before offering them to the *Great Buddha*. The colter of one plow is new, while the colter of the other is lacquered and painted in gold and silver, with the handle ornamented with decorative paintings applied on a gesso-like composition. Each plow bears an inscription saying that it was dedicated to the Todaiji on the Day of the Rat, first month, 758. The two *ne-no-hi* brooms are made of brushwood and are called beadbrooms, since originally they were "jeweled" with glass beads, though now only a few of the beads remain. There also survive broom stands, and batik-dyed plain silk sashs to tie the covers. On July 23, 760, the Empress Dowager Komyo died, and through her piety and munificence left an artistic legacy unique in the history of art.

Intrigue and conspiracy, stemming from the licentious behavior of the ex-Empress Koken and resulting in the disastrous rebellion of Emi-no-Oshikatsu, provided the motive for withdrawing a large quantity of arms and armor from the Repository on October 10, 764. The Empress Koken had abdicated in 758 in favor of the Emperor Jonin, but she continued to exercise her royal power. Her adviser was a monk named Dokyo, a capable but thoroughly unscrupulous man, whose rapid rise to power through the ex-Empress's favors aroused the jealousy of Fujiwara Nakamaro, known also as Oshikatsu, who supported the young Emperor, precipitating an open

July 23, 793, are inventory reports of the officials commissioned to examine the treasures at the airing. The second report contains a statement that the report was made in triplicate, one for the Imperial palace, a second for the office records of the Todaiji monastery, and a third for the Shosoin archives. An inspector's report of the treasures, dated October 15, 811, is the subject of another scroll, and it also was made in triplicate. The meticulous care expended in the compilation of these ancient inventories and other documents recording the entry, withdrawal, or return of various objects, together with the rebellion. An Imperial edict was issued requesting that the arms and armor kept in the Repository be sent to the Imperial palace. Accordingly on October 10, 764, ninety-nine suits of armor, eighty-eight swords, 103 bows, and ninety-six quivers completely equipped with arrows, and an additional 290 arrows were withdrawn from the Repository and never returned. As a result of Oshikatsu's revolt, the ex-Empress Koken once again ascended the throne, as the Empress Shotoku. The rebellion was finally crushed, but not before Oshikatsu and many of his followers were slain in 765. A visit paid to the Todaiji on March 6, 767, by the Empress Shotoku is noteworthy, for on that day she presented to the *Great Buddha* a handsome pair of silver jars decorated with chased bands of hunting scenes depicting horsemen with bows and arrows in pursuit of boar and deer, executed in a characteristic T'ang style.

The Emperor Konin, who succeeded the Empress Shotoku, was followed on his death in 782 by the Emperor Kwammu, who, soon after his accession, moved the capital from Nara, thus bringing to a close the glorious Nara period. One of the principal deciding factors prompting the removal of the capital was the growing political and economic power of Buddhism, a subject of grave concern to the aristocracy. The Emperor Kwammu wisely reasoned that if the court was to escape the domination of Buddhism, it was necessary to remove it from a city so rich in temples and monasteries supervised by wealthy and influential ecclesiastics. He accordingly removed the Imperial palace to Nagaoka in 784, but the court was to remain at Nara until the building of the city was completed. Almost a decade later, when the building of the city was nearing completion, an Imperial edict was issued ordering the removal of the capital from Nagaoka to Heian, the ancient name for Kyoto, which was only five miles distant. With the removal of the capital in 794 the scene of Imperial interest and activity shifted from the *Great Buddha* at Nara to Heian-kyo—"Capital (*kyo*) of Peace and Tranquillity"— which remained the capital for more than a thousand years, until it was moved to Tokyo in 1868. The history of the Shosoin from 794 until 950 is chiefly a record of withdrawals, returns, and substitutions and of airings and inspections by the Imperial commission, the more important aspects of which have to a large extent already been referred to. Actually very few presentations were made to the *Great Buddha* during this period. A *shaku*, which is a kind of flattened scepter used in ancient times by the court nobles as a form of memorandum pad but in later times carried as a mark of rank in the presence of the Emperor, is inscribed with the date, June 25, 905. Another gift is a silver bowl bearing the date December 30, 914. It is interesting to note that a report entitled *A True Record of Various Properties*, compiled in 856, exactly one hundred years after the original dedication to the *Great Buddha*,

Gilt-bronze chintaku, lozenge-shaped in section and ornamented with bosses near the top, with the tongue suspended by a metal piece having two openings to hold small bells as decoration. Eighth century. Shosoin, Nara.

indicates that the main part of the collection had virtually remained the same, despite the several changes, the principal ones of which have already been mentioned.

Until the year 950 the Shosoin contained only the offerings made by the Imperial family to the *Great Buddha*, and although these offerings were placed in the care of the Todaiji, they were under Imperial supervision and were Imperially sealed. In the year 950, however, the contents of a pair of ecclesiastically-sealed treasure houses of the Todaiji, which had been damaged in a violent storm, were moved into the South

Glass ewer with a slight tint of pale-green color and a narrow tapering neck terminating in a broad shallow leaf-shaped mouth and pouring lip. Eighth century. Shosoin, Nara.

to it at some later date, give the accession of these ecclesiastical treasures in 950 as the logical reason for enlarging the original Repository. The next milestone in the history of the Shosoin occurred in 1117 when, on September 4, the Emperor-Abdicant Shirakawa issued an order to make a detailed inventory of the ecclesiastic treasures stored in the South section. The report revealed that some of the important relics had been removed from the South section to the Imperially-sealed North and Middle sections. Thus, the offerings made to the Great Buddha by the people came to be intermingled with the Imperial presentations.

Undoubtedly the most interesting years in the art history of the Shosoin are the early years, until around the middle of the twelfth century. The "Tempyo Treasure" brush and "Tempyo Treasure" inkstick were taken out of the Repository on September 22, 1185, in order to be used the following day at the "eye-opening" ceremony of the *Great Buddha*, which was again observed for the new head of the *Great Buddha*. The "Tempyo" brush and inkstick were used for a third time on May 2, 1915, in the "eye-opening" ceremony of the *Great Buddha*, whose head had been completely reburnished. On September 30, 1261, the Emperor-Abdicant Gosaga inspected the Imperial relics and withdrew at the same time nine *kesa* or Buddhist robes, which he kept out for a year and several days. He finally returned them on October 5, 1262, because, according to the records, he had been severely reprimanded in a dream. It seems that these nine *kesa* were especially treasured by the Emperor Shomu and they also were the very first item in the long list of treasures offered to the *Great Buddha* in the *Kenmotsucho* of National Treasures. At the present time the top silk of two of these *kesa* is in almost perfect condition, and although the top silk in several examples has badly deteriorated, they still retain their original form without any trace of mending. Most of the original silk lining still remains in several of the *kesa*.

The later history of the Shosoin is chiefly a record of inspections and airings and of repairs to the building. In the years 1193 and 1230 the three sections were opened for the purpose of repairing the building. In 1243, as a result of rain leakage, repairs were started on the Imperially-sealed Repository and the treasures were stored temporarily in a storehouse belonging to the Todaiji. They were returned to the Shosoin three years later, in 1246. The building was again repaired in 1603, and also later in the same century in 1693, at which time some of the treasures, especially screen panels, were also repaired. Between the years 1833 and 1836 the entire building was reroofed, and urgent repairs were made on some of the treasures and the documents were put in order. In 1882 the present system of glass showcases with shelves was completed, and the treasures were arranged on them and catalogued.

section of the Shosoin, and the Imperial relics were moved into the North and Middle sections. Due to this change, the North and Middle sections of the Shosoin were Imperially sealed and the South section, containing offerings made by the people, was ecclesiastically sealed. The three sections continued to be sealed in this manner until probably 1872, when all three sections were Imperially sealed, and soon thereafter the link of the Repository with the Todaiji was completely severed. Finally in 1884 all three sections were put under the direct supervision of the Imperial Household Department. The supporters of the theory that the Middle section of the Shosoin was not a part of the original building, but was added

In the present arrangement of treasures, an attempt has been made to keep in the North section only those relics traceable to the original lists of offerings contained in the five *Kenmotsucho* and in other ancient documents, although there are some exceptions. In order to protect the Shosoin against a possible fire, a large tract of adjacent land was acquired in 1886 and enclosed within a wall, to which more ground outside the wall was added, totaling in all more than sixteen acres. Finally in March 1913, a provisional warehouse was built in the compound to contain the treasures temporarily while the Shosoin was being entirely taken apart and carefully reconstructed using all the available original materials. The reconstruction was finished in December of that same year, but the treasures were not returned until October 1914. The provisional warehouse still contains some of the empty ancient chests and fragments of textiles. There is also in the same compound a much smaller storehouse, also in the *azekura* style of building, called the Shogozo, which was offered as a gift by the Todaiji and formally accepted by the Imperial Household Department in 1894. This contains 4960 scrolls of ancient copies of sutras; some of which were copied in China in the Sui dynasty (589-618) and the subsequent T'ang dynasty (618-906), while almost fifteen hundred of the scrolls were copied in Japan during the Nara period (710-794). A new ferro-concrete repository has been built within the compound, and after various tests have been completed all the treasures will be moved into it from the old repository.

With respect to the treasures stored in the Shosoin, it should be mentioned that urgent repairs of objects are made from time to time and that replicas of certain treasures have been and are being made. The work of restoration as well as of putting in order countless things which have been left in confusion for centuries, such as an ancient chest containing more than sixty thousand colored glass beads used originally in different kinds of decoration, still continues. Of the treasures preserved in the Shosoin, some 532 objects are dated, of which 488 objects bear an eighth-century date. The inscription may be written on a tag attached to an article, on a bag in which the article is kept, or on the article itself. Some inscriptions are carved or incised, but the majority are written in black or occasionally red ink. Although some of the articles bear a post-Nara inspection date, the articles themselves are of the Nara period. Articles in the collection later than the eighth century are negligible, perhaps less than 2 per cent.

The debt of early Japanese art to China is indelibly written in this superlative collection of relics preserved intact in the Shosoin. The T'ang influence is clearly in evidence as it is in nearly all of the art of the Nara period, with the exception of a few examples having their provenance in Central Asia or in Persia. Many of the relics are so characteristically T'ang in form and in style of ornament that it is almost certain they were made in China. Some of the Imperial relics were undoubtedly gifts from the Chinese court to the reigning sovereigns of Japan, while other treasures were in all probability purchased in China by priests and scholars who, as members of missions, traveled extensively on the mainland. Other examples in the collection are directly inspired by Korean copies of Chinese work and it is presumed that they

Pottery bowl having a white body covered with a white glaze inside and outside streaked with green. The bowl is without a foot rim and cannot stand upright without support. Eighth century. Shosoin, Nara.

were executed by or under the direction of Korean artists. It must be remembered, however, that the artistic development in Japan under foreign tutelage after the seventh century was rapid and real. By the eighth century Japan had arrived at mature craftsmanship, so the collection contains many objects of sophisticated workmanship which were undoubtedly made in Japan, but by whose hand it is not possible to say. Notable are several examples of glass vessels, pottery jars, metalwork, and textiles that were either brought from Central Asia, or Persia, or Greece, or are fine reproductions of objects originating in those regions. China was then under the T'ang dynasty and, as perhaps the most powerful country in the world, possessed a civilization which was universally admired and emulated. Envoys from many countries—Turkey, Persia, Arabia, India—appeared at the Chinese court bearing gifts, so that Occidental influence, especially Persian and to a lesser extent Greek, is apparent in much of the art of the T'ang period. Ultimately some of these gifts of foreign origin or influence passed from the court in China to Japan and to the Imperial Repository. The thousands of relics stored in the Shosoin, their extraordinary variety, their antiquity, and their marvelous state of preservation make the collection unique. As examples of the arts and crafts of an ancient culture, they provide a picture of court life in the eighth century reflecting the pageantry of a brilliant, long-vanished civilization.

XXV Ainu Folk Art

THE PRIMITIVE ART and unique culture of the Ainu have been declining rapidly since the Meiji period, 1868-1912, and persons skilled in the old handicraft techniques are all but extinct. The Ainu race itself, numbering 16,000 in Hokkaido, will soon be extinct too. The Ainu, who have no racial affinities with the Japanese, are believed to have entered Japan from the north. Archaeological evidence shows that they were at one time spread over the whole archipelago before the arrival of the ancestors of the Japanese. Their origins remain unknown; some anthropologists regard them as Mongolians; others, as being remotely connected with early Caucasic races, perhaps a last remnant of the Neolithic peoples who ranged eastward in prehistoric times across the northern hemisphere to Manchuria and Japan. The Ainu are now confined to Hokkaido, Japan's northernmost island, Sakhalin, and part of the Kurile Islands.

Ainu handicraft, of which weaving is the most important, is characterized by designs peculiar to northern peoples who depend chiefly on hunting and fishing for their livelihood and whose primitive religious beliefs include an unseen world of gods, demons, and ancestral spirits. A peculiarity which distinguishes Ainu mythical rites is the worship of the bear and the curious Festival of the Bear, celebrated in the autumn of each year. Ainu designs appear to have been inspired by the complicated rope pattern which ornamented the Jomon-type earthenware of the Neolithic age in Japan, and by the decorative design and ornament on ancient Chinese ritual bronzes. Although Ainu designs appear to have been influenced by these design elements of early times, they have become true Ainu forms in character and feeling, and have nothing in common with those of other races or other countries. Perhaps it is because Ainu life has remained untouched by foreign or modern civilization that Ainu designs have retained their pure traditional forms.

Like the handicrafts of other primitive people, the custom of allotting work between men and women has prevailed for centuries. Specific jobs are assigned to each; those set apart for the men include the carved work in wood, bone and horn, and textile dyeing; while those allotted to the women are weaving, knitting, sewing, embroidery, and work in leather.

Beginning in early boyhood, Ainu men practice the art of carving decorative designs in wood with knives which they call *makiri*. The perfected designs are found in the carved decoration on a variety of articles in wood, such as arrow quivers, elliptical in section; peculiar ornaments of wood, shaped like the quivers but shorter, also elliptical in section, decorated at one end with flat disks of lead hammered into the wood, and used as mounts to hold a Japanese knife with its scabbard on the flattened side; wooden sword scabbards and knife sheaths inlaid with bone and horn; shallow wooden spoons of spatula shape for the ritual of serving sake to the gods; wooden sake vessels for rituals; bowls for food; weaver's shuttles, and other household utensils. Many of the motifs in these knife-carved designs were taken from nature. Others were inspired by the designs of centuries past in which they had their provenance. Characteristic Ainu male designs represent a harmonious combination of these stylistic elements, which remain distinguishable in the earlier work but have lost much of their original individuality in the examples of more recent times, while the component parts have become more obscure in their intermingling.

Unlike the male designs on the handicrafts of wood, bone, and horn, the female designs on textiles have remained almost unchanged in their original primitive forms, partly because the technical manner of the work does not allow the flexible expression so often found in wood carving, and because the weaver must observe certain religious precepts. There are no essential differences between the designs executed by men and women other than those which characteristically result from working in different techniques and different materials. From childhood, the Ainu woman practiced the art of drawing

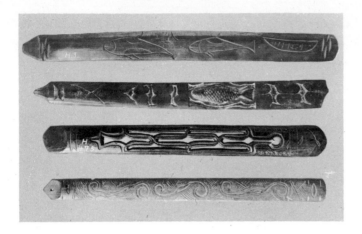

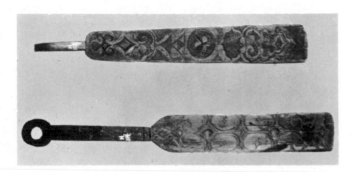

Ornamental quiver of carved wood. Ainu, first half of the nineteenth century. Courtesy Tokyo National Museum.

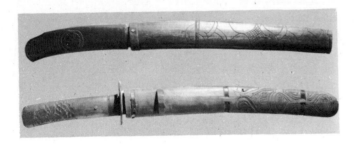

Top: Carved wood hige-bera or moustache raisers. Ainu, first half of the nineteenth century. Courtesy Tokyo National Museum.

Center: Carved wood spatula-shaped ritual spoons. Ainu, first half of the nineteenth century. Courtesy Tokyo National Museum.

Bottom: Swords with carved wood hilts and scabbards. Ainu, first half of the nineteenth century. Courtesy Tokyo National Museum.

symmetrical designs with her fingers on the foreshore of the beaches where the sand is left hard after the tide has gone out; drawing and erasing again and again until she has mastered a variety of designs. When she finds her future mate, she makes him clothing beautifully decorated with appliqué and embroidery work; and he in turn carves a wooden sheath for her woman's knife, called a *menoko makiri*, which is his most affectionate gift to her. The oldest truly native textiles of the Ainu which still exist are from the late Edo to the early Meiji periods, or from around the end of the eighteenth to the first half of the nineteenth centuries. In Ainu culture, the primitive age is prior to the Meiji period, 1868-1912, when the distinctive Ainu culture prevailed. During the era from the middle of the Meiji to the Taisho period, 1912-1926, the purity of their textile designs began to decline.

DESIGN MOTIFS

Ainu textile designs, illustrated most effectively on the robes and characterized by bold and striking geometric motifs, often in a labyrinthine manner, are executed in appliqué work.

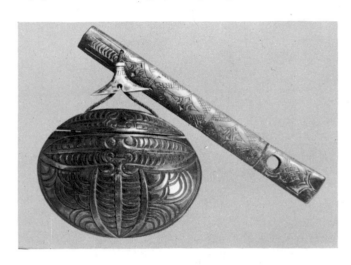

Left: Knives with carved wood hilts and sheaths. Ainu, first half of the nineteenth century. Courtesy Tokyo National Museum.

Below: Tobacco pouch and pipe case of carved wood. Ainu, first half of the nineteenth century. Courtesy Tokyo National Museum.

By this method the straight and curved lines handed down chiefly from the patterns on ancient Jomon pottery are more easily reproduced. The salient features of Ainu textile design have been classified into two categories; one is called *moreu*, meaning smoothly flowing, and is applied to the so-called spirals, which look much more like sharply pointed C scrolls; the other is called *aiushi*, or thorned, and is applied to brace-shaped patterns or geometrical designs in which the angles end in a thornlike projection made by a concluding stitch of the sewing thread. All these spirals and braces, with their thorns, are worked together in a vast number of design combinations to produce an endless variety of motifs. They are symmetrical even to the smallest detail, a distinctive feature thought to come from some ancient belief in which a design having mystical powers should protect all of the body evenly. A singular characteristic of the design on Ainu costume is that the motifs are usually applied only at the neck, the upper part of the back, around the skirt, and on the cuffs, most probably having its origin, too, in a mythological belief that all openings in the costume should be protected by magical designs having occult powers. These upper and lower designs are often expanded to become one continuous design covering the entire back of the robe, a feature seen more frequently in certain parts of the Ainu country than in others.

This quality of adhering to ancient religious beliefs gives simple power and remarkable character to Ainu textile designs. Many of the early extant robes are worked with double and triple appliqué ornament and frequently enhanced with embroidery. With the advance of time, the powerful effect of the traditional designs became weaker until decorative elaborateness all but replaced the early designs. The decorative motifs of later times have become inconsistent with the true principles of Ainu traditional design; some, wholly different in nature, mingle with pure Jomon patterns, and in others the motifs have been extended to such proportions that the original design is all but lost.

MATERIALS AND METHODS

The pliable native fabric used by the Ainu for clothing is a bark cloth. It is made from the fibers taken from the brownish bark of certain indigenous trees of Hokkaido such as the *shina-no-ki*, a kind of linden or basswood, and the *ohyotamo*, a kind

of elm; also from the bleached, soft white fibers from the bark of the *irakusa*, a genus of the nettle plant called *urtica* and found in Karafuto in the southern part of Sakhalin. The bark is stripped by the men, who bring it into the villages in lengths of about five feet, with the hard outer coating removed. The older women separate it into thin layers, which they split into very slender yarnlike strips, join the ends with tiny knots, and wind it into balls of about one pound each.

A number of fibers not native to the Ainu country of Hokkaido or the islands to the north are brought in from the main island of Honshu and the China mainland. They are cotton, silk, and ramie. But the fibers used in making the bands for the hanging swords are taken from the bark of the *tsuru-umemodoki*, or *Celastrus* shrubs and vines, and the fibers of the *ulmus* tree. These fibers are often used only as warp yarn, while the weft threads are made of the hair of the foetus or unborn seal dyed with the skin of the root of the *hamanashi*.

Ainu fabrics are always woven of pure vegetable-dyed yarn on which other yarn-dyed materials are appliquéd to form the designs or are worked with embroidery. Much of the yarn is dyed with the raw juice of certain fruits, but sometimes it is dyed by steeping it in coloring decoctions made by boiling certain parts of native plants found in the surrounding forests. Some of these colors are yellow, from the bark of the evergreen orange tree or yellowwood; brown, from the bark of the *han-no-ki*, or alder tree; blue-green, from leaves and stalks of the *ezotaisei* or common woad, which has been superseded by the indigo plant; purple, from the juice of the black, tasteless berry of the *gankoran* or crowberry; red, from the skin of the root of the *hamanashi*, the familiar shrub whose

Top: Bark-cloth robe with appliqué and embroidery. Ainu, early nineteenth century. Courtesy Japan Textile Color Design Center, Osaka; Collection Tokyo National Museum.

Center: Bark-cloth robe with appliqué and embroidery. Ainu, early nineteenth century. Courtesy Japan Textile Color Design Center. Osaka; Collection Prof. Sakuzaemon Kodama, Sapporo, Hokkaido.

Bottom: Ainu bark-cloth robe with appliqué and embroidery. Early nineteenth century. Courtesy Japan Textile Color Design Center, Osaka; Collection Mr. Hiromichi Kono.

deep-red, roselike flowers of summer and red berries of autumn are so colorful on the sandy beaches of northern Japan, where it is popularly called the *hamanasu*; another red from chips of wood of the *onko*, or yew tree; a yellow from the bark of the cork tree.

The weaving is done on a most primitive kind of loom called an *izari-bata*, or back-strap loom. The warp yarns are fastened to a stout hook fixed in the floor or, out of doors, to some sturdy object such as the trunk of a tree. The other warp ends are fastened to the waist of the weaver by a cord, the necessary tension being supplied by her body. The weaver sits on the floor or ground with the whole weaving arrangement attached to her waist. The loom consists of a comblike frame, resting on her ankles, through which the warp yarns pass; a beam which is raised by hand; a spatula-shaped wooden shuttle with a beautifully carved over-all design, and a roller on which the cloth is rolled as it is made. The warp yarns are about fifteen feet long, the width of the cloth about fifteen inches. The weaving is done with exactness. The knots in the bark yarn are carefully kept on the under side of the cloth, and as the weaving progresses, the weaver keeps moving her rigid position toward the fixed end of the warp. This feature has caused the weaving equipment to be called *izari-bata*, literally, a creeping-along loom.

Only patterns of simple vertical stripes were woven on such a device, but a rich variety of complex geometric designs were woven in with a kind of weft-patterned double weave on a ground of plain weave for sword hangers. This technique was perhaps derived from the Ainu method of weaving mats, which was more like braiding than weaving; each warp yarn was picked up individually with a pinlike tool. Except for this

Top: Ainu bark-cloth robe with embroidery design. Early nineteenth century. Courtesy Japan Textile Color Design Center, Osaka; Collection Tokyo National Museum.

Center: Bark-cloth robe with embroidery design. Ainu, early nineteenth century. Courtesy Japan Textile Color Design Center, Osaka; Collection Prof. Sakuzaemon Kodama, Sapporo, Hokkaido.

Bottom: Ainu bark-cloth robe of appliqué and patchwork. Early nineteenth century. Courtesy Japan Textile Color Design Center, Osaka; Collection Abashiri Kyodo Museum, Abashiri, Hokkaido.

337

method of pattern weaving, reserved for sword hangers, the Ainu used only appliqué work and embroidery to produce the designs for their textiles.

Ainu appliqué is divided into two categories. One is *nuno-oki*, or putting the cloth on, a method of stitching bands of cloth to the ground fabric according to a design already laid out. The other method is called *kiri-fuse*, or cutting and applying, or *kiri-nuki*, cutting out, in which a piece of cloth is cut according to a design previously drawn and stitched onto the ground fabric. In embroidery, there are two methods applied to Ainu textiles. In one, a stem or crewel stitch is used, as well as a buttonhole stitch, perhaps derived from their leather patchwork; also a satin stitch and a type of chain stitch which seems to have come from China. The other method is called *oki-nui*, or placing and sewing, a method in which thick yarns and sometimes bark or leather cords are laid on the fabric in a design and fixed with stitch work.

With their limited materials and primitive techniques, the Ainu have created remarkably well made textiles with splendid designs and harmonious color tones. Perhaps it is because of their ancient culture, untouched by the passage of time, and their pure religious beliefs, which they have clung to from remote antiquity, that they have been able to produce such unique work.

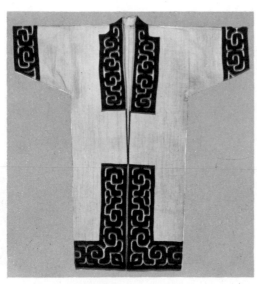

Ainu bark-cloth robe with appliqué design. Early nineteenth century. Courtesy Japan Textile Color Design Center, Osaka; Collection Hokkaido University.

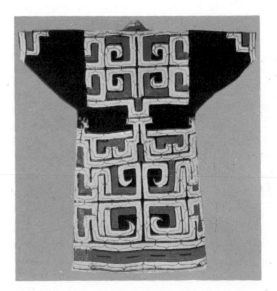

Appliqué and patchwork bark-cloth robe. Ainu, early nineteenth century. Courtesy Japan Textile Color Design Center, Osaka; Collection Tenri Museum, Tambaichi.

Bibliography

Akiyama, A. *Shinto and Its Architecture.* Tokyo, 1955.

Allen, Maude Rex. *Japanese Art Motives.* Chicago, 1917.

Anderson, William. *Japanese Wood Engravings, Their History, Technique and Characteristics.* London, 1895.

——. *The Pictorial Arts of Japan*, with a brief historical sketch of the associated arts and some remarks upon the pictorial art of the Chinese and Koreans. London, 1886.

Anesaki, Masaharu. *Art, Life and Nature in Japan.* Boston, 1933.

An Illustration of Japanese Coloured Porcelain. 2 Vols., Kyoto, 1953.

Asiatic Society of Japan, Transactions of. Yokohama, 1879–1955.

Audsley, George Ashdown. *Gems of Japanese Art and Handicraft.* London, 1913.

——. *The Ornamental Arts of Japan.* 2 Vols., New York, 1883–1884.

——, and Bowes, J. L. *Ceramic Art of Japan.* 2 Vols., Liverpool, 1875.

Binyon, Laurence. *A Catalogue of the Japanese and Chinese Wood-Cuts in the British Museum.* London, 1916.

——. *Painting in the Far East.* London, 1934.

——, and Sexton, J. J. O'Brien. *Japanese Colour Prints.* London, 1923.

Blunt, Wilfrid. *Japanese Colour Prints from Harunobu to Utamaro.* London, 1952.

Bowie, Henry P. *On the Laws of Japanese Painting.* London, 1911; reprinted, New York, 1951.

Brinkley, Frank. *Japan*, 5 Vols., Boston, 1904.

——. *Japan, Its History, Arts and Literature.* 8 Vols., Boston, 1901–1902.

——, with the collaboration of Baron Kikuchi. *A History of the Japanese People, from the Earliest Times to the End of the Meiji era.* New York, 1915.

Brockhaus, Albert. *Netsuke. Versuch einer Geschichte der japanischen Schnitzkunst.* Leipzig, 1909.

Brown, Louise Norton. *Block Printing and Book Illustration in Japan.* London, 1924.

Caiger, G. *Dolls on Display. An Illustrated Commentary of the Girls' and Boys' Festivals.* Tokyo, 1933.

Catalogue of the Imperial Treasures in the Shosoin. Published by the Imperial Household Museum, Tokyo, with the text by Professor Yoshinaga Oshima, translated into English by Jiro Harada. Vols. 1–18, Tokyo, 1929–1955.

Catalogue of Treasures in the Imperial Repository Shosoin. By Jiro Harada. Published by The Imperial Household Museum, Tokyo, 1932.

Conder, Josiah. *Landscape Gardening in Japan.* Tokyo, 1893.

——. *The Floral Art of Japan*, being a second and revised edition of *The Flowers of Japan and the Art of Floral Arrangement.* Tokyo, 1899.

——. *Theory of Japanese Flower Arrangement.* Kobe, 1935.

Dick, Stewart. *Arts and Crafts of Old Japan.* London, 1908.

Dresser, Christopher. *Japan, Its Architecture, Art and Art Manufactures.* London, 1882.

Du Cane, Florence. *The Flowers and Gardens of Japan, Painted by Ella Du Cane*, London, 1908.

Ema, Osamu. *A Historical Sketch of Japanese Customs and Costumes.* Tokyo, 1936.

——. *Kimono; One Hundred Masterpieces of Japanese Costumes*, 2 Vols., Tokyo.

Farrer, R. J. *The Garden of Asia.* 1904.

Ficke, Arthur Davison. *Chats on Japanese Prints.* London, 1915; reprinted, Tokyo, 1958.

Focillon, Henri. *Hokousai.* Paris, 1914.

Franks, Sir Augustus Wollaston. *Japanese Pottery.* London, 1880.

Fujii, Koji. *The Japanese Dwelling-House.* Tokyo, 1930.

Fujikake, Shizuya. *Japanese Wood-Block Prints.* Tokyo, 1954.

——. *Ukiyo-e no Kenkyu. A Study of Ukiyo-e.* 3 Vols., Tokyo, 1943.

Fukui, Kikusaburo. *Japanese Ceramic Art and National Characteristics.* Tokyo, 1926.

Fukukita, Yasunosuke. *Tea Cult of Japan.* Tokyo, 1957.

Fuku Sen Shiryo Kenkyi Kai (Specimens of Japanese Classical Dresses). Tokyo, 1935.

Goncourt, Edmond Louis Antoine Huot de. *Hokousai.* Paris, 1896.

——. *Outamaro le peintre de Maisons vertes; l'art Japonais du XVIII siècle.* Paris, 1891.

Gorham, Hazel H. *Japanese and Oriental Pottery.* Yokohama, ——.

——. *Japanese Netsuke.* Yokohama, 1957.

Harada, Jiro. *The Gardens of Japan.* Edited by C. Geoffrey Holme. London, 1928.

——. *The Lesson of Japanese Architecture.* Edited by C. Geoffrey Holme. London, 1936.

Hearn, Lafcadio. *Japan; An Attempt at Interpretation.* London, 1917.

——. *Japanese Fairy Tales.* New York, 1919.

Hillier, Jack Ronald. *Hokusai: Paintings, Drawings and Woodcuts.* New York, 1955.

——. *Japanese Masterpieces of the Colour Print.* London, 1954.

Hisamatsu, S. *Zen and Fine Arts.* Tokyo, 1958.

Holmes, Sir Charles John. *Hokusai.* London, 1899.

Howell-Smith, A. D., and Koop, Albert J. *A Guide to Japanese Textiles.* 2 Vols., London, 1919–1920.

Huish, Marcus C. *Japan and Its Art.* London, 1892.

Ienaga, Saburo. *History of Japan.* Tokyo, 1954.

Irigawa, Yasukichi, and Chadani, Tomoiro. *Bunraku, Japanese Puppet Theatre.* Tokyo, 1954.

Japan Society, London, Transactions and Proceedings of. Vol. 1 to Vol. 37 inclusive, first session 1892, 50th session 1941. London, 1893.

Japanese Temples and Their Treasures. Edited by His Imperial Majesty's Commission to the Panama-Pacific International Exposition. 3 Vols., Tokyo, 1915.

Joly, Henri Louis. *Japanese Sword Guards.* London, 1910.

——. *Legend in Japanese Art.* London, 1908.

——, and Tomita, Kumasaku. *Japanese Art and Handicraft.* An illustrated record of the loan exhibition held in aid of the British Red Cross in October-November 1915. 2 Vols., London, 1916.

Jonas, F. M. *Netsuke.* Kobe, 1928.

Kabuya, Okabe. *Japanese Sword Guards.* Boston, 1908.

Kanda, Matunosuke. *Japanese Lacquer.* Tokyo, 1941.

Kishida, Hideto. *Japanese Architecture.* Tokyo, 1936.

Koehn, Alfred. *Japanese Flower Symbolism.* Peiping, 1937.

——. *The Way of Japanese Flower Arrangement.* London, 1935.

Koizumi, Gunji. *Lacquer Work.* London, 1923.

Komatsu, Fumiko. *L'Evolution du Costume au Japon, depuis l'antiquité jusqu'à l'époque des Tokugawa.* Paris, 1942.

Kongo, Iwao. *The Costume of the No Play in Japan.* Tokyo.

——. *No-isho; Japanese No Play Costume.* Tokyo, 1934.

Kurth, Julius. *Masterpieces of Japanese Woodcuts from Moronobu to Hiroshige.* Berlin, 1924.

——. *Sharaku.* Leipzig, 1910.

——. *Suzuki Harunobu.* Leipzig, 1910.

——. *Utamaro.* Leipzig, 1907.

Lane, Richard. *Masters of the Japanese Print: Their World and Their Work*. New York, 1962.

Ledoux, Louis V. *An Essay on Japanese Prints*. New York, 1938.

Maeda, Taiji. *Japanese Decorative Design*. Tokyo, 1957.

Masterpieces of Japanese Puppetry. Edited by Seijiro Saito, Hoichi Yamaguchi, and Takao Yoshinaga. English adaption by Roy Andrew Miller. Tokyo, 1958.

Matsuki, Kihachiro. *Hiroshige Edo Fukei Hanga-shu* (A Collection of Hiroshige's Edo Landscapes). Tokyo, 1939.

Matsuoka, Asa. *Sacred Treasures of Nara in Shosoin and Kasuga Shrine*. Tokyo, 1935.

——. *Shoso-in, Ancient Storehouse of Treasures of Old Japan*. Japan Society of America. New York, 1931.

Mew, Egan. *Japanese Porcelain*. Masterpieces of Handicraft. London, 1909.

Michener, James A. *Japanese Prints, from the Early Masters to the Modern*. Tokyo, 1959.

——. *The Floating World*. New York, 1954.

——. *The Hokusai Sketchbooks: Selections from the Manga*. Tokyo, 1958.

Minamoto, Hoshu. *An Illustrated History of Japanese Art*. Kyoto, 1935.

Mitsuoka, Tadanari. *Ceramic Art of Japan*. Tokyo, 1949.

Morrison, Arthur. *The Painters of Old Japan*. 2 Vols., London, 1913.

Morse, Edward S. *Catalogue of the Morse Collection of Japanese Pottery*. Boston, 1901.

——. *Japanese Homes and Their Surroundings*. London, 1886.

Moslé Collection. Japanese works of art, selected from the Moslé collection, by Henri Louis Joly. Leipzig, 1914.

Munsterberg, Hugo. *The Arts of Japan*. Tokyo, 1957.

——. *The Landscape Painting of China and Japan*. Tokyo, 1955.

Murdoch, James. *A History of Japan*. Published by the Asiatic Society. Vols. 1–10. Yokohama, 1903–1926.

Nishikawa, Issotei. *Floral Art of Japan*. Tokyo, 1956.

Noguchi, Yonejiro. *Hiroshige and Japanese Landscapes*. Tokyo, 1934.

——. *Hosusai Kataushika*. Tokyo, 1931.

Noma, Seiroku. *Masks*. Tokyo, 1957.

Okada, Yuzuru. *Japanese Handicrafts*. Tokyo, 1956.

——. *Netsuke, a Miniature Art of Japan*. Tokyo, 1951.

——, Koyama and Hayashiya. *Japanese Ceramics*. Tokyo, 1954.

Okakura, Kakuzo. *The Book of Tea*. New York, 1912.

Oshikawa, Josui, and Gorham, Hazel H. *Manual of Japanese Flower Arrangement*. Tokyo, 1936.

Paine, Robert Treat, and Soper, Alexander Coburn. *The Art and Architecture of Japan*. Baltimore, 1955.

Piggott, Sir Francis Taylor. *Studies in the Decorative Art of Japan*. London, 1910,

——. *The Garden of Japan, A Year's Diary of Its Flowers*. London, 1892.

Revon, Michel. *Etude sur Hokousai*. Paris, 1898.

Rhead, George Wooliscroft. *History of the Fan*. London, 1910.

Rucker, R. H. *The Goda Collection of Japanese Sword Fittings*. New York, 1924.

Ryerson, Egerton. *Netsuke*. London, 1958.

Sadler, Arthur Lindsay. *A Short History of Japanese Architecture*. Sidney, 1941.

——. *The Art of Flower Arrangement in Japan: A Sketch of Its History and Development*. London, 1933.

Sagara, Tokuzo. *Japanese Fine Arts*. Tokyo, 1949.

Salway, Mrs. Charlotte M. *Fans of Japan*, With an introduction by William Anderson. London, 1894.

Sansom, George B. *Japan, A Short Cultural History*. Revised edition, New York, 1943.

Shigemori, K. *The Artistic Gardens of Japan*. 3 Vols., Tokyo, 1957.

Soper, Alexander Coburn. *The Evolution of Buddhist Architecture in Japan*. Princeton, 1942.

——, and Paine, Robert Treat. *The Art and Architecture of Japan*. Harmonsworth, England, and Baltimore, 1955.

Steward, Basil. *Subjects Portrayed in Japanese Color-Prints*. London, 1922.

Strange, Edward F. *Catalogue of Japanese Lacquer*. Victoria and Albert Museum, 2 Vols., London, 1924.

——. *The Colour-Prints of Hiroshige*. London, 1925.

Suzuki, Daisetz Teitaro. *Introduction to Zen Buddhism*. London, 1957.

——. *Zen and Japanese Culture*. Tokyo, 1958.

Tajima, Shiichi. *Masterpieces Selected from the Fine Art of the Far East*. 15 Vols., Tokyo, 1918–1920.

——. *Masterpieces Selected from the Ukiyo-e School*. 5 Vols., Tokyo, 1906–1909.

Takahashi, Sei-ichiro. *Ukiyo-e Nihyakugoju-nen* (Two Hundred and Fifty Years of Ukiyo-e). Tokyo, 1939.

Takahashi, Yoshio. *Taisho Meiki Kwan; The Ceremony Pottery of the Taisho Period*. 9 Vols., folio 4, Tokyo, 1921–1926.

Tamamura, K. *A Leaf from the Diary of a young Lady*. (Costume.) Yokohama.

Tamura, T. *Art of Landscape Garden in Japan*. Tokyo, 1935.

Tatsui, Matsunosuke. *Japanese Gardens*. Tokyo, 1949.

——. *Gardens of Japan, a Pictorial Record of Famous Palaces, Gardens and Tea-Gardens*. Tokyo, 1935.

Taut, Bruno. *Houses and People of Japan*. Tokyo, 1937.

Taylor, Basil, Mrs. *Japanese Gardens*. Pictures by Walter Tyndale. London, 1912.

Tessai. *Folio Volume of Colour Plates*. Kyoto, 1957.

Toda, Kenji. *Japanese Scroll Painting*. Chicago, 1935.

Tokyo National Museum. *Pageant of Japanese Art*. Edited by the Staff Members. 6 Vols., Tokyo, 1952–1954.

——. *Sotatsu Korin Hazuroku*. Tokyo.

Tsuda, Noritake. *Handbook of Japanese Art*. Tokyo, 1935.

——, *The Shosoin. The Art Treasure House Standing since the 8th Century in Japan*. Japan Society of America. New York.

Uemura, Rokuro. *Old Art Treasures from Japan's Needles and Looms*. Kyoto, 1949.

Ukiyo-e Taika Shusei (Grand Collection of Ukiyo-e Masters). 20 Vols., Tokyo, 1931–1932; supplement, 6 Vols., 1933.

Von Seidlitz, Waldemar. *History of Japanese Color Prints*. London, 1910.

Warner, Langdon. *The Crafts of the Japanese Sculptor*. New York, 1936.

——. *The Enduring Art of Japan*. Cambridge, 1952.

Yamada, Tokubei. *Japanese Dolls*. Tokyo, 1955.

Yamanobe, Tomoyuki. *Textiles*. Tokyo, 1957.

Yashiro, Yukio. *2000 Years of Japanese Art*. Edited by Peter C. Swann. New York, 1958.

Yoshida, Eiji. *Harunobu Zenshu* (Collected Works of Harunobu). Takamizawa Print Shop, Tokyo, 1942.

Yoshida, Tetsuro. *The Japanese House and Garden*. New York, 1955.

Yoshikawa, Kampo. *The Great Picture Collection of Japanese Costumes*. Kyoto, 1934.

Yoshinaga, Y. *Japanese Traditional Gardens*. Tokyo, 1958.

Yumoto, J. M. *The Samurai Sword: A Handbook*. Tokyo, 1958.

Index

Otowayama, Mount. *See* Kiyomizu temple
Otsu, 48, 49
otsu-e, 48, 49, 50
Owari, 21, 105
ox-drawn carriages, 261, 262
oyama-ningyo, 303
Oyamukui, 24
Oyashima, 13
Oyashiro (Izume-Taisha) shrine, 130, 131-32
oyashiro (*taisha*) style, 131, 132
oyoroi, 112
ozen, 217, 260

pagodas, 67, 137, 139-40, 145, 171. *See also taho-to*
Paikche, 14, 67, 70, 80
painters and painting, 20, 27-50 (*See also* specific painters); mediums and materials for, 49-50
palanquins, 261
paulownia tree. *See kiri* (wood)
peach blossom, 38, 204, 300
pegasus motif, 24
Peintre des Maisons Vertes (Goncourt), 59
peonies, 206
Petitions for Gold Dust and Cassia, 327
pewter, 94-95, 315
Phoenix Hall, 29, 76, 140, 141, 254
phoenix motif, 24, 254
picnic box, 261, 262
Picturesque Views of Famous Bridges in Several Provinces (Hokusai), 62
Pillow Book, 18, 289
Pine Breeze, The, 87
pine needles, 202
pine trees, 26, 167, 168, 174, 175
Pine Trees in Snow (Maruyama Okyo), 44
Pink and White Plum Blossoms (Korin Ogata), 43
pipes and smoking utensils, 91, 92, 261, 263, 274-75, 276, 335
pit houses, 129
plum, 26, 167, 168, 174, 204
Plum Tree and Birds (Sanraku), 39
poetry, 201, 225, 260, 273, 289, 310, 326
pommels, sword, 123
porcelain, 231-52, 301-4
pottery, 227-52, 331. *See also* specific objects
prehistoric culture, 8, 13-14. *See also* specific arts
prints, 23, 51-66; textiles, 283-86
protohistory, 8. *See also* specific arts
pruning, landscape gardening and, 168
puppets, 299, 305-6
Pure Land sect. *See* Jodo sect

Quail, 33
quivers, 116, 273, 334

ra, 278
raden, 264
raigo ceremony, 84
Raku pottery, 217, 229-30, 235-37, 243
Ramayana, 221
ramma, 151, 152, 154
rankan-bashi, 171
rankei-gata, 171
Record of Ancient Matters. *See* Kojiki
Reisho Tokaido, 63, 66
Renge-o-in (Sanju-Sangen-do), 78, 142

Rikei. *See* Koraizayemon
Rikishi mask, 81
Rikiu (*Rikyu*) *ogi*, 309-10
Rikka (Rikkwa) flower arrangement, 174-75, 193, 198
Rikyu, Sen-no-, 21, 211-12, 214, 217, 235, 292; and fans, 309; and flowers, 200, 211; and gardens, 165; and lacquer, 264; and pottery, 220, 228 ff., 236
Rinjo (Mitsuzane) Kanzayemon Goto, 121
Rinzai sect, 19
rinzu, 282
riobitsu, 121
Ritsuo (lacquer artist), 258
Riumon, 167
ro, 278
rocks, 163, 167, 172
ro-iro, 223, 225, 264, 267
roji, 164, 212, 213, 216
rokechi, 283, 284
Rokkakudo, 173
Rokubei family, 243
Rokuonji temple, 21
Rokusoan teahouse, 211
ronin, 121
roofs, 145-46. *See also* architecture
rope, 276; sacred Shinto, 14, 106, 147
roseitei, 211, 222
rozan, 167
Ryoanji temple, 163, 164
Ryobu, 16
Ryokei, Kano, 145
ryu. *See* dragons
Ryuko-in tearoom, 214
Ryumonji pottery, 237
ryusa netsuke, 272

sabi, 214
sabi-ji, 264
Sacred Rope of Shinto, 14, 106, 147
Sadamune (swordsmith), 106, 110
Sadatsune of Satsuma, 126
saddle, mulberry-wood, 316
Saffron Flower (Hishikawa Moronobu), 55
Saga, Emperor, 209
Saga (town), 248, 304
saga-ningyo, 302, 304-5
sagemono, 270 ff.
sage-o, 120
Saicho, 74-75, 209
Saihoji temple, 162, 163
Saijiro, Goto, 251
Saimyoji temple, 142, 144
Sakai, 280, 291
sakazuki, 258-60
sake and sake utensils, 217, 237, 255, 258-60. *See also* wine utensils
sakura. *See* cherry blossoms
Sakura-no-baba, 274
Sakyamuni, 68, 69, 75, 212; eight supernatural guardians of (*See* Hachibu-shu)
sambo-gin, 104
Samboin temple, 143, 166, 169
same, 119
same-nuri, 119
samisen, 305
Sammon gate, 145

Sampei, Kanae, 231
samurai, 19, 217, 276, 290, 301. *See also* arms and armor; feudal system
sandalwood, 152
sand-bowls, 175, 199
Sanetomo Minamoto, 18-19
san-gusoku, 100-1
Sanju-Sangen-do, 78, 142
Sanno-Sama, 24
Sanraku, Kano, 21, 39, 45, 143
san-san-kudo, 259
Sansetsu, Kano, 45
Sanshu-no-Shinki. *See* Three Sacred Treasures
sansui, 165-66
sarugaku, 85, 86, 87
saru-te, 123
sashi netsuke, 272
Satsuma, 103, 236, 237, 283
sawari, 103
scabbards, 119, 120, 122, 124
screens, 39 ff., 148, 157; garden, 171-72; at Shosoin Repository, 322, 323, 324
scrolls, 32-34, 326, 327, 331. *See also* kakemono
sculpture, 67-78. *See also* specific materials, objects
seals, 265
seasons, 26, 168, 197, 201. *See also* Five Seasons festivals
seigo, 279
Seiko (lake), 167
Sei Shonagon, 18
Seisuiji temple. *See* Kiyomizu temple
Sekigahara, 21
semba-sura, 25
sen, 108
Sengoku Jidai, 292
Senju-in of Yamato, 107
Sen-ke, 174
Sennin of Horaizan, 58
sentoku, 103
seppa, 121
seppa dqi, 121
Sesshu, 21, 33, 34, 35, 38, 39-40, 96
Seto ware, 228, 230, 231, 232-34, 235, 236, 243
setsubun (*tsuina*), 83, 85-86, 134, 170
setta, 297
seven gods of good luck, 25, 65, 240
sha, 278
shagetsu, 225
Shakamuni Butsu. *See* Sakyamuni
Shaka Nyorai. *See* Sakyamuni
shaku, 309, 329
shakudo, 92, 103-4, 118, 126
shakuhachi, 274
shakujo, 99, 100
Sharaku, Toshusai, 61
Shariden (Engakuji temple), 141, 143
shells, use in lacquer work, 264
shibori, 283, 285, 291
shibuichi, 93, 103, 104
shibumi, 23
shibu uchiwa, 310
shichifukujin (seven gods of good luck), 25, 65, 240
shichu (hipped-ridge) roofs, 145, 146
shi-ga-jiku, 38
Shigaraki palace, 72
Shigemasa (Hiroshige), 66